OCP
Oracle Certified Professional
Java SE 17 Developer
(Exam 1Z0-829)
Programmer's Guide

Volume I

OCP
Oracle Certified Professional
Java SE 17 Developer
(Exam 1Z0-829)
Programmer's Guide

Volume I

Khalid A. Mughal
Vasily A. Strelnikov

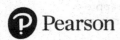 **Pearson**

Boston • Columbus • New York • San Francisco • Amsterdam • Cape Town
Dubai • London • Madrid • Milan • Munich • Paris • Montreal • Toronto • Delhi • Mexico City
São Paulo • Sydney • Hong Kong • Seoul • Singapore • Taipei • Tokyo

For information about buying this title in bulk quantities, or for special sales opportunities (which may include electronic versions; custom cover designs; and content particular to your business, training goals, marketing focus, or branding interests), please contact our corporate sales department at corpsales@pearsoned.com or (800) 382-3419.

For government sales inquiries, please contact governmentsales@pearsoned.com.

For questions about sales outside the U.S., please contact intlcs@pearson.com.

Visit us on the Web: informit.com

Library of Congress Control Number: 2022951639

ISBN-13: 978-0-13-799364-2
ISBN-10: 0-13-799364-1

1 2023

Pearson's Commitment to Diversity, Equity, and Inclusion

Pearson is dedicated to creating bias-free content that reflects the diversity of all learners. We embrace the many dimensions of diversity, including but not limited to race, ethnicity, gender, socioeconomic status, ability, age, sexual orientation, and religious or political beliefs.

Education is a powerful force for equity and change in our world. It has the potential to deliver opportunities that improve lives and enable economic mobility. As we work with authors to create content for every product and service, we acknowledge our responsibility to demonstrate inclusivity and incorporate diverse scholarship so that everyone can achieve their potential through learning. As the world's leading learning company, we have a duty to help drive change and live up to our purpose to help more people create a better life for themselves and to create a better world.

Our ambition is to purposefully contribute to a world where:

- Everyone has an equitable and lifelong opportunity to succeed through learning.
- Our educational products and services are inclusive and represent the rich diversity of learners.
- Our educational content accurately reflects the histories and experiences of the learners we serve.
- Our educational content prompts deeper discussions with learners and motivates them to expand their own learning (and worldview).

While we work hard to present unbiased content, we want to hear from you about any concerns or needs with this Pearson product so that we can investigate and address them.

- Please contact us with concerns about any potential bias at https://www.pearson.com/report-bias.html.

To the loving memory of my mother, Zubaida Begum,
and my father, Mohammed Azim.
And to the future generation: Tobias Albert, Ronja Johanne
and Serine Begum—with all my love.

—K.A.M.

Note to Reader

For ease of use, this print edition of *OCP Oracle Certified Professional Java SE 17 Developer (Exam 1Z0-829) Programmer's Guide* has been split into two volumes. Both volumes include a complete index of the book.

Contents Overview
Volume I (Chapters 1–15)

Contents Overview
Volume II (Chapters 16–Index)

Contents

Volumes I and II

Figures

Tables

Examples

Foreword

In over 25 years of teaching Java, one of the recurring questions I am asked is why one would bother to pursue Java certification. Obviously one answer is that it might be helpful in pursuit of a job, or a better job, as a Java programmer. But whether that is relevant is dependent on the job market. There is another answer that does not depend on the ever-changing ratio of applicants to vacancies, and it is the answer that I have always preferred. That answer is that it is good for anyone who claims to take a skill seriously to do two things. One is to be measured by the standards of one's peers, and the other is to push oneself to learn and improve continuously. Being satisfied with "good enough" must surely be a sign of some degree of mediocrity.

These days Java training is widely available from many sources (including video-based training that I offer). Each has its pros and cons, but what makes Khalid and Vasily's book stand out is probably the thoroughness of the treatment that is offered in these pages. Khalid has a long history teaching at the university level, and good teaching is a very different skill from merely being an expert. Far too much of what we are offered as training or self-study material these days is, on closer analysis, simply an enumeration of facts. Good teaching requires building not just knowledge but understanding, layer upon layer, so that it sticks.

One aspect of teaching and learning that is sadly little understood is how we learn. If you want to get better at lifting heavy weights, most of us would recognize that somewhere in the process, you have to do just that: lift heavy weights. That is essentially true of all human skills. We must practice (and practice diligently) those things at which we wish to succeed. In the case of learning, what we want to be able to do is to recall facts and apply them on demand. That means, quite literally, that we must practice the act of recalling those facts. To this end, you will find extensive review questions between these covers. These will provide you with the opportunity to practice the act of recall and thereby solidify your knowledge and understanding. That way, not only can you expect to pass what is undoubtedly a challenging exam, but you can also expect to become a better Java programmer.

Good luck in your study!

—*Simon Roberts*
President, Dancing Cloud Services, LLC

Preface

ooooooooooooooooooooooooooooooooooooooooooooooooooooooooooooooooooooo

Writing This Book

Java has been around for over 25 years. During this time, the Java ecosystem has evolved to become the platform of choice for developing software systems, and the Java certification has evolved with it. The goal of this book is twofold: to provide a comprehensive guide, not only for learning Java, and also to nail the Java certification exams.

This book provides extensive coverage for the following Java certifications:

- *Oracle Certified Professional (OCP), Java SE 17 Developer*, and its required exam, *Java SE 17 Developer (1Z0-829)* (for details, see Appendix B)
- *Oracle Certified Professional (OCP), Java SE 11 Developer*, and its required exam, *Java SE 11 Developer (1Z0-819)* (for details, see Appendix C)

The exam syllabus is defined by a set of *exam objectives*. The exam objectives have evolved to become more high-level, with a smattering of specific topics, leaving plenty of room for interpretation as to which topics are covered by an exam objective. The scope of the exam objectives is thus very difficult to define, and entails exhaustive coverage of the Java language features and its many APIs to be on the safe side. This factor is the major cause of the considerable size of this book.

Our approach to writing this book has not changed from the one we employed for our previous books, mainly because it has proved successful. The emphasis remains on analyzing code scenarios, rather than esoteric syntax of individual language constructs. The exam continues to require actual experience with the language, not just mere recitation of facts. We still claim that proficiency in the language is the key to success.

Since the exam emphasizes the core features of Java, this book provides in-depth coverage of topics related to those features.This book is also no different from our previous books in one other important aspect: It is a one-stop guide, providing a mixture of theory and practice that enables readers to prepare for the exam. It can be used to learn Java and to prepare for the exam. After the exam is passed, it can also be used as a handy reference for the Java language.

All elements found in our previous books (e.g., examples, figures, tables, review questions, mock exam questions) can be found in this one as well. We continue to use UML (Unified Modeling Language) extensively to illustrate concepts and language constructs, and all numbered examples continue to be complete Java programs ready for experimentation.

With that, dear reader, we wish you all the best should you decide to go down the path of Java certification. May your loops terminate and your exceptions get caught!

About This Book

This book provides extensive coverage of the core features of the Java programming language and its core application programming interface (API). The book is primarily intended for professionals who want to prepare for the *Java SE 17* or *Java SE 11 Developer Exams*, but it is readily accessible to any programmer who wants to master the language. For both purposes, it provides in-depth coverage of essential features of the language and its core API.

The demand for well-trained and highly skilled Java programmers remains unabated. Oracle offers many Java certifications that professionals can take to validate their skills (see https://education.oracle.com). The certification provides members of the IT industry with a standard to use when hiring such professionals, and it allows professionals to turn their Java skills into credentials that are important for career advancement.

The book provides extensive coverage of all the objectives defined by Oracle for both the *Java SE 17* and *Java SE 11 Developer Exams*. The exam objectives are selective, however, and do not include many of the essential features of Java. This book covers many additional topics that every Java programmer should master to be truly proficient. In this regard, the book is a comprehensive primer for learning the Java programming language. After mastering the language by working through this book, the reader can confidently sit for the exams.

This book is *not* a complete reference for Java, as it does not attempt to list every member of every class from the Java SE Platform API documentation. The purpose is not to document the Java SE Platform API. The emphasis is more on the Java programming language features—their syntax and correct usage through code examples—and less on teaching programming techniques.

The book assumes little background in programming. We believe the exam is accessible to any programmer who works through the book. A Java programmer can easily skip over material that is well understood and concentrate on parts that need reinforcing, whereas a programmer new to Java will find the concepts explained from basic principles.

Each topic is explained and discussed thoroughly with examples, and is backed by review questions to reinforce the concepts. The book is not biased toward any particular platform, but provides platform-specific details where necessary.

Using This Book

The reader can choose a linear or a nonlinear route through the book, depending on their programming background. Non-Java programmers wishing to migrate to Java can read Chapter 1, which provides a short introduction to object-oriented programming concepts, and the procedure for compiling and running Java applications. For those preparing for any of the Developer exams, the book has a separate appendix (Appendix A) providing all the pertinent information on preparing for and taking the exams.

Cross-references are provided where necessary to indicate the relationships among the various constructs of the language. To understand a language construct, all pertinent details are provided where the construct is covered, but in addition, cross-references are provided to indicate its relationship to other constructs. Sometimes it is necessary to postpone discussion of certain aspects of a topic if they depend on concepts that have not yet been covered in the book. A typical example is the consequences of object-oriented programming concepts (e.g., inheritance) on the member declarations that can occur in a class. This approach can result in forward references in the initial chapters of the book.

The table of contents; listings of tables, examples, and figures; and a comprehensive index facilitate locating topics discussed in the book.

In particular, we draw attention to the following features of the book:

 ## Chapter Topics

Each chapter starts with a short summary of the topics covered in the chapter, pointing out the major concepts that are introduced.

Developer Exam Objectives
[0.1] Exam objectives that are covered in each chapter are stated clearly at the beginning of every chapter.
[0.2] The number in front of the objective identifies the exam objective, as defined by Oracle. The objectives are organized into major sections, detailing the curriculum for the exam.
[0.3] The objectives for the *Java SE 17* and *Java SE 11 Developer Exams* are reproduced verbatim in Appendix B and Appendix C, respectively. These appendices also map each exam objective to relevant chapters and sections in the book.

Supplementary Topics
• Supplementary topics are Java topics that are *not* on the exam per se, but which the candidate is expected to know.
• Any supplementary topic is listed as a bullet at the beginning of the chapter.

Review Questions

Review questions are provided after every major topic to test and reinforce the material. The review questions predominantly reflect the kind of multiple-choice questions that can be asked on the actual exam. On the exam, the exact number of answers to choose for each question is explicitly stated. The review questions in this book follow that practice.

Many questions on the actual exam contain code snippets with line numbers to indicate that complete implementation is not provided, and that the necessary missing code to compile and run the code snippets can be assumed. The review questions in this book provide complete code implementations where possible, so that the code can be readily compiled and run.

Annotated answers to the review questions are provided in Appendix D.

Example 0.1   *Example Source Code*

We encourage readers to experiment with the code examples to reinforce the material in the book. The source code for the examples can be downloaded from the companion book website (see p. xlv), and readily imported into Eclipse IDE 2022-06.

Java code in the book is presented in a `monospaced` font. Lines of code in the examples or in code snippets are referenced in the text by a number, which is specified by using a single-line comment in the code. For example, in the following code snippet, the call to the method `doSomethingInteresting()` at (1) does something interesting:

```
// ...
doSomethingInteresting();                               // (1)
// ...
```

Names of classes and interfaces start with an uppercase letter. Names of packages, variables, and methods start with a lowercase letter. Constants are in all uppercase letters. Interface names begin with the prefix I, when it makes sense to distinguish them from class names. Coding conventions are followed, except when we have had to deviate from these conventions in the interest of space or clarity.

Mock Exam

The mock exam for Java SE 17 in Appendix E should be attempted when the reader feels confident about the topics on the exam. It is highly recommended to read Appendix A before attempting the mock exam, as Appendix A contains pertinent information about the questions to expect on the actual exam. Each multiple-choice question in the mock exam explicitly states how many answers are applicable for a given question, as is the case on the actual exam. Annotated answers to the questions in the mock exam are provided in Appendix F.

Java SE Platform API Documentation

A vertical gray bar is used to highlight methods and fields found in the classes of the Java SE Platform API.

Any explanation following the API information is also similarly highlighted.

To obtain the maximum benefit from using this book in preparing for the *Java SE 17* and *Java SE 11 Developer Exams*, we strongly recommend installing the latest version (Release 17 or newer) of the JDK and its accompanying API documentation. The book focuses solely on Java SE 17 and Java SE 11, and does not acknowledge other versions.

Book Website

This book is backed by a website:

https://www.mughal.no/jse17ocp/

Auxiliary material on the website includes the following:

- Source code for all the examples in the book
- Annotated answers to the reviews questions in the book
- Annotated answers to the mock exam in the book
- Table of contents, sample chapters, and index from the book
- Content specific for the *Java SE 17* and *Java SE 11 Developer Exams*
- Errata for the book
- Links to miscellaneous Java resources (e.g., certification, discussion groups, and tools)

Information about the Java Standard Edition (SE) and its documentation can be found at the following website:

www.oracle.com/technetwork/java/javase/overview/index.html

The current authoritative technical reference for the Java programming language, *The Java® Language Specification: Java SE 17 Edition*, can be found at this website:

http://docs.oracle.com/javase/specs/index.html

Request for Feedback

Considerable effort has been made to ensure the accuracy of the content of this book. All code examples (including code fragments) have been compiled and tested on various platforms. In the final analysis, any errors remaining are the sole responsibility of the principal author.

Any questions, comments, suggestions, and corrections are welcome. Let us know whether the book was helpful (or not) for your purpose. Any feedback is valuable.

The principal author and the co-author can be reached at the following email addresses, respectively:

```
khalid@mughal.no
vasiliy.a.strelnikov@oracle.com
```

About the Authors

Khalid A. Mughal

Khalid A. Mughal is the principal author of this book, primarily responsible for writing the material covering the Java topics. He is also the principal author of three other books on previous versions of the Java certification exam: Java SE 8 OCA (1Z0-808), Java SE 6 (1Z0-851), and SCPJ2 1.4 (CX-310-035).

Khalid is an associate professor emeritus at the Department of Informatics at the University of Bergen, Norway, where he was responsible for designing and implementing various courses in informatics. Over the years, he has taught programming (primarily Java), software engineering (object-oriented system development), databases (data modeling and database management systems), compiler techniques, web application development, and software security courses. For 15 years, he was responsible for developing and running web-based programming courses in Java, which were offered to off-campus students. He has also given numerous courses and seminars at various levels in object-oriented programming and system development using Java and Java-related technologies, both at the University of Bergen and various other universities in Norway and East Africa, and also for the IT industry.

Vasily A. Strelnikov

Vasily Strelnikov is primarily responsible for developing new review questions for the chapters contained in this book.

Vasily is a senior principal OCI (Oracle Cloud Infrastructure) solution specialist, working at Oracle for more than 26 years. He is a co-author of the Java EE 7, Java SE 8, Java SE 11, and Java SE 17 Certification exams. He has designed multiple Java courses that are offered by Oracle: Java SE 17 Programming Complete, Java SE 11 Programming Complete, and Java SE 8 Certification Preparation Seminar. He has also created the Developing Applications for the Java EE 7 Platform training at Oracle. Vasily has over 20 years of experience in Java. He specializes in Java middleware application development and web services.

Acknowledgments

First of all, we would like to acknowledge the contribution that Rolf W. Rasmussen at vizrt made in earlier Java certification books that we wrote together. Some of that contribution still permeates this edition as well.

At Pearson, senior executive editor Greg Doench was once again at the helm. He managed the long process of publishing this book. Senior content producer Julie Nahil was again the in-house contact at Pearson, professionally and efficiently managing production of the book. Audrey Doyle did a truly marvelous job copyediting the book. She scrutinized every sentence with a meticulous eye—and taught us a thing or two about the English language. The folks at codeMantra did the critical proofreading, endorsing the book with a quality assurance stamp. Rob Mauhar at The CIP Group performed the typesetting wizardry necessary to give the book its professional look. Our sincere thanks to Greg, Julie, Audrey, Rob, the folks at codeMantra, and all those behind the scenes at Pearson, who helped to make this publication see the light of day.

For the technical review of the book, we were lucky to have two Java gurus who agreed to take on the task.

- Mikalai Zaikin is a lead Java developer at IBA Lithuania, and is currently located in Vilnius. He has helped Oracle with development of Java certification exams and has also been a technical reviewer of several Java certification books. He also contributes to the Java Quiz column for Oracle's Java Magazine in collaboration with Simon Roberts.

- Ankit Garg is currently Vice President at Morgan-Stanley, Bengaluru, India, and a Sheriff (i.e., Moderator) for various Java Forums at coderanch.com. He is a Java developer with many years' experience in several Java-related technologies (e.g., Java SE, Java EE, and Spring). He is also a certified Java Programmer and Web Component Developer.

Without doubt, both Mikalai and Ankit have an eye for detail. It is no exaggeration to say that their feedback has been invaluable in improving the quality of this book at all levels. Our most sincere thanks to both Mikalai and Ankit for the many excellent comments and suggestions, and above all, for weeding out numerous pesky errors in the manuscript.

Kristian Berg and Morten Nygaard Åsnes were kind enough to review two chapters each and provide useful feedback, for which we are very grateful.

Great effort has been made to eliminate mistakes and errors in this book. We accept full responsibility for any remaining oversights. We hope that when our diligent readers find any, they will bring them to our attention.

Without family support this edition would still be a fantasy, and we are very grateful to our families for putting up with us when we were burning the midnight oil. Hopefully we can get our family life back now that this book is out the door.

—*Khalid A. Mughal*
December 2, 2022
Bergen, Norway

Basics of Java Programming

1

 Chapter Topics

- Factors and features of the Java ecosystem that have contributed to its evolution and success
- Basic terminology and concepts in Java, and how the language supports object-oriented programming (OOP)
- Understand the distinction between a class and an object
- Basics of how to create objects, access their fields and call methods on them
- Essential elements of a Java program
- Compiling and running Java programs
- Executing single-file source-code programs
- Brief introduction to the Java Shell tool (jshell)
- Formatting and printing values to the terminal window

Java SE 17 Developer Exam Objectives	
[3.2] Create classes and records, and define and use instance and static fields and methods, constructors, and instance and static initializers	§1.2, p. 5 §1.3, p. 8 §1.4, p. 9 §1.5, p. 10
○ Basic terminology for declaring and using classes and class members is introduced in this chapter.	
○ For details on classes, fields, methods, and constructors, see Chapter 3, p. 97.	
○ For record classes, see §5.14, p. 299.	
○ For instance and static initializers, see §10.5, p. 540.	

Java SE 11 Developer Exam Objectives	
[3.2] Define and use fields and methods, including instance, static and overloaded methods	§1.2, p. 5 §1.3, p. 8 §1.4, p. 9 §1.5, p. 10
○ Basic terminology for declaring and using classes and class members is introduced in this chapter.	
○ For details on classes, fields, methods, and constructors, see Chapter 3, p. 97.	

Before embarking on the road to Java certification, it is important to understand the basic terminology and concepts in Java. No particular exam objective is covered in this chapter. The emphasis is on providing an introduction to Java and core concepts in object-oriented programming (OOP). In-depth coverage of the concepts introduced will follow in due course in subsequent chapters.

The basic elements of a Java program are introduced in this chapter. The old adage that practice makes perfect is certainly true when learning a programming language. We highly encourage programming on the computer. The mechanics of compiling and running a Java program are provided in this chapter. We begin with an overview of factors that make Java the platform of choice for enterprises and developers.

1.1 The Java Ecosystem

Since its initial release as Java Development Kit 1.0 (JDK 1.0) in 1996, the name Java has become synonymous with a thriving ecosystem that provides the components and the tools necessary for developing systems for today's multicore world. Its diverse community, comprising a multitude of volunteers, organizations, and corporations, continues to fuel its evolution and grow with its success. Many free and open source technologies now exist that are well proven, mature, and supported, making their adoption less daunting. These tools and frameworks provide support for all phases of the software development lifecycle and beyond.

There are different Java platforms, each targeting different application domains:

- Java SE (Standard Edition): designed for developing desktop and server environments
- Java EE, also known as Jakarta EE (Enterprise Edition): designed for developing enterprise applications
- Java ME (Micro Edition): designed for embedded systems, such as mobile devices and set-top boxes
- Java Card: designed for tiny memory footprint devices, such as smart cards

Each platform provides a hardware/operating system–specific JVM and an API (*application programming interface*) to develop applications for that platform. The Java SE platform provides the core functionality of the language. The Java EE platform is a superset of the Java SE platform and, as the most extensive of the three platforms, targets enterprise application development. The Java ME platform is a subset of the Java SE platform, having a small footprint, and is suitable for developing mobile and embedded applications. The Java Card platform allows development of embedded applications that have a very tiny memory footprint, targeting devices like smart cards. The upshot of this classification is that a Java program developed for one Java platform will not necessarily run under the JVM of another Java platform. The JVM must be compatible with the Java platform that was used to develop the application.

The API and the tools for developing and running Java applications are bundled together as the JDK. Starting with Java 11, JRE (Java Runtime Environment) is no longer available as a stand-alone bundle providing runtime support for execution of Java programs, but it continues to be a subset of the now modular JDK. As before, one needs to install the JDK to both develop and run Java programs. However, to deploy Java programs, the JDK tool `jlink` can be used to create a runtime image that includes the program code and the necessary runtime support to run the program—a topic that we will get to when we discuss modules.

We highly recommend installing the JDK for Java SE 17 depending on the hardware and operating system. Although newer versions of Java are released periodically, Java SE 17 is readily available as an LTS (*long-term support*) release, and is the subject of this book.

As of Java SE 17, Oracle is making the Oracle JDK available for free under the *Oracle No-Fee Terms and Conditions* (NFTC) license. Although subject to the conditions, it permits free use for *all* users.

Key Features of Java

The rest of this section summarizes some of the factors that have contributed to the evolution of Java from an object-oriented programming language to a full-fledged ecosystem for developing all sorts of systems, including large-scale business systems and embedded systems for portable computing devices. A lot of jargon is used in this section and it might be difficult to understand at the first reading, so we recommend coming back after working through the book to appreciate the factors that have contributed to the success of Java.

Multi-paradigm Programming

The Java programming language supports the *object-oriented programming paradigm*, in which the properties of an object and its behavior are encapsulated in the object. The properties and the behavior are represented by the fields and the methods of the object, respectively. The objects communicate through method calls in a procedural manner—in other words, Java also incorporates the *procedural programming paradigm*. Encapsulation ensures that objects are immune to tampering except when manipulated through their public interface. Encapsulation exposes only *what* an object does and not *how* it does it, so that its implementation can be changed with minimal impact on its clients. The later sections in this chapter provide an overview of basic concepts of object-oriented programming, such as inheritance and aggregation, and subsequent chapters will expand on this topic.

Java has also evolved to support the *functional-style programming paradigm* with the introduction of lambda expressions and their implementation using functional interfaces. This topic will be thoroughly explored in this book.

Above all, object-oriented system development promotes code reuse where existing classes can be reused to implement new classes. Its module facility facilitates implementation of large systems, allowing their decomposition into manageable subsystems, as we will see when we discuss modules.

Bytecode Interpreted by the JVM

Java programs are compiled to bytecode that is interpreted by the JVM. Various optimization technologies (e.g., just-in-time [JIT] delivery) have led to the JVM becoming a lean and mean virtual machine with regard to performance, stability, and security. Many other languages, such as Scala, Groovy, and Clojure, now compile to bytecode and seamlessly execute on the JVM. The JVM has thus evolved into an ecosystem in its own right.

Architecture-Neutral and Portable Bytecode

The often-cited slogan "Write once, run everywhere" is true only if a compatible JVM is available for the hardware and software platform. In other words, to run Java SE applications under Windows 10 on a 64-bit hardware architecture, the right JVM must be installed. Fortunately, the JVM has been ported to run under most platforms and operating systems that exist today, including hardware devices such as smart cards, mobile devices, and home appliances.

The specification of the bytecode is architecture neutral, meaning it is independent of any hardware architecture. It is executed by a readily available hardware and operating system–specific JVM. The portability of the Java bytecode thus eases the burden of cross-platform system development.

Simplicity

The language design of Java has been driven by a desire to simplify the programming process. Although Java borrows heavily from the C++ programming language, certain features that were deemed problematic were not incorporated into its design. For example, Java does not have a preprocessor, and it does not allow pointer handling, user-defined operator overloading, or multiple class inheritance.

Java opted for automatic garbage collection, which frees the programmer from dealing with many issues related to memory management, such as memory leaks.

However, the jury is still out on whether the syntax of nested classes or introduction of wild cards for generics can be considered simple.

The introduction of functional-style features has enhanced Java's appeal, and the potential of its module system is yet to be seen.

Dynamic and Distributed

The JVM can dynamically load class libraries from the local file system as well as from machines on the network, when those libraries are needed at runtime. This feature facilitates linking the code as and when necessary during the execution of a program. It is also possible to programmatically query a class or an object at runtime about its meta-information, such as its methods and fields.

Java provides extensive support for networking to build distributed systems, where objects are able to communicate across networks using various communication protocols and technologies, such as Remote Method Invocation (RMI) and socket connections.

Robust and Secure

Java promotes the development of reliable, robust, and secure systems. It is a strong statically typed language: The compiler guarantees runtime execution if the code compiles without errors. Runtime index checks for arrays and strings, automatic garbage collection, and elimination of pointers are some of the features of Java that promote reliability. The exception handling feature of Java is without a doubt the main factor that facilitates the development of robust systems. And the module system further enhances encapsulation and configuration.

Java provides multilevel protection from malicious code. The language does not allow direct access to memory. A bytecode verifier determines whether any untrusted code loaded in the JVM is safe. The sandbox model is used to confine and execute any untrusted code, limiting the damage that such code can cause. These features, among others, are provided by a comprehensive Java security model to ensure that application code executes securely in the JVM.

High Performance and Multithreaded

The performance of Java programs has improved significantly with various optimizations that are applied to the bytecode at runtime by the JVM. The JIT feature monitors the program at runtime to identify performance-critical bytecode (called *hotspots*) that can be optimized. Such code is usually translated to machine code to boost performance. The performance achieved by the JVM is a balance between native code execution and interpretation of fully scripted languages, which fortunately is adequate for many applications.

Java has always provided high-level support for multithreading, allowing multiple threads of execution to perform different tasks concurrently in an application. It has risen to the new challenges that have emerged in recent years to harness the increased computing power made available by multicore architectures. Functional programming, in which computation is treated as side-effects-free evaluation of functions, is seen as a boon to meet these challenges. Java brings elements of functional-style programming into the language, providing language constructs (lambda expressions and functional interfaces) and API support (through its Concurrent and Stream APIs) to efficiently utilize the many cores to process large amounts of data in parallel.

1.2 Classes

One of the fundamental ways in which we handle complexity is by using *abstractions*. An abstraction denotes the essential properties and behaviors of an object that differentiate it from other objects. The essence of OOP is modeling abstractions, using classes and objects. The hardest part of this endeavor is coming up with the right abstractions.

A *class* denotes a category of objects, and acts as a blueprint for creating objects. A class models an abstraction by defining the properties and behaviors of the objects representing the abstraction. An *object* exhibits the *properties* and *behaviors* defined by its class. The properties of an object of a class are also called *attributes*, and are defined by fields in Java. A *field* in a class is a variable that can store a value that represents a particular property of an object. The behaviors of an object of a class are also known as *operations*, and are defined using *methods* in Java. Fields and methods in a class declaration are collectively called *members*.

An important distinction is made between the *contract* and the *implementation* that a class provides for its objects. The contract defines *which* services are provided, and the implementation defines *how* these services are provided by the class. Clients (i.e., other objects) need only know the contract of an object, and not its implementation, to avail themselves of the object's services.

As an example, we will implement a class that models the abstraction of a point as (x, y)-coordinates in a two-dimensional plane. The class Point2D will use two int fields x and y to store the coordinates. Using simplified Unified Modeling Language (UML) notation, the class Point2D is graphically depicted in Figure 1.1, which models the abstraction. Both fields, with their type and method names and their return value type, are shown in Figure 1.1a.

Figure 1.1   *UML Notation for Classes*

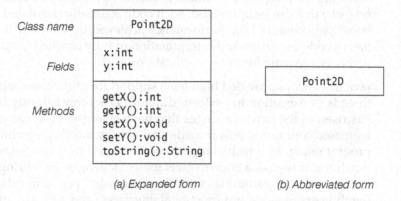

(a) Expanded form   (b) Abbreviated form

Declaring Members: Fields and Methods

Example 1.1 shows the declaration of the class Point2D depicted in Figure 1.1. Its intention is to illustrate the salient features of a class declaration in Java, rather than an industrial-strength implementation. We will come back to the nitty-gritty of the Java syntax in subsequent chapters.

In Example 1.1, the character sequence // in the code indicates the start of a *single-line comment* that can be used to document the code. All characters after this sequence and to the end of the line are ignored by the compiler.

A class declaration can contain member declarations that define the fields and the methods of the objects the class represents. In the case of the class Point2D, it has the following two fields declared at (1):

- x, which is the x-coordinate of a point
- y, which is the y-coordinate of a point

The class Point2D has five methods, declared at (3), that implement the essential operations provided by a point:

- getX() returns the x-coordinate of the point.
- getY() returns the y-coordinate of the point.
- setX() sets the x-coordinate to the value passed to the method.
- setY() sets the y-coordinate to the value passed to the method.
- toString() returns a string with the coordinate values formatted as "(x,y)".

The class declaration also has a method-like declaration at (2) with the same name as the class. Such declarations are called *constructors*. As we shall see, a constructor is executed when an object is created from the class. However, the implementation details in the example are not important for the present discussion.

Example 1.1   *Basic Elements of a Class Declaration*

```java
// File: Point2D.java
public class Point2D {              // Class name
  // Class Member Declarations

  // Fields:                                                (1)
  private int x;      // The x-coordinate
  private int y;      // The y-coordinate

  // Constructor:                                           (2)
  public Point2D(int xCoord, int yCoord) {
    x = xCoord;
    y = yCoord;
  }

  // Methods:                                               (3)
  public int  getX()            { return x; }
  public int  getY()            { return y; }
  public void setX(int xCoord) { x = xCoord; }
  public void setY(int yCoord) { y = yCoord; }
  public String toString() { return "(" + x + "," + y + ")"; } // Format: (x,y)
}
```

1.3 Objects

Class Instantiation, Reference Values, and References

The process of creating objects from a class is called *instantiation*. An *object* is an instance of a class. The object is constructed using the class as a blueprint and is a concrete instance of the abstraction that the class represents. An object must be created before it can be used in a program.

A *reference value* is returned when an object is created. A reference value uniquely denotes a particular object. A *variable* denotes a location in memory where a value can be stored. An *object reference* (or simply *reference*) is a variable that can store a reference value. Thus a reference provides a handle to an object, as it can indirectly denote an object whose reference value it holds. In Java, an object can only be manipulated by a reference that holds its reference value. Direct access to the reference value is not permitted.

This setup for manipulating objects requires that a reference be declared, a class be instantiated to create an object, and the reference value of the object created be stored in the reference. These steps are accomplished by a *declaration statement*:

```
Point2D p1 = new Point2D(10, 20);  // A point with coordinates (10,20)
```

In the preceding declaration statement, the left-hand side of the *assignment operator* (=) declares that p1 is a reference of class Point2D. The reference p1, therefore, can refer to objects of class Point2D.

The right-hand side of the assignment operator creates an object of class Point2D. This step involves using the new operator in conjunction with a call to a constructor of the class (new Point2D(10, 20)). The new operator creates an instance of the Point2D class and returns the reference value of this instance. The arguments passed in the constructor call are used to initialize the x and the y fields, respectively. The assignment operator stores the reference value in the reference p1 declared on the left-hand side of the assignment operator. The reference p1 can now be used to manipulate the object whose reference value it holds.

Analogously, the following declaration statement declares the reference p2 to be of class Point2D, creates an object of class Point2D, and assigns its reference value to the reference p2:

```
Point2D p2 = new Point2D(5, 15);  // A point with coordinates (5,15)
```

Each object that is created has its own copy of the fields declared in the class declaration. That is, the two point objects, referenced by p1 and p2, will have their own x and y fields. The fields of an object are also called *instance variables*. The values of the instance variables in an object constitute its *state*. Two distinct objects can have the same state if their instance variables have the same values.

The purpose of the constructor call on the right-hand side of the new operator is to initialize the fields of the newly created object. In this particular case, for each new

Point2D object created using the new operator, the constructor at (2) in Example 1.1 creates the x and y fields and initializes them with the arguments passed.

Figure 1.2 shows the UML notation for objects. The graphical representation of an object is very similar to that of a class. Figure 1.2 shows the canonical notation, where the name of the reference denoting the object is prefixed to the class name with a colon (:). If the name of the reference is omitted, as in Figure 1.2b, this denotes an anonymous object. Since objects in Java do not have names, but rather are denoted by references, a more elaborate notation is shown in Figure 1.2c, where references of the Point2D class explicitly refer to Point2D objects. In most cases, the more compact notation will suffice.

Figure 1.2 *UML Notation for Objects*

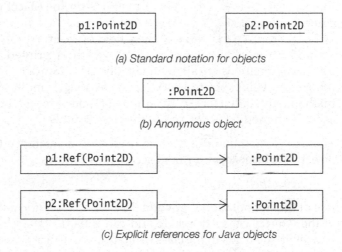

The methods of an object define its behavior; such methods are called *instance methods*. It is important to note that these methods pertain to each object of the class. In contrast to the instance variables, the *implementation* of the methods is shared by all instances of the class. Instance variables and instance methods, which belong to objects, are collectively called *instance members*, to distinguish them from *static members* (p. 10), which only belong to the class.

Invoking Methods

Objects communicate by calling methods on each other. As a consequence, an object can be made to exhibit a particular behavior by calling the appropriate method on the object. This is achieved by a *method call* whose basic form is the following: a reference that refers to the object, the binary dot (.) operator, and the

1.4 Instance Members

name of method to be invoked, together with a list of any arguments required by
the method.

reference.methodName(listOfArguments)

The method invoked on the object can also return results back to its caller, via a single return value. The method called must be one that is defined for the object;
otherwise, the compiler reports an error.

```
Point2D point = new Point2D(-1, -4);    // Creates a point with coordinates (-1,-4)
point.setX(-2);                         // (1) The x field is set to the value -2
int yCoord = point.getY();              // (2) Returns the value -4 of the y field
System.out.println(point.toString());   // (3) Prints: (-2,-4)
point.distanceFromOrigin();             // (4) Compile-time error: No such method.
```

The sample code above invokes methods on the object denoted by the reference
point. The method call at (1) sets the value of the x field of point, and the method
call at (2) returns the value of the y field of point. At (3), the call to the toString()
method returns the string "(-2,-4)" which is printed. The setX(), getY(), and
toString() methods are all defined in the class Point2D. The setX() method does not
return any value, but the getY() and toString() methods do. Trying to invoke a
method named distanceFromOrigin() at (4) on point results in a compile-time error,
as no such method is defined in the class Point2D.

The dot (.) notation can also be used with a reference to access the fields of an
object. The basic form for field access is as follows:

reference.fieldName

Use of the dot notation is governed by the *accessibility* of the member. The methods
of the Point2D class are public and can thus be called by the clients of the class.
However, the fields in the class Point2D have private access, indicating that they are
not accessible from outside the class. Thus the code below at (1) in a client of the
Point2D class will not compile. Typically, a class provides public methods to access
values in its private fields, as class Point2D does.

```
System.out.println(point.x);        // (1) Compile-time error: x is not accessible.
System.out.println(point.getX());   // OK.
```

1.5 Static Members

In some cases, certain members should belong only to the class; that is, they should
not be part of any instance of the class. Such members are called *static members*. Fields
and methods that are static members are easily distinguishable in a class declaration as
they must always be declared with the keyword static.

Figure 1.3 shows the class diagram for the class Point2D. It has been augmented by
three static members, whose names are underlined to distinguish them from
instance members. The augmented declaration of the Point2D class is given in
Example 1.2.

Figure 1.3   *Class Diagram Showing Static Members of a Class*

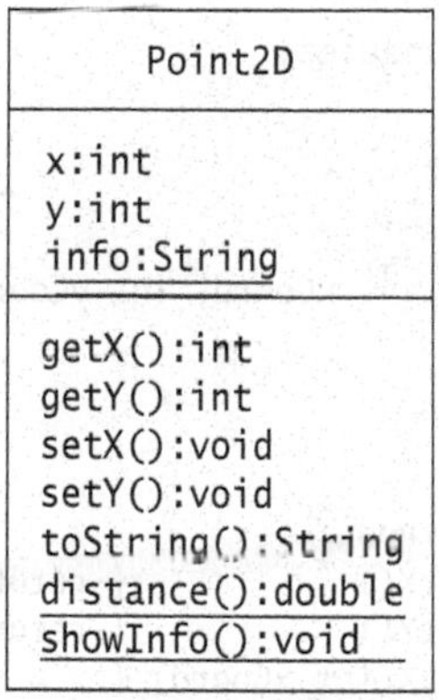

```
┌─────────────────────────┐
│         Point2D         │
├─────────────────────────┤
│ x:int                   │
│ y:int                   │
│ info:String             │
├─────────────────────────┤
│ getX():int              │
│ getY():int              │
│ setX():void             │
│ setY():void             │
│ toString():String       │
│ distance():double       │
│ showInfo():void         │
└─────────────────────────┘
```

In Example 1.2, the field info at (1) is declared as a *static variable*. This field has information about the purpose of the class that the class can share with its clients. A static variable belongs to the class, rather than to any specific object of the class. It will be allocated in the class and initialized to the string specified in its declaration when the class is loaded. Declaring the info field as static makes sense, as it is unnecessary that every object of the class Point2D should have a copy of this information.

```
private static String info = "A point represented by (x,y)-coordinates.";
```

In Example 1.2, the two methods distance() and showInfo() at (5) are *static methods* belonging to the class. Both are declared with the keyword static. The static method distance() calculates and returns the distance between two points passed as arguments to the method. The static method showInfo() prints the string with the information referenced by the static variable info. These methods belong to the class, rather than to any specific objects of the class.

Clients can access static members in the class by using the class name. The following code invokes the static method distance() in the class Point2D:

```
double d = Point2D.distance(p1, p2); // Class name to invoke static method
```

Static members can also be accessed via object references, although doing so is not encouraged:

```
p1.showInfo();                      // Reference invokes static method
```

Static members in a class can be accessed both by the class name and via object references, but instance members can be accessed only by object references.

- -

Example 1.2   *Static Members in Class Declaration*

```
// File: Point2D.java
public class Point2D {                  // Class name
  // Class Member Declarations
```

```
// Static variable:                                               (1)
private static String info = "A 2D point represented by (x,y)-coordinates.";

// Instance variables:                                            (2)
private int x;
private int y;

// Constructor:                                                   (3)
public Point2D(int xCoord, int yCoord) {
  x = xCoord;
  y = yCoord;
}

// Instance methods:                                              (4)
public int  getX()            { return x; }
public int  getY()            { return y; }
public void setX(int xCoord) { x = xCoord; }
public void setY(int yCoord) { y = yCoord; }
public String toString() { return "(" + x + "," + y + ")"; } // Format: (x,y)

// Static methods:                                                (5)
public static double distance(Point2D p1, Point2D p2) {
  int xDiff = p1.x - p2.x;
  int yDiff = p1.y - p2.y;
  return Math.sqrt(xDiff*xDiff + yDiff*yDiff);
}
public static void showInfo() { System.out.println(info); }
}
```

Figure 1.4 shows the classification of the members in the class Point2D, using the terminology we have introduced so far. Table 1.1 provides a summary of the terminology used in defining members of a class.

Figure 1.4 *Members of a Class*

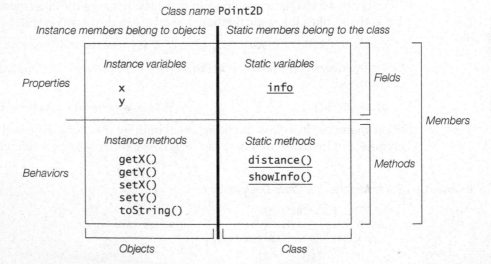

Table 1.1 *Terminology for Class Members*

Instance members	The instance variables and instance methods of an object. They can be accessed or invoked only through an object reference.
Instance variable	A field that is allocated when the class is instantiated (i.e., when an object of the class is created). Also called a *non-static field* or just a *field* when the context is obvious.
Instance method	A method that belongs to an instance of the class. Objects of the same class share its implementation.
Static members	The static variables and static methods of a class. They can be accessed or invoked either by using the class name or through an object reference.
Static variable	A field that is allocated when the class is loaded. It belongs to the class, and not to any specific object of the class. Also called a *static field* or a *class variable*.
Static method	A method that belongs to the class, and not to any object of the class. Also called a *class method*.

1.6 Inheritance

There are two fundamental mechanisms for building new classes from existing ones: *inheritance* and *aggregation* (p. 16). It makes sense to *inherit* from an existing class Vehicle to define a class Car, since a car is a vehicle. The class Vehicle has several *parts*; therefore, it makes sense to define a *composite object* of the class Vehicle that has *constituent objects* of such classes as Engine, Axle, and GearBox, which make up a vehicle.

Inheritance is illustrated here by an example that implements a point in three-dimensional space—that is, a 3D point represented by (x, y, z)-coordinates. We can derive the 3D point from the Point2D class. This 3D point will have all the properties and behaviors of the Point2D class, along with the additional third dimension. This relationship is shown in Figure 1.5 and implemented in Example 1.3. The class Point3D is called the *subclass*, and the class Point2D is called the *superclass*. The Point2D class is a *generalization* for points, whereas the class Point3D is a *specialization* of points that have three coordinates.

In Java, deriving a new class from an existing class requires the use of the extends clause in the subclass declaration. A subclass can *extend* only one superclass. The subclass Point3D extends the Point2D class, shown at (1).

```
public class Point3D extends Point2D {          // (1) Uses extends clause
    // ...
}
```

The Point3D class only declares the z-coordinate at (3), as every object of the subclass will have the x and y fields that are specified in its superclass Point2D. Note that

Figure 1.5   *Class Diagram Depicting Inheritance Relationship*

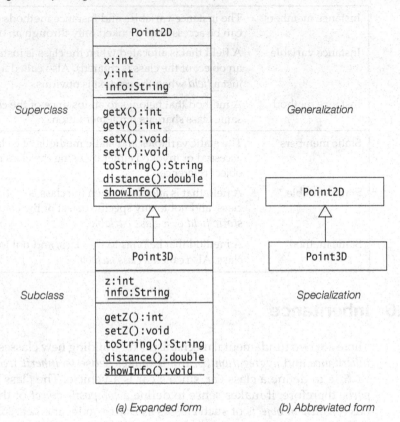

(a) Expanded form   (b) Abbreviated form

these fields are declared private in the superclass Point2D, but they are accessible to a Point3D object indirectly through the public get and set methods for the x- and the y-coordinates in the superclass Point2D. These methods are *inherited* by the Point3D class.

The constructor of the Point3D class at (4) takes three arguments corresponding to the x-, y-, and z-coordinates. The call to super() at (5) results in the constructor of the superclass Point2D being called to initialize the x- and y-coordinates.

It addition, the Point3D class declares methods at (6) to get and set the z-coordinate. It provides its own version of the toString() method to format a point that has three coordinates.

Since calculating the distance is also different in three-dimensional space from that in a two-dimensional plane, the Point3D class provides its own distance() static method at (7). As its objects represent 3D points, it declares its own static field info and provides its own static method showInfo() to print this information.

Example 1.3 *Defining a Subclass*

```java
// File: Point2D.java
public class Point2D {
  // Same as in Example 1.2.
}
```

```java
// File: Point3D.java
public class Point3D extends Point2D {                    // (1) Uses extends clause

  // Static variable:                                               (2)
  private static String info = "A 3D point represented by (x,y,z)-coordinates.";

  // Instance variable:                                             (3)
  private int z;

  // Constructor:                                                   (4)
  public Point3D(int xCoord, int yCoord, int zCoord) {
    super(xCoord, yCoord);                                // (5)
    z = zCoord;
  }

  // Instance methods:                                              (6)
  public int  getZ()          { return z; }
  public void setZ(int zCoord) { z = zCoord; }
  @Override
  public String toString() {
    return "(" + getX() + "," + getY() + "," + z + ")"; // Format: (x,y,z)
  }

  // Static methods:                                                (7)
  public static double distance(Point3D p1, Point3D p2) {
    int xDiff = p1.getX() - p2.getX();
    int yDiff = p1.getY() - p2.getY();
    int zDiff = p1.getZ() - p2.getZ();
    return Math.sqrt(xDiff*xDiff + yDiff*yDiff + zDiff*zDiff);
  }
  public static void showInfo() { System.out.println(info); }
}
```

Objects of the Point3D class will respond just like objects of the Point2D class, but they also have the additional functionality defined in the subclass. References of the class Point3D are used in the code below. The comments indicate in which class a method is invoked. Note that the subclass reference can invoke the inherited get and set methods in the superclass.

```java
Point3D p3A = new Point3D(10, 20, 30);
System.out.println(p3A.toString());          // (10,20,30)      (Point3D)
System.out.println("x: " + p3A.getX());      // x: 10           (Point2D)
System.out.println("y: " + p3A.getY());      // y: 20           (Point2D)
System.out.println("z: " + p3A.getZ());      // z: 30           (Point3D)
```

```
p3A.setX(-10); p3A.setY(-20); p3A.setZ(-30);
System.out.println(p3A.toString());                    // (-10,-20,-30)      (Point3D)

Point3D p3B = new Point3D(30, 20, 10);
System.out.println(p3B.toString());                    // (30,20,10)         (Point3D)
System.out.println(Point3D.distance(p3A, p3B));        // 69.2820323027551 (Point3D)
Point3D.showInfo(); // A 3D point represented by (x,y,z)-coordinates. (Point3D)
```

1.7 Aggregation

An *association* defines a static relationship between objects of two classes. One such association, called *aggregation* (also known as *composition*), expresses how an object uses other objects. Java supports aggregation of objects by reference, since objects cannot contain other objects explicitly. The aggregate object usually has fields that denote its constituent objects. By default, Java uses aggregation when fields denoting objects are declared in a class declaration. Typically, an aggregate object delegates its tasks to its constituent objects.

We illustrate aggregation by implementing a finite-length straight line that has two end points in a two-dimensional plane. We would like to use the class Point2D to implement such a line. A class Line could be implemented by having fields for two Point2D objects that would represent the end points of a line. This aggregate relationship is depicted in Figure 1.6, which shows that a Line object has two Point2D objects, indicated by the diamond notation. The complete declaration of the Line class is shown in Example 1.4. The two fields endPoint1 and endPoint2 declared at (1) represent the two end points. In particular, note the length() method at (2) which delegates the computation of the length to the Point2D.distance() method.

The following code shows how a Line object can be manipulated:

```
Line line1 = new Line(new Point2D(5,6), new Point2D(7,8));
System.out.println(line1.toString());                  // Line[(5,6),(7,8)]
line1.setEndPoint1(new Point2D(11, 12));
line1.setEndPoint2(new Point2D(13, 14));
System.out.println(line1.toString());                  // Line[(11,12),(13,14)]
System.out.println("Length: " + line1.length());       // Length: 2.8284271247461903
```

Figure 1.6 *Class Diagram Depicting Aggregation*

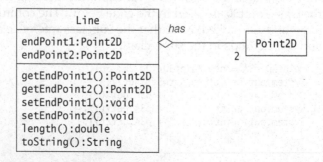

Example 1.4   *Using Aggregation*

```java
// File: Point2D.java
public class Point2D {
  // Same as in Example 1.2.
}
```

```java
// File: Line.java
public class Line {

  // Instance variables:                                                        (1)
  private Point2D endPoint1;
  private Point2D endPoint2;

  // Constructor:
  public Line(Point2D p1, Point2D p2) {
    endPoint1 = p1;
    endPoint2 = p2;
  }

  // Methods:
  public Point2D getEndPoint1() { return endPoint1; }
  public Point2D getEndPoint2() { return endPoint2; }
  public void setEndPoint1(Point2D p1) { endPoint1 = p1; }
  public void setEndPoint2(Point2D p2) { endPoint2 = p2; }
  public double length() {                                          // (2)
    return Point2D.distance(endPoint1, endPoint2);
  }
  public String toString()  {
    return "Line[" + endPoint1 + "," + endPoint2 + "]";
  }
}
```

 Review Questions

1.1   Which statement is true about methods?
Select the one correct answer.

(a) A method is an attribute defining a particular property of an abstraction.
(b) A method is a category of objects.
(c) A method is an operation defining a particular behavior of an abstraction.
(d) A method is a blueprint for defining operations.

1.2   Which statement is true about objects?
Select the one correct answer.

(a) An object is what classes are instantiated from.
(b) An object is an instance of a class.

(c) An object is a blueprint for creating concrete realization of abstractions.
(d) An object is a reference.
(e) An object is a variable.

1.3   Which is the first line of a constructor declaration in the following code?

```
public class Counter {                                          // (1)
  int current, step;
  public Counter(int startValue, int stepValue) {               // (2)
    setCurrent(startValue);                                     // (3)
    setStep(stepValue);
  }
  public int  getCurrent()          { return current; }         // (4)
  public void setCurrent(int value) { current = value; }        // (5)
  public void setStep(int stepValue) { step = stepValue; }      // (6)
}
```

Select the one correct answer.

(a) (1)
(b) (2)
(c) (3)
(d) (4)
(e) (5)
(f) (6)

1.4   Given that Thing is a class, how many objects are created and how many references are declared by the following code?

```
Thing item, stuff;
item = new Thing();
Thing entity = new Thing();
```

Select the two correct answers.

(a) One object is created.
(b) Two objects are created.
(c) Three objects are created.
(d) One reference is declared.
(e) Two references are declared.
(f) Three references are declared.

1.5   Which statement is true about instance members?
Select the one correct answer.

(a) An instance member is also called a static member.
(b) An instance member is always a field.
(c) An instance member is never a method.
(d) An instance member is always a part of an instance.
(e) An instance member always represents an operation.

1.6 How do objects communicate with each other in Java?
Select the one correct answer.

(a) They communicate by modifying each other's fields.
(b) They communicate by modifying the static variables of each other's classes.
(c) They communicate by calling each other's instance methods.
(d) They communicate by calling static methods of each other's classes.

1.7 Given the following code, which of the following statements are true?

```
class A {
  protected int value1;
}

class B extends A {
  int value2;
}
```

Select the two correct answers.

(a) Class A extends class B.
(b) Class B is the superclass of class A.
(c) Class A inherits from class B.
(d) Class B is a subclass of class A.
(e) Objects of class A have a field named value2.
(f) Objects of class B have a field named value1.

1.8 Sample Java Program

The term *program* refers to source code that is compiled and directly executed. The terms *program* and *application* are often used synonymously, and are so used in this book. To create a program in Java, the program must have a class that defines a method named main, which is invoked at runtime to start the execution of the program. The class with this main() method is known as the *entry point of the program*.

Essential Elements of a Java Program

Example 1.5 comprises three classes: Point2D, Point3D, and TestPoint3D. The public class TestPoint3D in the file TestPoint3D.java is the entry point of the program. It defines a method with the name main. The *method header* of this main() method must be declared as shown in the following method stub:

```
public static void main(String[] args)    // Method header
{ /* Implementation */ }
```

The main() method has public access—that is, it is accessible from any class. The keyword static means the method belongs to the class. The keyword void indicates that the method does not return any value. The parameter args is an array of strings that can be used to pass information to the main() method when execution starts.

Example 1.5   *A Sample Program*

```java
// File: Point2D.java
public class Point2D {
  // Same as in Example 1.2.
}
```

```java
// File: Point3D.java
public class Point3D extends Point2D {
  // Same as in Example 1.3.
}
```

```java
// File: TestPoint3D.java
public class TestPoint3D {
  public static void main(String[] args) {
    Point3D p3A = new Point3D(10, 20, 30);
    System.out.println("p3A: " + p3A.toString());
    System.out.println("x: " + p3A.getX());
    System.out.println("y: " + p3A.getY());
    System.out.println("z: " + p3A.getZ());
    p3A.setX(-10); p3A.setY(-20); p3A.setZ(-30);
    System.out.println("p3A: " + p3A.toString());

    Point3D p3B = new Point3D(30, 20, 10);
    System.out.println("p3B: " + p3B.toString());
    System.out.println("Distance between p3A and p3B: " +
                       Point3D.distance(p3A, p3B));
    Point3D.showInfo();
  }
}
```

Output from the program:

```
p3A: (10,20,30)
x: 10
y: 20
z: 30
p3A: (-10,-20,-30)
p3B: (30,20,10)
Distance between p3A and p3B: 69.2820323027551
A 3D point represented by (x,y,z)-coordinates.
```

Compiling a Program

The JDK provides tools for compiling and running programs. The classes in the Java SE Platform API are already compiled, and the JDK tools know where to find them.

Java source files can be compiled using the *Java Language Compiler*, javac, which is part of the JDK. Each source file name has the extension .java. Each class declaration in a source file is compiled into a separate *class file*, containing its *Java bytecode*. The name of this file comprises the name of the class with .class as its extension.

The source files Point2D.java, Point3D.java, and TestPoint3D.java contain the declarations of the Point2D, Point3D, and TestPoint3D classes, respectively. The respective source files are in the same directory. The source files can be compiled by giving the following javac command on the command line (the character > is the command prompt and we will use bold type for anything typed on the command line):

```
>javac Point2D.java Point3D.java TestPoint3D.java
```

This javac command creates the class files Point2D.class, Point3D.class, and TestPoint3D.class containing the Java bytecode for the Point2D, Point3D, and TestPoint3D classes, respectively. The command creates the class files in the same directory as the source files.

Although a Java source file can contain more than one class declaration, the Java compiler enforces the rule that there can only be *at the most* one class in the source file that has public access. If there is a public class in the source file, the name of the source file must be the name of the public class with .java as its extension. In the absence of a public class in the source file, the name of the file can be arbitrary, but still with the .java extension. Regardless, each class declaration in a source file is compiled into a separate .class file.

Running a Program

It is the bytecode in the class files that is executed when a Java program is run—the source code is immaterial in this regard. A Java program is run by the *Java Application Launcher*, java, which is also part of the JDK. The java command creates an instance of the JVM that executes the bytecode.

The following java command on the command line will launch the program in Example 1.5:

```
>java TestPoint3D
p3A: (10,20,30)
...
```

Note that only the name of the class that is the entry point of the program is specified, resulting in the execution starting in the main() method of the specified class. This main() method is found in the *class* file of the TestPoint3D class. The program in Example 1.5 terminates when the execution of the main() method is completed.

Running a Single-File Source-Code Program

Typically, Java source code is first compiled by the javac command to Java bytecode in class files and then the bytecode in the class files is executed by the java command. The compilation step can be omitted if the complete source code of the program is contained in a *single* source file, meaning that all class declarations that comprise the program are declared in one source file.

In Example 1.5, the program is composed of three source files: Point2D.java, Point3D.java, and TestPoint3D.java, containing the declarations of the Point2D, Point3D, and TestPoint3D classes, respectively. In Example 1.6, the class declarations are now contained in the Demo-App.java file; in other words, the complete source code of the program is now in a single source file. We can run the program with the following java command, without compiling the source code first:

```
>java Demo-App.java
p3A: (10,20,30)
...
```

The full name of the single source file is specified in the command line. Full program output is shown in Example 1.6.

Note that no class files are created. The source code is compiled fully in memory and executed.

In order to run a single-file source-code program, the following conditions must be met:

- The single source file must contain *all* source code for the program.
- Although there can be several class declarations in the source file, the *first* class declaration in the source file must provide the main() method; that is, it must be the entry point of the program.
- There must not exist *class* files corresponding to the class declarations in the single source file that are accessible by the java command.

Unlike the javac command, the name of the single source file (e.g., Demo-App.java) need not be a valid class name, but it must have the .java extension. Also unlike the javac command, the java command allows several public classes in the single source file (only public classes in the Demo-App.java file).

Examples of single-file source-code programs can be found throughout the book.

- -

Example 1.6   *A Single-File Source-Code Program*

```
// File: Demo-App.java
public class TestPoint3D {
  // Same as in Example 1.5.
  // Provides the main() method and is the first class declaration in the file.
}

public class Point2D {
  // Same as in Example 1.2.
}

public class Point3D extends Point2D {
  // Same as in Example 1.3.
}
```

Running the program:

```
>java Demo-App.java
p3A: (10,20,30)
x: 10
y: 20
z: 30
p3A: (-10,-20,-30)
p3B: (30,20,10)
Distance between p3A and p3B: 69.2820323027551
A 3D point represented by (x,y,z)-coordinates.
```

The Java Shell Tool (jshell)

This subsection is not on any Java Developer Exam. Its sole purpose is to introduce a JDK tool that is an excellent aid in learning Java programming.

The interactive command-line tool jshell is excellent when it comes to learning the Java programming language. It is a *Read-Evaluate-Print Loop* (REPL) tool, meaning that it continuously reads what is typed at the terminal, evaluates the input, and prints the results. It evaluates such language constructs as declarations, statements, and expressions as they are entered at the terminal, and shows the results immediately. It provides access to the Java SE Platform API. Pressing the TAB key results in auto-completion of the snippet, and if that fails, suggests possible options. It is an ideal tool for quickly testing code snippets. We also encourage the reader to consult the documentation for the jshell JDK tool.

The following is an example of a session with the jshell tool:

```
>jshell
|  Welcome to JShell -- Version 17.0.2
|  For an introduction type: /help intro

jshell> int i = 20
i ==> 20

jshell> Math.sqrt(i)
$6 ==> 4.47213595499958

jshell> 3 + 4 * 5
$7 ==> 23

jshell> (3 + 4) * 5
$8 ==> 35

jshell> /exit
|  Goodbye
>
```

1.9 Program Output

Data produced by a program is called *output*. This output can be sent to different devices. The examples presented in this book usually send their output to a terminal window, where the output is printed as a line of characters with a cursor that advances as the characters are printed. A Java program can send its output to the terminal window using an object called *standard out*. This object, which can be accessed using the public static final field out in the System class, is an object of the class java.io.PrintStream. This class provides methods for printing values. These methods convert values to their text representation and print the resulting string.

The print methods convert a primitive value to a string that represents its literal value, and then print the resulting string.

```
System.out.println(2022);                              // 2022
```

An object is first converted to its text representation by calling its toString() method implicitly, if it is not already called explicitly on the object. The print statements below will print the same text representation of the Point2D object denoted by the reference origin:

```
Point2D origin = new Point2D(0, 0);
System.out.println(origin.toString());                 // (0,0)
System.out.println(origin);                            // (0,0)
```

The toString() method called on a String object returns the String object itself. As string literals are String objects, the following statements will print the same result:

```
System.out.println("Stranger Strings".toString());     // Stranger Strings
System.out.println("Stranger Strings");                // Stranger Strings
```

The println() method always terminates the current line, which results in the cursor being moved to the beginning of the next line. The print() method prints its argument to the terminal window, but it does not terminate the current line:

```
System.out.print("Don't terminate this line!");
```

To terminate a line without printing any values, we can use the no-argument println() method:

```
System.out.println();
```

Formatted Output

This subsection is not on any Java Developer Exam. It is solely included because many examples in this book format their output to aid in understanding the computed results.

For more control over how the values are printed, we can format the output. The following method of the java.io.PrintStream class can be used for this purpose:

```
PrintStream printf(String format, Object... args)
```

The `String` parameter format specifies how formatting will be done. It contains *format specifications* that determine how each subsequent value in the parameter args will be formatted and printed. The parameter declaration `Object...` args represents an array of zero or more arguments to be formatted and printed. The resulting string from the formatting will be printed to the *destination stream*. (`System.out` will print to the *standard out* object.)

Any error in the format string will result in a runtime exception.

This method returns the `PrintStream` on which the method is invoked, and can be ignored, as in the examples here.

The following call to the `printf()` method on the standard out object formats and prints three values:

```
System.out.printf("Formatted values|%5d|%8.3f|%5s|%n", // Format string
                  2016, Math.PI, "Hi");                 // Values to format
```

At runtime, the following line is printed in the terminal window:

```
Formatted values| 2016|   3.142|   Hi|
```

The format string is the first argument in the method call. It contains four *format specifiers*. The first three are `%5d`, `%8.3f`, and `%5s`, which specify how the three arguments should be processed. The letter in the format specifier indicates the type of value to format. Their location in the format string specifies where the text representation of the arguments should be inserted. The fourth format specifier, `%n`, is a platform-specific line separator. Its occurrence causes the current line to be terminated, with the cursor moving to the start of the next line. All other text in the format string is fixed, including any other spaces or punctuation, and is printed verbatim.

In the preceding example, the first value is formatted according to the first format specifier, the second value is formatted according to the second format specifier, and so on. The | character has been used in the format string to show how many character positions are taken up by the text representation of each value. The output shows that the `int` value was written right-justified, spanning five character positions using the format specifier `%5d`; the `double` value of `Math.PI` took up eight character positions and was rounded to three decimal places using the format specifier `%8.3f`; and the `String` value was written right-justified, spanning five character positions using the format specifier `%5s`. The format specifier `%n` terminates the current line. All other characters in the format string are printed verbatim.

Table 1.2 shows examples of some selected format specifiers that can be used to format values.

Table 1.2 *Format Specifier Examples*

Parameter value	Format spec	Example value	String printed	Description
Integer value	"%d"	123	"123"	Occupies as many character positions as needed.
	"%6d"	123	" 123"	Occupies six character positions and is right-justified. The printed string is padded with leading spaces, if necessary.
Floating-point value	"%f"	4.567	"4.567000"	Occupies as many character positions as needed, but always includes six decimal places.
	"%.2f"	4.567	"4.57"	Occupies as many character positions as needed, but includes only two decimal places. The value is rounded in the output, if necessary.
	"%6.2f"	4.567	" 4.57"	Occupies six character positions, including the decimal point, and uses two decimal places. The value is rounded in the output, if necessary.
Any object	"%s"	"Hi!"	"Hi!"	The text representation of the object occupies as many character positions as needed.
	"%6s"	"Hi!"	" Hi!"	The text representation of the object occupies six character positions and is right-justified.
	"%-6s"	"Hi!"	"Hi! "	The text representation of the object occupies six character positions and is left-justified.

 Review Questions

1.8   Which command from the JDK will create a class file with the bytecode of the following source code contained in a file named SmallProg.java?

```java
public class SmallProg {
    public static void main(String[] args) { System.out.println("Good luck!"); }
}
```

Select the one correct answer.

(a) java SmallProg
(b) javac SmallProg
(c) java SmallProg.java
(d) javac SmallProg.java
(e) java SmallProg main

1.9 Which command from the JDK should be used to execute the main() method of a class named SmallProg that has been compiled?
Select the one correct answer.

(a) java SmallProg
(b) javac SmallProg
(c) java SmallProg.java
(d) java SmallProg.class
(e) java SmallProg.main()

1.10 Which of the following statements are true about a single-file source-code program?
Select the two correct answers.

(a) It can be composed of multiple class declarations in the source file, where the first class declaration must provide the main() method.
(b) It can access previously compiled user-defined classes.
(c) It can be composed of multiple source files.
(d) It can accept program arguments on the command line.

1.11 Which statement is true about Java?
Select the one correct answer.

(a) A Java program can be executed by any JVM.
(b) Java bytecode cannot be translated to machine code.
(c) Only Java programs can be executed by a JVM.
(d) A Java program can create and destroy objects.
(e) None of the above

Basic Elements, Primitive Data Types, and Operators

2

 Chapter Topics

- Overview of basic language elements in Java: identifiers, keywords, separators, literals, whitespace, and comments

- Overview of primitive data types defined in Java: integral, floating-point, and boolgean

- Representing integers in different number systems and in memory

- Understanding type conversion categories and conversion contexts, and which conversions are permissible in each conversion context

- Defining and evaluating arithmetic and boolean expressions, and the order in which operands and operators are evaluated

- Using Java operators, including precedence and associativity rules for expression evaluation

Java SE 17 Developer Exam Objectives	
[1.1] Use primitives and wrapper classes including Math API, parentheses, type promotion, and casting to evaluate arithmetic and boolean expressions ○ *Primitive types, operators, expression evaluation, and type conversions are covered in this chapter.* ○ *For wrapper classes, see §8.3, p. 429.* ○ *For Math API, see §8.6, p. 478.*	*§2.2, p. 41* *to* *§2.19, p. 92*
Java SE 11 Developer Exam Objectives	
[1.1] Use primitives and wrapper classes, including, operators, the use of parentheses, type promotion and casting ○ *Primitive types, operators, expression evaluation, and type conversions are covered in this chapter.* ○ *For wrapper classes, see §8.3, p. 429.*	*§2.2, p. 41* *to* *§2.19, p. 92*

This chapter covers the low-level language elements from which high-level constructs are formed, the primitive data types that are provided by the language, and the operators that can be used to compose expressions. In addition to how expressions are evaluated, an understanding of which type conversions can be applied in which context is also essential.

2.1   Basic Language Elements

Like any other programming language, the Java programming language is defined by *grammar rules* that specify how *syntactically* legal constructs can be formed using the language elements, and by a *semantic definition* that specifies the *meaning* of syntactically legal constructs.

Lexical Tokens

The low-level language elements are called *lexical tokens* (or just *tokens*) and are the building blocks for more complex constructs. Identifiers, numbers, operators, and special characters are all examples of tokens that can be used to build high-level constructs like expressions, statements, methods, and classes.

Identifiers

A name in a program is called an *identifier*. Identifiers can be used to denote classes, methods, variables, and labels.

In Java, an *identifier* is composed of a sequence of characters, where each character can be either a *letter* or a *digit*. However, the first character in an identifier must always be a letter, as explained later.

Since Java programs are written in the Unicode character set (p. 37), characters allowed in identifier names are interpreted according to this character set. Use of the Unicode character set opens up the possibility of writing identifier names in many writing scripts used around the world. As one would expect, the characters A to Z and a to z are letters and the characters 0 to 9 are digits. A *connecting punctuation character* (such as *underscore _*) and any *currency symbol* (such as $, ¢, ¥, or £) are also allowed as letters in identifier names, but these characters should be used judiciously. Note also that the underscore (_) on its own is *not* a legal identifier name, but a keyword (Table 2.1, p. 31).

Identifiers in Java are *case sensitive*. For example, price and Price are two different identifiers.

Examples of Legal Identifiers

```
number, Number, sum_$, bingo, $$_100, _007, mål, grüß
```

Examples of Illegal Identifiers

```
48chevy, all@hands, grand-sum, _
```

The name 48chevy is not a legal identifier because it starts with a digit. The character @ is not a legal character in an identifier. It is also not a legal operator, so all@hands cannot be interpreted as a legal expression with two operands. The character - is not a legal character in an identifier, but it is a legal operator; thus grand-sum could be interpreted as a legal expression with two operands. An underscore (_) by itself is not a legal identifier.

Keywords

Keywords are reserved words or identifiers that are predefined in the language and cannot be used to denote other entities. All Java keywords are lowercase, and incorrect usage results in compile-time errors.

Keywords currently defined in the language are listed in Table 2.1. The keyword strictfp is obsolete as of Java SE 17, and its use is discouraged in new code. *Contextual keywords* that are restricted in certain contexts are listed in Table 2.2. Keywords currently reserved, but *not in use*, are listed in Table 2.3. In addition, three identifiers are reserved as predefined *literals* in the language: the null literal, and the boolean literals true and false (Table 2.4). A keyword cannot be used as an identifier. A contextual keyword cannot be used as an identifier in certain contexts. The index at the end of the book contains references to relevant sections where currently used keywords are explained.

Table 2.1 *Keywords in Java*

abstract	default	if	private	this
assert	do	implements	protected	throw
boolean	double	import	public	throws
break	else	instanceof	return	transient
byte	enum	int	short	try
case	extends	interface	static	void
catch	final	long	strictfp	volatile
char	finally	native	super	while
class	float	new	switch	_ (underscore)
continue	for	package	synchronized	

Table 2.2 *Contextual Keywords*

exports	opens	requires	uses
module	permits	sealed	var
non-sealed	provides	to	with
open	record	transitive	yield

Table 2.3 *Reserved Keywords Not Currently in Use*

const	goto

Table 2.4 *Reserved Literals in Java*

null	true	false

Separators

Separators (also known as *punctuators*) are tokens that have meaning depending on the context in which they are used; they aid the compiler in performing syntax and semantic analysis of a program (Table 2.5). The semicolon (;) is used to terminate a statement. A pair of curly brackets, {}, can be used to group several statements. See the index entries for these separators for more details.

Table 2.5 *Separators in Java*

{	}	[	]	(	)
.	;	,	...	@	::

Literals

A *literal* denotes a constant value; in other words, the value that a literal represents remains unchanged in the program. Literals represent numerical (integer or floating-point), character, boolean, and string values. In addition, the literal null represents the null reference. Table 2.6 shows examples of literals in Java.

Table 2.6 *Examples of Literals*

Integer	2000	0	-7			
Floating-point	3.14	-3.14	.5	0.5		
Character	'a'	'A'	'0'	':'	'-'	')'
Boolean	true	false				
String	"abba"	"3.14"	"for"	"a piece of the action"		

Integer Literals

Integer data types comprise the following primitive data types: int, long, byte, and short (p. 41).

The default data type of an integer literal is always int, but it can be specified as long by appending the suffix L (or l) to the integer value. The suffix L is often preferred because the suffix l and the digit 1 can be hard to distinguish. Without the suffix, the long literals 2020L and 0L will be interpreted as int literals. There is no direct way to specify a short or a byte literal.

In addition to the decimal number system, integer literals can be specified in the binary (*base* 2, *digits* 0–1), octal (*base* 8, *digits* 0–7), and hexadecimal (*base* 16, *digits* 0–9 and a–f) number systems. The digits a to f in the hexadecimal system correspond to decimal values 10 to 15. Binary, octal, and hexadecimal numbers are specified with 0b (or 0B), 0, and 0x (or 0X) as the base or radix prefix, respectively.

Examples of decimal, binary, octal, and hexadecimal literals are shown in Table 2.7. Note that the leading 0 (zero) digit is not the uppercase letter O. The hexadecimal digits from a to f can also be specified with the corresponding uppercase forms (A–F). Negative integers (e.g., -90) can be specified by prefixing the minus sign (-) to the magnitude of the integer regardless of the number system (e.g., -0b1011010, -0132, or -0X5a).

Table 2.7 *Examples of Decimal, Binary, Octal, and Hexadecimal Literals*

Decimal	Binary	Octal	Hexadecimal
8	0b1000	010	0x8
10L	0b1010L	012L	0xaL
16	0b10000	020	0x10
27	0b11011	033	0x1b
90L	0b1011010L	0132L	0x5aL
-90	-0b1011010 or 0b11111111111111111111111 1110100110	-0132 or 037777777646	-0x5a or 0xffffffa6
-1	-0b1 or 0b11111111111111111111111 1111111111	-01 or 037777777777	-0x1 or 0xffffffff
2147483647 (i.e., $2^{31} - 1$)	0b01111111111111111111111 1111111111	017777777777	0x7fffffff
-2147483648 (i.e., -2^{31})	0b10000000000000000000000 0000000000	020000000000	0x80000000
1125899906842624L (i.e., 2^{50})	0b10000000000000000000000 00000000000000000000000000 00000L	040000000000000000000L	0x4000000000000L

Representing Integers

Integer data types in Java represent *signed* integer values, meaning both positive and negative integer values. The values of type char can effectively be regarded as *unsigned* 16-bit integers.

Values of type byte are represented as shown in Table 2.8. A value of type byte requires 8 bits. With 8 bits, we can represent 2^8 or 256 values. Java uses two's complement (explained later) to store signed values of integer data types. For the byte data type, this means values are in the range –128 (i.e., -2^7) to +127 (i.e., $2^7 - 1$), inclusive.

Bits in an integral value are usually numbered from right to left, starting with the least significant bit 0 (also called the *rightmost bit*). The representation of the signed types sets the most significant bit to 1, indicating negative values. Adding 1 to the maximum int value 2147483647 results in the minimum value -2147483648, such that the values wrap around for integers and no overflow or underflow is indicated.

Table 2.8   *Representing Signed byte Values Using Two's Complement*

Decimal value	Binary representation (8 bit)	Binary value with prefix 0b	Octal value with prefix 0	Hexadecimal value with prefix 0x
127	01111111	0b1111111	0177	0x7f
126	01111110	0b1111110	0176	0x7e
...	...	...	...	...
41	00101001	0b101001	051	0x29
...	...	...	...	...
2	00000010	0b10	02	0x2
1	00000001	0b1	01	0x1
0	00000000	0b0	00	0x0
−1	11111111	0b11111111	0377	0xff
−2	11111110	0b11111110	0376	0xfe
...	...	...	...	...
−41	11010111	0b11010111	0327	0xd7
...	...	...	...	...
−127	10000001	0b10000001	0201	0x81
−128	10000000	0b10000000	0200	0x80

Calculating Two's Complement

Before we look at two's complement, we need to understand one's complement. The one's complement of a binary integer is computed by inverting the bits in the number. Thus the one's complement of the binary number 00101001 is 11010110. The one's complement of a binary number N_2 is denoted as $\sim N_2$. The following relations hold between a binary integer N_2, its one's complement $\sim N_2$, and its two's complement $-N_2$:

$$-N_2 = \sim N_2 + 1$$

$$0 = -N_2 + N_2$$

If N_2 is a positive binary integer, then $-N_2$ denotes its negative binary value, and vice versa. The second relation states that adding a binary integer N_2 to its two's complement $-N_2$ equals 0.

Given a positive byte value, say 41, the binary representation of -41 can be found as follows:

	Binary representation	Decimal value
Given a value, N_2:	00101001	41
Form one's complement, $\sim N_2$:	11010110	
Add 1:	00000001	
Result is two's complement, $-N_2$:	11010111	-41

Adding a number N_2 to its two's complement $-N_2$ gives 0, and the carry bit from the addition of the most significant bits (after any necessary extension of the operands) is ignored:

	Binary representation	Decimal value
Given a value, N_2:	00101001	41
Add two's complement, $-N_2$:	11010111	-41
Sum:	00000000	0

Subtraction between two integers is also computed as addition with two's complement:

$N_2 - M_2 = N_2 + (-M_2)$

For example, the expression $41_{10} - 3_{10}$ (with the correct result 38_{10}) is computed as follows:

	Binary representation	Decimal value
Given a value, N_2:	00101001	41
Add $-M_2$ (i.e., subtract M_2):	11111101	-3
Result:	00100110	38

The previous discussion of byte values applies equally to values of other integer types: short, int, and long. These types have their values represented by two's complement in 16, 32, and 64 bits, respectively.

Floating-Point Literals

Floating-point data types come in two flavors: `float` and `double`.

The default data type of a floating-point literal is `double`, but it can be explicitly designated by appending the suffix D (or d) to the value. A floating-point literal can also be specified to be a `float` by appending the suffix F (or f).

Floating-point literals can also be specified in scientific notation, where E (or e) stands for *exponent*. For example, the `double` literal 194.9E-2 in scientific notation is interpreted as 194.9×10^{-2} (i.e., 1.949).

Examples of double *Literals*

```
0.0       0.0d      0D
0.49      .49       .49D
49.0      49.       49D
4.9E+1    4.9E+1D   4.9e1d    4900e-2   .49E2
```

Examples of float *Literals*

```
0.0F      0f
0.49F     .49F
49.0F     49.F      49F
4.9E+1F   4900e-2f  .49E2F
```

Note that the decimal point and the exponent are optional, and that at least one digit must be specified. Also, for the examples of `float` literals presented here, the suffix F is mandatory; if it were omitted, they would be interpreted as `double` literals.

Underscores in Numerical Literals

The underscore character (_) can be used to improve the readability of numerical literals in the source code. Any number of underscores can be inserted *between the digits* that make up the numerical literal. This rules out underscores adjacent to the sign (+, -), the radix prefix (0b, 0B, 0x, 0X), the decimal point (.), the exponent (e, E), and the data type suffix (l, L, d, D, f, F), as well as before the first digit and after the last digit. Note that octal radix prefix 0 is part of the definition of an octal literal and is therefore considered the first digit of an octal literal.

Underscores in identifiers are treated as letters. For example, the names _XXL and _XXL_ are two distinct legal identifiers. In contrast, underscores are used as a notational convenience for numerical literals and are ignored by the compiler when used in such literals. In other words, a numerical literal can be specified in the source code using underscores between digits, such that 2_0_2_2 and 20__22 represent the same numerical literal 2022 in source code.

Examples of Legal Use of Underscores in Numerical Literals

```
0b0111_1111_1111_1111_1111_1111_1111_1111
0_377_777_777              0xff_ff_ff_ff
-123_456.00                1_2.345_678e1_2
2009__08__13               49_03_01d
```

Examples of Illegal Use of Underscores in Numerical Literals

```
_0_b_0111111111111111111111111111111111_
_0377777777_               _0_x_ffffffff_
+_123456_._00_             _12_._345678_e_12_
_20090813_                 _490301_d_
```

Boolean Literals

The primitive data type boolean represents the truth values *true* and *false* that are denoted by the reserved literals true and false, respectively.

Character Literals

A character literal is quoted in single quotes ('). All character literals have the primitive data type char.

A character literal is represented according to the 16-bit Unicode character set, which subsumes the 8-bit ISO Latin-1 and the 7-bit ASCII characters. In Table 2.9, note that digits (0–9), uppercase letters (A–Z), and lowercase letters (a–z) have contiguous Unicode values. A Unicode character can always be specified as a four-digit hexadecimal number (i.e., 16 bits) with the prefix \u.

Table 2.9 *Examples of Character Literals*

Character literal	Character literal using Unicode value	Character
' '	'\u0020'	*Space*
'0'	'\u0030'	0
'1'	'\u0031'	1
'9'	'\u0039'	9
'A'	'\u0041'	A
'B'	'\u0042'	B
'Z'	'\u005a'	Z
'a'	'\u0061'	a
'b'	'\u0062'	b
'z'	'\u007a'	z
'Ñ'	'\u0084'	Ñ
'å'	'\u008c'	å
'ß'	'\u00a7'	ß

Escape Sequences

Certain *escape sequences* define special characters, as shown in Table 2.10. These escape sequences allow representation of some special characters in character literals, string literals (p. 39), and text blocks (§8.4, p. 458). These escape sequences can be single-quoted to define character literals, or included in string literals and text blocks. For example, the escape sequence \t and the Unicode value \u0009 are equivalent. However, the Unicode values \u000a and \u000d should not be used to represent a newline and a carriage return in the source code. These values are interpreted as line-terminator characters by the compiler and will cause compile-time errors. You should use the escape sequences \n and \r, respectively, for correct interpretation of these characters in the source code.

Table 2.10   *Escape Sequences*

Escape sequence	Unicode value	Character
\b	\u0008	Backspace (BS)
\t	\u0009	Horizontal tab (HT or TAB)
\n	\u000a	Linefeed (LF), also known as newline (NL)
\f	\u000c	Form feed (FF)
\r	\u000d	Carriage return (CR)
\s	\u0020	Space (SP)
Line terminator	–	Line continuation in a text block
\'	\u0027	Apostrophe-quote, also known as single quote
\"	\u0022	Quotation mark, also known as double quote
\\	\u005c	Backslash

We can also use the escape sequence \ddd to specify a character literal as an octal value, where each digit d can be any octal digit (0–7), as shown in Table 2.11. The number of digits must be three or fewer, and the octal value cannot exceed \377; in other words, only the first 256 characters can be specified with this notation.

Table 2.11   *Examples of Escape Sequence* \ddd

Escape sequence \ddd	Character literal
'\141'	'a'
'\46'	'&'
'\60'	'0'

String Literals

A *string literal* is a sequence of characters that must be enclosed in double quotes and must occur on a single line. All string literals are objects of the class String (§8.4, p. 439).

Escape sequences as well as Unicode values can appear in string literals:

```
"Here comes a tab.\t And here comes another one\u0009!"          (1)
"What's on the menu?"                                            (2)
"\"String literals are double-quoted.\""                         (3)
"Left!\nRight!"                                                  (4)
"Don't split                                                     (5)
me up!"
```

In (1), the tab character is specified using the escape sequence and the Unicode value, respectively. In (2), the single quote need not be escaped in strings, but it would be if specified as a character literal ('\''). In (3), the double quotes in the string must be escaped. In (4), we use the escape sequence \n to insert a newline. The expression in (5) generates a compile-time error, as the string literal is split over several lines. Printing the strings from (1) to (4) will give the following result:

```
Here comes a tab.     And here comes another one     !
What's on the menu?
"String literals are double-quoted."
Left!
Right!
```

One should also use the escape sequences \n and \r, respectively, for correct interpretation of the characters \u000a (newline) and \u000d (form feed) in string literals.

Whitespace

Whitespace is a sequence of spaces, tabs, form feeds, and line terminator characters in a Java source file. Line terminators include the newline, carriage return, and carriage return–newline sequence.

A Java program is a free-format sequence of characters that is *tokenized* by the compiler—that is, broken into a stream of tokens for further analysis. Separators and operators help to distinguish tokens, but sometimes whitespace has to be inserted explicitly as a separator. For example, the identifier classRoom will be interpreted as a single token, unless whitespace is inserted to distinguish the keyword class from the identifier Room.

Whitespace aids not only in separating tokens, but also in formatting the program so that it is easy to read. The compiler ignores the whitespace once the tokens are identified.

Comments

A program can be documented by inserting comments at relevant places in the source code. These comments are for documentation purposes only and are ignored by the compiler.

Java provides three types of comments that can be used to document a program:

- A single-line comment: `// ... to the end of the line`
- A multiple-line comment: `/* ... */`
- A documentation (Javadoc) comment: `/** ... */`'

Single-Line Comment

All characters after the comment-start sequence `//` through to the end of the line constitute a *single-line comment*.

```
// This comment ends at the end of this line.
int age;        // From comment-start sequence to the end of the line is a comment.
```

Multiple-Line Comment

A *multiple-line comment*, as the name suggests, can span several lines. Such a comment starts with the sequence `/*` and ends with the sequence `*/`.

```
/* A comment
   on several
   lines.
*/
```

The comment-start sequences (`//`, `/*`, `/**`) are not treated differently from other characters when occurring within comments, so they are ignored. This means that trying to nest multiple-line comments will result in a compile-time error:

```
/* Formula for alchemy.
   gold = wizard.makeGold(stone);
   /* But it only works on Sundays. */
*/
```

The second occurrence of the comment-start sequence `/*` is ignored. The last occurrence of the sequence `*/` in the code is now unmatched, resulting in a syntax error.

Documentation Comment

A *documentation comment* is a special-purpose multiple-line comment that is used by the javadoc tool to generate HTML documentation for the program. Documentation comments are usually placed in front of classes, interfaces, methods, and field definitions. Special tags can be used inside a documentation comment to provide more specific information. Such a comment starts with the sequence /** and ends with the sequence */:

```
/**
 *  This class implements a gizmo.
 *  @author K.A.M.
 *  @version 4.0
 */
```

For details on the javadoc tool, see the tools documentation provided by the JDK.

2.2 Primitive Data Types

Figure 2.1 gives an overview of the *primitive data types* in Java.

Primitive data types in Java can be divided into three main categories:

- *Integral types*: represent signed integers (byte, short, int, long) and unsigned character values (char)
- *Floating-point types* (float, double): represent fractional signed numbers
- *Boolean type* (boolean): represents logical values

Figure 2.1 *Primitive Data Types in Java*

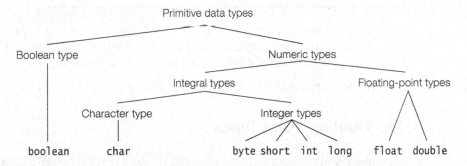

Each primitive data type defines the range of values in the data type, and operations on these values are defined by special operators in the language (p. 51).

Primitive data values are not objects, but each primitive data type has a corresponding *wrapper* class that can be used to represent a primitive value as an object. Wrapper classes are discussed in §8.3, p. 429.

The Integer Types

The integer data types are byte, short, int, and long (Table 2.12). Their values are signed integers represented by two's complement (p. 34).

Table 2.12   *Range of Integer Values*

Data type	Width (bits)	Minimum value MIN_VALUE	Maximum value MAX_VALUE
byte	8	-2^7 (−128)	$2^7 - 1$ (+127)
short	16	-2^{15} (−32768)	$2^{15} - 1$ (+32767)
int	32	-2^{31} (−2147483648)	$2^{31} - 1$ (+2147483647)
long	64	-2^{63} (−9223372036854775808L)	$2^{63} - 1$ (+9223372036854775807L)

The char Type

The data type char represents characters (Table 2.13). Their values are unsigned integers that denote all of the 65,536 (2^{16}) characters in the 16-bit Unicode character set. This set includes letters, digits, and special characters.

Table 2.13   *Range of Character Values*

Data type	Width (bits)	Minimum Unicode value	Maximum Unicode value
char	16	0x0 (\u0000)	0xffff (\uffff)

The first 128 characters of the Unicode set are the same as the 128 characters of the 7-bit ASCII character set, and the first 256 characters of the Unicode set correspond to the 256 characters of the 8-bit ISO Latin-1 character set.

The integer types and the char type are collectively called *integral types*.

The Floating-Point Types

Floating-point numbers are represented by the float and double data types.

Floating-point numbers conform to the IEEE 754-1985 binary floating-point standard. Table 2.14 shows the range of values for positive floating-point numbers, but these apply equally to negative floating-point numbers with the minus sign (-) as a prefix. Zero can be either 0.0 or -0.0. The range of values represented by the double data type is wider than that of the float data type.

Table 2.14   *Range of Floating-Point Values*

Data type	Width (bits)	Minimum positive value MIN_VALUE	Maximum positive value MAX_VALUE
float	32	1.401298464324817E-45f	3.402823476638528860e+38f
double	64	4.94065645841246544e-324	1.79769313486231570e+308

Since the size for representation is a finite number of bits, certain floating-point numbers can be represented only as approximations. For example, the value of the expression (1.0/3.0) is represented as an approximation due to the finite number of bits used to represent floating-point numbers.

The boolean Type

The data type boolean represents the two logical values denoted by the literals true and false (Table 2.15).

Table 2.15   *Boolean Values*

Data type	Width	True value literal	False value literal
boolean	Not applicable	true	false

Boolean values are results of all *relational* (p. 74), *conditional* (p. 80), and *boolean* (p. 78) *logical operators*.

Table 2.16 summarizes the pertinent facts about the primitive data types: their width or size, which indicates the number of bits required to store a primitive value; their range of legal values, which is specified by the minimum and maximum values permissible; and the name of the corresponding wrapper class (§8.3, p. 429).

Table 2.16   *Summary of Primitive Data Types*

Data type	Width (bits)	Minimum value, maximum value	Wrapper class
boolean	Not applicable	true, false	Boolean
byte	8	$-2^7, 2^7 - 1$	Byte
short	16	$-2^{15}, 2^{15} - 1$	Short
char	16	0x0, 0xffff	Character
int	32	$-2^{31}, 2^{31} - 1$	Integer
long	64	$-2^{63}, 2^{63} - 1$	Long
float	32	±1.40129846432481707e-45f, ±3.402823476638528860e+38f	Float
double	64	±4.94065645841246544e-324, ±1.79769313486231570e+308	Double

2.3 Conversions

In this section we discuss the different kinds of *type conversions* that can be applied to values; in the next section we discuss the *contexts* in which these conversions are permitted. Some type conversions must be *explicitly* stated in the program, while others are performed *implicitly.* Some type conversions can be checked at compile time to guarantee their validity at runtime, while others will require an extra check at runtime.

Widening and Narrowing Primitive Conversions

For the primitive data types, the value of a *narrower* data type can be converted to a value of a *wider* data type. This is called a *widening primitive conversion.* Widening conversions from one primitive type to the next wider primitive type are summarized in Figure 2.2. The conversions shown are transitive. For example, an int can be directly converted to a double without first having to convert it to a long and a float.

Note that the target type of a widening primitive conversion has a *wider range* of values than the source type—for example, the range of the long type subsumes the range of the int type. In widening conversions between *integral* types, the source value remains intact, with no loss of magnitude information. However, a widening conversion from an int or a long value to a float value, or from a long value to a double value, may result in a *loss of precision.* The floating-point value in the target type is then a correctly rounded approximation of the integer value. Note that precision relates to the number of significant bits in the value, and must not be confused with *magnitude*, which relates to how large the represented value can be.

Figure 2.2   *Widening Primitive Conversions*

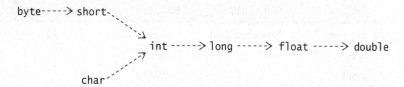

Converting from a wider primitive type to a narrower primitive type is called a *narrowing primitive conversion;* it can result in a loss of magnitude information, and possibly in a loss of precision as well. Any conversion that is not a widening primitive conversion according to Figure 2.2 is a narrowing primitive conversion. The target type of a narrowing primitive conversion has a *narrower range* of values than the source type—for example, the range of the int type does not include all the values in the range of the long type.

Note that all conversions between char and the two integer types byte and short are considered narrowing primitive conversions. The reason is that the conversions between the unsigned type char and the signed types byte and short can result in a loss of information. These narrowing conversions are done in two steps: first converting the source value to the int type, and then converting the int value to the target type.

Widening primitive conversions are usually done implicitly, whereas narrowing primitive conversions usually require a *cast* (p. 48). It is not illegal to use a cast for a widening conversion. However, the compiler will flag any conversion that requires a cast if none has been specified. Regardless of any loss of magnitude or precision, widening and narrowing primitive conversions *never* result in a runtime exception.

```
long year = 2020;    // (1) Implicit widening: long <----- int, assigned 2020L

int pi = (int) 3.14; // (2) Narrowing requires cast: int <----- double, assigned 3
```

Ample examples of widening and narrowing primitive conversions can be found in this chapter.

Widening and Narrowing Reference Conversions

The *subtype–supertype* relationship between reference types determines which conversions are permissible between them (§5.1, p. 191). Conversions *up* the *type hierarchy* are called *widening reference conversions* (also called *upcasting*). Such a conversion converts from a subtype to a supertype:

```
Object obj = "Upcast me";  // (1) Widening: Object <----- String
```

Conversions *down* the type hierarchy represent *narrowing reference conversions* (also called *downcasting*):

```
String str = (String) obj; // (2) Narrowing requires cast: String <----- Object
```

A subtype is a *narrower* type than its supertype in the sense that it is a specialization of its supertype. Contexts under which reference conversions can occur are discussed in §5.8, p. 261.

Widening reference conversions are usually done implicitly, whereas narrowing reference conversions usually require a cast, as illustrated in the second declaration statement above. The compiler will reject casts that are not legal or will issue an *unchecked warning* under certain circumstances if type-safety cannot be guaranteed.

Widening reference conversions do not require any runtime checks and never result in an exception during execution. This is not the case for narrowing reference conversions, which require a runtime check and can throw a ClassCastException if the conversion is not legal.

Boxing and Unboxing Conversions

Boxing and unboxing conversions allow interoperability between primitive values and their representation as objects of the wrapper types (§8.3, p. 429).

A *boxing conversion* converts the value of a primitive type to a corresponding value of its wrapper type, and an *unboxing conversion* converts the value of a wrapper type to a value of its corresponding primitive type. Both boxing and unboxing conversion are applied implicitly in the right context, but the wrapper classes also provide the static method valueOf() to explicitly box a primitive value in a wrapper object, and the method *primitiveType*Value() to explicitly unbox the value in a wrapper object as a value of *primitiveType*.

```
Integer iRef = 10;                    // (1) Implicit boxing: Integer <----- int
Double dRef = Double.valueOf(3.14);   // (2) Explicit boxing: Double <----- double

int i = iRef;                         // (3) Implicit unboxing: int <----- Integer
double d = dRef.doubleValue();        // (4) Explicit unboxing: double <----- Double
```

At (1) above, the int value 10 results in an object of type Integer implicitly being created; this object contains the int value 10. We say that the int value 10 has been *boxed* in an object of the wrapper type Integer. This implicit boxing conversion is also called *autoboxing*. An explicit boxing by the valueOf() method of the wrapper classes is used at (2) to box a double value.

Unboxing conversion is illustrated by (3) and (4) above. Implicit unboxing is applied at (3) to unbox the value in the Integer object, and explicit unboxing is applied at (4) by calling the doubleValue() method of the Double class.

Note that both boxing and unboxing are done implicitly in the right context. Boxing allows primitive values to be used where an object of their wrapper type is expected, and unboxing allows the converse. Unboxing makes it possible to use a Boolean wrapper object as a boolean value in a boolean expression, and to use an integral wrapper object as an integral primitive value in an arithmetic expression. Unboxing a wrapper reference that has the null value results in a NullPointer-Exception. Ample examples of boxing and unboxing can be found in this chapter and in §5.8, p. 261.

Other Conversions

Here we briefly mention some other conversions.

* *Identity conversions* allow conversions from a type to that same type. An identity conversion is always permitted.

```
int i = (int) 10;             // int <---- int
String str = (String) "Hi";   // String <---- String
```

* *String conversions* allow a value of any other type to be converted to a String type in the context of the string concatenation operator + (p. 67).

* *Unchecked conversions* are permitted to facilitate operability between legacy and generic code (§11.2, p. 575).

2.4 Type Conversion Contexts

Selected conversion contexts and the conversions that are applicable in these contexts are summarized in Table 2.17. The conversions shown in each context occur *implicitly*, without the program having to take any special action. For other conversion contexts, see §2.3, p. 46.

Table 2.17 *Selected Conversion Contexts and Conversion Categories*

Conversion categories	Conversion contexts			
	Assignment	Method invocation	Casting	Numeric promotion
Widening/ narrowing *primitive* conversions	Widening Narrowing for *constant expressions* of non-long integral type, with optional boxing	Widening	Both	Widening
Widening/ narrowing *reference* conversions	Widening	Widening	Both, followed by optional unchecked conversion	Not applicable
Boxing/ unboxing conversions	Unboxing, followed by optional widening *primitive* conversion Boxing, followed by optional widening *reference* conversion	Unboxing, followed by optional widening *primitive* conversion Boxing, followed by optional widening *reference* conversion	Both	Unboxing, followed by optional widening *primitive* conversion

Assignment Context

Assignment conversions that can occur in an assignment context are shown in the second column of Table 2.17. An assignment conversion converts the type of an expression to the type of a target variable.

An expression (or its value) is *assignable* to the target variable, if the type of the expression can be converted to the type of the target variable by an assignment conversion. Equivalently, the type of the expression is *assignment compatible* with the type of the target variable.

For assignment conversion involving primitive data types, see §2.7, p. 54. Note the special case where a narrowing conversion occurs when assigning a non-long integer constant expression:

```
byte b = 10;   // Narrowing conversion: byte <--- int
```

For assignment conversions involving reference types, see §5.8, p. 261.

Method Invocation Context

Method invocation conversions that can occur in a method invocation context are shown in the third column of Table 2.17. Note that method invocation and assignment conversions differ in one respect: Method invocation conversions do not include the implicit narrowing conversion performed for non-long integral constant expressions.

```
// Assignment: (1) Implicit narrowing followed by (2) boxing.
Character space1 = 32;      // Character <-(2)-- char <-(1)-- int

// Invocation of method with signature: valueOf(char)
Character space2 = Character.valueOf(32);       // Compile-time error!
                                                // Call signature: valueOf(int)
Character space3 = Character.valueOf((char)32); // OK!
                                                // Call signature: valueOf(char)
```

A method invocation conversion involves converting each argument value in a method or constructor call to the type of the corresponding formal parameter in the method or constructor declaration.

Method invocation conversions involving parameters of primitive data types are discussed in §3.10, p. 129, and those involving reference types are discussed in §5.8, p. 261.

Casting Context of the Unary Type Cast Operator (*type*)

Java, being a *strongly typed* language, checks for *type compatibility* (i.e., it checks whether a type can substitute for another type in a given context) at compile time. However, some checks are possible only at runtime (e.g., which type of object a reference actually denotes during execution). In cases where an operator would have incompatible operands (e.g., assigning a double to an int), Java demands that a *type cast* be used to *explicitly* indicate the type conversion. The type cast construct has the following syntax:

(*type*) *expression*

The *cast operator* (*type*) is applied to the value of the *expression*. At runtime, a cast results in a new value of *type*, which best represents the value of the *expression* in the old type. We use the term *casting* to mean applying the cast operator for *explicit* type conversion.

However, in the context of casting, *implicit* casting conversions can take place. These casting conversions are shown in the fourth column of Table 2.17. Casting conversions include more conversion categories than the assignment or the method invocation conversions. In the code that follows, the comments indicate the category of the conversion that takes place because of the cast operator on the right-hand side of each assignment—although casts are only necessary for the sake of the assignment at (1) and (2).

```
long l = (long) 10;         // Widening primitive conversion: long <--- int
int i = (int) l;            // (1) Narrowing primitive conversion: int <--- long
Object obj = (Object) "7Up"; // Widening ref conversion: Object <--- String
String str = (String) obj;  // (2) Narrowing ref conversion: String <--- Object
Integer iRef = (Integer) i; // Boxing: Integer <--- int
i = (int) iRef;             // Unboxing: int <--- Integer
```

A casting conversion is applied to the value of the operand *expression* of a cast operator. Casting can be applied to primitive values as well as references. Casting between primitive data types and reference types is not permitted, except where boxing and unboxing is applicable. Boolean values cannot be cast to other data values, and vice versa. The reference literal null can be cast to any reference type.

Examples of casting between primitive data types are provided in this chapter. Casting reference values is discussed in §5.11, p. 269.

Numeric Promotion Context

Numeric operators allow only operands of certain types. Numeric promotion results in conversions being applied to the operands to convert them to permissible types. *Numeric promotion conversions* that can occur in a numeric promotion context are shown in the fifth column of Table 2.17. Permissible conversion categories are widening primitive conversions and unboxing conversions. A distinction is made between unary and binary numeric promotion.

Unary Numeric Promotion

Unary numeric promotion proceeds as follows:

- If the single operand is of type Byte, Short, Character, or Integer, it is unboxed. If the resulting value is narrower than int, it is promoted to a value of type int by a widening conversion.
- Otherwise, if the single operand is of type Long, Float, or Double, it is unboxed.
- Otherwise, if the single operand is of a type narrower than int, its value is promoted to a value of type int by a widening conversion.
- Otherwise, the operand remains unchanged.

In other words, *unary numeric promotion results in an operand value that is either* int *or wider.*

Unary numeric promotion is applied in the following expressions:

- Operand of the unary arithmetic operators + and - (p. 58)
- Array creation expression; for example, new int[20], where the dimension expression (in this case, 20) must evaluate to an int value (§3.9, p. 117)
- Indexing array elements; for example, objArray['a'], where the index expression (in this case, 'a') must evaluate to an int value (§3.9, p. 120)

Binary Numeric Promotion

Binary numeric promotion implicitly applies appropriate widening primitive conversions so that the widest numeric type of a pair of operands is always at least int. If T is the widest numeric type of two operands after any unboxing conversions have been performed, the operands are promoted as follows during binary numeric promotion:

> If T is wider than int, both operands are converted to T; otherwise, both operands are converted to int.

This means that *the resulting type of the operands is at least* int.

Binary numeric promotion is applied in the following expressions:

- Operands of the arithmetic operators *, /, %, +, and - (p. 58)
- Operands of the relational operators <, <=, >, and >= (p. 74)
- Operands of the numerical equality operators == and != (p. 75)
- Operands of the conditional operator ? :, under certain circumstances (p. 90)

2.5 Precedence and Associativity Rules for Operators

Precedence and associativity rules are necessary for deterministic evaluation of expressions. The operators are summarized in Table 2.18. The majority of them are discussed in subsequent sections in this chapter. See also the index entries for these operators.

The following remarks apply to Table 2.18:

- The operators are shown with decreasing precedence from the top of the table.
- Operators within the same row have the same precedence.
- Parentheses, (), can be used to override precedence and associativity.
- The *unary operators*, which require one operand, include the following: the postfix increment (++) and decrement (--) operators from the first row, all the prefix operators (+, -, ++, --, ~, !) in the second row, and the prefix operators (object creation operator new, cast operator (*type*)) in the third row.
- The conditional operator (? :) is *ternary*—that is, it requires three operands.
- All operators not identified previously as unary or ternary are *binary*—that is, they require two operands.
- All binary operators, except for the relational and assignment operators, associate from left to right. The relational operators are nonassociative.
- Except for unary postfix increment and decrement operators, all unary operators, all assignment operators, and the ternary conditional operator associate from right to left.

Depending on the context, brackets ([]), parentheses (()), the colon (:), and the dot operator (.) can also be interpreted as *separators* (p. 32). See the index entries for these separators for more details.

Table 2.18 *Operator Summary*

Array element access, member access, method invocation	`[expression] . (args)`
Unary postfix operators	`expression++ expression--`
Unary prefix operators	`~ ! ++expression --expression +expression -expression`
Unary prefix creation and cast	`new (type)`
Multiplicative	`* / %`
Additive	`+ -`
Shift	`<< >> >>>`
Relational	`< <= > >= instanceof`
Equality	`== !=`
Bitwise/logical AND	`&`
Bitwise/logical XOR	`^`
Bitwise/logical OR	`|`
Conditional AND	`&&`
Conditional OR	`||`
Conditional	`?:`
Arrow operator	`->`
Assignment	`= += -= *= /= %= <<= >>= >>>= &= ^= |=`

Precedence rules are used to determine which operator should be applied first if there are two operators with a *different* precedence, and these operators follow each other in the expression. In such a case, the operator with the highest precedence is applied first.

The expression 2 + 3 * 4 is evaluated as 2 + (3 * 4) (with the result 14) since * has higher precedence than +.

Associativity rules are used to determine which operator should be applied first if there are two operators with the *same* precedence, and these operators follow each other in the expression.

Left associativity implies grouping from left to right: The expression 7 - 4 + 2 is interpreted as ((7 - 4) + 2), since the binary operators + and - both have the same precedence and left associativity.

Right associativity implies grouping from right to left: The expression - - 4 is interpreted as (- (- 4)) (with the result 4), since the unary operator - has right associativity.

The precedence and associativity rules together determine the *evaluation order of the operators*.

2.6 Evaluation Order of Operands

To understand the result returned by an operator, it is important to understand the *evaluation order of its operands*. In general, the operands of operators are evaluated from left to right. The evaluation order also respects any parentheses, and the precedence and associativity rules of operators.

Examples illustrating how the operand evaluation order influences the result returned by an operator can be found in §2.7, p. 54, and §2.10, p. 69.

Left-Hand Operand Evaluation First

The left-hand operand of a binary operator is fully evaluated before the right-hand operand is evaluated.

The evaluation of the left-hand operand can have side effects that can influence the value of the right-hand operand. For example, in the code

```
int b = 10;
System.out.println((b=3) + b);
```

the value printed will be 6 and not 13. The evaluation proceeds as follows:

```
(b=3) + b
  3   + b        b is assigned the value 3
  3   + 3
  6
```

If evaluation of the left-hand operand of a binary operator throws an exception (§7.1, p. 365), we cannot rely on the presumption that the right-hand operand has been evaluated.

Operand Evaluation before Operation Execution

Java guarantees that *all* operands of an operator are fully evaluated *before* the actual operation is performed. This rule does *not* apply to the short-circuit conditional operators &&, ||, and ?:.

This rule also applies to operators that throw an exception (the integer division operator / and the integer remainder operator %). The operation is performed only if the operands evaluate normally. Any side effects of the right-hand operand will have been effectuated before the operator throws an exception.

Example 2.1 illustrates the evaluation order of the operands and precedence rules for arithmetic expressions. We use the eval() method at (3) in Example 2.1 to demonstrate integer expression evaluation. The first argument to this method is the operand value that is returned by the method, and the second argument is a string to identify the evaluation order.

The argument to the println() method in the statement at (1) is an integer expression to evaluate 2 + 3 * 4. The evaluation of each operand in the expression at (1) results in a call of the eval() method declared at (3).

```
out.println(eval(j++, " + ") + eval(j++, " * ") * eval(j, "\n"));  // (1)
```

The output from Example 2.1 shows that the operands were evaluated first, from left to right, before operator execution, and that the expression was evaluated as (2 + (3 * 4)), respecting the precedence rules for arithmetic expression evaluation. Note how the value of variable j changes successively from left to right as the first two operands are evaluated.

Example 2.1 *Evaluation Order of Operands and Arguments*

```
import static java.lang.System.out;

public class EvalOrder{
  public static void main(String[] args){

    int j = 2;
    out.println("Evaluation order of operands:");
    out.println(eval(j++, " + ") + eval(j++, " * ") * eval(j, "\n"));     // (1)

    int i = 1;
    out.println("Evaluation order of arguments:");
    add3(eval(i++, ", "), eval(i++, ", "), eval(i, "\n")); // (2) Three arguments.
  }

  public static int eval(int operand, String str) {       // (3)
    out.print(operand + str);        // Print int operand and String str.
    return operand;                  // Return int operand.
  }

  public static void add3(int operand1, int operand2, int operand3) {    // (4)
    out.print(operand1 + operand2 + operand3);
  }
}
```

Output from the program:

```
Evaluation order of operands:
2 + 3 * 4
14
Evaluation order of arguments:
1, 2, 3
6
```

Left-to-Right Evaluation of Argument Lists

In a method or constructor invocation, each argument expression in the argument list is fully evaluated before any argument expression to its right.

If evaluation of an argument expression does not complete normally, we cannot presume that any argument expression to its right has been evaluated.

We can use the add3() method at (4) in Example 2.1, which takes three arguments, to demonstrate the order in which the arguments in a method call are evaluated. The method call at (2)

```
add3(eval(i++, ", "), eval(i++, ", "), eval(i, "\n"));  // (2) Three arguments.
```

results in the following output, clearly indicating that the arguments were evaluated from left to right, before being passed to the method:

```
1, 2, 3
6
```

Note how the value of variable i changes successively from left to right as the first two arguments are evaluated.

2.7 The Simple Assignment Operator =

The assignment statement has the following syntax:

variable = *expression*

which can be read as "the target, *variable*, gets the value of the source, *expression*." The previous value of the target variable is overwritten by the assignment operator =.

The target *variable* and the source *expression* must be assignment compatible. The target variable must also have been declared. Since variables can store either primitive values or reference values, *expression* evaluates to either a primitive value or a reference value.

Assigning Primitive Values

The following examples illustrate assignment of primitive values:

```
int j, k;
j = 0b10;          // j gets the value 2.
j = 5;             // j gets the value 5. Previous value is overwritten.
k = j;             // k gets the value 5.
```

The assignment operator has the lowest precedence, so the expression on the right-hand side is evaluated before the assignment is done.

```
int i;
i = 5;             // i gets the value 5.
i = i + 1;         // i gets the value 6. + has higher precedence than =.
i = 20 - i * 2;    // i gets the value 8: (20 - (i * 2))
```

Assigning References

Copying reference values by assignment creates *aliases*. Below, the variable `pizza1` is a reference to a pizza that is hot and spicy, and `pizza2` is a reference to a pizza that is sweet and sour.

```
Pizza pizza1 = new Pizza("Hot&Spicy");
Pizza pizza2 = new Pizza("Sweet&Sour");

pizza2 = pizza1;
```

Assigning `pizza1` to `pizza2` means that `pizza2` now refers to the same pizza as `pizza1`, the hot and spicy one. After the assignment, these variables are aliases and either one can be used to manipulate the hot and spicy `Pizza` object.

Assigning a reference value does *not* create a copy of the source object denoted by the reference variable on the right-hand side. It merely assigns the reference value of the variable on the right-hand side to the variable on the left-hand side so that they denote the same object. Reference assignment also does not copy the *state* of the source object to any object denoted by the reference variable on the left-hand side.

A more detailed discussion of reference assignment can be found in §5.8, p. 261.

Multiple Assignments

The assignment statement is an *expression statement*, which means that application of the binary assignment operator returns the value of the expression on the *right-hand* side.

```
int j, k;
j = 10;     // (1) j gets the value 10, which is returned
k = j;      // (2) k gets the value of j, which is 10, and this value is returned
```

The value returned by an assignment statement is usually discarded, as in the two assignment statements above. We can verify the value returned as follows:

```
System.out.println(j = 10);   // j gets the value 10, which is printed.
System.out.println(k = j);    // k gets the value of j, i.e. 10, which is printed
```

The two assignments (1) and (2) above can be written as multiple assignments, illustrating the right associativity of the assignment operator:

```
k = j = 10;     // (k = (j = 10))
```

Multiple assignments are equally valid with references:

```
Pizza pizzaOne, pizzaTwo;
pizzaOne = pizzaTwo = new Pizza("Supreme"); // Aliases
```

The following example shows the effect of operand evaluation order:

```
int[] a = {10, 20, 30, 40, 50}; // An array of int (§3.9, p. 119)
int index = 4;
a[index] = index = 2;           // (1)
```

What is the value of index, and which array element a[index] is assigned a value in the multiple assignment statement at (1)? The evaluation proceeds as follows:

```
a[index] = index = 2;
a[4]     = index = 2;
a[4]     = (index = 2);        // index gets the value 2. = is right associative.
a[4]     =      2;             // The value of a[4] is changed from 50 to 2.
```

The following declaration statement will not compile, as the variable v2 has not been declared:

```
int v1 = v2 = 2016;           // Only v1 is declared. Compile-time error!
```

Type Conversions in an Assignment Context

If the target and the source have the same type in an assignment, then obviously the source and the target are assignment compatible and the source value need not be converted. Otherwise, if a widening primitive conversion is permissible, then the widening conversion is applied implicitly; that is, the source type is converted to the target type in an assignment context.

```
// Widening Primitive Conversions
int    smallOne = 1234;               // No widening necessary.
long   bigOne   = 2020;               // Widening: int to long.
double largeOne = bigOne;             // Widening: long to double.
double hugeOne  = (double) bigOne;    // Cast redundant but allowed.
```

A widening primitive conversion can result in loss of *precision*. In the next example, the precision of the least significant bits of the long value may be lost when it is converted to a float value:

```
long bigInteger = 98765432112345678L;
float fpNum = bigInteger;  // Widening but loss of precision: 9.8765436E16
```

Additionally, *implicit narrowing primitive conversions* on assignment can occur in cases where *all* of the following conditions are fulfilled:

- The source is a *constant expression* of type byte, short, char, or int.
- The target type is of type byte, short, or char.
- The value of the source is determined to be in the range of the target type at compile time.

A *constant expression* is an expression that denotes either a primitive or a String literal; it is composed of operands that can be only *literals* or *constant variables*, and operators that can be evaluated only at compile time (e.g., arithmetic and numerical comparison operators, but not increment/decrement operators and method calls). A *constant variable* is a final variable of either a primitive type or the String type that is initialized with a constant expression.

```
int result = 100;                 // Not a constant variable. Not declared final.
final char finalGrade = 'A';      // Constant variable. 'A'
```

```
System.out.printf("%d%n%s%n%d%n%.2f%n%b%n%d%n%d%n",
    2022,                       // Constant expression. 2022
    "Trust " + "me!",           // Constant expression. "Trust me"
    2 + 3 * 4,                  // Constant expression. 14
    Math.PI * Math.PI * 10.0,   // Constant expression. 98.70
    finalGrade == 'A',          // Constant expression. true
    Math.min(2020, 2021),       // Not constant expression. Method call.
    ++result                    // Not constant expression. Increment operator.
);
```

Here are some examples that illustrate how the conditions mentioned previously affect narrowing primitive conversions:

```
// Conditions fulfilled for implicit narrowing primitive conversions.
short s1 = 10;        // int value in range.
short s2 = 'a';       // char value in range.
char c1 = 32;         // int value in range.
char c2 = (byte)35;   // byte value in range. (int value in range, without cast.)
byte b1 = 40;         // int value in range.
byte b2 = (short)40;  // short value in range. (int value in range, without cast.)
final int i1 = 20;    // Constant variable
byte b3 = i1;         // final value of i1 in range.
```

All other narrowing primitive conversions will produce a compile-time error on assignment and will explicitly require a cast. Here are some examples:

```
// Conditions not fulfilled for implicit narrowing primitive conversions.
// A cast is required.
int i2 = -20;            // i2 is not a constant variable. i2 is not final.
final int i3 = i2;       // i3 is not a constant variable, since i2 is not.
final int i4 = 200;      // i4 is a constant variable.
final int i5;            // i5 is not a constant variable.
short s3 = (short) i2;   // Not constant expression.
char  c3 = (char)  i3;   // Final value of i3 not determinable at compile time.
char  c4 = (char)  i2;   // Not constant expression.
byte  b4 = (byte)  128;  // int value not in range.
byte  b5 = (byte)  i4;   // Value of constant variable i4 is not in range.
i5 = 100;                // Initialized at runtime.
short s4 = (short) i5;   // Final value of i5 not determinable at compile time.
```

Floating-point values are truncated when cast to integral values.

```
// The value is truncated to fit the size of the target type.
float huge   = (float) 1.7976931348623157d;  // double to float.
long  giant  = (long)  4415961481999.03D;     // (1) double to long.
int   big    = (int)   giant;                 // (2) long to int.
short small  = (short) big;                   // (3) int to short.
byte  tiny   = (byte)  small;                 // (4) short to byte.
char  symbol = (char)  112.5F;                // (5) float to char.
```

Table 2.19 shows how the values are truncated for assignments from (1) to (5).

The discussion of numeric assignment conversions also applies to numeric parameter values at method invocation (§3.10, p. 129), except for the narrowing conversions, which always require a cast.

Table 2.19 *Examples of Truncated Values*

Binary	Decimal	
0000000000000000000001000000010000101011110100001100001100001111	4415961481999	(1)
00101011110100001100001100001111	735101711	(2)
1100001100001111	-15601	(3)
00001111	15	(4)
0000000001110000	'p'	(5)

The following examples illustrate boxing and unboxing in an assignment context:

```
Boolean   boolRef = true;   // Boxing.
Byte      bRef = 2;         // Constant in range: narrowing, then boxing.
// Byte  bRef2 =  257;      // Constant not in range. Compile-time error!

short s = 10;               // Narrowing from int to short.
// Integer   iRef1 = s;     // short not assignable to Integer.
Integer iRef3 = (int) s;    // Explicit widening with cast to int and boxing

boolean bv1 = boolRef;      // Unboxing.
byte  b1 = bRef;            // Unboxing.
int   iVal = bRef;          // Unboxing and widening.

Integer iRefVal = null;             // Always allowed.
// int j = iRefVal;                 // NullPointerException at runtime.
if (iRef3 != null) iVal = iRef3;    // Avoids exception at runtime.
```

2.8 Arithmetic Operators: *, /, %, +, -

Arithmetic operators are used to construct mathematical expressions as in algebra. Their operands are of a numeric type (which includes the char type).

Floating-point operations are now consistently *strict*; that is, they are executed in accordance with the IEEE-754 32-bit (float) and 64-bit (double) standard formats. This means that floating-point arithmetic operations give the same results on any JVM implementation. The keyword strictfp used to enforce strict behavior for floating-point arithmetic is now obsolete and should not be used in new code.

Arithmetic Operator Precedence and Associativity

In Table 2.20, the precedence of the operators appears in decreasing order, starting from the top row, which has the highest precedence. Unary subtraction has higher precedence than multiplication. The operators in the same row have the same precedence. Binary multiplication, division, and remainder operators have the same precedence. The unary operators have right associativity, and the binary operators have left associativity.

Table 2.20 *Arithmetic Operators*

Unary	+ *Plus*	− *Minus*	
Binary	* *Multiplication*	/ *Division*	% *Remainder*
	+ *Addition*	− *Subtraction*	

Evaluation Order in Arithmetic Expressions

Java guarantees that the operands are fully evaluated from left to right before an arithmetic binary operator is applied. If evaluation of an operand results in an error, the subsequent operands will not be evaluated.

In the expression a + b * c, the operand a will always be fully evaluated before the operand b, which will always be fully evaluated before the operand c. However, the multiplication operator * will be applied before the addition operator +, respecting the precedence rules. Note that a, b, and c are arbitrary arithmetic expressions that have been determined to be the operands of the operators.

Example 2.1, p. 53, illustrates the evaluation order and precedence rules for arithmetic expressions.

Range of Numeric Values

As we have seen, all numeric types have a range of valid values (p. 41). This range is given by the constants named MAX_VALUE and MIN_VALUE, which are defined in each numeric wrapper type.

The arithmetic operators are overloaded, meaning that the operation of an operator varies depending on the type of its operands. Floating-point arithmetic is performed if any operand of an operator is of floating-point type; otherwise, integer arithmetic is performed.

Values that are out of range or are the results of invalid expressions are handled differently depending on whether integer or floating-point arithmetic is performed.

Integer Arithmetic

Integer arithmetic always returns a value that is in range, except in the case of integer division by zero and remainder by zero, which cause an ArithmeticException (see the later discussion of the division operator / and the remainder operator %). A valid value does not necessarily mean that the result is correct, as demonstrated by the following examples:

```
int tooBig   = Integer.MAX_VALUE + 1;    // -2147483648 which is Integer.MIN_VALUE.
int tooSmall = Integer.MIN_VALUE - 1;    //  2147483647 which is Integer.MAX_VALUE.
```

These results should be values that are out of range. However, integer arithmetic *wraps around* the result if it is out of range; that is, the result is reduced modulo in the range of the result type. To avoid wrapping around out-of-range values, programs should use either explicit checks or a wider type. If the type long were used in the earlier examples, the results would be correct in the long range:

```
long notTooBig   = Integer.MAX_VALUE + 1L;   // 2147483648L in range.
long notTooSmall = Integer.MIN_VALUE - 1L;   // -2147483649L in range.
```

Floating-Point Arithmetic

Certain floating-point operations result in values that are out of range. Typically, adding or multiplying two very large floating-point numbers can result in an out-of-range value that is represented by *infinity* (Figure 2.3). Attempting floating-point division by zero also returns infinity. The following examples show how this value is printed as signed infinity:

```
System.out.println( 4.0 / 0.0);        // Prints:  Infinity
System.out.println(-4.0 / 0.0);        // Prints:  -Infinity
```

Both positive and negative infinity represent *overflow* to infinity; that is, the value is too large to be represented as a double or float (Figure 2.3). Signed infinity is represented by the named constants POSITIVE_INFINITY and NEGATIVE_INFINITY in the wrapper classes java.lang.Float and java.lang.Double. A value can be compared with these constants to detect overflow.

Figure 2.3   *Overflow and Underflow in Floating-Point Arithmetic*

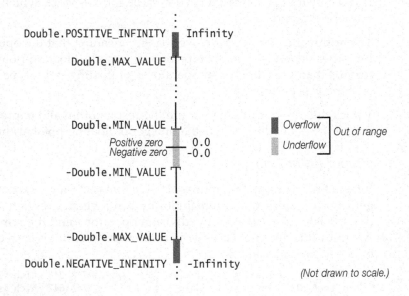

Floating-point arithmetic can also result in *underflow* to zero, when the value is too small to be represented as a double or float (Figure 2.3). Underflow occurs in the following situations:

- The result is between Double.MIN_VALUE (or Float.MIN_VALUE) and zero, as with the result of (5.1E-324 - 4.9E-324). Underflow then returns positive zero 0.0 (or 0.0F).
- The result is between -Double.MIN_VALUE (or -Float.MIN_VALUE) and zero, as with the result of (-Double.MIN_VALUE * 1E-1). Underflow then returns negative zero -0.0 (or -0.0F).

Negative zero compares equal to positive zero; in other words, (-0.0 == 0.0) is true.

Certain operations have no mathematical result, and are represented by *NaN* (*Not-a-Number*). For example, calculating the square root of –1 results in a NaN. Another example is (floating-point) dividing zero by zero:

```
System.out.println(0.0 / 0.0);        // Prints: NaN
```

NaN is represented by the constant named NaN in the wrapper classes java.lang.Float and java.lang.Double. Any operation involving NaN produces NaN. Any comparison (except inequality, !=) involving NaN and any other value (including NaN) returns false. An inequality comparison of NaN with another value (including NaN) always returns true. However, the recommended way of checking a value for NaN is to use the static method isNaN() defined in both wrapper classes, java.lang.Float and java.lang.Double.

Unary Arithmetic Operators: -, +

The unary operators have the highest precedence of all the arithmetic operators. The unary operator - negates the numeric value of its operand. The following example illustrates the right associativity of the unary operators:

```
int value = - -10;             // (-(-10)) is 10
```

Notice the blank space needed to separate the unary operators; without the blank space, these would be interpreted as the decrement operator -- (p. 69), which would result in a compile-time error because a literal cannot be decremented. The unary operator + has no effect on the evaluation of the operand value.

Multiplicative Binary Operators: *, /, %

Multiplication Operator: *

The multiplication operator * multiplies two numbers, as one would expect.

```
int    sameSigns     = -4   * -8;   // result: 32
double oppositeSigns = 4    * -8.0; // Widening of int 4 to double. result: -32.0
int    zero          = 0    * -0;   // result:  0
```

Division Operator: /

The division operator / is overloaded. If its operands are integral, the operation results in *integer division*.

```
int    i1 = 4  / 5;   // result: 0
int    i2 = 8  / 8;   // result: 1
double d1 = 12 / 8;   // result: 1.0; integer division, then widening conversion
```

Integer division always returns the quotient as an integer value; that is, the result is truncated toward zero. Note that the division performed is integer division if the operands have integral values, even if the result will be stored in a floating-point type. The integer value is subjected to a widening conversion in the assignment context.

An ArithmeticException is thrown when integer division with zero is attempted, meaning that integer division by zero is an illegal operation.

If any of the operands is a floating-point type, the operation performs *floating-point division*, where relevant operand values undergo binary numeric promotion:

```
double d2 = 4.0 / 8;      // result: 0.5
double d3 = 8 / 8.0;      // result: 1.0
float d4  = 12.0F / 8;    // result: 1.5F

double result1 = 12.0 / 4.0 * 3.0;    // ((12.0 / 4.0) * 3.0) which is 9.0
double result2 = 12.0 * 3.0 / 4.0;    // ((12.0 * 3.0) / 4.0) which is 9.0
```

Remainder Operator: %

In mathematics, when we divide a number (the *dividend*) by another number (the *divisor*), the result can be expressed in terms of a *quotient* and a *remainder*. For example, when 7 is divided by 5, the quotient is 1 and the remainder is 2. The remainder operator % returns the remainder of the division performed on the operands.

```
int quotient  = 7 / 5;    // Integer division operation: 1
int remainder = 7 % 5;    // Integer remainder operation: 2
```

For *integer remainder operation*, where only integer operands are involved, evaluation of the expression (x % y) always satisfies the following relation:

$$x == (x / y) * y + (x \% y)$$

In other words, the right-hand side yields a value that is always equal to the value of the dividend. The following examples show how we can calculate the remainder so that this relation is satisfied:

Calculating (7 % 5):

```
7 == (7 / 5) * 5 + (7 % 5)
  == (  1  ) * 5 + (7 % 5)
  ==             5 + (7 % 5)
2 ==                 (7 % 5)          (7 % 5) is equal to 2
```

Calculating (7 % –5):

```
7 == (7 / -5) * -5 + (7 % -5)
  == (  -1  ) * -5 + (7 % -5)
  ==              5 + (7 % -5)
2 ==                (7 % -5)
```
(7 % –5) is equal to 2

Calculating (–7 % 5):

```
-7 == (-7 / 5) * 5 + (-7 % 5)
   == (  -1  ) * 5 + (-7 % 5)
   ==            -5 + (-7 % 5)
-2 ==              (-7 % 5)
```
(–7 % 5) is equal to –2

Calculating (–7 % –5):

```
-7 == (-7 / -5) * -5 + (-7 % -5)
   == (   1  ) * -5 + (-7 % -5)
   ==             -5 + (-7 % -5)
-2 ==               (-7 % -5)
```
(–7 % –5) is equal to –2

The remainder can be negative only if the dividend is negative, and the sign of the divisor is irrelevant. A shortcut to evaluating the remainder involving negative operands is the following: Ignore the signs of the operands, calculate the remainder, and negate the remainder if the dividend is negative.

```
int  r0 =   7 %  7;    //  0
int  r1 =   7 %  5;    //  2
long r2 =  7L % -5L;   //  2L
int  r3 =  -7 %  5;    // -2
long r4 = -7L % -5L;   // -2L
boolean relation = -7L == (-7L / -5L) * -5L + r4;  // true
```

An ArithmeticException is thrown if the divisor evaluates to zero.

Note that the remainder operator accepts not only integral operands, but also floating-point operands. The *floating-point remainder* r is defined by the relation

$$r == a - (b * q)$$

where a and b are the dividend and the divisor, respectively, and q is the *integer* quotient of (a/b). The following examples illustrate a floating-point remainder operation:

```
double dr0 =  7.0  %  7.0;    //  0.0
float  fr1 =  7.0F %  5.0F;   //  2.0F
double dr1 =  7.0  % -5.0;    //  2.0
float  fr2 = -7.0F %  5.0F;   // -2.0F
double dr2 = -7.0  % -5.0;    // -2.0
boolean fpRelation = dr2 == (-7.0) - (-5.0) * (long)(-7.0 / -5.0);  // true
float  fr3 = -7.0F %  0.0F;   // NaN
```

Additive Binary Operators: +, -

The addition operator + and the subtraction operator - behave as their names imply: They add and subtract values, respectively. The binary operator + also acts as *string concatenation* if any of its operands is a string (p. 67).

Additive operators have lower precedence than all the other arithmetic operators. Table 2.21 includes examples that show how precedence and associativity are used in arithmetic expression evaluation.

Table 2.21   *Examples of Arithmetic Expression Evaluation*

Arithmetic expression	Evaluation	Result when printed
3 + 2 - 1	((3 + 2) - 1)	4
2 + 6 * 7	(2 + (6 * 7))	44
-5 + 7 - -6	(((-5) + 7) - (-6))	8
2 + 4 / 5	(2 + (4 / 5))	2
13 % 5	(13 % 5)	3
11.5 % 2.5	(11.5 % 2.5)	1.5
10 / 0		ArithmeticException
2 + 4.0 / 5	(2.0 + (4.0 / 5.0))	2.8
4.0 / 0.0	(4.0 / 0.0)	Infinity
-4.0 / 0.0	((-4.0) / 0.0)	-Infinity
0.0 / 0.0	(0.0 / 0.0)	NaN

Numeric Promotions in Arithmetic Expressions

Unary numeric promotion is applied to the single operand of the unary arithmetic operators - and +. When a unary arithmetic operator is applied to an operand whose type is narrower than int, the operand is promoted to a value of type int, with the operation resulting in an int value. If the conditions for implicit narrowing conversion are not fulfilled (p. 56), assigning the int result to a variable of a narrower type will require a cast. This is demonstrated by the following example, where the byte operand b is promoted to an int in the expression (-b):

```
byte b = 3;        // int literal in range. Narrowing conversion.
b = (byte) -b;     // Cast required on assignment.
```

Binary numeric promotion is applied to operands of binary arithmetic operators. Its application leads to type promotion for the operands, as explained in §2.4, p. 49. The result is of the promoted type, which is always type int or wider. For the expression at (1) in Example 2.2, numeric promotions proceed as shown in Figure 2.4. Note the integer division performed in evaluating the subexpression (c / s).

Example 2.2   *Numeric Promotion in Arithmetic Expressions*

```
public class NumPromotion {
  public static void main(String[] args) {
    byte   b = 32;
```

```
        char   c = 'z';                      // Unicode value 122 (\u007a)
        short  s = 256;
        int    i = 10000;
        float  f = 3.5F;
        double d = 0.5;
        double v = (d * i) + (f * -b) - (c / s);    // (1) 4888.0D
        System.out.println("Value of v: " + v);
    }
}
```

Output from the program:

```
Value of v: 4888.0
```

Figure 2.4 *Numeric Promotion in Arithmetic Expressions*

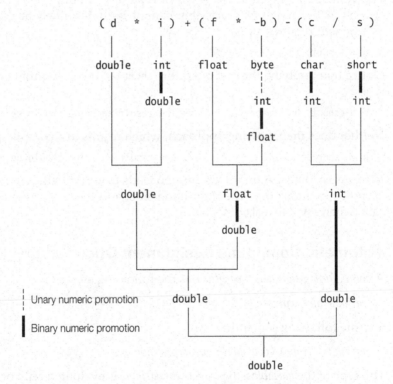

In addition to the binary numeric promotions in arithmetic expression evaluation, the resulting value can undergo an implicit widening conversion if assigned to a variable. In the first two declaration statements that follow, only assignment conversions take place. Numeric promotions take place in the evaluation of the right-hand expression in the other declaration statements.

```
Byte   b = 10;      // Constant in range: narrowing and boxing on assignment.
Short  s = 20;      // Constant in range: narrowing and boxing on assignment.
```

```
char   c = 'z';        // 122 (\u007a)
int    i = s * b;      // Values in s and b promoted to int: unboxing, widening.
long   n = 20L + s;    // Value in s promoted to long: unboxing, widening.
float  r = s + c;      // Value in s is unboxed. This short value and the char
                       // value in c are promoted to int, followed by implicit
                       // widening conversion of int to float on assignment.
double d = r + i;      // Value in i promoted to float, followed by implicit
                       // widening conversion of float to double on assignment.
```

Binary numeric promotion for operands of binary operators implies that each operand of a binary operator is promoted to type int or a broader numeric type, if necessary. As with unary operators, care must be exercised in assigning the value resulting from applying a binary operator to operands of these types.

```
short h = 40;          // OK: int converted to short. Implicit narrowing.
h = h + 2;             // Error: cannot assign an int to short.
```

The value of the expression h + 2 is of type int. Although the result of the expression is in the range of short, this cannot be determined at compile time. The assignment requires a cast.

```
h = (short) (h + 2);   // OK
```

Notice that applying the cast operator (short) to the individual operands does not work:

```
h = (short) h + (short) 2;      // The resulting value should be cast.
```

Neither does the following approach, which results in a compile-time error:

```
h = (short) h + 2;              // The resulting value should be cast.
```

In this case, binary numeric promotion leads to an int value as the result of evaluating the expression on the right-hand side, and therefore, requires an additional cast to narrow it to a short value.

Arithmetic Compound Assignment Operators: *=, /=, %=, +=, -=

A *compound assignment operator* has the following syntax:

variable op= expression

and the following semantics:

variable = (type) ((variable) op (expression))

The type of the *variable* is *type* and the *variable* is evaluated only once. Note the cast and the parentheses implied in the semantics. Here *op=* can be any of the compound assignment operators specified in Table 2.18. The compound assignment operators have the lowest precedence of all the operators in Java, allowing the expression on the right-hand side to be evaluated before the assignment. Table 2.22 defines the arithmetic compound assignment operators.

Table 2.22 *Arithmetic Compound Assignment Operators*

Expression	Given T as the numeric type of x, the expression is evaluated as:
x *= a	x = (T) ((x) * (a))
x /= a	x = (T) ((x) / (a))
x %= a	x = (T) ((x) % (a))
x += a	x = (T) ((x) + (a))
x -= a	x = (T) ((x) - (a))

The implied cast operator, (T), in the compound assignments becomes necessary when the result must be narrowed to the target type. This is illustrated by the following examples:

```
int i = 2;
i *= i + 4;             // (1) Evaluated as i = (int) ((i) * (i + 4)).

Integer iRef = 2;
iRef *= iRef + 4;       // (2) Evaluated as iRef = (Integer) ((iRef) * (iRef + 4)).

byte b = 2;
b += 10;                // (3) Evaluated as b = (byte) (b + 10).
b = b + 10;             // (4) Will not compile. Cast is required.
```

At (1) the source int value is assigned to the target int variable, and the cast operator (int) in this case is an *identity conversion* (i.e., conversion from a type to the same type). Such casts are permitted. The assignment at (2) entails unboxing to evaluate the expression on the right-hand side, followed by boxing to assign the int value. However, at (3), as the source value is an int value because the byte value in b is promoted to int to carry out the addition, assigning it to a target byte variable requires an implicit narrowing conversion. The situation at (4) with simple assignment will not compile because implicit narrowing conversion is not applicable.

The *variable* is evaluated only once in the expression, not twice, as one might infer from the definition of the compound assignment operator. In the following assignment, a[i] is evaluated just once:

```
int[] a = new int[] { 2020, 2030, 2040 };
int i = 2;
a[i] += 1;      // Evaluates as a[2] = a[2] + 1, and a[2] gets the value 2041.
```

Implicit narrowing conversions are also applied to increment and decrement operators (p. 69).

Boolean logical compound assignment operators are covered in §2.14, p. 78.

2.9 The Binary String Concatenation Operator +

The binary operator + is overloaded in the sense that the operation performed is determined by the type of the operands. When one of the operands is a String object, a string concatenation is performed rather than numeric addition. String concatenation results in a newly created String object in which the characters in the text representation of the left-hand operand precede the characters in the text representation of the right-hand operand. It might be necessary to perform a *string conversion* on the non-String operand before the string concatenation can be performed. The String class is discussed in §8.4, p. 439.

A *string conversion* is performed on the non-String operand as follows:

- For an operand of a primitive data type, its value is converted to a text representation.

- For all reference value operands, a text representation is constructed by calling the no-argument toString() method on the referred object. Most classes override this method from the Object class so as to provide a more meaningful text representation of their objects. Discussion of the toString() method can be found in §8.2, p. 425.

- Values like true, false, and null have text representations that correspond to their names. A reference variable with the value null also has the text representation "null" in this context.

The operator + is left associative and has the same precedence level as the additive operators, whether it is performed as a string concatenation or as a numeric addition.

```
String strVal = "" + 2020;              // (1) "2020"
String theName = " Uranium";
theName = " Pure" + theName;            // (2) " Pure Uranium"
String trademark1 = 100 + "%" + theName;  // (3) "100% Pure Uranium"
```

Since the + operator is left-associative, the evaluation at (3) proceeds as follows: The int value 100 is concatenated with the string literal "%", followed by concatenation with the contents of the String object referred to by the theName reference.

Note that using the character literal '%' instead of the string literal "%" in line (2) does not give the same result:

```
String trademark2 = 100 + '%' + theName;    // (4) "137 Pure Uranium"
```

Integer addition is performed by the first + operator: 100 + '%'; that is, (100 + 37).

Caution should be exercised because the + operator might not be applied as intended, as shown by the following example:

```
System.out.println("We can put two and two together and get " + 2 + 2);    // (5)
```

This statement prints "We can put two and two together and get 22". String concatenation proceeds from left to right: The String literal is concatenated with the first int literal 2, followed by concatenation with the second int literal 2. Both occurrences of the + operator are treated as string concatenation. To convey the intended meaning of the sentence, parentheses are necessary:

```
System.out.println("We can put two and two together and get " + (2 + 2)); // (6)
```

This statement prints "We can put two and two together and get 4", since the parentheses enforce integer addition in the expression (2 + 2) before string concatenation is performed with the contents of the String operand.

The following statement will print the correct result, even without the parentheses, because the * operator has higher precedence than the + operator:

```
System.out.println("2 * 2 = " + 2 * 2);       // (7) 2 * 2 = 4
```

Creation of temporary String objects might be necessary to store the results of performing successive string concatenations in a String-valued expression. For a String-valued *constant expression* ((1), (5), (6), and (7) in the preceding examples), the compiler computes such an expression at compile time, and the result is treated as a string literal in the program. The compiler uses a *string builder* to avoid the overhead of temporary String objects when applying the string concatenation operator (+) in String-valued non-constant expressions ((2), (3), and (4) in the preceding examples), as explained in §8.5, p. 469.

2.10 Variable Increment and Decrement Operators: ++, --

Variable increment (++) and decrement (--) operators come in two flavors: *prefix* and *postfix*. These unary operators have the side effect of changing the value of the arithmetic operand, which must evaluate to a variable. Depending on the operator used, the variable is either incremented by 1 or decremented by 1.

These operators cannot be applied to a variable that is declared final and that has been initialized, as the side effect would change the value in such a variable.

These operators are useful for updating variables in loops where only the side effect of the operator is of interest.

The Increment Operator ++

The prefix increment operator has the following semantics: ++i adds 1 to the value in i, and stores the new value in i. It returns the *new* value as the value of the expression. It is equivalent to the following statements:

```
i += 1;
result = i;
return result;
```

The postfix increment operator has the following semantics: j++ adds 1 to the value in j, and stores the new value in j. It returns the *original* value that was in j as the value of the expression. It is equivalent to the following statements:

```
result = j;
j += 1;
return result;
```

The Decrement Operator --

The prefix decrement operator has the following semantics: --i subtracts 1 from the value of i, and stores the new value in i. It returns the *new* value as the value of the expression. It is equivalent to the following statements:

```
i -= 1;
result = i;
return result;
```

The postfix decrement operator has the following semantics: j-- subtracts 1 from the value of j, and stores the new value in j. It returns the *original* value that was in j as the value of the expression. It is equivalent to the following statements:

```
result = j;
j -= 1;
return result;
```

This behavior of decrement and increment operators applies to any variable whose type is a numeric primitive type or its corresponding numeric wrapper type. Necessary numeric promotions are performed on the value 1 and the value of the variable. Before the new value is assigned to the variable, it is subjected to any narrowing primitive conversion and/or boxing that might be necessary.

Here are some examples that illustrate the behavior of increment and decrement operators:

```
// (1) Prefix order: increment/decrement operand before use.
int i = 10;
int k = ++i + --i;    // ((++i) + (--i)). k gets the value 21 and i becomes 10.
--i;                  // Only side effect utilized. i is 9. (expression statement)

Integer iRef = 11;    // Boxing on assignment
--iRef;               // Only side effect utilized. iRef refers to an Integer
                      // object with the value 10. (expression statement)
k = ++iRef + --iRef;// ((++iRef) + (--iRef)). k gets the value 21 and
                      // iRef refers to an Integer object with the value 10.

// (2) Postfix order: increment/decrement operand after use.
long j = 10;
long n = j++ + j--; // ((j++) + (j--)). n gets the value 21L and j becomes 10L.
j++;                  // Only side effect utilized. j is 11L. (expression statement)
```

An increment or decrement operator, together with its operand, can be used as an *expression statement* (§3.3, p. 101).

Execution of the assignment in the second declaration statement under (1) proceeds as follows:

```
k = ((++i) + (--i))          Operands are evaluated from left to right.
k = ( 11   + (--i))          Side effect: i += 1, i gets the value 11.
k = ( 11   + 10)             Side effect: i -= 1, i gets the value 10.
k = 21
```

Execution of the expression statement `--iRef;` under (1) proceeds as follows:

- The value in the `Integer` object referred to by the reference `iRef` is unboxed, resulting in the `int` value 11.
- The value 11 is decremented, resulting in the value 10.
- The value 10 is boxed in an `Integer` object, and this object's reference value is assigned to the reference `iRef`.
- The `int` value 10 of the expression statement is discarded.

Expressions where variables are modified multiple times during the evaluation should be avoided because the order of evaluation is not always immediately apparent.

We cannot associate increment and decrement operators. Given that a is a variable, we cannot write (++(++a)). The reason is that any operand to ++ must evaluate to a variable, but the evaluation of (++a) results in a value.

In the next example, both binary numeric promotion and an implicit narrowing conversion are performed to achieve the side effect of modifying the value of the operand. The `int` value of the expression (++b) (i.e., 11) is assigned to the `int` variable i. The side effect of incrementing the value of the byte variable b requires binary numeric promotion to perform `int` addition, followed by an implicit narrowing conversion of the `int` value to byte to assign the value to variable b.

```
byte b = 10;
int  i = ++b;        // i is 11, and so is b.
```

The following example illustrates applying the increment operator to a floating-point operand. The side effect of the ++ operator is overwritten by the assignment.

```
double x = 4.5;
x = x + ++x;         // x gets the value 10.0.
```

 ## Review Questions

2.1 Which of the following is not a legal comment in Java?
Select the one correct answer.

(a) `/* // */`
(b) `/* */ //`
(c) `// /* */`
(d) `/* /* */`
(e) `/* /* */ */`
(f) `// //`

2.2 What will be the result of compiling and running the following program?

```
public class Assignment {
  public static void main(String[] args) {
    int a, b, c;
    b = 10;
```

```
      a = b = c = 20;
      System.out.println(a);
    }
  }
```

Select the one correct answer.

(a) The code will fail to compile because the compiler will report that the variable
    c in the multiple assignment statement a = b = c = 20; has not been
    initialized.
(b) The code will fail to compile because the multiple assignment statement a = b
    = c = 20; is illegal.
(c) The code will compile and print 10 at runtime.
(d) The code will compile and print 20 at runtime.

2.3 What will be the result of compiling and running the following program?

```
public class MyClass {
  public static void main(String[] args) {
    String a, b, c;
    c = new String("mouse");
    a = new String("cat");
    b = a;
    a = new String("dog");
    c = b;

    System.out.println(c);
  }
}
```

Select the one correct answer.

(a) The program will fail to compile.
(b) The program will print mouse at runtime.
(c) The program will print cat at runtime.
(d) The program will print dog at runtime.
(e) The program will randomly print either cat or dog at runtime.

2.4 Which of the following expressions evaluate to a floating-point value?
Select the three correct answers.

(a) 2.0 * 3
(b) 2 * 3
(c) 2/3 + 5/7
(d) 2.4 + 1.6
(e) 0x10 * 1L * 300.0

2.5 What is the value of the expression (1 / 2 + 3 / 2 + 0.1)?
Select the one correct answer.

(a) 1
(b) 1.1
(c) 1.6
(d) 2
(e) 2.1

2.6 What is the value of evaluating the following expression: (- -1-3 * 10 / 5-1)? Select the one correct answer.
(a) –8
(b) –6
(c) 7
(d) 8
(e) 10
(f) None of the above

2.7 What is the result of compiling and running the following program?

```java
public class Prog1 {
  public static void main(String[] args) {
    int k = 1;
    int i = ++k + k++ + + k;      // (1)
    System.out.println(i);
  }
}
```

Select the one correct answer.
(a) The program will fail to compile because of errors in the expression at (1).
(b) The program will print the value 3 at runtime.
(c) The program will print the value 4 at runtime.
(d) The program will print the value 7 at runtime.
(e) The program will print the value 8 at runtime.

2.8 Which is the first line that will cause a compile-time error in the following program?

```java
public class MyClass {
  public static void main(String[] args) {
    char c;
    int i;
    c = 'a'; // (1)
    i = c;   // (2)
    i++;     // (3)
    c = i;   // (4)
    c++;     // (5)
  }
}
```

Select the one correct answer.
(a) (1)
(b) (2)
(c) (3)
(d) (4)
(e) (5)
(f) None of the above. The compiler will not report any errors.

2.9 What will be the result of compiling and running the following program?

```java
public class EvaluationOrder {
  public static void main(String[] args) {
    int[] array = { 4, 8, 16 };
```

```
    int i = 1;
    array[++i] = --i;
    System.out.println(array[0] + array[1] + array[2]);
  }
}
```

Select the one correct answer.

(a) 13
(b) 14
(c) 20
(d) 21
(e) 24

2.11 Boolean Expressions

As the name implies, a boolean expression has the boolean data type and can only evaluate to the value true or false. Boolean expressions, when used as conditionals in control statements, allow the program flow to be controlled during execution.

Boolean expressions can be formed using *relational operators* (p. 74), *equality operators* (p. 75), *boolean logical operators* (p. 78), *conditional operators* (p. 80), the *assignment operator* (p. 54), and the instanceof operator (§5.11, p. 269).

2.12 Relational Operators: <, <=, >, >=

Given that a and b represent numeric expressions, the relational (also called *comparison*) operators are defined as shown in Table 2.23.

Table 2.23 *Relational Operators*

a < b	a less than b?
a <= b	a less than or equal to b?
a > b	a greater than b?
a >= b	a greater than or equal to b?

All relational operators are binary operators and their operands are numeric expressions. Binary numeric promotion is applied to the operands of these operators. The evaluation results in a boolean value. Relational operators have lower precedence than arithmetic operators, but higher than that of the assignment operators.

```
double hours = 45.5;
Double time = 18.0;              // Boxing of double value.
boolean overtime = hours >= 35; // true. Binary numeric promotion: double <-- int.
boolean beforeMidnight = time < 24.0;// true. Unboxing of value in time reference.
char letterA = 'A';
boolean order = letterA < 'a';  // true. Binary numeric promotion: int <-- char.
```

Relational operators are nonassociative. Mathematical expressions like $a \leq b \leq c$ must be written using relational and boolean logical/conditional operators.

```
int a = 1, b = 7, c = 10;
boolean illegal = a <= b <= c;      // (1) Illegal. Compile-time error!
boolean valid2 = a <= b && b <= c;  // (2) OK.
```

Since relational operators have left associativity, the evaluation of the expression a <= b <= c at (1) in these examples would proceed as follows: ((a <= b) <= c). Evaluation of (a <= b) would yield a boolean value that is not permitted as an operand of a relational operator; that is, (*boolean value* <= c) would be illegal.

2.13 Equality

We distinguish between *primitive data value equality*, *object reference equality*, and *object value equality*.

The equality operators have lower precedence than the relational operators, but higher precedence than the assignment operators.

Primitive Data Value Equality: ==, !=

Given that a and b represent operands of primitive data types, the primitive data value equality operators are defined as shown in Table 2.24.

Table 2.24 *Primitive Data Value Equality Operators*

| a == b | Determines whether a and b are equal—that is, have the same primitive value (*equality*). |
| a != b | Determines whether a and b are not equal—that is, do not have the same primitive value (*inequality*). |

The equality operator == and the inequality operator != can be used to compare primitive data values, including boolean values. Binary numeric promotion may be applied to the non-boolean operands of these equality operators.

```
int year = 2002;
boolean isEven   = year % 2 == 0;    // true.
boolean compare  = '1' == 1;         // false. Binary numeric promotion applied.
boolean test     = compare == false; // true.
```

Care must be exercised when comparing floating-point numbers for equality, as an infinite number of floating-point values can be stored only as approximations in a finite number of bits. For example, the expression (1.0 - 2.0/3.0 == 1.0/3.0) returns false, although mathematically the result should be true.

Analogous to the discussion for relational operators, mathematical expressions like $a = b = c$ must be written using relational and logical/conditional operators. Since equality operators have left associativity, the evaluation of the expression a == b == c would proceed as follows: ((a == b) == c). Evaluation of (a == b) would yield a boolean value that *is* permitted as an operand of a data value equality operator, but (*boolean value* == c) would be illegal if c had a numeric type. This problem is illustrated in the following examples. The expression at (1) is illegal, but those at (2) and (3) are legal.

```
int a, b, c;
a = b = c = 5;
boolean illegal = a == b == c;          // (1) Illegal.
boolean valid2 = a == b && b == c;      // (2) Legal.
boolean valid3 = a == b == true;        // (3) Legal.
```

Object Reference Equality: ==, !=

The equality operator == and the inequality operator != can be applied to reference variables to test whether they refer to the same object. Given that r and s are reference variables, the reference equality operators are defined as shown in Table 2.25.

Table 2.25 *Reference Equality Operators*

r == s	Determines whether r and s are equal—that is, have the same reference value and therefore refer to the same object (also called *aliases*) (*equality*).
r != s	Determines whether r and s are not equal—that is, do not have the same reference value and therefore refer to different objects (*inequality*).

The operands must be cast compatible: It must be possible to cast the reference value of the one into the other's type; otherwise a compile-time error will result. Casting of references is discussed in §5.8, p. 261.

```
Pizza pizzaA = new Pizza("Sweet&Sour");    // new object
Pizza pizzaB = new Pizza("Sweet&Sour");    // new object
Pizza pizzaC = new Pizza("Hot&Spicy");     // new object

String banner = "Come and get it!";        // new object

boolean test  = banner == pizzaA;          // (1) Compile-time error
boolean test1 = pizzaA == pizzaB;          // false
boolean test2 = pizzaA == pizzaC;          // false

pizzaA = pizzaB;                           // Denote the same object; are aliases
boolean test3 = pizzaA == pizzaB;          // true
```

The comparison banner == pizzaA at (1) is illegal because the String and Pizza types are incompatible operand types as the reference value of one type cannot be cast to the other type. The values of test1 and test2 are false because the three references denote different objects, regardless of the fact that pizzaA and pizzaB are both sweet and sour pizzas. The value of test3 is true because now both pizzaA and pizzaB denote the same object.

The equality and inequality operators are applied to object references to check whether two references denote the same object. The state of the objects that the references denote is not compared. This is the same as testing whether the references are *aliases*, meaning that they denote the same object.

The `null` literal can be assigned to any reference variable, and the reference value in a reference variable can be compared for equality with the `null` literal. The comparison can be used to avoid inadvertent use of a reference variable that does not denote any object.

```
if (objRef != null) {
    // ... use objRef ...
}
```

Note that only when the type of *both* operands is either a reference type or the `null` type do these operators test for object reference equality. Otherwise, they test for primitive data equality (see also §8.3, p. 432). In the following code snippet, binary numeric promotion involving unboxing is performed at (1):

```
Integer iRef = 10;
boolean b1 = iRef == null;        // Object reference equality
boolean b2 = iRef == 10;          // (1) Primitive data value equality
boolean b3 = null == 10;          // Compile-time error!
```

Object Value Equality

The `Object` class provides the method `public boolean equals(Object obj)`, which can be *overridden* (§5.1, p. 196) to give the right semantics of *object value equality*. The default implementation of this method in the `Object` class returns `true` only if the object is compared with itself, as if the equality operator `==` had been used to compare aliases of an object. Consequently, if a class does not override the semantics of the `equals()` method from the `Object` class, object value equality is the same as object reference equality.

Certain classes in the Java SE API override the `equals()` method, such as `java.lang.String` and the wrapper classes for the primitive data types. For two `String` objects, value equality means they contain identical character sequences. For the wrapper classes, value equality means the wrapper objects have the same primitive value and are of the same wrapper type (see also §8.3, p. 432).

```
// Equality for String objects means identical character sequences.
String movie1 = new String("The Revenge of the Exception Handler");
String movie2 = new String("High Noon at the Java Corral");
String movie3 = new String("The Revenge of the Exception Handler");
boolean test0 = movie1.equals(movie2);          // false.
boolean test1 = movie1.equals(movie3);          // true.

// Equality for wrapper classes means same type and same primitive value.
Boolean flag1 = true;                           // Boxing.
Boolean flag2 = false;                          // Boxing.
boolean test2 = flag1.equals("true");           // false. Not same type.
boolean test3 = flag1.equals(!flag2);           // true. Same type and value.

Integer iRef = 100;                             // Boxing.
Short sRef = 100;                               // Boxing <--- short <--- int
boolean test4 = iRef.equals(100);               // true. Same type and value.
boolean test5 = iRef.equals(sRef);              // false. Not same type.
boolean test6 = iRef.equals(3.14);              // false. Not same type.
```

```
// The Pizza class does not override the equals() method, so we can use either
// equals() method inherited from the Object class or equality operator ==.
Pizza pizza1 = new Pizza("Veggies Delight");
Pizza pizza2 = new Pizza("Veggies Delight");
Pizza pizza3 = new Pizza("Cheese Delight");
boolean test7 = pizza1.equals(pizza2);              // false.
boolean test8 = pizza1.equals(pizza3);              // false.
boolean test9 = pizza1 == pizza2;                   // false.
pizza1 = pizza2;                                    // Creates aliases.
boolean test10 = pizza1.equals(pizza2);             // true.
boolean test11 = pizza1 == pizza2;                  // true.
```

2.14 Boolean Logical Operators: !, ∧, &, |

Boolean logical operators include the unary operator ! (*logical complement*) and the binary operators & (*logical* AND), | (*logical inclusive* OR), and ∧ (*logical exclusive* OR, also called *logical* XOR). These operators can be applied to boolean or Boolean operands, returning a boolean value. The operators &, |, and ∧ can also be applied to integral operands to perform *bitwise* logical operations (p. 82).

Given that *x* and *y* represent boolean expressions, the boolean logical operators are defined in Table 2.26. The precedence of the operators decreases from left to right in the table.

These operators always evaluate *both* of the operands, unlike their counterpart *conditional operators* && and || (p. 80). Unboxing is applied to the operand values, if necessary. Truth values for boolean logical operators are shown in Table 2.26, where x and y are either of type boolean or Boolean.

Table 2.26   *Truth Values for Boolean Logical Operators*

x	y	Complement !x	AND x & y	XOR x ∧ y	OR x | y
true	true	false	true	false	true
true	false	false	false	true	true
false	true	true	false	true	true
false	false	true	false	false	false

Operand Evaluation for Boolean Logical Operators

In the evaluation of boolean expressions involving boolean logical AND, XOR, and OR operators, both the operands are evaluated. The order of operand evaluation is always from left to right.

```
if (i > 0 & i++ < 10) {/*...*/} // i will be incremented, regardless of value in i.
```

The binary boolean logical operators have lower precedence than the arithmetic and relational operators, but higher precedence than the assignment, conditional AND, and OR operators (p. 80). This is illustrated in the following examples:

```
boolean b1, b2, b3 = false, b4 = false;
Boolean b5 = true;
b1 = 4 == 2 & 1 < 4;              // false, evaluated as (b1 = ((4 == 2) & (1 < 4)))
b2 = b1 | !(2.5 >= 8);           // true
b3 = b3 ^ b5;                    // true, unboxing conversion on b5
b4 = b4 | b1 & b2;               // false
```

Here, the order of evaluation is illustrated for the last expression statement:

$\qquad$ (b4 = (b4 | (b1 & b2)))

$\Longrightarrow$ (b4 = (false | (b1 & b2)))

$\Longrightarrow$ (b4 = (false | (false & b2)))

$\Longrightarrow$ (b4 = (false | (false & true)))

$\Longrightarrow$ (b4 = (false | false))

$\Longrightarrow$ (b4 = false)

$\Longrightarrow$ false

Note that b2 was evaluated, although strictly speaking, it was not necessary. This behavior is guaranteed for boolean logical operators.

Boolean Logical Compound Assignment Operators: &=, ^=, |=

Compound assignment operators for the boolean logical operators are defined in Table 2.27. The left-hand operand must be a boolean variable, and the right-hand operand must be a boolean expression. An identity conversion is applied implicitly on assignment. These operators can also be applied to integral operands to perform *bitwise* compound assignments (p. 82). See also the discussion on arithmetic compound assignment operators (p. 66).

Table 2.27 *Boolean Logical Compound Assignment Operators*

Expression	Given a and b are of type boolean or Boolean, the expression is evaluated as:
b &= a	b = (b & (a))
b ^= a	b = (b ^ (a))
b |= a	b = (b | (a))

Here are some examples to illustrate the behavior of boolean logical compound assignment operators:

```
boolean b1 = false, b2 = true, b3 = false;
Boolean b4 = false;
b1 |= true;                      // true
b4 ^= b1;                        // (1) true, unboxing in (b4 ^ (b1)), boxing on assignment
b3 &= b1 | b2;                   // (2) false, b3 = (b3 & (b1 | b2))
b3 = b3 & b1 | b2;               // (3) true,  b3 = ((b3 & b1) | b2)
```

The assignment at (1) entails unboxing to evaluate the expression on the right-hand side, followed by boxing to assign the boolean result. It is also instructive to compare how the assignments at (2) and (3) are performed, as they lead to different results with the same values of the operands, showing how the precedence affects the evaluation.

2.15 Conditional Operators: &&, ||

The conditional operators && and || are similar to their counterpart logical operators & and |, except that their evaluation is *short-circuited*. Given that x and y represent values of boolean or Boolean expressions, the conditional operators are defined in Table 2.28. In the table, the operators are listed in decreasing order of precedence.

Table 2.28 *Conditional Operators*

Conditional AND	x && y	true if both operands are true; otherwise false.
Conditional OR	x || y	true if either or both operands are true; otherwise false.

Unlike their logical counterparts & and |, which can also be applied to integral operands for bitwise operations, the conditional operators && and || can be applied to only boolean operands. Their evaluation results in a boolean value. Truth values for conditional operators are shown in Table 2.29. Not surprisingly, the conditional operators have the same truth values as their counterpart logical operators. However, unlike with their logical counterparts, there are no compound assignment operators for the conditional operators.

Table 2.29 *Truth Values for Conditional Operators*

x	y	AND x && y	OR x || y
true	true	true	true
true	false	false	true
false	true	false	true
false	false	false	false

Short-Circuit Evaluation

In the evaluation of boolean expressions involving conditional AND and OR, the left-hand operand is evaluated before the right-hand operand, and the evaluation is short-circuited (i.e., if the result of the boolean expression can be determined from the left-hand operand, the right-hand operand is not evaluated). In other words, the right-hand operand is evaluated conditionally.

The binary conditional operators have lower precedence than the arithmetic, relational, and logical operators, but higher precedence than the assignment operators.

Unboxing of the operand value takes place when necessary, before the operation is performed. The following examples illustrate usage of conditional operators:

```
Boolean b1 = 4 == 2 && 1 < 4;    // false, short-circuit evaluated as
                                 // (b1 = ((4 == 2) && (1 < 4)))
boolean b2 = !b1 || 2.5 > 8;     // true, short-circuit evaluated as
                                 // (b2 = ((!b1) || (2.5 > 8)))
Boolean b3 = !(b1 && b2);        // true
boolean b4 = b1 || !b3 && b2;    // false, short-circuit evaluated as
                                 // (b4 = (b1 || ((!b3) && b2)))
```

The order of evaluation for computing the value stored in the boolean variable b4 proceeds as follows:

```
   (b4 = (b1 || ((!b3) && b2)))
⟹ (b4 = (false || ((!b3) && b2)))
⟹ (b4 = (false || ((!true) && b2)))
⟹ (b4 = (false || ((false) && b2)))
⟹ (b4 = (false || false))
⟹ (b4 = false)
```

Note that b2 is not evaluated, short-circuiting the evaluation. Example 2.3 illustrates the short-circuit evaluation of the initialization expressions in the declaration statements given in the code snippet above. In addition, it shows an evaluation (see the declaration of b5) involving boolean logical operators that always evaluate both operands. The output shows how many operands were evaluated for each expression. See also Example 2.1, p. 53, which uses a similar approach to illustrate the order of operand evaluation in arithmetic expressions.

Example 2.3 *Short-Circuit Evaluation Involving Conditional Operators*

```java
public class ShortCircuit {
  public static void main(String[] args) {
    // Boolean b1 = 4 == 2 && 1 < 4;
    Boolean b1 = operandEval(1, 4 == 2) && operandEval(2, 1 < 4);
    System.out.println("Value of b1: " + b1);

    // boolean b2 = !b1 || 2.5 > 8;
    boolean b2 = !operandEval(1, b1) || operandEval(2, 2.5 > 8);
    System.out.println("Value of b2: " + b2);

    // Boolean b3 = !(b1 && b2);
    Boolean b3 = !(operandEval(1, b1) && operandEval(2, b2));
    System.out.println("Value of b3: " + b3);

    // boolean b4 = b1 || !b3 && b2;
    boolean b4 = operandEval(1, b1) || !operandEval(2, b3) && operandEval(3, b2);
    System.out.println("Value of b4: " + b4);

    // boolean b5 = b1 | !b3 & b2;    // Using boolean logical operators
    boolean b5 = operandEval(1, b1) | !operandEval(2, b3) & operandEval(3, b2);
    System.out.println("Value of b5: " + b5);
  }
```

```
    static boolean operandEval(int opNum, boolean operand) {          // (1)
        System.out.println(opNum);
        return operand;
    }
}
```

Output from the program:

```
1
Value of b1: false
1
Value of b2: true
1
Value of b3: true
1
2
Value of b4: false
1
2
3
Value of b5: false
```

Short-circuit evaluation can be used to ensure that a reference variable denotes an object before it is used.

```
if (objRef != null && objRef.equals(other)) { /*...*/ }
```

The method call is now conditionally dependent on the left-hand operand and will not be executed if the variable objRef has the null reference. If we use the logical & operator and the variable objRef has the null reference, evaluation of the right-hand operand will result in a NullPointerException.

In summary, we employ the conditional operators && and || if the evaluation of the right-hand operand is conditionally dependent on the left-hand operand. We use the boolean logical operators & and | if both operands must be evaluated. The subtlety of conditional operators is illustrated by the following examples:

```
if (i > 0 && i++ < 10) {/*...*/}   // i is not incremented if i > 0 is false.
if (i > 0 || i++ < 10) {/*...*/}   // i is not incremented if i > 0 is true.
```

2.16 Integer Bitwise Operators: ~, &, |, ∧

A review of integer representation (p. 33) is recommended before continuing with this section on how integer bitwise operators can be applied to values of *integral* data types.

Integer bitwise operators include the unary operator ~ (*bitwise complement*) and the binary operators & (*bitwise* AND), | (*bitwise inclusive* OR), and ∧ (*bitwise exclusive* OR, also known as *bitwise* XOR). The operators &, |, and ∧ are overloaded, as they can be applied to boolean or Boolean operands to perform *boolean* logical operations (p. 78).

The binary bitwise operators perform bitwise operations between corresponding individual bit values in the operands. Unary numeric promotion is applied to the operand of the unary bitwise complement operator ~, and binary numeric promotion is applied to the operands of the binary bitwise operators. The result is a new integer value of the promoted type, which can be either int or long.

Given that A and B are corresponding bit values (either 0 or 1) in the left-hand and right-hand operands, respectively, these bitwise operators are defined as shown in Table 2.30. The operators are listed in order of decreasing precedence.

Table 2.30 *Integer Bitwise Operators*

Operator name	Notation	Effect on each bit of the binary representation
Bitwise complement	~A	Invert the bit value: 1 to 0, 0 to 1.
Bitwise AND	A & B	1 if both bits are 1; otherwise 0.
Bitwise OR	A | B	1 if either or both bits are 1; otherwise 0.
Bitwise XOR	A ^ B	1 if and only if one of the bits is 1; otherwise 0.

The result of applying bitwise operators between two corresponding bits in the operands is shown in Table 2.31, where A and B are corresponding bit values in the left-hand and right-hand operands, respectively. Table 2.31 is analogous to Table 2.26 for boolean logical operators, if we consider bit value 1 to represent true and bit value 0 to represent false.

Table 2.31 *Result Table for Bitwise Operators*

A	B	Complement ~A	AND A & B	XOR A ^ B	OR A | B
1	1	0	1	0	1
1	0	0	0	1	1
0	1	1	0	1	1
0	0	1	0	0	0

Examples of Bitwise Operator Application

```
char v1 = ')';           // Unicode value 41
byte v2 = 13;

int result1 = ~v1;       // -42
int result2 = v1 & v2;   // 9
int result3 = v1 | v2;   // 45
int result4 = v1 ^ v2;   // 36
```

Table 2.32 shows how the result is calculated. Unary and binary numeric promotions are applied first, converting the operands to int in these cases. Note that the operator semantics are applied to corresponding individual bits—that is, the first bit of the left-hand operand and the first bit of the right-hand operand, the second bit of the left-hand operand and the second bit of the right-hand operand, and so on.

Table 2.32   *Examples of Bitwise Operations*

~v1	v1 & v2	v1 | v2	v1 ^ v2
~ 0...0010 1001	0...0010 1001	0...0010 1001	0...0010 1001
	& 0...0000 1101	| 0...0000 1101	^ 0...0000 1101
= 1...1101 0110	= 0...0000 1001	= 0...0010 1101	= 0...0010 0100
= 0xffffffd6	= 0x00000009	= 0x0000002d	= 0x00000024
= -42	= 9	= 45	= 36

It is instructive to run examples and print the result of a bitwise operation in different notations, as shown in Example 2.4. The integer bitwise operators support a programming technique called *bit masking*. The value v2 is usually called a *bit mask*. Depending on the bitwise operation performed on the value v1 and the mask v2, we see how the resulting value reflects the bitwise operation performed between the individual corresponding bits of the value v1 and the mask v2. By choosing appropriate values for the bits in the mask v2 and the right bitwise operation, it is possible to extract, set, and toggle specific bits in the value v1.

Methods for converting integers to strings in different notations can be found in the Integer class (§8.3, p. 435).

Example 2.4   *Bitwise Operations*

```
public class BitOperations {
  public static void main(String[] args) {
    char v1 = ')';                      // Unicode value 41
    byte v2 = 13;
    printIntToStr("v1:", v1);           // 41
    printIntToStr("v2:", v2);           // 13
    printIntToStr("~v1:", ~v1);         // -42
    printIntToStr("v1 & v2:", v1 & v2); // 9
    printIntToStr("v1 | v2:", v1 | v2); // 45
    printIntToStr("v1 ^ v2:", v1 ^ v2); // 36
  }

  public static void printIntToStr(String label, int result) {
    System.out.println(label);
    System.out.println("    Binary:  " + Integer.toBinaryString(result));
    System.out.println("    Hex:     " + Integer.toHexString(result));
    System.out.println("    Decimal: " + result);
  }
}
```

Output from the program:

```
v1:
    Binary:  101001
```

```
        Hex:      29
        Decimal: 41
  v2:
        Binary:  1101
        Hex:      d
        Decimal: 13
  ~v1:
        Binary:  11111111111111111111111111010110
        Hex:      ffffffd6
        Decimal: -42
  v1 & v2:
        Binary:  1001
        Hex:      9
        Decimal: 9
  v1 | v2:
        Binary:  101101
        Hex:      2d
        Decimal: 45
  v1 ∧ v2:
        Binary:  100100
        Hex:      24
        Decimal: 36
```

Bitwise Compound Assignment Operators: &=, ∧=, |=

Bitwise compound assignment operators for the bitwise operators are defined in Table 2.33. Type conversions for these operators, when applied to integral operands, are the same as for other compound assignment operators: An implicit narrowing conversion is performed on assignment when the destination data type is either byte, short, or char. These operators can also be applied to boolean operands to perform logical compound assignments (p. 79).

Table 2.33 *Bitwise Compound Assignment Operators*

Expression	Given T is the integral type of b, the expression is evaluated as:
b &= a	b = (T) ((b) & (a))
b ∧= a	b = (T) ((b) ∧ (a))
b |= a	b = (T) ((b)	(a))

Examples of Bitwise Compound Assignment

```
int  v0 = -42;
char v1 = ')';   // 41
byte v2 = 13;

v0 &= 15;        //     1...1101 0110 & 0...0000 1111 => 0...0000 0110 (= 6)
v1 |= v2;        // (1) 0...0010 1001 | 0...0000 1101 => 0...0010 1101 (= 45, '-')
```

At (1) in these examples, both the char value in v1 and the byte value in v2 are first promoted to int. The result is implicitly narrowed to the destination type char on assignment.

2.17 Shift Operators: <<, >>, >>>

The binary shift operators return a new value formed by shifting bits either left or right a specified number of times in a given integral value. The number of shifts (also called the *shift distance*) is given by the right-hand operand, and the value that is to be shifted is given by the left-hand operand. Note that *unary* numeric promotion is applied to each operand *individually*. The value returned has the promoted type of the left-hand operand. Also, the value of the left-hand operand is *not* affected by applying the shift operator.

The shift distance is calculated by AND-ing the value of the right-hand operand with a mask value of 0x1f (31) if the left-hand operand has the promoted type int, or using a mask value of 0x3f (63) if the left-hand operand has the promoted type long. This effectively means masking the five lower bits of the right-hand operand in the case of an int left-hand operand, and masking the six lower bits of the right-hand operand in the case of a long left-hand operand. Thus the shift distance is always in the range 0 to 31 when the promoted type of the left-hand operand is int (which has size 32 bits), and in the range 0 to 63 when the promoted type of the left-hand operand is long (which has size 64 bits).

Given that v contains the value whose bits are to be shifted and n specifies the number of bits to shift, the bitwise operators are defined in Table 2.34. It is implied that the value n in Table 2.34 is subject to the shift distance calculation outlined above, and that the shift operations are always performed on the value of the left-hand operand represented in two's complement.

Table 2.34 *Shift Operators*

Shift left	v << n	Shift all bits in v left n times, filling with 0 from the right.
Shift right with sign bit	v >> n	Shift all bits in v right n times, filling with the sign bit from the left.
Shift right with zero fill	v >>> n	Shift all bits in v right n times, filling with 0 from the left.

Since char, byte, and short operands are promoted to int, the result of applying these bitwise operators is always either an int or a long value. Care must be taken in employing a cast to narrow the resulting value, as this can result in a loss of information as the upper bits are discarded during conversion.

Note that regardless of the promotion of the values in the operands or determination of the shift distance, the operands v and n are not affected by these three shift operators. However, the shift compound assignment operators, discussed in this section, can change the value of the left-hand operand v.

Bit values shifted out (*falling off*) from bit 0 or the most significant bit are lost. Since bits can be shifted both left and right, a positive value when shifted can result in a negative value, and vice versa.

The Shift-Left Operator <<

As the bits are shifted left, zeros are always filled in from the right.

```
int i = 12;
int result = i << 4;    // 192
```

The bits in the int value for i are shifted left four places as follows:

```
i << 4
= 0000 0000 0000 0000 0000 0000 0000 1100 << 4
= 0000 0000 0000 0000 0000 0000 1100 0000
= 0x000000c0
= 192
```

Each left-shift corresponds to multiplication of the value by 2. In the above example, $12 * 2^4$ is 192.

The sign bit of a byte or short value is extended to fill the higher bits when the value is promoted, as illustrated by the example below:

```
byte  b = -42;          // 11010110
short n = 4;
int   result = b << n;  // -672
```

The values of the two operands, b and n, in the previous example are promoted individually. The short value in n is promoted to int. The byte value in b, after promotion to int, is shifted left 4 places:

```
b << n
= 1101 0110 << 0000 0000 0000 0100
= 1111 1111 1111 1111 1111 1111 1101 0110 <<0000 0000 0000 0000 0000 0000 0000 0100
= 1111 1111 1111 1111 1111 1111 1101 0110 << 4
= 1111 1111 1111 1111 1111 1101 0110 0000
= 0xfffffd60
= -672
```

In the above example, $-42 * 2^4$ is -672.

Care must also be taken when assigning the result of a shift operator to a narrower data type.

```
byte a = 32;
int  j = a << 3;          // 256
byte b = (byte) (a << 3); // 0. Cast mandatory.
```

The result of (a << 3) is 256.

```
a << 3
= 0000 0000 0000 0000 0000 0000 0010 0000 << 3
= 0000 0000 0000 0000 0000 0001 0000 0000
= 0x00000100
= 256
```

The value that j gets is 256, but the value that b gets is 0, as the higher bits are discarded in the explicit narrowing conversion.

The examples above do not show how the shift distance is determined. It is obvious from the value of the right-hand operand, which is within the range 0 to 31, inclusive. An example with the shift-left operator, where the value of the right-hand operand is out of range, is shown below.

```
12 << 36
= 0000 0000 0000 0000 0000 0000 0000 1100 << (0...0010 0100 & 0001 1111)
= 0000 0000 0000 0000 0000 0000 0000 1100 << 0...0000 0100
= 0000 0000 0000 0000 0000 0000 0000 1100 << 4
= 0000 0000 0000 0000 0000 0000 1100 0000
= 0x000000c0
= 192
```

The value of the right-hand operand, 36, is AND-ed with the mask 11111 (i.e., 31, 0x1f), giving the shift distance 4. This is the same as (36 % 32). It is not surprising that (12 << 36) is equal to (12 << 4) (i.e., 192).

The Shift-Right-with-Sign-Fill Operator >>

As the bits are shifted right, the sign bit (the most significant bit) is used to fill in from the left. So, if the left-hand operand is a positive value, zeros are filled in from the left, but if the operand is a negative value, ones are filled in from the left.

```
int i = 12;
int result = i >> 2;      // 3
```

The value for i is shifted right with sign-fill two places.

```
i >> 2
= 0000 0000 0000 0000 0000 0000 0000 1100 >> 2
= 0000 0000 0000 0000 0000 0000 0000 0011
= 0x00000003
= 3
```

Each right-shift corresponds to integer division of the value by 2, but this can give unexpected results if care is not exercised, as bits start falling off. In the above example, $12 / 2^2$ is 3.

Similarly, when a negative value is shifted right, ones are filled in from the left.

```
byte b = -42;             // 11010110
int result = b >> 4;      // -3
```

The byte value for b, after promotion to int, is shifted right with sign-fill four places.

```
b >> 4
= 1111 1111 1111 1111 1111 1111 1101 0110 >> 4
= 1111 1111 1111 1111 1111 1111 1111 1101
= 0xfffffffd
= -3
```

In the following example, the right-hand operand has a negative value:

```
-42 >> -4
= 1111 1111 1111 1111 1111 1111 1101 0110 >> (1...1111 1100 & 0001 1111)
= 1111 1111 1111 1111 1111 1111 1101 0110 >> 0...0001 1100
= 1111 1111 1111 1111 1111 1111 1101 0110 >> 28
= 1111 1111 1111 1111 1111 1111 1111 1111
= 0xffffffff
= -1
```

The value of the right-hand operand, -4, is AND-ed with the mask 11111 (i.e., 31, 0x1f), giving the shift distance 28. This is the same as (-4 % 32). The value of (-42 >> -4) is equivalent to (-42 >> 28).

The Shift-Right-with-Zero-Fill Operator >>>

As the bits are shifted right, zeros are filled in from the left, regardless of whether the operand has a positive or a negative value.

Obviously, for positive values, the shift-right-with-zero-fill >>> and shift-right-with-
sign-fill >> operators are equivalent. The expression (12 >> 2) and the expression (12 >>> 2) return the same value:

```
12 >>> 2
= 0000 0000 0000 0000 0000 0000 0000 1100 >>> 2
= 0000 0000 0000 0000 0000 0000 0000 0011
= 0x00000003
= 3
```

Individual unary numeric promotion of the left-hand operand is shown in the following example:

```
byte b = -42;          // 1101 0110
int result = b >>> 4;  // 268435453
```

It is instructive to compare the value of the expression (-42 >>> 4) with that of the expression (-42 >> 4), which has the value -3. The byte value for b, after unary numeric promotion to int, is shifted right with zero-fill four places.

```
b >>> 4
= 1111 1111 1111 1111 1111 1111 1101 0110 >>> 4
= 0000 1111 1111 1111 1111 1111 1111 1101
= 0x0ffffffd
= 268435453
```

In the following example, the value of the right-hand operand is out of range, resulting in a shift distance of 28 (as we have seen before):

```
-42 >>> -4
= 1111 1111 1111 1111 1111 1111 1101 0110 >>> 28
= 0000 0000 0000 0000 0000 0000 0000 1111
= 0x0000000f
= 15
```

Shift Compound Assignment Operators: <<=, >>=, >>>=

Table 2.35 lists shift compound assignment operators. Type conversions for these operators, when applied to integral operands, are the same as for other compound assignment operators: An implicit narrowing conversion is performed on assignment when the destination data type is either byte, short, or char.

Table 2.35 *Shift Compound Assignment Operators*

Expression	Given T as the integral type of v, the expression is evaluated as:
v <<= n	v = (T) ((v) << (n))
v >>= n	v = (T) ((v) >> (n))
v >>>= n	v = (T) ((v) >>> (n))

Examples of Shift Compound Assignment Operators

```
int i = -42;
i >>= 4;                 // 1...1101 0110 >> 4 => 1...1111 1101 (= -3).

byte a = 12;
a <<= 5;                 // (1) -128. Evaluated as a = (byte)((int)a << 5)
a = a << 5;              // Compile-time error! Needs explicit cast.
```

The example at (1) illustrates the truncation that takes place on narrowing to the destination type. The byte value in a is first promoted to int (by applying unary numeric promotion in this case), then shifted left five places, followed by implicit narrowing to byte:

```
a = (byte) (a << 5)
  = (byte) (0000 0000 0000 0000 0000 0000 0000 1100 << 5)
  = (byte)  0000 0000 0000 0000 0000 0001 1000 0000
  = 1000 0000
  = 0x80
  = -128
```

2.18 The Conditional Operator ?:

The ternary conditional operator ?: allows *conditional expressions* to be defined. The conditional expression has the following syntax:

    condition ? *expression*$_1$: *expression*$_2$

It is called ternary because it has three operands. If the boolean expression *condition* is true, then *expression₁* is evaluated; otherwise, *expression₂* is evaluated. Both *expression₁* and *expression₂* must evaluate to values that can be converted to the *type* of the conditional expression. This type is determined from the types of the two expressions. The value of the evaluated expression is converted to the type of the conditional expression, and may involve autoboxing and unboxing.

Evaluation of a conditional expression is an example of short-circuit evaluation. As only one of the two expressions is evaluated, one should be wary of any side effects in a conditional expression.

In the following code snippet at (1), both expressions in the conditional expression are of type byte. The type of the conditional expression is therefore byte. That a value of type byte can be converted to an int by an implicit widening numeric conversion to be assignment compatible with the int variable daysInFebruary is secondary in determining the type of the conditional expression. Note that the conditional operator at (1) has higher precedence than the assignment operator =, making it unnecessary to enclose the conditional expression in parentheses.

```
boolean leapYear = false;
byte v29 = 29;
byte v28 = 28;
int daysInFebruary = leapYear ? v29 : v28;    // (1)
```

The following examples illustrate the use of conditional expressions. The type of the conditional expression at (2) is int, and no conversion of any expression value is necessary. The type of the conditional expression at (3) is double, due to binary numeric promotion: The int value of the first expression is promoted to a double. The compiler reports an error because a double cannot be assigned to an int variable. The type of the conditional expression at (4) is also double as at (3), but now the double value is assignment compatible with the double variable minDoubleValue.

```
int i = 3;
int j = 4;
int minValue1 = i < j ? i : j;                  // (2) int
int minValue2 = i < j ? i : Double.MIN_VALUE;   // (3) double. Not OK.
double minDoubleValue = i < j ? i : Double.MIN_VALUE; // (4) double
```

At (5) below, the primitive values of the expressions can be boxed and assigned to an Object reference. At (6), the int value of the first expression can be boxed in an Integer. The println() method creates and prints a text representation of any object whose reference value is passed as a parameter.

```
// Assume i and j are of type int and initialized correctly.
Object obj = i < j ? i : true;        // (5) value of i boxed in Integer or
                                      //      literal true boxed in Boolean
System.out.println(i < j ? i : "Hi"); // (6) value of i boxed in Integer or
                                      //      String object "Hi"
```

The conditional expression is *not* an expression statement. The following code will not compile:

```
(i < j) ? i : j;    // Compile-time error!
```

The conditional expression can be nested, and the conditional operator associates from right to left.

a?b:c?d:e?f:g evaluates as (a?b:(c?d:(e?f:g)))

The value of this conditional expression is g if, and only if, a, c, and e are false. A nested conditional expression is used in the next example. As a convention, the condition in a conditional expression is enclosed in parentheses to aid in reading the code. Typically, a conditional expression is used when it makes the code easier to read, especially when the expressions are short and without side effects.

```
int n = 3;
String msg = (n==0) ? "no cookies." : (n==1) ? "one cookie." : "many cookies.";
System.out.println("You get " + msg); // You get many cookies.
```

The conditional operator is the expression equivalent of the if-else statement (§4.1, p. 153).

2.19 Other Operators: new, [], instanceof, ->

The new operator is used to create objects, such as instances of classes and arrays. It is used with a constructor call to instantiate classes (§5.11, p. 269) and with the [] notation to create arrays (§3.9, p. 119). It is also used to instantiate anonymous arrays (§3.9, p. 122).

```
Pizza onePizza = new Pizza();       // Create an instance of the Pizza class.
```

The [] notation is used to declare and construct arrays, and is also used to access array elements (§3.9, p. 120).

```
int[] anArray = new int[5];// Declare and construct an int array of 5 elements.
anArray[4] = anArray[3];   // Element at index 4 gets value of element at index 3.
```

The boolean, binary, and infix operator instanceof is used for either type comparison or pattern matching (§5.11, p. 269).

```
Pizza myPizza = new Pizza();
boolean test1 = myPizza instanceof Pizza; // true.
boolean test2 = "Pizza" instanceof Pizza; // Compile-time error. Incompatible
                                          // operand types.
boolean test3 = null instanceof Pizza; // Always false. null is not an instance.
```

The arrow operator -> is used in a switch statement (§4.2, p. 155), in a switch expression (§4.3, p. 164), and in the definition of a lambda expression (§13.2, p. 679).

```
java.util.function.Predicate<String> predicate = str -> str.length() % 2 == 0;
boolean test4 = predicate.test("The lambda strikes back!");    // true.
```

Review Questions

2.10 Which of the following statements are true?
Select the two correct answers.

(a) The remainder operator % can be used only with integral operands.
(b) Short-circuit evaluation occurs with boolean logical operators.
(c) The arithmetic operators *, /, and % have the same level of precedence.
(d) A short value ranges from -128 to +127, inclusive.
(e) (+15) is a legal expression.

2.11 Which of the following statements are true about the lines of output printed by the following program?

```java
public class BoolOp {
    static void op(boolean a, boolean b) {
        boolean c = a != b;
        boolean d = a ^ b;
        boolean e = c == d;
        System.out.println(e);
    }

    public static void main(String[] args) {
        op(false, false);
        op(true, false);
        op(false, true);
        op(true, true);
    }
}
```

Select the three correct answers.

(a) All lines printed are the same.
(b) At least one line contains false.
(c) At least one line contains true.
(d) The first line contains false.
(e) The last line contains true.

2.12 What is the result of running the following program?

```java
public class OperandOrder {
    public static void main(String[] args) {
        int i = 0;
        int[] a = {3, 6};
        a[i] = i = 9;
        System.out.println(i + " " + a[0] + " " + a[1]);
    }
}
```

Select the one correct answer.

(a) When run, the program throws an ArrayIndexOutOfBoundsException.
(b) When run, the program will print 9 9 6.

(c) When run, the program will print 9 0 6.

(d) When run, the program will print 9 3 6.

(e) When run, the program will print 9 3 9.

2.13 Which of the following statements are true about the output from the following program?

```java
public class Logic {
  public static void main(String[] args) {
    int i = 0;
    int j = 0;

    boolean t = true;
    boolean r;

    r = (t &  0 < (i+=1));
    r = (t && 0 < (i+=2));
    r = (t |  0 < (j+=1));
    r = (t || 0 < (j+=2));
    System.out.println(i + " " + j);
  }
}
```

Select the two correct answers.

(a) The first digit printed is 1.

(b) The first digit printed is 2.

(c) The first digit printed is 3.

(d) The second digit printed is 1.

(e) The second digit printed is 2.

(f) The second digit printed is 3.

2.14 Given the following code:

```java
int x = 1, y = 2, z = 3;
if (x < y || ++z > 4) {
  System.out.println("a" + x + y + z);
}
if (x < y && ++z > 4) {
  System.out.println("b" + x + y + z);
}
```

What will be the output?

Select the one correct answer.

(a) a124
   b125

(b) a123

(c) a123
   b124

2.15 Which of the following statements when inserted at (1) will not result in a compile-time error?

```
public class RQ05A200 {
  public static void main(String[] args) {
    int i = 20;
    int j = 30;
    // (1) INSERT STATEMENT HERE
  }
}
```

Select the three correct answers.

(a) `int result1 = i < j ? i : j * 10d;`
(b) `int result2 = i < j ? { ++i } : { ++j };`
(c) `Number number = i < j ? i : j * 10D;`
(d) `System.out.println(i < j ? i);`
(e) `System.out.println(i < j ? ++i : ++j);`
(f) `System.out.println(i == j ? i == j : "i not equal to j");`

2.16 Which of the following statements are true about the following code?

```
public class RQ05A100 {
  public static void main(String[] args) {
    int n1 = 10, n2 = 10;
    int m1 = 20, m2 = 30;
    int result = n1 != n2? n1 : m1 != m2? m1 : m2;
    System.out.println(result);
  }
}
```

Select the one correct answer.

(a) The program will fail to compile.
(b) The program will throw an `ArithmeticException` at runtime.
(c) The program will compile and print 10 when run.
(d) The program will compile and print 20 when run.
(e) The program will compile and print 30 when run.

Declarations

3

 Chapter Topics

- An overview of declarations that can be specified in a class
- How to declare and initialize variables
- Using default values for instance variables and static variables
- Understanding lifetime of instance variables, static variables, and local variables
- Using arrays: declaration, construction, initialization, and usage of both simple and multidimensional arrays, including anonymous arrays
- Writing methods, usage of the `this` reference in an instance method, and method overloading
- Understanding the role of constructors, usage of the default constructor, and constructor overloading
- Understanding parameter passing, both primitive values and object references, including arrays and array elements; and declaring `final` parameters0
- Declaring and calling methods with variable arity
- Declaring the `main()` method whose execution starts the application
- Passing program arguments to the `main()` method on the command line
- Declaring and using local variable type inference with var

Java SE 17 Developer Exam Objectives	
[3.2] Create classes and records, and define and use instance and static fields and methods, constructors, and instance and static initializers ○ *Declaring normal classes and defining class members and constructors are covered in this chapter.* ○ *For record classes, see §5.14, p. 299.* ○ *For instance and static initializers, see Chapter 10, p. 531.*	§3.1, p. 99 *to* §3.8, p. 112
[3.3] Implement overloading, including var-arg methods ○ *Method overloading and varargs methods are covered in this chapter.* ○ *For comparing overloading and overriding, see §5.1, p. 202.*	§3.6, p. 108 §3.11, p. 136
[3.4] Understand variable scopes, use local variable type inference, apply encapsulation, and make objects immutable ○ *Local variable type inference is covered in this chapter.* ○ *For detailed coverage of lambda expressions, see §13.2, p. 679.* ○ *For variable scope, encapsulation, and immutability, see Chapter 6, p. 323.*	§3.13, p. 142
[5.1] Create Java arrays, List, Set, Map and Deque collections, and add, remove, update, retrieve and sort their elements ○ *Arrays are covered in this chapter.* ○ *For Collections and Maps, see Chapter 15, p. 781.*	§3.9, p. 117
Java SE 11 Developer Exam Objectives	
[1.3] Use local variable type inference, including as lambda parameters ○ *Local variable type inference is covered in this chapter.* ○ *For detailed coverage of lambda expressions, see §13.2, p. 679.*	§3.13, p. 142
[3.2] Define and use fields and methods, including instance, static and overloaded methods	§3.1, p. 99 *to* §3.8, p. 112
[3.3] Initialize objects and their members using instance and static initialiser statements and constructors	§3.4, p. 102 §3.7, p. 109
[5.2] Use a Java array and List, Set, Map and Deque collections, including convenience methods ○ *Arrays are covered in this chapter.* ○ *For collections and maps, see Chapter 15, p. 781.*	§3.9, p. 117

This chapter covers declaration of classes, methods, constructors, and variables, including array types. Other declarations (e.g., modules, packages, interfaces, enum types, and nested types) will be covered in due course in later chapters.

A *declaration* is a language construct that includes an identifier which can be used to refer to this declaration in the program. Examples include a class declaration that can be referred to by its class name and a method declaration that can be referred to by its method name.

3.1 Class Declarations

A class declaration introduces a new *reference type* and has the following syntax:

class_modifiers class *class_name extends_clause implements_clause* // Class header
{ // Class body
    field_declarations
    method_declarations
    constructor_declarations
    member_type_declarations
}

In the class header, the name of the class is preceded by the keyword class. In addition, the class header can specify the following information:

* The following *class modifiers*:
    o *Access modifiers*: public, protected, private (§6.5, p. 345)
    o *Non-access class modifiers*: abstract (§5.4, p. 218), final (§5.5, p. 225), static (§9.2, p. 495), sealed and non-sealed (§5.15, p. 311)
* Any class it *extends* using the extends clause (§5.1, p. 191)
* Any interfaces it *implements* using the implements clause (§5.6, p. 237)

The class body, enclosed in curly brackets ({}), can contain *member declarations*, which comprise the following:

* *Field declarations* (p. 102)
* *Method declarations* (p. 100)
* *Constructor declarations* (p. 109)
* *Member type declarations* (§9.1, p. 491)

The declarations can appear in any order in the class body. The only mandatory parts of the class declaration syntax are the keyword class, the class name, and the class body curly brackets ({}), as exemplified by the following class declaration:

class X { }

To understand which code can be legally declared in a class, we distinguish between *static context* and *non-static context*. A static context is defined by static methods, static field initializers, and static initializer blocks. A non-static context is defined by instance methods, instance field initializers, instance initializer blocks, and constructors. By *static code*, we mean expressions and statements in a static context; by *non-static code*, we mean expressions and statements in a non-static context. One crucial difference between the two contexts is that *static code in a class can only refer to other static members* in the class, whereas *non-static code can refer to any member of the class.*

3.2 Method Declarations

A method declaration has the following syntax:

method_modifiers return_type method_name
        (*formal_parameter_list*) *throws_clause* // Method header

{ // Method body
    local_variable_declarations
    statements
}

In addition to the name of the method, the method header can specify the following information:

- The following *method modifiers*:
    - ○ *Access modifiers*: public, protected, private (§6.5, p. 347)
    - ○ *Non-access method modifiers*: static (p. 115), abstract (§5.4, p. 224), final (§5.5, p. 226), synchronized (§22.4, p. 1388)
- The *type* of the *return value*, or void if the method does not return any value

    A non-void method must either use a return statement (§4.13, p. 184) to return a value or throw an exception to terminate its execution.

- A *formal parameter list*

    The *formal parameter list* is a comma-separated list of parameters for passing information to the method when the method is invoked by a *method call* (p. 127). An empty parameter list must be specified by ( ). Each parameter is a simple variable declaration consisting of its type and name:

    optional_parameter_modifier type parameter_name

    The parameter names are local to the method (§6.6, p. 354). The *optional parameter modifier* final is discussed in §3.10, p. 135. It is recommended to use the @param tag in a Javadoc comment to document the formal parameters of a method.

    The *type* in the parameter declaration *cannot* be designated by the var reserved type name, as illustrated in the method declaration below. At compile time, it is not possible to determine the type of the newSpeed formal parameter.

    ```
    void setSpeed(var newSpeed) {}          // var not permitted. Compile-time error!
    ```
- Any *exceptions* thrown by the method, which are specified in a throws clause (§7.5, p. 388)

The method body is a *block* ({}) containing the *local variable declarations* (p. 102) and the *statements* (p. 101) of the method. The return statement in the body of a method is of particular importance as it terminates the execution of the method and can optionally return a value to the caller of the method (§4.13, p. 184).

The mandatory parts of a method declaration are the return type, the method name, and the method body curly brackets ({}), as exemplified by the following method declaration:

```
void noAction() {}
```

Member methods are characterized as one of two types: *instance methods* (p. 106) and *static methods* (p. 112).

The *signature* of a method comprises the name of the method and the types of the formal parameters only. The following method:

```
double cubeVolume(double length, double width, double height) {}
```

has the signature:

```
cubeVolume(double, double, double)
```

3.3 Statements

Statements in Java can be grouped into various categories. Variable declarations, optionally specified with an initialization expression, are called *declaration statements* (p. 102). Other basic forms of statements are *control flow statements* (Chapter 4, p. 151) and *expression statements*.

An *expression statement* is an expression terminated by a semicolon (;). Any value returned by the expression is discarded. Only certain types of expressions have meaning as statements:

- Assignments (§2.7, p. 54)
- Increment and decrement operators (§2.10, p. 69)
- Method calls (p. 127)
- Object creation expressions with the new operator (§2.19, p. 92)

A solitary semicolon denotes the *empty statement*, which does nothing.

A block, {}, is a *compound* statement that can be used to group zero or more local declarations and statements (§6.6, p. 354). Blocks can be nested, since a block is a statement that can contain other statements. A block can be used in any context where a simple statement is permitted. The compound statement that is embodied in a block begins at the left curly bracket ({) and ends with a matching right curly bracket (}). Such a block must not be confused with an array initializer in declaration statements (p. 119).

Labeled statements are discussed in §4.10, p. 179.

3.4 Variable Declarations

A *variable* stores a value of a particular type. A variable has a name, a type, and a value associated with it. In Java, variables can store only values of primitive data types and reference values of objects. Variables that store reference values of objects are called *reference variables* (or *object references* or simply *references*).

We distinguish between two kinds of variables: *field variables* and *local variables*. Field variables are variables that are declared in *type declarations* (*classes*, *interfaces*, and *enums*). Local variables are variables that are declared in *methods*, *constructors*, and *blocks*. Local variables declared with the var type name are discussed in §3.13, p. 142.

Declaring and Initializing Variables

Variable declarations (technically called *declaration statements*) are used to *declare* variables, meaning they are used to specify the type and the name of variables. This implicitly determines their memory allocation and the values that can be stored in them. Examples of declaring variables that can store primitive values follow:

```
char a, b, c;          // a, b, and c are character variables.
double area;           // area is a floating-point variable.
boolean flag;          // flag is a boolean variable.
```

The first declaration is equivalent to the following three declarations:

```
char a;
char b;
char c;
```

A declaration can also be combined with an *initialization expression* to specify an appropriate initial value for the variable.

```
int i = 10,            // i is an int variable with initial value 10.
    j = 0b101;         // j is an int variable with initial value 5.
long big = 2147483648L;  // big is a long variable with specified initial value.
```

Reference Variables

A *reference variable* can store the reference value of an object, and can be used to manipulate the object denoted by the reference value.

A variable declaration that specifies a *reference type* (i.e., a class, an array, an interface name, or an enum type) declares a reference variable. Analogous to the declaration of variables of primitive data types, the simplest form of reference variable declaration specifies the name and the reference type only. The declaration determines which objects can be referenced by a reference variable. Before we can use a reference variable to manipulate an object, it must be declared and initialized with the reference value of the object.

```
Pizza yummyPizza;    // Variable yummyPizza can reference objects of class Pizza.
Hamburger bigOne,    // Variable bigOne can reference objects of class Hamburger,
          smallOne;  // and so can variable smallOne.
```

It is important to note that the preceding declarations do not create any objects of class Pizza or Hamburger. Rather, they simply create variables that can store reference values of objects of the specified classes.

A declaration can also be combined with an *initializer expression* to create an object whose reference value can be assigned to the reference variable:

```
Pizza yummyPizza = new Pizza("Hot&Spicy"); // Declaration statement
```

The reference variable yummyPizza can reference objects of class Pizza. The keyword new, together with the *constructor call* Pizza("Hot&Spicy"), creates an object of the class Pizza. The reference value of this object is assigned to the variable yummyPizza. The newly created object of class Pizza can now be manipulated through the reference variable yummyPizza.

Initial Values for Variables

This section discusses what value, if any, is assigned to a variable when no explicit initial value is provided in the declaration.

Default Values for Fields

Default values for fields of primitive data types and reference types are listed in Table 3.1. The value assigned depends on the type of the field.

Table 3.1 *Default Values*

Data type	Default value
boolean	false
char	'\u0000'
Integer (byte, short, int, long)	0L for long, 0 for others
Floating-point (float, double)	0.0F or 0.0D
Reference types	null

If no explicit initialization is provided for a static variable, it is initialized with the default value of its type when the class is loaded. Similarly, if no initialization is provided for an instance variable, it is initialized with the default value of its type when the class is instantiated. The fields of reference types are always initialized with the null reference value if no initialization is provided.

Example 3.1 illustrates the default initialization of fields. Note that static variables are initialized when the class is loaded the first time, and instance variables are initialized accordingly in *every* object created from the class Light.

Example 3.1   *Default Values for Fields*

```java
public class Light {
  // Static variable
  static int counter;        // Default value 0 when class is loaded

  // Instance variables:
  int      noOfWatts = 100;  // Explicitly set to 100
  boolean indicator;         // Implicitly set to default value false
  String  location;          // Implicitly set to default value null

  public static void main(String[] args) {
    Light bulb = new Light();
    System.out.println("Static variable counter:      " + Light.counter);
    System.out.println("Instance variable noOfWatts: " + bulb.noOfWatts);
    System.out.println("Instance variable indicator: " + bulb.indicator);
    System.out.println("Instance variable location:  " + bulb.location);
  }
}
```

Output from the program:

```
Static variable counter:     0
Instance variable noOfWatts: 100
Instance variable indicator: false
Instance variable location:  null
```

Initializing Local Variables of Primitive Data Types

Local variables are variables that are declared in *methods*, *constructors*, and *blocks*. They are *not* initialized implicitly when they are allocated memory at method invocation—that is, when the execution of a method begins. The same applies to local variables in constructors and blocks. Local variables must be explicitly initialized before being used. The compiler will report an error only if an attempt is made to *use* an uninitialized local variable.

Example 3.2   *Flagging Uninitialized Local Variables of Primitive Data Types*

```java
public class TooSmartClass {
  public static void main(String[] args) {
    double weight = 10.0, thePrice;                    // (1) Local variables

    if (weight <  10.0) thePrice = 20.50;
    if (weight >  50.0) thePrice = 399.00;
    if (weight >= 10.0) thePrice = weight * 10.0;      // (2) Always executed
    System.out.println("The price is: " + thePrice);   // (3) Compile-time error!
  }
}
```

In Example 3.2, the compiler complains that the local variable thePrice used in the print statement at (3) may not have been initialized. If allowed to compile and execute, the local variable thePrice will get the value 100.0 in the last if statement at (2), before it is used in the print statement. However, in Example 3.2, the compiler cannot guarantee that code in the body of any of the if statements will be executed and thereby the local variable thePrice is initialized, as it cannot determine whether the condition in any of the if statements is true at compile time.

We will not go into the details of *definite assignment analysis* that the compiler performs to guarantee that a local variable is initialized before it is used. In essence, the compiler determines whether a variable is initialized on a path of control flow from where it is declared to where it is used. This analysis can at times be conservative, as in Example 3.2.

The program will compile correctly if the local variable thePrice is initialized in the declaration, or if an unconditional assignment is made to it. Replacing the declaration of the local variables at (1) in Example 3.2 with the following declaration solves the problem:

```
double weight = 10.0, thePrice = 0.0;    // (1') Both local variables initialized
```

Replacing the condition in any of the if statements with a *constant expression* that evaluates to true will also allow the compiler to ensure that the local variable thePrice is initialized before use in the print statement.

Initializing Local Reference Variables

Local reference variables are bound by the same initialization rules as local variables of primitive data types.

Example 3.3   *Flagging Uninitialized Local Reference Variables*

```
public class VerySmartClass {
  public static void main(String[] args) {
    String importantMessage;        // Local reference variable

    System.out.println("The message length is: " +
                        importantMessage.length());  // Compile-time error!
  }
}
```

In Example 3.3, the compiler complains that the local variable importantMessage used in the println statement may not be initialized. If the variable importantMessage is set to the value null, the program will compile. However, a runtime error (NullPointerException) will occur when the code is executed because the variable importantMessage will not denote any object. The golden rule is to ensure that a reference variable, whether local or not, is assigned a reference value denoting an object before it is used—that is, to ensure that it does not have the value null.

The program compiles and runs if we replace the declaration with the following declaration of the local variable, which creates a string literal and assigns its reference value to the local reference variable importantMessage:

```
String importantMessage = "Initialize before use!";
```

Arrays and their default values are discussed in §3.9, p. 119.

Lifetime of Variables

The *lifetime* of a variable—that is, the time a variable is accessible during execution—is determined by the context in which it is declared. The lifetime of a variable, which is also called its *scope*, is discussed in more detail in §6.6, p. 352. We distinguish among the lifetime of variables in the following three contexts:

- *Instance variables*: members of a class, which are created for each object of the class. In other words, every object of the class will have its own copies of these variables, which are local to the object. The values of these variables at any given time constitute the *state* of the object. Instance variables exist as long as the object they belong to is in use at runtime.

- *Static variables*: members of a class, but which are not created for any specific object of the class, and therefore, belong only to the class. They are created when the class is loaded at runtime and exist as long as the class is available at runtime.

- *Local variables* (also called *method automatic variables*): declared in methods, constructors, and blocks, and created for each execution of the method, constructor, or block. After the execution of the method, constructor, or block completes, local variables are no longer accessible.

3.5 Instance Methods and the Object Reference this

Instance methods belong to every object of the class and can be invoked only on objects. All members defined in the class, both static and non-static, are accessible in the context of an instance method. The reason is that all instance methods are passed an implicit reference to the *current object*—that is, the object on which the method is being invoked.

The current object can be referenced in the body of the instance method by the keyword this. In the body of the method, the this reference can be used like any other object reference to access members of the object. In fact, the keyword this can be used in any non-static context. The this reference can be used as a normal reference to reference the current object, but the reference cannot be modified—it is a final reference (§5.5, p. 225).

The this reference to the current object is useful in situations where a local variable hides, or *shadows*, a field with the same name. In Example 3.4, the two parameters noOfWatts and indicator in the constructor of the Light class have the same names as the fields in the class. The example also declares a local variable location, which has the same name as one of the fields. The reference this can be used to distinguish the fields from the local variables. At (1), the this reference is used to identify the field noOfWatts, which is assigned the value of the parameter noOfWatts. Without the this reference at (2), the value of the parameter indicator is assigned back to this parameter, and not to the field by the same name, resulting in a logical error. Similarly at (3), without the this reference, it is the local variable location that is assigned the value of the parameter site, and not the field with the same name.

Example 3.4   *Using the* this *Reference*

```java
public class Light {
  // Fields:
  int     noOfWatts;      // Wattage
  boolean indicator;      // On or off
  String  location;       // Placement

  // Constructor:
  public Light(int noOfWatts, boolean indicator, String site) {
    String location;

    this.noOfWatts = noOfWatts;  // (1) Assignment to field
    indicator = indicator;       // (2) Assignment to parameter
    location = site;             // (3) Assignment to local variable
    this.superfluous();          // (4)
    superfluous();               // equivalent to call at (4)
  }

  // Instance method:
  public void superfluous() {
    System.out.printf("Current object: %s%n", this); // (5)
  }

  // Static method:
  public static void main(String[] args) {
    Light light = new Light(100, true, "loft");
    System.out.println("No. of watts: " + light.noOfWatts);
    System.out.println("Indicator:    " + light.indicator);
    System.out.println("Location:     " + light.location);
  }
}
```

Probable output from the program:

```
Current object: Light@1bc4459
Current object: Light@1bc4459
No. of watts: 100
Indicator:    false
Location:     null
```

If a member is not shadowed by a local declaration, the simple name member is considered a shorthand notation for this.member. In particular, the this reference can be used explicitly to invoke other methods in the class. This usage is illustrated at (4) in Example 3.4, where the method superfluous() is called.

If, for some reason, a method needs to pass the current object to another method, it can do so using the `this` reference. This approach is illustrated at (5) in Example 3.4, where the current object is passed to the `printf()` method. The `printf()` method prints the text representation of the current object (which comprises the name of the class of the current object and the hexadecimal representation of the current object's hash code). The *hash code* of an object is an `int` value that uniquely identifies the object.

Note that the `this` reference cannot be used in a static context, as static code is not executed in the context of any object.

3.6 Method Overloading

Each method has a *signature*, which comprises the name of the method plus the types and order of the parameters in the formal parameter list. Several method implementations may have the same name, as long as the method signatures differ. This practice is called *method overloading*. Because overloaded methods have the same name, their parameter lists must be different.

Rather than inventing new method names, method overloading can be used when the same logical operation requires multiple implementations. The Java SE Platform API makes heavy use of method overloading. For example, the class `java.lang.Math` contains an overloaded method `min()`, which returns the minimum of two numeric values.

```
public static double min(double a, double b)
public static float min(float a, float b)
public static int min(int a, int b)
public static long min(long a, long b)
```

In the following examples, five implementations of the method `methodA` are shown:

```
void methodA(int a, double b) { /* ... */ }     // (1)
int  methodA(int a)           { return a; }     // (2)
int  methodA()                { return 1; }     // (3)
long methodA(double a, int b) { return b; }     // (4)
long methodA(int x, double y) { return x; }     // (5) Not OK.
```

The corresponding signatures of the five methods are as follows:

```
methodA(int, double)          1'
methodA(int)j                 2': Number of parameters
methodA()                     3': Number of parameters
methodA(double, int)          4': Order of parameters
methodA(int, double)          5': Same as 1'
```

The first four implementations of the method named `methodA` are overloaded correctly, each time with a different parameter list and, therefore, different signatures. The declaration at (5) has the same signature `methodA(int, double)` as the declaration at (1), and therefore, is not a valid overloading of this method.

```
void bake(Cake k)  { /* ... */ }                // (1)
void bake(Pizza p) { /* ... */ }                // (2)

int    halfIt(int a) { return a/2; }            // (3)
double halfIt(int a) { return a/2.0; }          // (4) Not OK. Same signature.
```

The method named bake is correctly overloaded at (1) and (2), with two different parameter lists. In the implementation, changing just the return type (as shown at (3) and (4) in the preceding example) is not enough to overload a method and will be flagged as a compile-time error. The parameter list in the declarations must be different.

Only methods declared in the same class and those that are inherited by the class can be overloaded. Overloaded methods should be considered to be individual methods that just happen to have the same name. Methods with the same name are allowed, since methods are identified by their signature. At compile time, the right implementation of an overloaded method is chosen, based on the signature of the method call. Details of method overloading resolution can be found in §5.10, p. 265. Method overloading should not be confused with *method overriding* (§5.1, p. 196).

3.7 Constructors

The main purpose of constructors is to set the initial state of an object, when the object is created by using the new operator.

The following simplified syntax is the canonical declaration of a constructor:

access_modifier class_name (formal_parameter_list)
                    throws_clause // Constructor header
    { // Constructor body
        local_variable_declarations
        statements
    }

Constructor declarations are very much like method declarations. However, the following restrictions on constructors should be noted:

- Modifiers other than an access modifier are not permitted in the constructor header. For more on access modifiers for constructors, see §6.5, p. 345.
- Constructors cannot return a value, and therefore, do not specify a return type, not even void, in the constructor header. But their declaration can use the return statement (without the return value) in the constructor body (§4.13, p. 184).
- The constructor name must be the same as the class name.

Class names and method names exist in different *namespaces*. Thus there are no name conflicts in Example 3.5, where a method declared at (2) has the same name as the constructor declared at (1). The method Name() at (2) is also breaking the convention of starting a method name with a lowercase character. A method must always specify a return type, whereas a constructor does not. However, using such naming schemes is strongly discouraged.

A constructor that has no parameters, like the one at (1) in Example 3.5, is called a *no-argument constructor*.

Example 3.5 *Namespaces*

```java
public class Name {

  Name() {                            // (1) No-argument constructor
    System.out.println("Constructor");
  }

  void Name() {                       // (2) Instance method
    System.out.println("Method");
  }

  public static void main(String[] args) {
    new Name().Name();              // (3) Constructor call followed by method call
  }
}
```

Output from the program:

```
Constructor
Method
```

The Default Constructor

If a class does not specify *any* constructors, then a *default constructor* is generated for the class by the compiler. The default constructor is equivalent to the following implementation:

```java
class_name() { super(); }   // No parameters. Calls superclass constructor.
```

A default constructor is a no-argument constructor. The only action taken by the default constructor is to call the superclass constructor. This ensures that the inherited state of the object is initialized properly (§5.3, p. 209). In addition, all instance variables in the object are set to the default value of their type, barring those that are initialized by an initialization expression in their declaration.

In the following code, the class Light does not specify any constructors:

```java
class Light {
  // Fields:
  int    noOfWatts;       // Wattage
  boolean indicator;      // On or off
  String  location;       // Placement

  // No constructors
  //...
}

class Greenhouse {
  // ...
```

```
                    Light oneLight = new Light();      // (1) Call to default constructor
        }
```

In this code, the following default constructor is called when a Light object is created by the object creation expression at (1):

```
        Light() { super(); }
```

Creating an object using the new operator with the default constructor, as at (1), will initialize the fields of the object to their *default values* (i.e., the fields noOfWatts, indicator, and location in a Light object will be initialized to 0, false, and null, respectively).

A class can choose to provide its own constructors, rather than relying on the default constructor. In the following example, the class Light provides a no-argument constructor at (1).

```
        class Light {
          // ...
          Light() {                               // (1) No-argument constructor
            noOfWatts = 50;
            indicator = true;
            location  = "X";
          }
          //...
        }

        class Greenhouse {
          // ...
          Light extraLight = new Light();     // (2) Call to no-argument constructor
        }
```

The no-argument constructor ensures that any object created with the object creation expression new Light(), as at (2), will have its fields noOfWatts, indicator, and location initialized to 50, true, and "X", respectively.

If a class defines *any* constructor, the default constructor is not generated. If such a class requires a no-argument constructor, it must provide its own implementation, as in the preceding example. In the next example, the class Light does not provide a no-argument constructor, but rather includes a non-zero argument constructor at (1). It is called at (2) when an object of the class Light is created with the new operator. Any attempt to call the default constructor will be flagged as a compile-time error, as shown at (3).

```
        class Light {
          // ...
          // Only non-zero argument constructor:
          Light(int noOfWatts, boolean indicator, String location) {        // (1)
            this.noOfWatts = noOfWatts;
            this.indicator = indicator;
            this.location  = location;
          }
          //...
        }
```

```java
class Greenhouse {
  // ...
  Light moreLight  = new Light(100, true, "Greenhouse");// (2) OK
  Light firstLight = new Light();                        // (3) Compile-time error
}
```

Overloaded Constructors

Like methods, constructors can be overloaded. Since the constructors in a class all have the same name as the class, their signatures are differentiated by their parameter lists. In the following example, the class Light now provides explicit implementation of the no-argument constructor at (1) and that of a non-zero argument constructor at (2). The constructors are overloaded, as is evident by their signatures. The non-zero argument constructor at (2) is called when an object of the class Light is created at (4), and the no-argument constructor is likewise called at (3). Overloading of constructors allows appropriate initialization of objects on creation, depending on the constructor invoked (see chaining of constructors in §5.3, p. 209). It is recommended to use the @param tag in a Javadoc comment to document the formal parameters of a constructor.

```java
class Light {
  // ...
  // No-argument constructor:
  Light() {                                              // (1)
    noOfWatts = 50;
    indicator = true;
    location  = "X";
  }

  // Non-zero argument constructor:
  Light(int noOfWatts, boolean indicator, String location) { // (2)
    this.noOfWatts = noOfWatts;
    this.indicator = indicator;
    this.location  = location;
  }
  //...
}

class Greenhouse {
  // ...
  Light firstLight = new Light();                        // (3) OK. Calls (1)
  Light moreLight  = new Light(100, true, "Greenhouse"); // (4) OK. Calls (2)
}
```

3.8 Static Member Declarations

In this section we look at static members in classes, but in general, the keyword static is used in the following contexts:

• Declaring static fields in classes (p. 113), enum types (§5.13, p. 290) and interfaces (§5.6, p. 254)

- Declaring static methods in classes (p. 115), enum types (§5.13, p. 290) and interfaces (§5.6, p. 251)
- Declaring static initializer blocks in classes (§10.7, p. 545) and enum types (§5.13, p. 290)
- Declaring nested static member types (§9.2, p. 495)

Static Members in Classes

Static members belong to the class in which they are declared and are not part of any instance of the class. The declaration of static members is prefixed by the keyword static to distinguish them from instance members.

Static code inside a class can access a static member in the following three ways:

- By the static member's simple name
- By using the class name with the static member's name
- By using an object reference of the static member's class with the static member's name

Depending on the access modifier of the static members declared in a class, clients can only access these members by using the class name or using an object reference of their class.

The class need not be instantiated to access its static members. This is in contrast to instance members of the class which can only be accessed by references that actually refer to an instance of the class.

Static Fields in Classes

Static fields (also called *static variables* and *class variables*) exist only in the class in which they are defined. When the class is loaded, static fields are initialized to their default values if no explicit initialization is specified. They are not created when an instance of the class is created. In other words, the values of these fields are not a part of the state of any object. Static fields are akin to global variables that can be shared with all objects of the class and with other clients, if necessary.

- -

Example 3.6   *Accessing Static Members in a Class*

```java
// File: StaticTest.java
import static java.lang.System.out;

class Light {

  // Static field:
  static int counter;                    // (1) No initializer expression

  // Static method:
  public static void printStatic() {
    Light myLight = null;
    out.printf("%s, %s, %s%n", counter, Light.counter, myLight.counter); // (2)
```

```
        long counter = 10;                       // (3) Local variable shadows static field
        out.println("Local counter: " + counter);        // (4) Local variable accessed
        out.println("Static counter: " + Light.counter);// (5) Static field accessed

//    out.println(this.counter);                 // (6) Cannot use this in static context
//    printNonStatic();                          // (7) Cannot call non-static method
    }

    // Non-static method:
    public void printNonStatic() {
      out.printf("%s, %s, %s%n", counter, this.counter, Light.counter);      // (8)
    }
}
//_____
public class StaticTest {                  // Client of class Light
  public static void main(String[] args) {
    Light.counter++;                       // (9) Using class name
    Light dimLight = null;
    dimLight.counter++;                    // (10) Using object reference

    out.print("Light.counter == dimLight.counter: ");
    out.println(Light.counter == dimLight.counter);//(11) Aliases for static field

    out.println("Calling static method using class name:");
    Light.printStatic();                   // (12) Using class name
    out.println("Calling static method using object reference:");
    dimLight.printStatic();                // (13) Using object reference
  }
}
```

Output from the program:

```
Light.counter == dimLight.counter: true
Calling static method using class name:
2, 2, 2
Local counter: 10
Static counter: 2
Calling static method using object reference:
2, 2, 2
Local counter: 10
Static counter: 2
```

In Example 3.6, the static field counter at (1) will be initialized to the default value 0 when the class is loaded at runtime, since no initializer expression is specified. The print statement at (2) in the static method printCount() shows how this static field can be accessed in three different ways, respectively: simple name counter, the class name Light, and object reference myLight of class Light, although no object has been created.

Shadowing of fields by local variables is different from *hiding* of fields by field declarations in subclasses. In Example 3.6, a local variable is declared at (3) that has the same name as the static field. Since this local variable *shadows* the static field, the simple name at (4) now refers to the local variable, as shown by the output from the program. The shadowed static field can of course be accessed using the class name, as shown at (5). It is the local variable that is accessed by its simple name as long as it is in scope.

Trying to access the static field with the this reference at (6) results in a compile-time error, since the this reference cannot be used in static code. Invoking the non-static method at (7) also results in a compile-time error, since static code cannot refer to non-static members by its simple name in the class.

The print statement at (8) in the method printNonStatic() illustrates referring to static members in non-static code: It refers to the static field counter by its simple name, with the this reference, and using the class name.

In Example 3.6, the class StaticTest is a client of the class Light. The client must use the class name or an object reference of class Light at (9) and (10), respectively, to access the static field counter in the class Light. The result from the print statement at (11) shows that these two ways of accessing a static field are equivalent.

Static Methods in Classes

Static methods are also known as *class methods*. A static method in a class can directly access other static members in the class by their simple name. It cannot access instance (i.e., non-static) members of the class directly, as there is no notion of an object associated with a static method.

A typical static method might perform some task on behalf of the whole class or for objects of the class. Static methods are often used to implement *utility classes* that provide common and frequently used functions. A good example of a utility class is the java.lang.Math class in the Java platform SE API that provides common mathematical functions.

Static methods can be overloaded analogous to instance methods. Static methods in a superclass cannot be overridden in a subclass as instance methods can, but they can be *hidden* by static methods in a subclass (§5.1, p. 203).

A type parameter of a generic class or interface cannot be used in a static method (§11.2, p. 567).

Example 3.6 shows how the static method printCount() of the class Light can be invoked using the class name and via an object reference of the class Light at (12) and (13), respectively.

 Review Questions

3.1 In which of these variable declarations will the variable remain uninitialized unless it is explicitly initialized?
Select the one correct answer.

(a) Declaration of an instance variable of type int
(b) Declaration of a static variable of type float

(c) Declaration of a local variable of type float
(d) Declaration of a static variable of type Object
(e) Declaration of an instance variable of type int[]

3.2   What will be the result of compiling and running the following program?

```java
public class Init {

    String title;
    boolean published;

    static int total;
    static double maxPrice;

    public static void main(String[] args) {
        Init initMe = new Init();
        double price;
        if (true)
            price = 100.00;
        System.out.println("|" + initMe.title + "|" + initMe.published + "|" +
                          Init.total + "|" + Init.maxPrice + "|" + price + "|");
    }
}
```

Select the one correct answer.

(a) The program will fail to compile.
(b) The program will print |null|false|0|0.0|0.0| at runtime.
(c) The program will print |null|true|0|0.0|100.0| at runtime.
(d) The program will print | |false|0|0.0|0.0| at runtime.
(e) The program will print |null|false|0|0.0|100.0| at runtime.

3.3   Given that the following pairs of method are declared in the same class, which of the following statements are true?

```java
void fly(int distance) {}
int  fly(int time, int speed) { return time*speed; }

void fall(int time) {}
int  fall(int distance) { return distance; }

void glide(int time) {}
void Glide(int time) {}
```

Select the two correct answers.

(a) The first pair of methods will compile and will overload the method name fly.
(b) The second pair of methods will compile and will overload the method name fall.
(c) The third pair of methods will compile and will overload the method name glide.
(d) The first pair of methods will fail to compile.
(e) The second pair of methods will fail to compile.
(f) The third pair of methods will fail to compile.

3.4 Which of the following statements are true?
Select the two correct answers.

(a) A class must define a constructor.
(b) A constructor can be declared private.
(c) A constructor can return a value.
(d) A constructor must initialize all fields when a class is instantiated.
(e) A constructor can access the non-static members of a class.

3.5 What will be the result of compiling the following program?

```
public class MyClass {
  long var;

  public void MyClass(long param) { var = param; }  // (1)

  public static void main(String[] args) {
    MyClass a, b;
    a = new MyClass();                                // (2)
    b = new MyClass(5);                               // (3)
  }
}
```

Select the one correct answer.

(a) A compile-time error will occur at (1).
(b) A compile-time error will occur at (2).
(c) A compile-time error will occur at (3).
(d) The program will compile without errors.

3.6 Which statement is true?
Select the one correct answer.

(a) A static method can call other non-static methods in the same class by using the this keyword.
(b) A class may contain both static and non-static variables, and both static and non-static methods.
(c) Each object of a class has its own instance of the static variables declared in the class.
(d) Instance methods may access local variables of static methods.
(e) All methods in a class are implicitly passed the this reference as an argument, when invoked.

3.9 Arrays

An *array* is a data structure that defines an indexed collection with a fixed number of data elements that all have the *same type*. A position in the array is indicated by a non-negative integer value called the *index*. An element at a given position in the array is accessed using the index. The size of an array is fixed and cannot be changed after the array has been created.

In Java, arrays are objects. Arrays can be of primitive data types or reference types. In the former case, all elements in the array are of a specific primitive data type. In the latter case, all elements are references of a specific reference type. References in the array can then denote objects of this reference type or its subtypes. Each array object has a `public final` field called `length`, which specifies the array size (i.e., the number of elements the array can accommodate). The first element is always at index 0 and the last element at index $n - 1$, where n is the value of the `length` field in the array.

Simple arrays are *one-dimensional arrays*—that is, a simple list of values. Since arrays can store reference values, the objects referenced can also be array objects. Thus a multidimensional arrays is implemented as an *array of arrays* (p. 124).

Passing array references as parameters is discussed in §3.10, p. 127. Type conversions for array references on assignment and on method invocation are discussed in §5.9, p. 261, and §5.10, p. 265, respectively.

Declaring Array Variables

A one-dimensional array variable declaration has either of the following syntaxes:

> *element_type*[] *array_name*;

or

> *element_type array_name*[];

where *element_type* can be a primitive data type or a reference type. The array variable *array_name* has the type *element_type*[]. Note that the array size is not specified. As a consequence, the array variable *array_name* can be assigned the reference value of an array of any length, as long as its elements have *element_type*.

It is important to understand that the declaration does not actually create an array. Instead, it simply declares a *reference* that can refer to an array object. The [] notation can also be specified after a variable name to declare it as an array variable, but then it applies to just that variable.

```
int anIntArray[], oneInteger;
Pizza[] mediumPizzas, largePizzas;
```

These two declarations declare `anIntArray` and `mediumPizzas` to be reference variables that can refer to arrays of `int` values and arrays of `Pizza` objects, respectively. The variable `largePizzas` can denote an array of `Pizza` objects, but the variable `oneInteger` cannot denote an array of `int` values—it is a simple variable of the type `int`.

An array variable that is declared as a field in a class, but is not explicitly initialized to any array, will be initialized to the default reference value `null`. This default initialization does *not* apply to *local* reference variables, and therefore, does not apply to local array variables either. This behavior should not be confused with initialization of the elements of an array during array construction.

Constructing an Array

An array can be constructed for a fixed number of elements of a specific type, using the new operator. The reference value of the resulting array can be assigned to an array variable of the corresponding type. The syntax of the *array creation expression* is shown on the right-hand side of the following assignment statement:

    array_name = new element_type[array_size];

The minimum value of *array_size* is 0; in other words, zero-length arrays can be constructed in Java. If the array size is negative, a NegativeArraySizeException is thrown at runtime.

Given the declarations

    int anIntArray[], oneInteger;
    Pizza[] mediumPizzas, largePizzas;

the three arrays in the declarations can be constructed as follows:

    anIntArray   = new int[10];   // array for 10 integers
    mediumPizzas = new Pizza[5];   // array of 5 pizzas
    largePizzas = new Pizza[3];   // array of 3 pizzas

The array declaration and construction can be combined.

    element_type₁[] array_name = new element_type₂[array_size];

In the preceding syntax, the array type *element_type₂[]* must be *assignable* to the array type *element_type₁[]* (§5.8, p. 261). When the array is constructed, all of its elements are initialized to the default value for *element_type₂*. This is true for both member and local arrays when they are constructed.

In the following examples, the code constructs the array, and the array elements are implicitly initialized to their default values. For example, all elements of the array anIntArray get the value 0, and all elements of the array mediumPizzas get the value null when the arrays are constructed.

    int[] anIntArray = new int[10];   // Default element value: 0
    Pizza[] mediumPizzas = new Pizza[5];   // Default element value: null

The value of the field length in each array is set to the number of elements specified during the construction of the array; for example, mediumPizzas.length has the value 5.

Once an array has been constructed, its elements can also be explicitly initialized individually—for example, in a loop. The examples in the rest of this section make use of a loop to iterate over the elements of an array for various purposes.

Initializing an Array

Java provides the means to declare, construct, and explicitly initialize an array in one declaration statement:

    element_type[] array_name = { array_initialize_list };

This form of initialization applies to fields as well as to local arrays. The *array_initialize_list* is a comma-separated list of zero or more expressions. Such an array initializer results in the construction and initialization of the array.

```
int[] anIntArray = {13, 49, 267, 15, 215};
```

In the declaration statement above, the variable anIntArray is declared as a reference to an array of ints. The array initializer results in the construction of an array to hold five elements (equal to the length of the list of expressions in the block), where the first element is initialized to the value of the first expression (13), the second element to the value of the second expression (49), and so on.

```
Pizza[] pizzaOrder = { new Pizza(), new Pizza(), null };
```

In this declaration statement, the variable pizzaOrder is declared as a reference to an array of Pizza objects. The array initializer constructs an array to hold three elements. The initialization code sets the first two elements of the array to refer to two Pizza objects, while the last element is initialized to the null reference. The reference value of the array of Pizza objects is assigned to the reference pizzaOrder. Note also that this declaration statement actually creates *three* objects: the array object with three references and the two Pizza objects.

The expressions in the *array_initialize_list* are evaluated from left to right, and the array name obviously cannot occur in any of the expressions in the list. In the preceding examples, the *array_initialize_list* is terminated by the right curly bracket, }, of the block. The list can also be legally terminated by a comma. The following array has length 2, and not 3:

```
Topping[] pizzaToppings = { new Topping("cheese"), new Topping("tomato"), };
```

The declaration statement at (1) in the following code defines an array of four String objects, while the declaration statement at (2) shows that a String object is not the same as an array of char.

```
// Array with 4 String objects:
String[] pets = {"crocodiles", "elephants", "crocophants", "elediles"}; // (1)

// Array of 3 characters:
char[] charArray = {'a', 'h', 'a'};     // (2) Not the same as "aha"
```

Using an Array

The array object is referenced by the array name, but individual array elements are accessed by specifying an index with the [] operator. The array element access expression has the following syntax:

array_name [*index_expression*]

Each individual element is treated as a simple variable of the element type. The *index* is specified by the *index_expression*, whose value should be promotable to an int value; otherwise, a compile-time error is flagged. Since the lower bound of an array index is always 0, the upper bound is 1 less than the array size—that is, *array_name*.length-1. The ith element in the array has index (i-1). At runtime, the index value is automatically checked to ensure that it is within the array index bounds. If the index value is less than 0, or greater than or equal to *array_name*.length, an ArrayIndexOutOfBoundsException is thrown. A program can either explicitly check that the index value is within the array index bounds or catch the runtime exception that is thrown if it is invalid (§7.3, p. 375), but an illegal index is typically an indication of a programming error.

In the array element access expression, the *array_name* can be any expression that returns a reference to an array. For example, the expression on the right-hand side of the following assignment statement returns the character 'H' at index 1 in the character array returned by a call to the toCharArray() method of the String class:

```
char letter = "AHA".toCharArray()[1];      // 'H'
```

The array operator [] is used to declare array types (Topping[]), specify the array size (new Topping[3]), and access array elements (toppings[1]). This operator is not used when the array reference is manipulated, such as in an array reference assignment, or when the array reference is passed as an actual parameter in a method call (p. 132).

Example 3.7 shows traversal of arrays using for loops (§4.7, p. 174 and p. 176). A for(;;) loop at (3) in the main() method initializes the local array trialArray declared at (2) five times with pseudorandom numbers (from 0.0 to 100.0), by calling the method randomize() declared at (5). The minimum value in the array is found by calling the method findMinimum() declared at (6), and is stored in the array storeMinimum declared at (1). Both of these methods also use a for(;;) loop. The loop variable is initialized to a start value—0 at (3) and (5), and 1 at (6). The loop condition tests whether the loop variable is less than the length of the array; this guarantees that the loop will terminate when the last element has been accessed. The loop variable is incremented after each iteration to access the next element.

A for(:) loop at (4) in the main() method is used to print the minimum values from the trials, as elements are read consecutively from the array, without keeping track of an index value.

Example 3.7   *Using Arrays*

```
public class Trials {
  public static void main(String[] args) {
    // Declare and construct the local arrays:
    double[] storeMinimum = new double[5];                // (1)
    double[] trialArray = new double[15];                 // (2)
    for (int i = 0; i < storeMinimum.length; ++i) {       // (3)
      // Initialize the array.
      randomize(trialArray);

      // Find and store the minimum value.
      storeMinimum[i] = findMinimum(trialArray);
    }
```

```java
    // Print the minimum values:                        (4)
    for (double minValue : storeMinimum)
      System.out.printf("%.4f%n", minValue);
  }

  public static void randomize(double[] valArray) {       // (5)
    for (int i = 0; i < valArray.length; ++i)
      valArray[i] = Math.random() * 100.0;
  }

  public static double findMinimum(double[] valArray) {  // (6)
    // Assume the array has at least one element.
    double minValue = valArray[0];
    for (int i = 1; i < valArray.length; ++i)
      minValue = Math.min(minValue, valArray[i]);
    return minValue;
  }
}
```

Probable output from the program:

```
6.9330
2.7819
6.7427
18.0849
26.2462
```

Anonymous Arrays

As shown earlier in this section, the following declaration statement can be used to construct arrays using an array creation expression:

$element\_type_1$[] $array\_name$ = new $element\_type_2$[$array\_size$];   // (1)

int[] intArray = new int[5];

The size of the array is specified in the array creation expression, which creates the array and initializes the array elements to their default values. By comparison, the following declaration statement both creates the array and initializes the array elements to specific values given in the array initializer:

$element\_type$[] $array\_name$ = { $array\_initialize\_list$ };   // (2)

int[] intArray = {3, 5, 2, 8, 6};

However, the array initializer is *not* an expression. Java has another array creation expression, called an *anonymous array*, which allows the concept of the array creation expression from (1) to be combined with the array initializer from (2), so as to create and initialize an array:

new $element\_type$[] { $array\_initialize\_list$ }

new int[] {3, 5, 2, 8, 6}

This construct has enough information to create a nameless array of a specific type and specific length. Neither the name of the array nor the size of the array is specified. The construct returns the reference value of the newly created array, which can be assigned to references and passed as arguments in method calls. In particular, the following declaration statements are equivalent:

```
int[] intArray = {3, 5, 2, 8, 6};                              // (1)
int[] intArray = new int[] {3, 5, 2, 8, 6};                    // (2)
```

At (1), an array initializer is used to create and initialize the elements. At (2), an anonymous array expression is used. It is tempting to use the array initializer as an expression—for example, in an assignment statement, as a shortcut for assigning values to array elements in one go. However, this is not allowed; instead, an anonymous array expression should be used. The concept of the anonymous array combines the definition and the creation of the array into one operation.

```
int[] daysInMonth;
daysInMonth = {31, 28, 31, 30, 31, 30,
               31, 31, 30, 31, 30, 31};                        // Compile-time error
daysInMonth = new int[] {31, 28, 31, 30, 31, 30, 31, 31, 30, 31, 30, 31}; // OK
```

In Example 3.8, an anonymous array is constructed at (1), and passed as an actual parameter to the static method findMinimum() defined at (2). Note that no array name or array size is specified for the anonymous array.

Example 3.8 *Using Anonymous Arrays*

```
public class AnonArray {
  public static void main(String[] args) {
    System.out.println("Minimum value: " +
       findMinimum(new int[] {3, 5, 2, 8, 6}));                // (1)
  }

  public static int findMinimum(int[] dataSeq) {               // (2)
    // Assume the array has at least one element.
    int min = dataSeq[0];
    for (int index = 1; index < dataSeq.length; ++index)
      if (dataSeq[index] < min)
        min = dataSeq[index];
    return min;
  }
}
```

Output from the program:

```
Minimum value: 2
```

Multidimensional Arrays

Since an array element can be an object reference and arrays are objects, array elements can themselves refer to other arrays. In Java, an array of arrays can be defined as follows:

element_type[][]...[] *array_name*;

or

element_type array_name[][]...[];

In fact, the sequence of square bracket pairs, [], indicating the number of dimensions, can be distributed as a postfix to both the element type and the array name. Arrays of arrays are often called *multidimensional arrays*.

The following declarations are all equivalent:

```
int[][] mXnArray;       // two-dimensional array
int[]   mXnArray[];     // two-dimensional array
int     mXnArray[][];   // two-dimensional array
```

It is customary to combine the declaration with the construction of the multidimensional array.

```
int[][] mXnArray = new int[4][5];    // 4 x 5 matrix of ints
```

The previous declaration constructs an array mXnArray of four elements, where each element is an array (row) of five int values. The concept of rows and columns is often used to describe the dimensions of a two-dimensional array, which is often called a *matrix*. However, such an interpretation is not dictated by the Java language.

Each row in the previous matrix is denoted by mXnArray[i], where $0 \leq i < 4$. Each element in the ith row, mXnArray[i], is accessed by mXnArray[i][j], where $0 \leq j < 5$. The number of rows is given by mXnArray.length, in this case 4, and the number of values in the ith row is given by mXnArray[i].length, in this case 5 for all the rows, where $0 \leq i < 4$.

Multidimensional arrays can also be constructed and explicitly initialized using the array initializers discussed for simple arrays. Note that each row is an array that uses an array initializer to specify its values:

```
double[][] identityMatrix = {
  {1.0, 0.0, 0.0, 0.0 }, // 1. row
  {0.0, 1.0, 0.0, 0.0 }, // 2. row
  {0.0, 0.0, 1.0, 0.0 }, // 3. row
  {0.0, 0.0, 0.0, 1.0 }  // 4. row
}; // 4 x 4 floating-point matrix
```

Arrays in a multidimensional array need not have the same length; in which case, they are called *ragged arrays*. The array of arrays pizzaGalore in the following code has five rows; the first four rows have different lengths but the fifth row is left unconstructed:

```
Pizza[][] pizzaGalore = {
  { new Pizza(), null, new Pizza() },    // 1. row is an array of 3 elements.
  { null, new Pizza()},                  // 2. row is an array of 2 elements.
  new Pizza[1],                          // 3. row is an array of 1 element.
  {},                                    // 4. row is an array of 0 elements.
  null                                   // 5. row is not constructed.
};
```

When constructing multidimensional arrays with the new operator, the length of the deeply nested arrays may be omitted. In such a case, these arrays are left unconstructed. For example, an array of arrays to represent a room (defined by class HotelRoom) on a floor in a hotel on a street in a city can have the type HotelRoom[][][][]. From left to right, the square brackets represent indices for street, hotel, floor, and room, respectively. This four-dimensional array of arrays can be constructed piecemeal, starting with the leftmost dimension and proceeding to the rightmost successively.

```
HotelRoom[][][][] rooms = new HotelRoom[10][5][][];  // Just streets and hotels.
```

The preceding declaration constructs the array of arrays rooms partially with 10 streets, where each street has five hotels. Floors and rooms can be added to a particular hotel on a particular street:

```
rooms[0][0]       = new HotelRoom[3][]; // 3 floors in 1st hotel on 1st street.
rooms[0][0][0]    = new HotelRoom[8];   // 8 rooms on 1st floor in this hotel.
rooms[0][0][0][0] = new HotelRoom();    // Initializes 1st room on this floor.
```

The next code snippet constructs an array of arrays matrix, where the first row has one element, the second row has two elements, and the third row has three elements. Note that the outer array is constructed first. The second dimension is constructed in a loop that constructs the array in each row. The elements in the multidimensional array will be implicitly initialized to the default double value (0.0D). In Figure 3.1, the array of arrays matrix is depicted after the elements have been explicitly initialized.

```
double[][] matrix = new double[3][];      // (1) Number of rows.

for (int i = 0; i < matrix.length; ++i)
  matrix[i] = new double[i + 1];          // Construct a row.
```

The type of the variable matrix is double[][] at (1), a two-dimensional array of double values. The type of the variable matrix[i] (where $0 \leq i <$ matrix.length) is double[], a one-dimensional array of double values. The type of the variable matrix[i][j] (where $0 \leq i <$ matrix.length and $0 \leq j <$ matrix[i].length) is double, a simple variable of type double.

Figure 3.1 *Array of Arrays*

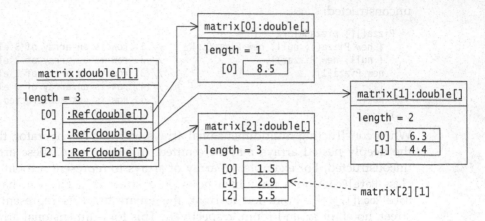

Two other ways of initializing such an array of arrays are shown next. The first approach uses array initializers, and the second uses an anonymous array of arrays.

```
double[][] matrix2 = {      // (2) Using array initializers.
  {1.0},                    // 1. row
  {1.0, 2.0},               // 2. row
  {1.0, 2.0, 3.0}           // 3. row
};

double[][] matrix3 = new double[][] { // (3) Using an anonymous array of arrays.
  {1.0},                    // 1. row
  {1.0, 2.0},               // 2. row
  {1.0, 2.0, 1.0}           // 3. row
};
```

Nested loops are a natural match for manipulating multidimensional arrays. In Example 3.9, a rectangular 4 × 3 int matrix is declared and constructed at (1). The program finds the minimum value in the matrix. The outer loop at (2) iterates over the rows (mXnArray[i], where $0 \leq i <$ mXnArray.length), and the inner loop at (3) iterates over the elements in each row in turn (mXnArray[i][j], where $0 \leq j <$ mXnArray[i].length). The outer loop is executed mXnArray.length times, or four times, and the inner loop is executed (mXnArray.length) × (mXnArray[i].length), or 12 times, since all rows have the same length 3.

The for(:) loop also provides a safe and convenient way of iterating over an array. Several examples of its use are provided in §4.8, p. 176.

Example 3.9 *Using Multidimensional Arrays*

```
public class MultiArrays {

  public static void main(String[] args) {
    // Declare and construct the M X N matrix.
    int[][] mXnArray = {                                      // (1)
```

```
              {16,  7, 12}, // 1. row
              { 9, 20, 18}, // 2. row
              {14, 11,  5}, // 3. row
              { 8,  5, 10} // 4. row
           }; // 4 x 3 int matrix

           // Find the minimum value in an M X N matrix:
           int min = mXnArray[0][0];
           for (int i = 0; i < mXnArray.length; ++i)                              // (2)
               // Find min in mXnArray[i], in the row given by index i:
               for (int j = 0; j < mXnArray[i].length; ++j)                       // (3)
               min = Math.min(min, mXnArray[i][j]);

           System.out.println("Minimum value: " + min);
        }
    }
```

Output from the program:

```
Minimum value: 5
```

3.10 Parameter Passing

Objects communicate by calling methods on each other. A *method call* is used to invoke a method on an object. Parameters in the method call provide one way of exchanging information between the caller object and the callee object (which need not be different).

The syntax of a method call can be any one of the following:

   object_reference.*method_name*(*actual_parameter_list*)

   class_name.*static_method_name*(*actual_parameter_list*)

   method_name(*actual_parameter_list*)

The *object_reference* must be an expression that evaluates to a reference value denoting the object on which the method is called. If the caller and the callee are the same, *object reference* can be omitted (see the discussion of the this reference on p. 106). The *class_name* can be the *fully qualified name* (§6.3, p. 326) of the class. The *actual_parameter_list* is *comma-separated* if there is more than one parameter. The parentheses are mandatory even if the actual parameter list is empty. This distinguishes the method call from field access. One can specify fully qualified names for classes and packages using the *dot operator* (.).

```
objRef.doIt(time, place);          // Explicit object reference
int i = java.lang.Math.abs(-1);    // Fully qualified class name
int j = Math.abs(-1);              // Simple class name
someMethod(ofValue);               // Object or class is implied
someObjRef.make().make().make();   // make() returns a reference value
```

The dot operator (.) has left associativity. In the last line of the preceding code, the first call of the make() method returns a reference value that denotes the object on which to execute the next call, and so on. This is an example of *call chaining*.

Each *actual parameter* (also called an *argument*) is an expression that is evaluated, and whose value is passed to the method when the method is invoked. Its value can vary from invocation to invocation. *Formal parameters* are parameters defined in the *method declaration* and are *local* to the method.

It should also be stressed that each invocation of a method has its own copies of the formal parameters, as is the case for any local variables in the method. The JVM uses a *stack* to keep track of method execution and a *heap* to manage the objects that are created by the program (§7.1, p. 365). Values of local variables and those passed to the method as parameters, together with any temporary values computed during the execution of the method, are always stored on the stack. Thus only primitive values and reference values are stored on the stack, and only these can be passed as parameters in a method call, but never any object from the heap.

In Java, all parameters are *passed by value*—that is, an actual parameter is evaluated and its value from the stack is assigned to the corresponding formal parameter. Table 3.2 summarizes the value that is passed depending on the type of the parameters. In the case of primitive data types, the data value of the actual parameter is passed. If the actual parameter is a reference to an object, the reference value of the denoted object is passed and not the object itself. Analogously, if the actual parameter is an array element of a primitive data type, its data value is passed, and if the array element is a reference to an object, then its reference value is passed.

Table 3.2   *Parameter Passing by Value*

Data type of the formal parameter	Value passed
Primitive data type	Primitive data value of the actual parameter
Reference type (i.e., class, interface, array, or enum type)	Reference value of the actual parameter

The order of evaluation in the actual parameter list is always *from left to right*. The evaluation of an actual parameter can be influenced by an earlier evaluation of an actual parameter. Given the following declaration:

```
int i = 4;
```

the method call

```
leftRight(i++, i);
```

is effectively the same as

```
leftRight(4, 5);
```

and not the same as

```
leftRight(4, 4);
```

An overview of the conversions that can take place in a method invocation context is provided in §2.4, p. 48. Method invocation conversions for primitive values are discussed in the next subsection (p. 129), and those for reference types are discussed in §5.10, p. 265. Calling variable arity methods is discussed in the next section (p. 136).

For the sake of simplicity, the examples in subsequent sections primarily show method invocation on the same object or the same class. The parameter passing mechanism is no different when different objects or classes are involved.

Passing Primitive Data Values

An actual parameter is an expression that is evaluated first, with the resulting value then being assigned to the corresponding formal parameter at method invocation. The use of this value in the method has no influence on the actual parameter. In particular, when the actual parameter is a variable of a primitive data type, the value of the variable from the stack is copied to the formal parameter at method invocation. Since formal parameters are local to the method, any changes made to the formal parameter will not be reflected in the actual parameter after the call completes.

Legal type conversions between actual parameters and formal parameters of *primitive data types* are summarized here from Table 2.17, p. 47:

- Primitive widening conversion
- Unboxing conversion, followed by an optional widening primitive conversion

These conversions are illustrated by invoking the following method

```
static void doIt(long i) { /* ... */ }
```

with the following code:

```
Integer intRef = 34;
Long longRef = 34L;
doIt(34);          // (1) Primitive widening conversion: long <-- int
doIt(longRef);     // (2) Unboxing: long <-- Long
doIt(intRef);      // (3) Unboxing, followed by primitive widening conversion:
                   //     long <-- int <-- Integer
```

However, for parameter passing, there are no implicit narrowing conversions for integer constant expressions (§2.4, p. 48).

Example 3.10 *Passing Primitive Values*

```
public class CustomerOne {
  public static void main (String[] args) {
    PizzaFactory pizzaHouse = new PizzaFactory();
    int pricePrPizza = 15;
    System.out.println("Value of pricePrPizza before call: " + pricePrPizza);
    double totPrice = pizzaHouse.calcPrice(4, pricePrPizza);          // (1)
    System.out.println("Value of pricePrPizza after call: " + pricePrPizza);
  }
}
```

```
class PizzaFactory {
  public double calcPrice(int numberOfPizzas, double pizzaPrice) {        // (2)
    pizzaPrice = pizzaPrice / 2.0;         // Changes price.
    System.out.println("Changed pizza price in the method: " + pizzaPrice);
    return numberOfPizzas * pizzaPrice;
  }
}
```

Output from the program:

```
Value of pricePrPizza before call: 15
Changed pizza price in the method: 7.5
Value of pricePrPizza after call: 15
```

In Example 3.10, the method calcPrice() is defined in the class PizzaFactory at (2). It is called from the CustomerOne.main() method at (1). The value of the first actual parameter, 4, is copied to the int formal parameter numberOfPizzas. Note that the second actual parameter pricePrPizza is of the type int, while the corresponding formal parameter pizzaPrice is of the type double. Before the value of the actual parameter pricePrPizza is copied to the formal parameter pizzaPrice, it is implicitly widened to a double. The passing of primitive values is illustrated in Figure 3.2.

Figure 3.2 *Parameter Passing: Primitive Data Values*

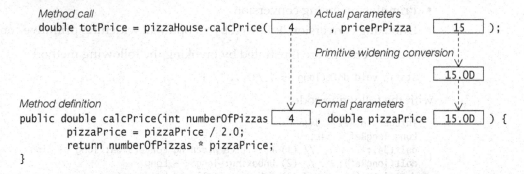

The value of the formal parameter pizzaPrice is changed in the calcPrice() method, but this does not affect the value of the actual parameter pricePrPizza on return. It still has the value 15. The bottom line is that the formal parameter is a local variable, and changing its value does not affect the value of the actual parameter.

Passing Reference Values

If the actual parameter expression evaluates to a reference value, the resulting reference value on the stack is assigned to the corresponding formal parameter reference at method invocation. In particular, if an actual parameter is a reference to an object, the reference value stored in the actual parameter is passed. Consequently, both the actual parameter and the formal parameter are aliases to the object denoted by this reference value during the invocation of the method. In particular, this implies that changes made to the object via the formal parameter *will* be apparent after the call returns.

Type conversions between actual and formal parameters of reference types are discussed in §5.10, p. 265.

In Example 3.11, a Pizza object is created at (1). Any object of the class Pizza created using the class declaration at (5) always results in a beef pizza. In the call to the bake() method at (2), the reference value of the object referenced by the actual parameter favoritePizza is assigned to the formal parameter pizzaToBeBaked in the declaration of the bake() method at (3).

Example 3.11   *Passing Reference Values*

```
public class CustomerTwo {
  public static void main (String[] args) {
    Pizza favoritePizza = new Pizza();              // (1)
    System.out.println("Meat on pizza before baking: " + favoritePizza.meat);
    bake(favoritePizza);                            // (2)
    System.out.println("Meat on pizza after baking: " + favoritePizza.meat);
  }
  public static void bake(Pizza pizzaToBeBaked) {   // (3)
    pizzaToBeBaked.meat = "chicken";  // Change the meat on the pizza.
    pizzaToBeBaked = null;                          // (4)
  }
}

class Pizza {                                       // (5)
  String meat = "beef";
}
```

Output from the program:

```
Meat on pizza before baking: beef
Meat on pizza after baking: chicken
```

One particular consequence of passing reference values to formal parameters is that any changes made to the object via formal parameters will be reflected back in the calling method when the call returns. In this case, the reference favoritePizza will show that chicken has been substituted for beef on the pizza. Setting the formal parameter pizzaToBeBaked to null at (4) does not change the reference value in the actual parameter favoritePizza. The situation at method invocation, and just before the return from method bake(), is illustrated in Figure 3.3.

In summary, the formal parameter can only change the *state* of the object whose reference value was passed to the method.

The parameter passing strategy in Java is *call by value* and not *call by reference*, regardless of the type of the parameter. Call by reference would have allowed values in the actual parameters to be changed via formal parameters; that is, the value in pricePrPizza would be halved in Example 3.10 and favoritePizza would be set to null in Example 3.11. However, this cannot be directly implemented in Java.

Figure 3.3 *Parameter Passing: Reference Values*

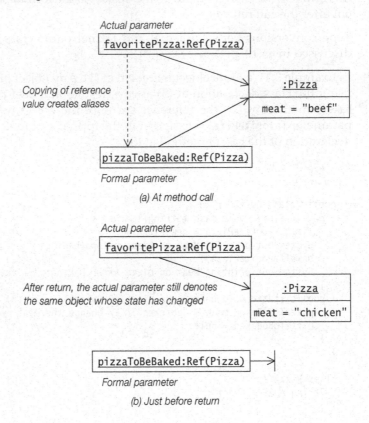

(a) At method call

(b) Just before return

Passing Arrays

The discussion of passing reference values in the previous section is equally valid for arrays, as arrays are objects in Java. Method invocation conversions for array types are discussed along with those for other reference types in §5.10, p. 265.

In Example 3.12, the idea is to repeatedly swap neighboring elements in an integer array until the largest element in the array *percolates* to the last position in the array.

Example 3.12 *Passing Arrays*

```java
public class Percolate {

    public static void main (String[] args) {
        int[] dataSeq = {8,4,6,2,1};    // Create and initialize an array.

        // Write array before percolation:
        printIntArray(dataSeq);

        // Percolate:
        for (int index = 1; index < dataSeq.length; ++index)
```

```
            if (dataSeq[index-1] > dataSeq[index])
                swap(dataSeq, index-1, index);                    // (1)

        // Write array after percolation:
        printIntArray(dataSeq);
    }

    public static void swap(int[] intArray, int i, int j) { // (2)
        int tmp = intArray[i]; intArray[i] = intArray[j]; intArray[j] = tmp;
    }

    public static void swap(int v1, int v2) {                 // (3) Logical error!
        int tmp = v1; v1 = v2; v2 = tmp;
    }

    public static void printIntArray(int[] array) {           // (4)
        for (int value : array)
          System.out.print(" " + value);
        System.out.println();
    }
}
```

Output from the program:

```
8 4 6 2 1
4 6 2 1 8
```

Note that in the declaration of the method swap() at (2), the formal parameter intArray is of the array type int[]. The other two parameters are of type int. They denote the values in the array that should be swapped. The signature of the method is

swap(int[], int, int)

This swap() method is called in the main() method at (1), where one of the actual parameters is the array variable dataSeq. The reference value of the array variable dataSeq is assigned to the array variable intArray at method invocation. After return from the call to the swap() method, the array variable dataSeq will reflect the changes made to the array via the corresponding formal parameter. This situation is depicted in Figure 3.4 at the first call and return from the swap() method, indicating how the values of the elements at indices 0 and 1 in the array have been swapped.

Figure 3.4 *Parameter Passing: Arrays*

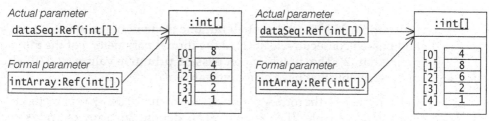

(a) *At first call to the* swap() *method*   (b) *Just before first return from the* swap() *method*

However, the declaration of the swap() method at (3) will *not* swap two values. The method call

```
swap(dataSeq[index-1], dataSeq[index]); // Call signature: swap(int, int)
```

will result in the swap() method at (3) to be invoked. Its execution will have no effect on the array elements, as the swapping is done on the values of the formal parameters.

The method printIntArray() at (4) also has a formal parameter of array type int[]. Note that the formal parameter is specified as an array reference using the [] notation, but this notation is not used when an array is passed as an actual parameter.

Array Elements as Actual Parameters

Array elements, like other variables, can store values of primitive data types or reference values of objects. In the latter case, they can also be arrays—that is, arrays of arrays (p. 124). If an array element is of a primitive data type, its data value is passed; if it is a reference to an object, the reference value is passed. The method invocation conversions apply to the values of array elements as well.

Example 3.13 *Array Elements as Primitive Data Values*

```java
public class FindMinimum {

  public static void main(String[] args) {
    int[] dataSeq = {6,4,8,2,1};

    int minValue = dataSeq[0];
    for (int index = 1; index < dataSeq.length; ++index)
      minValue = minimum(minValue, dataSeq[index]);            // (1)

    System.out.println("Minimum value: " + minValue);
  }

  public static int minimum(int i, int j) {                   // (2)
    return (i <= j) ? i : j;
  }
}
```

Output from the program:

```
Minimum value: 1
```

In Example 3.13, the value of all but one element of the array dataSeq is retrieved and passed consecutively at (1) to the formal parameter j of the minimum() method defined at (2). The discussion on passing primitive values (p. 129) also applies to array elements that have primitive values.

In Example 3.14, the formal parameter seq of the findMinimum() method defined at (4) is an array variable. The variable matrix denotes an array of arrays declared at (1) simulating a multidimensional array that has three rows, where each row is a simple array. The first row, denoted by matrix[0], is passed to the findMinimum() method in the call at (2). Each remaining row is passed by its reference value in the call to the findMinimum() method at (3).

Example 3.14   *Array Elements as Reference Values*

```java
public class FindMinimumMxN {

  public static void main(String[] args) {
    int[][] matrix = { {8,4},{6,3,2},{7} };                    // (1)

    int min = findMinimum(matrix[0]);                          // (2)
    for (int i = 1; i < matrix.length; ++i) {
      int minInRow = findMinimum(matrix[i]);                   // (3)
      min = Math.min(min, minInRow);
    }
    System.out.println("Minimum value in matrix: " + min);
  }

  public static int findMinimum(int[] seq) {                   // (4)
    int min = seq[0];
    for (int i = 1; i < seq.length; ++i)
      min = Math.min(min, seq[i]);
    return min;
  }
}
```

Output from the program:

```
Minimum value in matrix: 2
```

final **Parameters**

A formal parameter can be declared with the keyword final preceding the parameter declaration in the method declaration. A final parameter is also known as a *blank final variable*; that is, it is blank (uninitialized) until a value is assigned to it, (e.g., at method invocation) and then the value in the variable cannot be changed during the lifetime of the variable (see also the discussion in §6.6, p. 352). The compiler can treat final variables as constants for code optimization purposes. Declaring parameters as final prevents their values from being changed inadvertently. A formal parameter's declaration as final does not affect the caller's code.

The declaration of the method calcPrice() from Example 3.10 is shown next, with the formal parameter pizzaPrice declared as final:

```java
public double calcPrice(int numberOfPizzas, final double pizzaPrice) {  // (2')
  pizzaPrice = pizzaPrice/2.0;        // (3) Not allowed. Compile-time error!
  return numberOfPizzas * pizzaPrice;
}
```

If this declaration of the calcPrice() method is compiled, the compiler will not allow the value of the final parameter pizzaPrice to be changed at (3) in the body of the method.

As another example, the declaration of the method bake() from Example 3.11 is shown here, with the formal parameter pizzaToBeBaked declared as final:

```
public static void bake(final Pizza pizzaToBeBaked) { // (3)
   pizzaToBeBaked.meat = "chicken";    // (3a) Allowed
   pizzaToBeBaked = null;              // (4) Not allowed. Compile-time error!
}
```

If this declaration of the bake() method is compiled, the compiler will not allow the reference value of the final parameter pizzaToBeBaked to be changed at (4) in the body of the method. Note that this applies to the reference value in the final parameter, but not to the object denoted by this parameter. The state of the object can be changed as before, as shown at (3a).

For use of the final keyword in other contexts, see §5.5, p. 225.

3.11 Variable Arity Methods

A *fixed arity* method must be called with the same number of actual parameters (also called *arguments*) as the number of formal parameters specified in its declaration. If the method declaration specifies two formal parameters, every call of this method must specify exactly two arguments. We say that the arity of this method is 2. In other words, the arity of such a method is fixed, and it is equal to the number of formal parameters specified in the method declaration.

Java also allows declaration of *variable arity* methods (also called *varargs* methods), meaning that the number of arguments in its call can be *varied*. As we shall see, invocations of such a method may contain more actual parameters than formal parameters. Variable arity methods are heavily employed in formatting text representation of values, as demonstrated by the variable arity method System.out.printf() that is used in many examples for this purpose.

The *last* formal parameter in a variable arity method declaration is declared as follows:

type... *formal_parameter_name*

The ellipsis (...) is specified between the *type* and the *formal_parameter_name*. The *type* can be a primitive type, a reference type, or a type parameter. Whitespace can be specified on both sides of the ellipsis. Such a parameter is usually called a *variable arity parameter* (also known as a *varargs* parameter).

Apart from the variable arity parameter, a variable arity method is identical to a fixed arity method. The method publish() below is a variable arity method:

```
public static void publish(int n, String... data) {      // (int, String[])
   System.out.println("n: " + n + ", data size: " + data.length);
}
```

The variable arity parameter in a variable arity method is always interpreted as having an array type:

type[]

In the body of the publish() method, the variable arity parameter data has the type String[], so it is a simple array of Strings.

Only *one* variable arity parameter is permitted in the formal parameter list, and it is always the *last* parameter in the list. Given that the method declaration has n formal parameters and the method call has k actual parameters, k must be equal to or greater than $n - 1$. The last $k - n + 1$ actual parameters are evaluated and stored in an array whose reference value is passed as the value of the actual parameter. In the case of the publish() method, n is equal to 2, so k can be 1, 2, 3, and so on. The following invocations of the publish() method show which arguments are passed in each method call:

```
publish(1);                   // (1, new String[] {})
publish(2, "two");            // (2, new String[] {"two"})
publish(3, "two", "three");   // (3, new String[] {"two", "three"})
```

Each method call results in an *implicit* array being created and passed as an argument. This array can contain zero or more argument values that do *not* correspond to the formal parameters preceding the variable arity parameter. This array is referenced by the variable arity parameter data in the method declaration. The preceding calls would result in the publish() method printing the following output:

```
n: 1, data size: 0
n: 2, data size: 1
n: 3, data size: 2
```

To overload a variable arity method, it is not enough to change the type of the variable arity parameter to an explicit array type. The compiler will complain if an attempt is made to overload the method transmit(), as shown in the following code:

```
public static void transmit(String... data) { }  // Compile-time error!
public static void transmit(String[] data) { }    // Compile-time error!
```

Both methods above have the signature transmit(String[]). These declarations would result in two methods with equivalent signatures in the same class, which is not permitted.

Overloading and overriding of methods with variable arity are discussed in §5.10, p. 265.

Calling a Variable Arity Method

Example 3.15 illustrates various aspects of calling a variable arity method. The method flexiPrint() in the VarargsDemo class has a variable arity parameter:

```
public static void flexiPrint(Object... data) { // Object[]
  //...
}
```

The variable arity method prints the name of the Class object representing the *actual array* that is passed at runtime. It prints the number of elements in this array as well as the text representation of each element in the array.

The method flexiPrint() is called in the main() method. First it is called with the values of primitive types and Strings ((1) to (8)), and then it is called with the program arguments (p. 141) supplied on the command line ((9) to (11)).

Compiling the program results in a *warning* at (9), which we ignore for the time being. The program can still be run, as shown in Example 3.15. The numbers at the end of the lines in the output relate to numbers in the code, and are not printed by the program.

Example 3.15 *Calling a Variable Arity Method*

```java
public class VarargsDemo {
  public static void flexiPrint(Object... data) { // Object[]
    // Print the name of the Class object for the varargs parameter.
    System.out.print("Type: " + data.getClass().getName());

    System.out.println("  No. of elements: " + data.length);

    System.out.print("Element values: ");
    for(Object element : data)
      System.out.print(element + " ");
    System.out.println();
  }

  public static void main(String... args) {
    int    day      = 13;
    String monthName = "August";
    int    year     = 2009;

    // Passing primitives and non-array types:
    flexiPrint();                       // (1) new Object[] {}
    flexiPrint(day);                    // (2) new Object[] {Integer.valueOf(day)}
    flexiPrint(day, monthName);         // (3) new Object[] {Integer.valueOf(day),
                                        //                   monthName}
    flexiPrint(day, monthName, year);   // (4) new Object[] {Integer.valueOf(day),
                                        //                   monthName,
                                        //                   Integer.valueOf(year)}
    System.out.println();

    // Passing an array type:
    Object[] dateInfo = {day,           // (5) new Object[] {Integer.valueOf(day),
                         monthName,      //                   monthName,
                         year};          //                   Integer.valueOf(year)}
    flexiPrint(dateInfo);               // (6) Non-varargs call
    flexiPrint((Object) dateInfo);      // (7) new Object[] {(Object) dateInfo}
    flexiPrint(new Object[]{dateInfo}); // (8) Non-varargs call
    System.out.println();
```

```
        // Explicit varargs or non-varargs call:
        flexiPrint(args);                    // (9) Warning!
        flexiPrint((Object) args);           // (10) Explicit varargs call
        flexiPrint((Object[]) args);         // (11) Explicit non-varargs call
    }
}
```

Compiling the program:

```
>javac VarargsDemo.java
VarargsDemo.java:41: warning: non-varargs call of varargs method with inexact
argument type for last parameter;
    flexiPrint(args);                        // (9) Warning!
              ^
    cast to Object for a varargs call
    cast to Object[] for a non-varargs call and to suppress this warning
1 warning
```

Running the program:

```
>java VarargsDemo To arg or not to arg
Type: [Ljava.lang.Object;  No. of elements: 0         (1)
Element values:
Type: [Ljava.lang.Object;  No. of elements: 1         (2)
Element values: 13
Type: [Ljava.lang.Object;  No. of elements: 2         (3)
Element values: 13 August
Type: [Ljava.lang.Object;  No. of elements: 3         (4)
Element values: 13 August 2009

Type: [Ljava.lang.Object;  No. of elements: 3         (6)
Element values: 13 August 2009
Type: [Ljava.lang.Object;  No. of elements: 1         (7)
Element values: [Ljava.lang.Object;@1eed786
Type: [Ljava.lang.Object;  No. of elements: 1         (8)
Element values: [Ljava.lang.Object;@1eed786

Type: [Ljava.lang.String;  No. of elements: 6         (9)
Element values: To arg or not to arg
Type: [Ljava.lang.Object;  No. of elements: 1         (10)
Element values: [Ljava.lang.String;@187aeca
Type: [Ljava.lang.String;  No. of elements: 6         (11)
Element values: To arg or not to arg
```

- -

Variable Arity and Fixed Arity Method Calls

The calls at (1) to (4) in Example 3.15 are all *variable arity calls*, as an implicit Object array is created in which the values of the actual parameters are stored. The reference value of this array is passed to the method. The printout shows that the type of the parameter is actually an array of Objects ([Ljava.lang.Object;).

The call at (6) differs from the previous calls in that the actual parameter is an array that has the *same* type (Object[]) as the variable arity parameter, without having to create an implicit array. In such a case, *no* implicit array is created, and the reference value of the array dateInfo is passed to the method. See also the result from this call at (6) in the output. The call at (6) is a *fixed arity call* (also called a *non-varargs call*), where no implicit array is created:

```
flexiPrint(dateInfo);                    // (6) Non-varargs call
```

However, if the actual parameter is cast to the type Object as at (7), a *variable arity* call is executed:

```
flexiPrint((Object) dateInfo);       // (7) new Object[] {(Object) dateInfo}
```

The type of the actual argument (Object) is now *not* the same as that of the variable arity parameter (Object[]), resulting in an array of the type Object[] being created in which the array dateInfo is stored as an element. The printout at (7) shows that only the text representation of the dateInfo array is printed, and not its elements, as it is the sole element of the implicit array.

The call at (8) is a *fixed arity* call, for the same reason as the call at (6). Now, however, the array dateInfo is explicitly stored as an element in an array of the type Object[] that matches the type of the variable arity parameter:

```
flexiPrint(new Object[]{dateInfo});// (8) Non-varargs call
```

The output from (8) is the same as the output from (7), where the array dateInfo was passed as an element in an implicitly created array of type Object[].

The compiler issues a *warning* for the call at (9):

```
flexiPrint(args);                        // (9) Warning!
```

The actual parameter args is an array of the type String[], which is a *subtype* of Object[]—the type of the variable arity parameter. The array args can be passed in a fixed arity call as an array of the type String[], or in a variable arity call as *an element* in an implicitly created array of the type Object[]. *Both* calls are feasible and valid in this case. Note that the compiler chooses a fixed arity call rather than a variable arity call, but also issues a warning. The result at (9) confirms this course of action. A warning at compile time is not the same as a compile-time error. The former does not prevent the program from being run, whereas the latter does.

At (10), the array args of the type String[] is explicitly passed as an Object in a variable arity call, similar to the call at (7):

```
flexiPrint((Object) args);           // (10) Explicit varargs call
```

At (11), the array args of type String[] is explicitly passed as an array of the type Object[] in a fixed arity call. This call is equivalent to the call at (9), where the widening reference conversion is implicit, but now without a warning at compile time. The two calls print the same information, as is evident from the output at (9) and (11):

```
flexiPrint((Object[]) args);         // (11) Explicit non-varargs call
```

3.12 The main() Method

The mechanics of compiling and running Java applications using the JDK are outlined in §1.8, p. 19. The java command executes a method called main in the class specified on the command line. This class designates the *entry point of the application*. Any class can have a main() method, but only the main() method of the class specified in the java command starts the execution of a Java application.

The main() method must have public access so that the JVM can call this method (§6.5, p. 345). It is a static method belonging to the class, so no object of the class is required to start its execution. It does not return a value; that is, it is declared as void. It has an array of String objects as its only formal parameter. This array contains any arguments passed to the program on the command line (see the next subsection). The following method header declarations fit the bill, and any one of them can be used for the main() method:

```
public static void main(String[] args)      // Method header
public static void main(String args[])       // Method header
public static void main(String... args)      // Method header
```

The three modifiers can occur in any order in the method header. The requirements given in these examples do not exclude specification of other non-access modifiers like final (§5.5, p. 226) or a throws clause (§7.5, p. 388). The main() method can also be overloaded like any other method. The JVM ensures that the main() method having the correct method header is the starting point of program execution.

Program Arguments

Any arguments passed to the program on the command line can be accessed in the main() method of the class specified on the command line. These arguments are passed to the main() method via its formal parameter args of type String[]. These arguments are called *program arguments*.

In Example 3.16, the program prints the arguments passed to the main() method from the following command line:

```
>java Colors red yellow green "blue velvet"
```

The program prints the total number of arguments given by the field length of the String array args. Each string in args, which corresponds to a program argument, is printed together with its length inside a for loop. From the output, we see that there are four program arguments. On the command line, the arguments can be separated by one or more spaces between them, but these are not part of any argument. The last argument shows that we can quote the argument if spaces are to be included as part of the argument.

When no arguments are specified on the command line, a String array of zero length is created and passed to the main() method. Thus the reference value of the formal parameter in the main() method is never null.

Note that the command name java and the class name Colors are not passed to the main() method of the class Colors, nor are any other options that are specified on the command line.

As program arguments can only be passed as strings, they must be explicitly converted to other values by the program, if necessary.

Program arguments supply information to the application, which can be used to tailor the runtime behavior of the application according to user requirements.

Example 3.16 *Passing Program Arguments*

```
public class Colors {
    synchronized public static void main(String[] args) {
        System.out.println("No. of program arguments: " + args.length);
        for (int i = 0; i < args.length; i++)
            System.out.println("Argument no. " + i + " (" + args[i] + ") has " +
                               args[i].length() + " characters.");
    }
}
```

Running the program:

```
>java Colors red yellow green "blue velvet"
No. of program arguments: 4
Argument no. 0 (red) has 3 characters.
Argument no. 1 (yellow) has 6 characters.
Argument no. 2 (green) has 5 characters.
Argument no. 3 (blue velvet) has 11 characters.
```

3.13 Local Variable Type Inference

A variable declaration requires the *type* of the variable to be specified in the declaration. However, in the case of *local variables*, the type can be specified by the reserved type name var, if the local declaration also specifies an *initialization expression* in the declaration. The compiler uses the type of the initialization expression to *infer* the type of the local variable. The restricted type name var denotes this inferred type in the local declaration. This is an example of *type inference*, where the type of a variable or an expression is derived from the context in which it is used. If the compiler cannot infer the type, it reports a compile-time error. A local variable declaration that uses var is also called a var *declaration*. A local variable declared this way is no different from any other local variable.

It is important to note that the type of the local variable is *solely* inferred from the initialization expression specified in the declaration. The following variable declaration in a local context (e.g., body of a method) is declared using the reserved type name var:

```
var year = 2022;
```

The compiler is able to infer that the type of the initialization expression 2022 is int in the above declaration, and therefore the variable year has the type int. The declaration above is equivalent to the declaration below, where the type is explicitly specified:

```
int year = 2022;
```

A cautionary note going forward: This subsection refers to many concepts and constructs that might not be familiar at this stage. It might be a good idea to get an overview now and to come back later for a more thorough review of this topic. The exhaustive index at the end of the book can of course be used at any time to look up a topic.

The class ValidLVTI in Example 3.17 illustrates valid uses of the restricted type name var. The comments in the code should be self-explanatory.

The var restricted type name is allowed in local variable declarations in *blocks* (including *initializer blocks*), *constructors*, and *methods*, as can be seen in the class ValidLVTI at (1a), (1b), and (2) and the method main(), respectively.

Note that at (3b) and (3c), the compiler is able to infer the type of the local variable from the return type of the method on the right-hand side.

It is worth noting that the *cast operator*, (), can be necessary to indicate the desired type, as shown at (5) and (7).

For array variables, the initialization expression must be an *array creation expression* that allows the array size and the array element type to be inferred, as shown at (11a), (11b), (11c), and (11d). A local declaration with var requires an initialization expression, which in the case of local arrays must be either an array creation expression or an anonymous array expression. In other words, it should be possible to infer both the array element type and the size of the array. It cannot be an array initializer.

The bodies (and the headers) of the for(;;) and for(:) *loops* can define their own local variables in their *block scope*. The type of the local variable vowel at (13) is inferred to be char from the array vowels (of type char[]) in the header of the for(:) loop. The type of the local variable i in the header of the for(;;) loop at (16) is determined to be int from the initial value. The switch statement also defines its own block scope in which local variables can be declared, as shown at (18).

Example 3.17   *Illustrating Local Variable Type Reference*

```
// Class ValidLVTI illustrates valid use of the restricted type name var.
public class ValidLVTI {

  // Static initializer block:
  static {
    var slogan = "Keep calm and code Java.";        // (1a) Allowed in static
  }                                                  //       initializer block
```

```java
// Instance initializer block:
{
  var banner = "Keep calm and catch exceptions."; // (1b) Allowed in instance
}                                                  //      initializer block

// Constructor:
public ValidLVTI() {
  var luckyNumber = 13;                            // (2) Allowed in a constructor.
}

// Method:
public static void main(String[] args) {

  var virus = "COVID-19";                          // (3a) Type of virus is String.
  var acronym = virus.substring(0, 5);             // (3b) Type of acronym is String.
  var num = Integer.parseInt(virus.substring(6));  // (3c) Type of num is int.

  var obj = new Object();                          // (4) Type of obj is Object.
  var title = (String) null; // (5) Initialization expression type is String.
                             //     Type of title is String.
  var sqrtOfNumber = Math.sqrt(100); // (6) Type of sqrtOfNumber is double,
                                     //     since the method returns
                                     //     a double value.

  var tvSize  = (short) 55;  // (7) Type of tvSize is short.
  var tvSize2 = 65;          // (8) Type of tvSize2 is int.

  var diameter = 10.0;       // (9) Type of diameter is double.
  var radius = 2.5F;         // (10) Type of radius is float.

  // Arrays:
  var vowels = new char[] {'a', 'e', 'i', 'o', 'u' }; // (11a) Type of vowels
                                                      //  is char[]. Size is 5.
  var zodiacSigns = new String[12]; // (11b) Type of zodiacSigns is String[].
                                    //       Size is 12.
  var a_2x3 = new int[2][3]; // (11c) Type of a_2x3 is int[][]. Size is 2x3.
  var a_2xn = new int[2][];  // (11d) Type of a_2xn is int[][]. Size is 2x?,
                             //       where second dimension can be undefined.

  // The for(:) loop:
  var word1 = "";            // (12) Type of word2 is String.
  for (var vowel : vowels) { // (13) Type of vowel is char in the for(:)loop.
    var letter = vowel;      // (14) Type of letter is char.
    word1 += letter;
  }

  // The for(;;) loop:
  var word2 = "";                        // (15) Type of word2 is String.
  for (var i = 0; i < vowels.length; i++) { // (16) Type of i is int in
                                         //      the for loop.
    var letter = vowels[i];              // (17) Type of letter is char.
    word2 += letter;
  }
```

```
        // switch-statement:
        switch(virus) {
          case "Covid-19":
            var flag = "Needs to be tested.";      // (18) Type is String.
            // Do testing.
            break;
          default: // Do nothing.
        }
      }
    }
```

// Class InvalidLVTI illustrates invalid use of the restricted type name var.
```
public class InvalidLVTI {

    var javaVendor = "Oracle"; // (19) Not allowed in instance variable declaration.

    static var javaVersion = 11; // (20) Not allowed in static variable declaration.

    public static void main(var args) { // (21) Not allowed for method parameters.

        var name;                // (22) Not allowed without initialization expression.

        var objRef = null;       // (23) Literal null not allowed.

        var x = 10.0, y = 20.0, z = 40;    // (24) Not allowed in compound declaration.

        var vowelsOnly = {'a', 'e', 'i', 'o', 'u' }; // (25) Array initializer not
                                             //       allowed.
        var attendance = new int[];        // (26) Non-empty dimension required.
        var array3Dim = new String[][2][]; // (27) Cannot specify an empty dimension
                                           //       before a non-empty dimension.
        var letters[] = new char[]{'a', 'e', 'i', 'o', 'u' }; // (28) var not allowed
                                                   //         as element type.

        var prompt = prompt + 1;           // (29) Self-reference not allowed in
                                           //       initialization expression.
    }

    public static var getPlatformName() { // (30) Not allowed as return type.
      return "JDK";
    }
}
```

The following examples of invalid uses of the restricted type name var are shown in the class InvalidLVTI in Example 3.17:

• *Not allowed in field variable declarations*

The var restricted type name is not allowed in field variable declarations, as shown at (19) and (20).

- *Not allowed in declaring formal parameters*

  Formal parameters in methods and constructors cannot be declared with var, as shown at (21) for the parameter args in the main() method.

- *Initialization expression is mandatory*

  The var restricted type name is not allowed in a local variable declaration if an initialization expression is not specified, as shown at (22).

- *Initialization expression cannot be the null literal value*

  Since the literal null can be assigned to any reference type, a specific type for objRef at (23) cannot be determined. At (5), the cast (String) specifies the type of the initialization expression.

- *Cannot use var in compound declarations*

  The reserved type name var cannot be used in a *compound declaration*—that is, a declaration that declares several variables, as shown at (24).

- *Cannot use var when an array initializer is specified*

  As shown at (25), an *array initializer* cannot be used in a var declaration. However, an *array initialization expression* is allowed, as at (11a).

- *Array creation expression must specify the size*

  As in the case when an explicit type is specified for an array variable, the array creation expressions in the declaration must also specify the array size when using var; otherwise, the compiler will issue an error, as at (26) and (27). Valid array creation expressions specifying correct size are shown at (11b), (11c), and (11d).

- *Cannot use var as an array element type*

  The square brackets ([]) on the left-hand side at (28) are not allowed, as they indicate that the local variable is an array. Array type and size are solely determined from the initialization expression, as at (11a), (11b), (11c), and (11d).

- *Cannot have a self-reference in an initialization expression*

  As in the case when an explicit type is specified for the local variable, the initialization expression cannot refer to the local variable being declared, as at (29), where the variable is not initialized before use.

- *Cannot use var as the return type of a method*

  The method declaration at (30) cannot specify the return type using var.

- *A type cannot be a named var*

  As var is a reserved type name, it is *not* a valid name for a reference type; that is, a class, an interface, or an enum cannot be named var. In other contexts, it can be used as an identifier, but this is not recommended.

```
public class var {}   // var is not permitted as a class name. Compile-time error!
```

The reserved type name var should be used judiciously as the code can become difficult to understand. When reading the local declaration below, the initialization expression does not divulge any information about the type, and the names are not too helpful:

```
var x = gizmo.get();
```

Unless it is intuitively obvious, a human reader will have to resort to the API documentation in order to infer the type. Using intuitive names becomes even more important when using the reserved type name var.

We will revisit the restricted type name var when discussing *exception handling with try-with-resources* (§7.7, p. 407), using *generics* in local variable declarations (§11.2, p. 571), and specifying *inferred-type lambda parameters* (§13.2, p. 680).

 ## Review Questions

3.7 How many of the following array declaration statements are legal?

```
int []aa[]  = new int [4][4];
int bb[][]  = new int [4][4];
int cc[][]  = new int [][4];
int []dd[]  = new int [4][];
int [][]ee  = new int [4][4];
```

Select the one correct answer.

(a) 0
(b) 1
(c) 2
(d) 3
(e) 4
(f) 5

3.8 Which of these array declaration statements are legal?
Select the three correct answers.

(a) `int[] i[] = { { 1, 2 }, { 1 }, {}, { 1, 2, 3 } };`
(b) `int i[] = new int[2] {1, 2};`
(c) `int i[][] = new int[][] { {1, 2, 3}, {4, 5, 6} };`
(d) `int[][] i = { { 1, 2 }, new int[2] };`
(e) `int i[4] = { 1, 2, 3, 4 };`

3.9 What would be the result of compiling and running the following program?

```
public class MyClass {
  public static void main(String[] args) {
    int size = 20;
    int[] arr = new int[ size ];
```

```
        for (int i = 0; i < size; ++i) {
          System.out.println(arr[i]);
        }
      }
    }
```

Select the one correct answer.

(a) The code will fail to compile because the array type int[] is incorrect.
(b) The program will compile, but it will throw an ArrayIndexOutOfBoundsException
    when run.
(c) The program will compile and run without error, but it will produce no
    output.
(d) The program will compile and run without error and will print the numbers 0
    through 19.
(e) The program will compile and run without error and will print 0 twenty
    times.
(f) The program will compile and run without error and will print null twenty
    times.

3.10   What would be the result of compiling and running the following program?

```
        public class DefaultValuesTest {
          int[] ia = new int[1];
          boolean b;
          int i;
          Object o;

          public static void main(String[] args) {
            DefaultValuesTest instance = new DefaultValuesTest();
            instance.print();
          }

          public void print() {
            System.out.println(ia[0] + " " + b + " " + i + " " + o);
          }
        }
```

Select the one correct answer.

(a) The program will fail to compile because of uninitialized variables.
(b) The program will throw a java.lang.NullPointerException when run.
(c) The program will print 0 false NaN null.
(d) The program will print 0 false 0 null.
(e) The program will print null 0 0 null.
(f) The program will print null false 0 null.

3.11   What will be the result of attempting to compile and run the following program?

```
        public class ParameterPass {
          public static void main(String[] args) {
            int i = 0;
            addTwo(i++);
            System.out.println(i);
          }
```

```
static void addTwo(int i) {
    i += 2;
  }
}
```

Select the one correct answer.

(a) 0
(b) 1
(c) 2
(d) 3

3.12 What will be the result of compiling and running the following program?

```
public class Passing {
  public static void main(String[] args) {
    int a = 0; int b = 0;
    int[] bArr = new int[1]; bArr[0] = b;

    inc1(a); inc2(bArr);

    System.out.println("a=" + a + " b=" + b + " bArr[0]=" + bArr[0]);
  }

  public static void inc1(int x) { x++; }

  public static void inc2(int[] x) { x[0]++; }
}
```

Select the one correct answer.

(a) The code will fail to compile, since x[0]++; is not a legal statement.
(b) The code will compile and will print a=1 b=1 bArr[0]=1 at runtime.
(c) The code will compile and will print a=0 b=1 bArr[0]=1 at runtime.
(d) The code will compile and will print a=0 b=0 bArr[0]=1 at runtime.
(e) The code will compile and will print a=0 b=0 bArr[0]=0 at runtime.

3.13 Given the following code:

```
public class RQ810A40 {
  static void print(Object... obj) {
    System.out.println("Object...: " + obj[0]);
  }
  public static void main(String[] args) {
    // (1) INSERT METHOD CALL HERE
  }
}
```

Which method call, when inserted at (1), will not result in the following output from the program?

```
Object...: 9
```

Select the one correct answer.

(a) print("9", "1", "1");
(b) print(9, 1, 1);
(c) print(new int[] {9, 1, 1});

(d) print(new Integer[] {9, 1, 1});
(e) print(new String[] {"9", "1", "1"});
(f) print(new Object[] {"9", "1", "1"});
(g) None of the above

3.14   Which statement is true about the following program?

```
public class Test {
  public static int add(int x, int y)  {
    var z = x + y;      // (1)
    return z;
  }
  public static void main(String[] args) {
    var a = 2, b = 3;  // (2)
    var z = add(a,b);  // (3)
  }
}
```

Select the one correct answer.

(a) Line (1) will fail to compile.
(b) Line (2) will fail to compile.
(c) Line (3) will fail to compile.
(d) The code will compile successfully.

3.15   Given the following code:

```
public class TestMe {
  /* (1) INSERT METHOD HEADER HERE */ {
    return (double)x / y;
  }
  public static void main(String[] args) {
    double x = divide(2, 3);
  }
}
```

Which method headers, when inserted individually at (1), will allow the code to compile?
Select the three correct answers.

(a) public static var divide(double x, double y)
(b) public static double divide(double x, var y)
(c) public static double divide(var x, double y)
(d) public static double divide(int x, int y)
(e) public static double divide(int x, double y)
(f) public static double divide(double x, int y)

Control Flow

4

Chapter Topics

- Choosing between alternative actions with the selection statements: the if statement, the if-else statement, the switch statement, and the switch expression

- Repeatedly executing code with the iteration statements: the for loop (for(;;)), the enhanced for loop (for(:)), the while loop, and the do-while loop

- Understanding control transfer with the yield, break, continue, and return statements, including labeled statements

Java SE 17 Developer Exam Objectives	
[2.1] Create program flow control constructs including if/else, switch statements and expressions, loops, and break and continue statements	§4.1, p. 152 to §4.13, p. 184
Java SE 11 Developer Exam Objectives	
[2.1] Create and use loops, if/else, and switch statements	§4.1, p. 152 to §4.8, p. 176

Control flow statements determine *the flow of control* in a program during execution, meaning the order in which statements are executed in a running program. There are three main categories of control flow statements:

- *Selection* statements: `if`, `if-else`, and `switch`
- *Iteration* statements: `while`, `do-while`, basic `for`, and enhanced `for` loops
- *Transfer* statements: `yield`, `break`, `continue`, and `return`

Each category of statements is discussed in subsequent sections.

4.1 Selection Statements

Java provides selection statements that allow the program to choose between alternative actions during execution. The choice is based on criteria specified in the selection statement. These selection statements are

- The simple `if` statement
- The `if-else` statement
- The `switch` statement and the `switch` expression

The Simple `if` Statement

The simple `if` statement has the following syntax:

```
if (condition)
    statement
```

It is used to decide whether an action is to be performed or not, based on a *condition*. The action to be performed is specified by *statement*, which can be a single statement or a code block. The *condition* must evaluate to a `boolean` or `Boolean` value. In the latter case, the `Boolean` value is unboxed to the corresponding `boolean` value.

The semantics of the simple `if` statement are straightforward. The *condition* is evaluated first. If its value is `true`, *statement* (called the `if` block) is executed and then execution continues with the rest of the program. If the value is `false`, the `if` block is skipped and execution continues with the rest of the program. The semantics are illustrated by the activity diagram in Figure 4.1a.

In the following examples of the `if` statement, it is assumed that the variables and the methods have been appropriately defined:

```
if (emergency)             // emergency is a boolean variable
    operate();

if (temperature > critical)
    soundAlarm();
```

```
if (isLeapYear() && endOfCentury())
    celebrate();

if (catIsAway()) {           // Block
    getFishingRod();
    goFishing();
}
```

Figure 4.1 *Activity Diagram for* if *Statements*

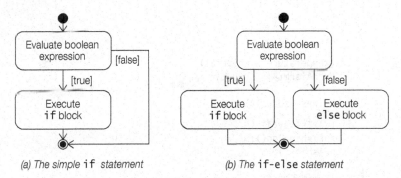

(a) *The simple* if *statement*   (b) *The* if-else *statement*

Note that *statement* can be a *block*, and the block notation is necessary if more than one statement is to be executed when the *condition* is true.

Since the *condition* evaluates to a boolean value, it avoids a common programming error: using an expression of the form (a=b) as the condition, where inadvertently an assignment operator is used instead of a relational operator. The compiler will flag this as an error, unless both a and b are boolean.

Note that the if block can be any valid statement. In particular, it can be the empty statement (;) or the empty block ({}). A common programming error is inadvertent use of the empty statement.

```
if (emergency); // Empty if block
    operate();     // Executed regardless of whether it was an emergency
```

The if-else **Statement**

The if-else statement is used to decide between two actions, based on a *condition*. It has the following syntax:

```
if (condition)
    statement₁
else
    statement₂
```

The *condition* is evaluated first. If its value is true (or unboxed to true), *statement₁* (the if block) is executed and then execution continues with the rest of the program. If the value is false (or unboxed to false), *statement₂* (the else block) is executed and then execution continues with the rest of the program. In other words, one of two mutually exclusive actions is performed. The else clause is optional; if omitted, the construct is equivalent to the simple if statement. The semantics are illustrated by the activity diagram in Figure 4.1b.

In the following examples of the if-else statement, it is assumed that all variables and methods have been appropriately defined:

```
if (emergency)
  operate();
else
  joinQueue();

if (temperature > critical)
  soundAlarm();
else
  businessAsUsual();

if (catIsAway()) {
  getFishingRod();
  goFishing();
} else
  playWithCat();
```

Since actions can be arbitrary statements, the if statements can be nested.

```
if (temperature >= upperLimit) {      // (1)
  if (danger)                         // (2) Simple if.
    soundAlarm();
  if (critical)                       // (3)
    evacuate();
  else                                // Goes with if at (3).
    turnHeaterOff();
} else                                // Goes with if at (1).
  turnHeaterOn();
```

The use of block notation, {}, can be critical to the execution of if statements. The if statements (A) and (B) in the following examples do *not* have the same meaning. The if statements (B) and (C) are the same, with extra indentation used in (C) to make the meaning evident. Leaving out the block notation in this case could have catastrophic consequences: The heater could be turned on when the temperature is above the upper limit.

```
// (A):
if (temperature > upperLimit) {       // (1) Block notation.
  if (danger) soundAlarm();           // (2)
} else                                // Goes with if at (1).
  turnHeaterOn();

// (B):
if (temperature > upperLimit)         // (1) Without block notation.
  if (danger) soundAlarm();           // (2)
else turnHeaterOn();                  // Goes with if at (2).

// (C):
if (temperature > upperLimit)         // (1)
```

```
    if (danger)                               // (2)
      soundAlarm();
    else                                      // Goes with if at (2).
      turnHeaterOn();
```

The rule for matching an else clause is that an else clause always refers to the nearest if that is not already associated with another else clause. Block notation and proper indentation can be used to make the meaning obvious.

Cascading of if-else statements comprises a sequence of nested if-else statements where the if block of the next if-else statement is joined to the else clause of the previous if-else statement. The decision to execute a block is then based on all the conditions evaluated so far.

```
    if (temperature >= upperLimit) {          // (1)
      soundAlarm();
      turnHeaterOff();
    } else if (temperature < lowerLimit) {    // (2)
      soundAlarm();
      turnHeaterOn();
    } else if (temperature == (upperLimit-lowerLimit)/2) {   // (3)
      doingFine();
    } else                                    // (4)
      noCauseToWorry();
```

The block corresponding to the first if condition that evaluates to true is executed, and the remaining if statements are skipped. In the preceding example, the block at (3) will execute only if the conditions at (1) and (2) are false and the condition at (3) is true. If none of the conditions is true, the block associated with the last else clause is executed. If there is no last else clause, no actions are performed.

4.2 The switch Statement

The switch construct implements a *multi-way branch* that allows program control to be transferred to a specific entry point in the code of the switch block based on a computed value. Java has two variants of the switch construct (the switch *statement* and the switch *expression*), and each of them can be written in two different ways (one using the *colon notation* and the other using the *arrow notation*). This section covers the two forms of the switch statement. Particular details of the switch expression are covered in the next section (p. 164).

The switch Statement with the Colon (:) Notation

We will first look at the switch *statement* defined using the *colon notation*, illustrated in Figure 4.2.

Conceptually, the switch statement can be used to choose one among many alternative actions, based on the value of an expression. The syntax of the switch statement

Figure 4.2 *Form of the* switch *Statement with the Colon Notation*

```
switch (selector_expression) {
  // Switch block with statement groups defined using colon notation:
  case CC:                            statements
  case CC₁: case CC₂: ... case CCₙ:  statements
  case CC₃, CC₄, ..., CCₘ:           statements
  ...
  default: ...
}
```

comprises a *selector expression* followed by a switch *block*. The selector expression must evaluate to a value whose type must be one of the following:

- A primitive data type: char, byte, short, or int
- A wrapper type: Character, Byte, Short, or Integer
- An enum type (§5.13, p. 287)
- The type String (§8.4, p. 439)

Note that the type of the selector expression cannot be boolean, long, or floating-point. The statements in the switch block can have case *labels*, where each case label specifies one or more case *constants* (CC), thereby defining entry points in the switch block where control can be transferred depending on the value of the selector expression. The switch block must be compatible with the type of the selector expression, otherwise a compile-time error occurs.

The execution of the switch statement proceeds as follows:

- The selector expression is evaluated first. If the value is a wrapper type, an unboxing conversion is performed (§2.3, p. 45). If the selector expression evaluates to null, a NullPointerException is thrown.
- The value of the selector expression is compared with the constants in the case labels. Control is transferred to the start of the *statements* associated with the case label that has a case constant whose value is equal to the value of the selector expression. Note that a colon (:) prefixes the associated statements that can be any *group of statements*, including a statement block. After execution of the associated statements, control *falls through* to the *next* group of statements, unless this was the last group of statements declared or control was transferred out of the switch statement.
- If no case label has a case constant that is equal to the value of the selector expression, the statements associated with the default label are executed. After execution of the associated statements, control *falls through* to the *next* group of statements, unless this was the last group of statements declared or control was transferred out of the switch statement.

Figure 4.3 illustrates the flow of control through a switch statement where the default label is declared last and control is not transferred out of the switch statement in the preceding group of statements.

Figure 4.3   *Activity Diagram for the* switch *Statement with the Colon Notation*

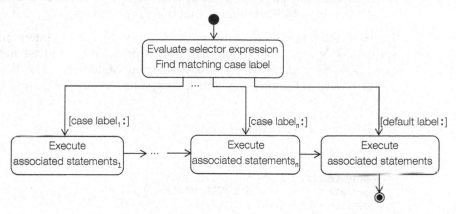

All case labels (including the default label) are optional and can be defined in any order in the switch block. All case labels and the default label are separated from their associated group of statements by a colon (:). A list of case labels can be associated with the same statements, and a case label can specify a comma-separated list of case constants. At most, one default label can be present in a switch statement. If no valid case labels are found and the default label is omitted, the whole switch statement is skipped.

The case *constants* (CC) in the case labels are constant expressions whose values must be unique, meaning no duplicate values are allowed. In fact, a case constant must be a compile-time constant expression whose value is *assignable* to the type of the selector expression (§2.4, p. 46). In particular, all case constant values must be in the range of the type of the selector expression. The type of a case constant cannot be boolean, long, or floating-point.

The compiler is able to generate efficient code for a switch statement, as this statement only tests for *equality* between the selector expression and the constant expressions of the case labels, so as to determine which code to execute at runtime. In contrast, a sequence of if statements determines the flow of control at runtime, based on arbitrary conditions which might be determinable only at runtime.

In Example 4.1, depending on the value of the howMuchAdvice parameter, different advice is printed in the switch statement at (1) in the method dispenseAdvice(). The example shows the output when the value of the howMuchAdvice parameter is LOTS_OF_ADVICE. In the switch statement, the associated statement at (2) is executed, giving one piece of advice. Control then falls through to the statement at (3), giving the second piece of advice. Control next falls through to (4), dispensing the third piece of advice, and finally execution of the break statement at (5) causes control to exit the switch statement. Without the break statement at (5), control would continue to fall through the remaining statements—in this case, to the statement at (6) being executed. Execution of the break statement in a switch block transfers control out of the switch statement (p. 180). If the parameter howMuchAdvice has the value MORE_ADVICE, then the advice at both (3) and (4) is given. The value LITTLE_ADVICE results in only one piece of advice at (4) being given. Any other value results in the default action, which announces that there is no advice.

The associated statement of a case label can be a *group* of statements (which need *not* be a statement block). The case label is prefixed to the first statement in each case. This is illustrated by the associated statements for the case constant LITTLE_ADVICE in Example 4.1, which comprises statements (4) and (5).

Example 4.1   *Fall-Through in a* switch *Statement with the Colon Notation*

```
public class Advice {

  private static final int LITTLE_ADVICE = 0;
  private static final int MORE_ADVICE = 1;
  private static final int LOTS_OF_ADVICE = 2;

  public static void main(String[] args) {
    dispenseAdvice(LOTS_OF_ADVICE);
  }

  public static void dispenseAdvice(int howMuchAdvice) {
    switch (howMuchAdvice) {                                   // (1)
      case LOTS_OF_ADVICE: System.out.println("See no evil.");   // (2)
      case MORE_ADVICE:    System.out.println("Speak no evil."); // (3)
      case LITTLE_ADVICE:  System.out.println("Hear no evil.");  // (4)
                           break;                              // (5)
      default:             System.out.println("No advice.");   // (6)
    }
  }
}
```

Output from the program:

```
See no evil.
Speak no evil.
Hear no evil.
```

Several case labels can prefix the same group of statements. This is the equivalent of specifying the same case constants in a single case label. The latter syntax is preferable as it is more concise than the former. Such case constants will result in the associated group of statements being executed. This behavior is illustrated in Example 4.2 for the switch statement at (1).

At (2) in Example 4.2, three case labels are defined that are associated with the same action. At (3), (4), and (5), a list of case constants is defined for some of the case labels. Note also the use of the break statement to stop fall-through in the switch block after the statements associated with a case label are executed.

The first statement in the switch block must always have a case or default label; otherwise, it will be unreachable. This statement will never be executed because control can never be transferred to it. The compiler will flag this case (no pun intended) as an error. An empty switch block is perfectly legal, but not of much use.

Since each group of statements associated with a case label can be any arbitrary statement, it can also be another switch statement. In other words, switch statements can be nested. Since a switch statement defines its own local block, the case labels in an inner block do not conflict with any case labels in an outer block. Labels can be redefined in nested blocks; in contrast, variables cannot be redeclared in nested blocks (§6.6, p. 354). In Example 4.2, an inner switch statement is defined at (6), which allows further refinement of the action to take on the value of the selector expression in cases where multiple case labels are used in the outer switch statement. A break statement terminates the innermost switch statement in which it is executed.

The print statement at (7) is always executed for the case constants 9, 10, and 11.

Note that the break statement is the last statement in the group of statements associated with each case label. It is easy to think that the break statement is a part of the switch statement syntax, but technically it is not.

Example 4.2   *Nested* switch *Statements with the Colon Notation*

```java
public class Seasons {
  public static void main(String[] args) {
    int monthNumber = 11;
    switch(monthNumber) {                                   // (1) Outer
      case 12: case 1: case 2:                              // (2)
        System.out.println("Snow in the winter.");
        break;
      case 3, 4: case 5:                                    // (3)
        System.out.println("Green grass in the spring.");
        break;
      case 6, 7, 8:                                         // (4)
        System.out.println("Sunshine in the summer.");
        break;
      case 9, 10, 11:                                       // (5)
        switch(monthNumber) { // Nested switch                 (6) Inner
          case 10:
            System.out.println("Halloween.");
            break;
          case 11:
            System.out.println("Thanksgiving.");
            break;
        } // End nested switch
        // Always printed for case constant 9, 10, 11
        System.out.println("Yellow leaves in the fall.");  // (7)
        break;
      default:
        System.out.println(monthNumber + " is not a valid month.");
    }
  }
}
```

Output from the program:

```
Thanksgiving.
Yellow leaves in the fall.
```

The switch Statement with the Arrow (->) Notation

The form of the switch statement with the arrow notation is shown in Figure 4.4. This form defines *switch rules* in which each case label is associated with a corresponding action using the arrow (->) notation.

Figure 4.4 *Form of the switch Statement with the Arrow Notation*

```
switch (selector_expression) {
    // Switch block with switch rules defined using arrow notation:
    case CC                    -> expression_statement;
    case CC₁, CC₂, ..., CCₘ  -> block
    case CC₄                   -> throw_statement
    ...
    default                    -> ...
}
```

Compared to the switch statement with the colon notation (Figure 4.2), there are a few things to note.

First, although the case labels (and the default label) are specified similarly, the arrow notation does not allow multiple case labels to be associated with a common action. However, the same result can be achieved by specifying a single case label with a list of case constants, thereby associating the case constants with a common action.

Second, the action that can be associated with the case labels in switch rules is restricted. The switch statement with the colon notation allows a group of statements, but the switch statement with the arrow notation only allows the following actions to be associated with case labels:

- *An expression statement (§3.3, p. 101)*

  By far, the canonical action of a case label in a switch rule is an expression statement. Such an expression statement is always terminated by a semicolon (;). Typically, the value returned by the expression statement is discarded. In the examples below, what is important is the side effect of evaluating the expression statements.

  ```
  ...
  case PASSED -> ++numbersPassed;
  case FAILED -> ++numbersFailed;
  ...
  ```

- *A block (§6.6, p. 354)*

  A block of statements can be used if program logic should be refined.

  ```
  ...
  case ALARM ->  { soundTheAlarm();
                   callTheFireDepartment(); }
  ...
  ```

- *Throw an exception (§7.4, p. 386)*

  The switch rule below throws an exception when the value of the selector expression does not match any case constants:

  ```
  ...
  default -> throw new IllegalArgumentException("Not a valid value");
  ...
  ```

Third, the execution of the switch rules is *mutually exclusive* (Figure 4.5). Once the action in the switch rule has completed execution, the execution of the switch statement terminates. This is illustrated in Figure 4.5 where only one expression statement is executed, after which the switch statement also terminates. There is no fall-through and the break statement is not necessary.

Figure 4.5   *Activity Diagram for the* switch *Statement with the Arrow Notation*

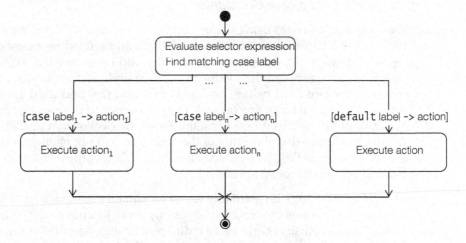

Example 4.3 is a refactoring of Example 4.2 with a switch statement with the arrow notation. At (2), (3), (4), and (8), the action executed is an expression statement, whereas at (5), the action executed is a block. Using switch rules results in compact and elegant code that also improves the readability of the switch statement.

Example 4.3   *Nested* switch *Statements with the Arrow Notation*

```
public class SeasonsII {
  public static void main(String[] args) {
    int monthNumber = 11;
```

```
    switch(monthNumber) {                                               // (1) Outer
       case 12, 1,  2 -> System.out.println("Snow in the winter.");     // (2)
       case 3,  4,  5 -> System.out.println("Green grass in the spring.");  // (3)
       case 6,  7,  8 -> System.out.println("Sunshine in the summer.");    // (4)
       case 9, 10, 11 -> {                                              // (5)
         switch(monthNumber) { // Nested switch                            (6) Inner
           case 10 -> System.out.println("Halloween.");
           case 11 -> System.out.println("Thanksgiving.");
         }
         // Always printed for case constants 9, 10, 11:
         System.out.println("Yellow leaves in the fall.");             // (7)
       }
       default -> throw new IllegalArgumentException(monthNumber +
                                       " is not a valid month.");// (8)
    }
  }
}
```

Output from the program:

```
Thanksgiving.
Yellow leaves in the fall.
```

Using Strings as case Constants

Example 4.4 illustrates using strings in a switch statement. The thing to note is what constitutes a constant string expression that can be used as a case constant. The case constants at (3), (4), (5), and (6) are all valid *constant string expressions*, as the compiler can figure out their value at compile time. String literals, used at (3) and (6), and constant field values, declared at (1) and (2a) and used at (4) and (5), are all valid case constants. In contrast, the HOT reference from declarations (2b) and (2c) cannot be used as a case constant. From the declaration at (2a), the compiler cannot guarantee that the value of the reference will not change at runtime. From the declaration at (2c), it cannot deduce the value at compile time, as the constructor must be run to construct the value.

Switching on strings is essentially based on equality comparison of integer values that are hash values of strings, followed by an object equality test to rule out the possibility of collision between two different strings having the same hash value. Switching on strings should be used judiciously, as it is less efficient than switching on integers. Switching on strings is not advisable if the values being switched on are not already strings.

Example 4.4 *Strings in a* switch *Statement*

```
public class SwitchingOnAString {
  public static final String MEDIUM = "Medium";      // (1)
  public static final String HOT = "Hot";            // (2a)
//public static        String HOT = "Hot";           // (2b) Not OK as case label
//public static final String HOT = new String("Hot"); // (2c) Not OK as case label
```

```
      public static void main(String[] args) {
        String spiceLevel = "Medium_Hot";
        switch (spiceLevel) {
          case "Mild",                                                      // (3)
               MEDIUM + "_" + HOT -> System.out.println("Enjoy your meal!"); // (4)
          case HOT                -> System.out.println("Have fun!");        // (5)
          case "Suicide"          -> System.out.println("Good luck!");       // (6)
          default                 -> System.out.println("You being funny?");
        }
      }
    }
```

Output from the program:

```
Enjoy your meal!
```

Using Enum Constants as case Constants

Example 4.5 illustrates the use of enum types (§5.13, p. 287) in a switch statement with the arrow notation. The enum type SpiceGrade is defined at (1). The type of the selector expression at (2) is the enum type SpiceGrade. Note that the enum constants are *not* specified with their fully qualified name (see (3a)). Using the fully qualified name results in a compile-time error, as shown at (3b). Only enum constants that have the same enum type as the selector expression can be specified as case label values.

The semantics of the switch statement are the same as described earlier. Switching on enum values is essentially based on equality comparison of unique integer values that are ordinal values assigned by the compiler to the constants of an enum type.

When the switch rules cover *all* values of the selector expression type, the switch statement is said to be *exhaustive*. Non-exhaustive switch statements are a common cause of programming errors. It is up to the programmer to ensure that the switch statement is exhaustive, as the compiler does not provide any help in this regard for the switch statement. Judicious use of the default label should be considered, as illustrated in the examples provided in this section that use the switch statement.

Example 4.5   *Enums in a switch Statement*

```
      enum SpiceGrade { MILD, MEDIUM, MEDIUM_HOT, HOT, SUICIDE; }   // (1)

      public class SwitchingFun {
        public static void main(String[] args) {
          SpiceGrade spicing = SpiceGrade.HOT;
          switch (spicing) {                                // (2)
            case HOT ->  System.out.println("Have fun!");   // (3a) OK!
      //    case SpiceGrade.HOT                             // (3b) Compile-time error!
      //         -> System.out.println("Have fun!");
            case SUICIDE -> System.out.println("Good luck!");
```

```
        default -> System.out.println("Enjoy your meal!");
      }
    }
  }
```

Output from the program:

```
Have fun!
```

- -

4.3 The switch Expression

A switch expression evaluates to a value, as opposed to a switch statement that does not. Conceptually we can think of a switch expression as an augmented switch statement that returns a value. We look at both forms of the switch expression, defined using the colon notation and the arrow notation, how it yields a value, and compare it to the switch statement. The switch expression is analogous to the switch statement, except for the provision to return a value.

The yield Statement

The yield statement in a switch expression is analogous to the break statement in a switch statement. It can only be used in a switch expression, where the identifier yield is a *contextual keyword* only having a special meaning in the context of a switch expression.

    yield *expression*;

Execution of the yield statement results in the expression being evaluated, and its value being returned as the value of the switch expression.

The switch Expression with the Colon (:) Notation

The switch expression with the colon notation has the same form as the switch statement with the colon notation (Figure 4.2), except that the execution of the switch body results in a value (or it throws an exception).

Example 4.6 is a reworking of Example 4.2 with seasons, where the group of statements associated with a case label print information about the season and return a constant of the enum type Season that is defined at (1). Note that the yield statement is the last statement in the group of statements associated with each case label. Execution of the yield statement results in its expression being evaluated, and its value being returned as the value of the switch expression, thereby also terminating the execution of the switch expression. Not surprisingly, a break or a return statement is not allowed in a switch expression. Note that the switch expression is on the right-hand side of the assignment statement defined at (2) and is terminated by a semicolon (;).

The *fall-through* of execution in the switch expression with the colon notation is analogous to that of the switch statement with the colon notation (Figure 4.3). If a group of statements associated with a case label does not end in a yield statement, execution continues with the next group of statements, if any.

The switch expression with the colon notation must be *exhaustive*, meaning the case labels, and if necessary the default label, must cover *all* values of the selector expression type. Non-exhaustive switch expressions will result in a compile-time error. The default label is typically used to make the switch expression exhaustive. In Example 4.6, the type of the selector expression is int, but the case labels only cover the int values from 1 to 12. A default label is necessary to cover the other int values or to throw an exception, as in this case, and make the switch expression exhaustive.

Example 4.6   *A* yield *Statement in a* switch *Expression with the Colon Notation*

```
public class SeasonsIII {

  enum Season { WINTER, SPRING, SUMMER, FALL }              // (1)

  public static void main(String[] args) {
    int monthNumber = 11;
    Season season = switch(monthNumber) {                   // (2)
      case 12: case 1: case 2:                              // (3)
        System.out.println("Snow in the winter.");
        yield Season.WINTER;                                // (4)
      case 3, 4: case 5:                                    // (5)
        System.out.println("Green grass in the spring.");
        yield Season.SPRING;                                // (6)
      case 6, 7, 8:                                         // (7)
        System.out.println("Sunshine in the summer.");
        yield Season.SUMMER;                                // (8)
      case 9, 10, 11:                                       // (9)
        System.out.println("Yellow leaves in the fall.");
        yield Season.FALL;                                  // (10)
      default:                                              // (11)
        throw new IllegalArgumentException(monthNumber + " not a valid month.");
    };                                                      // (12)
    System.out.println(season);
  }
}
```

Output from the program:

```
Yellow leaves in the fall.
FALL
```

The `switch` Expression with the Arrow (->) Notation

The `switch` expression with the arrow notation also has the same form as the `switch` statement with the arrow notation (Figure 4.4), except that the execution of the `switch` body must result in a value (or it must throw an exception).

The execution of the switch rules in a `switch` expression is *mutually exclusive*, analogous to the switch rules in a `switch` statement (Figure 4.5). Once the action in the switch rule has completed execution, the value computed by the action is returned and the execution of the `switch` expression terminates. There is no fall-through and no break statement is allowed.

Whereas the actions in the switch rules of a `switch` statement only allowed an *expression statement* (Figure 4.5), the actions in the switch rules of a `switch` expression allow *any expression*, in addition to allowing a block or throwing an exception, as in the switch rules of a `switch` statement.

- *Any expression (Chapter 2, p. 29)*

  By far, the canonical action of a case label in a switch rule of a `switch` expression is an arbitrary expression. Such an expression is always terminated by a semicolon (`;`). The expression value is returned as the value of the `switch` expression whose execution is then terminated. Note that no `yield` statement is necessary or allowed.

  ```
  ...
  case 1 -> "ONE";
  case 2 -> yield "two";        // Compile-time error!
  ...
  ```

- *A block (§6.6, p. 354)*

  A *block* of statements can be used if program logic should be refined, but the last statement in the block should be a `yield` statement to return its value and terminate the execution of the `switch` expression (alternatively, the last statement can be a `throw` statement). In a `switch` expression with the arrow notation, the `yield` statement is only allowed as the last statement in a block that constitutes the action in a switch rule.

  ```
  ...
  case ALARM      -> { soundTheAlarm();
                       callTheFireDepartment();
                       yield Status.EVACUATE; }  // OK

  case ALL_CLEAR -> { yield Status.NORMAL; // Compile-time error: not last statement
                      standDown(); }       //                      in the block.
  ...
  ```

- *Throw an exception (§7.4, p. 386)*

  As the switch rules must be *exhaustive*, one way to achieve exhaustiveness is to throw an exception as the action in the `default` label.

  ```
  ...
  default -> throw new IllegalArgumentException("Not a valid value");
  ...
  ```

Example 4.6 has been refactored to use the switch expression with the arrow notation in Example 4.7. Each action associated with a case label of a switch rule is a block of statements, where a yield statement is the last statement in a block. If this is not the case, the code will not compile.

The switch expression with the arrow notation must also be *exhaustive*. Again a non-exhaustive switch expression with the arrow notation will result in a compile-time error. In Example 4.7, the type of the selector expression is int, but the switch rules only cover the int values from 1 to 12. A default label is necessary to make the switch expression exhaustive, as shown at (11).

Example 4.7 *Statement Blocks in a switch Expression with the Arrow Notation*

```
public class SeasonsIV {
  enum Season { WINTER, SPRING, SUMMER, FALL }            // (1)

  public static void main(String[] args) {
    int monthNumber = 11;
    Season season = switch(monthNumber) {                 // (2)
      case 12, 1, 2 -> {                                  // (3)
        System.out.println("Snow in the winter.");
        yield Season.WINTER;                              // (4)
      }
      case 3, 4, 5 -> {                                   // (5)
        System.out.println("Green grass in the spring.");
        yield Season.SPRING;                              // (6)
      }
      case 6, 7, 8 -> {                                   // (7)
        System.out.println("Sunshine in the summer.");
        yield Season.SUMMER;                              // (8)
      }
      case 9, 10, 11 -> {                                 // (9)
        System.out.println("Yellow leaves in the fall.");
        yield Season.FALL;                                // (10)
      }
      default ->                                          // (11)
        throw new IllegalArgumentException(monthNumber + " not a valid month.");
    };                                                    // (12)
    System.out.println(season);
  }
}
```

Output from the program:

```
Yellow leaves in the fall.
FALL
```

Example 4.8 is a reworking of Example 4.7 that defines *expressions* as the actions in the switch rules. No yield statement is necessary or allowed in this case. The switch expression is also exhaustive.

Example 4.8   *Expression Actions in a* switch *Expression with the Arrow Notation*

```
public class SeasonsV {
  enum Season { WINTER, SPRING, SUMMER, FALL }                    // (1)

  public static void main(String[] args) {
    int monthNumber = 11;
    Season season = switch(monthNumber) {                         // (2)
    case 12,  1,  2 -> Season.WINTER;                             // (3)
    case  3,  4,  5 -> Season.SPRING;                             // (4)
    case  6,  7,  8 -> Season.SUMMER;                             // (5)
    case  9, 10, 11 -> Season.FALL;                              // (6)
    default         -> throw new IllegalArgumentException(monthNumber +
                                                 " not a valid month.");
    };
    System.out.println(season);
  }
}
```

Output from the program:

```
FALL
```

The switch expression can only evaluate to a single value. Multiple values can be returned by constructing an object with the required values and returning the object as a result of evaluating the switch expression. Record classes are particularly suited for this purpose (§5.14, p. 299). The switch expression at (3) in Example 4.9 returns an object of the record class SeasonInfo, defined at (2), to return the month number and the season in which it occurs.

Example 4.9   *Returning Multiple Values as a Record from a* switch *Expression*

```
public class SeasonsVI {

  enum Season { WINTER, SPRING, SUMMER, FALL }                    // (1)
  record SeasonInfo(int month, Season season) {}                 // (2)

  public static void main(String[] args) {
    int monthNumber = 11;
    SeasonInfo seasonInfo = switch(monthNumber) {                 // (3)
    case 12,  1,  2 -> new SeasonInfo(monthNumber, Season.WINTER);  // (4)
    case  3,  4,  5 -> new SeasonInfo(monthNumber, Season.SPRING);  // (5)
    case  6,  7,  8 -> new SeasonInfo(monthNumber, Season.SUMMER);  // (6)
    case  9, 10, 11 -> new SeasonInfo(monthNumber, Season.FALL);    // (7)
    default         -> throw new IllegalArgumentException(monthNumber +
                                                 " not a valid month.");
    };
    System.out.println(seasonInfo);
  }
}
```

Output from the program:

```
SeasonInfo[month=11, season=FALL]
```

Local Variable Scope in the switch Body

The *scope* of a local variable declared in a switch statement or a switch expression is the *entire* switch block. Any local block in the switch body introduces a new *local scope*. Any local variable declared in it has *block scope*, and therefore, is only accessible in that block. A local variable declared in an enclosing local scope cannot be redeclared in a nested local scope (§6.6, p. 354).

Summary of the switch Statement and the switch Expression

Table 4.1 summarizes the features of the switch statement and the switch expression, and provides a comparison of the two constructs.

Table 4.1   *Comparing the* switch *Statement and the* switch *Expression*

Notation	The switch statement	The switch expression
The colon (:) notation: case *label*: *statements*	• Executes statements associated with the matching case label. • Fall-through can occur. • No compile-time check for exhaustiveness. • Only break and return statements allowed to control fall-through.	• Executes statements associated with the matching case label, but must have a yield statement to return a value. • Fall-through can occur. • Compile-time check for exhaustiveness. • No break or return statement allowed.
The arrow (->) notation: case *label* -> *action*	• Action associated with a switch rule can be *an expression statement*, can be a *block*, or can *throw an exception*. • Mutually exclusive switch rules: no fall-through can occur. • No compile-time check for exhaustiveness. • break and return statements allowed.	• Action associated with a switch rule can be *any expression*, can be a *block*, or can *throw an exception*. • Mutually exclusive switch rules: no fall-through can occur. • Compile-time check for exhaustiveness. • No break or return statement allowed. • Must return a value that is either the value of a stand-alone *expression* or the value of the expression in a yield statement that can occur as the last statement in a *block*.

Review Questions

4.1   What will be the result of attempting to compile and run the following class?

```
public class IfTest {
  public static void main(String[] args) {
    if (true)
    if (false)
    System.out.println("a");
    else
    System.out.println("b");
  }
}
```

Select the one correct answer.

(a) The code will fail to compile because the syntax of the `if` statement is incorrect.

(b) The code will fail to compile because the compiler will not be able to determine which `if` statement the `else` clause belongs to.

(c) The code will compile correctly and will display the letter a at runtime.

(d) The code will compile correctly and will display the letter b at runtime.

(e) The code will compile correctly but will not display any output.

4.2   What will be the result of attempting to compile and run the following program?

```
public class Switching {
  public static void main(String[] args) {
    final int iLoc = 3;
    switch (6) {
      case 1:
      case iLoc:
      case 2 * iLoc:
        System.out.println("I am not OK.");
      default:
        System.out.println("You are OK.");
      case 4:
        System.out.println("It's OK.");
    }
  }
}
```

Select the one correct answer.

(a) The code will fail to compile because of the case label value 2 * iLoc.

(b) The code will fail to compile because the `default` label is not specified last in the `switch` statement.

(c) The code will compile correctly and will print the following at runtime:
```
I am not OK.
You are OK.
It's OK.
```

    (d) The code will compile correctly and will print the following at runtime:
```
You are OK.
It's OK.
```

    (e) The code will compile correctly and will print the following at runtime:
```
It's OK.
```

4.3   Which code option will print the string "Prime"?
Select the one correct answer.

    (a)
```
char value = 3;
String result = "Unknown";
switch (value) {
    case 2,3,5,7:   result = "Prime";
    case 1,4,6,8,9: result = "Composite";
}
System.out.println(result);
```

    (b)
```
char value = 3;
String result =
switch (value) {
    case 2,3,5,7:   yield "Prime";
    case 1,4,6,8,9: yield "Composite";
};
System.out.println(result);
```

    (c)
```
char value = 3;
String yield =
switch (value) {
    case 2,3,5,7:   yield "Prime";
    case 1,4,6,8,9: yield "Composite";
    default:        yield "Unknown";
};
System.out.println(yield);
```

    (d)
```
char value = 3;
String result =
switch (value) {
    case 2,3,5,7  -> "Prime";
    case 1,4,6,8,9 -> "Composite";
    default: { yield "Unknown"; }
};
System.out.println(result);
```

4.4   Given the following code:

```
public class RQ462 {
  public static void main(String[] args) {
    int price = 1;
    int discount = switch (price) {
      case 5, 1, 2 -> price - 1;
      case 4, 3, 6 -> price - 2;
      default      -> 0;
    };
```

```
        System.out.println(discount);
    }
}
```

What is the result?
Select the one correct answer.

(a) 0
(b) 1
(c) -1
(d) -2
(e) The program will throw an exception at runtime.
(f) The program will fail to compile.

4.4 Iteration Statements

Loops allow a single statement or a statement block to be executed repeatedly (i.e., iterated). A boolean condition (called the *loop condition*) is commonly used to determine when to terminate the loop. The statements executed in the loop constitute the *loop body*.

Java provides four language constructs for loop construction:

- The while statement
- The do-while statement
- The *basic* for statement
- The *enhanced* for statement

These loops differ in the order in which they execute the loop body and test the loop condition. The while loop and the basic for loop test the loop condition *before* executing the loop body, whereas the do-while loop tests the loop condition *after* execution of the loop body.

The *enhanced* for loop (also called the *for-each* loop) simplifies iterating over arrays and collections. We will use the notations for(;;) and for(:) to designate the basic for loop and the enhanced for loop, respectively.

4.5 The while Statement

The syntax of the while loop is

```
while (loop_condition)
    loop_body
```

The *loop condition* is evaluated before executing the *loop body*. The while statement executes the *loop body* as long as the *loop condition* is true. When the *loop condition* becomes false, the loop is terminated and execution continues with any statement immediately following the loop. If the *loop condition* is false to begin with, the *loop body* is not executed at all. In other words, a while loop can execute zero or more times. The *loop condition* must evaluate to a boolean or a Boolean value. In the latter case, the reference value is unboxed to a boolean value. The flow of control in a while statement is shown in Figure 4.6.

Figure 4.6   *Activity Diagram for the while Statement*

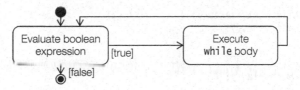

The while statement is normally used when the number of iterations is not known.

```
while (noSignOfLife())
    keepLooking();
```

Since the *loop body* can be any valid statement, inadvertently terminating each line with the empty statement (;) can give unintended results. Always using a block statement as the *loop body* helps to avoid such problems.

```
while (noSignOfLife());      // Empty statement as loop body!
    keepLooking();           // Statement not in the loop body.
```

4.6   The do-while **Statement**

The syntax of the do-while loop is

```
do
    loop_body
while (loop_condition);
```

In a do-while statement, the *loop condition* is evaluated *after* executing the *loop body*. The *loop condition* must evaluate to a boolean or Boolean value. The value of the *loop condition* is subjected to unboxing if it is of the type Boolean. The do-while statement executes the *loop body* until the *loop condition* becomes false. When the *loop condition* becomes false, the loop is terminated and execution continues with any statement immediately following the loop. Note that the *loop body* is executed at least once. Figure 4.7 illustrates the flow of control in a do-while statement.

The *loop body* in a do-while loop is invariably a statement block. It is instructive to compare the while and do-while loops. In the examples that follow, the mice might never get to play if the cat is not away, as in the loop at (1). The mice do get to play at least once (at the peril of losing their life) in the loop at (2).

Figure 4.7 *Activity Diagram for the* do-while *Statement*

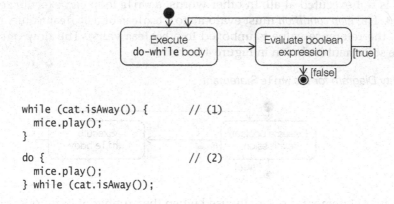

```
while (cat.isAway()) {          // (1)
  mice.play();
}

do {                            // (2)
  mice.play();
} while (cat.isAway());
```

4.7 The for(;;) Statement

The for(;;) loop is the most general of all the loops. It is mostly used for *counter-controlled loops*, in which the number of iterations is known beforehand.

The syntax of the loop is as follows:

for (*initialization*; *loop_condition*; *update_expression*)
 loop_body

The *initialization* usually declares and initializes a *loop variable* that controls the execution of the *loop body*. The loop body can be a single statement or a statement block. The *loop condition* must evaluate to a boolean or Boolean value. In the latter case, the reference value is converted to a boolean value by unboxing. The *loop condition* usually involves the loop variable, and if the loop condition is true, the *loop body* is executed; otherwise, execution continues with any statement following the for(;;) loop. After each iteration (i.e., execution of the loop body), the *update expression* is executed. This usually modifies the value of the loop variable to ensure eventual loop termination. The *loop condition* is then tested to determine whether the loop body should be executed again. Note that the *initialization* is executed only once, on entry into the loop. The semantics of the for(;;) loop are illustrated in Figure 4.8, and are summarized by the following equivalent while loop code template:

initialization
while (*loop_condition*) {
 loop_body
 update_expression
}

Figure 4.8 *Activity Diagram for the* for *Statement*

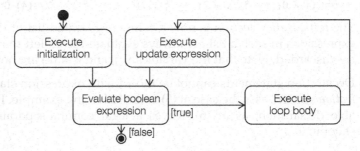

The following code creates an int array and sums the values in the array:

```
int sum = 0;
int[] array = {12, 23, 5, 7, 19};
for (int index = 0; index < array.length; index++)   // (1)
    sum += array[index];
```

The loop variable index is declared and initialized in the *initialization* section of the loop. It is incremented in the *update expression* section. This loop is an example of a *forward* for(;;) loop, where the loop variable is incremented.

The next code snippet is an example of a *backward* for(;;) loop, where the loop variable is decremented to sum the values in the array:

```
int sum = 0;
int[] array = {12, 23, 5, 7, 19};
for (int index = array.length - 1; index >= 0; index--)
    sum += array[index];
```

It is instructive to compare the specification of the loop header in the forward and backward for(;;) loops in these examples.

The loop at (1) earlier showed how a declaration statement can be specified in the *initialization* section. Such a declaration statement can also specify a comma-separated list of variables:

```
for (int i = 0, j = 1, k = 2; ... ; ...) ...;      // (2)
```

The variables i, j, and k in the declaration statement all have type int. All variables declared in the *initialization* section are local variables in the for(;;) statement and obey the scope rules for local blocks, as do any variables declared in the *loop body*. The following code will not compile, however, as variable declarations of different types (in this case, int and String) require declaration statements that are terminated by semicolons:

```
for (int i = 0, String str = "@"; ... ; ...) ...;  // (3) Compile-time error
```

The *initialization* section can also be a comma-separated list of *expression* statements (§3.3, p. 101). Any value returned by an expression statement is discarded. For example, the loop at (2) can be rewritten by factoring out the variable declarations:

```
int i, j, k;                                // Variable declaration
for (i = 0, j = 1, k = 2; ... ; ...) ...;   // (4) Only initialization
```

The *initialization* section is now a comma-separated list of three expressions. The expressions in such a list are always evaluated from left to right, and their values are discarded. Note that the variables i, j, and k at (4) are not local to the loop.

Declaration statements cannot be mixed with expression statements in the *initialization* section, as is the case at (5) in the following example. Factoring out the variable declaration, as at (6), leaves a legal comma-separated list of expression statements.

```
// (5) Not legal and ugly:
for (int i = 0, System.out.println("This won't do!"); flag; i++) { // Error!
  // loop body
}

// (6) Legal, but still ugly:
int i;                                      // Declaration factored out.
for (i = 0, System.out.println("This is legal!"); flag; i++) {    // OK.
  // loop body
}
```

The *update expression* can also be a comma-separated list of expression statements. The following code specifies a for(;;) loop that has a comma-separated list of three variables in the *initialization* section, and a comma-separated list of two expressions in the *update expression* section:

```
// Legal usage but not recommended, as it can affect code comprehension.
int[][] sqMatrix = { {3, 4, 6}, {5, 7, 4}, {5, 8, 9} };
for (int i = 0, j = sqMatrix[0].length - 1, asymDiagonal = 0;  // initialization
     i < sqMatrix.length;                                      // loop condition
     i++, j--)                                                 // update expression
  asymDiagonal += sqMatrix[i][j];                              // loop body
```

All sections in the for(;;) header are optional. Any or all of them can be left empty, but the two semicolons are mandatory. In particular, leaving out the *loop condition* signifies that the loop condition is true. The "crab", (;;), can be used to construct an infinite loop, where termination is presumably achieved through code in the loop body (see the next section on transfer statements):

```
for (;;) doProgramming();        // Infinite loop
```

4.8 The for(:) Statement

The enhanced for loop is convenient when we need to iterate over an array or a collection, especially when some operation needs to be performed on each element of the array or collection. In this section we discuss iterating over arrays. In §15.2, p. 795, we take a look at the for(:) loop for iterating over collections.

Earlier in this chapter we used a for(;;) loop to sum the values of elements in an int array:

```
    int sum = 0;
    int[] intArray = {12, 23, 5, 7, 19};
    for (int index = 0; index < intArray.length; index++) { // (1) using for(;;) loop
        sum += intArray[index];
    }
```

The for(;;) loop at (1) is rewritten using the for(:) loop in Figure 4.9.

Figure 4.9 *Enhanced* for *Statement*

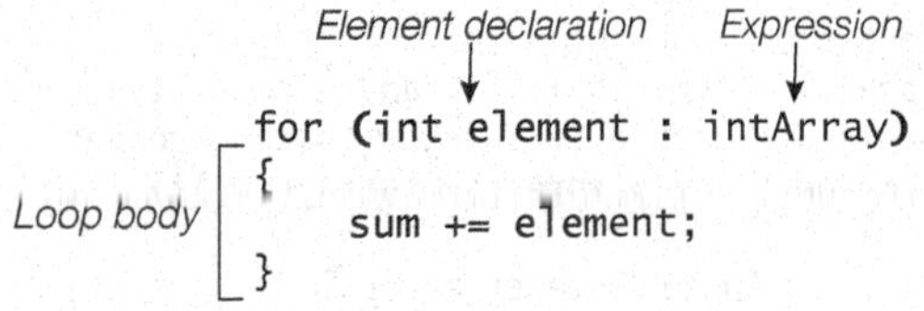

The body of the loop is executed for each element in the array, where the variable element successively denotes the current element in the array intArray. When the loop terminates, the variable sum will contain the sum of all elements in the array. We do not care about the *position* of the elements in the array, just that the loop iterates over *all* elements of the array.

From Figure 4.9 we see that the for(:) loop header has two parts. The *expression* must evaluate to a reference value that refers to an *array* (or an object which implements the Iterable<E> interface (§15.2, p. 791)). The array can be an array of primitive values or objects, or even an array of arrays. The *expression* is evaluated only once. The *element declaration* specifies a local variable that can be assigned a value of the element type of the array. The type of the array intArray in Figure 4.9 is int[], and the element type is int. The element variable of type int can be assigned int values from the array of int. However, this assignment might require either a boxing or an unboxing conversion, with optional widening conversion.

The element variable is local to the loop block and is not accessible after the loop terminates. Also, changing the value of the current variable does *not* change any value in the array. The *loop body*, which can be a simple statement or a statement block, is executed for each element in the array and there is no danger of any out-of-bounds errors.

The for(:) loop has its limitations. Specifically, we cannot change element values, and this kind of loop does not provide any provision for positional access using an index. The for(:) loop only increments by one and always in a forward direction. It does not allow iterations over several arrays simultaneously. Under such circumstances, the for(;;) loop can be more convenient.

Here are some code examples of legal for(:) loops:

```
// Some one-dim arrays:
int[]     intArray =    {10, 20, 30};
Integer[] intObjArray = {10, 20, 30};
String[]  strArray =    {"one", "two"};
```

```
// Some two-dim arrays:
Object[][] objArrayOfArrays = {intObjArray, strArray};
Number[][] numArrayOfArrays = {{1.5, 2.5}, intObjArray, {100L, 200L}};
int[][]    intArrayOfArrays = {{20}, intArray, {40}};

// Iterate over a String array.
// Expression type is String[], and element type is String.
// String is assignable to Object (widening conversion).
for (Object obj : strArray) {}

// Iterate over an int array.
// Expression type is int[], and element type is int.
// int is assignable to Integer (boxing conversion)
for (Integer iRef : intArrayOfArrays[0]){}

// Iterate over an Integer array.
// Expression type is Integer[], and element type is Integer.
// Integer is assignable to int (unboxing conversion)
for (int i : intObjArray){}

// Iterate over a two-dim int array.
// Outer loop: expression type is int[][], and element type is int[].
// Inner loop: expression type is int[], and element type is int.
for (int[] row : intArrayOfArrays)
  for (int val : row) {}

// Iterate over a two-dim Number array.
// Outer loop: expression type is Number[][], and element type is Number[].
// Outer loop: Number[] is assignable to Object[] (widening conversion).
// Inner loop: expression type is Object[], and element type is Object.
for (Object[] row : numArrayOfArrays)
  for (Object obj : row) {}

// Outer loop: expression type is Integer[][], and element type is Integer[].
// Outer loop: Integer[] is assignable to Number[].
// Inner loop: expression type is int[], and element type is int.
// Inner loop: int is assignable to double.
for (Number[] row : new Integer[][] {intObjArray, intObjArray, intObjArray})
  for (double num : intArray) {}
```

Here are some code examples of for(:) loops that are not legal:

```
// Expression type is Number[][], and element type is Number[].
// Number[] is not assignable to Number.
for (Number num : numArrayOfArrays) {}        // Compile-time error!

// Expression type is Number[], and element type is Number.
// Number is not assignable to int.
for (int row : numArrayOfArrays[0]) {}        // Compile-time error!

// Outer loop: expression type is int[][], and element type is int[].
// int[] is not assignable to Integer[].
for (Integer[] row : intArrayOfArrays)        // Compile-time error!
  for (int val : row) {}
```

```
// Expression type is Object[][], and element type is Object[].
// Object[] is not assignable to Integer[].
for (Integer[] row : objArrayOfArrays) {}     // Compile-time error!

// Outer loop: expression type is String[], and element type is String.
// Inner loop: expression type is String, which is not legal here. Not an array.
for (String str : strArray)
  for (char val : str) {}                      // Compile-time error!
```

When using the for(:) loop to iterate over an array, the two main causes of errors are an expression in the loop header that does not represent an array and/or an element type of the array that is not assignable to the local variable declared in the loop header.

4.9 Transfer Statements

Java provides the following language constructs for transferring control in a program:

- The yield statement (p. 164)
- The break statement
- The continue statement
- The return statement

The throw statement can also transfer control in a program (§7.4, p. 386).

4.10 Labeled Statements

A statement may have a *label*:

   label : statement

A label is any valid identifier; it always immediately precedes the statement. Label names exist in their own namespace, so that they do not conflict with names of packages, classes, interfaces, methods, fields, and local variables. The scope of a label is the statement prefixed by the label, meaning that it cannot be redeclared as a label inside the labeled statement—analogous to the scope of local variables.

```
L1: if (i > 0) {
  L1: System.out.println(i);     // (1) Not OK. Label L1 redeclared.
}

L1: while (i < 0) {              // (2) OK.
  L2: System.out.println(i);
}

L1: {                            // (3) OK. Labeled block.
  int j = 10;
```

```
    System.out.println(j);
  }

  L1: try {                         // (4) OK. Labeled try-catch-finally block.
    int j = 10, k = 0;
    L2: System.out.println(j/k);
  } catch (ArithmeticException ae) {
    L3: ae.printStackTrace();
  } finally {
    L4: System.out.println("Finally done.");
  }
```

A statement can have multiple labels:

```
LabelA: LabelB: System.out.println("Multiple labels. Use judiciously.");
```

A declaration statement cannot have a label:

```
L0: int i = 0;                      // Compile-time error!
```

A labeled statement is executed as if it were unlabeled, unless it is the break or continue statement. This behavior is discussed in the next two subsections.

4.11 The break Statement

The break statement comes in two forms: *unlabeled* and *labeled*.

```
break;              // the unlabeled form
break label;        // the labeled form
```

The unlabeled break statement terminates loops (for(;;), for(:), while, do-while) and switch statements, and transfers control out of the current context (i.e., the closest enclosing block). The rest of the statement body is skipped, and execution continues after the enclosing statement.

In Example 4.10, the break statement at (1) is used to terminate a for(;;) loop. Control is transferred to (2) when the value of i is equal to 4 at (1), skipping the rest of the loop body and terminating the loop.

Example 4.10 also shows that the unlabeled break statement terminates only the innermost loop or switch statement that contains the break statement. The break statement at (3) terminates the inner for(;;) loop when j is equal to 2, and execution continues in the outer switch statement at (4) after the for(;;) loop.

Example 4.10   *The break Statement*

```
class BreakOut {

  public static void main(String[] args) {
    System.out.println("i    sqrt(i)");
    for (int i = 1; i <= 5; ++i) {
```

```
        if (i == 4)
          break;                                      // (1) Terminate loop. Control to (2).
        // Rest of loop body skipped when i gets the value 4.
        System.out.printf("%d     %.2f%n", i, Math.sqrt(i));
      } // end for
      // (2) Continue here.
      int n = 2;
      switch (n) {
        case 1:
          System.out.println(n);
          break;
        case 2:
          System.out.println("Inner for(;;) loop: ");
          for (int j = 0; j <= n; j++) {
            if (j == 2)
              break;                                  // (3) Terminate loop. Control to (4).
            System.out.println("j = " + j);
          }
        default:
          System.out.println("default: n = " + n); // (4) Continue here.
      }
    }
  }
```

Output from the program:

```
i     sqrt(i)
1     1.00
2     1.41
3     1.73
Inner for(;;) loop:
j = 0
j = 1
default: n = 2
```

A labeled break statement can be used to terminate *any* labeled statement that contains the break statement. Control is then transferred to the statement following the enclosing labeled statement. In the case of a labeled block, the rest of the block is skipped and execution continues with the statement following the block:

```
out:                            // Label.
{                               // (1) Labeled block.
    // ...
    if (j == 10) break out;     // (2) Terminate block. Control to (3).
    System.out.println(j);      // Rest of the block not executed if j == 10.
    // ...
}
// (3) Continue here.
```

In Example 4.11, the program continues to add the elements below the diagonal of a square matrix until the sum is greater than 10. Two nested for loops are defined at (1) and (2). The outer loop is labeled outer at (1). The unlabeled break statement at (3) transfers control to (5) when it is executed; that is, it terminates the inner loop and control is transferred to the statement after the inner loop. The labeled break statement at (4) transfers control to (6) when it is executed; that is, it terminates both the inner and outer loops, transferring control to the statement after the loop labeled outer.

Example 4.11   *Labeled* break *Statement*

```
class LabeledBreakOut {
  public static void main(String[] args) {
    int[][] squareMatrix = {{4, 3, 5}, {2, 1, 6}, {9, 7, 8}};
    int sum = 0;
    outer: for (int i = 0; i < squareMatrix.length; ++i){    // (1) label
        for (int j = 0; j < squareMatrix[i].length; ++j) {   // (2)
            if (j == i) break;          // (3) Terminate inner loop. Control to (5).
            System.out.println("Element[" + i + ", " + j + "]: " +
                                    squareMatrix[i][j]);
            sum += squareMatrix[i][j];
            if (sum > 10) break outer;  // (4) Terminate both loops. Control to (6).
        } // end inner loop
        // (5) Continue with update expression in the outer loop header.
    } // end outer loop
    // (6) Continue here.
    System.out.println("sum: " + sum);
  }
}
```

Output from the program:

```
Element[1, 0]: 2
Element[2, 0]: 9
sum: 11
```

4.12 The continue **Statement**

Like the break statement, the continue statement comes in two forms: *unlabeled* and *labeled*.

```
continue;          // the unlabeled form
continue label;    // the labeled form
```

The continue statement can be used only in a for(;;), for(:), while, or do-while loop to prematurely stop the current iteration of the loop body and proceed with the next iteration, if possible. In the case of the while and do-while loops, the rest of the loop body is skipped—that is, the current iteration is stopped, with execution continuing with the *loop condition*. In the case of the for(;;) loop, the rest of the loop body is skipped, with execution continuing with the *update expression*.

In Example 4.12, an unlabeled continue statement is used to skip an iteration in a for(;;) loop. Control is transferred to (2) when the value of i is equal to 4 at (1), skipping the rest of the loop body and continuing with the *update expression* in the for(;;) statement.

Example 4.12   *The continue Statement*

```
class Skip {
  public static void main(String[] args) {
    System.out.println("i    sqrt(i)");
    for (int i = 1; i <= 5; ++i) {
      if (i == 4) continue;                // (1) Control to (2).
      // Rest of loop body skipped when i has the value 4.
      System.out.printf("%d    %.2f%n", i, Math.sqrt(i));
      // (2) Continue with update expression in the loop header.
    } // end for
  }
}
```

Output from the program:

```
i    sqrt(i)
1    1.00
2    1.41
3    1.73
5    2.24
```

A labeled continue statement must occur within a labeled loop that has the same label. Execution of the labeled continue statement then transfers control to the end of that enclosing labeled loop. In Example 4.13, the unlabeled continue statement at (3) transfers control to (5) when it is executed; that is, the rest of the loop body is skipped and execution continues with the update expression in the inner loop. The labeled continue statement at (4) transfers control to (6) when it is executed; that is, it terminates the inner loop but execution continues with the update expression in the loop labeled outer. It is instructive to compare the output from Example 4.11 (labeled break) with that from Example 4.13 (labeled continue).

Example 4.13   *Labeled continue Statement*

```
class LabeledSkip {
  public static void main(String[] args) {
    int[][] squareMatrix = {{4, 3, 5}, {2, 1, 6}, {9, 7, 8}};
    int sum = 0;
    outer: for (int i = 0; i < squareMatrix.length; ++i){    // (1) label
      for (int j = 0; j < squareMatrix[i].length; ++j) {  // (2)
        if (j == i) continue;                              // (3) Control to (5).
        System.out.println("Element[" + i + ", " + j + "]: " +
          squareMatrix[i][j]);
        sum += squareMatrix[i][j];
        if (sum > 10) continue outer;                      // (4) Control to (6).
        // (5) Continue with update expression in the inner loop header.
      } // end inner loop
      // (6) Continue with update expression in the outer loop header.
```

```
        } // end outer loop
      System.out.println("sum: " + sum);
    }
  }
```

Output from the program:

```
Element[0, 1]: 3
Element[0, 2]: 5
Element[1, 0]: 2
Element[1, 2]: 6
Element[2, 0]: 9
sum: 25
```

4.13 The `return` **Statement**

The `return` statement is used to stop execution of a method (or a constructor) and transfer control back to the calling code (also called the *caller* or *invoker*). The usage of the two forms of the `return` statement is dictated by whether that statement is used in a `void` or a non-void method (Table 4.2). The first form does not return any value to the calling code, but the second form does. Note that the keyword void does not represent any type.

In Table 4.2, the *expression* must evaluate to a primitive value or a reference value, and its type must be *assignable* to the *return type* specified in the method header (§2.7, p. 54, and §5.9, p. 261). See also the discussion on covariant return in connection with method overriding in §5.1, p. 201.

As can be seen from Table 4.2, a `void` method need not have a `return` statement—in which case the control typically returns to the caller after the last statement in the method body has been executed. However, a `void` method can specify only the first form of the `return` statement. This form of the `return` statement can also be used in constructors, as they likewise do not return a value.

Table 4.2 also shows that the first form of the `return` statement is not allowed in a non-void method. The second form of the return statement is mandatory in a non-void method, if the method execution is not terminated programmatically—for example, by throwing an exception. Example 4.14 illustrates the use of the `return` statement summarized in Table 4.2. A recommended best practice is to document the value returned by a method in a Javadoc comment using the `@return` tag.

Table 4.2 *The `return` Statement*

Form of return statement	In void method or in constructor	In non-void method
`return;`	Optional	Not allowed
`return` *expression*`;`	Not allowed	Mandatory, if the method is not terminated explicitly

Example 4.14 *The* return *Statement*

```java
public class ReturnDemo {

  public static void main (String[] args) { // (1) void method can use return.
    if (args.length == 0) return;
    output(checkValue(args.length));
  }

  static void output(int value) {  // (2) void method need not use return.
    System.out.println(value);
    return 'a';                    // Not OK. Cannot return a value.
  }

  static int checkValue(int i) {   // (3) Non-void method: Any return statement
                                   //     must return a value.
    if (i > 3)
      return i;                    // OK.
    else
      return 2.0;                  // Not OK. double not assignable to int.
  }

  static int absentMinded() {      // (4) Non-void method.
    throw new RuntimeException();  // OK: No return statement provided, but
                                   // method terminates by throwing an exception.
  }
}
```

 Review Questions

4.5 What will be the result of attempting to compile and run the following code?

```java
class MyClass {
  public static void main(String[] args) {
    boolean b = false;
    int i = 1;
    do {
      i++;
      b = ! b;
    } while (b);
    System.out.println(i);
  }
}
```

Select the one correct answer.

(a) The code will fail to compile because b is an invalid condition for the do-while statement.
(b) The code will fail to compile because the assignment b = ! b is not allowed.
(c) The code will compile without error and will print 1 at runtime.
(d) The code will compile without error and will print 2 at runtime.
(e) The code will compile without error and will print 3 at runtime.

4.6   What will be the output when running the following program?

```java
public class StillMyClass {
  public static void main(String[] args) {
    int i = 0;
    int j;
    for (j = 0; j < 10; ++j) { i++; }
    System.out.println(i + " " + j);
  }
}
```

Select the two correct answers.

(a) The first number printed will be 9.
(b) The first number printed will be 10.
(c) The first number printed will be 11.
(d) The second number printed will be 9.
(e) The second number printed will be 10.
(f) The second number printed will be 11.

4.7   What will be the result of attempting to compile and run the following program?

```java
class AnotherClass {
  public static void main(String[] args) {
    int i = 0;
    for (; i < 10; i++) ;        // (1)
    for (i = 0;; i++) break;     // (2)
    for (i = 0; i < 10;) i++;    // (3)
    for (;;) ;                   // (4)
  }
}
```

Select the one correct answer.

(a) The code will fail to compile because of errors in the for loop at (1).
(b) The code will fail to compile because of errors in the for loop at (2).
(c) The code will fail to compile because of errors in the for loop at (3).
(d) The code will fail to compile because of errors in the for loop at (4).
(e) The code will compile without error, and the program will run and terminate without any output.
(f) The code will compile without error, but will never terminate when run.

4.8   Given the following code fragment, which of the following lines will be a part of the output?

```java
outer:
for (int i = 0; i < 3; i++) {
  for (int j = 0; j < 2; j++) {
    if (i == j) {
      continue outer;
    }
    System.out.println("i=" + i + ", j=" + j);
  }
}
```

Select the two correct answers.

(a) i=1, j=0
(b) i=0, j=1
(c) i=1, j=2
(d) i=2, j=1
(e) i=2, j=2
(f) i=3, j=3
(g) i=3, j=2

4.9 Which declarations, when inserted at (1), will result in the program compiling and printing 90 at runtime?

```
public class RQ400A10 {
  public static void main(String[] args) {
    // (1) INSERT DECLARATION HERE
    int sum = 0;
    for (int i : nums)
      sum += i;
    System.out.println(sum);
  }
}
```

Select the two correct answers.

(a) `Object[] nums = {20, 30, 40};`
(b) `Number[] nums = {20, 30, 40};`
(c) `Integer[] nums = {20, 30, 40};`
(d) `int[] nums = {20, 30, 40};`
(e) None of the above

4.10 Which method declarations, when inserted at (1), will result in the program compiling and printing 90 when run?

```
public class RQ400A30 {
  public static void main(String[] args) {
    doIt();
  }
  // (1) INSERT METHOD DECLARATION HERE
}
```

Select the two correct answers.

(a) ```
public static void doIt() {
  int[] nums = {20, 30, 40};
  for (int sum = 0, i : nums)
    sum += i;
  System.out.println(sum);
}
```
(b) ```
public static void doIt() {
  for (int sum = 0, i : {20, 30, 40})
    sum += i;
  System.out.println(sum);
}
```

```
(c) public static void doIt() {
      int sum = 0;
      for (int i : {20, 30, 40})
        sum += i;
      System.out.println(sum);
    }
(d) public static void doIt() {
      int sum = 0;
      for (int i : new int[] {20, 30, 40})
        sum += i;
      System.out.println(sum);
    }
(e) public static void doIt() {
      int[] nums = {20, 30, 40};
      int sum = 0;
      for (int i : nums)
        sum += i;
      System.out.println(sum);
    }
```

4.11   Which of the following statements are true about the following for(:) loop?

```
for (type variable : expression) statement
```

Select the three correct answers.

(a) The *variable* is only accessible in the for(:) loop body.
(b) The *expression* is only evaluated once.
(c) The type of the expression must be java.lang.Iterable<E> or an array type.
(d) Changing the value of the *variable* in the loop body affects the data structure represented by the *expression*.
(e) The loop runs backward if the *expression* is negated as follows: !*expression*.
(f) We can iterate over several data structures simultaneously in a for(:) loop.

Object-Oriented
Programming

5

 Chapter Topics

- Implementing inheritance and its implications in object-oriented programming
- Implications of the subtype–supertype relationship
- Differentiating between inheritance (*is-a*) and aggregation (*has-a*)
- Distinguishing between static and dynamic types of a reference
- Overriding and hiding superclass members
- Understanding method overriding and comparing it with method overloading
- Using the super reference to access superclass members
- Using the this() and super() calls for constructor chaining
- Declaring abstract classes and methods
- Using the final modifier to declare classes, methods, fields, and local variables
- Declaring interfaces, and the implications of multiple interface inheritance
- Understanding the implications of subtyping for reference arrays
- Understanding conversions when assigning, casting, and passing references
- Understanding resolution of overloaded methods
- Identifying the type of objects and pattern matching using the instanceof operator
- Taking advantage of polymorphism and how dynamic method lookup works
- Declaring and using enum types
- Declaring and using record classes
- Declaring and using sealed classes and interfaces

Java SE 17 Developer Exam Objectives	

[3.2] Create classes and records, and define and use instance and static fields and methods, constructors, and instance and static initializers
  o *Record classes are covered in this chapter.*
  o *For creating normal classes and defining class members and constructors, see Chapter 3, p. 97.*
  o *For instance and static initializers, see Chapter 10.5, p. 540.*
	§5.14, p. 299

[3.3] Implement overloading, including var-arg methods
  o *Comparing overloading and overriding is covered in this chapter.*
  o *For overloading methods, including varargs methods, see Chapter 3, p. 97.*
	§5.1, p. 202

[3.5] Implement inheritance, including abstract and sealed classes. Override methods, including that of Object class. Implement polymorphism and differentiate object type versus reference type. Perform type casting, identify object types using instanceof operator and pattern matching
  o *Inheritance, abstract and sealed classes, overriding methods, polymorphism and type casting, static and dynamic types of a reference, and* instanceof *type comparison and pattern match operators are covered in this chapter.*
  o *For overriding methods of the* Object *class, see §14.1, p. 743.*
	§5.1, p. 191
	to
	§5.4, p. 218
	§5.11, p. 269
	§5.12, p. 278
	§5.15, p. 311

[3.6] Create and use interfaces, identify functional interfaces, and utilize private, static, and default interface methods
  o *Only nonfunctional interfaces are covered in this chapter.*
  o *For functional interfaces, see §13.1, p. 675.*
	§5.6, p. 237

[3.7] Create and use enumerations with fields, methods and constructors	*§5.13, p. 287*
Java SE 11 Developer Exam Objectives	
[3.5] Create and use subclasses and superclasses, including abstract classes	*§5.1, p. 191* *to* *§5.4, p. 218*
[3.6] Utilize polymorphism and casting to call methods, differentiating object type versus reference type	*§5.11, p. 269* *§5.12, p. 278*

[3.7] Create and use interfaces, identify functional interfaces, and utilize private, static, and default methods
  o *Only nonfunctional interfaces are covered in this chapter.*
  o *For functional interfaces, see §13.1, p. 675.*
	§5.6, p. 237

[3.8] Create and use enumerations	*§5.13, p. 287*

This chapter delves into two of the main pillars of object-oriented programming (OOP): inheritance and polymorphism. The discussion of the other two OOP concepts, abstraction and encapsulation, can be found in §1.2, p. 5, and §6.1, p. 324, respectively.

Many Java features relating to OOP are covered in this chapter: subtype–supertype relationship, abstract classes and methods, final declarations, interfaces, reference conversions, enum types, record classes, and sealed classes and interfaces. There is a lot of ground to cover in this chapter, so take a deep breath and dive in.

5.1 Implementing Inheritance

Inheritance is one of the fundamental mechanisms for code reuse in OOP. It allows new classes to be derived from existing ones. The new class (also called a *subclass, subtype, derived class,* or *child class*) can inherit members from the old class (also called a *superclass, supertype, base class,* or *parent class*). The subclass can add new behavior and properties and, under certain circumstances, modify its inherited behavior.

A subclass specifies the name of its superclass in the subclass header using the extends clause.

```
class TubeLight extends Light { ... }   // TubeLight is a subclass of Light.
```

The subclass specifies only the additional new and modified members in its class body. The rest of its declaration is made up of its inherited members. If no extends clause is specified in the header of a class declaration, the class implicitly inherits from the java.lang.Object class. Selected methods inherited by all objects from the Object class are covered in connection with object comparison (Chapter 14, p. 741) and thread synchronization (§22.4, p. 1396).

Inheritance of members is closely tied to their declared *accessibility*. If a superclass member is accessible by its simple name in the subclass (without the use of any extra syntax, like super), that member is considered inherited. Conversely, private, overridden, and hidden members of the superclass are *not* inherited. Inheritance should not be confused with the *existence* of such members in the state of a subclass object.

The declaration of the Light class at (1) in Example 5.1 implicitly extends the java.lang.Object class, as no explicit extends clause is specified. Also in Example 5.1, the subclass TubeLight at (2) explicitly uses the extends clause and specifies only members other than those that it already inherits from the superclass Light (which, in turn, inherits from the Object class). Members of the superclass Light, which are accessible by their simple names in the subclass TubeLight, are inherited by the subclass, as evident from the output in Example 5.1.

Members of the superclass that have private access are not inherited by the subclass and can only be accessed indirectly. The private field indicator of the superclass Light is not inherited, but exists in the subclass object and is indirectly accessible through public methods.

Using appropriate access modifiers, the superclass can limit which members can be accessed directly, and therefore, inherited by its subclasses. As shown in Example 5.1, the subclass can use the inherited members as if they were declared in its own class body. This is not the case for members that are declared as private in the superclass, as shown at (3), (4), and (5). Members that have package accessibility in the superclass are also not inherited by subclasses in other packages, as these members are accessible by their simple names only in subclasses within the same package as the superclass.

Since constructors are *not* members of a class, they are *not* inherited by a subclass.

Example 5.1   *Extending Classes: Inheritance and Accessibility*

```java
// File: Utility.java
class Light {                               // (1)
  // Instance fields:
            int    noOfWatts;               // Wattage
  private   boolean indicator;              // On or off
  protected String  location;              // Placement

  // Static field:
  private static int counter;               // Number of Light objects created

  // Non-zero argument constructor:
  Light(int noOfWatts, boolean indicator, String location) {
    this.noOfWatts = noOfWatts;
    this.indicator = indicator;
    this.location  = location;
    ++counter;                              // Increment counter.
  }

  // Instance methods:
  public  void    switchOn()  { indicator = true; }
  public  void    switchOff() { indicator = false; }
  public  boolean isOn()      { return indicator; }
  private String  getLocation() { return location; }

  // Static methods:
  public static int getCount() { return counter; }
}
//_____
class TubeLight extends Light {             // (2) Subclass uses the extends clause.
  // Instance fields:
  private int tubeLength;                    // Length in millimeters
  private int tubeDiameter;                  // Diameter in millimeters

  // Non-zero argument constructor
  TubeLight(int noOfWatts, boolean indicator, String location,
            int tubeLength, int tubeDiameter) {
    super(noOfWatts, indicator, location);  // Calling constructor in superclass.
    this.tubeLength = tubeLength;
    this.tubeDiameter = tubeDiameter;
  }
```

```
     // Instance methods:
     public int getTubeLength() { return tubeLength; }

     public void printInfo() {
        System.out.println("From the subclass:");
        System.out.println("Tube length (mm): " + getTubeLength());
        System.out.println("Tube diameter (mm): " + tubeDiameter);
        System.out.println();
        System.out.println("From the superclass:");
        System.out.println("Wattage: "       + noOfWatts);      // Inherited.
//      System.out.println("Indicator: "     + indicator);      // (3) Not inherited.
        System.out.println("Location: "      + location);       // Inherited.
//      System.out.println("Counter: "    + counter);           // (4) Not inherited.
        switchOn();                                             // Inherited
        switchOff();                                            // Inherited
        System.out.println("Indicator: "     + isOn());         // Inherited.
//      System.out.println("Location: " + getLocation());       // (5) Not inherited.
        System.out.println("Number of lights: " + getCount());// Inherited.
     }
  }
//_____
public class Utility {
   public static void main(String[] args) {
      TubeLight loftLight = new TubeLight(18, true, "Loft", 590, 26);
      loftLight.printInfo();
   }
}
```

Output from the program:

```
From the subclass:
Tube length (mm): 590
Tube diameter (mm): 26

From the superclass:
Wattage: 18
Location: Loft
Indicator: false
Number of lights: 1
```

In Java, a class can extend only *one* class; that is, it can have only one direct super-class. This kind of inheritance is sometimes called *single* or *linear implementation inheritance*. The name is appropriate, as the subclass inherits the *implementation* of its superclass. Java only allows *single inheritance of implementation* using the extends clause. *Multiple inheritance of implementation* occurs when a class inherits multiple implementations from the interfaces it implements, but this is *not* allowed in Java (p. 240).

The inheritance relationship can be depicted as an *inheritance hierarchy* (also called a *class hierarchy*), where each subclass is connected by the inheritance arrow to its direct superclass. The java.lang.Object class is always at the top (the *root*) of any Java inheritance hierarchy, as all classes extend (either directly or indirectly) this class. The path from a subclass in the inheritance hierarchy to the root traces all the superclasses that the subclass inherits from. Classes up in the hierarchy are more *generalized* (often called *broader*), as they abstract the class behavior. Classes lower in the hierarchy are more *specialized* (often called *narrower*), as they customize the inherited behavior by additional properties and behavior. Figure 5.1 illustrates the inheritance relationship between the class Light, which represents the more general abstraction, and its more specialized subclasses. The class SpotLightBulb inherits from the classes LightBulb, Light, and Object.

Figure 5.1   *Inheritance Hierarchy*

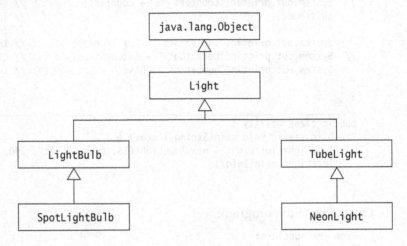

Relationships: *is-a* and *has-a*

The inheritance relationship between a subclass and its superclass is embodied by the *is-a* relationship. Since a subclass inherits from its superclass, a subclass object *is-a* superclass object, and can be used wherever an object of the superclass can be used. It has particular consequences for how objects can be used. An object of the TubeLight class *is-an* object of the superclass Light. Referring to Figure 5.1, an object of the TubeLight class can be used wherever an object of the superclass Light can be used.

The inheritance relationship is *transitive*: If class B extends class A and class C extends class B, then class C will also inherit from class A via class B. In Figure 5.1, an object of the SpotLightBulb class *is-an* object of the class Light. The *is-a* relationship does not hold between peer classes: An object of the LightBulb class is *not* an object of the class TubeLight, and vice versa.

Whereas inheritance defines the relationship *is-a* between a superclass and its subclasses, *aggregation* defines the relationship *has-a* (also called the *whole–part* relationship) between an instance of a class and its constituents (also called *parts*). Aggregation comprises the *usage* of objects.

A class declaration with instance field references implements an aggregate object. The class Light is declared with three instance fields: an instance field to store its wattage (noOfWatts), an instance field to store whether it is on or off (indicator), and an instance field reference (location) to a String object to store its location (in fact, its only constituent object). An instance of class Light *has* (or *uses*) an object of class String. In Java, a composite object cannot contain other objects. It can only store *reference values* of its constituent objects in its fields. This relationship defines an *aggregation hierarchy* (also called *object hierarchy*) that embodies the *has-a* relationship. Constituent objects can be shared between objects. If their lifetimes are dependent on the lifetime of the aggregate object, then this relationship is called *composition*, and implies strong ownership of the parts by the composite object.

Choosing between inheritance and aggregation to model relationships can be a crucial design decision. A good design strategy advocates that inheritance should be used only if the relationship *is-a* is unequivocally maintained throughout the lifetime of the objects involved; otherwise, aggregation is the best choice. A *role* is often confused with an *is-a* relationship. For example, given the class Employee, it would not be a good idea to model the roles that an employee can play (such as manager or cashier) by inheritance, if these roles change intermittently. Changing roles would involve a new object to represent the new role every time this happens.

Code reuse is also best achieved by aggregation when there is no *is-a* relationship. Enforcing an artificial *is-a* relationship that is not naturally present is usually not a good idea. Methods that contradict the abstraction represented by the subclass can be invoked. Using aggregation in such a case results in a better solution.

Both inheritance and aggregation promote encapsulation of *implementation*. Changes in the implementation of constituent objects generally have minimal impact on the clients of the composite object, since these clients do not directly deal with the underlying objects. However, changing the *contract* of a superclass can have consequences for the subclasses (called the *ripple effect*) as well as for clients that are dependent on a particular behavior of the subclasses. For this reason, aggregation provides stronger encapsulation than inheritance.

The Subtype–Supertype Relationship

A class defines a *reference type*, a data type whose objects can be accessed only by references. Therefore, the inheritance hierarchy can be regarded as a *type hierarchy*, embodying the *subtype–supertype relationship* between reference types. The *subclass–superclass* relationship is a special case of the subtype–supertype relationship that is between classes. The subclass–superclass relationship allows *single inheritance of type*, meaning that the subclass inherits the *type* of its direct superclass. This is in contrast to a class that implements several interfaces, resulting in *multiple inheritance of type*—that is, a class inherits the *type* of all interfaces it implements.

In the context of Java, the subtype–supertype relationship implies that the reference value of a subtype object can be assigned to a supertype reference because a subtype object can be substituted for a supertype object. This assignment involves a *widening reference conversion*, as references are assigned *up* the inheritance hierarchy. Using the reference types in Example 5.1, the following code assigns the reference value of an object of the subtype TubeLight to the reference light of the supertype Light:

```
Light light = new TubeLight(36, false, "Basement",
                            1200, 26);      // (1) widening reference conversion
```

An implicit widening conversion takes place under assignment, as the reference value of a narrower type (subtype TubeLight) object is being assigned to a reference of a broader type (supertype Light). We can now use the reference light to invoke those methods on the subtype object that are inherited from the supertype Light:

```
light.switchOn();                                    // (2)
```

Note that the compiler only knows about the *static type* (also called the *declared type*) of the reference light, which is Light, and ensures that only methods from this type can be called using the reference light. However, at runtime, the reference light will refer to an object of the subtype TubeLight when the call to the method switchOn() is executed. It is the *type of the object* that the reference refers to at runtime that determines which method is executed. The subtype object inherits the switchOn() method from its supertype Light, so this method is executed. The type of the object that the reference refers to at runtime is called the *dynamic type* (a.k.a. the *runtime type* or the *object type*) of the reference.

One might be tempted to invoke methods exclusive to the TubeLight subtype via the supertype reference light:

```
light.getTubeLength();                               // (3) Compile-time error!
```

This code will not work, as the compiler does not know which object the reference light will denote at runtime; it only knows the declared type of the reference. As the declaration of the class Light does not have a method called getTubeLength(), this method call at (3) results in a compile-time error. Eliciting subtype-specific behavior using a supertype reference requires a *narrowing reference conversion* with an explicit cast (p. 278).

Overriding Instance Methods

Under certain circumstances, a subclass can *override instance methods* from its superclass. Overriding such a method allows the subclass to provide its *own* implementation of the method. The overridden method in the superclass is *not* inherited by the subclass. When the method is invoked on an object of the subclass, it is the method implementation in the subclass that is executed. The new method in the subclass must abide by the following rules of method overriding:

- The new method definition in the subclass must have the same *method signature*. In other words, the method name, and the types and the number of parameters, including their order, must be the same as in the overridden method of the superclass.

Whether parameters in the overriding method should be `final` is at the discretion of the subclass. A method's signature does not comprise the `final` modifier of parameters, only their types and order.

- The return type of the overriding method can be a *subtype* of the return type of the overridden method (called *covariant return*, p. 201).

- The new method definition cannot *narrow* the accessibility of the method, but it can *widen* it.

- The new method definition can throw either all or none, or a subset of the *checked* exceptions (including their subclasses) that are specified in the `throws` clause of the overridden method in the superclass (§7.5, p. 388)—that is, the overriding method may not throw any checked exception that is *wider* than the checked exceptions thrown by the overridden method. However, the overriding method may throw any *unchecked* exceptions.

The criteria for overriding methods also apply to interfaces, where a subinterface can override `abstract` and `default` method declarations from its superinterfaces (p. 237).

Figure 5.2   *Inheritance Hierarchy for Example 5.2*

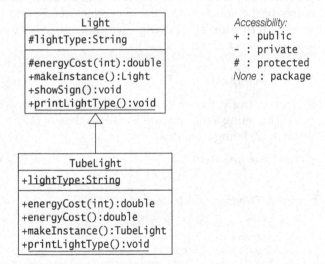

The canonical examples of method overriding in Java are the `equals()`, `hashCode()`, and `toString()` methods of the `Object` class. The wrapper classes and the `String` class all override these methods (Chapter 8, p. 423). Overriding these methods in user-defined classes is thoroughly covered in connection with object comparison (Chapter 14, p. 741).

Example 5.2 illustrates overriding, overloading, and hiding of members in a class. Figure 5.2 gives an overview of the two main classes in Example 5.2. The new definition of the `energyCost()` method at (7) in the subclass `TubeLight` has the same signature and the same return type as the method at (2) in the superclass `Light`. The new definition specifies a subset of the exceptions (ZeroHoursException) thrown by the overridden method (the exception class InvalidHoursException is a superclass of NegativeHoursException and ZeroHoursException). The new definition also widens the accessibility (public) from what it was in the overridden definition (protected). The overriding method declares the parameter to be final, but this has no bearing on overriding the method.

```
// The overridden method in the superclass Light:
protected double energyCost(int noOfHours)      // (2) Instance method
    throws InvalidHoursException { ... }

// The overriding method in the subclass TubeLight:
@Override
public double energyCost(final int noOfHours)   // (7) Overriding instance
    throws ZeroHoursException { ... }            //     method at (2).
```

The astute reader will have noticed the @Override annotation preceding the method definition at (7). The compiler will now report an error if the method definition at (7) does *not* override an inherited method. The annotation helps to ensure that the method definition overrides the inherited method, rather than overloading another method silently.

Invocation of the method energyCost() on an object of subclass TubeLight using references of the subclass and the superclass at (15) and (16), respectively, results in the new definition at (7) being executed, since both references are aliases of the TubeLight object created at (12).

```
    tubeLight.energyCost(50);                    // (15) Invokes method at (7).
    light1.energyCost(50);                       // (16) Invokes method at (7).
```

Not surprisingly, the invocation of the method energyCost() on an object of superclass Light, using a reference of the superclass at (17), results in the overridden definition at (2) being executed:

```
    light2.energyCost(50);                       // (17) Invokes method at (2).
```

Example 5.2   *Overriding, Overloading, and Hiding*

```
// File: Client2.java
// Exceptions
class InvalidHoursException extends Exception {}
class NegativeHoursException extends InvalidHoursException {}
class ZeroHoursException extends InvalidHoursException {}

class Light {

  protected String lightType = "Generic Light";   // (1) Instance field

  protected double energyCost(int noOfHours)       // (2) Instance method
      throws InvalidHoursException {
    System.out.print(">> Light.energyCost(int): ");
    if (noOfHours < 0)
      throw new NegativeHoursException();
```

```
      double cost = 00.20 * noOfHours;
      System.out.println("Energy cost for " + lightType + ": " + cost);
      return cost;
    }

    public Light makeInstance() {                    // (3) Instance method
      System.out.print(">> Light.makeInstance(): ");
      return new Light();
    }

    public void showSign() {                         // (4) Instance method
      System.out.print(">> Light.showSign(): ");
      System.out.println("Let there be light!");
    }

    public static void printLightType() {            // (5) Static method
      System.out.print(">> Static Light.printLightType(): ");
      System.out.println("Generic Light");
    }
  }
}
//_____
class TubeLight extends Light {

  public static String lightType = "Tube Light";  // (6) Hiding field at (1).

  @Override
  public double energyCost(final int noOfHours)    // (7) Overriding instance
      throws ZeroHoursException {                   //      method at (2).
    System.out.print(">> TubeLight.energyCost(int): ");
    if (noOfHours == 0)
      throw new ZeroHoursException();
    double cost = 00.10 * noOfHours;
    System.out.println("Energy cost for " + lightType + ": " + cost);
    return cost;
  }

  public double energyCost() {            // (8) Overloading method at (7).
    System.out.print(">> TubeLight.energyCost(): ");
    double flatrate = 20.00;
    System.out.println("Energy cost for " + lightType + ": " + flatrate);
    return flatrate;
  }

  @Override
  public TubeLight makeInstance() {       // (9) Overriding instance method at (3).
    System.out.print(">> TubeLight.makeInstance(): ");
    return new TubeLight();
  }

  public static void printLightType() { // (10) Hiding static method at (5).
    System.out.print(">> Static TubeLight.printLightType(): ");
    System.out.println(lightType);
  }
}
//_____
```

```java
public class Client2 {
  public static void main(String[] args)            // (11)
      throws InvalidHoursException {

    TubeLight tubeLight = new TubeLight();           // (12)
    Light     light1    = tubeLight;                 // (13) Aliases.
    Light     light2    = new Light();               // (14)

    System.out.println("Invoke overridden instance method:");
    tubeLight.energyCost(50);                        // (15) Invokes method at (7).
    light1.energyCost(50);                           // (16) Invokes method at (7).
    light2.energyCost(50);                           // (17) Invokes method at (2).

    System.out.println(
        "\nInvoke overridden instance method with covariant return:");
    System.out.println(
        light2.makeInstance().getClass());           // (18) Invokes method at (3).
    System.out.println(
        tubeLight.makeInstance().getClass());        // (19) Invokes method at (9).

    System.out.println("\nAccess hidden field:");
    System.out.println(tubeLight.lightType);         // (20) Accesses field at (6).
    System.out.println(light1.lightType);            // (21) Accesses field at (1).
    System.out.println(light2.lightType);            // (22) Accesses field at (1).

    System.out.println("\nInvoke hidden static method:");
    tubeLight.printLightType();                      // (23) Invokes method at (10).
    light1.printLightType();                         // (24) Invokes method at (5).
    light2.printLightType();                         // (25) Invokes method at (5).

    System.out.println("\nInvoke overloaded method:");
    tubeLight.energyCost();                          // (26) Invokes method at (8).
  }
}
```

Output from the program:

```
Invoke overridden instance method:
>> TubeLight.energyCost(int): Energy cost for Tube Light: 5.0
>> TubeLight.energyCost(int): Energy cost for Tube Light: 5.0
>> Light.energyCost(int): Energy cost for Generic Light: 10.0

Invoke overridden instance method with covariant return:
>> Light.makeInstance(): class Light
>> TubeLight.makeInstance(): class TubeLight

Access hidden field:
Tube Light
Generic Light
Generic Light

Invoke hidden static method:
>> Static TubeLight.printLightType(): Tube Light
>> Static Light.printLightType(): Generic Light
>> Static Light.printLightType(): Generic Light
```

```
Invoke overloaded method:
>> TubeLight.energyCost(): Energy cost for Tube Light: 20.0
```

Here are a few more facts to note about overriding.

- A subclass must use the keyword super to invoke an overridden method in the superclass.

- A final method cannot be overridden because the modifier final prevents method overriding. An attempt to override a final method will result in a compile-time error. An abstract method, in contrast, requires the non-abstract subclasses to override the method so as to provide an implementation. Abstract and final methods are discussed in §5.4, p. 224, and §5.5, p. 226, respectively.

- The access modifier private for a method means that the method is not accessible outside the class in which it is defined; therefore, a subclass cannot override it. However, a subclass can give its own definition of such a method, which may have the same signature as the method in its superclass.

- A subclass within the same package as the superclass can override any non-final methods declared in the superclass. However, a subclass in a different package can override only the non-final methods that are declared as either public or protected in the superclass.

- An instance method in a subclass cannot override a static method in the superclass. The compiler will flag such an attempt as an error. A static method is class specific and not part of any object, while overriding methods are invoked on behalf of objects of the subclass. However, a static method in a subclass can *hide* a static method in the superclass, as we shall see (p. 203), but it cannot hide an instance method in the superclass.

- Constructors, since they are not inherited, cannot be overridden.

Covariant return in Overriding Methods

In Example 5.2, the definition of the method makeInstance() at (9) overrides the method definition at (3).

```
// The overridden method in the superclass Light:
public Light makeInstance() { ... }      // (3) Instance method
```

```
// The overriding method in the subclass TubeLight:
@Override
public TubeLight makeInstance() { ... } // (9) Overriding instance method at (3).
```

Note that the method signatures are the same, but the return type at (9) is a subtype of the return type at (3). The method at (9) returns an object of the subtype Tube-Light, whereas the method at (3) returns an object of the supertype Light. This is an example of *covariant return*.

Depending on whether we call the method makeInstance() on an object of the subtype TubeLight or an object of the supertype Light, the respective method definition will be executed. The code at (18) and (19) illustrates which object is returned by the method, depending on which method definition is executed.

Note that covariant return applies only to *reference* types, not to primitive types. For example, changing the return type of the energyCost() method at (7) to float will result in a compile-time error. There is no subtype–supertype relationship between primitive types.

Overriding versus Overloading

Method overriding should not be confused with *method overloading* (§3.6, p. 108). Method overriding always requires the same method signature (name and parameter types) and the same or covariant return types. Overloading occurs when the method names are the same, but the parameter lists differ. Therefore, to overload methods, the parameters must differ in either type, order, or number. As the return type is not a part of the method signature, use of different return types is not sufficient to overload methods. Although methods can be overloaded, as shown at (1) and (2) in Example 5.3, a call to such an overloaded method can be *ambiguous*, as shown at (3). It is not possible to determine which method should be called, (1) or (2). Disambiguation can be done by making the types of the arguments in the call more specific, as shown at (4) and (5).

Example 5.3 *Ambiguous Call to Overloaded Methods*

```java
public class Overloader {

  static final void callMe(long x, Integer y) {        // (1) Overloaded by (2)
    System.out.println("long, Integer");
  }
  static void callMe(Integer x, long y) {         // (2) Overloaded by (1)
    System.out.println("Integer, long");
  }

  public static void main(String[] args) {
//  callMe(20, 17);                      // (3) Ambiguous call: Box 1st or 2nd argument?
    callMe(20, Integer.valueOf(17));   // (4) Calls (1): long, Integer
    callMe(Integer.valueOf(20), 17);   // (5) Calls (2): Integer, long
  }
}
```

Output from the program:

```
long, Integer
Integer, long
```

Only non-final instance methods in the superclass that are directly accessible from the subclass using their simple name can be overridden. In contrast, both non-private instance and static methods can be overloaded in the class they are defined in or are in a subclass of the class they are defined in.

Depending on the arguments passed in a call to an overloaded method, the appropriate method implementation is invoked. In Example 5.2, the method energy-Cost() at (2) in superclass Light is overridden in subclass TubeLight at (7) and overloaded at (8). When invoked at (26), the overloaded declaration at (8) is executed.

For overloaded and static methods, which method implementation will be executed at runtime is determined at *compile time*. In contrast, for overridden methods, the method implementation to be executed is determined at *runtime* (p. 278).

Hiding Fields

A subclass cannot override inherited *fields* of the superclass, but it can *hide* them. The subclass can define fields with the same name as in the superclass. If this is the case, the fields in the superclass cannot be accessed in the subclass by their simple names; therefore, they are not inherited by the subclass. A hidden static field can always be accessed by using the superclass name in the subclass declaration. Additionally, the keyword super can be used in non-static code in the subclass declaration to access hidden static fields.

The following distinction between invoking instance methods on an object and accessing fields of an object must be noted. When an instance method is invoked on an object using a reference, it is the *dynamic type* of the reference (i.e., *the type of the current object* denoted by the reference at runtime), not the declared type of the reference, that determines which method implementation will be executed. In Example 5.2 at (15), (16), and (17), this is evident from invoking the overridden method energyCost(): The method from the class corresponding to the current object is executed, regardless of the declared reference type.

When a field of an object is accessed using a reference, it is the *declared type* of the reference, not the type of the current object denoted by the reference, that determines which field will actually be accessed. In Example 5.2 at (20), (21), and (22), this is evident from accessing the hidden field lightType: The field accessed is the one declared in the class corresponding to the declared reference type, regardless of the object denoted by the reference at runtime.

In contrast to method overriding, where an instance method cannot override a static method, there are no such restrictions on the hiding of fields. The field lightType is static in the subclass, but not in the superclass. The declared type of the fields need not be the same either—only the field name matters in the hiding of fields.

Hiding Static Methods

Only instance methods in an object can be overridden. However, a static method in a subclass can *hide* a static method from the superclass. Hiding a static method is analogous to overriding an instance method except for one important aspect: Calls to static methods are *bound at compile time* as opposed to runtime for calls to overridden instance methods, and therefore do *not* exhibit polymorphic behavior exhibited by calls to overridden instance methods (p. 278).

When hiding a static method, the compiler will flag an error if the signatures are the same, but the other requirements regarding the return type, throws clause, and accessibility are not met. If the signatures are different, the method name is over-loaded, not hidden.

A static method in the subclass can only hide a static method in the superclass. Analogous to an overridden instance method, a hidden superclass static method is *not* inherited. Analogous to accessing hidden static fields, a hidden static method in the superclass can always be invoked by using the superclass name or by using the keyword super in non-static code in the subclass declaration.

Example 5.2 illustrates invocation of static methods using references. Analogous to accessing fields, the static method invoked at (23), (24), and (25) is determined by the *declared type* of the reference. At (23), the declared reference type is TubeLight; therefore, the static method printLightType() at (10) in this class is invoked. At (24) and (25), the declared reference type is Light, and the hidden static method print-LightType() at (5) in that class is invoked. This is borne out by the output from the program.

In summary, a subclass can do any of the following:

- Access inherited members using their simple names
- Override a non-final instance method with the same signature as in the super-class
- Overload a static or instance method with the same name as in the superclass
- Hide a static non-final method with the same signature as in the superclass
- Hide a static or instance field with the same name as in the superclass
- Declare new members that are not in the superclass
- Declare constructors that can invoke constructors in the superclass implicitly, or use the super() construct with the appropriate arguments to invoke them explicitly (p. 209)

Table 5.1 provides a comparison between overriding, hiding, and overloading of methods.

Table 5.1 *Overriding, Hiding, and Overloading of Methods*

Comparison criteria	Overriding of instance methods/Hiding of static methods	Overloading of instance and static methods
Method name	Must be the same.	Must be the same.
Argument list	Must be the same.	Must be different.

Table 5.1   *Overriding, Hiding, and Overloading of Methods (Continued)*

Comparison criteria	Overriding of instance methods/Hiding of static methods	Overloading of instance and static methods
Return type	Can be the same type or a covariant type.	Can be different.
throws clause	Can be restrictive about checked exceptions thrown. Must not throw new checked exceptions, but can include subclasses of exceptions thrown.	Can be different.
Accessibility	Can make it less restrictive, but not more restrictive.	Can be different.
final modifier	A final instance/static method cannot be overridden/hidden. Compile-time error if final instance/static method is defined in a subclass.	Can be overloaded in the same class or in a subclass.
private modifier	A private instance/static method cannot be overridden/hidden. No compile-time error if private instance/static method is defined in a subclass.	Can be overloaded only in the same class.
Declaration context	An instance/static method can only be overridden/hidden in a subclass.	An instance or static method can be overloaded in the same class or in a subclass.
Binding of method call/ polymorphic behavior	Calls to overridden instance methods are bound at runtime, and therefore exhibit polymorphic behavior. Calls to hidden static methods are bound at compile time and do *not* exhibit polymorphic behavior.	Calls are bound at compile time and do *not* exhibit polymorphic behavior.

5.2 **The Object Reference** super

The this reference can be used in non-static code to refer to the current object (§3.5, p. 106). The keyword super, in contrast, can be used in non-static code to access fields and invoke methods from the superclass. The keyword super provides a reference to the current object as an instance of its superclass. In method invocations with super, the method from the superclass is invoked regardless of what the actual type of the current object is or whether the current class overrides the method. This approach is typically used to invoke methods that are overridden and to access members that are hidden to the subclass. Unlike the this keyword, the super keyword cannot be used as an ordinary reference. For example, it cannot be assigned to other references or cast to other reference types.

Example 5.4 uses the superclass Light and its subclass TubeLight from Example 5.2, which are also shown in Figure 5.2. In Example 5.4, the class NeonLight extends the class TubeLight. The declaration of the method demonstrate() at (11) in the class NeonLight makes use of the super keyword to access members higher in its inheritance hierarchy. This is the case when the showSign() method is invoked at (12). This method is defined at (4) in the class Light, rather than in the direct superclass TubeLight of the subclass NeonLight. The overridden method energyCost() at (7) and its overloaded version at (8) in the class TubeLight are invoked, using the object reference super at (13) and (14), respectively.

The superclass Light has a field named lightType and a method named energyCost defined at (1) and (2), respectively. One might be tempted to use the syntax super.super.energyCost(20) in the subclass NeonLight to invoke this method, but this is not a valid construct. One might also be tempted to cast the this reference to the class Light and try again, as shown at (15). The output shows that the method energyCost() at (7) in the class TubeLight was executed, not the one from the class Light. The reason is that a cast simply changes the type of the reference (in this case to Light), not the class of the object (which is still NeonLight). Method invocation is determined by the class of the current object, resulting in the inherited method energyCost() in the class TubeLight being executed. There is no way to invoke the method energyCost() in the class Light from the subclass NeonLight, without declaring a reference of the type Light.

At (16), the keyword super is used to access the field lightType at (6) in the class TubeLight, but the keyword super is redundant in this case. At (17), the field light-Type from the class Light is accessed successfully by casting the this reference, because it is the type of the reference that determines which field is accessed. From non-static code in a subclass, it is possible to directly access fields in a class higher in the inheritance hierarchy by casting the this reference. However, it is futile to cast the this reference to invoke instance methods in a class higher in the inheritance hierarchy, as illustrated earlier for the overridden method energyCost().

Finally, the calls to the static methods at (18) and (19) using the super and this references, respectively, exhibit runtime behavior analogous to accessing fields, as discussed previously.

Example 5.4   *Using the* super *Keyword*

```java
// File: Client3.java
//Exceptions
class InvalidHoursException extends Exception {}
class NegativeHoursException extends InvalidHoursException {}
class ZeroHoursException extends InvalidHoursException {}

class Light {

  protected String lightType = "Generic Light";   // (1) Instance field

  protected double energyCost(int noOfHours)       // (2) Instance method
      throws InvalidHoursException {
    System.out.print(">> Light.energyCost(int): ");
    if (noOfHours < 0)
      throw new NegativeHoursException();
    double cost = 00.20 * noOfHours;
    System.out.println("Energy cost for " + lightType + ": " + cost);
    return cost;
  }

  public Light makeInstance() {                    // (3) Instance method
    System.out.print(">> Light.makeInstance(): ");
    return new Light();
  }

  public void showSign() {                         // (4) Instance method
    System.out.print(">> Light.showSign(): ");
    System.out.println("Let there be light!");
  }

  public static void printLightType() {            // (5) Static method
    System.out.print(">> Static Light.printLightType(): ");
    System.out.println("Generic Light");
  }
}
//_____
class TubeLight extends Light {

  public static String lightType = "Tube Light";   // (6) Hiding field at (1).

  @Override
  public double energyCost(final int noOfHours)    // (7) Overriding instance
      throws ZeroHoursException {                  //        method at (2).
    System.out.print(">> TubeLight.energyCost(int): ");
    if (noOfHours == 0)
      throw new ZeroHoursException();
    double cost = 00.10 * noOfHours;
    System.out.println("Energy cost for " + lightType + ": " + cost);
    return cost;
  }

  public double energyCost() {            // (8) Overloading method at (7).
    System.out.print(">> TubeLight.energyCost(): ");
```

```java
      double flatrate = 20.00;
      System.out.println("Energy cost for " + lightType + ": " + flatrate);
      return flatrate;
    }

    @Override
    public TubeLight makeInstance() {      // (9) Overriding instance method at (3).
      System.out.print(">> TubeLight.makeInstance(): ");
      return new TubeLight();
    }

    public static void printLightType() { // (10) Hiding static method at (5).
      System.out.print(">> Static TubeLight.printLightType(): ");
      System.out.println(lightType);
    }
  }
//_____
class NeonLight extends TubeLight {
  // ...
  public void demonstrate()                        // (11)
      throws InvalidHoursException {
    super.showSign();                              // (12) Invokes method at (4)
    super.energyCost(50);                          // (13) Invokes method at (7)
    super.energyCost();                            // (14) Invokes method at (8)

    ((Light) this).energyCost(50);                 // (15) Invokes method at (7)

    System.out.println(super.lightType);           // (16) Accesses field at (6)
    System.out.println(((Light) this).lightType);  // (17) Accesses field at (1)

    super.printLightType();                        // (18) Invokes method at (10)
    ((Light) this).printLightType();               // (19) Invokes method at (5)
  }
}
//_____
public class Client3 {
  public static void main(String[] args)
      throws InvalidHoursException {
    NeonLight neonRef = new NeonLight();
    neonRef.demonstrate();
  }
}
```

Output from the program:

```
>> Light.showSign(): Let there be light!
>> TubeLight.energyCost(int): Energy cost for Tube Light: 5.0
>> TubeLight.energyCost(): Energy cost for Tube Light: 20.0
>> TubeLight.energyCost(int): Energy cost for Tube Light: 5.0
Tube Light
Generic Light
>> Static TubeLight.printLightType(): Tube Light
>> Static Light.printLightType(): Generic Light
```

5.3 Chaining Constructors Using `this()` and `super()`

A basic understanding of constructors (§3.7, p. 109) is beneficent for the discussion in this section.

The `this()` Constructor Call

Constructors cannot be inherited or overridden. They can be overloaded, but only in the same class. Since a constructor always has the same name as the class, each parameter list must be different when defining more than one constructor for a class. In Example 5.5, the class `Light` has three overloaded constructors. In the constructor at (3), the `this` reference is used to access the fields shadowed by the parameters. In the `main()` method at (4), the appropriate constructor is invoked depending on the arguments in the constructor call, as illustrated by the program output.

Example 5.5 *Constructor Overloading*

```
// File: DemoConstructorCall.java
class Light {
  // Fields:
  private int    noOfWatts;     // wattage
  private boolean indicator;    // on or off
  private String  location;     // placement

  // Constructors:
  Light() {                                    // (1) No-argument constructor
    noOfWatts = 0;
    indicator = false;
    location  = "X";
    System.out.println("Returning from no-argument constructor no. 1.");
  }
  Light(int watts, boolean onOffState) {                      // (2)
    noOfWatts = watts;
    indicator = onOffState;
    location  = "X";
    System.out.println("Returning from constructor no. 2.");
  }
  Light(int noOfWatts, boolean indicator, String location) {  // (3)
    this.noOfWatts = noOfWatts;
    this.indicator = indicator;
    this.location  = location;
    System.out.println("Returning from constructor no. 3.");
  }
}
//_____
public class DemoConstructorCall {
  public static void main(String[] args) {                   // (4)
    System.out.println("Creating Light object no. 1.");
    Light light1 = new Light();
    System.out.println("Creating Light object no. 2.");
    Light light2 = new Light(250, true);
```

```
        System.out.println("Creating Light object no. 3.");
        Light light3 = new Light(250, true, "attic");
    }
}
```

Output from the program:

```
Creating Light object no. 1.
Returning from no-argument constructor no. 1.
Creating Light object no. 2.
Returning from constructor no. 2.
Creating Light object no. 3.
Returning from constructor no. 3.
```

Example 5.6 illustrates the use of the this() construct, which is used to implement *local chaining* of constructors in the class when an instance of the class is created. The first two constructors at (1) and (2) from Example 5.5 have been rewritten using the this() construct in Example 5.6 at (1) and (2), respectively. The this() construct can be regarded as being locally overloaded, since its parameters (and hence its signature) can vary, as shown in the body of the constructors at (1) and (2). The this() call invokes the local constructor with the corresponding parameter list. In the main() method at (4), the appropriate constructor is invoked depending on the arguments in the constructor call when each of the three Light objects are created. Calling the no-argument constructor at (1) to create a Light object results in the constructors at (2) and (3) being executed as well. This is confirmed by the output from the program. In this case, the output shows that the constructor at (3) completed first, followed by the constructor at (2), and finally by the no-argument constructor at (1) that was called first. Bearing in mind the definition of the constructors, the constructors are invoked in the *reverse* order; that is, invocation of the no-argument constructor immediately leads to invocation of the constructor at (2) by the call this(0, false), and its invocation leads to the constructor at (3) being called immediately by the call this(watt, ind, "X"), with the completion of the execution in the reverse order of their invocation. Similarly, calling the constructor at (2) to create an instance of the Light class results in the constructor at (3) being executed as well.

If the this() call is specified, it must occur as the *first* statement in a constructor. The this() call can be followed by any other relevant code. This restriction is due to Java's handling of constructor invocation in the superclass when an object of the subclass is created. This mechanism is explained in the next subsection.

Example 5.6   *The* this() *Constructor Call*

```
// File: DemoThisCall.java
class Light {
// Fields:
  private int     noOfWatts;
  private boolean indicator;
  private String  location;
```

```
      // Constructors:
      Light() {                                     // (1) No-argument constructor
        this(0, false);
        System.out.println("Returning from no-argument constructor no. 1.");
      }
      Light(int watt, boolean ind) {                // (2)
        this(watt, ind, "X");
        System.out.println("Returning from constructor no. 2.");
      }
      Light(int noOfWatts, boolean indicator, String location) { // (3)
        this.noOfWatts = noOfWatts;
        this.indicator = indicator;
        this.location  = location;
        System.out.println("Returning from constructor no. 3.");
      }
    }
    //_____
    public class DemoThisCall {
      public static void main(String[] args) {              // (4)
        System.out.println("Creating Light object no. 1.");
        Light light1 = new Light();                         // (5)
        System.out.println("Creating Light object no. 2.");
        Light light2 = new Light(250, true);                // (6)
        System.out.println("Creating Light object no. 3.");
        Light light3 = new Light(250, true, "attic");       // (7)
      }
    }
```

Output from the program:

```
Creating Light object no. 1.
Returning from constructor no. 3.
Returning from constructor no. 2.
Returning from no-argument constructor no. 1.
Creating Light object no. 2.
Returning from constructor no. 3.
Returning from constructor no. 2.
Creating Light object no. 3.
Returning from constructor no. 3.
```

The super() Constructor Call

The constructor call super() is used in a subclass constructor to invoke a constructor in the *direct* superclass. This allows the subclass to influence the initialization of its inherited state when an object of the subclass is created. A super() call in the constructor of a subclass will result in the execution of the relevant constructor from the superclass, based on the signature of the call. Since the superclass name is known in the subclass declaration, the compiler can determine the superclass constructor invoked from the signature of the parameter list.

A constructor in a subclass can access the class's inherited members by their simple names. The keyword super can also be used in a subclass constructor to access

inherited members via its superclass. One might be tempted to use the super keyword in a constructor to specify initial values for inherited fields. However, the
super() construct provides a better solution to initialize the inherited state.

In Example 5.7, the constructor at (3) of the class Light has a super() call (with no
arguments) at (4). Although the constructor is not strictly necessary, as the compiler
will insert one—as explained later—it is included here for expositional purposes.
The constructor at (6) of the class TubeLight has a super() call (with three arguments) at (7). This super() call will match the constructor at (3) of the superclass
Light. This is evident from the program output.

Example 5.7   *The* super() *Constructor Call*

```java
// File: ChainingConstructors.java
class Light {
  // Fields:
  private int     noOfWatts;
  private boolean indicator;
  private String  location;

  // Constructors:
  Light() {                                   // (1) No-argument constructor
    this(0, false);
    System.out.println(
    "Returning from no-argument constructor no. 1 in class Light");
  }
  Light(int watt, boolean ind) {                            // (2)
    this(watt, ind, "X");
    System.out.println(
    "Returning from constructor no. 2 in class Light");
  }
  Light(int noOfWatts, boolean indicator, String location) {  // (3)
    super();                                                  // (4)
    this.noOfWatts = noOfWatts;
    this.indicator = indicator;
    this.location  = location;
    System.out.println(
        "Returning from constructor no. 3 in class Light");
  }
}
//_____
class TubeLight extends Light {
  // Instance variables:
  private int tubeLength;
  private int colorNo;

  // Constructors:
  TubeLight(int tubeLength, int colorNo) {                    // (5)
    this(tubeLength, colorNo, 100, true, "Unknown");
    System.out.println(
        "Returning from constructor no. 1 in class TubeLight");
  }
  TubeLight(int tubeLength, int colorNo, int noOfWatts,
          boolean indicator, String location) {              // (6)
```

```
        super(noOfWatts, indicator, location);                    // (7)
        this.tubeLength = tubeLength;
        this.colorNo    = colorNo;
        System.out.println(
                "Returning from constructor no. 2 in class TubeLight");
    }
}
//_____
public class ChainingConstructors {
    public static void main(String[] args) {
        System.out.println("Creating a TubeLight object.");
        TubeLight tubeLightRef = new TubeLight(20, 5);            // (8)
    }
}
```

Output from the program:

```
Creating a TubeLight object.
Returning from constructor no. 3 in class Light
Returning from constructor no. 2 in class TubeLight
Returning from constructor no. 1 in class TubeLight
```

The super() construct has the same restrictions as the this() construct: If used, the super() call must occur as the *first* statement in a constructor, and it can only be used in a constructor declaration. This implies that this() and super() calls cannot both occur in the same constructor. The this() construct is used to *chain* constructors in the *same* class. The constructor at the end of such a chain can invoke a superclass constructor using the super() construct. Just as the this() construct leads to chaining of constructors in the same class, so the super() construct leads to chaining of subclass constructors to superclass constructors. This chaining behavior guarantees that all superclass constructors are called, starting with the constructor of the class being instantiated, all the way to the top of the inheritance hierarchy, which is always the Object class. Note that the body of the constructor is executed in the reverse order to the call order, as the super() call can occur only as the first statement in a constructor. This order of execution ensures that the constructor from the Object class is completed first, followed by the constructors in the other classes down to the class being instantiated in the inheritance hierarchy. This is called (subclass–superclass) *constructor chaining*. The output from Example 5.7 clearly illustrates this chain of events when an object of the class TubeLight is created.

If a constructor at the end of a this() chain (which may not be a chain at all if no this() call is invoked) does not have an explicit call to super(), the call super() (without the parameters) is implicitly inserted by the compiler to invoke the no-argument constructor of the superclass. In other words, if a constructor has neither a this() call nor a super() call as its first statement, the compiler inserts a super() call to the no-argument constructor in the superclass. The code

```
class A {
  A() {}                    // No-argument constructor.
  // ...
}
```

```
class B extends A {    // No constructors.
  // ...
}
```

is equivalent to

```
class A {
  A() { super(); }    // (1) Call to no-argument superclass constructor inserted.
  // ...
}

class B extends A {
  B() { super(); }    // (2) Default constructor inserted.
  // ...
}
```

where the compiler inserts a super() call in the no-argument constructor for class A at (1) and inserts the default constructor for class B at (2). The super() call at (2) will result in a call to the no-argument constructor in A at (1), and the super() call at (1) will result in a call to the no-argument constructor in the superclass of A—that is, the Object class.

If a superclass defines just non-zero argument constructors (i.e., only constructors with parameters), its subclasses cannot rely on the implicit super() call being inserted. This will be flagged as a compile-time error. The subclasses must then explicitly call a superclass constructor, using the super() construct with the right arguments.

```
class NeonLight extends TubeLight {
  // Field
  private String sign;

  NeonLight() {                          // (1)
    super(10, 2, 100, true, "Roof-top"); // (2) Cannot be commented out.
    sign = "All will be revealed!";
  }
  // ...
}
```

The preceding declaration of the subclass NeonLight provides a no-argument constructor at (1). The call of the constructor at (2) in the superclass TubeLight cannot be omitted. If it is omitted, any insertion of a super() call (with no arguments) in this constructor will try to match a no-argument constructor in the superclass Tube-Light, which provides only non-zero argument constructors. The class NeonLight will not compile unless an explicit valid super() call is inserted at (2).

If the superclass provides just non-zero argument constructors (i.e., it does not have a no-argument constructor), this has implications for its subclasses. A subclass that relies on its default constructor will fail to compile because the default constructor of the subclass will attempt to call the (nonexistent) no-argument constructor in the superclass. A constructor in a subclass must explicitly use the super() call, with the appropriate arguments, to invoke a non-zero argument constructor in the superclass. This call is necessary because the constructor in the subclass cannot rely on an implicit super() call to the no-argument constructor in the superclass.

Review Questions

5.1   Given the following class declarations:

```java
// Classes
class Foo {
  private int i;
  public void f() { /* ... */ }
  public void g() { /* ... */ }
}

class Bar extends Foo {
  public int j;
  public void g() { /* ... */ }
}

public class Main {
  public static void main(String[] args) {
    Foo a = new Bar();
    Bar b = new Bar()
    // (1) INSERT STATEMENT HERE
  }
}
```

Which of the following statements can be inserted at (1) without causing a compile-time error?
Select the two correct answers.

(a) b.f();
(b) a.j = 5;
(c) a.g();
(d) b.i = 3;

5.2   Given the following code:

```java
class A {
  void doIt() {}
}

class B extends A {
  void doIt() {}
}

class C extends B {
  void doIt() {}
  void callUp() {
    // (1) INSERT EXPRESSION HERE
  }
}
```

insert the expression that would call the doIt() method in A.
Select the one correct answer.

(a) doIt();
(b) super.doIt();
(c) super.super.doIt();

(d) `this.super.doIt();`

(e) `A.this.doIt();`

(f) `((A) this).doIt();`

(g) It is not possible.

5.3   What would be the result of compiling and running the following program?

```
class A {
  int max(int x, int y) { (x>y) ? x : y; }
}

class B extends A {
  int max(int x, int y) { return super.max(y, x) - 10; }
}

class C extends B {
  int max(int x, int y) { return super.max(x+10, y+10); }

}

public class UserClass {
  public static void main(String[] args) {
    B b = new C();
    System.out.println(b.max(13, 29));
  }
}
```

Select the one correct answer.

(a) The code will fail to compile.

(b) The code will compile, but it will throw an exception at runtime.

(c) The code will compile and print 13 at runtime.

(d) The code will compile and print 23 at runtime.

(e) The code will compile and print 29 at runtime.

(f) The code will compile and print 39 at runtime.

5.4   What would be the result of compiling and running the following program?

```
class Vehicle {
  static public String getModelName() { return "Volvo"; }
  public long getRegNo() { return 12345; }
}

class Car extends Vehicle {
  static public String getModelName() { return "Toyota"; }
  public long getRegNo() { return 54321; }
}

public class TakeARide {
  public static void main(String[] args) {
    Car c = new Car();
    Vehicle v = c;

    System.out.println("|" + v.getModelName() + "|" + c.getModelName() +
                      "|" + v.getRegNo()     + "|" + c.getRegNo() + "|");
  }
}
```

Select the one correct answer.

(a) The code will fail to compile.
(b) The code will compile and print |Toyota|Volvo|12345|54321| at runtime.
(c) The code will compile and print |Volvo|Toyota|12345|54321| at runtime.
(d) The code will compile and print |Toyota|Toyota|12345|12345| at runtime.
(e) The code will compile and print |Volvo|Volvo|12345|54321| at runtime.
(f) The code will compile and print |Toyota|Toyota|12345|12345| at runtime.
(g) The code will compile and print |Volvo|Toyota|54321|54321| at runtime.

5.5 Which constructors can be inserted at (1) in MySub without causing a compile-time error?

```
class MySuper {
  int number;
  MySuper(int i) { number = i; }
}

class MySub extends MySuper {
  int count;
  MySub(int count, int num) {
    super(num);
    this.count = count;
  }

  // (1) INSERT CONSTRUCTOR HERE
}
```

Select the one correct answer.

(a) MySub() {}
(b) MySub(int count) { this.count = count; }
(c) MySub(int count) { super(); this.count = count; }
(d) MySub(int count) { this.count = count; super(count); }
(e) MySub(int count) { this(count, count); }
(f) MySub(int count) { super(count); this(count, 0); }

5.6 Which of the following statements is true?
Select the one correct answer.

(a) A super() or this() call must always be provided explicitly as the first statement in the body of a constructor.
(b) If both a subclass and its superclass do not have any declared constructors, the implicit default constructor of the subclass will call super() when run.
(c) If neither super() nor this() is specified as the first statement in the body of a constructor, this() will implicitly be inserted as the first statement.
(d) If super() is the first statement in the body of a constructor, this() can be declared as the second statement.
(e) Calling super() as the first statement in the body of a constructor of a subclass will always work, since all superclasses have a default constructor.

5.7   What will the following program print when run?

```java
public class MyClass {
  public static void main(String[] args) {
    B b = new B("Test");
  }
}

class A {
  A() { this("1", "2"); }

  A(String s, String t) { this(s + t); }

  A(String s) { System.out.println(s); }
}

class B extends A {
  B(String s) { System.out.println(s); }

  B(String s, String t) { this(t + s + "3"); }

  B() { super("4"); };
}
```

Select the one correct answer.

(a) It will just print Test.
(b) It will print Test followed by Test.
(c) It will print 123 followed by Test.
(d) It will print 12 followed by Test.
(e) It will print 4 followed by Test.

5.4   Abstract Classes and Methods

The keyword abstract is used in the following contexts in Java:

- Declaring abstract classes
- Declaring abstract methods in classes (p. 224), in interfaces (p. 240), and in enum types (p. 294)

Abstract Classes

A *concrete* class is one that defines, by virtue of its public methods, a *contract* for services it guarantees its clients and provides the *implementation for all the methods* necessary to fulfill that contract. Clients can readily instantiate a concrete class and use its objects.

In certain cases, a class might want to define the contract for the services, but only provide *partial implementation* for its contract. Such a design decision might be necessary if the abstraction the class represents is so general that certain aspects need to be specialized by subclasses to be of practical use, but at the same time guarantee that these *will* be implemented by the subclasses. This design strategy can be implemented by using *abstract classes*. Clients cannot instantiate an abstract class, but now its concrete subclasses must be instantiated to provide the necessary objects.

The class Vehicle might be declared as an abstract class with a partially implemented contract to represent the general abstraction of a vehicle, as creating instances of the class would not make much sense. Its non-abstract subclasses, like Car or Bus, would then provide the implementation necessary to fulfill the contract of the superclass Vehicle, making the abstraction more concrete and useful.

The Java SE Platform API contains many abstract classes. The abstract class java.lang.Number is the superclass of wrapper classes that represent numeric values as objects (§8.3, p. 434). The Java Collections Framework makes heavy use of abstract classes in implementing commonly used collection data structures (§15.1, p. 783).

Declaring an abstract Class

An abstract class is declared with the modifier abstract in its class header. In Example 5.8, the class Light at (1) is declared as an abstract class. It also declares an abstract method energyCost() at (2), which has no method body and is essentially a method header (p. 224).

```
abstract class Light {                                   // (1) Abstract class
    //...
    // Abstract instance method:
    protected abstract double energyCost(int noOfHours)   // (2) Method header
        throws InvalidHoursException;                     // No method body
}
```

If a class has one or more abstract methods, it must be declared as abstract, as it is *incomplete*. In Example 5.8, if the abstract keyword is omitted from the header of the class Light at (1), the compiler will issue an error, as the class declares an abstract method and is therefore incomplete.

Like a normal class, an abstract class can declare class members, constructors, and initializers. The abstract class Light in Example 5.8 declares three instance fields—one non-zero argument constructor and three instance methods—in addition to the abstract method at (2).

A class that is declared absract cannot be instantiated, regardless of whether it has abstract methods or not.

```
Light porchLight = new Light(21, true, "Porch");    // (5) Compile-time error!
```

The UML class diagram for the inheritance relationship in Example 5.8 is depicted in Figure 5.3. Note that an abstract class name and an abstract method name are shown in *italics* to distinguish them from concrete classes and methods.

Figure 5.3   *Class Diagram for Example 5.8*

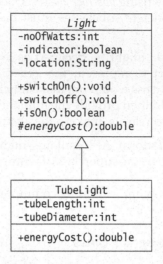

Extending an abstract *Class*

A class might choose the design strategy with abstract methods to dictate certain behavior, but allow its subclasses the freedom to provide the relevant implementation. An abstract class forces its subclasses to provide the subclass-specific functionality stipulated by its abstract methods, which is needed to fully implement its abstraction. In other words, subclasses of the abstract class have to take a stand and provide implementations of any inherited abstract methods before objects can be created. In Example 5.8, since the class Light is abstract, it forces its *concrete* (i.e., non-abstract) subclass to provide an implementation for the abstract method energyCost(). The concrete subclass TubeLight provides an implementation for this method at (3).

```
class TubeLight extends Light {
  // ...
  // Implementation of the abstract method from the superclass.
  @Override public double energyCost(int noOfHours) {      // (3)
    return  0.15 * noOfHours;
  }
}
```

Creating an object of a subclass results in the fields of all its superclasses, whether these classes are abstract or not, to be created and initialized—that is, they *exist* in the subclass object. As with normal classes, the inheritance relationship between classes allows references of the abstract superclass type to be declared and used to refer to objects of their subclasses—that is, these references exhibit polymorphic behavior (p. 278).

In Example 5.8, the class Factory creates an instance of the subclass TubeLight at (6). The private fields declared in the abstract superclass Light can be accessed indirectly by invoking the public methods it provides on objects of the subclass TubeLight. The subclass reference cellarLight is used to invoke public methods in the superclass in the following code:

```
TubeLight cellarLight = new TubeLight(18, true, "Cellar", 590, 26);  // (6)
cellarLight.switchOff();                          // Method in superclass
System.out.println(cellarLight.isOn());           // Method in superclass: false
```

The subclass reference cellarLight of course can be used to invoke subclass-specific methods, as shown at (7).

```
System.out.printf("Energy cost ($): %2.2f%n",
    cellarLight.energyCost(40));                  // (7) Using subclass reference
```

References of an abstract superclass can be declared and assigned reference values of its subclass objects, as shown at (8). Superclass references can be used to manipulate subclass objects, as shown at (9), where the energyCost() method from the subclass TubeLight is executed.

```
Light nightLight = new TubeLight(15, false, "Bedroom", 850, 15);    // (8)
System.out.printf("Energy cost ($): %2.2f%n",
    nightLight.energyCost(30));                   // (9) Using superclass reference
                                                  // Invokes method in subclass
                                                  // Requires throws clause at (4)
```

Note that using the subclass reference cellarLight at (7) to invoke the method energyCost() cannot throw a checked exception, as readily seen from its declaration in the subclass TubeLight. However, using the superclass reference nightLight at (9) to invoke the method energyCost() can throw a checked exception, as seen from the method declaration in the superclass Light. At compile time, only the static type of the reference is known, namely Light, and the method energyCost() in this class throws a checked InvalidHoursException (§7.2, p. 374). The throws clause in the main() method at (4) specifies this exception—otherwise, the code will not compile.

In the code below, the class AbstractArt at (2) must be declared as abstract as it does not implement the abstract method paint() from its superclass Art at (1).

```
abstract class Art { abstract void paint(); }          // (1) Abstract class

abstract class AbstractArt extends Art {}              // (2) Must be abstract

class MinimalistArt extends AbstractArt {              // (3) Concrete class
  @Override void paint() { System.out.println(":-)"); } // (4) Concrete method
}

abstract class PostModernMinimalistArt
                          extends MinimalistArt { // (5) Abstract class
  @Override void paint() { System.out.println(":-("); } // (6) Concrete method
                                                  //      overrides (4)
}

class ArtsyFartsy extends PostModernMinimalistArt {}   // (7) Concrete class
```

Analogous to a normal class, an abstract class can only extend a single non-final class that can be either concrete or abstract. In the code above, the abstract class AbstractArt at (2) extends the abstract class Art, and the abstract class PostModern-MinimalistArt at (5) extends the concrete class MinimalistArt.

A non-final concrete class, which by definition has no abstract methods, can be *considered incomplete* by declaring it as abstract. The PostModernMinimalistArt class at (5) is declared abstract and considered incomplete, even though it is concrete. It cannot be instantiated. However, its subclass ArtsyFartsy at (7) is a concrete class, as it inherits the concrete method paint() from its abstract superclass PostModern-MinimalistArt.

A class cannot be declared both final and abstract—that would be a contradiction in terms: A final class cannot be extended, but an abstract class is incomplete or considered to be incomplete and must be extended.

An abstract class should not be used to implement a class that cannot be instantiated. The recommended practice is to only provide a zero-argument constructor that is private, thus making sure that it is never invoked in the class.

In many ways abstract classes and interfaces are similar, and interfaces can be used with advantage in many cases. However, if private state should be maintained with instance members, then abstract classes are preferred, as interfaces do not have any notion of state.

Analogous to a normal class, an abstract class can implement multiple interfaces (p. 240).

Example 5.8   *Using Abstract Classes*

```java
// File: Factory.java
// Checked exceptions:
class InvalidHoursException extends Exception {}
class NegativeHoursException extends InvalidHoursException {}
class ZeroHoursException extends InvalidHoursException {}

abstract class Light {                                            // (1) Abstract class
  // Fields:
  private int     noOfWatts;      // Wattage
  private boolean indicator;      // On or off
  private String  location;       // Placement

  // Non-zero argument constructor:
  Light(int noOfWatts, boolean indicator, String location) {
    this.noOfWatts = noOfWatts;
    this.indicator = indicator;
    this.location  = location;
  }

  // Instance methods:
  public void switchOn()  { indicator = true; }
```

```java
        public void switchOff() { indicator = false; }
        public boolean isOn()    { return indicator; }

        // Abstract instance method:
        protected abstract double energyCost(int noOfHours)       // (2) Method header
            throws InvalidHoursException;                         // No method body
    }
//_____
class TubeLight extends Light {
    // Instance fields:
    private int tubeLength;                                       // millimeters
    private int tubeDiameter;                                     // millimeters

    // Non-zero argument constructor
    TubeLight(int noOfWatts, boolean indicator, String location,
                int tubeLength, int tubeDiameter) {
        super(noOfWatts, indicator, location);  // Calling constructor in superclass.
        this.tubeLength = tubeLength;
        this.tubeDiameter = tubeDiameter;
    }

    // Implementation of the abstract method from the superclass.
    @Override public double energyCost(int noOfHours) {        // (3)
        return  0.15 * noOfHours;
    }
}
//_____
public class Factory {
    public static void main(String[] args) throws InvalidHoursException {  // (4)
//   Light porchLight = new Light(21, true, "Porch");       // (5) Compile-time error!
     TubeLight cellarLight = new TubeLight(18, true, "Cellar", 590, 26);  // (6)
     cellarLight.switchOff();
     System.out.println(cellarLight.isOn());          // false
     System.out.printf("Energy cost ($): %2.2f%n",
         cellarLight.energyCost(40));                 // (7) Using subclass reference
     Light nightLight = new TubeLight(15, false, "Bedroom", 850, 15);      // (8)
     System.out.printf("Energy cost ($): %2.2f%n",
         nightLight.energyCost(30));                  // (9) Using superclass reference
                                                      // Invokes method in subclass
                                                      // Requires throws clause in (4)

    }
}
```

Output from the program:

```
false
Energy cost ($): 6.00
Energy cost ($): 4.50
```

Abstract Methods in Classes

In this subsection we discuss in more detail declaring and overriding abstract methods in classes.

Declaring an abstract Method

An abstract method in an abstract class has the following syntax:

access_modifier abstract *return_type method_name (formal_parameter_list)*
throws_clause;

An abstract method does not have an implementation; that is, no method body is defined for an abstract method, and only the *method header* is provided in the class declaration. The keyword abstract is mandatory in the header of an abstract method declared in a class. Its class is then incomplete and must be explicitly declared as abstract. Subclasses of an abstract class must then override the abstract method to provide the method implementation; otherwise, they must also be declared as abstract.

Overriding an abstract Method

When overriding an abstract method from the superclass, the notation @Override should always be used in the overriding method in the subclass. The compiler will issue an error if the override criteria are not satisfied.

The accessibility of an abstract method declared in a top-level class cannot be private, as subclasses would not be able to override the method and provide an implementation. Thus an abstract method in a top-level class can only have public, protected, or package accessibility.

In Example 5.8, the abstract instance method in the abstract superclass Light has the following declaration:

```
protected abstract double energyCost(int noOfHours)     // (2) Method header
    throws InvalidHoursException;                        // No method body
```

It has protected access and has type double as the return type. Its method signature is energyCost(int), and it throws the checked InvalidHoursException.

The implementation of the abstract method in the subclass TubeLight has the following declaration:

```
@Override public double energyCost(int noOfHours) {      // (3)
    return  0.15 * noOfHours;
}
```

It has public access and has type double as the return type. Its method signature is energyCost(int), and it has no throws clause. Widening the access to public access and throwing no checked exceptions are allowed according to the override criteria.

Since an abstract method must be overridden to provide an implementation, only an instance method can be declared as abstract. Since static methods cannot be overridden, declaring an abstract static method makes no sense, and the compiler will report an error.

An abstract method can be overloaded just like a normal method. The following method declaration in either the superclass or the subclass overloads the method named energyCost, as it has a different signature: energyCost().

```
public double energyCost() {          // Overloaded
    return 1.75;
}
```

If an attempt to override or overload an abstract method fails, the compiler will issue an error. If either of these two methods is declared in a subclass of the Light class, the compiler will issue an error.

```
@Override
double energyCost(int numOfHours) {    // Not overridden! Narrows accessibility!
    return 2.0 * numOfHours;

}

public Double energyCost(int numOfHours) {  // Not overloaded! Duplicate method!
    return 3.5 * numOfHours;
}
```

An abstract method or a non-final concrete method in a class can be overridden by an abstract method in a subclass. This is governed by the same rules for method overriding.

A method cannot be both final and abstract—that would be a contradiction in terms: A final method cannot be overridden, but an abstract method must be overridden to provide an implementation.

For a discussion of abstract methods in top-level interfaces, see §5.6, p. 240. Abstract methods can also be declared in an enum type, if the enum type contains constant-specific class bodies that implement these methods (p. 294).

5.5 Final Declarations

The keyword final can be used in the following contexts in Java:

- Declaring final classes (p. 225)
- Declaring final members in classes (p. 226), and in enum types (p. 294)
- Declaring final local variables in methods and blocks (p. 231)
- Declaring final static variables in interfaces (p. 254)

Final Classes

A class can be declared final to indicate that it cannot be extended—that is, one cannot define subclasses of a final class. In other words, the class behavior cannot be changed by extending the class. This implies that one cannot override or hide any methods declared in such a class. Its methods behave as final methods (p. 226). A final class marks the lower boundary of its *implementation inheritance hierarchy*.

A *concrete* class is a class that has only *concrete* methods—that is, methods that are non-abstract, and therefore have an implementation. Only a concrete class can be declared final. If it is decided that the class TubeLight at (12) in Example 5.9 may not be extended, it can be declared final. Any attempt to specify the class name TubeLight in an extends clause will result in a compile-time error.

```
final class TubeLight extends Light {               // (12)
  // ...
}

class NeonLight extends TubeLight {                 // Compile-time error!
  // ...
}
```

A final class must be complete, whereas an abstract class is considered incomplete. Classes, therefore, cannot be both final and abstract at the same time. Interfaces are implicitly abstract, and therefore cannot be declared as final. A final class and an interface with only abstract methods represent two diametrical strategies when it comes to providing an implementation: the former with all the methods implemented and the latter with none. An abstract class or an interface with partial implementation represents a compromise between these two strategies.

The Java SE Platform API includes many final classes—for example, the java.lang.String class and the wrapper classes for primitive values.

Final Methods in Classes

A final method in a class is a *concrete* method (i.e., has an implementation) and cannot be overridden or hidden in any subclass. Any normal class can declare a final method. The class need not be declared final.

In Example 5.9, the non-final class Light defines the final method setWatts() at (10).

```
class Light {                                       // (1)
  // ...
  public final void setWatts(int watt) {            // (10) Final instance method
    noOfWatts = watt;
  }
}
```

The subclass TubeLight attempts to override the final method setWatts() from the superclass Light at (14), which is not permitted.

```
class TubeLight extends Light {                     // (12)
  // ...
  @Override
  public void setWatts(int watt) {    // (14) Cannot override final method at (10)!
    noOfWatts = 2*watt;
  }
}
```

A call to a final method is bound at compile time; as such, a method cannot be overridden by a subclass and therefore there is no dynamic lookup to perform at runtime. A method that is declared final allows the compiler to do code optimization by replacing its method call with the code of its method body, a technique called *inlining*. Use of the final keyword for exceptional performance enhancement is not recommended, as the compiler is too smart to fall for that trick.

A subclass cannot override or hide a private method from its superclass. However, it can define a new method using the same method signature as the private method, without regard to the other criteria for overriding: the return type and the throws clause. Defining a new method using the same method signature is *not* possible with a final method which cannot be overridden or hidden. Declaring a private method as final in addition is redundant.

Although a constructor cannot be overridden, it also *cannot* be declared final.

The java.lang.Object class—the superclass of all classes—defines a number of final methods (notify(), notifyAll(), and wait()—mostly to synchronize the running of threads) that all objects inherit, but cannot override.

Example 5.9 *Using the* final *Modifier*

```
import java.util.Arrays;
import static java.lang.System.out;

class Light {                                    // (1)
  // Static final variables:
  public static final double KWH_PRICE = 3.25;   // (2) Constant static variable
  public static final String MANUFACTURER;       // (3) Blank final static field

  static {                                       // Static initializer block
    MANUFACTURER = "Ozam";                       // (4) Initializes (3)
  }

  // Instance variables:
  int noOfWatts;                                 // (5)
  final String color;                            // (6) Blank final instance field
  final String energyRating;                     // (7) Blank final instance field

  {                                              // Instance initializer block
    color = "off white";                         // (8) Initializes (6)
  }

  // Constructor:
  Light() {
    energyRating = "A++";                        // (9) Initializes (7)
  }

  public final void setWatts(int watt) {         // (10) Final instance method
    this.noOfWatts = watt;
  }
```

```
      public static void setKWH(double rate) {
//    KWH_PRICE = rate;                                  // (11) Not OK. Final field.
    }
}
//_____
class TubeLight extends Light {                          // (12)
    static StringBuilder color = new StringBuilder("green");      // (13) Hiding (6)

//@Override
//public void setWatts(int watt) {    // (14) Cannot override final method at (10)!
//    noOfWatts = 2*watt;
//}
}
//_____
public class Warehouse {
    public static void main(final String[] args) { // (15) Final parameter

        final Light workLight = new Light(); // (16) Non-blank final local variable.
        workLight.setWatts(100);             // (17) OK. Changing object state.
//      workLight.color = "pink";            // (18) Not OK. Final instance field.
//      workLight = new Light();             // (19) Not OK. Changing final reference.

        final Light alarmLight;              // (20) Blank final local variable.
//      alarmLight.setWatts(200);            // (21) Not OK. Not initialized.

        Light carLight;                      // (22) Non-final local variable.
//      carLight.setWatts(10);               // (23) Not OK. Not initialized.

        out.println("Accessing final static fields in class Light:");
        out.println("KWH_PRICE:    " + Light.KWH_PRICE);
        out.println("MANUFACTURER: " + Light.MANUFACTURER);

        out.println("Accessing final instance fields in an object of class Light:");
        out.println("noOfWatts:    " + workLight.noOfWatts);
        out.println("color:        " + workLight.color);
        out.println("energyRating: " + workLight.energyRating);

        out.println("Fun with final parameter args:");
        out.println(Arrays.toString(args));  // Print array.
        out.println("args length: " + args.length);
        args[0] = "1";                       // (24) OK. Modifying array state.
        out.println(Arrays.toString(args));  // Print array.
//      args = null;                         // (25) Not OK. Final parameter.
//      args.length = 10;                    // (26) Not OK. Final instance field.
    }
}
```

Output from the program when run with the following command:

```
>java Warehouse One Two Three
Accessing final static fields in class Light:
KWH_PRICE:    3.25
MANUFACTURER: Ozam
Accessing final instance fields in an object of class Light:
noOfWatts:    100
color:        off white
```

```
energyRating: A++
Fun with final parameter args:
[One, Two, Three]
args length: 3
[1, Two, Three]
```

Final Variables

A final *variable* is a variable whose value cannot be changed during its lifetime once it has been initialized. A final variable is declared with the keyword final in its declaration. Any attempt to reassign a value will result in a compile-time error.

Declaring a variable as final has the following implications:

- A final variable of a primitive data type cannot change its value once it has been initialized.
- A final variable of a reference type cannot change its reference value once it has been initialized. This effectively means that a final reference will always refer to the same object. However, the keyword final has no bearing on whether the *state of the object* denoted by the reference can be changed.
- The compiler may perform code optimizations for final variables, as certain assumptions can be made about such code.

For all paths of execution through the code, the compiler checks that a final variable is assigned only once before it is accessed, and when in doubt, the compiler issues an error (p. 232).

A *blank* final *variable* is a final variable whose declaration does not specify an initializer expression.

A *constant variable* is a final variable of either a primitive type or type String that is initialized with a *constant expression*. Constant variables can be used as case labels of a switch statement.

We distinguish between two kinds of final variables: final *fields* that are members in a class declaration and final *local variables* that can be declared in methods and blocks. A final *field* is either static or non-static depending on whether it is declared as a static or non-static member in the class.

Example 5.9 provides examples of different kinds of final variables. The declarations from Example 5.9 are shown here.

```
class Light {                                 // (1)
  public static final double KWH_PRICE = 3.25;  // (2) Constant static variable
  public static final String MANUFACTURER;      // (3) Blank final static field

  int noOfWatts;                                // (5) Non-final instance field
  final String color;                           // (6) Blank final instance field
  final String energyRating;                    // (7) Blank final instance field
  // ...
}
```

```
public class Warehouse {
  public static void main(final String[] args) { // (15) Final parameter

    final Light workLight = new Light(); // (16) Non-blank final local variable.

    final Light alarmLight;              // (20) Blank final local variable.

    Light carLight;                      // (22) Non-final local variable.
    // ...
  }
}
```

In the next two subsections we elaborate on final fields in classes and final local variables that can be declared in methods and blocks.

Final Fields in Classes

A final field must be explicitly initialized only once with an initializer expression, either in its declaration or in an initializer block. A final instance field can also be initialized in a constructor. After the class completes initialization, the final static fields of the class are all guaranteed to be initialized. After a constructor completes execution, the final instance fields of the current object are all guaranteed to be initialized. The compiler ensures that the class provides the appropriate code to initialize the final fields.

In Example 5.9, the class Light defines two final static fields at (2) and (3). The field KWH_PRICE is a constant variable that is initialized by the constant expression 3.25 in the declaration at (2). The field MANUFACTURER is a blank final static field that is initialized in the static initializer block at (4). All static initializer blocks are executed at class initialization. Note that a blank final static field *must* be initialized in a static initializer block; otherwise, the compiler will issue an error. An attempt to change the value of the final static field KWH_PRICE at (11) in a method results in a compile-time error.

In Example 5.9, the class Light also defines two final instance fields at (6) and (7). The instance field color is a blank final instance field that is initialized in the instance initializer block at (8), and the instance field energyRating is a blank final instance field that is initialized in the constructor at (9). If either the assignment at (8) in the instance initializer block or the assignment at (9) in the constructor is removed, it will result in a compile-time error.

Note that a blank final instance field *must* be initialized either in an instance initializer block or in a constructor; otherwise, the code will not compile. Each time an object is created using the new operator with a constructor call, all instance initializer blocks are executed, but not necessarily all constructors, as this depends on constructor chaining. If the class has several constructors, code must make sure that a blank final instance field is initialized no matter which constructor is called to initialize the object.

Since final static fields are initialized at class initialization time and final instance fields are initialized at object creation time, the compiler will issue an error if an attempt is made to assign a value to a final field inside any method.

Analogous to a non-final field, a final field with the same name *can* be hidden in a subclass—in contrast to final methods that can neither be overridden nor hidden. In Example 5.9, the blank final instance field color of type String at (6) in class Light is hidden by the static field color of type StringBuilder at (13) in subclass TubeLight.

Fields that are final and static are commonly used to define *manifest constants* (also called *named constants*). For example, the minimum and maximum values of the numerical primitive types are defined by final static fields in the respective wrapper classes. The final static field Integer.MAX_VALUE defines the maximum int value. The field java.lang.System.out is a final static field. Fields defined in an interface are implicitly final static fields (p. 254), as are the enum constants of an enum type (p. 287).

Final Local Variables in Methods

A final local variable need not be initialized in its declaration—that is, it can be a blank final local variable—but it must be initialized in the code before it is accessed. However, the compiler does not complain as long as the local variable is not accessed—this is in contrast to final fields that must be explicitly assigned a value, whether they are accessed or not.

In Example 5.9, the main() method at (15) in the class Warehouse defines a final local reference workLight at (16). The state of the object denoted by the reference workLight is changed at (17), but an attempt to change the value of the final instance field color of this object at (18) does not succeed. The compiler also reports an error at (19), since the reference value of the final local variable work-Light cannot be changed. A blank final local reference alarmLight is declared at (20). The compiler reports an error when an attempt is made to use this reference at (21) before it is initialized. The non-final local reference carLight at (22) also cannot be accessed at (22) before it is initialized. However, note that the compiler does not complain as long as the local variables at (20) and (22) are not accessed.

```
   final Light workLight = new Light(); // (16) Final local variable.
   workLight.setWatts(100);             // (17) OK. Changing object state.
// workLight.color = "pink";           // (18) Not OK. Final instance field.
// workLight = new Light();            // (19) Not OK. Changing final reference.

   final Light alarmLight;              // (20) Blank final local variable.
// alarmLight.setWatts(200);           // (21) Not OK. Not initialized.

   Light carLight;                      // (22) Non-final local variable.
// carLight.setWatts(10);              // (23) Not OK. Not initialized.
```

Local variables in certain contexts are considered to be *implicitly declared* final: an exception parameter of a multi-catch clause (§7.6, p. 397) and a local variable that refers to a resource in a try-with-resources statement (§7.7, p. 407).

final **Parameters**

A formal parameter can be declared with the keyword final preceding the parameter declaration in the method header. A final parameter is a special case of a blank final local variable. It is initialized with the value of the corresponding argument in the method call, before the code in the body of the method is executed. Declaring parameters as final prevents their values from being changed inadvertently in the method. A formal parameter's declaration as final does not affect the caller's code.

In the declaration of the main() method at (15) in Example 5.9, the parameter args is declared as final. The array args will be initialized with the program arguments on the command line when execution starts.

```
public static void main(final String[] args) {  // (15) Final parameter
  // ...
  out.println("Fun with final parameter args:");
  out.println(Arrays.toString(args));          // (24) Print array.
  out.println("args length: " + args.length); // (25) Access final field
  args[0] = "1";                               // (26) OK. Modifying array state.
  out.println(Arrays.toString(args));          // Print array.
//args = null;                                 // (27) Not OK. Final parameter.
//args.length = 10;                            // (28) Not OK. Final instance field.
}
```

The state of the array object args is printed at (24). Its final field length is accessed at (25). The state of the args array is changed at (26), and is printed again. However, the compiler will not allow the reference value of the final parameter args to be changed at (27), nor will it allow the value of the final instance field args.length to be changed at (28).

Definite Assignment Analysis for Final Variables

The *name* of a final variable can occur in the following contexts: in its declaration when it is declared, in the context of an assignment when it is assigned a value, and in the context where its value is accessed in an expression.

The analysis performed by the compiler determines whether the blank final variable is initialized *before* its value is accessed. This involves checking whether a blank final variable has been assigned a value on any possible path of execution to where the value of the variable is accessed. In technical terms, this means a blank final variable must be *definitely assigned* before any access.

```
final int k;              // Declaration: blank final local variable
k = 10;                   // (1) Assignment
System.out.println(k);    // (2) Access: k is definitely assigned.

boolean status = true;    // Non-constant variable.
final int j;              // Declaration: blank final local variable
if (status) {             // (3) Value of conditional expression not evaluated
  j = 5;                  // (4) Conditional assignment
}
System.out.println(j);    // (5) Access: j is not definitely assigned!
```

The blank final local variable k is accessed at (2) after it has been assigned a value at (1). It is *definitely assigned* before access at (2). The situation is different at (5). The compiler can deduce that the blank final local variable j can be assigned a value in the if block, depending on the conditional expression in the if statement. In other words, the structure of the if statement is considered in the analysis, but not the non-constant conditional expression. The compiler cannot guarantee that the assignment at (4) will be executed. The conclusion being that the blank final local variable j is *not definitely assigned* before access at (5). The statement at (5) does not compile. However, if the conditional expression in the if statement at (3) is replaced with the boolean literal true, the compiler can determine that the assignment at (4) will be executed and the variable j at (5) becomes definitely assigned before access.

The flow analysis performed is conservative. The compiler does not always evaluate all expressions, particularly method calls. However, it does evaluate boolean-valued constant expressions, and it also takes into consideration the syntax of statements and expressions, including the use of the conditional operators !, &&, ||, and ? :.

For each assignment to a blank final variable, the compiler must also determine that it is assigned *exactly once*—in other words, it has not already been assigned a value. This means that, given an assignment to a blank final local variable, there should not be any other assignment to this variable on any possible path of execution prior to this assignment. In technical terms, this means a blank final variable must be *definitely unassigned* before any assignment.

```
int n = 5;
final int k;            // Declaration: blank final local variable
if (n >= 4) {           // (1) Value of conditional expression not evaluated
  k = 6;                // (2) Conditional assignment: k is definitely unassigned
}
k = 12;                 // (3) Assignment: k is not definitely unassigned!
System.out.println(k);  // (4) Access: k is definitely assigned
```

The blank final local variable k in the assignment at (2) is definitely unassigned, as there is no other assignment on a path of execution before this assignment. However, the variable k at (3) is *not* definitely unassigned, as the assignment at (2) in the if statement can be executed on a path of execution before the assignment at (3). The compiler reports that the variable k at (3) may already have been assigned a value. The assignment at (3) does not compile. Note that the variable k at (4) is definitely assigned before the access, because of the assignment at (3). Removing the assignment statement at (3) makes the variable k at (4) *not* definitely assigned, as in the previous example.

If the code is modified by replacing the if statement at (3) with an if-else statement, where the assignment at (3) is done in the else block, the variable k at (3) also becomes definitely unassigned—there is no assignment to the variable k before this assignment. Regardless of which assignment executes in the if-else statement, the variable k at (4) is definitely assigned before access.

```
int n = 5;
final int k;              // Declaration: blank final local variable
if (n >= 4) {             // (1) Value of conditional expression not evaluated
  k = 6;                  // (2) Conditional assignment: k is definitely unassigned
} else {
  k = 12;                 // (3) Conditional assignment: k is definitely unassigned
}
System.out.println(k);    // (4) Access: k is definitely assigned
```

The two rules of definitely assigned before an access and definitely unassigned before an assignment help to determine correct usage of blank final variables. For non-final *local variables*, the rule for definitely assigned before an access is sufficient, as the value of such variables can be changed.

The examples below shed more light on the usage of final variables.

```
{
  final int i = 10;
  i++;                    // Not OK. Side effect changes the value of i.
}


{
  for (int i = 0; i < 10; i++) {
    final int j = i; // OK. Final variable goes out of scope after each iteration.
  }
}


{
  final int j;
  for (int i = 0; i < 10; i++) {
    j = i;  // Not OK. Loop either not executed and j not initialized
            // or each iteration will assign a new value to j.
  }
  System.out.println(j); // Not OK. Not guaranteed that j is initialized.
}
```

Review Questions

5.8 Which one of the following class declarations is a valid declaration of a class that cannot be instantiated?
Select the one correct answer.

(a) `class Ghost          { abstract void haunt(); }`
(b) `abstract class Ghost { void haunt(); }`
(c) `abstract class Ghost { void haunt() {}; }`
(d) `abstract Ghost       { abstract void haunt(); }`
(e) `abstract class Ghost { abstract haunt(); }`

5.9 Given the following classes:

```
public class Animal {
  // (1)
}
```

```
public abstract class Cat extends Animal {
  // (2)
}
```

and the following method definition:

```
public abstract void eat();
```

where can this abstract method be inserted?
Select the one correct answer.

(a) It can be inserted at (1).
(b) It can be inserted at (2).
(c) It can be inserted at both (1) and (2).
(d) It cannot be inserted into any of the classes.

5.10 Which statement is true about an abstract class?
Select the one correct answer.

(a) An abstract class cannot have a constructor.
(b) An abstract class cannot have concrete methods.
(c) An abstract class cannot override methods from its supertypes.
(d) An abstract class cannot be instantiated with the new operator.

5.11 Which statement is true about the following classes?

```
abstract class LivingOrganism {
  public abstract void feed();
}

class Bacteria extends LivingOrganism {
  @Override
  public void feed()  {  }
  public void feed(int quantity)  {  }        // (1)
}

public class Lab {
  public static void main(String[] args) {
    LivingOrganism org = new Bacteria();       // (2)
    org.feed();
    ((Bacteria)org).feed(10);                  // (3)
  }
}
```

Select the one correct answer.

(a) Class Bacteria cannot overload the feed() method at (1).
(b) An @Overload annotation can be specified for the feed() method at (1).
(c) An @Override annotation can be specified for the feed() method at (1).
(d) An instance of Bacteria can be assigned to the org variable at (2).
(e) Class Lab at (3) cannot invoke the feed() method at (1).

5.12   Which of the following statements are true?
Select the two correct answers.

(a) In Java, the extends clause is used to specify the inheritance relationship.
(b) The subclass of a non-abstract class can be declared as abstract.
(c) All members of the superclass are inherited by the subclass.
(d) A `final` class can be abstract.
(e) A class in which all the members are declared `private` cannot be declared as `public`.

5.13   Which one of the following class declarations is a valid declaration of a class that cannot be extended?
Select the one correct answer.

(a) `class Link { }`
(b) `abstract class Link { }`
(c) `final class Link { }`
(d) `abstract final class Link { }`

5.14   Given the following source code, which comment line can be uncommented without introducing errors?

```
abstract class MyClass {
  abstract void f();
  final    void g() {}
//final    void h() {}                        // (1)

  protected static int i;
  private          int j;
}

final class MyOtherClass extends MyClass {
//MyOtherClass(int n) { m = n; }              // (2)

  public static void main(String[] args) {
    MyClass mc = new MyOtherClass();
  }

  void f() {}
  void h() {}
//void k() { i++; }                           // (3)
//void l() { j++; }                           // (4)

  int m;
}
```

Select the one correct answer.

(a) (1)
(b) (2)
(c) (3)
(d) (4)

5.15 Which of the following statements are true about modifiers?
Select the two correct answers.

(a) Abstract classes can declare `final` methods.
(b) Fields can be declared as abstract.
(c) Non-abstract methods can be declared in abstract classes.
(d) Abstract classes can declare `default` methods.
(e) Abstract classes can be declared as `final`.

5.16 Which statement is true about the following classes?

```
public abstract class Animal {
  public static final MAX_SIZE = 10;
  public abstract void measure(int size);
}

public class Cat extends Animal {
  private int size;
  @Override
  public final void measure(int size) {
    this.size = (size < Animal.MAX_SIZE) ? size : Animal.MAX_SIZE;
  }
}
```

Select the one correct answer.

(a) The compilation fails because of the `final` variable declaration in the abstract class.
(b) The compilation fails because of the `final` method overriding an abstract method.
(c) The compilation fails because `@Override` annotation cannot be applied to a `final` method.
(d) The compilation succeeds.

5.17 Which statement is true about `final` classes and methods?
Select the one correct answer.

(a) A `final` class cannot contain abstract methods.
(b) An abstract class cannot contain `final` methods.
(c) A `final` class cannot contain `final` methods.
(d) A `final` method cannot override an abstract method.

5.6 Interfaces

An interface defines a *contract* for services that classes can implement. Objects of such classes guarantee that this contract will be honored.

Before diving into interfaces, an overview of the inheritance relationship between *classes* can be useful. The extends clause in a class definition only allows *linear inheritance* between classes—that is, a subclass can only extend one superclass. A superclass reference can refer to objects of its own type and of its subclasses strictly according to the linear inheritance hierarchy. Note that this inheritance relationship between classes comprises both *inheritance of type* (i.e., a subclass inherits the type of its superclass and can act as such) and *inheritance of implementation* (i.e., a subclass inherits methods and fields from its superclass). Since this relationship is linear, it rules out *multiple inheritance of implementation*, in which a subclass can inherit implementation directly from more than one direct superclass.

As we shall see in this section, *interfaces* not only allow new named reference types to be introduced, but their usage can result in both *multiple inheritance of type* and *multiple inheritance of implementation*. As we shall also see, multiple inheritance of type does not pose any problems, but multiple inheritance of implementation does and is disallowed by the compiler.

Defining Interfaces

A top-level interface has the following syntax:

```
access_modifier interface interface_name
                        optional_type_parameter_list
                        optional_extends_interface_clause // Interface header
{ // Interface body
    abstract_method_declarations
    default_method_declarations
    static_method_declarations
    private_instance_method_declarations
    private_static_method_declarations
    constant_declarations
    member_type_declarations
}
```

In the interface header, the name of the interface is preceded by the keyword `interface`. In addition, the interface header can specify the following information:

- The *access modifier* can be `public` or `private`. Lack of an access modifier implies package accessibility.

- The *optional type parameter list* specifies a comma-separated list of any formal type parameters enclosed by angle brackets (<>) for declaring a *generic interface* (§11.2, p. 572).

- The *optional extends interface clause* specifies a comma-separated list of any superinterfaces that the interface extends (p. 244).

The interface body can contain *member declarations* that include any of the following:

- *Abstract method declarations* (p. 240)
- *Default method declarations* (p. 246)
- *Static method declarations* (p. 251)
- *Private instance and static method declarations* (p. 252)
- *Constant declarations* (p. 254)
- *Member type declarations* (§9.1, p. 491)

An interface is abstract by definition, which means that it cannot be instantiated. Declaring an interface as abstract is superfluous and seldom done in practice. It is the only non-access modifier that can be specified for a top-level interface.

The member declarations can appear in any order in the interface body, which can be empty. Since interfaces are meant to be implemented by classes, interface members implicitly have public access and the public modifier can be omitted. The following declaration is an example of a bare-bones interface that has an empty body:

```
interface Playable { }
```

Interfaces with empty bodies can be used as *markers* to *tag* classes as having a certain property or behavior. Such interfaces are also called *ability* interfaces. The Java SE Platform API provides several examples of such marker interfaces—for example, java.lang.Cloneable, java.io.Serializable (§20.5, p. 1261), and java.util.EventListener. However, *annotations* (Chapter 25, p. 1555) are a better solution than marker interfaces for attaching metadata to class definitions.

Table 5.2 and Table 5.3 summarize the salient properties of member declarations that can be included in an interface, and which we will elaborate on in this section.

Table 5.2 *Summary of Member Declarations in an Interface (Part I)*

Member declarations	Abstract instance method	Default instance method	Static method	Private instance method	Private static method
Access modifier:	Implicitly public	Implicitly public	Implicitly public	private mandatory	private mandatory
Non-access modifier:	Implicitly abstract	default mandatory	static mandatory	None	static mandatory
Implemented:	No	Yes	Yes	Yes	Yes
Can be inherited:	If not overridden	If not overridden	No	No	No

Table 5.3 *Summary of Member Declarations in an Interface (Part II)*

Member declarations	Constant	Member type declaration
Access modifier:	Implicitly public	Implicitly public
Non-access modifier:	Implicitly static and final	Implicitly static
Implemented:	Yes	Yes
Can be inherited:	If not hidden	If not hidden

Abstract Methods in Interfaces

An interface defines a *contract* by specifying a set of abstract and default method declarations, but provides implementations only for the default methods—not for the abstract methods. The abstract methods in an interface are all implicitly abstract and public by virtue of their definitions. Only the modifiers abstract and public are allowed, but these are invariably omitted. An abstract method declaration has the following simple form in a top-level interface:

   return_type method_name (formal_parameter_list) throws_clause;

An abstract method declaration is essentially a method header terminated by a semicolon (;). Note that an abstract method is an *instance method* whose implementation will be provided by a class that implements the interface in which the abstract method is declared. The throws *clause* is discussed in §7.5, p. 388.

The interface Playable shown below declares an abstract method play(). This method is implicitly declared to be public and abstract. The interface Playable defines a contract: To be Playable, an object must implement the method play().

```
interface Playable {
  void play();               // Abstract method: no implementation
}
```

An interface that has no direct superinterfaces implicitly includes a public abstract method declaration for each public instance method from the java.lang.Object class (e.g., equals(), toString(), hashCode()). These methods are *not* inherited from the java.lang.Object class, as only abstract method declarations are included in the interface. Their inclusion allows these methods to be called using an interface reference, and their implementation is always guaranteed at runtime as they are either inherited or overridden by all classes.

In contrast to the syntax of abstract methods in top-level interfaces, abstract methods in top-level classes must be explicitly specified with the keyword abstract, and can have public, protected, or package accessibility.

Functional interfaces, meaning interfaces with a single abstract method, are discussed together with lambda expressions in §13.1, p. 675.

The rest of this chapter provides numerous examples of declaring, implementing, and using interfaces.

Implementing Interfaces

A class can implement, wholly or partially, any number of interfaces. A class specifies the interfaces it implements as a comma-separated list of unique interface names in an implements clause in the class header. Implementing an interface essentially means that the class must provide implementation for the abstract methods declared in the interface. In fact, an abstract method declaration is overridden when an implementation is provided by a class. Optionally, the class can also override any default methods if necessary.

The criteria for overriding methods in classes also apply when implementing abstract and any default methods from interfaces. A class must provide a method implementation with the same method signature and (covariant) return type as the declaration in the interface, and it can neither narrow the public access of the method nor specify new exceptions in the method's throws clause, as attempting to do so would amount to altering the interface's contract, which is illegal.

Best practice advocates using the @Override annotation on the implementations of abstract and default methods (Example 5.10). The compiler checks that such a method satisfies the criteria for overriding another method. This check ensures that the method is not inadvertently overloaded by catching the error at compile time. The annotations also aid in the readability of the code, making obvious which methods are overridden.

It is not enough for a class to provide implementations of methods declared in an interface. The class must also specify the interface name in its implements clause in order to reap the benefits of interfaces.

In Example 5.10, the class Stack at (2) implements the interface IStack. It both specifies the interface name using the implements clause in its class header at (2) and provides the implementation for the abstract methods in the interface at (3) and (4). Changing the public access of these methods in the class will result in a compile-time error, as this would narrow their accessibility.

Example 5.10   *Implementing Interfaces*

```
// File: StackUser.java
interface IStack {                                                   // (1)
  void   push(Object item);
  Object pop();
}
//_____
class Stack implements IStack {                                      // (2)
  protected Object[] elements;
  protected int       tos;  // top of stack

  public Stack(int capacity) {
    elements = new Object[capacity];
    tos       = -1;
  }

  @Override
  public void push(Object item) { elements[++tos] = item; }          // (3)

  @Override
  public Object pop() {                                              // (4)
    Object objRef = elements[tos];
    elements[tos] = null;
    tos--;
    return objRef;
  }
}
```

```
    public Object peek() { return elements[tos]; }
  }
  //_____
  interface ISafeStack extends IStack {                              // (5)
    boolean isEmpty();
    boolean isFull();
  }
  //_____
  class SafeStack extends Stack implements ISafeStack {              // (6)

    public SafeStack(int capacity) { super(capacity); }
    @Override public boolean isEmpty() { return tos < 0; }          // (7)
    @Override public boolean isFull()  { return tos >= elements.length-1; } // (8)
  }
  //_____
  public class StackUser {

    public static void main(String[] args) {                         // (9)
      SafeStack   safeStackRef  = new SafeStack(10);
      Stack       stackRef      = safeStackRef;
      ISafeStack isafeStackRef = safeStackRef;
      IStack      istackRef     = safeStackRef;
      Object      objRef        = safeStackRef;

      safeStackRef.push("Dollars");                                  // (10)
      stackRef.push("Kroner");
      System.out.println(isafeStackRef.pop());
      System.out.println(istackRef.pop());
      System.out.println(objRef.getClass());
    }
  }
```

Output from the program:

```
Kroner
Dollars
class SafeStack
```

A class can choose to implement only some of the abstract methods of its interfaces (i.e., give a partial implementation of its interfaces). The class must then be declared as abstract. Note that abstract methods cannot be declared as static, because they comprise the contract fulfilled by the *objects* of the class implementing the interface. Abstract methods are always implemented as instance methods.

The interfaces that a class implements and the classes that it extends (directly or indirectly) are called *supertypes* of the class. Conversely, the class is a *subtype* of its supertypes. A class can now inherit from multiple interfaces. Even so, regardless of how many interfaces a class implements directly or indirectly, it provides just a *single* implementation of any abstract method declared in multiple interfaces.

Single implementation of an abstract method is illustrated by the following code, where the Worker class at (5) provides only one implementation of the doIt()

method that is declared in both interfaces, at (1) and (2). The class Worker fulfills the contract for both interfaces, as the doIt() method declarations at (1) and (2) have the same method signature and return type. However, the class Combined at (3) declares that it implements the two interfaces, but does not provide any implementation of the doIt() method; consequently, it must be declared as abstract.

```java
interface IA { int doIt(); }                    // (1)

interface IB { int doIt(); }                    // (2)

abstract class Combined implements IA, IB { }   // (3)

public class Worker implements IA, IB {         // (4)
  @Override
  public int doIt() { return 0; }               // (5)
}
```

Multiple declarations of the same abstract method in several interfaces implemented by a class do *not* result in multiple inheritance of implementation, as no implementation is inherited for such methods. The abstract method doIt() has only one implementation in the Worker class. Multiple inheritance of type is also *not* a problem, as the class is a subtype of all interfaces it implements.

If the doIt() methods in the two previous interfaces at (1) and (2) had the same signatures but different return types, the Worker class would not be able to implement both interfaces. This is illustrated by the code below. The doIt() methods at (1) and (2) have the same signature, but different return types. The ChallengedWorker class provides two implementations of the doIt() method at (5) and (6), which results in compile-time errors because a class cannot have two methods with the same signature but different return types. Removing either implementation from the ChallengedWorker class will be flagged as a compile-time error because the ChallengedWorker class will not be implementing both interfaces. There is no way the ChallengedWorker class can implement both interfaces, given the declarations shown in the code. In addition, the abstract class Combined at (3) will not compile because it will be inheriting two methods with conflicting abstract method declarations. In fact, the compiler complains of duplicate methods.

```java
interface IA { int doIt(); }                    // (1)

interface IB { double doIt(); }                 // (2)

abstract class Combined implements IA, IB { }   // (3) Compile-time error!

public class ChallengedWorker implements IA, IB {  // (4)
  @Override
  public int doIt() { return 0; }               // (5) Compile-time error!
  @Override
  public double doIt() {                         // (6) Compile-time error!
    System.out.println("Sorry!");
    return = 0.0;
  }
}
```

An enum type (p. 298) can also implement interfaces. The discussion above on classes implementing interfaces also applies to enum types, but with the following caveat. Since an enum type can never be abstract, each abstract method of its declared interfaces must be implemented as an instance member either in the enum type or in *all* constant-specific class bodies defined in the enum type—otherwise, the code will not compile.

Extending Interfaces

An interface can extend other interfaces, using the extends clause. Unlike when extending classes, an interface can extend several interfaces. The interfaces extended by an interface (directly or indirectly) are called *superinterfaces*. Conversely, the interface is a *subinterface* of its superinterfaces. Since interfaces define new reference types, superinterfaces and subinterfaces are also supertypes and subtypes, respectively.

A subinterface inherits from its superinterfaces all members of those superinterfaces, *except* for the following:

* Any abstract or default methods that it overrides from its superinterfaces (p. 240 and p. 246)
* Any static methods declared in its superinterfaces (p. 251)
* Any static constants that it hides from its superinterfaces (p. 254)
* Any static member types that it hides from its superinterfaces (§9.2, p. 495)

Barring any conflicts, a subinterface inherits abstract and default method declarations that are not overridden, as well as constants and static member types that it does not hide in its superinterfaces. In addition, abstract, static, and default method declarations can be overloaded, analogous to method overloading in classes. For a detailed discussion of overriding abstract methods from multiple superinterfaces, see §11.12, p. 621.

Example 5.10 illustrates the relationships between classes and interfaces. In Example 5.10, the interface ISafeStack extends the interface IStack at (5). The class SafeStack both extends the Stack class and implements the ISafeStack interface at (6). Inheritance hierarchies for classes and interfaces defined in Example 5.10 are shown in Figure 5.4.

In UML, an interface resembles a class. One way to differentiate between them is to use an *«interface»* stereotype, as in Figure 5.4. The association between a class and any interface it implements is called a *realization* in UML. Realization is depicted in a similar manner to extending classes, but is indicated by an unbroken inheritance arrow. In Figure 5.4, there are two explicit realizations: The class Stack implements the IStack interface and the class SafeStack implements the ISafeStack interface.

It is instructive to consider how the class SafeStack transitively also implements the IStack interface in Example 5.10. This is evident from the diamond shape of the inheritance hierarchy in Figure 5.4. The class SafeStack inherits the implementations of the push() and pop() methods from its superclass Stack, which itself implements the

Figure 5.4   *Inheritance Hierarchies for Classes and Interfaces in Example 5.10*

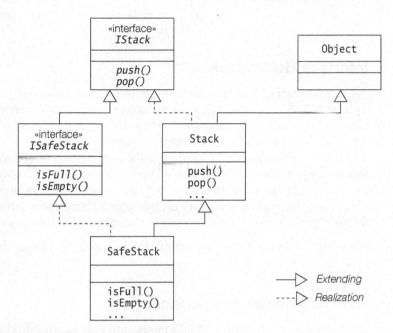

IStack interface in which these two methods are declared. The class SafeStack also implements the IStack interface via the ISafeStack interface. The class SafeStack provides its own implementation of the isFull() and isEmpty() methods declared in the ISafeStack interface, and has inherited implementations of the push() and pop() methods whose declarations the ISafeStack interface inherits from its super-interface IStack. Note that there is only one *implementation* of a method that is inherited by the class SafeStack—from its superclass Stack.

Thinking in terms of types, every reference type in Java is a subtype of the java.lang.Object class. In turn, any interface type is also a subtype of the Object class, but it does *not* inherit any implementation from the Object class. As mentioned earlier, an interface that has *no direct superinterfaces* implicitly declares a public abstract method for *each* public instance method in the Object class. These abstract method declarations are inherited by all subinterfaces of such an interface. Note that this does not mean any *implementation* is inherited by the subinterfaces. The implicit public abstract method declarations in an interface allow public instance methods in the Object class to be invoked on objects referenced by an interface reference. All classes implement these methods, whether they are inherited or overridden from the Object class. Any interface can also provide *explicit* public abstract method declarations for *non-final* public instance methods in the Object class.

```
interface IStack {                                              // (1)
    void    push(Object item);
    Object pop();
```

```
    @Override boolean equals(Object other);          // public method in Object class.
    @Override String toString();                     // public method in Object class.
  //@Override Class getClass(); // Compile-time error! final method in Object class.
  }
```

Interface References

Although interfaces cannot be instantiated, references of an interface type can be declared. The reference value of an object can be assigned to references of the object's supertypes. In Example 5.10, an object of the class SafeStack is created in the main() method of the class StackUser at (9). The reference value of the object is assigned to references of all the object's supertypes, which are used to manipulate the object. The references are aliases to the same SafeStack object, but they can only be used to manipulate this object as an object of the reference type. For example, calling the method isFull() on this object using the stackRef reference will be flagged as a compile-time error, as the class Stack does not provide such a method.

Polymorphic behavior of supertype references is discussed later in this chapter (p. 278).

Default Methods in Interfaces

Only interfaces can define default methods. A default method is an *instance method* declared with the keyword default and whose implementation is provided by the interface. However, a default method in a top-level interface always has public access, whether the keyword public is specified or not.

```
default return_type method_name (formal_parameter_list) throws_clause {
    implementaion_of_method_body
}
```

A class implementing an interface can optionally decide to override any default method in the interface, as can a subinterface of the interface. If a default method is not overridden to provide a new implementation, the default implementation provided by the interface is inherited by the class or the subinterface.

No other non-access modifiers, such as abstract, final, or static, are allowed in a default method declaration. A default method is not abstract because it provides an implementation; is not final because it can be overridden; and is not static because it can be invoked only on instances of a class that implements the interface in which the default method is declared.

Note that a default method can only be implemented in terms of the values of its local variables (including those passed as parameters) and calls to other methods accessible in the interface, but without reference to any persistent state, as there is none associated with an interface.

The keyword default in the context of a default method should not be confused with default or package accessibility of a method in a class, which is implied in the absence of any access modifier.

Example 5.11 illustrates the use of default methods. The default method printSlogan() at (1) in the interface ISlogan is overridden at (2) in the class JavaGuru, and is inherited by the class JavaGeek at (3). The output from the program shows that this is the case.

Example 5.11 *Default Methods in Interfaces*

```java
// File: JavaParty.java
interface ISlogan {
  default void printSlogan() {                         // (1)
    System.out.println("Happiness is getting certified!");
  }
}
//_____
class JavaGuru implements ISlogan {
  @Override
  public void printSlogan() {                          // (2) overrides (1)
    System.out.println("Happiness is catching all the exceptions!");
  }
}
//_____
class JavaGeek implements ISlogan { }                  // (3) inherits (1)
//_____
public class JavaParty {
  public static void main(String[] args) {
    JavaGuru guru = new JavaGuru();
    guru.printSlogan();                                // (4)
    JavaGeek geek = new JavaGeek();
    geek.printSlogan();                                // (5)
  }
}
```

Output from the program:

```
Happiness is catching all the exceptions!
Happiness is getting certified!
```

Overriding Default Methods

Overriding a default method from an interface does not necessarily imply that a new implementation is being provided. The default method can also be overridden by providing an abstract method declaration, as illustrated by the code below. The default method printSlogan() at (1) in the interface ISlogan is overridden by an abstract method declaration at (2) and (3) in the interface INewSlogan and the abstract class JavaMaster, respectively. This strategy effectively forces the subtypes of the interface INewSlogan and of the abstract class JavaMaster to provide a new concrete implementation for the method, as one would expect for an abstract method.

```java
interface ISlogan {
  default void printSlogan() {            // (1) Default method.
```

```
        System.out.println("Happiness is getting certified!");
    }
}

interface INewSlogan extends ISlogan {
    @Override
    abstract void printSlogan();          // (2) overrides (1) with abstract method.
}

abstract class JavaMaster implements ISlogan {
    @Override
    public abstract void printSlogan();   // (3) overrides (1) with abstract method.
}
```

Conflict Resolution for Default Methods

Conflicts with multiple inheritance of implementation can arise when default methods are inherited from unrelated interfaces.

Example 5.12 illustrates the case where two interfaces define a default method with the same signature. The default method printSlogan() is declared at (1) and (2) in the interfaces ICheapSlogan and IFunnySlogan, respectively. The two method declarations have the same signature. The interface IAvailableSlogan at (3) tries to extend the two interfaces ICheapSlogan and IFunnySlogan. If this were allowed, the interface IAvailableSlogan would inherit two implementations of a method with the same signature, which of course is not allowed—so the compiler flags it as an error. By the same token, the compiler flags an error at (4), indicating that the abstract class Wholesaler cannot inherit two default methods with the same signature.

A way out of this dilemma is to override the conflicting default methods. The abstract class RetailSeller that implements the interfaces ICheapSlogan and IFunnySlogan overrides the conflicting methods by providing an abstract method declaration of the default method printSlogan() at (5). Similarly, the class NetSeller that implements the interfaces ICheapSlogan and IFunnySlogan overrides the conflicting methods by providing an implementation of the default method printSlogan() at (6).

The upshot of this solution is that clients of the classes RetailSeller and NetSeller now have to deal with the new declarations of the printSlogan() method provided by these classes. One such client is the class MultipleInheritance at (10), which calls the method printSlogan() on an instance of class NetSeller at (11). Not surprisingly, the program output shows that the method in the NetSeller class was executed.

What if the class NetSeller wanted to invoke the default method printSlogan() in the interfaces it implements? The overridden default method can be called by the overriding subtype (in this case, NetSeller) using the keyword super in conjunction with the fully qualified name of the interface and the name of the method, as shown at (8) and (9). This syntax works for calling overridden default methods in the *direct* superinterface, but not at any higher level in the inheritance hierarchy. The class NetSeller can call only default methods in its direct superinterfaces

ICheapSlogan and IFunnySlogan. It would not be possible for the class NetSeller to call any default methods inherited by these superinterfaces, even if they had any.

Example 5.12   *Inheriting Default Method Implementations from Superinterfaces*

```java
// File: MultipleInheritance.java
interface ICheapSlogan {
  default void printSlogan() {          // (1)
    System.out.println("Override, don't overload.");
  }
}
//_____
interface IFunnySlogan {
  default void printSlogan() {          // (2)
    System.out.println("Catch exceptions, not bugs.");
  }
}
//_____
interface IAvailableSlogan                 // (3) Compile-time error.
          extends ICheapSlogan, IFunnySlogan { }
//_____
abstract class Wholesaler                  // (4) Compile-time error.
          implements ICheapSlogan, IFunnySlogan { }
//_____
abstract class RetailSeller implements ICheapSlogan, IFunnySlogan {
  @Override                                // Abstract method.
  public abstract void printSlogan();      // (5) overrides (1) and (2).
}
//_____
class NetSeller implements ICheapSlogan, IFunnySlogan {
  @Override                                // Concrete method.
  public void printSlogan() {              // (6) overrides (1) and (2).
    System.out.println("Think outside of the class.");
  }

  public void invokeDirect() {             // (7)
    ICheapSlogan.super.printSlogan();      // (8) calls ICheapSlogan.printSlogan()
    IFunnySlogan.super.printSlogan();      // (9) calls IFunnySlogan.printSlogan()
  }
}
//_____
public class MultipleInheritance {         // (10)
  public static void main(String[] args) {
    NetSeller seller = new NetSeller();
    seller.printSlogan();                  // (11)
    seller.invokeDirect();
  }
}
```

Output from the program:

```
Think outside of the class.
Override, don't overload.
Catch exceptions, not bugs.
```

Example 5.13 illustrates the case where a concrete method at (1) in the class Slogan and a default method at (2) in the interface ISlogan have the same signature. The subclass MySlogan at (3) extends the superclass Slogan and implements the super-interface ISlogan. The class MySlogan compiles even though it looks like two implementations of the printSlogan() method are being inherited. In this special case there is no multiple inheritance of implementation, as only the implementation from the superclass Slogan is inherited. The implementation of the default method at (2) is ignored. This is borne out by the program output when the method printSlogan() is called at (5) on an object of class MySlogan.

Interface Evolution

Augmenting an existing interface with an abstract method will break all classes that implement this interface, as they will no longer implement the old interface. These classes will need to be modified and recompiled in order to work with the augmented interface.

Augmenting an existing interface with a default method does not pose this problem. Classes that implement the old interface will work with the augmented interface *without modifying or recompiling* them. Thus interfaces can evolve without affecting classes that worked with the old interface. This is also true for static methods (p. 251) added to existing interfaces.

Example 5.13 *Inheriting Method Implementations from Supertypes*

```java
// File: MultipleInheritance2.java
class Slogan {
  public void printSlogan() {                        // (1) Concrete method
    System.out.println("Superclass wins!");
  }
}
//_____
interface ISlogan {
  default void printSlogan() {                       // (2) Default method
    System.out.println("Superinterface wins!");
  }
}
//_____
class MySlogan extends Slogan implements ISlogan { } // (3)
//_____
public class MultipleInheritance2 {                  // (4)
  public static void main(String[] args) {
    MySlogan slogan = new MySlogan();
    slogan.printSlogan();                            // (5)
  }
}
```

Output from the program:

```
Superclass wins!
```

Static Methods in Interfaces

A common practice in designing APIs has been to provide an interface that classes can implement and a separate *utility class* providing static methods for common operations on objects of these classes. Typical examples are the java.util.Collection interface and the java.util.Collections utility class (Chapter 15, p. 781). Another example is the Path interface and the Paths utility class in the java.nio.file package (Chapter 21, p. 1285). However, now an interface can also declare static methods, and there is no need for a separate utility class.

Static method declarations in a top-level interface are declared analogous to static method declarations in a class. However, a static method in a top-level interface always has public access, whether the keyword public is specified or not. As with static methods in a class, the keyword static is mandatory; otherwise, the code will not compile. Without the keyword static, the method declaration is identical to that of an instance method, but such instance methods cannot be declared in an interface and the compiler will flag an error.

```
static return_type method_name (formal_parameter_list) throws_clause {
    implementaion_of_method_body
}
```

Static methods in an interface differ from those in a class in one important respect: Static methods in an interface *cannot* be inherited, unlike static methods in classes. This essentially means that such methods cannot be invoked directly by calling the method in subinterfaces or in classes that extend or implement interfaces containing such methods, respectively. A static method can be invoked only by using its qualified name—that is, the name of the interface in which it is declared, together with its simple name, using the dot notation (.).

Example 5.14 illustrates the use of static methods in interfaces. The static method getNumOfCylinders() at (1) is declared in the IMaxEngineSize interface. There are two implementations of the method getEngineSize(), at (2) and (3), in the interface IMaxEngineSize and its subinterface INewEngineSize, respectively. The class CarRace implements the subinterface INewEngineSize.

It is not possible to invoke the static method getNumOfCylinders() directly, as shown at (4). It is also not possible to invoke directly the static method getEngineSize() from either interface, as shown at (6). The respective implementations of the static methods can be invoked only by using their qualified names, as shown at (5), (7), and (8). It does not matter that a static method is redeclared in a subinterface; the static method is not inherited. Each static method declaration in Example 5.14 is a new method.

- -

Example 5.14 *Static Methods in Interfaces*

```
// File: CarRace.java
import static java.lang.System.out;
```

```java
interface IMaxEngineSize {
  static int getNumOfCylinders() { return 6; }        // (1) Static method
  static double getEngineSize() { return 1.6; }       // (2) Static method
}
//_____
interface INewEngineSize extends IMaxEngineSize {
  static double getEngineSize() { return 2.4; }       // (3) Static method
}
//_____
public class CarRace implements INewEngineSize {
  public static void main(String[] args) {
// out.println("No. of cylinders: " +
//             getNumOfCylinders());                  // (4) Compile-time error.
    out.println("No. of cylinders: " +
        IMaxEngineSize.getNumOfCylinders());          // (5)
// out.println("Engine size: " + getEngineSize());    // (6) Compile-time error.
    out.println("Max engine size: " + IMaxEngineSize.getEngineSize()); // (7)
    out.println("New engine size: " + INewEngineSize.getEngineSize()); // (8)
  }
}
```

Output from the program:

```
No. of cylinders: 6
Max engine size: 1.6
New engine size: 2.4
```

Private Methods in Interfaces

Private methods in interfaces are no different from private methods in classes. As such, they can only be accessed inside the interface, acting as *helper* or *auxiliary methods* for non-abstract methods declared in the interface. They allow code to be shared between the non-abstract methods in the interface, thus promoting code reuse and avoiding code duplicity.

Private methods in an interface are governed by the following rules:

- Not surprisingly, a private method must be declared with the private modifier in its header.

- A private method can only be accessed inside the interface itself.

- A private method cannot be declared with the abstract or the default modifier, but can be declared either as a private instance method or a private static method.

- A private static method can be invoked in any non-abstract method in the interface.

- A private instance method can only be invoked in default and private instance methods of the interface, and not in any static methods of the interface.

The above rules stem from accessibility of a private member in a type declaration in which the code is accessible in static and non-static contexts.

Example 5.15 illustrates declaring private methods in an interface. The default method getSalePrice() at (2) and the static method startSale() at (5) call the private instance method wrapUp() at (4) and the private static method showSaleItems() at (7), respectively.

Example 5.15 *Private Methods in Interfaces*

```java
/** Interface with private methods. */
public interface IShopper {

  // Abstract method:
  double getItemPrice();                               // (1)

  // Default method:
  default double getSalePrice(double price) {          // (2)
    var salePrice = (80.0/100.0)*price;
    System.out.println("Default method: " + "Sale price is " + salePrice);
    wrapUp();                   // (3) Calls the private instance method at (4)
    return salePrice;
  }

  // Private instance method:
  private void wrapUp() {                              // 4)
    System.out.println("Private method: " + "Wrapping up!");
  }

  // Static method:
  static void startSale() {                           // (5)
    System.out.println("Static method: " + "Amazing savings!");
    showSaleItems();            // (6) Calls the private static method at (7)
  }

  // Private static method:
  private static void showSaleItems() {               // (7)
    System.out.println("Private static method: " + "Sorry. No items on sale!");
  }
}
```

```java
/** Class Shopper implements IShopper interface */
public class Shopper implements IShopper {

  @Override
  public double getItemPrice() {
    return 100.00;
  }

  public static void main(String[] args) {
    Shopper customer = new Shopper();
    var price = customer.getItemPrice();
    System.out.println("Item price: " + price);
    var salePrice = customer.getSalePrice(price); // Calls default method at (2)
    System.out.println();
```

```
      IShopper.startSale();                          // Calls static method at (5)
    }
  }
```

Output from the program:

```
Item price: 100.0
Default method: Sale price is 80.0
Private method: Wrapping up!

Static method: Amazing savings!
Private static method: Sorry. No items on sale!
```

Constants in Interfaces

A field declaration in an interface defines a *named constant*. Naming conventions recommend using uppercase letters, with multiple words in the name being separated by underscores. Such constants are considered to be public, static, and final. These modifiers are usually omitted from the declaration, but can be specified in any order. Such a constant must be initialized with an initializer expression.

An interface constant can be accessed by any client (a class or interface) using its qualified name, regardless of whether the client extends or implements its interface. However, if the client is a class that implements this interface or is an interface that extends this interface, then the client can also access such constants directly by their simple names. Such a client inherits the interface constants. Typical usage of constants in interfaces is illustrated in Example 5.16, showing access both by the constant's simple name and its qualified name in the print statements at (1) and (2), respectively.

Example 5.16 *Constants in Interfaces*

```
// File: Client.java
interface Constants {
  double PI_APPROXIMATION = 3.14;
  String AREA_UNITS      = "sq.cm.";
  String LENGTH_UNITS    = "cm.";
}
//_____
public class Client implements Constants {
  public static void main(String[] args) {
    double radius = 1.5;

    // (1) Using simple name:
    System.out.printf("Area of circle is %.2f %s%n",
            PI_APPROXIMATION * radius*radius, AREA_UNITS);

    // (2) Using qualified name:
    System.out.printf("Circumference of circle is %.2f %s%n",
            2.0 * Constants.PI_APPROXIMATION * radius, Constants.LENGTH_UNITS);
  }
}
```

Output from the program:

```
Area of circle is 7.06 sq.cm.
Circumference of circle is 9.42 cm.
```

Extending an interface that has constants is analogous to extending a class that has static variables. This is illustrated in Figure 5.5 and Example 5.17. Note the diamond shape of the inheritance hierarchy, indicating the presence of multiple inheritance paths through which constants can be inherited. The constants IDLE and BUSY at (1) and (2) in the interface IBaseStates are inherited by the subinterface IAllStates via both the interface IExtStatesA and the interface IExtStatesB. In such cases, the constant is considered to be inherited only once and can be accessed by its simple name, as shown at (12) in Example 5.17.

Figure 5.5 *Inheritance Relationships for Interface Constants*

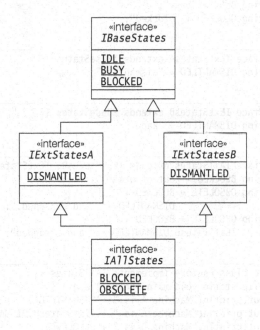

Constants can be *hidden* by the subinterfaces. The declaration of the constant BLOCKED at (6) in the interface IAllStates hides the declaration of the constant at (2) in the interface IBaseStates. The new declaration can be accessed by its simple name in a class implementing the interface IAllStates, as shown at (10) in Example 5.17. The hidden constant declaration can always be accessed by using its qualified name as shown at (11) in Example 5.17.

In the case of multiple inheritance of interface constants, any name conflicts can be resolved by using the qualified name to access the constants. This is illustrated by the constant DISMANTLED, which is declared in both the IExtStatesA and IExtStatesB interfaces. Both declarations are inherited by the subinterface IAllStates. Such declarations are said to be *ambiguous*. The compiler will report an error only if such constants are accessed by their simple names, as shown at (7) and (8) for the constant DISMANTLED. Only the qualified name can be used to disambiguate such constants and resolve the conflict, as shown at (7a) and (8a) for the constant DISMANTLED.

When defining a *set of related constants*, the recommended practice is to use an enum type, rather than named constants in an interface.

Example 5.17   *Inheriting Constants in Interfaces*

```
// File: Factory.java
import static java.lang.System.out;

interface IBaseStates {
  String IDLE = "idle";                                // (1)
  String BUSY = "busy";                                // (2)
  String BLOCKED = "blocked";                          // (3)
}
//_____
interface IExtStatesA extends IBaseStates {
  String DISMANTLED = "dismantled";                    // (4)
}
//_____
interface IExtStatesB extends IBaseStates {
  String DISMANTLED = "kaput";                         // (5)
}
//_____
interface IAllStates extends IExtStatesB, IExtStatesA {
  String BLOCKED = "out of order";                     // (6) hides (3)
//String OBSOLETE = BLOCKED + ", " +
//                  DISMANTLED + " and scrapped.";     // (7) Ambiguous
  String OBSOLETE = BLOCKED + ", " +
        IExtStatesB.DISMANTLED + " and scrapped";      // (7a)
}
//_____
public class Factory implements IAllStates {
  public static void main(String[] args) {
// out.println("Machine A is " + DISMANTLED);                // (8) Ambiguous.
   out.println("Machine A is " + IExtStatesB.DISMANTLED); // (8a)
   out.println("Machine B is " + OBSOLETE);           // (9) IAllStates.OBSOLETE
   out.println("Machine C is " + BLOCKED);            // (10) IAllStates.BLOCKED
   out.println("Machine D is " + IBaseStates.BLOCKED);// (11)
   out.println("Machine E is " + BUSY);               // (12) Simple name
  }
}
```

Output from the program:

```
Machine A is kaput
Machine B is out of order, kaput and scrapped
Machine C is out of order
Machine D is blocked
Machine E is busy
```

Review Questions

5.18 Which modifiers are not allowed for methods in an interface ?
Select the two correct answers.

(a) public
(b) protected
(c) private
(d) default
(e) abstract
(f) static
(g) final

5.19 Which method call can be inserted at both (1) and (2) so that the following code will
still compile?

```
interface INewSlogan {
  String SLOGAN = "Trouble shared is trouble halved!";
  static void printSlogan() { System.out.println(SLOGAN); }
}
//_____
public class Firm implements INewSlogan {
  public static void main(String[] args) {
    Firm co = new Firm();
    INewSlogan sl = co;
    // (1) INSERT STATEMENT EXPRESSION HERE
  }

  void testSlogan() {
    Firm co = new Firm();
    INewSlogan sl = co;
    // (2) INSERT STATEMENT EXPRESSION HERE
  }
}
```

Select the one correct answer.

(a) printSlogan();
(b) co.printSlogan();
(c) sl.printSlogan();
(d) Firm.printSlogan();
(e) INewSlogan.printSlogan();

5.20 What will be the result of compiling and running the following program?

```
interface IJogger {
  default boolean justDoIt(String msg) { return false; }  // (1)
  static  boolean justDoIt(int i)      { return true; }   // (2)
}
```

```
class Athlete implements IJogger {
  public boolean justDoIt(String msg)  { return true; }   // (3)
  public boolean justDoIt(int i)       { return false; }  // (4)
}

public class RaceA {
  public static void main(String[] args) {
    Athlete athlete = new Athlete();
    IJogger jogger = athlete;
    System.out.print(jogger.justDoIt("Run"));              // (5)
    System.out.println("|" + athlete.justDoIt(10));        // (6)
  }
}
```

Select the one correct answer.

(a) The program will fail to compile.
(b) true|true
(c) true|false
(d) false|true
(e) false|false

5.21   Which statement is true about the following code?

```
abstract class MyClass implements Interface1, Interface2 {
  public void f() { }
  public void g() { }
}

interface Interface1 {
  int VAL_A = 1;
  int VAL_B = 2;

  void f();
  void g();
}

interface Interface2 {
  int VAL_B = 3;
  int VAL_C = 4;

  void g();
  void h();
}
```

Select the one correct answer.

(a) MyClass implements only Interface1; the implementation for void h() from Interface2 is missing.
(b) The declarations of void g() in the two interfaces are in conflict, so the code will fail to compile.
(c) The declarations of int VAL_B in the two interfaces are in conflict, so the code will fail to compile.
(d) Nothing is wrong with the code; it will compile without errors.

5.7 Arrays and Subtyping

Table 5.4 summarizes the types found in Java. Only primitive data and reference values can be stored in variables. Only class and array types can be explicitly instantiated to create objects.

Table 5.4 *Types and Values*

Types	Values
Primitive data types	Primitive data values
Class, interface, enum, and array types (*reference types*)	Reference values

Arrays and Subtype Covariance

Arrays are objects in Java. Array types (`boolean[]`, `Object[]`, `Stack[]`) implicitly augment the inheritance hierarchy. The inheritance hierarchy depicted in Figure 5.4, for example, can be augmented by the corresponding array types to produce the *type hierarchy* shown in Figure 5.6. An array type is shown as a "class" with the [] notation appended to the name of the element type. The class SafeStack is a subclass of the class Stack. The corresponding array types, SafeStack[] and Stack[], are shown as the subtype and the supertype, respectively, in the type hierarchy. Figure 5.6 also shows array types corresponding to some of the primitive data types.

Figure 5.6 *Reference Type Hierarchy: Arrays and Subtype Covariance*

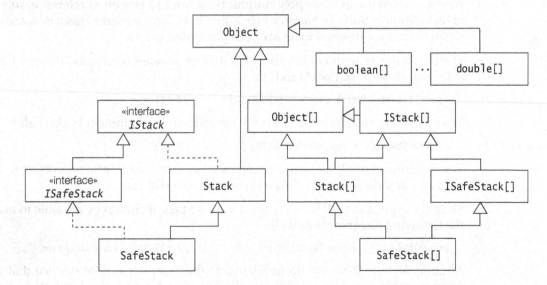

From the type hierarchy in Figure 5.6, the following facts are apparent:

- *All* reference types are subtypes of the Object type. This applies to classes, interfaces, enums, and array types, as these are all reference types.
- All arrays of reference types are also subtypes of the array type Object[], but arrays of primitive data types are not. Note that the array type Object[] is also a subtype of the Object type.
- If a non-generic reference type is a subtype of another non-generic reference type, the corresponding array types also have an analogous subtype–supertype relationship. This is called the *subtype covariance relationship*.
- There is no subtype–supertype relationship between a type and its corresponding array type.

We can create an array of an interface type, but we cannot instantiate an interface (as is the case with abstract classes). In the following declaration statement, the reference arrayOfISafeStack has type ISafeStack[] (i.e., an array of the interface type ISafeStack):

```
ISafeStack[] arrayOfISafeStack = new ISafeStack[5];
```

The array creation expression creates an array whose element type is ISafeStack. The array object can accommodate five references of the type ISafeStack. The declaration statement does not initialize these references to refer to any objects; instead, they are initialized to the default value null.

Array Store Check

An array reference exhibits polymorphic behavior like any other reference, subject to its location in the type hierarchy (p. 278). However, a runtime check is necessary when objects are inserted in an array, as illustrated below.

The following assignment is valid, as a supertype reference (Stack[]) can refer to objects of its subtype (SafeStack[]):

```
Stack[] arrayOfStack = new SafeStack[2];      // (1)
```

Since Stack is a supertype of SafeStack, the following assignment is also valid:

```
arrayOfStack[0] = new SafeStack(10);          // (2)
```

The assignment at (2) assigns the reference value of a new SafeStack object to the reference at index 0 in the SafeStack[] object created at (1).

Since the type of arrayOfStack[i], (0 ≤ i < 2), is Stack, it should be possible to make the following assignment as well:

```
arrayOfStack[1] = new Stack(20);              // (3) ArrayStoreException
```

At compile time there are no problems, as the compiler cannot deduce that the array variable arrayOfStack will actually denote a SafeStack[] object at runtime. However, the assignment at (3) results in an ArrayStoreException being thrown at runtime because an array of SafeStack objects cannot possibly contain objects of its supertype Stack.

The array store check at runtime ensures that an object being stored in the array is assignment compatible (p. 264) with the element type of the array. To make the array store check feasible at runtime, the array retains information about its declared element type at runtime.

5.8 Reference Values and Conversions

A review of conversions (§2.3, p. 43) is recommended before proceeding with this section.

Reference values, like primitive values, can be assigned, cast, and passed as arguments. Conversions can occur in the following contexts:

- Assignment
- Method invocation
- Casting

The rule of thumb for the primitive data types is that widening conversions are permitted, but narrowing conversions require an explicit cast. The rule of thumb for reference values is that widening conversions up the type hierarchy are permitted, but narrowing conversions down the hierarchy require an explicit cast. In other words, conversions that are from a subtype to its supertypes are allowed, but other conversions require an explicit cast or are otherwise illegal. There is no notion of promotion for reference values.

5.9 Reference Value Assignment Conversions

In the context of assignments, the following conversions are permitted (Table 2.17, p. 47):

- Widening primitive and reference conversions (long ← int, Object ← String)
- Boxing conversion of primitive values, followed by optional widening reference conversion (Integer ← int, Number ← Integer ← int)
- Unboxing conversion of a primitive value wrapper object, followed by optional widening primitive conversion (long ← int ← Integer)

In addition, for assignment conversions only, the following conversion is also possible:

- Narrowing conversion for constant expressions of non-long integer types, with optional boxing (Byte ← byte ← int)

Note that these rules imply that a widening conversion *cannot* be followed by any boxing conversion, but the converse is permitted.

Widening reference conversions typically occur during assignment *up* the type hierarchy, with implicit conversion of the source reference value to that of the destination reference type:

```java
Object obj = "Up the tree";     // Widening reference conversion: Object <-- String
String str1 = obj;              // Not OK. Narrowing reference conversion requires a cast.
String str2 = Integer.valueOf(10); // Illegal. No relation between
                               //             String and Integer.
```

The source value can be a primitive value, in which case the value is boxed in a wrapper object corresponding to the primitive type. If the destination reference type is a supertype of the wrapper type, a widening reference conversion can occur:

```java
Integer iRef = 10;  // Only boxing
Number num = 10L;   // Boxing, followed by widening: Number <--- Long <--- long
Object obj = 100;   // Boxing, followed by widening: Object <--- Integer <--- int
```

More examples of boxing during assignment can be found in §2.3, p. 45.

Example 5.18   *Assigning and Passing Reference Values*

```java
// See Example 5.10, p. 241, for type declarations.
interface IStack
interface ISafeStack extends IStack
class Stack implements IStack
class SafeStack extends Stack implements ISafeStack
```

```java
public class ReferenceConversion {

  public static void main(String[] args) {
    // Reference declarations:
    Object       objRef;
    Stack        stackRef;
    SafeStack    safeStackRef;
    IStack       iStackRef;
    ISafeStack   iSafeStackRef;

    // SourceType is a class type:
    safeStackRef  = new SafeStack(10);
    objRef        = safeStackRef;    // (1) Always possible
    stackRef      = safeStackRef;    // (2) Subclass to superclass assignment
    iStackRef     = stackRef;        // (3) Stack implements IStack
    iSafeStackRef = safeStackRef;    // (4) SafeStack implements ISafeStack

    // SourceType is an interface type:
    objRef    = iStackRef;           // (5) Always possible
    iStackRef = iSafeStackRef;       // (6) Sub- to superinterface assignment

    // SourceType is an array type:
    Object[]      objArray        = new Object[3];
    Stack[]       arrayOfStack    = new Stack[3];
    SafeStack[]   arrayOfSafeStack = new SafeStack[5];
    ISafeStack[]  arrayOfISafeStack = new ISafeStack[5];
    int[]         intArray        = new int[10];
```

```
            // Reference value assignments:
            objRef     = objArray;         // (7) Always possible
            objRef     = arrayOfStack;     // (8) Always possible
            objArray   = arrayOfStack;     // (9) Always possible
            objArray   = arrayOfISafeStack; // (10) Always possible
            objRef     = intArray;         // (11) Always possible
            // objArray   = intArray;      // (12) Compile-time error:
                                           //      int[] not subtype of Object[]
            arrayOfStack = arrayOfSafeStack; // (13) Subclass array to superclass array
            arrayOfISafeStack = arrayOfSafeStack; // (14) SafeStack implements
                                              //      ISafeStack

            // Method invocation conversions:
            System.out.println("First call:");
            sendParams(stackRef, safeStackRef, iStackRef,
                    arrayOfSafeStack, arrayOfISafeStack);                    // (15)
            // Call Signature: sendParams(Stack, SafeStack, IStack,
            //                            SafeStack[], ISafeStack[]);

            System.out.println("Second call:");
            sendParams(arrayOfISafeStack, stackRef, iSafeStackRef,
                    arrayOfStack, arrayOfSafeStack);                         // (16)
            // Call Signature: sendParams(ISafeStack[], Stack, ISafeStack,
            //                            Stack[], SafeStack[]);
        }

        public static void sendParams(Object objRefParam, Stack stackRefParam,
            IStack iStackRefParam, Stack[] arrayOfStackParam,
            IStack[] arrayOfIStackParam) {                                    // (17)
            // Signature: sendParams(Object, Stack, IStack, Stack[], IStack[])
            // Print class name of object denoted by the reference at runtime.
            System.out.println(objRefParam.getClass());
            System.out.println(stackRefParam.getClass());
            System.out.println(iStackRefParam.getClass());
            System.out.println(arrayOfStackParam.getClass());
            System.out.println(arrayOfIStackParam.getClass());
        }
    }
```

Output from the program:

```
    First call:
    class SafeStack
    class SafeStack
    class SafeStack
    class [LSafeStack;
    class [LSafeStack;
    Second call:
    class [LSafeStack;
    class SafeStack
    class SafeStack
    class [LSafeStack;
    class [LSafeStack;
```

The rules for reference value assignment are stated in this section, based on the following code:

```
SourceType srcRef;
// srcRef is appropriately initialized.
DestinationType destRef = srcRef;
```

If an assignment is legal, the reference value of srcRef is said to be *assignable* (or *assignment compatible*) to the reference of DestinationType. The rules are illustrated by concrete cases from Example 5.18. Note that the code in Example 5.18 uses reference types from Example 5.10, p. 241.

- If the SourceType is a *class type*, the reference value in srcRef may be assigned to the destRef reference, provided the DestinationType is one of the following:
  - ○ DestinationType is a superclass of the subclass SourceType.
  - ○ DestinationType is an interface type that is implemented by the class SourceType.

```
objRef        = safeStackRef;   // (1) Always possible
stackRef      = safeStackRef;   // (2) Subclass to superclass assignment
iStackRef     = stackRef;       // (3) Stack implements IStack
iSafeStackRef = safeStackRef;   // (4) SafeStack implements ISafeStack
```

- If the SourceType is an *interface type*, the reference value in srcRef may be assigned to the destRef reference, provided the DestinationType is one of the following:
  - ○ DestinationType is the Object class.
  - ○ DestinationType is a superinterface of the subinterface SourceType.

```
objRef    = iStackRef;     // (5) Always possible
iStackRef = iSafeStackRef; // (6) Subinterface to superinterface assignment
```

- If the SourceType is an *array type*, the reference value in srcRef may be assigned to the destRef reference, provided the DestinationType is one of the following:
  - ○ DestinationType is the Object class.
  - ○ DestinationType is an array type, where the element type of the SourceType is assignable to the element type of the DestinationType.

```
objRef        = objArray;          // (7) Always possible
objRef        = arrayOfStack;      // (8) Always possible
objArray      = arrayOfStack;      // (9) Always possible
objArray      = arrayOfISafeStack; // (10) Always possible
objRef        = intArray;          // (11) Always possible
// objArray   = intArray;          // (12) Compile-time error:
                                   //      int[] not subtype of Object[]
arrayOfStack = arrayOfSafeStack; // (13) Subclass array to superclass array
arrayOfISafeStack = arrayOfSafeStack; // (14) SafeStack implements
                                   //      ISafeStack
```

The rules for assignment are enforced at compile time, guaranteeing that no type conversion error will occur during assignment at runtime. Such conversions are *type-safe*. The reason the rules can be enforced at compile time is that they concern the *declared type* of the reference (which is always known at compile time) rather than the actual type of the object being referenced (which is known at runtime).

5.10 Method Invocation Conversions Involving References

The conversions for reference value assignment are also applicable to *method invocation conversions*, except for the narrowing conversion for constant expressions of non-long integer type (Table 2.17, p. 47). This is reasonable, as parameters in Java are passed by value (§3.10, p. 127), requiring that values of the actual parameters must be assignable to formal parameters of the compatible types.

In Example 5.18, the method `sendParams()` at (17) has the following signature, showing the types of the formal parameters:

```
sendParams(Object, Stack, IStack, Stack[], IStack[])
```

The method call at (15) has the following signature, showing the types of the actual parameters:

```
sendParams(Stack, SafeStack, IStack, SafeStack[], ISafeStack[]);   // Compile time
```

At runtime, the actual type of the objects whose reference values are passed at (15) is the following:

```
sendParams(SafeStack, SafeStack, SafeStack, SafeStack[], SafeStack[]); // Runtime
```

Note that the assignment of the values of the actual parameters to the corresponding formal parameters is legal, according to the rules for assignment discussed earlier. The method call at (16) provides another example of the parameter-passing conversion. It has the following signature:

```
sendParams(ISafeStack[], Stack, ISafeStack, Stack[], SafeStack[]); // Compile time
```

At runtime, the actual type of the objects whose reference values are passed at (16) is the following:

```
sendParams(SafeStack[], SafeStack, SafeStack, SafeStack[], SafeStack[]);// Runtime
```

Analogous to assignment, the rules for parameter-passing conversions are based on the reference type of the parameters and are enforced at compile time. It is instructive to compare the type of a formal parameter with the type of its corresponding actual parameter at compile time, and the type of the object whose reference value is actually passed at runtime. The output in Example 5.18 shows the class of the actual objects referenced by the formal parameters at runtime, which in this case turns out to be either `SafeStack` or `SafeStack[]`. The characters [L in the output indicate a one-dimensional array of a class or interface type (see the `Class.getName()` method in the Java SE Platform API documentation).

Overloaded Method Resolution

In this subsection, we take a look at some aspects regarding *overloaded method resolution*—that is, how the compiler determines which overloaded method will be invoked by a given method call at runtime.

Resolution of overloaded methods selects the *most specific* method for execution. One method is considered more specific than another method if all actual parameters that can be accepted by the one method can be accepted by the other method. If more than one such method is present, the call is described as *ambiguous*. The following overloaded methods illustrate this situation:

```
private static void flipFlop(String str, int i, Integer iRef) { // (1)
    out.println(str + " ==> (String, int, Integer)");
}
private static void flipFlop(String str, int i, int j) {         // (2)
    out.println(str + " ==> (String, int, int)");
}
```

Their method signatures are as follows:

```
flipFlop(String, int, Integer)                                  // See (1)
flipFlop(String, int, int)                                      // See (2)
```

The following method call is ambiguous:

```
flipFlop("(String, Integer, int)",
         Integer.valueOf(4), 2020);                             // (3) Ambiguous call
```

It has the call signature:

```
flipFlop(String, Integer, int)                                  // See (3)
```

The method at (1) can be called with the second argument unboxed and the third argument boxed, as can the method at (2) with only the second argument unboxed. In other words, for the call at (3), none of the methods is more specific than the other.

Example 5.19 illustrates a simple case of how method resolution is done to choose the most specific overloaded method. The method testIfOn() is overloaded at (1) and (2) in the class Overload. The call client.testIfOn(tubeLight) at (3) *satisfies* the parameter lists in both implementations given at (1) and (2), as the reference tubeLight can also be assigned to a reference of its superclass Light. The *most specific* method, (2), is chosen, resulting in false being written on the terminal. The call client.testIfOn(light) at (4) satisfies only the parameter list in the implementation given at (1), resulting in true being written on the terminal. This is also the case at (5). The object referred to by the argument in the call at runtime is irrelevant; rather, it is the *type* of the argument that is important for overloaded method resolution.

Example 5.19 *Choosing the Most Specific Method (Simple Case)*

```
class Light { /* ... */ }

class TubeLight extends Light { /* ... */ }

public class Overload {
    boolean testIfOn(Light aLight)          { return true; }   // (1)
    boolean testIfOn(TubeLight aTubeLight) { return false; }   // (2)
```

```
    public static void main(String[] args) {

        TubeLight tubeLight = new TubeLight();
        Light     light     = new Light();
        Light     light2    = new TubeLight();

        Overload client = new Overload();
        System.out.println(client.testIfOn(tubeLight)); // (3) ==> method at (2)
        System.out.println(client.testIfOn(light));     // (4) ==> method at (1)
        System.out.println(client.testIfOn(light2));    // (5) ==> method at (2)
    }
}
```

Output from the program:

```
false
true
true
```

The algorithm used by the compiler for the resolution of overloaded methods incorporates the following phases:

1. The compiler performs overload resolution without permitting boxing, unboxing, or the use of a variable arity call.

2. If phase (1) fails, the compiler performs overload resolution allowing boxing and unboxing, but excluding the use of a variable arity call.

3. If phase (2) fails, the compiler performs overload resolution combining a variable arity call, boxing, and unboxing.

Example 5.20 provides some insight into how the compiler determines the most specific overloaded method using these three phases. The example has six overloaded declarations of the method action(). The signature of each method is given by the local variable signature in each method. The first formal parameter of each method is the *signature of the call* that invoked the method. The printout from each method allows us to see which method call resolved to which method. The main() method contains 10 calls, (8) to (17), of the action() method. In each call, the first argument is the signature of that method call.

An important point to note is that the compiler chooses a *fixed arity* call over a variable arity call, as seen in the calls from (8) to (12):

(String) => (String)	(8) calls (1)
(String, int) => (String, int)	(9) calls (2)
(String, Integer) => (String, int)	(10) calls (2)
(String, int, byte) => (String, int, int)	(11) calls (3)
(String, int, int) => (String, int, int)	(12) calls (3)

An unboxing conversion (Integer to int) takes place for the call at (10). A widening primitive conversion (byte to int) takes place for the call at (11).

Variable arity calls are chosen from (13) to (17):

(String, int, long) => (String, Number[])	(13) calls (5)
(String, int, int, int) => (String, Integer[])	(14) calls (4)
(String, int, double) => (String, Number[])	(15) calls (5)
(String, int, String) => (String, Object[])	(16) calls (6)
(String, boolean) => (String, Object[])	(17) calls (6)

When a variable arity call is chosen, the method determined has the most specific variable arity parameter that is applicable for the actual argument. For example, in the method call at (14), the type Integer[] is more specific than either Number[] or Object[]. Note also the boxing of the elements of the implicitly created array in the calls from (13) to (17).

Example 5.20 *Overloaded Method Resolution*

```java
import static java.lang.System.out;

class OverloadResolution {

  public void action(String str) {                    // (1)
    String signature = "(String)";
    out.println(str + " => " + signature);
  }

  public void action(String str, int m) {             // (2)
    String signature = "(String, int)";
    out.println(str + " => " + signature);
  }

  public void action(String str, int m, int n) {     // (3)
    String signature = "(String, int, int)";
    out.println(str + " => " + signature);
  }

  public void action(String str, Integer... data) { // (4)
    String signature = "(String, Integer[])";
    out.println(str + " => " + signature);
  }

  public void action(String str, Number... data) {  // (5)
    String signature = "(String, Number[])";
    out.println(str + " => " + signature);
  }

  public void action(String str, Object... data) {  // (6)
    String signature = "(String, Object[])";
    out.println(str + " => " + signature);
  }

  public static void main(String[] args) {
    OverloadResolution ref = new OverloadResolution();
    ref.action("(String)");                                 // (8)  calls (1)
    ref.action("(String, int)",        10);                 // (9)  calls (2)
```

```
    ref.action("(String, Integer)",    Integer.valueOf(10));  // (10) calls (2)
    ref.action("(String, int, byte)",     10, (byte)20);      // (11) calls (3)
    ref.action("(String, int, int)",      10, 20);            // (12) calls (3)
    ref.action("(String, int, long)",     10, 20L);           // (13) calls (5)
    ref.action("(String, int, int, int)", 10, 20, 30);        // (14) calls (4)
    ref.action("(String, int, double)",   10, 20.0);          // (15) calls (5)
    ref.action("(String, int, String)",   10, "what?");       // (16) calls (6)
    ref.action("(String, boolean)",          false);          // (17) calls (6)
  }
}
```

For output from the program, see the explanation for Example 5.20 in the text.

5.11 Reference Casting and the instanceof Operator

In this section we explore *type casting of references* and the instanceof operator that can be used to perform either *type comparison* or *pattern matching*.

The Cast Operator

The basic form of the type cast expression for reference types has the following syntax:

(*destination_type*) *reference_expression*

where the *reference expression* evaluates to a reference value of an object of some reference type. A type cast expression checks that the reference value refers to an object whose type is compatible with the *destination type*, meaning that its type is a subtype of the *destination type*. The construct (*destination_type*) is usually called the *cast operator*. The result of a type cast expression for references is always a reference value of an object. The literal null can be cast to any reference type.

The code below illustrates the various scenarios that arise when using the cast operator. In this discussion, it is the type cast expression that is important, not the evaluation of the assignment operator in the declaration statements. At (1), the cast is from the superclass Object to the subclass String; the code compiles and at runtime this cast is permitted, as the reference obj will denote an object of class String. At (2), the cast is from the superclass Object to the subclass Integer; the code compiles, but at runtime this cast results in a ClassCastException, since the reference obj will denote an object of class String, which cannot be converted to an Integer. At (3), the cast is from the class String to the class Integer. As these two classes are unrelated, the compiler flags an error for the cast.

```
Object  obj = new String("Cast me!");
String  str = (String) obj;        // (1) Cast from Object to String.
Integer iRef1 = (Integer) obj;     // (2) Cast from Object to Integer, but
                                   //     ClassCastException at runtime.
Integer iRef2 = (Integer) str;     // (3) Compile-time error!
                                   //     Cast between unrelated types.
```

The following conversions can be applied to the operand of a cast operator:

- Both widening and narrowing reference conversions, followed optionally by an unchecked conversion (§11.2, p. 575)
- Both boxing and unboxing conversions

Boxing and unboxing conversions that can occur during casting are illustrated by the following code. Again, it is the type cast expression that is important in this discussion, rather than whether the assignment operator requires one in the declaration statements.

```
// (1) Boxing and casting: Number <-- Integer <-- int:
Number num = (Number) 100;
// (2) Casting, boxing, casting: Object <-- Integer <-- int <-- double:
Object obj = (Object) (int) 10.5;
// (3) Casting, unboxing, casting: double <--- int <-- Integer <-- Object:
double d = (double) (Integer) obj;
```

Note that the resulting object at (1) and (2) is an Integer, but the resulting value at (3) is a double. The boxing conversions from int to Integer at (1) and (2) are implicit, and the unboxing conversion from Integer to int at (3) is also implicit.

Casting to a supertype is always permitted, but redundant, since a supertype reference can always refer to an object of its subtype.

The instanceof Type Comparison Operator

The binary instanceof operator can be used for comparing *types*. It has the following syntax when used as a type comparison operator (note that the keyword is composed of lowercase letters only):

reference_expression instanceof *destination_type*

The instanceof type comparison operator returns true if the left-hand operand (i.e., the reference value that results from the evaluation of *reference expression*) can be a *subtype* of the right-hand operand (*destination type*). It always returns false if the left-hand operand is null. If the instanceof operator returns true, the corresponding type cast expression (*destination_type*) applied to the left-hand operand *reference_expression* will always be valid:

(*destination_type*) *reference_expression*

Both the type cast expression and the instanceof type comparison operator require a compile-time check and a runtime check. The compile-time check determines whether there is a subtype–supertype relationship between the source and destination types. Given that the type of the *reference expression* is *source type*, the compiler determines whether a reference of *source type* and a reference of *destination type* can refer to objects of a reference type that is a *common subtype* of both *source type* and *destination type* in the type hierarchy. If this is not the case, then obviously there is no relationship between the types, and neither the cast nor the instanceof type comparison operator application would be valid. At runtime, the *reference expression* evaluates to a reference value of an object. The instanceof type comparison operator determines whether the type of this object is a subtype of the *destination type*.

With the classes Light and String as *source type* and *destination type*, respectively, there is no subtype–supertype relationship between *source type* and *destination type*. The compiler would reject casting a reference of type Light to type String or applying the instanceof operator, as shown at (2) and (3) in Example 5.21. References of the classes Light and TubeLight can refer to objects of the class TubeLight (or its subclasses) in the inheritance hierarchy depicted in Figure 5.1, p. 194. Therefore, it makes sense to apply the instanceof type comparison operator or to cast a reference of the type Light to the type TubeLight as shown at (4) and (5), respectively, in Example 5.21.

At runtime, the result of applying the instanceof type comparison operator at (4) is false because the reference light1 of the class Light will actually denote an object of the subclass LightBulb, and this object cannot be denoted by a reference of the peer class TubeLight. Applying the cast at (5) results in a ClassCastException for the same reason. This is the reason why cast conversions are said to be *unsafe*, as they may throw a ClassCastException at runtime. Note that if the result of the instanceof type comparison operator is false, the cast involving the operands will throw a ClassCastException.

In Example 5.21, the result of applying the instanceof type comparison operator at (6) is also false because the reference light1 will still denote an object of the class LightBulb, whose objects cannot be denoted by a reference of its subclass SpotLightBulb. Thus applying the cast at (7) causes a ClassCastException to be thrown at runtime.

The situation shown at (8), (9), and (10) illustrates typical usage of the instanceof type comparison operator to determine which object a reference is denoting so that it can be cast for the purpose of carrying out some specific action—as we will see later, the instanceof pattern match operator provides a better solution for this particular case (p. 274). The reference light1 of the class Light is initialized to an object of the subclass NeonLight at (8). The result of the instanceof type comparison operator at (9) is true because the reference light1 will denote an object of the subclass NeonLight, whose objects can also be denoted by a reference of its superclass TubeLight. By the same token, the cast at (10) is valid. If the result of the instanceof type comparison operator is true, the cast involving the operands will be valid as well.

So far in Example 5.21, the *static* type of the reference in the left-hand operand of the instanceof comparison operator has been a *supertype* of the destination type. At (12), the *static* type (SpotLightBulb) of the reference in the left-hand operand of the instanceof comparison operator is a *subtype* of the destination type (Light). Since the *dynamic* type of the object is SpotLightBulb, which is a subtype of the destination type Light, the instanceof comparison operator returns true. The reference value of the object can be trivially assigned to a reference of the supertype Light, and the cast shown at (13) is actually redundant. This behavior of the instanceof comparison operator is allowed because of backward compatibility.

Example 5.21 *The* instanceof *Type Comparison and Cast Operators*

```java
// See Figure 5.1, p. 194, for inheritance hierarchy.
class Light { /* ... */ }
class LightBulb extends Light { /* ... */ }
class SpotLightBulb extends LightBulb { /* ... */ }
class TubeLight extends Light { /* ... */ }
class NeonLight extends TubeLight { /* ... */ }

public class WhoAmI {
  public static void main(String[] args) {
    boolean result1, result2, result3, result4;
    Light light1 = new LightBulb();                  // (1)
    //  String str = (String) light1;                // (2) Compile-time error!
    //   result1 = light1 instanceof String;         // (3) Compile-time error!

    result2 = light1 instanceof TubeLight;           // (4) false: peer class.
    //  TubeLight tubeLight1 = (TubeLight) light1;    // (5) ClassCastException!

    result3 = light1 instanceof SpotLightBulb;       // (6) false: superclass.
    //  SpotLightBulb spotRef = (SpotLightBulb) light1;// (7) ClassCastException!

    light1 = new NeonLight();                         // (8)
    if (light1 instanceof TubeLight) {                // (9) true.
      TubeLight tubeLight2 = (TubeLight) light1;      // (10) OK.
      // Can now use tubeLight2 to access an object of the class NeonLight,
      // but only those members that the object inherits or overrides
      // from the superclass TubeLight.
    }

    SpotLightBulb light2 = new SpotLightBulb();        // (11)
    result4 = light2 instanceof Light;                 // (12) true.
    Light light = (Light) light2;                      // (13) OK. Redundant cast.
  }
}
```

As we have seen, the instanceof type comparison operator effectively determines whether the reference value in the reference on the left-hand side refers to an object whose class is a subtype of the type specified on the right-hand side. At runtime, it is the type of the actual object denoted by the reference on the left-hand side that is compared with the type specified on the right-hand side. In other words, what matters at runtime is the type of the actual object denoted by the reference, not the declared or static type of the reference.

Example 5.22 provides more examples of the instanceof type comparison operator. It is instructive to go through the print statements and understand the results printed by the program. The following facts should be noted:

- The literal null is not an instance of any reference type, as shown in the print statements at (1), (2), and (16).
- An instance of a superclass is not an instance of its subclass, as shown in the print statement at (4).
- An instance of a class is not an instance of a totally unrelated class, as shown in the print statement at (10).
- An instance of a class is not an instance of an interface type that the class does not implement, as shown in the print statement at (6).
- Any array of a non-primitive type is an instance of both Object and Object[] types, as shown in the print statements at (14) and (15), respectively.

Example 5.22   *Using the* instanceof *Type Comparison Operator*

```
// See Figure 5.4, p. 245, for inheritance hierarchy.
interface IStack
interface ISafeStack extends IStack
class Stack implements IStack
class SafeStack extends Stack implements ISafeStack
```

```
public class Identification {
  public static void main(String[] args) {
    Object obj = new Object();
    Stack stack = new Stack(10);
    SafeStack safeStack = new SafeStack(5);
    IStack iStack;

    String strFormat = "(%d)  %-25s instance of %-25s: %s%n";
    System.out.printf(strFormat, 1,
        null, Object.class, null instanceof Object);      // Always false.
    System.out.printf(strFormat, 2,
        null, IStack.class, null instanceof IStack);      // Always false.

    System.out.printf(strFormat, 3, stack.getClass(), Object.class,
        stack instanceof Object);      // true: instance of subclass of Object.
    System.out.printf(strFormat, 4, obj.getClass(), Stack.class,
        obj instanceof Stack);         // false: Object not subtype of Stack.
    System.out.printf(strFormat, 5, stack.getClass(), Stack.class,
        stack instanceof Stack);       // true: instance of Stack.
    System.out.printf(strFormat, 6, obj.getClass(), IStack.class,
        obj instanceof IStack);        // false: Object does not implement IStack.
    System.out.printf(strFormat, 7, safeStack.getClass(), IStack.class,
        safeStack instanceof IStack); // true: SafeStack implements IStack.

    obj = stack;          // No cast required: assigning subclass to superclass.
    System.out.printf(strFormat, 8, obj.getClass(), Stack.class,
        obj instanceof Stack);         // true: instance of Stack.
    System.out.printf(strFormat, 9, obj.getClass(), IStack.class,
        obj instanceof IStack);        // true: Stack implements IStack.
    System.out.printf(strFormat, 10, obj.getClass(), String.class,
        obj instanceof String);        // false: no relationship.
```

```
        iStack = (IStack) obj; // Cast required: assigning superclass to subclass.
        System.out.printf(strFormat, 11, iStack.getClass(), Object.class,
            iStack instanceof Object);        // true: instance of subclass of Object.
        System.out.printf(strFormat, 12, iStack.getClass(), Stack.class,
            iStack instanceof Stack);         // true: instance of Stack.

        String[] strArray = new String[10];
//      System.out.printf(strFormat, 13, strArray.getClass(), String.class,
//          strArray instanceof String);      // Compile-time error: no relationship.
        System.out.printf(strFormat, 14, strArray.getClass(), Object.class,
            strArray instanceof Object);      // true: array subclass of Object.
        System.out.printf(strFormat, 15, strArray.getClass(), Object[].class,
            strArray instanceof Object[]);    // true: array subclass of Object[].
        System.out.printf(strFormat, 16, strArray[0], Object.class,
            strArray[0] instanceof Object);   // false: strArray[0] is null.
        System.out.printf(strFormat, 17, strArray.getClass(), String[].class,
            strArray instanceof String[]);    // true: array of String.

        strArray[0] = "Amoeba strip";
        System.out.printf(strFormat, 18, strArray[0].getClass(), String.class,
            strArray[0] instanceof String);   // true: strArray[0] instance of String.
    }
}
```

Output from the program:

```
(1)   null                      instance of class java.lang.Object    : false
(2)   null                      instance of interface IStack          : false
(3)   class Stack               instance of class java.lang.Object    : true
(4)   class java.lang.Object    instance of class Stack               : false
(5)   class Stack               instance of class Stack               : true
(6)   class java.lang.Object    instance of interface IStack          : false
(7)   class SafeStack           instance of interface IStack          : true
(8)   class Stack               instance of class Stack               : true
(9)   class Stack               instance of interface IStack          : true
(10)  class Stack               instance of class java.lang.String    : false
(11)  class Stack               instance of class java.lang.Object    : true
(12)  class Stack               instance of class Stack               : true
(14)  class [Ljava.lang.String; instance of class java.lang.Object    : true
(15)  class [Ljava.lang.String; instance of class [Ljava.lang.Object;: true
(16)  null                      instance of class java.lang.Object    : false
(17)  class [Ljava.lang.String; instance of class [Ljava.lang.String;: true
(18)  class java.lang.String    instance of class java.lang.String    : true
```

The instanceof Pattern Match Operator

The instanceof operator can also be used for *pattern matching,* as explained below.
It has the following syntax when used as a *pattern match operator:*

$$
\underset{\underbrace{\textit{destination\_type}\ \textit{pattern\_variable}}_{\textit{type\_pattern}}}{\textit{reference\_expression}\ \texttt{instanceof}}
$$

Note that the syntax of the instanceof pattern match operator augments the syntax of the instanceof type comparison operator with a *pattern variable*. The *type pattern* comprises a *local reference variable declaration*. The instanceof pattern match operator essentially combines the instanceof type comparison operator with a type cast and initialization of a *pattern variable*.

As with the instanceof type comparison operator, a compile-time check determines whether there is a subtype–supertype relationship between the static type of the left-hand operand and the *destination type*. However, as opposed to the instanceof type comparison operator, the compiler flags an error if the *destination type* is *not* a *subtype* of the *static* type of the left-hand operand.

At runtime, if the reference value of the object resulting from the evaluation of the *reference expression* can be *cast* to the *destination type* (i.e., the dynamic type of the resulting object is a *subtype* of the *destination type*), the object is said to *match* the *type pattern*. Only in this case does the instanceof pattern match operator return true and, as a side effect, *the reference value of the object is cast to the destination type and assigned to the pattern variable*. The *pattern variable* is never created or initialized if the instanceof pattern match operator returns false. It always returns false if the left-hand operand is null.

We assume the following types in the discussion below. See Example 5.10, p. 241, for type declarations.

```
interface IStack                  (defines methods push() and pop())
interface ISafeStack extends IStack (with boolean methods isEmpty() and isFull())
class Stack implements IStack
class SafeStack extends Stack implements ISafeStack
```

The instanceof-and-cast idiom is commonly used to elicit the subtype-specific behavior of an object referenced by a supertype reference. The code below at (1) and (2) is equivalent. However, this idiom can be expressed compactly with the instanceof pattern match operator as it type checks the object and casts its reference value that is assigned to the pattern variable. When this operator returns true, it is said to *introduce* a *pattern variable* into a well-defined scope, which in this case is the if block.

```
IStack stack = new SafeStack(20); // Supertype reference denotes subtype object.

// Using the instanceof type comparison operator. (1)
if (stack instanceof SafeStack) {                // Correct subtype?
  SafeStack safestack = (SafeStack) stack;       // Cast to subtype.
  System.out.println(safestack.isFull());        // Call subtype-specific method.
}

// Using the instanceof pattern match operator.   (2)
if (stack instanceof SafeStack safestack) {
  System.out.println(safestack.isFull());
}
```

In contrast to the instanceof type comparison operator, the destination type in the instanceof pattern match operator *must* be a subtype of the static type of the left-hand operand. In other words, the reference value of the object is always cast to a subtype by the operator. In the code below, the compiler complains that the expression type (ISafeStack) cannot be a subtype of the pattern types ISafeStack and IStack, respectively, at (1) and (2), in the context of the instanceof pattern match operator.

```
ISafeStack safestack = new SafeStack(20);
if (safestack instanceof ISafeStack stack) {      // (1) Compile-time error!
    stack.push("Hi");
}
if (safestack instanceof IStack stack) {          // (2) Compile-time error!
    stack.push("Howdy");
}
```

A pattern variable *cannot* shadow another local variable by the same name—that is, it cannot be redeclared in a pattern if the local variable of the same name is still in scope.

```
IStack stack = new SafeStack(20);
SafeStack safestack = new SafeStack(5);        // Local variable safestack

if (stack instanceof SafeStack safestack) {    // Error: safestack redeclared.
  System.out.println(safestack.isFull());
}
```

A pattern variable introduced by the instanceof pattern match operator can shadow a *field* of the same name in the class.

```
// Field declaration:
private static IStack myStack = new Stack(10);

...

IStack stack = new SafeStack(20);
if (stack instanceof SafeStack myStack) {    // Local variable introduced.
  System.out.println(myStack.isFull());      // Shadows field reference.
}
myStack.push("Hello");                       // Field reference.
```

A pattern variable is not final in its scope unless it is declared final—in other words, the pattern variable can be declared with the modifier final, as shown at (1). Changing the value of a final pattern variable is flagged as a compile-time error, as shown at (2).

```
IStack stack = new SafeStack(
if (stack instanceof final SafeStack safestack) {  // (1) final pattern variable.
  safestack = new SafeStack(100);                  // (2) Compile-time error!
  System.out.println(safestack.isFull());
}
```

Scope of Pattern Variables

We first examine the scope of a pattern variable in an if-else statement. If the instanceof pattern match operator returns true in the conditional of an if statement, the pattern variable is introduced and its scope is the if block. Not surprisingly, this is also the case for the if-else statement. The pattern variable is *not* accessible in the else block.

```
IStack stack = new SafeStack(20);
if (stack instanceof SafeStack safestack) {
  System.out.println(safestack.isFull());    // Pattern variable in scope.
} else {
  System.out.println(safestack.isEmpty());  // Compile-time error!
}
```

It is important to keep in mind that the instanceof pattern match operator introduces a pattern variable if and only if it returns true. In the if-else statement below, the if block is only executed if the conditional is true—that is, if the instanceof pattern match operator returns false. In that case, no pattern variable is introduced, and thus no pattern variable is ever accessible in the if block. However, if the conditional is false, the instanceof pattern match operator must be true, and thus introduces a pattern variable that is guaranteed to be accessible in the else block.

```
IStack stack = new SafeStack(20);
if (!(stack instanceof SafeStack safestack)) { // Logical complement operator (!)
  System.out.println(safestack.isFull());        // Compile-time error.
} else {
  System.out.println(safestack.isFull());        // Pattern variable in scope.
}
```

In fact, if the if block does *not complete normally* (e.g., by executing a return, a break, or a continue statement) as shown at (1), the pattern variable introduced is accessible in the else block and in code after the if-else statement.

```
IStack stack = new SafeStack(20);
if (!(stack instanceof SafeStack safestack)) {
  System.out.println("No safestack here");
  return;                                      // (1) Does not complete normally.
} else {
  System.out.println(safestack.isFull());      // Pattern variable in scope.
}
System.out.println(safestack.isEmpty());       // Pattern variable still in scope.
```

The instanceof pattern match operator can also introduce a pattern variable in certain boolean expressions. The conditional in the if statement below uses the conditional-AND operator (&&). The short-circuit evaluation of the && operator ensures that the right-hand operand is only executed if the left-hand operand evaluates to true, thereby introducing the pattern variable that is then in scope in the right-hand operand. The pattern variable will be in scope in the if block if the conditional evaluates to true—that is, both operands of the && operator return true. Applying the logical complement (!) operator to the conditional expression below works the same way as we have seen earlier with the if-else statement.

```
IStack stack = new SafeStack(20);
if (stack instanceof SafeStack safestack && safestack.isFull()) {
  System.out.println("safestack is full");
  Object obj = safestack.pop();
}
```

The conditional-OR operator (||) does *not* introduce a pattern variable in the if block. Because of short-circuit evaluation of the || operator, the right-side operand of the conditional is only evaluated if the left-side operand is false, but then no pattern variable has been introduced in the boolean expression by the instanceof pattern match operator.

```
IStack stack = new SafeStack(20);
if (stack instanceof SafeStack safestack || safestack.isFull()) { // Compile-time
                                                                         error.
  System.out.println("safestack is full");
  Object obj = safestack.pop();                              // Compile-time error.
}
```

Using the same pattern variable in instanceof expressions below results in a compile-time error, as this is analogous to redeclaring a local variable.

```
IStack stack = new SafeStack(20);
if (stack instanceof SafeStack safestack &&  // Compile-time error!
    stack instanceof ISafeStack safestack) { // Duplicate variable safestack
  System.out.println(safestack);
}
```

The instanceof pattern match operator can be used in the conditional (ternary) operator, and it's semantics are analogous to those of the if-else statement:

```
IStack stack = new SafeStack(20);
boolean result = stack instanceof SafeStack safestack ? safestack.isEmpty()
                                                       : false;
```

The instanceof pattern match operator can also introduce a pattern variable in loops—for example, in for and while statements. This allows conditional processing of objects where loop termination is controlled by the boolean value of the instanceof pattern match operator and the pattern variable referring to the next object for processing.

Using the instanceof pattern match operator makes the code concise and safe, as it combines three tasks into a single operation: subtype checking, reference casting, and assignment to a local variable.

5.12 Polymorphism

A supertype reference can denote an object of its subtypes—conversely, a subtype object can act as an object of its supertypes. This is because there is an *is-a* relationship between a subtype and its supertypes.

Since a supertype reference can denote objects of different types at different times during execution, a supertype reference is said to exhibit *polymorphic* behavior (meaning *has many forms*). A subtype object also exhibits polymorphic behavior, since it can act as any object of its supertypes.

When a non-private instance method is called, the method definition executed is determined by *dynamic method lookup*, based on *the type of the object* denoted by the reference at runtime. Dynamic method lookup (also known as *late binding*, *dynamic binding,* and *virtual method invocation*) is the process of determining which method definition a method call signature denotes at runtime. It is performed starting in the class of the object on which the method is invoked, and moves up the inheritance hierarchy to find the supertype with the appropriate method definition.

For *a call to an overridden method using a supertype reference,* dynamic method lookup can determine a different method definition to execute at different times depending on the type of the object that is denoted by the supertype reference during execution. The overridden method is said to exhibit polymorphic behavior. Exploiting this polymorphic behavior is illustrated next.

The inheritance hierarchy depicted in Figure 5.7 is implemented in Example 5.23. Note that both the draw() and area() methods are overridden in Figure 5.7. The abstract method draw() in the IDrawable interface at (1) is implemented in all subclasses of the abstract class Shape. It is also implemented by the class Graph. The invocation of the draw() method in the three loops at (3), (4), and (6) in Example 5.23 relies on the polymorphic behavior of references and dynamic method lookup. The array drawables holds IDrawable references that can be assigned the reference value of an object whose class implements the IDrawable interface: a Square, a Circle, a Rectangle, and a Graph, as shown at (2). At runtime, dynamic lookup determines the draw() method implementation that will execute, based on the type of the object denoted by each element in the array.

Figure 5.7 *Type Hierarchy to Illustrate Polymorphism*

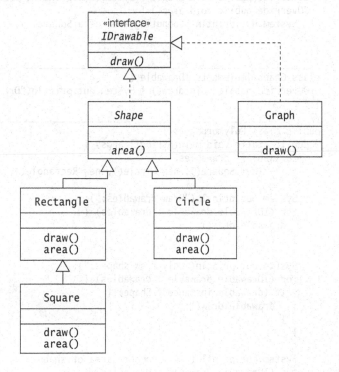

Example 5.23 *Using Polymorphism*

```java
// File: PolymorphRefs.java
interface IDrawable {                                                    // (1)
  void draw();
}
//_____
abstract class Shape implements IDrawable {
  abstract public void area();
}
//_____
class Circle extends Shape {
  @Override public void draw() { System.out.println("Drawing a Circle."); }
  @Override public void area() {
    System.out.println("Computing area of a Circle.");
  }
}
//_____
class Rectangle extends Shape {
  @Override public void draw() { System.out.println("Drawing a Rectangle."); }
  @Override public void area() {
    System.out.println("Computing area of a Rectangle.");
  }
}
//_____
class Square extends Rectangle {
  @Override public void draw() { System.out.println("Drawing a Square."); }
  @Override public void area() {
    System.out.println("Computing area of a Square.");
  }
}
//_____
class Graph implements IDrawable {
  @Override public void draw() { System.out.println("Drawing a Graph."); }
}
//_____
public class PolymorphRefs {
  public static void main(String[] args) {
    IDrawable[] drawables
      = {new Square(), new Circle(), new Rectangle(), new Graph()};      // (2)

    System.out.println("Draw drawables:");
    for (IDrawable drawable : drawables) {                               // (3)
      drawable.draw();
    }

    System.out.println("Only draw shapes:");
    for (IDrawable drawable : drawables) {                               // (4)
      if (drawable instanceof Shape) {                                   // (5)
        drawable.draw();
      }
    }

    System.out.println("Only compute area of shapes:");
    for (IDrawable drawable : drawables) {                               // (6)
```

```
        if (drawable instanceof Shape shape) {                            // (7)
          shape.area();                                                   // (8)
        }
      }
    }
  }
}
```

Output from the program:

```
Draw drawables:
Drawing a Square.
Drawing a Circle.
Drawing a Rectangle.
Drawing a Graph.
Only draw shapes:
Drawing a Square.
Drawing a Circle.
Drawing a Rectangle.
Only compute area of shapes:
Computing area of a Square.
Computing area of a Circle.
Computing area of a Rectangle.
```

In the for(:) loop at (3) in Example 5.23, depending on the type of the object
denoted by the loop variable drawable, the call to the draw() method will result in
the draw() method of this object to be executed.

The instanceof type comparison operator returns true if the reference specified as
its left-hand operand at runtime denotes an object whose type is the same as or is
a subtype of the reference type specified in its right-hand operand. If the types of
the operands are unrelated, the compiler issues an error.

```
IDrawable d1 = new Rectangle();
System.out.println(d1 instanceof IDrawable); // true. Rectangle is an IDrawable.
System.out.println(d1 instanceof Shape);     // true. Rectangle is a Shape.
System.out.println(d1 instanceof Rectangle); // true. Rectangle is a Rectangle.
System.out.println(d1 instanceof Circle);    // false. Rectangle is not a Circle.
System.out.println(d1 instanceof Graph);     // false. Rectangle is not a Graph.
// System.out.println(d1 instanceof String); // Unrelated. Compile-time error.
```

In Example 5.23, the abstract method area() of the abstract class Shape is implemented by all subclasses of the superclass Shape. The code below does not compile,
as the compiler determines that the method area() is not defined by the interface
IDrawable.

```
IDrawable d2 = new Square();  // Subtype object denoted by supertype reference.
d2.area();          // Method not defined for type IDrawable. Compile-time error!
```

In order to elicit subtype-specific behavior in an object that is denoted by a supertype reference, the reference must be *cast* to the subtype. The cast is specified as
(*reference_type*). The cast in this case applies a narrowing reference conversion
from a supertype to a subtype. The cast appeases the compiler. At runtime, the type
of the object still determines which area() method will be executed.

```
((Square) d2).area();           // Prints "Computing area of a Square."
((Shape) d2).area();            // Prints "Computing area of a Square."
```

The code above executes normally because the reference d2 at runtime denotes an object whose type defines the appropriate area() method. The code below shows that the cast alone is not enough to guarantee that the execution will proceed normally, even though there was no compile-time error. The Graph object denoted by the reference d3 at runtime does not define the area() method.

```
IDrawable d3 = new Graph();      // No compile-time error.
((Shape) d3).area();             // Throws a ClassCastException!
```

Guaranteeing the correct subtype and casting to a subtype reference safely can be accomplished using the instanceof pattern match operator.

```
if (d2 instanceof Shape shape) {          // true
  shape.area();                           // Prints "Computing area of a Square."
} else {
  System.out.println(d2.getClass().getName() + " is not a Shape." );
}

if (d3 instanceof Shape shape) {          // false
  shape.area();
} else {
  System.out.println(d3.getClass().getName() +
                " is not a Shape." ); // Prints "Graph is not a Shape."
}
```

In the for(:) loop at (4) in Example 5.23, we are only interested in drawing objects from the drawables array that are of type Shape. The binary instanceof type comparison operator in the conditional of the if statement at (5) is used to determine whether the type of an object in the drawables array is of type Shape. The draw() method is only called on objects that satisfy this condition.

The for(:) loop at (6) in Example 5.23 uses the instanceof pattern match operator at (7) to select those IDrawable objects whose type is Shape, and invoke the area() method on them.

A private instance method does not exhibit polymorphic behavior. A call to such a method can occur only within the class and gets bound to the private method implementation at compile time.

Overloaded instance methods do not exhibit polymorphic behavior, as their calls are bound at compile time, unless an overloaded method is also overridden and invoked by a supertype reference.

Static methods also do not exhibit polymorphic behavior, as these methods do not belong to objects.

Polymorphism is achieved through inheritance and interface implementation. Code relying on polymorphic behavior will still work without any change if new subclasses or new classes implementing the interface are added. If no obvious is-a relationship is present, polymorphism is best achieved by using aggregation with interface implementation.

Polymorphism and dynamic method lookup form a powerful programming paradigm that simplifies client definitions, encourages object decoupling, and supports dynamically changing relationships between objects at runtime.

 Review Questions

5.22 Given the following class and reference declarations, what can be said about the statement y = (Sub) x?

```
// Class declarations:
class Super {}
class Sub extends Super {}

// Reference declarations:
  Super x = null;
  Sub y = null;
```

Select the one correct answer.

(a) It is illegal at compile time.
(b) It is legal at compile time, but it might throw a ClassCastException at runtime.
(c) It is definitely legal at runtime, but the cast operator (Sub) is not strictly needed.
(d) It is definitely legal at runtime, and the cast operator (Sub) is needed.

5.23 Given the following code:

```
class A { }
class B extends A { }
class C extends B { }
```

Which boolean expression is true only when the reference o refers to an object of class B, and not to an object of class A or class C?
Select the one correct answer.

(a) (o instanceof B) && (!(o instanceof A))
(b) (o instanceof B) && (!(o instanceof C))
(c) !((o instanceof A) || (o instanceof B))
(d) (o instanceof B)
(e) (o instanceof B) && !((o instanceof A) || (o instanceof C))

5.24 What will the following program print when run?

```
interface I{}
interface J{}
class C implements I {}
class D extends C implements J {}

public class RQ07A100 {
  public static void main(String[] args) {
    I x = new D();
    if (x instanceof I) System.out.print("I");
    if (x instanceof J) System.out.print("J");
    if (x instanceof C) System.out.print("C");
    if (x instanceof D) System.out.print("D");
```

```
      System.out.println();
    }
  }
```

Select the one correct answer.

(a) The program will not print any letters.
(b) ICD
(c) IJD
(d) IJCD
(e) ID

5.25 What will be the result of compiling and running the following program?

```
public class RQ800A20 {
  static void compute(int... ia) {                          // (1)
    System.out.print("|");
    for(int i : ia) {
      System.out.print(i + "|");
    }
    System.out.println();
  }
  static void compute(int[] ia1, int... ia2) {              // (2)
    compute(ia1);
    compute(ia2);
  }
  static void compute(int[] ia1, int[]... ia2d) {           // (3)
    for(int[] ia : ia2d) {
      compute(ia);
    }
  }
  public static void main(String[] args) {
    compute(new int[] {10, 11}, new int[] {12, 13, 14});    // (4)
    compute(15, 16);                                        // (5)
    compute(new int[] {17, 18}, new int[][] {{19}, {20}});  // (6)
    compute(null, new int[][] {{21}, {22}});                // (7)
  }
}
```

Select the one correct answer.

(a) The program will fail to compile because of errors in one or more calls to the compute() method.
(b) The program compiles, but it throws a NullPointerException when run.
(c) The program compiles and prints:
```
|10|11|
|12|13|14|
|15|16|
|19|
|20|
|21|
|22|
```
(d) The program compiles and prints:
```
|12|13|14|
|15|16|
```

```
|10|11|
|19|
|20|
|21|
|22|
```

5.26   Given the following code:

```java
public class RQ43 {
  public static void main(String[] args) {
    Object x = "acme";
    if (x instanceof String s && s.length() > 5) {
      x = s.equals("acme") ? "1" : "2";
    } else {
      x = s.equals("acme") ? "3" : "4";
    }
    System.out.println(x);
  }
}
```

What is the result?
Select the one correct answer.

(a) 1

(b) 2

(c) 3

(d) 4

(e) The program will throw an exception at runtime.

(f) The program will fail to compile.

5.27   Which option will compile without errors?
Select the one correct answer.

(a) ```java
     Integer x = Integer.valueOf(42);
     if (x instanceof Integer s) {
         System.out.print(s.intValue());
     }
     ```

(b)  ```java
     var x = Integer.valueOf(42);
     if (x instanceof Integer s) {
         System.out.print(s.intValue());
     }
     ```

(c) ```java
     var x = Integer.valueOf(42);
     if (x instanceof String s) {
         System.out.print(s.toUpperCase());
     }
     ```

(d)  ```java
     Number x = Integer.valueOf(42);
     if (x instanceof Integer s) {
         System.out.print(s.intValue());
     }
     ```

(e) ```java
     Integer x = Integer.valueOf(42);
     if (x instanceof Number s) {
         System.out.print(s.intValue());
     }
     ```
     ```

5.28   Which of the following statements are true?
Select the two correct answers.

(a) The instanceof pattern match operator does not throw a NullPointerException
if its left operand is null.
(b) The instanceof pattern match operator throws a NullPointerException if its left
operand is null.
(c) A pattern variable is only introduced when the instanceof pattern match
operator returns true.
(d) A pattern variable is only introduced when the instanceof pattern match
operator returns false.

5.29   What will be the result of compiling and running the following program?

```
class A              { int f() { return 0; } }
class B extends A { int f() { return 1; } }
class C extends B { int f() { return 2; } }

public class Polymorphism {
  public static void main(String[] args) {
    A ref1 = new C();
    B ref2 = (B) ref1;
    System.out.println(ref2.f());
  }
}
```

Select the one correct answer.

(a) The program will fail to compile.
(b) The program will compile, but it will throw a ClassCastException at runtime.
(c) The program will compile and print 0 when run.
(d) The program will compile and print 1 when run.
(e) The program will compile and print 2 when run.

5.30   What will be the result of compiling and running the following program?

```
class A {
  private int f() { return 0; }
  public int g() { return 3; }
}
class B extends A {
  private int f() { return 1; }
  public int g() { return f(); }
}
class C extends B {
  public int f() { return 2; }
}

public class Polymorphism2 {
  public static void main(String[] args) {
    A ref1 = new C();
    B ref2 = (B) ref1;
    System.out.println(ref2.g());
  }
}
```

Select the one correct answer.

(a) The program will fail to compile.
(b) The program will compile and print 0 when run.
(c) The program will compile and print 1 when run.
(d) The program will compile and print 2 when run.
(e) The program will compile and print 3 when run.

5.31 Which of the following statements about the following program are true?

```java
public interface HeavenlyBody { String describe(); }

class Star {
  String starName;
  public String describe() { return "star " + starName; }
}

class Planet extends Star {
  String name;
  public String describe() {
    return "planet " + name + " orbiting star " + starName;
  }
}
```

Select the three correct answers:

(a) The code will fail to compile.
(b) The code defines a Planet *is-a* Star relationship.
(c) The code will fail to compile if the name starName is replaced with the name bodyName throughout the declaration of the Star class.
(d) The code will fail to compile if the name starName is replaced with the name name throughout the declaration of the Star class.
(e) An instance of Planet is a valid instance of HeavenlyBody.
(f) The code defines a Planet *has-a* Star relationship.

5.13 Enum Types

An *enum type* is a special-purpose class that defines *a finite set of symbolic names and their values*. These symbolic names are usually called *enum constants* or *named constants*. An enum type is also synonymously referred to as an *enum class*.

Before the introduction of enum types in the Java programming language, such constants were typically declared as final, static variables in a class (or an interface) declaration:

```java
public class MachineState {
  public static final int BUSY = 1;
  public static final int IDLE = 0;
  public static final int BLOCKED = -1;
}
```

Such constants are not type-safe, as *any* int value can be used where we need to use a constant declared in the MachineState class. Such a constant must be qualified by the class (or interface) name, unless the class is extended (or the interface is implemented). When such a constant is printed, only its value (e.g., 0), and not its name (e.g., IDLE) is printed. A constant also needs recompiling if its value is changed, as the values of such constants are compiled into the client code.

An enum type in Java is a special kind of class that is much more powerful than the approach outlined above for defining named constants.

Declaring Type-Safe Enums

The canonical form of declaring an enum type is shown below.

```
access_modifier enum enum_type_name    // Enum header
{                                      // Enum body
    EC1, EC2, ..., ECk                 // Enum constants
}
```

The following declaration is an example of an enum type:

```
public enum MachineState              // Enum header
{                                     // Enum body
    BUSY, IDLE, BLOCKED               // Enum constants

}
```

The keyword enum is used to declare an enum type, as opposed to the keyword class for a class declaration. The basic notation requires the *enum type name* in the enum header, and *a comma-separated list of enum constants* (EC_1, EC2, ..., ECk) can be specified in the enum body. In the example enum declaration, the name of the enum type is MachineState. It defines three enum constants with explicit names: BUSY, IDLE, and BLOCKED. An enum constant can be any legal Java identifier, but the convention is to use uppercase letters in the name.

Essentially, an enum declaration defines a *reference type* that has a *finite number of permissible values* referenced by the enum constants, and the compiler ensures they are used in a type-safe manner.

Analogous to a top-level class, a top-level enum type can be declared with either public or package accessibility. However, an enum type declared as a static member of a reference type can be declared with any accessibility.

As we shall see later, other member declarations can be specified in the body of an enum type. If this is the case, the enum constant list must be terminated by a semicolon (;). Analogous to a class declaration, an enum type is compiled to Java bytecode that is placed in a separate class file.

The Java SE Platform API contains numerous enum types. We mention two enum types here: java.time.Month and java.time.DayOfWeek. As we would expect, the Month enum type represents the months from JANUARY to DECEMBER, and the DayOfWeek enum type represents the days of the week from MONDAY to SUNDAY. Examples of their usage can be found in §17.2, p. 1027.

Some additional examples of enum types are given below.

```
public enum MarchingOrders { LEFT, RIGHT }

public enum TrafficLightState { RED, YELLOW, GREEN; }

enum MealType { BREAKFAST, LUNCH, DINNER }
```

Using Type-Safe Enums

Example 5.24 illustrates using enum constants. An enum type is essentially used as any other reference type, and the restrictions are noted later in this section. Enum constants are actually final, static variables of the enum type, and they are implicitly initialized with instances of the enum type when the enum type is loaded at runtime. Since the enum constants are static members, they can be accessed using the name of the enum type—analogous to accessing static members in a class.

Example 5.24 shows a machine client that uses a machine whose state is an enum constant. In this example, we see that an enum constant can be passed as an argument, as shown at (1), and we can declare references whose type is an enum type, as shown at (3), but we *cannot* create new constants (i.e., objects) of the enum type MachineState. An attempt to do so at (5) results in a compile-time error.

The text representation of an enum constant is its name, as shown at (4). Note that it is not possible to pass a value of a type other than a MachineState enum constant in the call to the method setState() of the Machine class, as shown at (2).

Example 5.24 *Using Enums*

```
// File: MachineState.java
public enum MachineState { BUSY, IDLE, BLOCKED }
```

```
// File: Machine.java
public class Machine {

  private MachineState state;

  public void setState(MachineState state) { this.state = state; }
  public MachineState getState()           { return this.state; }
}
```

```
// File: MachineClient.java
public class MachineClient {
  public static void main(String[] args) {

    Machine machine = new Machine();
    machine.setState(MachineState.IDLE);          // (1) Passed as a value.
    // machine.setState(1);                         // (2) Compile error!
```

```
    MachineState state = machine.getState();        // (3) Declaring a reference.
    System.out.println(
        "Current machine state: " + state            // (4) Printing the enum name.
    );

    // MachineState newState = new MachineState();   // (5) Compile error!

    System.out.println("All machine states:");
    for (MachineState ms : MachineState.values()) {  // (6) Traversing over enum
      System.out.println(ms + ":" + ms.ordinal());   //     contants.
    }

    System.out.println("Comparison:");
    MachineState state1 = MachineState.BUSY;
    MachineState state2 = state1;
    MachineState state3 = MachineState.BLOCKED;

    System.out.println(state1 + " == " + state2 + ": " +
                        (state1 == state2));                          // (7)
    System.out.println(state1 + " is equal to " + state2 + ": " +
                        (state1.equals(state2)));                     // (8)
    System.out.println(state1 + " is less than " + state3 + ": " +
                        (state1.compareTo(state3) < 0));              // (9)
  }
}
```

Output from the program:

```
Current machine state: IDLE
All machine states:
BUSY:0
IDLE:1
BLOCKED:2
Comparison:
BUSY == BUSY: true
BUSY is equal to BUSY: true
BUSY is less than BLOCKED: true
```

Declaring Enum Constructors and Members

An enum type can declare constructors and other members as in an ordinary class, but the enum constants must be declared before any other declarations (see the declaration of the enum type Meal in Example 5.25). The list of enum constants must be terminated by a semicolon (;) if followed by any constructor or member declaration. Each enum constant name can be followed by an argument list that is passed to the constructor of the enum type having the matching parameter signature.

In Example 5.25, the enum type Meal contains a constructor declaration at (2) with the following signature:

```
Meal(int, int)
```

Each enum constant is specified with an argument list with the signature (int, int) that matches the non-zero argument constructor signature. The enum constant list is also terminated by a semicolon, as the enum declaration contains other members: two fields for the meal time at (3), and three instance methods to retrieve meal time information at (4).

When the enum type is loaded at runtime, the constructor is run for each enum constant, passing the argument values specified for the enum constant. For the Meal enum type, three objects are created that are initialized with the specified argument values, and are referenced by the three enum constant names, respectively. Note that each enum constant is a final, static reference that stores the reference value of an object of the enum type, and methods of the enum type can be called on this object by using the enum constant name. This is illustrated at (5) in Example 5.25 by calling methods on the object referenced by the enum constant Meal.BREAKFAST.

A default constructor is created if no constructors are provided for the enum type, analogous to a class. As mentioned earlier, an enum type cannot be instantiated using the new operator. The constructors cannot be called explicitly. Thus the only access modifier allowed for a constructor is private, as a constructor is understood to be implicitly declared private if no access modifier is specified.

Static initializer blocks can also be declared in an enum type, analogous to those in a class (§10.7, p. 545).

Example 5.25 *Declaring Enum Constructors and Members*

```java
// File: Meal.java
public enum Meal {
  BREAKFAST(7,30), LUNCH(12,15), DINNER(19,45);              // (1)

  // Non-zero argument constructor                            (2)
  Meal(int hh, int mm) {
    this.hh = hh;
    this.mm = mm;
  }

  // Fields for the meal time:                                (3)
  private int hh;
  private int mm;

  // Instance methods:                                        (4)
  public int getHour() { return this.hh; }
  public int getMins() { return this.mm; }
  public String getTimeString() {                     // "hh:mm"
    return String.format("%02d:%02d", this.hh, this.mm);
  }
}
```

```java
// File: MealAdministrator.java
public class MealAdministrator {
  public static void main(String[] args) {

    System.out.printf(                                          // (5)
        "Please note that no eggs will be served at %s, %s.%n",
        Meal.BREAKFAST, Meal.BREAKFAST.getTimeString()
    );

    System.out.println("Meal times are as follows:");
    Meal[] meals = Meal.values();                               // (6)
    for (Meal meal : meals) {                                   // (7)
      System.out.printf("%s served at %s%n", meal, meal.getTimeString());
    }

    Meal formalDinner = Meal.valueOf("DINNER");                 // (8)
    System.out.printf("Formal dress is required for %s at %s.%n",
        formalDinner, formalDinner.getTimeString()
    );
  }
}
```

Output from the program:

```
Please note that no eggs will be served at BREAKFAST, 07:30.
Meal times are as follows:
BREAKFAST served at 07:30
LUNCH served at 12:15
DINNER served at 19:45
Formal dress is required for DINNER at 19:45.
```

Implicit Static Methods for Enum Types

All enum types implicitly have the following static methods, and methods with these names *cannot* be declared in an enum type declaration:

static *EnumTypeName*[] values()

Returns an array containing the enum constants of this enum type, *in the order they are specified*.

static *EnumTypeName* valueOf(String name)

Returns the enum constant with the specified name. An IllegalArgumentException is thrown if the specified name does not match the name of an enum constant. The specified name is *not* qualified with the enum type name.

The static method values() is called at (6) in Example 5.25 to create an array of enum constants. This array is traversed in the for(:) loop at (7), printing the information about each meal.

The static method valueOf() is called at (8) in Example 5.25 to retrieve the enum constant that has the specified name "DINNER". A print statement is used to print the information about the meal denoted by this enum constant.

Inherited Methods from the java.lang.Enum Class

All enum types are subtypes of the java.lang.Enum class which implements the default behavior. All enum types are comparable (§14.4, p. 761) and serializable (§20.5, p. 1261).

All enum types inherit the following selected final methods from the java.lang.Enum class, and these methods therefore *cannot* be overridden by an enum type:

final int compareTo(E o)

The *natural order* of the enum constants in an enum type is according to their *ordinal values* (see the ordinal() method below). The compareTo() method in the Comparable interface is discussed in §14.4, p. 761.

final boolean equals(Object other)

Returns true if the specified object is equal to this enum constant (§14.2, p. 744).

final int hashCode()

Returns a hash code for this enum constant (§14.3, p. 753).

final String name()

Returns the name of this enum constant, exactly as it is declared in its enum declaration.

final int ordinal()

Returns the *ordinal value* of this enum constant (i.e., its position in its enum type declaration). The first enum constant is assigned an ordinal value of zero. If the ordinal value of an enum constant is less than the ordinal value of another enum constant of the same enum type, the former occurs before the latter in the enum type declaration.

Note that the equality test implemented by the equals() method is based on reference equality (==) of the enum constants, not on object value equality. Comparing two enum references for equality meanss determining whether they store the reference value of the same enum constant—that is, whether the references are aliases. Thus for any two enum references, meal1 and meal2, the expressions meal1.equals(meal2) and meal1 == meal2 are equivalent.

The java.lang.Enum class also overrides the toString() method from the Object class. The toString() method returns the name of the enum constant, but it is *not* final and can be overridden by an enum type—but that is rarely done. Examples in this subsection illustrate the use of these methods.

Extending Enum Types: Constant-Specific Class Bodies

Constant-specific class bodies define anonymous classes (§9.6, p. 521) inside an enum type—they implicitly extend the enclosing enum type creating new subtypes. The enum type Meal in Example 5.26 declares constant-specific class bodies for its constants. The following skeletal code declares the constant-specific class body for the enum constant BREAKFAST:

```
BREAKFAST(7,30) {                       // (1) Start of constant-specific class body
  @Override
  public double mealPrice(Day day) {  // (2) Overriding abstract method
    ...
  }
  @Override
  public String toString() {          // (3) Overriding method from the Enum class
    ...
  }
}                                       // (4) End of constant-specific class body
```

The constant-specific class body, as the name implies, is a class body that is specific to a particular enum constant. As for any class body, it is enclosed in curly brackets, { }. It is declared immediately after the enum constant and any constructor arguments. In the code above, it starts at (1) and ends at (4). Like any class body, it can contain member declarations. In the above case, the body contains two method declarations: an implementation of the method mealPrice() at (2) that overrides the abstract method declaration at (7) in the enclosing enum supertype Meal, and an implementation of the toString() method at (3) that overrides the one inherited by the Meal enum type from the superclass java.lang.Enum. The @Override annotation used on these overriding methods ensures that the compiler will issue an error message if such a method declaration does not satisfy the criteria for overriding.

The constant-specific class body is an anonymous class—that is, a class with no name. Each constant-specific class body defines a distinct, albeit anonymous, subtype of the enclosing enum type. In the code above, the constant-specific class body defines a subtype of the Meal enum type. It inherits members of the enclosing enum supertype that are not private, overridden, or hidden. When the enum type Meal is loaded at runtime, this constant-specific class body is instantiated, and the reference value of the instance is assigned to the enum constant BREAKFAST. Note that the type of the enum constant is Meal, which is the supertype of the anonymous subtype represented by the constant-specific class body. Since supertype references can refer to subtype objects, this assignment is legal.

Each enum constant overrides the abstract method mealPrice() declared in the enclosing enum supertype—that is, provides an implementation for the method. The compiler will report an error if this is not the case. Although the enum type declaration specifies an abstract method, the enum type declaration is *not* declared abstract—contrary to an abstract class. Given that the references meal and day are of the enum types Meal and Day from Example 5.26, respectively, the method call

```
meal.mealPrice(day)
```

will execute the mealPrice() method from the constant-specific body of the enum constant denoted by the reference meal.

Two constant-specific class bodies, associated with the enum constants BREAKFAST and LUNCH, override the toString() method from the java.lang.Enum class. Note that the toString() method is not overridden in the Meal enum type, but in the anonymous classes represented by two constant-specific class bodies. The third enum constant, DINNER, relies on the toString() method inherited from the java.lang.Enum class.

Constructors, abstract methods, and static methods cannot be declared in a constant-specific class body. Instance methods declared in constant-specific class bodies are only accessible if they override methods in the enclosing enum supertype.

Example 5.26 *Declaring Constant-Specific Class Bodies*

```java
// File: Day.java
public enum Day {
  MONDAY, TUESDAY, WEDNESDAY, THURSDAY, FRIDAY, SATURDAY, SUNDAY
}
```

```java
// File: Meal.java
public enum Meal {
  // Each enum constant defines a constant-specific class body
  BREAKFAST(7,30) {                                                        // (1)
    @Override
    public double mealPrice(Day day) {                                     // (2)
      double breakfastPrice = 10.50;
      if (day.equals(Day.SATURDAY) || day == Day.SUNDAY)
        breakfastPrice *= 1.5;
      return breakfastPrice;
    }
    @Override
    public String toString() {                                            // (3)
      return "Breakfast";
    }
  },                                                                       // (4)
  LUNCH(12,15) {
    @Override
    public double mealPrice(Day day) {                                    // (5)
      double lunchPrice = 20.50;
      switch (day) {
        case SATURDAY: case SUNDAY:
          lunchPrice *= 2.0;
      }
      return lunchPrice;
    }
    @Override
    public String toString() {
      return "Lunch";
    }
  },
```

```java
    DINNER(19,45) {
      @Override
      public double mealPrice(Day day) {                              // (6)
        double dinnerPrice = 25.50;
        if (day.compareTo(Day.SATURDAY) >= 0 && day.compareTo(Day.SUNDAY) <= 0)
          dinnerPrice *= 2.5;
        return dinnerPrice;
      }
    };

    // Abstract method implemented in constant-specific class bodies.
    abstract double mealPrice(Day day);                               // (7)

    // Enum constructor:
    Meal(int hh, int mm) {
      this.hh = hh;
      this.mm = mm;
    }

    // Instance fields: Time for the meal.
    private int hh;
    private int mm;

    // Instance methods:
    public int getHour() { return this.hh; }
    public int getMins() { return this.mm; }
    public String getTimeString() {                                  // "hh:mm"
      return String.format("%02d:%02d", this.hh, this.mm);
    }
  }

// File: MealPrices.java
public class MealPrices {

  public static void main(String[] args) {                          // (8)
    System.out.printf(
        "Please note that %s, %s, on %s costs $%.2f.%n",
        Meal.BREAKFAST.name(),                                       // (9)
        Meal.BREAKFAST.getTimeString(),
        Day.MONDAY,
        Meal.BREAKFAST.mealPrice(Day.MONDAY)                         // (10)
    );

    System.out.println("Meal prices on " + Day.SATURDAY + " are as follows:");
    Meal[] meals = Meal.values();
    for (Meal meal : meals) {
      System.out.printf(
          "%s costs $%.2f.%n", meal, meal.mealPrice(Day.SATURDAY)    // (11)
      );
    }
  }
}
```

Output from the program:

```
Please note that BREAKFAST, 07:30, on MONDAY costs $10.50.
```

```
Meal prices on SATURDAY are as follows:
Breakfast costs $15.75.
Lunch costs $41.00.
DINNER costs $63.75.
```

In Example 5.26, the `mealPrice()` method declaration at (2) uses both the `equals()` method and the `==` operator to compare enum constants for equality. The `mealPrice()` method declaration at (5) uses enum constants in a `switch` statement. Note that the case labels in the `switch` statement are enum constant names, without the enum type name. The `mealPrice()` method declaration at (6) uses the `compareTo()` method to compare enum constants.

The `main()` method at (8) in Example 5.26 demonstrates calling the `mealPrice()` method in the constant-specific class bodies. The `mealPrice()` method is called at (10) and (11). Example 5.26 also illustrates the difference between the `name()` and the `toString()` methods of the enum types. The `name()` method is called at (9), and the `toString()` method is called implicitly at (11) on `Meal` enum values. The `name()` method always prints the enum constant name exactly as it was declared. Which `toString()` method is executed depends on whether the `toString()` method from the `java.lang.Enum` class is overridden. Only the constant-specific class bodies of the enum constants BREAKFAST and LUNCH override this method. The output from the program confirms this to be the case.

Enum Values in Exhaustive switch Expressions

A `switch` expression is always *exhaustive*—that is, the cases defined in the `switch` expression must cover *all* values of the selector expression type or the code will not compile (§4.2, p. 160).

The `switch` expression below at (1) is exhaustive, as all values of the enum type Day are covered by the two switch rules at (2) and (3). Deleting any one or both of these switch rules will result in a compile-time error.

```
Day day = Day.MONDAY;            // See Example 5.26, p. 295, for enum type Day.
String typeOfDay = switch (day) {                                        // (1)
  case MONDAY, TUESDAY, WEDNESDAY, THURSDAY, FRIDAY -> "Weekday";        // (2)
  case SATURDAY, SUNDAY                             -> "Weekend";        // (3)
};
```

The `switch` expression below at (4) is also exhaustive, as all values of the enum type Day are collectively covered by the case label at (5) and the `default` label at (6). Deleting the case label at (5) does *not* result in a compile-time error, as the `default` label will then cover all values of the selector expression—but it may result in a wrong value being returned by the `switch` expression. However, deleting the `default` label at (6) will result in a compile-time error, as the case label at (5) only covers a subset of the values for the Day enum type. Compile-time checking of exhaustiveness of a `switch` expression whose switch rules are defined by the arrow notation results in robust and secure code.

```
typeOfDay = switch (day) {                                    // (4)
  case SATURDAY, SUNDAY -> "Weekend";                         // (5)
  default -> "Weekday";                                       // (6)
}
```

Declaring Type-Safe Enums, Revisited

We have seen declarations of enum types as top-level types, but they can also be nested as static member and static local types (§9.1, p. 491). Although nested enum types are implicitly static, they can be declared with the keyword static. The following skeletal code shows the two enum types Day and Meal declared as static member types in the class MealPrices:

```
public class MealPrices {
  public enum Day { /* ... */ }                          // Static member

  public static enum Meal { /* ... */ }                  // Static member

  public static void main(String[] args) { /* ... */ }   // Static method
}
```

An enum type cannot be explicitly extended using the extends clause. An enum type is implicitly final, unless it contains constant-specific class bodies. If it declares constant-specific class bodies, it is implicitly extended. No matter what, it cannot be explicitly declared final.

An enum class is either *implicitly* final if its declaration contains no enum constants that have a class body, or *implicitly* sealed if its declaration contains at least one enum constant that has a class body. Since an enum type can be either implicitly final or implicitly sealed, it can implement a sealed interface—in which case, it must be specified in the permits clause of the sealed interface (p. 311).

An enum type *cannot* be declared abstract, regardless of whether each abstract method is overridden in the constant-specific class body of every enum constant.

Like a class, an enum can implement interfaces.

```
public interface ITimeInfo {
  public int getHour();
  public int getMins();
}
public enum Meal implements ITimeInfo {
  // ...
  @Override public int getHour() { return this.hh; }
  @Override public int getMins() { return this.mm; }
  // ...
}
```

The Java Collections Framework provides a special-purpose *set* implementation (java.util.EnumSet) and a special-purpose *map* implementation (java.util.EnumMap) for use with enum types. These implementations provide better performance for enum types than their general-purpose counterparts, and are worth checking out.

5.14 Record Classes

Exchanging *plain data* between programs is a common task. *Plain data objects* allow efficient *aggregation* of data and provide transparent *access* to it. In the literature, such data objects are referred to by different names; the acronym *POJOs* (*Plain Old Java Objects*) is common in the Java community.

A *plain data class* can always be implemented as a normal class, but this is tedious and repetitive, entailing boilerplate code and full weight of the OOP programming model. In Example 5.27, the class CD_v1 represents the data for a CD. A full-fledged implementation of this data class requires declaration of its instance fields that constitute the data, an appropriate constructor to initialize the data fields, *get methods* to allow access to the data, and overriding the pertinent methods from the Object class to make CD objects more meaningful and useful. (For details on overriding methods from the Object class, see Chapter 14, p. 741). Although most IDEs can generate the code necessary to implement such data objects, they lack the incremental validation required when changes are made to the data model of the normal class.

Example 5.27   *The CD Class*

```
package record.basics;
// The different genres in music.
public enum Genre {POP, JAZZ, OTHER}
```

```
package record.basics;
import java.time.Year;
import java.util.Objects;

/** A class that represents a CD. */
public class CD_v1 {

    // Instance fields:
    private final String artist;        // Name of the artist.
    private final String title;         // Title of the CD.
    private final int    noOfTracks;    // Number of tracks on the CD.
    private final Year   year;          // Year the CD was released.
    private final Genre  genre;         // Music genre of the CD.

    // Non-zero argument constructor:
    public CD_v1(String artist, String title, int noOfTracks,
                 Year year, Genre genre) {
        this.artist     = artist;
        this.title      = title;
        this.noOfTracks = noOfTracks;
        this.year       = year;
        this.genre      = genre;
    }
```

```
    // Get methods:
    public String getArtist()    { return this.artist; }
    public String getTitle()     { return this.title; }
    public int    getNoOfTracks() { return this.noOfTracks; }
    public Year   getYear()      { return this.year; }
    public Genre  getGenre()     { return this.genre; }

    // Overridden methods from the Object class:
    @Override public String toString() {
      return String.format("<%s, \"%s\", %d, %s, %s>",
          this.artist, this.title, this.noOfTracks, this.year, this.genre);
    }

    @Override public boolean equals(Object obj) {
      return (this == obj)
          || (obj instanceof CD_v1 other
              && this.artist.equals(other.artist)
              && this.title.equals(other.title)
              && this.noOfTracks == other.noOfTracks
              && this.year == other.year
              && this.genre == other.genre);
    }

    @Override public int hashCode() {
      return Objects.hash(this.artist, this.title, this.noOfTracks,
                          this.year, this.genre);
    }
}
```

Record Class Basics

A *record class* in Java is a special-purpose class that simplifies declaration and handling of *an aggregate of values* that comprise the state of a plain data object. A record class defines immutable fields and the compiler generates the *get methods* (also called *getter* or *accessor methods*) necessary to access the values of fields in instances of the record class. A record class generally does not provide any heavy processing of the data; the primarily goal is to allow users to access the data.

The basic syntax for a record class is shown below. The *record header* of a top-level record class can specify the public access modifier, as in a top-level normal class. The contextual keyword record is used in the header to declare a record class. It has this special meaning only in this context. A record class has a *name*, similar to a normal class. The header specifies a comma-separated *component list* that comprises *field declarations* (called *record components*), where each field declaration specifies the *name* and the *type* of the field. For the basic record class declaration, the record body can be left empty.

```
access_modifier record record_name(component_list)     // Record header
{ }                                                    // Empty record body
```

The CD_v0 class in Example 5.27 can be declared as a record class, as shown in Example 5.28. The public record class CD declared at (1) in Example 5.28 is equivalent to the normal class CD_v1 in Example 5.27. The compiler automatically generates the necessary fields, contructor, and method declarations for the record class CD. The client class DataUser in Example 5.28 utilizes data objects of record class CD.

Example 5.28 *The CD Record Class*

```java
package record.basics;
import java.time.Year;

/** A record class that represents a CD. */
public record CD(String artist, String title, int noOfTracks,        // (1)
                 Year year, Genre genre) { /* Empty body */ }
```

```java
package record.basics;
import java.time.Year;

public class DataUser {
  public static void main(String[] args) {
    // Some ready-made CDs:                                            (2)
    CD cd0 = new CD("Jaav",      "Java Jive",      8, Year.of(2017), Genre.POP);
    CD cd1 = new CD("Jaav",      "Java Jam",       6, Year.of(2017), Genre.JAZZ);
    CD cd2 = new CD("Funkies",   "Lambda Dancing", 10, Year.of(2018), Genre.POP);
    CD cd3 = new CD("Genericos", "Keep on Erasing", 8, Year.of(2018), Genre.JAZZ);
    CD cd4 = new CD("Genericos", "Hot Generics",   10, Year.of(2018), Genre.JAZZ);

    // An array of CDs.
    CD[] cdArray = {cd0, cd1, cd2, cd3, cd4};

    System.out.println("    Artist    Title           No. Year Genre");
    for(int i = 0; i < cdArray.length; ++i) {
      CD cd = cdArray[i];
      String cdToString = String.format("%-10s%-16s%-4d%-5s%-5s",
              cd.artist(), cd.title(), cd.noOfTracks(),               // (3)
              cd.year(), cd.genre());
      System.out.printf("cd%d: %s%n", i, cdToString);
    }

    System.out.println();
    System.out.println(cd0.toString());                               // (4)

    CD cdX = new CD("Jaav",      "Java Jive",      8, Year.of(2017), Genre.POP);
    System.out.println("cd0.equals(cdX): " + cd0.equals(cdX));        // (5)
  }
}
```

Output from the program:

```
     Artist    Title           No. Year Genre
cd0: Jaav      Java Jive       8   2017 POP
cd1: Jaav      Java Jam        6   2017 JAZZ
cd2: Funkies   Lambda Dancing  10  2018 POP
```

```
cd3: Genericos Keep on Erasing 8    2018 JAZZ
cd4: Genericos Hot Generics      10 2018 JAZZ

cd0: CD[artist=Jaav, title=Java Jive, noOfTracks=8, year=2017, genre=POP]
cd0.equals(cdX): true
```

The compiler automatically generates the necessary declarations for a record class when it is declared according to the simplified syntax form, in particular, when the record body is empty.

- Each record component in the component list results in a private, final *instance field* in the record. In other words, these *component fields* pertain to objects of the record class, and their values constitute the state of a record. From the CD record class declaration, the following component fields are created: String artist, String title, int noOfTracks, Year year, and Genre genre. The component fields in the CD record class are equivalent to the instance field declarations in the CD_v0 class in Example 5.27.

  Fields being final means that once a final field is initialized, its value cannot be changed. However, if a field refers to a mutable object, this object can be modified, but the reference value of the object assigned to the field cannot be changed. Record classes are thus said to be *shallowly immutable*.

  The component fields in the CD record class have immutable values, as objects of String, Year, and Genre are immutable, as are primitive values. The CD record class is therefore immutable. (See also §6.7, p. 356, for a discussion on immutability.)

  As we shall see, the *order* of the record components in the component list has implications in the record class.

- Each record component results in a public zero-argument *get method* (also known as a *getter* method). It is important to note that the get method has the same name and return type as the corresponding record component. This does not create any problem, as method names and field names are in different *name spaces*.

  The compiler thus ensures that each record component has a corresponding private, final component field and a read-only public zero-argument get method that returns the value of this field.

  The following public zero-argument get methods are created for the CD record class: String artist(), String title(), int noOfTracks(), Year year(), and Genre genre(), each having the name and the return type as declared by the corresponding record component. As expected, calling a get method returns the value of the corresponding component field. In Example 5.28, the get methods are called at (3) to obtain the values of individual component fields in a CD record. Although their names are different, the get methods of the CD record class are equivalent to the get methods of the CD_v0 class in Example 5.27.

- In order to initialize all component fields properly, the compiler automatically creates a public constructor—called the *implicit canonical constructor*—that has a parameter list that corresponds to the record components in *name, type* and *order*. A call to the canonical constructor in a new expression results in the argument values being assigned to the corresponding component fields in the same order. The implicit canonical constructor of a record class functions analogously to the default constructor in a normal class.

The implementation of the implicit canonical constructor for the CD record class is equivalent to the non-zero argument normal constructor implemented in the CD_v0 class in Example 5.27.

Creating records is no different from creating objects of a normal class. In Example 5.28, CD records are constructed by calling the implicit canonical constructor at (2) in the new expression. Note that the order of the specified values corresponds to that of the record components in the component list.

```
CD cd0 = new CD("Jaav",      "Java Jive",        8, Year.of(2017), Genre.POP);
...
```

- The compiler also creates an implementation of the toString() method that is overridden from the Object class. The toString() method creates a default text representation of a record that includes the name of the record class and a textual list with name-value pairs for each component field in the order specified in the component list.

In Example 5.28, the toString() method is explicitly called in the print statement at (4), resulting in the following output:

```
CD[artist=Jaav, title=Java Jive, noOfTracks=8, year=2017, genre=POP]
```

- An implementation of the equals() method (§14.2, p. 744) that is overridden from the Object class is also created to compare two CD records for equality, based on the values of corresponding component fields in the two records. The method compares the component fields in the same order as specified in the component list, and returns true if the values in corresponding fields all match—analogous to the implementation of the equals() method in the CD_v0 class in Example 5.27. Overriding of the equals() method is essential if records are to be used in collections (§15.12, p. 866).

In Example 5.28, two records cd0 and cdX are compared for equality with the equals() method, showing that the two records are equal, since they have the same state.

- Lastly, the compiler generates an implementation of the hashCode() method (§14.3, p. 753) that is overridden from the Object class. The method returns a hash code that is computed based on the values of the component fields, in the same order as specified in the component list—analogous to the implementation of the hashCode() method in the CD_v0 class in Example 5.27. Overriding of the hashCode() method is essential if records are to be used in sets and maps (§15.8, p. 830).

Restrictions on Record Declarations

A record class is implemented as an implicitly `final` direct subclass of the `java.lang.Record` abstract class that defines the default inherited behavior of such classes. In particular, the `Record` class defines abstract methods that override the `equals()`, `hashCode()`, and `toString()` methods of the `Object` class. This means that every record class must implement these methods either explicitly or implicitly. We have seen in Example 5.28 that the compiler provides the implementation of these methods automatically when any of these methods is not declared explicitly in the record class.

A record class cannot have an explicit extends clause to declare a direct superclass, not even its direct superclass `Record`. Being `final` also means that a record class cannot be declared abstract. However, a record class is seldom declared explicitly `final`. As such, a record class is solely defined by its state and cannot be extended by any subclass.

Note also that the name of a record component in the component list cannot be the same as the name of any of the methods in the `Object` class, except `equals`.

Augmenting Basic Record Class Declaration

In the rest of this section, we explore how the basic declaration of a record class can be augmented and customized. The general syntax of a record class is shown below.

> *access_modifier* `record` *record_name*(*component_list*) *optional_implements_clause* {
>
> *optional_constructor_declarations*
>
> *optional_member_declarations*
>
> }

The basic declaration of a record class can be augmented with an `implements` clause in order to implement any interfaces. Constructors can be customized, as can the get methods corresponding to the component fields. New instance methods can be declared, as can static members and initializers, but new instance fields and initializers are not allowed in the record body.

Record Constructors

In this section we discuss three kinds of constructors that can be specified in a record class declaration:

- A *normal canonical record constructor*, if declared, supersedes the implicit canonical record constructor.
- If a normal canonical record constructor is not specified, a *compact canonical record constructor* can be declared. In this case, the implicit canonical record constructor is generated. Note that either the normal canonical record constructor or the compact canonical record constructor can be specified, but not both.

- Any number of *non-canonical record constructors* can be specified, whether or not any canonical constructor is provided.

Normal Canonical Record Constructor

In a basic record class declaration, the compiler generates the *implicit canonical record constructor* discussed earlier to ensure that component fields of a record are initialized properly. This canonical record constructor can be implemented *explicitly* when there is a need to process the argument values before they are assigned to the component fields. This explicit canonical record constructor is called the *normal canonical record constructor* as its declaration resembles the constructor of a normal class. If a record class implements the normal canonical record constructor, the implicit counterpart is *not* generated.

The normal canonical constructor must have the *same parameter list* as the implicit canonical record constructor, in *name, type,* and *order*. In the constructor, the component fields must be accessed with the this reference to distinguish them from the parameter names, and *all* component fields must be initialized in the constructor. In Example 5.29, the record class CD provides an implementation of the normal canonical constructor at (2). The parameter values are sanitized at (3) before being assigned to the component fields at (4). Running the DataUser class in Example 5.28 with the record class CD in Example 5.29 produces the same results.

Here are a few other restrictions to note regarding the normal canonical constructor:

- It must be at least as accessible as the record class. For example, for a top-level record class that has public accessibility, it must be declared public.
- It cannot be generic (§11.7, p. 593), or have a throws clause in its header (§7.5, p. 388). In other words, any checked exception thrown by the constructor must be handled in the body of the constructor.
- It cannot invoke another record constructor with the this() expression to chain constructors locally (p. 209), as is the case with normal constructors.

Example 5.29 *Normal Canonical Record Constructor*

```
package record.constructors.canonical;
import java.time.Year;

/** A record class that represents a CD. */
public record CD(String artist, String title, int noOfTracks,        // (1)
                 Year year, Genre genre) {

   // Normal canonical record constructor                            // (2)
   public CD(String artist, String title, int noOfTracks, Year year, Genre genre) {
      // Sanitize the parameter values:                              (3)
      artist = artist.strip();
      title = title.strip();
      noOfTracks = noOfTracks < 0 ? 0 : noOfTracks;
      year =  year.compareTo(Year.of(2022)) > 0? Year.of(2022) : year;
      genre = genre == null ? Genre.OTHER : genre;
```

```
        // Initialize all component fields:                              (4)
        this.artist     = artist;
        this.title      = title;
        this.noOfTracks = noOfTracks;
        this.year       = year;
        this.genre      = genre;
    }
}
```

Compact Canonical Record Constructor

The *compact canonical record constructor* is a more concise form of the normal canonical record constructor. It eliminates the need for a parameter list and the initialization of the component fields. The parameter list is derived from the component list declared in the record header, and the initialization of *all* component fields is left to the *implicit* canonical record constructor. In fact, the component fields cannot be accessed in the compact constructor, as the component names refer to the parameter names of the implicit canonical constructor. Note that the implicit canonical record constructor is generated when the compact constructor is provided in the record class declaration. The compact constructor is called in a new expression, exactly as any other constructor, passing the argument values in the call.

In Example 5.30, the compact canonical constructor for the record class CD is implemented at (2). It has no parameter list and it does *not* initialize the component fields. It only sanitizes the values passed to the constructor. Again running the DataUser class in Example 5.28 with the record class CD in Example 5.30 produces the same results.

The *implicit* canonical record constructor is called before exiting from the compact canonical constructor; therefore, a return statement is not allowed in the compact constructor. The compact constructor primarily functions as a validator for the data values before they are assigned to the component fields by the *implicit* canonical record constructor.

Previous restrictions mentioned for the normal canonical record constructor also apply to the compact canonical record constructor.

Example 5.30 *Compact Record Constructor and Non-Canonical Constructor*

```
        package record.constructors.compact;
        import java.time.Year;

        /** A record class that represents a CD. */
        public record CD(String artist, String title, int noOfTracks,       // (1)
                         Year year, Genre genre) {

            // Compact canonical record constructor                         (2)
            public CD {
                // Sanitize the values passed to the constructor:           (3)
                artist = artist.strip();
                title = title.strip();
                noOfTracks = noOfTracks < 0 ? 0 : noOfTracks;
```

```
      year =  year.compareTo(Year.of(2022)) > 0? Year.of(2022) : year;
      genre = genre == null ? Genre.OTHER : genre;

      // Cannot explicitly assign to component fields:                    (4)
      // this.artist = artist;                    // Compile-time error!
    }

    // A non-canonical record constructor                                 (5)
    public CD() {
      this(" Anonymous ", " No title ", 0, Year.of(2022), Genre.OTHER);  // (6)
    }
  }
```

Normal Non-Canonical Record Constructors

A record class declaration can specify any number of *non-canonical record constructors*—that is, constructors whose signature is *not* the same as that of the canonical constructor.

In Example 5.30, a non-canonical constructor for the record class CD is implemented at (5). It is a zero-argument non-canonical record constructor to create a record with default values for the component fields.

The first statement in the non-canonical constructor at (6) is an explicit invocation of the canonical constructor with the this() expression. The signature of the this() expression matches that of the canonical constructor in type and in order. The rule is that chaining of constructors with the this() expression (p. 209) must ultimately lead to the canonical constructor being invoked so that all component fields are initialized. In Example 5.30, the constructor invocation at (6) leads to the compact constructor being invoked, and whose execution in turn leads to the implicit canonical record constructor being invoked. Use of this non-canonical constructor is illustrated in the following print statement:

```
System.out.println(new CD());        // Calls the non-canonical constructor
```

Output from the print statement shows that the record was created after the string values were sanitized:

```
CD[artist=Anonymous, title=No title, noOfTracks=0, year=2022, genre=OTHER]
```

Non-canonical constructors are primarily used for creating specialized records.

The restrictions noted for the normal and the compact canonical constructors do *not* apply to a non-canonical constructor: It can be less accessible than its record class, be generic, and can specify a throws clause, but it must invoke another record constructor with the this() expression.

Member Declarations

The component fields of a record class are always automatically generated based on the field components specified in the component list. Thus a record class *cannot* declare any new instance fields in addition to those specified in the component list.

However, new instance methods can be declared in a record class. In Example 5.31, three new instance methods are declared at (8) in the record class to determine the genre of a CD.

Automatic generation of any get method or methods overridden from the Object class (equals(), hashCode(), and toString()) will be suppressed in a record class, if the record class provides an implementation for any of these methods.

In Example 5.31, the CD record class provides an implementation for the title() method at (9) that returns the uppercase version of the string in the title field. This explicit method will be invoked when called by a client to get the value of the title field in a CD record. An explicit get method can be annotated with the @Override annotation to enable validation of its method signature against that of the default get method that would otherwise be generated. Such an explicit get method must fulfill the following criteria:

- It must be an instance method that is declared public.
- It must have no formal parameters or a throws clause.
- Its return type must be the same as the declared type of its corresponding record component.
- It must not be a generic method.

When the object referenced by a field is mutable, its get method can be explicitly implemented to return a copy of the object so that the original object is never modified, maintaining the immutability of the record. As values of individual component fields cannot be changed, a new record with any modified values must be created.

Also, static fields, methods, and initializers (§10.7, p. 545) can be declared. In Example 5.31, the CD record class declares static fields to create some ready-made CD records. Argument values passed in the constructor call to create CD records will be sanitized by the compact constructor at (2) before being assigned to the component fields by the implicit canonical record constructor.

Nested static types can also be declared in a record class (Chapter 9, p. 489). In Example 5.31, the enum type Genre is declared as a static member of the CD record class at (11), and is used in the CD record class.

In Example 5.31, the client class DataUser2 uses some of the explicitly implemented methods in the CD record class. The CD.isOther() method is used at (13) to filter an array of CDs created at (12). The output from the program shows that the values passed in the constructor calls were sanitized.

An uppercase version of the string in the title field is printed when the title() method is explicitly invoked on a CD record. However, note that the automatically generated toString() method, called at (14), does not use the uppercase version of the title. The reason is that the fields are accessed directly by the generated methods in the record class, and not by calling the get methods. The toString() method accesses the title field directly, thereby accessing the original string in the field. In order to use the uppercase version of the string in all contexts, it can be converted to uppercase in the compact constructor by replacing line (4a) with (4b) so that the uppercase version of the string is assigned to the `title` field—and thereby making the `title()` method declared at (9) redundant.

Example 5.31 *Other Member Declarations in a Record Class*

```
package record.customize;
import java.time.Year;

/** A record class that represents a CD. */
public record CD(String artist, String title, int noOfTracks,            // (1)
                 Year year, Genre genre) {

  // Compact canonical record constructor                                 (2)
  public CD {
      // Sanitize the values passed to the constructor:                   (3)
      artist = artist.strip();
      title = title.strip();                                           // (4a)
  //  title = title.strip().toUpperCase();                             // (4b)
      noOfTracks = noOfTracks < 0 ? 0 : noOfTracks;
      year =  year.compareTo(Year.of(2022)) > 0? Year.of(2022) : year;
      genre = genre == null ? Genre.OTHER : genre;

  // Cannot explicitly assign to component fields:                        (5)
  // this.artist = artist;                              // Compile-time error!
  }

  // A non-canonical record constructor                                   (6)
  public CD() {
     this(" Anonymous ", " No title ", 0, Year.of(2022), Genre.OTHER);  // (7)
  }

  //  New instance methods:                                              (8)
  public boolean isPop()   { return this.genre == Genre.POP; }
  public boolean isJazz()  { return this.genre == Genre.JAZZ; }
  public boolean isOther() { return this.genre == Genre.OTHER; }

  // Customize a get method:                                             (9)
  @Override public String title() {
     return this.title.toUpperCase();
  }

  // Static fields with some ready-made CDs:                            (10)
  public final static CD cd0
      = new CD("  Jaav",      "Java Jive",        8, Year.of(2017), Genre.POP);
  public final static CD cd2
      = new CD("Funkies ",    " Lambda Dancing ", 10, Year.of(2024), null);
  public final static CD cd4
      = new CD("Genericos", "Hot Generics",   -5, Year.of(2018), Genre.JAZZ);

  // Declare a nested type:
  public enum Genre {POP, JAZZ, OTHER}                               // (11)
}
```

```
                        package record.customize;

                public class DataUser2 {
                  public static void main(String[] args) {
                    CD[] cdArray = {CD.cd0, CD.cd2, CD.cd4, new CD()};              // (12)
                    for(int i = 0; i < cdArray.length; ++i) {
                      CD cd = cdArray[i];
                      if (cd.isOther()) {                                            // (13)
                        System.out.println(cd.toString());                          // (14)
                      }
                    }
                    System.out.println("Title: " + cdArray[1].title());             // (15)
                  }
                }
```

Output from the program:

```
CD[artist=Funkies, title=Lambda Dancing, noOfTracks=10, year=2022, genre=OTHER]
CD[artist=Anonymous, title=No title, noOfTracks=0, year=2022, genre=OTHER]
Title: LAMBDA DANCING
```

Other Aspects of Record Classes

Some other aspects of record classes are mentioned below, and are covered in detail elsewhere in the book.

Implementing Interfaces

Records can implement interfaces, which is no different from a normal class implementing interfaces. As a record class is implicitly final, it cannot extend other classes. The CD record class below implements the Serializable interface and the Comparable<CD> interface. Example 20.6, p. 1263, uses the CD record class to demonstrate record serialization.

```
public record CD(String artist, String title, int noOfTracks,      // (1)
    Year year, Genre genre) implements Serializable and Comparable<CD> {

  @Override public int compareTo(CD other) { /* See Example 16.1, p. 883. */ }

  public enum Genre implements Serializable {POP, JAZZ, OTHER}
}
```

The CD record class in Example 16.1, p. 883, implements the Comparable<CD> interface so that CD records can be compared.

Record Serialization

Example 20.6, p. 1263, demonstrates serializing records to external storage. It is important to note that serialization of records cannot be customized, as with objects of normal classes, and that a record is always deserialized using the canonical constructor.

Generic Record Classes

Generic record classes can be delcared, analogous to generic classes (Chapter 11, p. 563). The generic record class Container below has one type parameter (T):

```
record Container<T>(T item) { /* Empty body */ }
```

We can create records by parameterizing the generic record class:

```
Container<String> p0 = new Container<>("Hi");
Container<Integer> p1 = new Container<>(Integer.valueOf(10));
```

Nested Record Classes

Record classes can be declared as nested record classes—in particular, as static *member types* and as static *local types*. For details on nested record classes, see Chapter 9, p. 489.

Direct Permitted Subtypes of Sealed Interfaces

A record class is only allowed in the permits clause of a *sealed interface*, if it implements the sealed interface. As a record class is implicitly final, it also fulfills the second criterion for a permitted direct subtype (p. 311).

Finally, it is worth noting that records in Java are designed so that the record state solely defines the representation of the record. Record classes require less effort to implement than normal classes and have an efficient memory footprint and runtime performance. Also, their immutability provides thread safety in concurrent applications.

5.15 Sealed Classes and Interfaces

Design by inheritance promotes code reuse in the OOP model—where subtypes can inherit code from their supertypes. Such an inheritance hierarchy is depicted in Figure 5.8, where the subclasses PrintedBook, Ebook, and Audiobook can inherit and reuse code from the superclass Book. The inheritance hierarchy of the Book superclass can also be regarded as a *domain model* for books (albeit greatly simplified for this exposition). However, this domain model as represented by the inheritance hierarchy in Figure 5.8 does not give the Book superclass much control over which classes can be classified as books. It can easily be exploited by clients to create their own subclasses of the Book superclass, thereby undermining the domain model represented by the inheritance hierarchy in Figure 5.8. If the PrintedBook subclass is not declared final, it can also be freely extended to define more kinds of books.

The superclass Book in Figure 5.8 cannot control which subclasses belong to the book domain, as it cannot control its extensibility. When it comes to domain modeling using inheritance, modifiers such as abstract and final are not adequate, nor are the accessibility modifiers to control the use of the superclass. In this section, we look at how sealed classes and interfaces aid in domain modeling that promotes accessibility of the superclass and allows control of extensibility of its subclasses. Sealed classes also have the additional benefits of resulting in secure hierarchies and aiding the compiler to provide better analysis of potential problems in the code.

Figure 5.8   *A Domain Model as Represented by Inheritance Hierarchy*

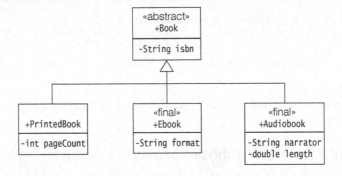

Sealed Classes

Sealing of classes and interfaces allows fine-grained control over the inheritance hierarchy of reference types in a given domain. A sealed class or interface only allows specific classes or interfaces to extend or implement its definition. To implement sealed classes, the language has introduced two new modifiers, sealed and non-sealed, and the permits clause—these three identifiers are *contextual keywords* that have special meaning only in the context of defining sealed types. As we shall see, the modifier final is also an integral part of defining sealed types.

We first look at sealed classes, and later we discuss sealed interfaces and compare the two (p. 315).

Going back to Figure 5.8 with the simplified domain model of books, we want to ensure that only the subclasses PrintedBook, Ebook, and Audiobook can *directly extend* the abstract superclass Book (i.e., ensure that the three subclasses are the only *permitted direct subclasses* of the sealed class Book). Figure 5.9 shows the modeling of the inheritance hierarchy with the required constraints. In this example, the classes involved are located in the same package. Skeletal code for the classes in shown in the discussion below, and complete class declarations can be found in Example 5.32.

A sealed class is declared using the modifier sealed and the optional permits clause in the class header. The permits clause is optional if a sealed class and its permitted direct subclasses are declared in the same compilation unit (p. 317). If a class specifies the permits clause, the class must be declared sealed. The permits clause, if specified, must appear after any extends and implements clauses in the class header.

The superclass Book is declared sealed and explicitly specifies a permits clause with a list of its permitted direct subclasses, as shown at (1) below. Keep in mind that

Figure 5.9   *Sealed Classes for Domain Modeling of Inheritance Hierarchy*

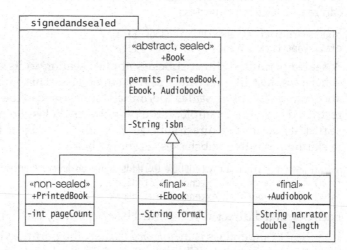

since these subclasses are `public`, they are declared in separate compilation units, but belong to the same package.

```
public abstract sealed class Book permits PrintedBook, Ebook, Audiobook {/*(1)*/}
```

Each *permitted direct subclass* of a sealed class is bound by the following *contract*:

- Each permitted direct subclass *must extend* its direct `sealed` superclass. Note that the sealing relationship is defined between two consecutive levels in the inheritance hierarchy: between a superclass and its direct subclasses. This is also the case for the permitted direct subclasses of the Book superclass:

```
public non-sealed class PrintedBook extends Book {/*...*/}

public final class Ebook extends Book {/*...*/}

public final class Audiobook extends Book {/*...*/}
```

- Each permitted direct subclass must be declared either `sealed`, `non-sealed`, or `final`. This avoids any unwanted subclassing to the inheritance hierarchy of a sealed class.

  A permitted direct subclass that is declared `final` cannot be extended, as in the case of a `final` normal class. This implies that the inheritance hierarchy of a `final` permitted subclass cannot be extended. The permitted direct subclasses `Ebook` and `Audiobook` are declared `final`. Any attempt to extend them would result in a compile-time error.

```
class EComicBook extends Ebook {}    // Compile-time error!
```

A permitted direct subclass that is declared `non-sealed` can be *freely extended*. This implies that the inheritance hierarchy of a `non-sealed` permitted subclass can be extended. Note that a class cannot be declared `non-sealed` unless it is a permitted direct subclass of a direct `sealed` superclass.

The permitted direct subclass `PrintedBook` is declared `non-sealed`. Client code can readily extend this class:

```
class Hardcover extends PrintedBook {}
class Paperback extends PrintedBook {}
```

A `sealed` permitted direct subclass applies sealing to its own permitted direct subclasses, just like its direct `sealed` superclass. This implies that the inheritance hierarchy of a `sealed` permitted subclass can be extended, but in a restricted way. For example, if the permitted subclass `PrintedBook` was declared `sealed`, its permitted direct subclasses would be subject to the same rules for declaring permitted subclasses, as shown below:

```
public sealed class PrintedBook extends Book permits Hardcover, Paperback {}
final class Hardcover extends PrintedBook {}
final class Paperback extends PrintedBook {}
```

- Each permitted direct subclass must be *accessible* by the direct `sealed` superclass.

If the `sealed` superclass is in a *named module*, the permitted subclasses must also be in the same module (Chapter 19, p. 1161). Note that this does not mean that they have to be in the same package in the named module. Their *fully qualified names* can be used in the `permits` clause to access the subclasses in their respective packages (§6.3, p. 326).

If the `sealed` superclass is in *the unnamed module*, the permitted subclasses must all be in either the *same named package* or *the unnamed package* as the `sealed` superclass. In Example 5.32, the `sealed` superclass `Book` is in a named package (but in the unnamed module), as are the permitted subclasses, specified using the package statement (§6.3, p. 326).

- -

Example 5.32 *Declaring* `sealed`, `non-sealed`, *and* `final` *Classes*

```
package signedandsealed;

public abstract sealed class Book permits PrintedBook, Ebook, Audiobook  { // (1)
  private String isbn;
  protected Book(String isbn) {
    this.isbn = isbn;
  }
  public String getIsbn() { return this.isbn; }
}
```

```
package signedandsealed;

public non-sealed class PrintedBook extends Book {                         // (2)
  private int pageCount;
  protected PrintedBook(String isbn, int pageCount) {
    super(isbn);
    this.pageCount = pageCount;
  }
  public int getPageCount() { return this.pageCount; }
}
```

```
package signedandsealed;

public final class Ebook extends Book {                                      // (3)
  private String format;
  public Ebook(String isbn, String format) {
    super(isbn);
    this.format = format;
  }
  public String getFormat() { return this.format; }
}
```

```
package signedandsealed;

public final class Audiobook extends Book {                                  // (4)
  private String narrator;
  private double length;
  public Audiobook(String isbn, String narrator, double length) {
    super(isbn);
    this.narrator = narrator;
    this.length = length;
  }
  public String getNarrator() { return this.narrator; }
  public double getLength() { return this.length; }
}
```

Sealed Interfaces

Analogous to sealed classes, sealed interfaces can also be defined. However, a sealed interface can have *both* subinterfaces and subclasses as its *permitted direct subtypes*. The permitted subtypes can be subclasses that *implement* the sealed interface and subinterfaces that *extend* the sealed interface. This is in contrast to a sealed class that can have direct subclasses, but not direct subinterfaces—as classes cannot be extended or implemented by interfaces.

Figure 5.10 shows the book domain from Figure 5.9 that has been augmented with a sealed interface that specifies its permitted direct subtypes in a permits clause:

```
public sealed interface Subscribable permits Ebook, Audiobook, VIPSubcribable {}
```

The sealed superinterface Subscribable has two final permitted direct subclasses (that implement the superinterface) and one non-sealed direct subinterface (that extends the superinterface). The declarations of the permitted direct subclasses Ebook and Audiobook have been updated accordingly so that they implement the direct superinterface Subscribable.

```
public final class Ebook extends Book implements Subscribable {}
public final class Audiobook extends Book implements Subscribable {}
public non-sealed interface VIPSubcribable extends Subscribable {}
```

The rest of the type declarations from Figure 5.9 remain the same in Figure 5.10:

```
public abstract sealed class Book permits PrintedBook, Ebook, Audiobook {}
public non-sealed class PrintedBook extends Book {}
```

Note that it is perfectly possible for a class or an interface to be a permitted direct subtype of more than one direct supertype—as is the case for the Ebook and the Audiobook subclasses in Figure 5.10.

Figure 5.10   *Sealed Classes and Interfaces*

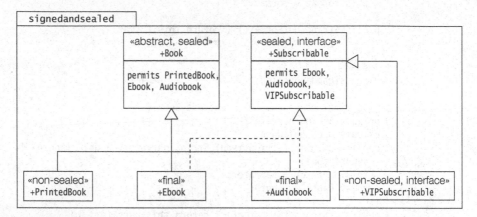

We see from the discussion above that the permitted direct subtypes of a sealed superinterface abide by the same *contract* rules as for sealed superclasses:

- A permitted direct subclass or subinterface must extend or implement its direct superinterface, respectively.

- Any permitted subclass of a sealed interface must be declared either sealed, non-sealed or final, but any permitted subinterface can only be declared either sealed or non-sealed. The modifier final is not allowed for interfaces.

- The same rules for locality also apply for sealed interfaces and their permitted direct subtypes: All are declared either in the same named module or in the same package (named or unnamed) in the unnamed module.

Enum and Record Types as Permitted Direct Subtypes

By definition, an enum type (p. 287) is either *implicitly* final (has *no* enum constants that have a class body, as shown at (2)) or *implicitly* sealed (has *at least one* enum constant with a class body that constitutes an implicitly declared direct subclass, as shown at (3) for the constant DVD_R that has an empty class body). Thus an enum type can be specified as a permitted direct subtype of a sealed superinterface, as shown at (1). The modifiers final and sealed cannot be explicitly specified in the enum type declaration.

```
sealed interface MediaStorage permits CD, DVD {}        // (1) Sealed interface
enum CD implements MediaStorage {CD_ROM, CD_R, CD_W}     // (2) Implicitly final
enum DVD implements MediaStorage {DVD_R {}, DVD_RW}      // (3) Implicitly sealed
```

Analogously, a record class (p. 299) is *implicitly* final, and can be specified as a permitted direct subtype of a sealed superinterface. The sealed interface MediaStorage at (1a) now permits the record class HardDisk as a direct subtype. Again note that the modifier final cannot be specified in the header of the HardDisk record class declared at (4).

```
sealed interface MediaStorage permits CD, DVD, HardDisk {}// (1a) Sealed interface
record HardDisk(double capacity) implements MediaStorage {}// (4) Implicitly final
```

Deriving Permitted Direct Subtypes of a Sealed Supertype

The permits clause of a sealed class or interface can be omitted, if all its permitted direct subtypes are declared in the *same compilation unit*—that is, are in the same source file. Since only one reference type can be declared public in a compilation unit, the accessibility of the other type declarations cannot be public.

The compiler can infer the permitted direct subtypes of any sealed class or interface in a compilation unit by checking whether a type declaration fulfills the contract for declaring a permitted direct subtype; that is, it extends/implements a sealed supertype and is declared either (implicitly) sealed, non-sealed, or (implicitly) final.

```
// File: Book.java (compilation unit)
public abstract sealed class Book {}          // Permitted subclasses are derived.
non-sealed class PrintedBook extends Book {}

sealed interface Subscribable {}              // Permitted subtypes are derived.
final class Ebook extends Book implements Subscribable {}
final class Audiobook extends Book implements Subscribable {}
non-sealed interface VIPSubcribable extends Subscribable {}
```

Given the type declarations in the compilation unit Book.java, the compiler is able to infer that PrintedBook, Ebook, and Audiobook are permitted direct subclasses of the sealed superclass Book, whereas Ebook, Audiobook, and VIPSubcribable are permitted direct subtypes of the sealed superinterface Subscribable.

Using Sealed Classes and Interfaces

As we have seen, sealed classes and interfaces restrict which other classes or interfaces can extend or implement them. Apart from providing the programmer with a language feature to develop improved domain models for libraries, the compiler can also leverage the sealed types to provide better analysis of potential problems in the code at compile time.

Example 5.33 is a client that uses the sealed classes and their permitted direct subclasses defined in Example 5.32. Typically, a reference of the sealed superclass is used to process a collection of objects of its permitted subtypes. The array books is such a collection created at (2). The objects of the permitted subtypes are processed by the enhanced for(:) loop at (3). Typically, a cascading if-else statement is used in the loop body to distinguish each object in the collection and process it accordingly. Any object of a permitted subclass can be processed by the code as long as the cascading if-else statement guarantees that the checks are exhaustive—that is, all permitted subtypes are covered. The compiler cannot help to ensure that this is the case, as it cannot extract the necessary information from the cascading if-else statement for this analysis. Note that the conditionals in the cascading if-else statement use the instanceof pattern match operator to make the code at least less verbose.

Example 5.33 *Using Sealed Classes*

```java
package signedandsealed;

public class BookAdmin {
  public static void main(String[] args) {
    // Create some books:                                      // (1)
    PrintedBook pBook = new PrintedBook("888-222", 340);
    Ebook eBook = new Ebook("999-777", "epub");
    Audiobook aBook = new Audiobook("333-555", "Fry", 300.0);

    // Create a book array:                                    // (2)
    Book[] books = {pBook, eBook, aBook};

    // Process the books:                                      // (3)
    for (Book book : books) {
      if (book instanceof PrintedBook pb) {                    // (4)
        System.out.printf("Printed book: %s, %d%n",
                            pb.getIsbn(), pb.getPageCount());
      } else if (book instanceof Ebook eb) {
        System.out.printf("Ebook: %s, %s%n", eb.getIsbn(), eb.getFormat());
      } else if (book instanceof Audiobook ab) {
        System.out.printf("Audiobook: %s, %s, %.1f%n",
                            ab.getIsbn(), ab.getNarrator(), ab.getLength());
      }
    }
  }
}
```

Output from the program:

```
Printed book: 888-222, 340
Ebook: 999-777, epub
Audiobook: 333-555, Fry, 300.0
```

 Review Questions

5.32   What will be the result of attempting to compile and run the following code?

```java
public enum Drill {
  ATTENTION("Attention!"), EYES_RIGHT("Eyes right!"),
  EYES_LEFT("Eyes left!"), AT_EASE("At ease!");

  private String command;

  Drill(String command) {
    this.command = command;
  }
```

```
    public static void main(String[] args) {
        System.out.println(ATTENTION);              // (1)
        System.out.println(AT_EASE);                // (2)
    }
}
```

Select the one correct answer.

(a) The code compiles, but it reports a ClassNotFoundException when run, since an enum type cannot be run as a stand-alone application.

(b) The compiler reports errors at (1) and (2), as the constants must be qualified by the enum type name Drill.

(c) The compiler reports errors at (1) and (2), as the constants cannot be accessed in a static context.

(d) The code compiles and prints:
    ATTENTION
    AT_EASE

(e) The code compiles and prints:
    Attention!
    At ease!

(f) None of the above

5.33 What will be the result of compiling and running the following code?

```
import java.util.Arrays;

public enum Priority {
    ONE(1) { public String toString() { return "LOW"; } },      // (1)
    TWO(2),
    THREE(3) { public String toString() { return "NORMAL"; } },  // (2)
    FOUR(4),
    FIVE(5) { public String toString() { return "HIGH"; } };     // (3)

    private int pValue;

    Priority(int pValue) {
        this.pValue = pValue;
    }

    public static void main(String[] args) {
        System.out.println(Arrays.toString(Priority.values()));
    }
}
```

Select the one correct answer.

(a) The compiler reports syntax errors at (1), (2), and (3).

(b) The code compiles and prints:
    [LOW, TWO, NORMAL, FOUR, HIGH]

(c) The code compiles and prints:
    [ONE, TWO, THREE, FOUR, FIVE]

(d) None of the above

5.34   What will be the result of compiling and running the following code?

```java
public enum TrafficLight {
  RED("Stop"), YELLOW("Caution"), GREEN("Go");

  private String action;

  TrafficLight(String action) {
    this.action = action;
  }

  public static void main(String[] args) {
    TrafficLight green = new TrafficLight("Go");
    System.out.println(GREEN.equals(green));
  }
}
```

Select the one correct answer.

(a) The code will compile and print true.
(b) The code will compile and print false.
(c) The code will fail to compile, as an enum type cannot be instantiated with the new operator.
(d) The code will fail to compile, as the enum type does not provide the equals() method.

5.35   Given the following code:

```java
public class RQ54 {
  public static void main(String[] args) {
    Product p = new Product(101, "Tea", 1.99);
    System.out.println(p);
  }
}
```

Which two record class definitions will cause this program to produce the following output?

```
Product[id=101, name=TEA, price=1.99]
```

Select the two correct answers.

(a)
```java
public record Product(int id, String name, double price) {
  public Product() {
    this.id = id;
    this.name = name.toUpperCase();
    this.price = price;
  }
}
```

(b)
```java
public record Product(int id, String name, double price) {
  public Product(int newId, String newName, double newPrice) {
    id = newId;
    name = newName.toUpperCase();
    price = newPrice;
  }
}
```

(c)
```
public record Product() {
    public Product(int id, String name, double price) {
        this.id = id;
        this.name = name.toUpperCase();
        this.price = price;
    }
}
```

(d)
```
public record Product(int id, String name, double price) {
    public Product {
        name = name.toUpperCase();
    }
}
```

(e)
```
public record Product(int id, String name, double price) {
    public String toString(){
        return "Product[id="+id+", name="+name.toUpperCase()+",
                price="+price+"]";
    }
}
```

(f)
```
public record Product(int id, String name, double price) {
    public String name() {
        return name.toUpperCase();
    }
    public String toString(){
        return "Product[id="+id+", name="+name+", price="+price+"]";
    }
}
```

5.36 Given the following code:

```
public record Employee(String name, double salary) { }
```

and

```
public class RQ55 {
    public static void main(String[] args) {
        Employee e1 = new Employee("Bob", 1234);
        Employee e2 = new Employee("Bob", 1234);
        System.out.print(e1.equals(e2));
        System.out.print(e1 == e2);
    }
}
```

What is the result?
Select the one correct answer.

(a) falsefalse

(b) truetrue

(c) falsetrue

(d) truefalse

5.37   Which statement is true?
Select the one correct answer.

(a) A record class cannot declare new fields, other than the ones in its header.
(b) A record class provides get and set methods for each component field.
(c) A record class cannot have an extends clause.
(d) A record class directly extends the class `Object`.

5.38   Which statement is true?
Select the one correct answer.

(a) A class marked as `sealed` cannot be abstract.
(b) A class marked as `non-sealed` cannot be abstract.
(c) A class marked as `sealed` cannot be freely extended.
(d) A class that extends a `sealed` class cannot be `sealed`.
(e) A class that extends a `sealed` class cannot be `non-sealed`.

5.39   Given the following code:

```
public sealed interface X permits Y, Z { }
```

Which of the following options provides a correct definition of the permitted sub-types Y and Z?
Select the one correct answer.

(a) ```
public final class Y implements X { }
public sealed interface Z extends X { }
```
(b) ```
public final class Y implements X { }
public interface Z extends X { }
```
(c) ```
public non-sealed class Y implements X, Z { }
public sealed interface Z extends X permits Y { }
```
(d) ```
public class Y implements X, Z { }
public non-sealed interface Z extends X { }
```

Access Control · 6

Chapter Topics

- Understanding the features in Java that aid encapsulation
- Knowing the structure of a Java compilation unit
- Creating and using packages
- Using class-path to search for types during program compilation and execution
- Compiling and running code from packages
- Applying accessibility rules for top-level reference types and their members
- Applying scope rules for class members and local variables
- Implementing immutability

Java SE 17 Developer Exam Objectives	
[3.4] Understand variable scopes, use local variable type inference, apply encapsulation, and make objects immutable ○ *Variable scope, encapsulation, and immutability are covered in this chapter.* ○ *For local variable type inference, see §3.13, p. 142.*	§6.1, p. 324 §6.6, p. 352 §6.7, p. 356

Java SE 11 Developer Exam Objectives	
[3.4] Understand variable scopes, applying encapsulation and make objects immutable	§6.1, p. 324 §6.6, p. 352 §6.7, p. 356

Java provides language features (such as classes, packages, and modules) that allow code to be encapsulated. This chapter covers creating and using packages, and compiling and running code from packages. Accessibility rules define how entities (e.g., classes and methods) are accessed in a Java program. Class scope rules define how class members are accessed in a class and block scope rules define how local variables are accessed in a block. Immutability of objects is a common class design strategy. The discussion in this chapter is based on *non-modular* code. Modules are discussed in Chapter 19, p. 1161.

6.1 Design Principle: Encapsulation

An object has properties and behaviors that are *encapsulated* inside the object. The services that the object offers to its clients make up its *contract*, or public interface. Only the contract defined by the object is available to the clients. The *implementation* of the object's properties and behavior is not a concern of the clients. Encapsulation helps to make clear the distinction between an object's contract and its implementation. This demarcation has major consequences for program development, as the implementation of an object can change without affecting the clients. Encapsulation also reduces complexity, as the internals of an object are hidden from the clients, which cannot alter its implementation.

Encapsulation is achieved through *information hiding*, by making judicious use of language features provided for this purpose. Information hiding in Java can be achieved at the following levels of granularity:

- *Method or block declaration*

  Localizing information in a method or a block hides it from the outside. Local variables can only be accessed in the method or the block according to their scope.

- *Reference type declaration*

  The accessibility of members declared in a reference type declaration (class, enum type, interface) can be controlled through access modifiers (p. 347). One much-advocated information-hiding practice is to prevent clients from having direct access to data maintained by an object. The fields of the object are private, and the object's contract defines public methods for the services provided by the object. Such tight encapsulation helps to separate the use from the implementation of a reference type.

- *Package declaration*

  Top-level reference types that belong together can be grouped into relevant packages by using the package statement. An import statement can be used to access types in other packages by their simple name. Inter-package accessibility of types can be controlled through public or package accessibility (p. 345).

- *Module declaration*

  Packages that are related can be grouped into a module by using a `module` declaration. How modules are created, accessed, compiled, and deployed is discussed in detail in Chapter 19, p. 1161.

Ample examples throughout the book illustrate how encapsulation can be achieved at different levels by using features provided by the Java programming language.

6.2 Java Source File Structure

The structure of a skeletal Java source file is depicted in Figure 6.1. A Java source file can have the following elements that, if present, must be specified in the following order:

1. An optional `package` declaration to specify a package name. Packages are discussed in §6.3, p. 326.

2. Zero or more `import` declarations. Since `import` declarations introduce type or static member names in the source code, they must be placed before any type declarations. Both type and static `import` declarations are discussed in §6.3, p. 329.

3. Any number of *top-level* type declarations. Class, enum, and interface declarations are collectively known as *type declarations*. Since these declarations belong to the same package, they are said to be defined at the *top level*, which is the package level.

    The type declarations can be defined in any order. Technically, a source file need not have any such declarations, but that is hardly useful.

    The JDK imposes the restriction that at most one `public` class declaration per source file can be defined. If a `public` class is defined, the file name must match this `public` class. For example, if the `public` class name is `NewApp`, the file name must be `NewApp.java`.

    Classes are discussed in §3.1, p. 99; interfaces are discussed in §5.6, p. 237; and enums are discussed in §5.13, p. 287.

Modules introduce another Java source file that contains a single module declaration (§19.3, p. 1168).

Note that except for the `package` and the `import` statements, all code is encapsulated in classes, interfaces, enums, and records. No such restriction applies to comments and whitespace.

Figure 6.1   *Java Source File Structure*

```
// File: NewApp.java
```

```
// PART 1: (OPTIONAL) package declaration
package com.company.project.fragilepackage;
// PART 2: (ZERO OR MORE) import declarations
import java.io.*;
import java.util.*;
import static java.lang.Math.*;
// PART 3: (ZERO OR MORE) top-level declarations
public class NewApp { }
class A { }
interface IX { }
record B() { }
enum C { }
```

```
// end of file
```

6.3 Packages

A package in Java is an encapsulation mechanism that can be used to group related classes, interfaces, enums, and records.

Figure 6.2 shows an example of a package hierarchy comprising a package called wizard that contains two other packages: pandorasbox and spells. The package pandorasbox has a class called Clown that implements an interface called Magic, also found in the same package. In addition, the package pandorasbox has a class called LovePotion and a subpackage called artifacts containing a class called Ailment. The package spells has two classes: Baldness and LovePotion. The class Baldness is a subclass of class Ailment found in the subpackage artifacts in the package pandorasbox.

The dot (.) notation is used to uniquely identify package members in the package hierarchy. The class wizard.pandorasbox.LovePotion, for example, is different from the class wizard.spells.LovePotion. The Ailment class can be easily identified by the name wizard.pandorasbox.artifacts.Ailment, which is known as the *fully qualified name* of the type. Note that the fully qualified name of the type in a named package comprises the fully qualified name of the package and the simple name of the type. The *simple type name* Ailment and the *fully qualified package name* wizard.pandorasbox .artifacts together define the *fully qualified type name* wizard.pandorasbox.artifacts .Ailment.

Java programming environments usually map the fully qualified name of packages to the underlying (hierarchical) file system. For example, on a Unix system, the class

Figure 6.2   *Package Structure*

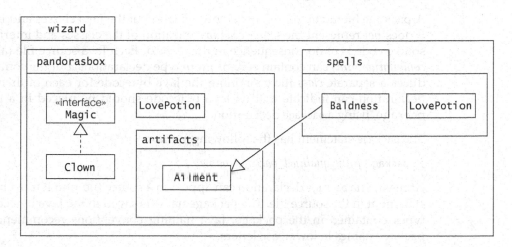

file `LovePotion.class` corresponding to the fully qualified name `wizard.pandorasbox`
`.LovePotion` would be found under the directory `wizard/pandorasbox`.

Conventionally, the *reverse* DNS (*Domain Name System*) notation based on the
Internet domain names is used to uniquely identify packages. If the package `wizard`
was implemented by a company called Sorcerers Limited that owns the domain
`sorcerersltd.com`, its fully qualified name would be

    com.sorcerersltd.wizard

Because domain names are unique, packages with this naming scheme are globally
identifiable. It is not advisable to use the top-level package names java and sun, as
these are reserved for the Java designers.

Note that each component of a package name must be a legal Java identifier. The
following package would be illegal:

    org.covid-19.2022.vaccine

The package name below is legal:

    org.covid_19._2022.vaccine

A subpackage would be located in a subdirectory of the directory corresponding
to its parent package. Apart from this locational relationship, a subpackage is an
independent package with no other relation to its parent package. The subpackage
`wizard.pandorasbox.artifacts` could easily have been placed elsewhere, as long as it
was uniquely identified. Subpackages in a package do not affect the accessibility
of the other package members. For all intents and purposes, subpackages are more
an *organizational* feature than a language feature. Accessibility of members defined
in type declarations is discussed in §6.5, p. 345.

Defining Packages

A package hierarchy represents an organization of the Java classes and interfaces. It does *not* represent the *source code* organization of the classes and interfaces. The source code is of no consequence in this regard. Each Java source file (also called *compilation unit*) can contain zero or more type declarations, but the compiler produces a separate *class* file containing the Java bytecode for each of them. A type declaration can indicate that its Java bytecode should be placed in a particular package, using a package declaration.

The package statement has the following syntax:

package *fully_qualified_package_name*;

At most, one package declaration can appear in a source file, and it must be the first statement in the source file. The package name is saved in the Java bytecode of the types contained in the package. Java naming conventions recommend writing package names in lowercase letters.

Note that this scheme has two consequences. First, all the classes and interfaces in a source file will be placed in the same package. Second, several source files can be used to specify the contents of a package.

If a package declaration is omitted in a compilation unit, the Java bytecode for the declarations in the compilation unit will belong to an *unnamed package* (also called the *default package*), which is typically synonymous with the current working directory on the host system.

Example 6.1 illustrates how the packages in Figure 6.2 can be defined using the package declaration. There are four compilation units. Each compilation unit has a package declaration, ensuring that the type declarations are compiled into the correct package. The complete code can be found in Example 6.7, p. 345.

Example 6.1 *Defining Packages and Using Type Import*

```
// File name: Clown.java                 // This file has 2 type declarations
package wizard.pandorasbox;              // Package declaration

import wizard.pandorasbox.artifacts.Ailment; // Importing specific class

public class Clown implements Magic { /* ... */ }

interface Magic { /* ... */ }
```

```
// File name: LovePotion.java
package wizard.pandorasbox;              // Package declaration

public class LovePotion { /* ... */ }
```

```
                    // File name: Ailment.java
                    package wizard.pandorasbox.artifacts;        // Package declaration

                    public class Ailment { /* ... */ }
```

```
                    // File name: Baldness.java                  // This file has 2 type declarations
                    package wizard.spells;                       // Package declaration

                    import wizard.pandorasbox.*;                 // (1) Type-import-on-demand
                    import wizard.pandorasbox.artifacts.*;       // (2) Import from subpackage

                    public class Baldness extends Ailment {      // Simple name for Ailment
                      wizard.pandorasbox.LovePotion tlcOne;      // (3) Fully qualified class name
                      LovePotion tlcTwo;                         // Class in same package
                      // ...
                    }

                    class LovePotion { /* ... */ }
```

Using Packages

The import facility in Java makes it easier to use the contents of packages. This sub-section discusses importing *reference types* and *static members of reference types* from packages.

Importing Reference Types

The accessibility of types (classes, interfaces, and enums) in a package determines their access from other packages. Given a reference type that is accessible from outside a package, the reference type can be accessed in two ways. One way is to use the fully qualified name of the type. However, writing long names can become tedious. The second way is to use the import declaration that provides a shorthand notation for specifying the name of the type, often called *type import*.

The import declarations must be the first statement after any package declaration in a source file. The simple form of the import declaration has the following syntax:

    import *fully_qualified_type_name*;

This is called *single-type-import*. As the name implies, such an import declaration provides a shorthand notation for a single type. The *simple* name of the type (i.e., its identifier) can now be used to access this particular type. Given the import declaration

    import wizard.pandorasbox.Clown;

the simple name Clown can be used in the source file to refer to this class.

Alternatively, the following form of the import declaration can be used:

    import *fully_qualified_package_name*.*;

This is called *type-import-on-demand*. It allows *any* type from the specified package to be accessed by its simple name. Given the import declaration

```
import wizard.pandorasbox.*;
```

the classes `Clown` and `LovePotion` and the interface `Magic` that are in the package `wizard.pandorasbox` can be accessed by their simple name in the source file.

An `import` declaration does not recursively import subpackages, as such nested packages are autonomous packages. The declaration also does not result in inclusion of the source code of the types; rather, it simply imports type names (i.e., it makes type names available to the code in a compilation unit).

All compilation units implicitly import the `java.lang` package (§8.1, p. 425). This is the reason why we can refer to the class `String` by its simple name, and need not use its fully qualified name `java.lang.String` all the time.

Import statements are *not* present in the compiled code, as all type names in the source code are replaced with their fully qualified names by the compiler.

Example 6.1 shows several usages of the `import` statement. Here we will draw attention to the class `Baldness` in the file `Baldness.java`. This class relies on two classes that have the same simple name `LovePotion` but are in different packages: `wizard.pandorasbox` and `wizard.spells`. To distinguish between the two classes, we can use their fully qualified names. However, since one of them is in the same package as the class `Baldness`, it is enough to fully qualify the class from the other package. This solution is used in Example 6.1 at (3). Note that the import of the `wizard.pandorasbox` package at (1) becomes redundant. Such name conflicts can usually be resolved by using variations of the `import` declaration together with fully qualified names.

The class `Baldness` extends the class `Ailment`, which is in the subpackage `artifacts` of the `wizard.pandorasbox` package. The `import` declaration at (2) is used to import the types from the subpackage `artifacts`.

The following example shows how a single-type-import declaration can be used to disambiguate a type name when access to the type is ambiguous by its simple name. The following `import` statement allows the simple name `List` to be used as shorthand for the `java.awt.List` type as expected:

```
import java.awt.*;          // imports all reference types from java.awt
```

Given the two `import` declarations

```
import java.awt.*;          // imports all type names from java.awt
import java.util.*;         // imports all type names from java.util
```

the simple name `List` is now ambiguous because both the types `java.util.List` and `java.awt.List` match.

Adding a single-type-import declaration for the `java.awt.List` type allows the simple name `List` to be used as a shorthand notation for this type:

```
import java.awt.*;        // imports all type names from java.awt
import java.util.*;       // imports all type names from java.util
import java.awt.List;     // imports the type List from java.awt explicitly
```

Importing Static Members of Reference Types

Analogous to the type import facility, Java also allows import of *static members* of reference types from packages, often called *static import*. Imported static members can be used by their simple names, and therefore need not be qualified. Importing static members of reference types from the unnamed package is not permissible.

The two forms of static import are shown here:

- *Single static import*: imports a specific static member from the designated type

  import static *fully_qualified_type_name*.*static_member_name*;

- *Static import on demand*: imports all static members in the designated type

  import static *fully_qualified_type_name*.*;

Both forms require the use of the keyword import followed by the keyword static, although the feature is called *static import*. In both cases, the *fully qualified name of the reference type* we are importing from is required.

The first form allows *single static import* of individual static members, and is demonstrated in Example 6.2. The constant PI, which is a static field in the class java.lang.Math, is imported at (1). Note the use of the fully qualified name of the type in the static import statement. The static method named sqrt from the class java.lang.Math is imported at (2). Only the *name* of the static method is specified in the static import statement; no parameters are listed. Use of any other static member from the Math class requires that the fully qualified name of the class be specified. Since types from the java.lang package are imported implicitly, the fully qualified name of the Math class is not necessary, as shown at (3).

Static import on demand is easily demonstrated by replacing the two import statements in Example 6.2 with the following import statement:

```
import static java.lang.Math.*;
```

We can also dispense with the use of the class name Math at (3), as all static members from the Math class are now imported:

```
double hypotenuse = hypot(x, y);   // (3') Type name can now be omitted.
```

- -

Example 6.2   *Single Static Import*

```
import static java.lang.Math.PI;        // (1) Static field
import static java.lang.Math.sqrt;       // (2) Static method
// Only specified static members are imported.

public class Calculate3 {
  public static void main(String[] args) {
    double x = 3.0, y = 4.0;
```

```
    double squareroot = sqrt(y);              // Simple name of static method
    double hypotenuse = Math.hypot(x, y);     // (3) Requires type name
    double area = PI * y * y;                 // Simple name of static field
    System.out.printf("Square root: %.2f, hypotenuse: %.2f, area: %.2f%n",
                      squareroot, hypotenuse, area);
  }
}
```

Output from the program:

```
Square root: 2.00, hypotenuse: 5.00, area: 50.27
```

Example 6.3 illustrates how static import can be used to access interface constants (§5.6, p. 254). The static import statement at (1) allows the interface constants in the package mypkg to be accessed by their simple names. The static import facility avoids the MyFactory class having to *implement* the interface so as to access the constants by their simple name (often referred to as the *interface constant antipattern*):

```
public class MyFactory implements mypkg.IMachineState {
  // ...
}
```

Example 6.3 *Avoiding the Interface Constant Antipattern*

```
package mypkg;

public interface IMachineState {
  // Fields are public, static, and final.
  int BUSY = 1;
  int IDLE = 0;
  int BLOCKED = -1;
}
```

```
import static mypkg.IMachineState.*;      // (1) Static import interface constants

public class MyFactory {
  public static void main(String[] args) {
    int[] states = { IDLE, BUSY, IDLE, BLOCKED }; // (2) Access by simple name
    for (int s : states)
      System.out.print(s + " ");
  }
}
```

Output from the program:

```
0 1 0 -1
```

Static import is ideal for importing enum constants from packages, as such constants are static members of an enum type (§5.13, p. 287). Example 6.4 combines type and static imports. The enum constants can be accessed at (5) using their simple names because of the static import statement at (2). The type import at (1) is required to access the enum type State by its simple name at (4) and (6).

Example 6.4   *Importing Enum Constants*

```
package mypkg;

public enum State { BUSY, IDLE, BLOCKED }
```

```
// File: Factory.java (in unnamed package)
import mypkg.State;                      // (1) Single type import

import static mypkg.State.*;             // (2) Static import on demand
import static java.lang.System.out;      // (3) Single static import

public class Factory {
  public static void main(String[] args) {
    State[] states = {                   // (4) Using type import implied by (1)
        IDLE, BUSY, IDLE, BLOCKED        // (5) Using static import implied by (2)
    };
    for (State s : states)               // (6) Using type import implied by (1)
      out.print(s + " ");                // (7) Using static import implied by (3)
  }
}
```

Output from the program:

```
IDLE BUSY IDLE BLOCKED
```

Identifiers in a class can *shadow* static members that are imported. Example 6.5 illustrates the case where the parameter out of the method writeInfo() has the same name as the statically imported field java.lang.System.out. The type of the parameter out is ShadowImport and that of the statically imported field out is PrintStream. Both classes PrintStream and ShadowImport define the method println() that is called in the program. The only way to access the imported field out in the method writeInfo() is to use its fully qualified name.

Example 6.5   *Shadowing Static Import*

```
import static java.lang.System.out;        // (1) Static import

public class ShadowImport {

  public static void main(String[] args) {
    out.println("Calling println() in java.lang.System.out");
    ShadowImport sbi = new ShadowImport();
    writeInfo(sbi);
  }
```

```java
    // Parameter out shadows java.lang.System.out:
    public static void writeInfo(ShadowImport out) {
      out.println("Calling println() in the parameter out");
      System.out.println("Calling println() in java.lang.System.out"); // Qualify
    }

    public void println(String msg) {
      out.println(msg + " of type ShadowImport");
    }
  }
```

Output from the program:

```
Calling println() in java.lang.System.out
Calling println() in the parameter out of type ShadowImport
Calling println() in java.lang.System.out
```

The next code snippet illustrates a common conflict that occurs when a static field with the same name is imported by *several* static import statements. This conflict is readily resolved by using the fully qualified name of the field. In the case shown here, we can use the simple name of the class in which the field is declared, as the java.lang package is implicitly imported by all compilation units.

```java
import static java.lang.Integer.MAX_VALUE;
import static java.lang.Double.MAX_VALUE;

public class StaticFieldConflict {
  public static void main(String[] args) {
    System.out.println(MAX_VALUE);          // (1) Ambiguous! Compile-time error!
    System.out.println(Integer.MAX_VALUE);  // OK
    System.out.println(Double.MAX_VALUE);   // OK
  }
}
```

Conflicts can also occur when a static method with the same signature is imported by several static import statements. In Example 6.6, a method named binarySearch is imported 21 times by the static import statements. This method is overloaded twice in the java.util.Collections class and 18 times in the java.util.Arrays class, in addition to one declaration in the mypkg.Auxiliary class. The classes java.util.Arrays and mypkg.Auxiliary have a declaration of this method with the *same signature* (binarySearch(int[], int)) that matches the method call at (2), resulting in a signature conflict that is flagged as a compile-time error. The conflict can again be resolved by specifying the fully qualified name of the method.

If the static import statement at (1) is removed, there is no conflict, as only the class java.util.Arrays has a method that matches the method call at (2). If the declaration of the method binarySearch() at (3) is allowed, there is also *no* conflict, as this method declaration will *shadow* the imported method whose signature it matches.

Example 6.6 *Conflict In Importing a Static Method with the Same Signature*

```java
package mypkg;

public class Auxiliary {
  public static int binarySearch(int[] a, int key) { // Same in java.util.Arrays
    // Implementation is omitted.
    return -1;
  }
}
```

```java
// File: MultipleStaticImport.java (in unnamed package)
import static java.util.Collections.binarySearch;  //   2 overloaded methods
import static java.util.Arrays.binarySearch;       // + 18 overloaded methods
import static mypkg.Auxiliary.binarySearch; // (1) Causes signature conflict

public class MultipleStaticImport {
  public static void main(String[] args) {
    int index = binarySearch(new int[] {10, 50, 100}, 50); // (2) Ambiguous!
    System.out.println(index);
  }

//public static int binarySearch(int[] a, int key) {       // (3)
//  return -1;
//}
}
```

Compiling Code into Package Directories

Conventions for specifying pathnames vary on different platforms. In this chapter, we will use pathname conventions used on a Unix-based platform. While trying out the examples in this section, attention should be paid to platform dependencies in this regard—especially the fact that the *separator characters* in *file paths* for the Unix-based and Windows platforms are / and \, respectively.

As mentioned earlier, a package can be mapped on a hierarchical file system. We can think of a package name as a pathname in the file system. Referring to Example 6.1, the package name wizard.pandorasbox corresponds to the pathname wizard/pandorasbox. The Java bytecode for all types declared in the source files Clown.java and LovePotion.java will be placed in the *package directory* with the pathname wizard/pandorasbox, as these source files have the following package declaration:

```java
package wizard.pandorasbox;
```

The *location* in the file system where the package directory should be created is specified using the -d option (d for *destination*) of the javac command. The term *destination directory* is a synonym for this location in the file system. The compiler will create the package directory with the pathname wizard/pandorasbox (including any subdirectories required) *under* the specified location, and will place the Java byte-code for the types declared in the source files Clown.java and LovePotion.java inside the package directory.

Assuming that the current directory (.) is the directory /pgjc/work, and the four source code files in Figure 6.3a (see also Example 6.1) are found in this directory, the following command issued in the current directory will create a file hierarchy (Figure 6.3b) under this directory that mirrors the package structure in Figure 6.2, p. 327:

```
>javac -d . Clown.java LovePotion.java Ailment.java Baldness.java
```

Note that two of the source code files in Figure 6.3a have multiple type declara-tions. Note also the subdirectories that are created for a fully qualified package name, and where the class files are located. In this command line, the space between the -d option and its argument is mandatory.

Figure 6.3   *Compiling Code into Package Directories*

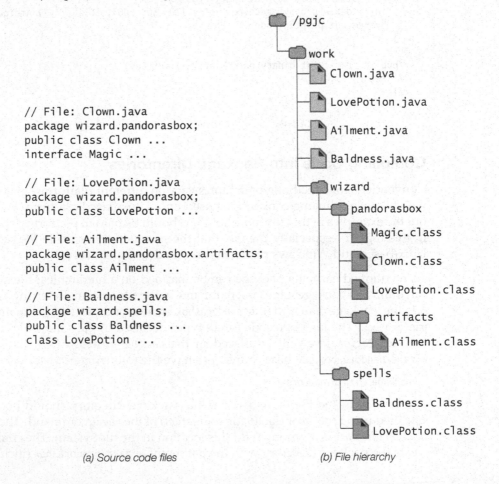

```
// File: Clown.java
package wizard.pandorasbox;
public class Clown ...
interface Magic ...

// File: LovePotion.java
package wizard.pandorasbox;
public class LovePotion ...

// File: Ailment.java
package wizard.pandorasbox.artifacts;
public class Ailment ...

// File: Baldness.java
package wizard.spells;
public class Baldness ...
class LovePotion ...
```

(a) Source code files   *(b) File hierarchy*

The wildcard * can be used to specify all Java source files to be compiled from a directory. It expands to the names of the Java source files in that directory. The two commands below are equivalent to the command above.

```
>javac -d . *.java
>javac -d . ./*.java
```

We can specify any *relative* pathname that designates the destination directory, or its *absolute* pathname:

```
>javac -d /pgjc/work Clown.java LovePotion.java Ailment.java Baldness.java
```

We can, of course, specify destinations other than the current directory where the class files with the bytecode should be stored. The following command in the current directory /pgjc/work will create the necessary packages with the class files under the destination directory /pgjc/myapp:

```
>javac -d ../myapp Clown.java LovePotion.java Ailment.java Baldness.java
```

Without the -d option, the default behavior of the javac compiler is to place all class files directly under the current directory (where the source files are located), rather than in the appropriate subdirectories corresponding to the packages.

The compiler will report an error if there is any problem with the destination directory specified with the -d option (e.g., if it does not exist or does not have the right file permissions).

Running Code from Packages

Referring to Example 6.1, if the current directory has the absolute pathname /pgjc/work and we want to run Clown.class in the directory with the pathname ./wizard/pandorasbox, the *fully qualified name* of the Clown class *must* be specified in the java command:

```
>java wizard.pandorasbox.Clown
```

This command will load the bytecode of the class Clown from the file with the pathname ./wizard/pandorasbox/Clown.class, and will start the execution of its main() method.

6.4 Searching for Classes on the Class Path

A program typically uses other precompiled classes and libraries, in addition to the ones provided by the Java standard libraries. In order for the JDK tools to find these files efficiently, the CLASSPATH environment variable or the -classpath option can be used, both of which are explained below.

In particular, the CLASSPATH environment variable can be used to specify the *class search path* (usually abbreviated to just *class path*), which is the *pathnames* or *locations* in the file system where JDK tools should look when searching for third-party and user-defined classes. Alternatively, the -classpath option (*short form* -cp) of the JDK tool commands can be used for the same purpose. The CLASSPATH environment variable is not recommended for this purpose, as its class path value affects *all* Java applications on the host platform, and any application can modify it. However, the -classpath option can be used to set the class path for each application individually. This way, an application cannot modify the class path for other applications. The class path specified in the -classpath option supersedes the path or paths set by the CLASSPATH environment variable while the JDK tool command is running. We will not discuss the CLASSPATH environment variable here, and will assume it to be undefined.

Basically, the JDK tools first look in the directories where the Java standard libraries are installed. If the class is not found in the standard libraries, the tool searches in the class path. When no class path is defined, the default value of the class path is assumed to be the current directory. If the -classpath option is used and the current directory should be searched by the JDK tool, the current directory must be specified as an entry in the class path, just like any other directory that should be searched. This is most conveniently done by including '.' as one of the entries in the class path.

We will use the file hierarchies shown in Figure 6.4 to illustrate some of the intricacies involved when searching for classes. The current directory has the absolute pathname /top/src, where the source files are stored. The package pkg will be created under the directory with the absolute pathname /top/bin. The source code in the two source files A.java and B.java is also shown in Figure 6.4.

Figure 6.4   *Searching for Classes*

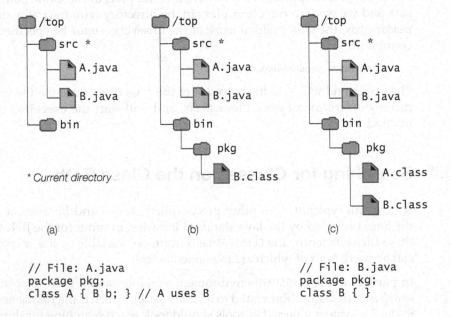

```
// File: A.java
package pkg;
class A { B b; } // A uses B
```

```
// File: B.java
package pkg;
class B { }
```

The file hierarchy before any files are compiled is shown in Figure 6.4a. Since the class B does not use any other classes, we compile it first with the following command, resulting in the file hierarchy shown in Figure 6.4b:

```
>javac -d ../bin B.java
```

Next, we try to compile the file A.java, and we get the following results:

```
>javac -d ../bin A.java
A.java:3: cannot find symbol
symbol  : class B
location: class pkg.A
public class A { B b; }
                 ^
1 error
```

The compiler cannot find the class B—that is, the file B.class containing the Java bytecode for the class B. In Figure 6.4b, we can see that it is in the package pkg under the directory bin, but the compiler cannot find it. This is hardly surprising, as there is no bytecode file for the class B in the current directory, which is the default value of the class path. The following command sets the value of the class path to be /top/bin, and compilation is successful (Figure 6.4c):

```
>javac -classpath /top/bin -d ../bin A.java
```

It is very important to understand that when we want the JDK tool to search in a *named package*, it is the *location* or the *root* of the package that is specified; in other words, the class path indicates the directory that *contains* the first component of the fully qualified package name. In Figure 6.4c, the package pkg is contained under the directory whose absolute path is /top/bin. The following command will *not* work, as the directory /top/bin/pkg does *not* contain a package with the name pkg that has a class B:

```
>javac -classpath /top/bin/pkg -d ../bin A.java
```

Also, the compiler is *not* using the class path to find the source file(s) that are specified in the command line. In the preceding command, the source file has the relative pathname ./A.java. Consequently, the compiler looks for the source file in the current directory. The class path is used to find the classes used by the class A, in this case, to find class B.

Given the file hierarchy in Figure 6.3, the following -classpath option sets the class path so that *all* packages (wizard.pandorasbox, wizard.pandorasbox.artifacts, wizard.spells) in Figure 6.3 will be searched, as all packages are located under the specified directory:

```
-classpath /pgjc/work
```

However, the following -classpath option will not help in finding *any* of the packages in Figure 6.3, as none of the *packages* are located under the specified directory:

```
>java -classpath /pgjc/work/wizard pandorasbox.Clown
```

This command also illustrates an important point about package names: The *fully qualified package name* should not be split. The package name for the class `wizard.pandorasbox.Clown` is `wizard.pandorasbox`, and must be specified fully. The following command will search all packages in Figure 6.3 for classes that are used by the class `wizard.pandorasbox.Clown`:

```
>java -classpath /pgjc/work wizard.pandorasbox.Clown
```

The class path can specify several *entries* (i.e., several locations), and the JDK tool searches them in the order they are specified, from left to right.

```
-classpath /pgjc/work:/top/bin:.
```

We have used the path-separator character ':' for Unix-based platforms to separate the entries, and also included the current directory (.) as an entry. There should be no whitespace on either side of the path-separator character. On the Windows platform, the path-separator character is a semicolon (;).

The search in the class path entries stops once the required class file is found. Therefore, the order in which entries are specified can be significant. If a class `B` is found in a package `pkg` located under the directory `/ext/lib1`, and also in a package `pkg` located under the directory `/ext/lib2`, the order in which the entries are specified in the two `-classpath` options shown below is significant. They will result in the class `pkg.B` being found under `/ext/lib1` and `/ext/lib2`, respectively.

```
-classpath /ext/lib1:/ext/lib2
-classpath /ext/lib2:/ext/lib1
```

The examples so far have used absolute pathnames for class path entries. We can, of course, use relative pathnames as well. If the current directory has the absolute pathname `/pgjc/work` in Figure 6.3, the following command will search the packages under the current directory:

```
>java -classpath . wizard.pandorasbox.Clown
```

If the current directory has the absolute pathname `/top/src` in Figure 6.4, the following command will compile the file `./A.java`:

```
>javac -classpath ../bin -d ../bin A.java
```

If the name of an entry in the class path includes whitespace, the name should be double-quoted so that it will be interpreted correctly:

```
-classpath "../new bin"
```

Table 6.1 summarizes the commands and options to compile and execute non-modular code. The tool documentation from Oracle provides more details on how to use the JDK development tools.

Table 6.1   *Compiling and Executing Non-Modular Java Code*

Operation	Command

Compiling non-modular code:	`javac --class-path classpath -d directory sourceFiles`
	`javac -classpath classpath -d directory sourceFiles`
	`javac -cp         classpath -d directory sourceFiles`

Executing non-modular code:	`java --class-path classpath qualifiedClassName`
	`java -classpath classpath qualifiedClassName`
	`java -cp         classpath qualifiedClassName`

 Review Questions

6.1   Which of the following statements are true about the following code in a source file?

```
package net.alphabet;
import java.util.ArrayList;
public class A {}
class B {}
```

Select the two correct answers.

(a)   Both class A and class B will be placed in the package net.alphabet.
(b)   Only class A will be placed in the package net.alphabet. Class B will be placed in the default package.
(c)   Both class A and class B can access the imported class java.util.ArrayList by its simple name.
(d)   Only class A can access the imported class java.util.ArrayList by its simple name.

6.2   Given the following code:

```
package app;
public class Window {
  final static String frame = "Top-frame";
}
```

```
package app;
// (1) INSERT IMPORT STATEMENT HERE
public class Canvas {
  private String str = frame;
}
```

Which import statement, when inserted at (1), will make the code compile? Select the one correct answer.

(a)   `import app.*;`
(b)   `import app.Window;`

    (c) `import java.lang.*;`
    (d) `import java.lang.String;`
    (e) `import static app.Window.frame;`

6.3   Given the following code:

```
package mainpkg.subpkg1;
public class Window {}
```

```
package mainpkg.subpkg2;
public class Window {}
```

```
package mainpkg;
// (1) INSERT IMPORT STATEMENTS HERE
public class Screen {
  private Window win;
}
```

Which import statement, when inserted independently at (1), will make the code compile?
Select the four correct answers.

    (a) `import mainpkg.*;`

    (b) `import mainpkg.subpkg1.*;`

    (c) `import mainpkg.subpkg2.*;`

    (d) `import mainpkg.subpkg1.*;`
        `import mainpkg.subpkg2.Window;`

    (e) `import mainpkg.subpkg1.Window;`
        `import mainpkg.subpkg2.*;`

    (f) `import mainpkg.subpkg1.*;`
        `import mainpkg.subpkg2.*;`

    (g) `import mainpkg.subpkg1.Window;`
        `import mainpkg.subpkg2.Window;`

6.4   Given the following code:

```
// (1) INSERT ONE IMPORT STATEMENT HERE
public class RQ700A20 {
  public static void main(String[] args) {
    System.out.println(sqrt(49));
  }
}
```

Which import statement, when inserted independently at (1), will make the program print 7 when the program is compiled and run?
Select the two correct answers.

    (a) `import static Math.*;`

    (b) `import static Math.sqrt;`

(c) `import static java.lang.Math.sqrt;`

(d) `import static java.lang.Math.sqrt();`

(e) `import static java.lang.Math.*;`

6.5 Given the following directory structure:

```
/top
 |--- wrk
        |--- pkg
               |--- A.java
               |--- B.java
```

assume that the two files `A.java` and `B.java` contain the following code, respectively:

```
package pkg;
class A { B b; }
```

```
package pkg;
class B {}
```

For which combinations of current directory and command is the compilation successful?

Select the two correct answers.

(a) Current directory: `/top/wrk`
Command: `javac -cp .:pkg A.java`

(b) Current directory: `/top/wrk`
Command: `javac -cp . pkg/A.java`

(c) Current directory: `/top/wrk`
Command: `javac -cp pkg A.java`

(d) Current directory: `/top/wrk`
Command: `javac -cp .:pkg pkg/A.java`

(e) Current directory: `/top/wrk/pkg`
Command: `javac A.java`

(f) Current directory: `/top/wrk/pkg`
Command: `javac -cp . A.java`

6.6 Given the following code:

```
package a.b;
public class X {
  public static int y = 100;
}
```

```
package a.b.c;
// (1) INSERT IMPORT STATEMENT HERE
public class Z {
  public void xyz() {
```

```
      int v = y;
    }
  }
```

Which import statement, when inserted individually at (1), will allow class Z to compile?
Select the two correct answers.

(a) `import a.b.*;`
(b) `import a.b.X.*;`
(c) `import static a.b.*;`
(d) `import static a.b.X.*;`
(e) `import static a.b.X.y;`

6.7 Given the following code:

```
package life.animals;
public class Cat { }
```

```
package life.animals;
public class Cow { }
```

```
package life.animals;
public class Dog { }
```

```
package habitat;
// (1) INSERT IMPORT STATEMENTS HERE
public class Farm {
  private Cat cat;
  private Cow cow;
}
```

Which import statements, when inserted individually at (1), will allow class Farm to compile?
Select the two correct answers.

(a) `import life.animals.*;`
(b) `import static life.animals.*;`
(c) `import static life.animals.Cat;`
    `import static life.animals.Cow;`
(d) `import life.animals.Cat;`
    `import life.animals.Cow;`

6.8 Which statement is true about `import` statements?
Select the one correct answer.

(a) Import of a package also imports all subpackages.
(b) Import of a package with a wildcard also imports all subpackages.
(c) Import statements are required to access code in other packages.
(d) All import statements are removed by the compiler.

6.5 Access Modifiers

In this section, we discuss accessibility of top-level type declarations that can be encapsulated into packages and accessibility of members that can be encapsulated in a top-level type declaration. A top-level reference type is a reference type (class, interface, enum, record) that is not declared inside another reference type.

Access modifiers are sometimes also called *visibility modifiers*.

Access Modifiers for Top-Level Type Declarations

The access modifier public can be used to declare top-level reference types that are accessible from everywhere, both from inside their own package and from inside other packages. If the access modifier is omitted, the reference types can be accessed only in their own package and not in any other packages—that is, they have *package access*, also called *package-private* or *default access*.

The packages shown in Figure 6.2, p. 327, are implemented by the code in Example 6.7. Class files with Java bytecode for top-level type declarations are placed in designated packages using the package statement. A top-level type declaration from one package can be accessed in another packages either by using the *fully qualified name* of the type or by using an import statement to import the type so that it can be accessed by its *simple name*.

Example 6.7 *Access Modifiers for Top-Level Reference Types*

```
// File: Clown.java
package wizard.pandorasbox;                    // Package declaration

import wizard.pandorasbox.artifacts.Ailment; // Importing class Ailment

public class Clown implements Magic {          // (1)
  LovePotion tlc;                              // Class in same package
  Ailment problem;                             // Simple class name
  Clown() {
    tlc = new LovePotion("passion");
    problem = new Ailment("flu");              // Simple class name
  }
  @Override public void levitate()  {          // (2)
    System.out.println("Levitating");
  }
  public void mixPotion()   { System.out.println("Mixing " + tlc); }
  public void healAilment() { System.out.println("Healing " + problem); }

  public static void main(String[] args) {
    Clown joker = new Clown();
    joker.levitate();
    joker.mixPotion();
    joker.healAilment();
  }
}
```

```
interface Magic { void levitate(); }            // (3)
```

```java
// File: LovePotion.java
package wizard.pandorasbox;                      // Package declaration

public class LovePotion {                        // (4) Accessible outside package
  String potionName;
  public LovePotion(String name) { potionName = name; }
  public String toString()        { return potionName; }
}
```

```java
// File: Ailment.java
package wizard.pandorasbox.artifacts;            // Package declaration

public class Ailment {                           // Accessible outside package
  String ailmentName;
  public Ailment(String name) { ailmentName = name; }
  public String toString() { return ailmentName; }
}
```

```java
// File: Baldness.java
package wizard.spells;                           // Package declaration

import wizard.pandorasbox.*;                      // Redundant
import wizard.pandorasbox.artifacts.*;            // Import of subpackage

public class Baldness extends Ailment {           // Simple name for Ailment
  wizard.pandorasbox.LovePotion tlcOne;           // Fully qualified name
  LovePotion tlcTwo;                              // Class in same package
  Baldness(String name) {
    super(name);
    tlcOne = new wizard.pandorasbox.             // Fully qualified name
                LovePotion("romance");
    tlcTwo = new LovePotion();                    // Class in same package
  }
}

class LovePotion /* implements Magic */ {         // (5) Magic is not accessible
  // @Override public void levitate() {}          // (6) Cannot override method
}
```

Compiling and running the program from the current directory gives the following results:

```
>javac -d . Clown.java LovePotion.java Ailment.java Baldness.java
>java wizard.pandorasbox.Clown
Levitating
Mixing passion
Healing flu
```

In Example 6.7, the class Clown at (1) and the interface Magic at (3) are placed in a package called wizard.pandorasbox. The public class Clown is accessible from everywhere. The Magic interface has package accessibility, and can only be accessed within the package wizard.pandorasbox. It is not accessible from other packages, not even from subpackages.

The class LovePotion at (4) is also placed in the package called wizard.pandorasbox. The class has public accessibility, and is therefore accessible from other packages. The two files Clown.java and LovePotion.java demonstrate how several compilation units can be used to group classes in the same package, as the type declarations in these two source files are placed in the package wizard.pandorasbox.

In the file Clown.java, the class Clown at (1) implements the interface Magic at (3) from the same package. We have used the annotation @Override in front of the declaration of the levitate() method at (2) so that the compiler can aid in checking that this method is declared correctly as required by the interface Magic.

In the file Baldness.java, the class LovePotion at (5) wishes to implement the interface Magic at (3) from the package wizard.pandorasbox, but this is not possible, although the source file imports from this package. The reason is that the interface Magic has package accessibility, and can therefore only be accessed within the package wizard.pandorasbox. The method levitate() of the Magic interface therefore cannot be overridden in class LovePotion at (6).

Table 6.2 summarizes accessibility of top-level reference types in a package. Just because a reference type is accessible does not necessarily mean that members of the type are also accessible. Accessibility of members is governed separately from type accessibility, as explained in the next subsection.

Table 6.2 *Access Modifiers for Top-Level Reference Types (Non-Modular)*

Modifiers	Top-level types
No modifier	Accessible in its own package (*package accessibility*)
public	Accessible anywhere

Access Modifiers for Class Members

By specifying member access modifiers, a class can control which information is accessible to clients (i.e., other classes). These modifiers help a class define a *contract* so that clients know exactly which services are offered by the class.

The accessibility of a member in a class can be any one of the following:

- public
- protected
- *package access* (also known as *package-private* and *default access*), when no access modifier is specified
- private

In the following discussion of access modifiers for members of a class, keep in mind that the member access modifier has meaning only if the class (or one of its subclasses) is accessible to the client. Also, note that only one access modifier can be specified for a member.

The discussion in this subsection applies to both instance and static members of top-level classes.

In UML notation, when applied to member names the prefixes +, #, and - indicate `public`, `protected`, and `private` member access, respectively. No access modifier indicates package access for class members.

The package hierarchy shown in Figure 6.5 is implemented by the code in Example 6.8. The class `Superclass1` at (1) in `pkg1` has two subclasses: `Subclass1` at (3) in `pkg1` and `Subclass2` at (5) in `pkg2`. The class `Superclass1` in `pkg1` is used by the other classes (designated as Client 1 to Client 4) in Figure 6.5.

Figure 6.5 *Accessibility of Class Members*

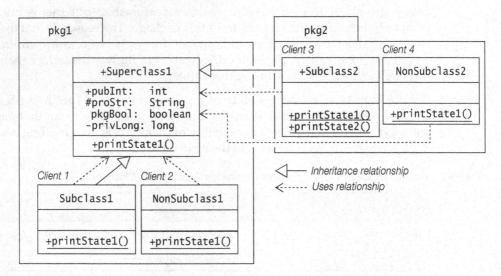

Accessibility of a member is illustrated in Example 6.8 by the four instance fields defined in the class `Superclass1` in `pkg1`, where each instance field has a different accessibility. These four instance fields are accessed in a `Superclass1` object created in the `static` method `printState1()` declared in five different contexts:

- Defining class: The class in which the member is declared—that is, `pkg1.Superclass1` in which the four instance fields being accessed are declared
- Client 1: From a subclass in the same package—that is, `pkg1.Subclass1`
- Client 2: From a non-subclass in the same package—that is, `pkg1.NonSubclass1`
- Client 3: From a subclass in another package—that is, `pkg2.Subclass2`
- Client 4: From a non-subclass in another package—that is, `pkg2.NonSubclass2`

Example 6.8 *Accessibility of Class Members*

```java
// File: Superclass1.java
package pkg1;

import static java.lang.System.out;

public class Superclass1 {                              // (1)

    // Instance fields with different accessibility:
    public    int     pubInt   = 2017;
    protected String  proStr   = "SuperDude";
              boolean pgkBool   = true;
    private   long    privLong = 0x7777;

    public static void printState1() {                  // (2)
      Superclass1 obj1 = new Superclass1();
      out.println(obj1.pubInt);
      out.println(obj1.proStr);
      out.println(obj1.pgkBool);
      out.println(obj1.privLong);
    }
}

// Client 1
class Subclass1 extends Superclass1 {                   // (3)
  public static void printState1() {
    Superclass1 obj1 = new Superclass1();
    out.println(obj1.pubInt);
    out.println(obj1.proStr);
    out.println(obj1.pgkBool);
    out.println(obj1.privLong);  // Compile-time error! Private access.
  }
}

// Client 2
class NonSubclass1 {                                    // (4)
  public static void printState1() {
    Superclass1 obj1 = new Superclass1();
    out.println(obj1.pubInt);
    out.println(obj1.proStr);
    out.println(obj1.pgkBool);
    out.println(obj1.privLong);  // Compile-time error! Private access.
  }
}
```

```java
// File: Subclass2.java
package pkg2;
import pkg1.Superclass1;

import static java.lang.System.out;
```

```java
// Client 3
public class Subclass2 extends Superclass1 {        // (5)

  public static void printState1() {                // (6)
    Superclass1 obj1 = new Superclass1();           // Object of Superclass1
    out.println(obj1.pubInt);
    out.println(obj1.proStr);    // (7) Compile-time error! Protected access.
    out.println(obj1.pgkBool);   // Compile-time error! Package access.
    out.println(obj1.privLong);  // Compile-time error! Private access.
  }

  public static void printState2() {                // (8)
    Subclass2 obj2 = new Subclass2();               // (9) Object of Subclass2
    out.println(obj2.pubInt);
    out.println(obj2.proStr);    // (10) OK! Protected access.
    out.println(obj2.pgkBool);   // Compile-time error! Package access.
    out.println(obj2.privLong);  // Compile-time error! Private access.
  }
}

// Client 4
class NonSubclass2 {                                 // (11)
  public static void printState1() {
    Superclass1 obj1 = new Superclass1();
    out.println(obj1.pubInt);
    out.println(obj1.proStr);    // Compile-time error! Protected access.
    out.println(obj1.pgkBool);   // Compile-time error! Package access.
    out.println(obj1.privLong);  // Compile-time error! Private access.
  }
}
```

public *Members*

Public access is the least restrictive of all the access modifiers. A public member is accessible from anywhere, both in the package containing its class and by other packages where its class is accessible.

In Example 6.8, the public instance field pubInt in an instance of the class Superclass1 is accessible by all four clients. Subclasses can access their inherited public members by their simple names, and all clients can access public members in an instance of the class Superclass1.

protected *Members*

A protected member is accessible in all classes in the same package, and by all subclasses of its class in any package where its class is accessible.

In other words, a protected member cannot be accessed by non-subclasses in other packages. This kind of access is more restrictive than public member access.

In Example 6.8, the protected instance field proStr in an instance of the class Superclass1 is accessible within pkg1 by Client 1 and Client 2. Also as expected,

Client 4—the class NonSubclass2 in pkg2—cannot access this protected member of the class Superclass1.

However, the compiler reports an error at (7) in the method printState1() of the class Subclass2 where the protected instance field proStr in an instance of the class Superclass1 *cannot* be accessed by the reference obj1.

In contrast, the method printState2() at (8) in the class Subclass2 uses the reference obj2 that refers to an instance of the class Subclass2 to access the instance fields declared in the class Superclass1, and now the protected instance field proStr in the superclass is accessible, as shown at (10).

This apparent anomaly is explained by the fact that a subclass in another package can only access protected instance members in the superclass via references of its own type—that is, protected instance members that are *inherited* by objects of the subclass. No inheritance from the superclass is involved in a subclass in another package when an object of the superclass is used.

Note that the above anomaly would *not* arise if a subclass in another package were to access any protected static members in the superclass, as such members are not part of any object of the superclass.

Members with Package Access

No access modifier implies package accessibility in this context. When no member access modifier is specified, the member is accessible only by other classes in the same package in which its class is declared. Even if its class is accessible in another package, the member is not accessible elsewhere. Package member access is more restrictive than protected member access.

In Example 6.8, the instance field pkgBool in an instance of the class Superclass1 has package access and is only accessible within pkg1, but not in any other packages—that is to say, it is accessible only by Client 1 and Client 2. Client 3 and Client 4 in pkg2 cannot access this field.

private *Members*

The private modifier is the most restrictive of all the access modifiers. Private members are not accessible by any other classes. This also applies to subclasses, whether they are in the same package or not. Since they are not accessible by their simple names in a subclass, they are also not inherited by the subclass. A standard design strategy for a class is to make all instance fields private and provide public get methods for such fields. Auxiliary methods are often declared as private, as they do not concern any client.

None of the clients in Figure 6.5 can access the private instance field privLong in an instance of the class Superclass1. This instance field is only accessible in the defining class—that is, in the class Superclass1.

Table 6.3 provides a summary of access modifiers for members in a class. References in parentheses refer to clients in Figure 6.5.

Table 6.3   *Accessibility of Members in a Class (Non-Modular)*

Member access	In the defining class Superclass1	In a subclass in the same package (Client 1)	In a non-subclass in the same package (Client 2)	In a subclass in a different package (Client 3)	In a non-subclass in a different package (Client 4)
public	Yes	Yes	Yes	Yes	Yes
protected	Yes	Yes	Yes	Yes	No
package	Yes	Yes	Yes	No	No
private	Yes	No	No	No	No

Additional Remarks on Accessibility

Access modifiers that can be specified for a class member apply equally to *constructors*. However, when no constructor is specified, the default constructor inserted by the compiler implicitly follows the accessibility of the class.

Accessibility of members declared in an enum type is analogous to those declared in a class, except for enum constants that are always public and constructors that are always private. A protected member in an enum type is only accessible in its own package, since an enum type is implicitly final. Member declarations in an enum type are discussed in §5.13, p. 290.

In contrast, the accessibility of members declared in an interface is always implicitly public (§5.6, p. 238). Omission of the public access modifier in this context does *not* imply package accessibility.

6.6 Scope Rules

Java provides explicit access modifiers to control the accessibility of members in a class by external clients, but in two areas access is governed by specific scope rules:

* Class scope for members: how member declarations are accessed within the class
* Block scope for local variables: how local variable declarations are accessed within a block

Class Scope for Members

Class scope concerns accessing members (including inherited ones) from code within a class. Table 6.4 gives an overview of how static and non-static code in a class can access members of the class, including those that are inherited. Table 6.4 assumes the following declarations:

```
class SuperClass {
  int instanceVarInSuper;
  static int staticVarInSuper;
```

```
              void instanceMethodInSuper()      { /* ... */ }
              static void staticMethodInSuper() { /* ... */ }
              // ...
          }

          class MyClass extends SuperClass {
            int instanceVar;
            static int staticVar;

            void instanceMethod()      { /* ... */ }
            static void staticMethod() { /* ... */ }
            // ...
          }
```

Table 6.1   *Accessing Members within a Class*

Member declarations	Non-static code in the class MyClass can refer to the member as	Static code in the class MyClass can refer to the member as

Instance variables	`instanceVar`
	`this.instanceVar`
	`instanceVarInSuper`
	`this.instanceVarInSuper`
	`super.instanceVarInSuper`
		Not possible

Instance methods	`instanceMethod()`
	`this.instanceMethod()`
	`instanceMethodInSuper()`
	`this.instanceMethodInSuper()`
	`super.instanceMethodInSuper()`
		Not possible

Static variables	`staticVar`
	`this.staticVar`
	`MyClass.staticVar`
	`staticVarInSuper`
	`this.staticVarInSuper`
	`super.staticVarInSuper`
	`MyClass.staticVarInSuper`
	`SuperClass.staticVarInSuper`
		`staticVar`
		
		`MyClass.staticVar`
		`staticVarInSuper`
		
		`MyClass.staticVarInSuper`
		`SuperClass.staticVarInSuper`

Static methods	`staticMethod()`
	`this.staticMethod()`
	`MyClass.staticMethod()`
	`staticMethodInSuper()`
	`this.staticMethodInSuper()`
	`super.staticMethodInSuper()`
	`MyClass.staticMethodInSuper()`
	`SuperClass.staticMethodInSuper()`
		`staticMethod()`
		
		`MyClass.staticMethod()`
		`staticMethodInSuper()`
		
		`MyClass.staticMethodInSuper()`
		`SuperClass.staticMethodInSuper()`

The golden rule is that static code can only access other static members by their simple names. Static code is not executed in the context of an object, so the references this and super are not available. An object has knowledge of its class, so static members are always accessible in a non-static context.

Note that using the class name to access static members within the class is no different from how external clients access these static members.

The following factors can all influence the scope of a member declaration:

* Shadowing of a field declaration, either by local variables (p. 354) or by declarations in the subclass (§5.1, p. 203)
* Overriding an instance method from a superclass (§5.1, p. 196)
* Hiding a static method declared in a superclass (§5.1, p. 203)

Within a class, references of the class can be declared and used to access *all* members in the class, regardless of their access modifiers. In Example 6.9, the method duplicateLight at (1) in the class Light has the parameter oldLight and the local variable newLight that are references of the class Light. Even though the fields of the class are private, they are accessible through the two references (oldLight and newLight) in the method duplicateLight(), as shown at (2), (3), and (4).

Example 6.9   *Class Scope*

```
class Light {
  // Instance variables:
  private int     noOfWatts;     // Wattage
  private boolean indicator;     // On or off
  private String  location;      // Placement

  // Instance methods:
  public void switchOn()  { indicator = true; }
  public void switchOff() { indicator = false; }
  public boolean isOn()   { return indicator; }

  public static Light duplicateLight(Light oldLight) {     // (1)
    Light newLight = new Light();
    newLight.noOfWatts = oldLight.noOfWatts;               // (2)
    newLight.indicator = oldLight.indicator;               // (3)
    newLight.location  = oldLight.location;                // (4)
    return newLight;
  }
}
```

Block Scope for Local Variables

Declarations and statements can be grouped into a *block* using curly brackets, {}. Blocks can be nested, and scope rules apply to local variable declarations in such blocks. A local declaration can appear anywhere in a block. The general rule is that a variable declared in a block is *in scope* in the block in which it is declared, but it is not accessible outside this block. It is not possible to redeclare a variable if a local variable of the same name is already declared in the current scope.

Local variables of a method include the formal parameters of the method and variables that are declared in the method body. The local variables in a method are created each time the method is invoked, and are therefore distinct from local variables in other invocations of the same method that might be executing (§7.1, p. 365).

Figure 6.6 illustrates *block scope* (also known as *lexical scope*) for local variables. It shows four blocks: Block 1 is the body of the method main(), Block 2 is the body of the for(;;) loop, Block 3 is the body of a switch statement, and Block 4 is the body of an if statement.

- Parameters cannot be redeclared in the method body, as shown at (1) in Block 1.
- A local variable—already declared in an enclosing block, and therefore visible in a nested block—cannot be redeclared in the nested block. These cases are shown at (3), (5), and (6).
- A local variable in a block can be redeclared in another block if the blocks are *disjoint*—that is, they do not overlap. This is the case for variable i at (2) in Block 3 and at (4) in Block 4, as these two blocks are disjoint.

The scope of a local variable declaration begins from where it is declared in the block and ends where this block terminates. The scope of the loop variable index is the entire Block 2. Even though Block 2 is nested in Block 1, the declaration of the variable index at (7) in Block 1 is valid. The scope of the variable index at (7) spans from its declaration to the end of Block 1, and it does not overlap with that of the loop variable index in Block 2.

Figure 6.6 *Block Scope*

```
public static void main(String[] args) {              // Block 1
//   String args = "";        // (1) Cannot redeclare parameters.
     char digit = 'z';

     for (int index = 0; index < 10; ++index) {        // Block 2
     {
         switch(digit) {                               // Block 3
             case 'a':
                 int i;      // (2)
             default:
             // int i;       // (3) Already declared in the same block
         } // end switch

         if (true) {                                   // Block 4
             int i;         // (4) OK
         // int digit;      // (5) Already declared in enclosing Block 1
         // int index;      // (6) Already declared in enclosing Block 2
         } // end if

     } // end for
     int index;             // (7) OK
} // end main
```

6.7 Implementing Immutability

Shared resources are typically implemented using synchronized code in order to guarantee thread safety of the shared resource (§22.4, p. 1387). However, if the shared resource is an immutable object, thread safety comes for free.

An object is *immutable* if its state cannot be changed once it has been constructed. Since its state can only be read, there can be no thread interference and the state is always consistent.

Some examples of immutable classes from the Java SE Platform API are listed in Table 6.5. Any method that seemingly modifies the state of an immutable object is in fact returning a new immutable object with the state modified appropriately based on the original object. Primitive values are of course always immutable.

Table 6.5 *Examples of Immutable Classes*

`java.lang.String`	This class implements immutable strings (§8.4, p. 439).
Wrapper classes in the `java.lang` package: `Boolean`, `Byte`, `Short`, `Character`, `Integer`, `Long`, `Float`, `Double`	Wrapper classes create immutable objects that wrap a value of their respective primitive type (§8.3, p. 429).
`java.nio.file.Path`	Objects of classes that implement this interface are immutable and represent a system-dependent file path (§21.2, p. 1289).
Temporal classes in the `java.time` package: `LocalDate`, `LocalTime`, `LocalDateTime`, `Instant`, `Period`, `Duration`, `ZonedDateTime`	These temporal classes create immutable objects that represent date-/time-based values (Chapter 17, p. 1023).
`java.time.format.DateTimeFormatter`	This class creates immutable objects with customized formatting and parsing capabilities for date-/time-based values (§18.6, p. 1134).
`java.util.Locale`	Immutable objects of this class represent a specific geographical, political, or cultural region (§18.1, p. 1096).

Example 6.10 *Implementing an Immutable Class*

```
import java.util.Arrays;

public final class WeeklyStats {          // (1) Class is final.

  private final String description;       // (2) Immutable string
  private final int weekNumber;           // (3) Immutable primitive value
  private final int[] stats;              // (4) Mutable int array
```

```java
    public WeeklyStats(String description, int weekNumber, int[] stats) {    // (5)
      if (weekNumber <= 0 || weekNumber > 52) {
        throw new IllegalArgumentException("Invalid week number: " + weekNumber);
      }
      if (stats.length != 7) {
        throw new IllegalArgumentException("Stats not for whole week: " +
                                           Arrays.toString(stats));
      }
      this.description = description;
      this.weekNumber = weekNumber;
      this.stats = Arrays.copyOf(stats, stats.length);    // Create a private copy.
    }

    public int getWeekNumber() {                    // (6) Returns immutable primitive.
      return weekNumber;
    }

    public String getDescription() {                // (7) Returns immutable string.
      return description;
    }

    public int getDayStats(int dayNumber) {     // (8) Returns stats for given day.
      return (0 <= dayNumber && dayNumber < 7) ? stats[dayNumber] : -1;
    }

    public int[] getStats() {                       // (9) Returns a copy of the stats.
      return Arrays.copyOf(this.stats, this.stats.length);
    }

    @Override
    public String toString() {
      return description + "(week " + weekNumber + "):" + Arrays.toString(stats);
    }
}
```

```java
public class StatsClient {
  public static void main(String[] args) {
    WeeklyStats ws1
        = new WeeklyStats("Appointments", 45, new int[] {5, 3, 8, 10, 7, 8, 9});
    System.out.println(ws1);
    WeeklyStats ws2
        = new WeeklyStats("E-mails", 47, new int[] {10, 5, 20, 7});
    System.out.println(ws2);
  }
}
```

Output from the program:

```
Appointments(week 45):[5, 3, 8, 10, 7, 8, 9]
Exception in thread "main" java.lang.IllegalArgumentException: Stats not for whole
week: [10, 5, 20, 7]
    at WeeklyStats.<init>(WeeklyStats.java:14)
    at StatsClient.main(StatsClient.java:7)
```

There are certain guidelines that can help to avoid common pitfalls when implementing immutable classes. We will illustrate implementing an immutable class called WeeklyStats in Example 6.10, whose instances, once created, cannot be modified. The class WeeklyStats creates an object with weekly statistics of a specified entity.

- *It should not be possible to extend the class.*

  Caution should be exercised in extending an immutable class to prevent any subclass from subverting the immutable nature of the superclass.

  A straightforward approach is to declare the class as final, as was done in Example 6.10 at (1) for the class WeeklyStats. Another approach is to declare the constructor as private and provide static factory methods to construct instances (discussed below). A static factory method is a static method whose sole purpose is to construct and return a new instance of the class—an alternative to calling the constructor directly.

- *All fields should be declared* final *and* private.

  Declaring the fields as private makes them accessible only inside the class, and other clients cannot access and modify them. This is the case for the fields in the WeeklyStats class at (2), (3), and (4).

  Declaring a field as final means the value stored in the field cannot be changed once initialized. However, if the final field is a reference to an object, the state of this object can be changed by other clients who might be sharing this object, unless the object is also immutable. See the last guideline on how to safeguard the state of an mutable object referenced by a field.

- *Check the consistency of the object state at the time the object is created.*

  Since it is not possible to change the state of an immutable object, the state should be checked for consistency when the object is created. If all relevant information to initialize the object is available when it is created, the state can be checked for consistency and any necessary measures taken. For example, a suitable exception can be thrown to signal illegal arguments.

  In the class WeeklyStats, the constructor at (5) is passed all the necessary values to initialize the object, and it checks whether they will result in a legal and consistent state for the object.

- *No set methods (a.k.a. setter or mutator methods) should be provided.*

  Set methods that change values in fields or objects referenced by fields should not be permitted. The class WeeklyStats does not have any set methods, and only provides get methods (a.k.a. *getter* or *assessor methods*).

  If a setter method is necessary, then the method should create a new instance of the class based on the modified state, and return that to the client, leaving the original instance unmodified. This approach has to be weighed against the cost of creating new instances, but is usually offset by other advantages associated with using immutable classes, like thread safety without synchronized code. Caching frequently used objects can alleviate some overhead of creating new objects, as exemplified by the immutable wrapper classes for primitive types. For example, the Boolean class has a static factory method valueOf() that always returns one of two objects, Boolean.TRUE or Boolean.FALSE, depending on whether its boolean argument was true or false, respectively. The Integer class interns values between −128 and 127 for efficiency so that there is only one Integer object to represent each int value in this range.

- *A client should not be able to access mutable objects referred to by any fields in the class.*

  The class should not provide any methods that can modify its mutable objects. The class WeeklyStats complies with this requirement.

  A class should also not share references to its mutable objects. The field at (4) has the type array of int that is mutable. An int array is passed as a parameter to the constructor at (5). The constructor in this case makes its own copy of this int array, so as not to share the array passed as an argument by the client. The getWeeklyStats() method at (8) does not return the reference value of the int array stored in the field stats. It creates and returns a new int array with values copied from its private int array. This technique is known as *defensive copying*. This way, the class avoids sharing references of its mutable objects with clients.

The class declaration below illustrates another approach to prevent a class from being extended. The class WeeklyStats is no longer declared final at (1), but now has a private constructor. This constructor at (5a) cannot be called by any client of the class to create an object. Instead, the class provides a static factory method at (5b) that creates an object by calling the private constructor. No subclass can be instantiated, as the superclass private constructor cannot be called, neither directly nor implicitly, in a subclass constructor.

```java
public class WeeklyStatsV2 {                           // (1) Class is not final.
  ...
  private WeeklyStatsV2(String description,
      int weekNumber, int[] stats) {                   // (5a) Private constructor
    this.description = description;
    this.weekNumber = weekNumber;
    this.stats = Arrays.copyOf(stats, stats.length); // Create a private copy.
  }

  // (5b) Static factory method to construct objects.
  public static WeeklyStatsV2 getNewWeeklyStats(String description,
                                      int weekNumber, int[] stats) {
    if (weekNumber <= 0 || weekNumber > 52) {
      throw new IllegalArgumentException("Invalid week number: " + weekNumber);
    }
    if (stats.length != 7) {
      throw new IllegalArgumentException("Stats not for whole week: " +
                                Arrays.toString(stats));
    }
    return new WeeklyStatsV2(description, weekNumber, stats);
  }
  ...
}
```

A class having just static methods is referred to as a *utility class*. Such a class cannot be instantiated and has no state, and is thus immutable. Examples of such classes in the Java API include the following: the java.lang.Math class, the java.util.Collections class, the java.util.Arrays class, and the java.util.concurrent.Executors class.

Apart from being thread safe, immutable objects have many other advantages. Once created, their state is guaranteed to be consistent throughout their lifetime. That makes them easy to reason about. Immutable classes are relatively simple to construct, amenable to testing, and easy to use compared to mutable classes. There is hardly any need to make or provide provisions for making copies of such objects. Their hash code value, once computed, can be cached for later use, as it will never change. Because of their immutable state, they are ideal candidates for keys in maps, and as elements in sets. They also are ideal building blocks for new and more complex objects.

A downside of using an immutable object is that if a value must be changed in its state, then a new object must be created, which can be costly if object construction is expensive.

 Review Questions

6.9   Which of the following statements are true about the use of modifiers?
      Select the two correct answers.
      (a) If no access modifier (public, protected, or private) is specified for a member declaration, the member is accessible only by classes in the package of its class and by subclasses of its class in any package.
      (b) You cannot specify accessibility of local variables. They are not accessible outside the block in which they are declared.
      (c) Subclasses of a class must reside in the same package as the class they extend.
      (d) Local variables can be declared as static.
      (e) The objects themselves do not have any access modifiers; only field references do.

6.10 Given the following declaration of a class, which field is accessible from outside the package com.corporation.project?

```
package com.corporation.project;

public class MyClass {
            int i;
   public    int j;
   protected int k;
   private   int l;
}
```

Select the one correct answer.
      (a) Field i is accessible in all classes in other packages.
      (b) Field j is accessible in all classes in other packages.

(c) Field k is accessible in all classes in other packages.
(d) Field k is accessible in subclasses only in other packages.
(e) Field 1 is accessible in all classes in other packages.
(f) Field 1 is accessible in subclasses only in other packages.

6.11   Which statement is true about the accessibility of members?
Select the one correct answer.

(a) A private member is always accessible within the same package.
(b) A private member can be accessed only in the class in which it is declared.
(c) A member with package access can be accessed by any subclass of the class in which it is declared.
(d) A private member cannot be accessed at all.
(e) Package accessibility for a member can be declared using the keyword default.

6.12   Which statement is true about immutability?
Select the one correct answer.

(a) Instances of a final class are immutable.
(b) Instances of a static class are immutable.
(c) All members of an immutable class are also immutable.
(d) None of the above

6.13   Which code modifications would make class Dog immutable?

```
public class Dog {
  String name;
  public Dog(String name) {
    this.name = name;
  }
  public void setName(String name) {
    this.name = name;
  }
  public String getName() {
    return name;
  }
}
```

Select the one correct answer.

(a) Mark the field name as private and remove the setName() method.
(b) Mark the field name as final and make the setName() method private.
(c) Mark the field name as final and initialize it in the declaration, then remove the setName() method.
(d) None of the above

Exception Handling 7

Chapter Topics

- Understanding program execution and the exception handling facility
- Recognizing the inheritance hierarchy of the Throwable class and its subclasses Exception, RuntimeException, and Error that define exception classes in Java
- Distinguishing between checked and unchecked exceptions
- Defining customized exception types
- Understanding the try-catch-finally construct and the control flow paths through it
- Using multiple catch clauses with the try statement
- Creating and throwing exceptions programmatically with the throw statement
- Using the throws clause to specify checked exceptions in the method header to propagate exceptions
- Using uni-catch and multi-catch clauses with the try statement to catch exceptions
- Rethrowing exceptions and handling chained exceptions
- Using the try-with-resources statement and implementing the AutoCloseable interface
- Handling suppressed exceptions

Java SE 11 Developer Exam Objectives	
[4.1] Handle exceptions in the Java program by using try/catch/ finally clauses, try-with-resource, and multi-catch statements	§7.3, p. 375 §7.6, p. 397 §7.7, p. 407
[4.2] Create and use custom exceptions	§7.2, p. 375

An exception in Java signals the occurrence of an event that disrupts the normal flow of program execution. Such an event typically occurs due to violation of some semantic constraint of the Java programming language during execution—for example, a requested file cannot be found, an array index is out of bounds, or a network link failed. Inserting explicit checks in the code for such events can easily result in less comprehensible code. Java provides an exception handling mechanism for systematically dealing with such events.

7.1 Stack-Based Execution and Exception Propagation

The exception mechanism is built around the *throw-and-catch* paradigm. To *throw* an exception is to signal that an unexpected event has occurred. To *catch* an exception is to take appropriate action to deal with the exception. An exception is caught by an *exception handler*, and the exception need not be caught in the same context in which it was thrown. The runtime behavior of the program determines which exceptions are thrown and how they are caught. The throw-and-catch principle is embedded in the try-catch-finally construct (p. 375).

Several threads can be executing at the same time in the JVM (§22.2, p. 1369). Each thread has its own *JVM stack* (also called a *runtime stack*, *call stack*, or *invocation stack* in the literature) that is used to handle execution of methods. Each element on the stack is called an *activation frame* or a *stack frame* and corresponds to a method call. Each new method call results in a new activation frame being pushed on the stack, which stores all the pertinent information such as the local variables. The method with the activation frame on the top of the stack is the one currently executing. When this method finishes executing, its activation frame is popped from the top of the stack. Execution then continues in the method corresponding to the activation frame that is now uncovered on the top of the stack. The methods on the stack are said to be *active*, as their execution has not completed. At any given time, the active methods on a JVM stack make up what is called the *stack trace* of a thread's execution.

Example 7.1 is a simple program to illustrate method execution. It calculates the average for a list of integers, given the sum of all the integers and the number of integers. It uses three methods:

- The method main() calls the method printAverage() with parameters supplying the total sum of the integers and the total number of integers, (1).

- The method printAverage() in turn calls the method computeAverage(), (3).

- The method computeAverage() uses integer division to calculate the average and returns the result, (7).

Example 7.1   *Method Execution*

```
public class Average1 {

  public static void main(String[] args) {
    printAverage(100, 20);                                    // (1)
```

```java
        System.out.println("Exit main().");                         // (2)
    }

    public static void printAverage(int totalSum, int totalCount) {
        int average = computeAverage(totalSum, totalCount);         // (3)
        System.out.println("Average = " +                           // (4)
            totalSum + " / " + totalCount + " = " + average);
        System.out.println("Exit printAverage().");                 // (5)
    }

    public static int computeAverage(int sum, int count) {
        System.out.println("Computing average.");                   // (6)
        return sum/count;                                           // (7)
    }
}
```

Output of program execution:
```
Computing average.
Average = 100 / 20 = 5
Exit printAverage().
Exit main().
```

- -

Execution of Example 7.1 is illustrated in Figure 7.1. Each method execution is shown as a box with the local variables declared in the method. The height of the box indicates how long a method is active. Before the call to the method System.out.println() at (6) in Figure 7.1, the stack trace comprises the three active methods: main(), printAverage(), and computeAverage(). The result 5 from the method computeAverage() is returned at (7) in Figure 7.1. The output from the program corresponds with the sequence of method calls in Figure 7.1. As the program terminates normally, this program behavior is called *normal execution*.

If the method call at (1) in Example 7.1

```java
    printAverage(100, 20);                                          // (1)
```

is replaced with

```java
    printAverage(100, 0);                                           // (1)
```

and the program is run again, the output is as follows:

```
Computing average.
Exception in thread "main" java.lang.ArithmeticException: / by zero
        at Average1.computeAverage(Average1.java:18)
        at Average1.printAverage(Average1.java:10)
        at Average1.main(Average1.java:5)
```

Figure 7.2 illustrates the program execution when the method printAverage() is called with the arguments 100 and 0 at (1). All goes well until the return statement at (7) in the method computeAverage() is executed. An error event occurs in calculating the expression sum/number because integer division by 0 is an illegal operation. This event is signaled by the JVM by *throwing* an ArithmeticException (p. 372). This exception is *propagated* by the JVM through the JVM stack as explained next.

Figure 7.1 *Normal Method Execution*

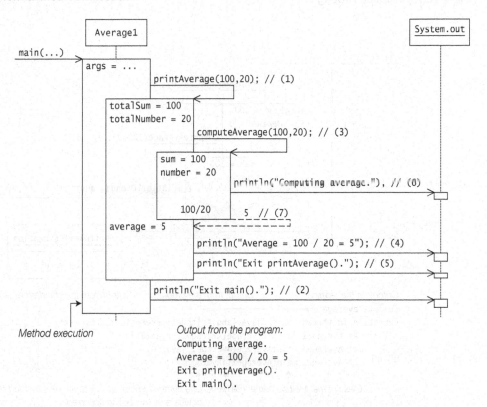

Output from the program:
Computing average.
Average = 100 / 20 = 5
Exit printAverage().
Exit main().

Figure 7.2 illustrates the case where an exception is thrown and the program does not take any explicit action to deal with the exception. In Figure 7.2, execution of the computeAverage() method is suspended at the point where the exception is thrown. The execution of the return statement at (7) never gets completed. Since this method does not have any code to deal with the exception, its execution is likewise terminated abruptly and its activation frame popped. We say that the method *completes abruptly.* The exception is then offered to the method whose activation is now on the top of the stack (printAverage()). This method does not have any code to deal with the exception either, so its execution completes abruptly. The statements at (4) and (5) in the method printAverage() never get executed. The exception now propagates to the last active method (main()). This does not deal with the exception either. The main() method also completes abruptly. The statement at (2) in the main() method never gets executed. Since the exception is not *caught* by any of the active methods, it is dealt with by the main thread's *default exception handler.* The default exception handler usually prints the name of the exception, with an explanatory message, followed by a printout of the stack trace at the time the exception was thrown. An uncaught exception, as in this case, results in the death of the thread in which the exception occurred.

Figure 7.2 *Exception Propagation*

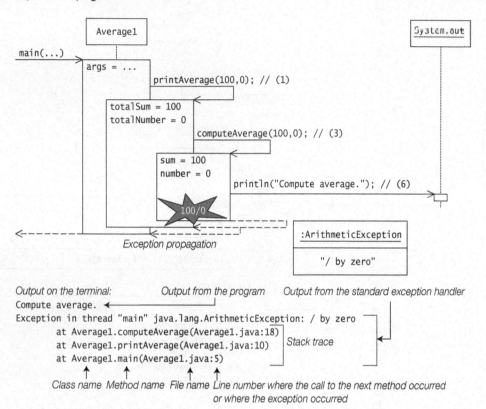

If an exception is thrown during the evaluation of the left-hand operand of a binary expression, then the right-hand operand is not evaluated. Similarly, if an exception is thrown during the evaluation of a list of expressions (e.g., a list of actual parameters in a method call), evaluation of the rest of the list is skipped.

If the line numbers in the stack trace are not printed in the output as shown previously, use the following command to run the program:

```
>java -Djava.compiler=NONE Average1
```

7.2 Exception Types

Exceptions in Java are objects. All exceptions are derived from the java.lang.Throwable class. Figure 7.3 shows a partial hierarchy of classes derived from the Throwable class. The two main subclasses Exception and Error constitute the main categories of *throwables*, the term used to refer to both exceptions and errors. Figure 7.3 also shows that not all exception classes are found in the java.lang package.

Figure 7.3 *Partial Exception Inheritance Hierarchy*

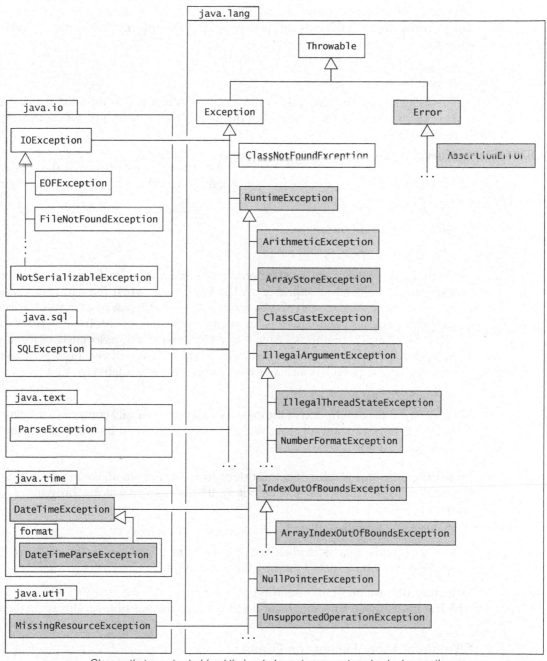

Classes that are shaded (and their subclasses) represent unchecked exceptions.

All throwable classes in the Java SE Platform API at least define a zero-argument constructor and a one-argument constructor that takes a `String` parameter. This parameter can be set to provide a *detail message* when an exception is constructed. The purpose of the detail message is to provide more information about the actual exception.

```
Throwable()
Throwable(String msg)
```

The first constructor constructs a throwable that has `null` as its detail message. The second constructor constructs a throwable that sets the specified string as its detail message.

Most exception types provide analogous constructors.

The class `Throwable` provides the following common methods to query an exception:

```
String getMessage()
```

Returns the detail message.

```
void printStackTrace()
```

Prints the stack trace on the standard error stream. The stack trace comprises the method invocation sequence on the JVM stack when the exception was thrown. The stack trace can also be written to a `PrintStream` or a `PrintWriter` by supplying such a destination as an argument to one of the two overloaded `printStackTrace()` methods. Any *suppressed exceptions* associated with an exception on the stack trace are also printed (p. 415). It will also print the *cause* of an exception (which is also an exception) if one is available (p. 405).

```
String toString()
```

Returns a short description of the exception, which typically comprises the class name of the exception together with the string returned by the `getMessage()` method.

In dealing with throwables, it is important to recognize *situations* in which a particular throwable can occur, and the *source* that is responsible for throwing it. By *source* we mean:

- The *JVM* that is responsible for throwing the throwable, or
- The throwable that is explicitly thrown *programmatically* by the code in the application or by any API used by the application.

In further discussion of exception types, we provide an overview of situations in which selected throwables can occur and the source responsible for throwing them.

The `java.lang.Exception` Class

The class `Exception` represents exceptions that a program would normally want to catch. Its subclass `java.lang.RuntimeException` represents many common programming errors that can manifest at runtime (see the next subsection). Other subclasses of the Exception class, excluding the RuntimeException class, define what are known as *checked exceptions* (p. 374) that particularly aid in building robust programs. Some common checked exceptions are presented below.

java.lang.ClassNotFoundException

The class ClassNotFoundException is a subclass of the Exception class that signals that the JVM tried to load a class by its string name, but the class could not be found. A typical example of this situation is when the class name is misspelled while starting program execution with the java command. The source in this case is the JVM throwing the exception to signal that the class cannot be found.

java.io.IOException

The class IOException is a subclass of the Exception class that represents I/O-related exceptions that are found in the java.io package (EOFException, FileNotFoundException, NotSerializableException). Chapter 20, p. 1231, and Chapter 21, p. 1285, provide ample examples of contexts in which I/O-related exceptions can occur.

java.io.EOFException

The class EOFException is a subclass of the IOException class that represents an exception that signals that an *end of file* (EOF) or end of stream was reached unexpectedly when more input was expected—that is, there is no more input available. Typically, this situation occurs when an attempt is made to read input from a file when all data from the file has already been read, often referred to as *reading past EOF*.

java.io.FileNotFoundException

The class FileNotFoundException is a subclass of the IOException class that represents an exception that signals an attempt to open a file by using a specific pathname failed—in other words, the file with the specified pathname does not exist. This exception can also occur when an I/O operation does not have the required permissions for accessing the file.

java.io.NotSerializableException

The class NotSerializableException is a subclass of the IOException class that represents an exception that signals that an object does not implement the Serializable interface that is required in order for the object to be serialized (§20.5, p. 1261).

java.sql.SQLException

The class SQLException is a subclass of the Exception class that represents an exception that can provide information about various database-related errors that can occur. Chapter 24 provides examples illustrating such situations.

java.text.ParseException

The class ParseException is a subclass of the Exception class that represents an exception that signals unexpected errors while parsing. Examples of parsing date, number, and currency where this exception is thrown can be found in §18.5, p. 1116.

The `java.lang.RuntimeException` Class

Runtime exceptions are all subclasses of the `java.lang.RuntimeException` class, which is a subclass of the `Exception` class. As these runtime exceptions are usually caused by program bugs that should not occur in the first place, it is usually more appropriate to treat them as faults in the program design and let them be handled by the default exception handler.

`java.lang.ArithmeticException`

This exception represents situations where an illegal arithmetic operation is attempted, such as integer division by 0. It is typically thrown by the JVM.

`java.lang.ArrayIndexOutOfBoundsException`

Java provides runtime checking of the array index value, meaning out-of-bounds array indices. The subclass `ArrayIndexOutOfBoundsException` of the `RuntimeException` class represents exceptions thrown by the JVM that signal out-of-bound errors specifically for arrays—that is, an error in which an invalid index is used to access an element in the array. The index value must satisfy the relation $0 \leq index\ value < length$ *of the array* (§3.9, p. 120).

`java.lang.ArrayStoreException`

This exception is thrown by the JVM when an attempt is made to store an object of the wrong type into an array of objects. The array store check at runtime ensures that an object being stored in the array is assignment compatible with the element type of the array (§5.7, p. 260). To make the array store check feasible at runtime, the array retains information about its declared element type at runtime.

`java.lang.ClassCastException`

This exception is thrown by the JVM to signal that an attempt was made to cast a reference value to a type that was not legal, such as casting the reference value of an `Integer` object to the `Long` type (§5.11, p. 269).

`java.lang.IllegalArgumentException`

The class `IllegalArgumentException` represents exceptions thrown to signal that a method was called with an illegal or inappropriate argument. For example, the `ofPattern(String pattern)` method in the `java.time.format.DateTimeFormatter` class throws an `IllegalArgumentException` when the letter pattern passed as an argument is invalid (§18.6, p. 1134).

java.lang.IllegalThreadStateException

The class IllegalThreadStateException is a subclass of the IllegalArgumentException class. Certain operations on a thread can only be executed when the thread is in an appropriate state (§22.4, p. 1380). This exception is thrown when this is not the case. For example, the start() method of a Thread object throws this exception if the thread has already been started (§22.3, p. 1370).

java.lang.NumberFormatException

The class NumberFormatException is a subclass of the IllegalArgumentException class that is specialized to signal problems when converting a string to a numeric value if the format of the characters in the string is not appropriate for the conversion. This exception is thrown programmatically. The numeric wrapper classes all have methods that throw this exception when conversion from a string to a numeric value is not possible (§8.3, p. 434).

java.lang.NullPointerException

This exception is typically thrown by the JVM when an attempt is made to use the null value as a reference value to refer to an object. This might involve calling an instance method using a reference that has the null value, or accessing a field using a reference that has the null value.

This programming error has made this exception one of the most frequently thrown exceptions by the JVM. The error message issued provides helpful information as to *where* and *which* reference raised the exception. However, inclusion of variables names in the message can be a potential security risk.

```
Exception in thread "main" java.lang.NullPointerException: Cannot invoke
"String.toLowerCase()" because "msg" is null
    at StringMethods.main(StringMethods.java:162)
```

java.lang.UnsupportedOperationException

This exception is thrown programmatically to indicate that an operation invoked on an object is not supported. Typically, a class implements an interface, but chooses not to provide certain operations specified in the interface. Methods in the class corresponding to these operations throw this exception to indicate that an operation is not supported by the objects of the class.

The API documentation of the java.util.Collection interface (§15.1, p. 783) in the Java Collections Framework states that certain methods are *optional*, meaning that a concrete collection class need not provide support for such operations, and if any such operation is not supported, then the method should throw this exception.

java.time.DateTimeException

In the Date and Time API, the class DateTimeException represents exceptions that signal problems with creating, querying, and manipulating date-time objects (§17.2, p. 1027).

`java.time.format.DateTimeParseException`

In the Date and Time API, the class DateTimeParseException is a subclass of the Date-
TimeException class that represents an exception that signals unexpected errors
when parsing date and time values (§18.6, p. 1127).

`java.util.MissingResourceException`

This exception is thrown programmatically, typically by the lookup methods of the
java.util.ResourceBundle class (§18.3, p. 1104). Get methods on resource bundles
typically throw this exception when no resource can be found for a given key. Static
lookup methods in this class also throw this exception when no resource bundle
can be found based on a specified base name for a resource bundle. Resource bundles are discussed in §18.3, p. 1102.

The `java.lang.Error` Class

The class Error and its subclasses define errors that are invariably never explicitly
caught and are usually irrecoverable. Not surprisingly, most such errors are signaled by the JVM. Apart from the subclass mentioned below, other subclasses of
the java.lang.Error class define different categories of errors.

The subclass VirtualMachineError represents virtual machine errors like stack overflow
(StackOverflowError) and out of memory for object allocation (OutOfMemoryError).
The subclass LinkageError represents class linkage errors like missing class definitions (NoClassDefFoundError). The subclass AssertionError of the Error class is used
by the Java assertion facility.

Checked and Unchecked Exceptions

Except for RuntimeException, Error, and their subclasses, all exceptions are *checked*
exceptions. A checked exception represents an unexpected event that is not under
the control of the program—for example, a file was not found. The compiler
ensures that if a method can throw a checked exception, directly or indirectly, the
method must either catch the exception and take the appropriate action, or pass the
exception on to its caller (p. 388).

Exceptions defined by the Error and RuntimeException classes and their subclasses
are known as *unchecked* exceptions, meaning that a method is not obliged to deal
with these kinds of exceptions (shown with gray color in Figure 7.3). Either they
are irrecoverable (exemplified by the Error class), in which case the program
should not attempt to deal with them, or they are programming errors (exemplified
by the RuntimeException class and its subclasses) and should usually be dealt with
as such, and not as exceptions.

Defining Customized Exceptions

Customized exceptions are usually defined to provide fine-grained categorization of error situations, instead of using existing exception classes with descriptive detail messages to differentiate among the various situations. New customized exceptions are usually defined by either extending the Exception class or one of its checked subclasses, thereby making the new exceptions checked, or extending the RuntimeException subclass or one of its subclasses to create new unchecked exceptions.

Customized exceptions, as any other Java classes, can declare fields, constructors, and methods, thereby providing more information as to their cause and remedy when they are thrown and caught. The super() call can be used in a constructor to set pertinent details about the exception: a detail message or the cause of the exception (p. 405), or both. Note that the exception class must be instantiated to create an exception object that can be thrown and subsequently caught and dealt with. The following code sketches a class declaration for an exception that can include all pertinent information about the exception. Typically, the new exception class provides a constructor to set the detail message.

```
public class EvacuateException extends Exception {
  // Fields
  private Date date;
  private Zone zone;
  private TransportMode transport;

  // Constructor
  public EvacuateException(Date d, Zone z, TransportMode t) {
    // Call the constructor of the superclass, usually passing a detail message.
    super("Evacuation of zone " + z);
    // ...
  }
  // Methods
  // ...
}
```

Several examples in subsequent sections illustrate exception handling.

7.3 Exception Handling: try, catch, and finally

The mechanism for handling exceptions is embedded in the try-catch-finally construct, which has the following basic form:

```
try {                                      // try block
  statements
} catch (exception_type₁ parameter₁) {     // uni-catch clause
  statements
}
...
  catch (exception_typeₙ parameterₙ) {     // uni-catch clause
  statements
```

```
    } finally {                                    // finally clause
        statements
    }
```

A few aspects about the syntax of this construct should be noted. For each try block, there can be zero or more catch clauses (i.e., it can have *multiple* catch clauses), but only one finally clause. The catch clauses and the finally clause must always appear in conjunction with a try block, and in the right order. A try block must be followed by at least one catch clause, or a finally clause must be specified—in contrast to the try-with-resources statement where neither a catch nor a finally clause is mandatory (p. 407). In addition to the try block, each catch clause and the finally clause specify a block, { }. The block notation is mandatory.

Exceptions thrown during execution of the try block can be caught and handled in a catch clause. Each catch clause defines an exception handler. The header of the catch clause specifies exactly one exception parameter. The exception type must be of the Throwable class or one of its subclasses; otherwise, the code will not compile. The type of the exception parameter of a catch clause is specified by a *single* exception type in the syntax shown earlier, and such a catch clause is called a *uni*-catch clause.

A finally clause is always executed, regardless of the cause of exit from the try block, or whether any catch clause was executed at all. The two exceptions to this scenario are if the JVM crashes or the System.exit() method is called. Figure 7.4 shows three typical scenarios of control flow through the try-catch-finally construct.

Figure 7.4   *The* try-catch-finally *Construct*

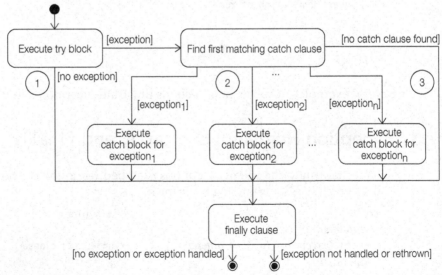

Normal execution continues after try-catch-finally construct   *Execution aborted and exception propagated*

The try block, the catch clause, and the finally clause of a try-catch-finally construct can contain arbitrary code, which means that a try-catch-finally construct can be nested in any block of the try-catch-finally construct. However, such nesting can easily make the code difficult to read and is best avoided, if possible.

The try Block

The try block establishes a context for exception handling. Termination of a try block occurs as a result of encountering an exception, or from successful execution of the code in the try block.

The catch clauses are skipped for all normal exits from the try block when no exceptions are thrown, and control is transferred to the finally clause if one is specified (Scenario 1 in Figure 7.4).

For all exits from the try block resulting from exceptions, control is transferred to the catch clauses—if any such clauses are specified—to find a matching catch clause (Scenario 2 in Figure 7.4). In the case when no catch clause is specified, control is transferred to the mandatory finally clause. If no catch clause matches the thrown exception, control is transferred to the finally clause if one is specified (Scenario 3 in Figure 7.4).

The catch Clause

Only an exit from a try block resulting from an exception can transfer control to a catch clause. A catch clause can catch the thrown exception only if the exception is assignable to the parameter in the catch clause. The code of the first such catch clause is executed, and all other catch clauses are ignored.

On exit from a catch clause, normal execution continues unless there is any uncaught exception that has been thrown and not handled. If this is the case, the method is aborted after the execution of any finally clause and the exception propagated up the JVM stack.

It is important to note that after a catch clause has been executed, control is always transferred to the finally clause if one is specified. This is true as long as there is a finally clause, regardless of whether the catch clause itself throws an exception.

In Example 7.2, the method printAverage() calls the method computeAverage() in a try-catch construct at (4). The catch clause is declared to catch exceptions of type ArithmeticException. The catch clause handles the exception by printing the stack trace and some additional information at (7) and (8), respectively. Normal execution of the program is illustrated in Figure 7.5, which shows that the try block is executed but no exceptions are thrown, with normal execution continuing after the try-catch construct. This corresponds to Scenario 1 in Figure 7.4.

Figure 7.5   *Exception Handling (Scenario 1)*

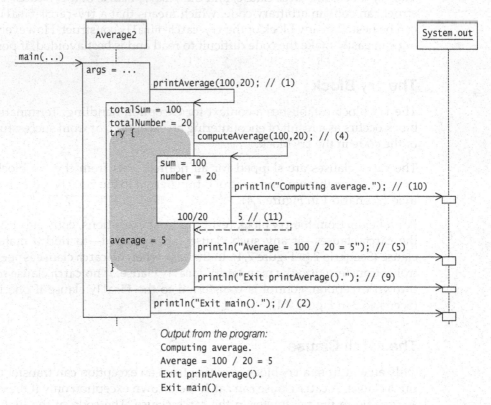

Output from the program:
Computing average.
Average = 100 / 20 = 5
Exit printAverage().
Exit main().

Example 7.2   *The* try-catch *Construct*

```java
public class Average2 {

    public static void main(String[] args) {
        printAverage(100, 20);                                        // (1)
        System.out.println("Exit main().");                          // (2)
    }

    public static void printAverage(int totalSum, int totalCount) {
        try {                                                         // (3)
            int average = computeAverage(totalSum, totalCount);      // (4)
            System.out.println("Average = " +                       // (5)
                totalSum + " / " + totalCount + " = " + average);
        } catch (ArithmeticException ae) {                           // (6)
            ae.printStackTrace();                                    // (7)
            System.out.println("Exception handled in printAverage().");  // (8)
        }
        System.out.println("Exit printAverage().");                 // (9)
    }
```

```
        public static int computeAverage(int sum, int count) {
          System.out.println("Computing average.");              // (10)
          return sum/count;                                      // (11)
        }
      }
```

Output from the program, with call `printAverage(100, 20)` at (1):

```
Computing average.
Average = 100 / 20 = 5
Exit printAverage().
Exit main().
```

Output from the program, with call `printAverage(100, 0)` at (1):

```
Computing average.
java.lang.ArithmeticException: / by zero
        at Average2.computeAverage(Average2.java:23)
        at Average2.printAverage(Average2.java:11)
        at Average2.main(Average2.java:5)
Exception handled in printAverage().
Exit printAverage().
Exit main().
```

However, if we run the program in Example 7.2 with the following call at (1):

```
printAverage(100, 0)
```

an ArithmeticException is thrown by the integer division operator in the method computeAverage(). In Figure 7.6 we see that the execution of the method compute-Average() is stopped and the exception propagated to method printAverage(), where it is handled by the catch clause at (6). Normal execution of the method continues at (9) after the try-catch construct, as witnessed by the output from the statements at (9) and (2). This corresponds to Scenario 2 in Figure 7.4.

In Example 7.3, the main() method calls the printAverage() method in a try-catch construct at (1). The catch clause at (3) is declared to catch exceptions of type ArithmeticException. The printAverage() method calls the computeAverage() method in a try-catch construct at (7), but here the catch clause is declared to catch exceptions of type IllegalArgumentException. Execution of the program is illustrated in Figure 7.7, which shows that the ArithmeticException is first propagated to the catch clause in the printAverage() method. Because this catch clause cannot handle this exception, it is propagated further to the catch clause in the main() method, where it is caught and handled. Normal execution continues at (6) after the exception is handled.

In Example 7.3, the execution of the try block at (7) in the printAverage() method is never completed: The statement at (9) is never executed. The catch clause at (10) is skipped. The execution of the printAverage() method is aborted: The statement at (13) is never executed, and the exception is propagated. This corresponds to Scenario 3 in Figure 7.4.

Figure 7.6 *Exception Handling (Scenario 2)*

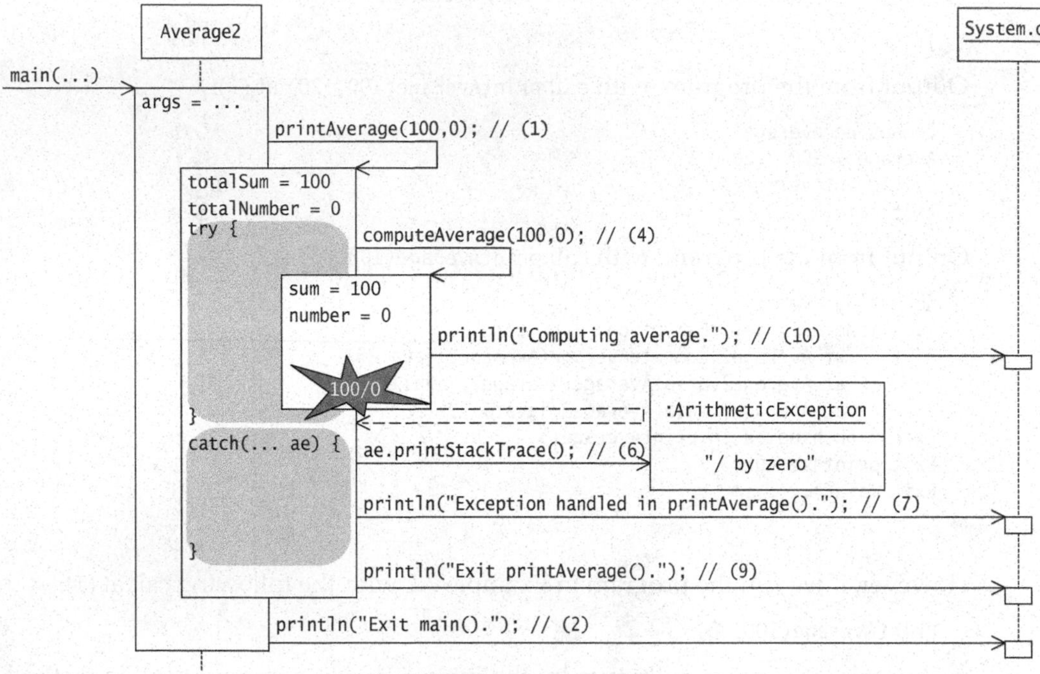

Output from the program:
```
Computing average.
java.lang.ArithmeticException: / by zero
        at Average2.computeAverage(Average2.java:23)
        at Average2.printAverage(Average2.java:11)
        at Average2.main(Average2.java:5)
Exception handled in printAverage().
Exit printAverage().
Exit main().
```

Example 7.3 *Exception Propagation*

```java
public class Average3 {

    public static void main(String[] args) {
        try {                                                    // (1)
            printAverage(100, 0);                                // (2)
        } catch (ArithmeticException ae) {                       // (3)
            ae.printStackTrace();                                // (4)
            System.out.println("Exception handled in main().");  // (5)
        }
        System.out.println("Exit main().");                      // (6)
    }

    public static void printAverage(int totalSum, int totalCount) {
        try {                                                    // (7)
            int average = computeAverage(totalSum, totalCount);  // (8)
            System.out.println("Average = " +                    // (9)
```

```
                       totalSum + " / " + totalCount + " = " + average);
          } catch (IllegalArgumentException iae) {                      // (10)
            iae.printStackTrace();                                      // (11)
            System.out.println("Exception handled in printAverage().");  // (12)
          }
          System.out.println("Exit printAverage().");                   // (13)
        }

        public static int computeAverage(int sum, int count) {
          System.out.println("Computing average.");                     // (14)
          return sum/count;                                             // (15)
        }
      }
```

Output from the program:

```
Computing average.
java.lang.ArithmeticException: / by zero
        at Average3.computeAverage(Average3.java:28)
        at Average3.printAverage(Average3.java:16)
        at Average3.main(Average3.java:6)
Exception handled in main().
Exit main().
```

The scope of the exception parameter name in the catch clause is the body of the catch clause—that is, it is a local variable in the body of the catch clause. As mentioned earlier, the type of the exception object must be *assignable* to the type of the argument in the catch clause. In the body of the catch clause, the exception object can be queried like any other object by using the parameter name.

The javac compiler complains if a catch clause for a superclass exception shadows the catch clause for a subclass exception, as the catch clause of the subclass exception will never be executed (a situation known as *unreachable code*). The following example shows incorrect order of the catch clauses at (1) and (2), which will result in a compile-time error at (2): The superclass Exception will shadow the subclass ArithmeticException.

```
try {
  // ...
} catch (Exception e) {            // (1) Superclass shadows subclass
  System.out.println(e);
} catch (ArithmeticException e) {  // (2) Compile-time error: Unreachable code
  System.out.println(e);
}
```

The compiler will also flag an error if the parameter of the catch clause has a *checked* exception type that cannot be thrown by the try block, as this would result in unreachable code.

```
try {
  throw new ArithmeticException();  // IOException never thrown in try block
} catch (IOException e) {           // Compile-time error: Unreachable code
  System.out.println(e);
}
```

Figure 7.7   *Exception Handling (Scenario 3)*

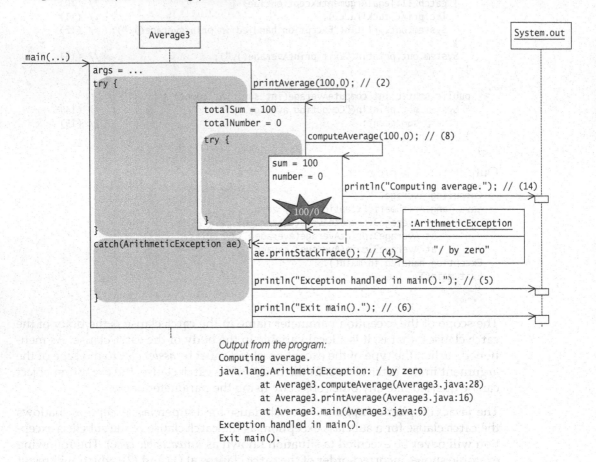

Output from the program:
```
Computing average.
java.lang.ArithmeticException: / by zero
        at Average3.computeAverage(Average3.java:28)
        at Average3.printAverage(Average3.java:16)
        at Average3.main(Average3.java:6)
Exception handled in main().
Exit main().
```

The `finally` Clause

If the try block executes, then the `finally` clause is guaranteed to be executed, regardless of whether any catch clause was executed, barring the two special cases (JVM crashes or the `System.exit()` method is called). Since the `finally` clause is always executed before control transfers to its final destination, the `finally` clause can be used to specify any clean-up code (e.g., to free resources such as files and network connections). However, the try-with-resources statement provides a better solution for handling resources, and eliminates the use of the `finally` clause in many cases (p. 407).

A try-finally construct can be used to control the interplay between two actions that must be executed in the correct order, possibly with other intervening actions. In the code below, the operation in the `calculateAverage()` method (called at (2)) is dependent on the success of the `sumNumbers()` method (called at (1)). The `if` statement at (2) checks the value of the sum variable before calling the `calculateAverage()` method:

```
int sum = 0;
try {
  sum = sumNumbers();              // (1)
  // other actions
} finally {
  if (sum > 0) calculateAverage();     // (2)
}
```

This code guarantees that if the try block is entered, the sumNumbers() method will be executed first, and later the calculateAverage() method will be executed in the finally clause, regardless of how execution proceeds in the try block. We can, if desired, include any catch clauses to handle any exceptions.

If the finally clause neither throws an exception nor executes a control transfer statement like a return or a labeled break, the execution of the try block or any catch clause determines how execution proceeds after the finally clause (Figure 7.4, p. 376).

- If no exception is thrown during execution of the try block or the exception has been handled in a catch clause, normal execution continues after the finally clause.

- If there is any uncaught exception (either because no matching catch clause was found or because the catch clause threw an exception), the method completes abruptly and the exception is propagated after the execution of the finally clause.

The output of Example 7.4 shows that the finally clause at (4) is executed, regardless of whether an exception is thrown in the try block at (2). If an ArithmeticException is thrown, it is caught and handled by the catch clause at (3). After the execution of the finally clause at (4), normal execution continues at (5).

- -

Example 7.4 *The* try-catch-finally *Construct*

```
public class Average4 {

  public static void main(String[] args) {
    printAverage(100, 20);                              // (1)
    System.out.println("Exit main().");
  }

  public static void printAverage(int totalSum, int totalCount) {
    try {                                              // (2)
      int average = computeAverage(totalSum, totalCount);
      System.out.println("Average = " +
        totalSum + " / " + totalCount + " = " + average);
    } catch (ArithmeticException ae) {                 // (3)
      ae.printStackTrace();
      System.out.println("Exception handled in printAverage().");
    } finally {                                        // (4)
      System.out.println("Finally done.");
    }
    System.out.println("Exit printAverage().");        // (5)
  }
```

```
    public static int computeAverage(int sum, int count) {
      System.out.println("Computing average.");
      return sum/count;
    }
  }
```

Output from the program, with the call printAverage(100, 20) at (1):

```
Computing average.
Average = 100 / 20 = 5
Finally done.
Exit printAverage().
Exit main().
```

Output from the program, with the call printAverage(100, 0) at (1):

```
Computing average.
java.lang.ArithmeticException: / by zero
        at Average4.computeAverage(Average4.java:24)
        at Average4.printAverage(Average4.java:10)
        at Average4.main(Average4.java:4)
Exception handled in printAverage().
Finally done.
Exit printAverage().
Exit main().
```

On exiting from the finally clause, if there is any uncaught exception, the method completes abruptly and the exception is propagated as explained earlier. This is illustrated in Example 7.5. The method printAverage() is aborted after the finally clause at (3) has been executed, as the ArithmeticException thrown at (4) is not caught by any method. In this case, the exception is handled by the default exception handler. Notice the difference in the output from Example 7.4 and Example 7.5.

Example 7.5   *The* try-finally *Construct*

```
public class Average5 {

  public static void main(String[] args) {
    printAverage(100, 0);                                          // (1)
    System.out.println("Exit main().");
  }

  public static void printAverage(int totalSum, int totalCount) {
    try {                                                          // (2)
      int average = computeAverage(totalSum, totalCount);
      System.out.println("Average = " +
          totalSum + " / " + totalCount + " = " + average);
    } finally {                                                    // (3)
      System.out.println("Finally done.");
    }
    System.out.println("Exit printAverage().");
  }
```

```
        public static int computeAverage(int sum, int count) {
          System.out.println("Computing average.");
          return sum/count;                                           // (4)
        }
      }
```

Output from the program:

```
Computing average.
Finally done.
Exception in thread "main" java.lang.ArithmeticException: / by zero
        at Average5.computeAverage(Average5.java:21)
        at Average5.printAverage(Average5.java:10)
        at Average5.main(Average5.java:4)
```

If the finally clause executes a control transfer statement, such as a return or a labeled break, this control transfer statement determines how the execution will proceed—regardless of how the try block or any catch clause was executed. In particular, a value returned by a return statement in the finally clause will supercede any value returned by a return statement in the try block or a catch clause.

Example 7.6 shows how the execution of a control transfer statement such as a return in the finally clause affects the program execution. The first output from the program shows that the average is computed but the value returned is from the return statement at (3) in the finally clause, not from the return statement at (2) in the try block. The second output shows that the ArithmeticException thrown in the computeAverage() method and propagated to the printAverage() method is suppressed by the return statement in the finally clause. Normal execution continues after the return statement at (3), with the value 0 being returned from the printAverage() method.

If the finally clause throws an exception, this exception is propagated with all its ramifications—regardless of how the try block or any catch clause was executed. In particular, the new exception overrules any previously uncaught exception (p. 415).

Example 7.6   *The* finally *Clause and the* return *Statement*

```
    public class Average6 {

      public static void main(String[] args) {
        System.out.println("Value: " + printAverage(100, 20));        // (1)
        System.out.println("Exit main().");
      }

      public static int printAverage(int totalSum, int totalCount) {
        int average = 0;
        try {
          average = computeAverage(totalSum, totalCount);
          System.out.println("Average = " +
              totalSum + " / " + totalCount + " = " + average);
```

```
        return average;                                           // (2)
      } finally {
        System.out.println("Finally done.");
        return average*2;                                         // (3)
      }
    }

    public static int computeAverage(int sum, int count) {
      System.out.println("Computing average.");
      return sum/count;
    }
  }
```

Output from the program, with call printAverage(100, 20) at (1):

```
Computing average.
Average = 100 / 20 = 5
Finally done.
Value: 10
Exit main().
```

Output from the program, with call printAverage(100, 0) at (1):

```
Computing average.
Finally done.
Value: 0
Exit main().
```

7.4 The throw Statement

Earlier examples in this chapter have shown how an exception can be thrown implicitly by the JVM during execution. Now we look at how an application can programmatically throw an exception using the throw statement. This statement can be used in a method, a constructor, or an initializer block. The general format of the throw statement is as follows:

throw *object_reference_expression*;

The compiler ensures that the type of the *object reference expression* is a Throwable or one of its subclasses. This ensures that a Throwable will always be propagated. At runtime a NullPointerException is thrown by the JVM if the *object reference expression* evaluates to null.

A detail message is often passed to the constructor when the exception object is created.

throw new ArithmeticException("Integer division by 0");

Propagation of a programmatically thrown exception is no different from one thrown implicitly by the JVM. When an exception is thrown, normal execution is suspended. The JVM proceeds to find a catch clause that can handle the exception.

The search starts in the context of the current try block, propagating to any enclosing try blocks and through the JVM stack to find a handler for the exception. Any associated finally clause of a try block encountered along the search path is executed. If no handler is found, then the exception is dealt with by the default exception handler at the top level. If a handler is found, normal execution resumes after the code in its catch clause has been executed, barring any rethrowing of an exception.

In Example 7.7, an exception is thrown by the throw statement at (4) as the count value is 0. This exception is propagated to the printAverage() method, where it is caught and handled by the catch clause at (1). Note that the finally clause at (2) is executed, followed by the resumption of normal execution, as evident from the output of the print statement at (3).

Example 7.7 *Throwing Exceptions Programmatically*

```
public class Average7 {

    public static void main(String[] args) {
        printAverage(100, 0);              // Calling with 0 number of values.
    }

    public static void printAverage(int totalSum, int totalCount) {
        System.out.println("Entering printAverage().");
        try {
            int average = computeAverage(totalSum, totalCount);
            System.out.println("Average = " +
                totalSum + " / " + totalCount + " = " + average);
        } catch (ArithmeticException ae) {                             // (1)
            ae.printStackTrace();
            System.out.println("Exception handled in printAverage().");
        } finally {                                                    // (2)
            System.out.println("Finally in printAverage().");
        }
        System.out.println("Exit printAverage().");                    // (3)
    }

    public static int computeAverage(int sum, int count) {
        System.out.println("Computing average.");
        if (count == 0)
            throw new ArithmeticException("Integer division by 0");    // (4)
        return sum/count;
    }
}
```

Output from the program:

```
Entering printAverage().
Computing average.
java.lang.ArithmeticException: Integer division by 0
        at Average7.computeAverage(Average7.java:26)
        at Average7.printAverage(Average7.java:11)
        at Average7.main(Average7.java:5)
```

```
Exception handled in printAverage().
Finally in printAverage().
Exit printAverage().
```

7.5 The throws Clause

A throws clause can be specified in a method or a constructor header to declare any checked exceptions that can be thrown by a statement in the body of a method or a constructor. It is declared immediately preceding the body of the method or the constructor.

... throws *ExceptionType*$_1$, *ExceptionType*$_2$,..., *ExceptionType*$_n$ { /* Body */ }

Each *ExceptionType*$_i$ is an *exception type* (i.e., a Throwable or one of its subclasses), although usually only checked exceptions are specified. The compiler enforces that if a checked exception can be thrown from the body of the method or the constructor, then either the type of this exception or a supertype of its exception type is specified in the throws clause of the method or the constructor. The throws clause can specify unchecked exceptions, but this is seldom done and the compiler does not enforce any restrictions on their usage.

The throws clause is part of the contract that a method or a constructor offers to its clients. The throws clause can specify any number of exception types in any order, even those that are not thrown by the method or the constructor. The compiler simply ensures that any checked exception that can actually be thrown in the method or constructor body is covered by the throws clause. Of course, any caller of the method or constructor cannot ignore the checked exceptions specified in the throws clause.

In a method or a constructor, a checked exception can be thrown directly by a throw statement, or indirectly by calling other methods or constructors that can throw a checked exception. If a checked exception is thrown, the code must obey the following rule (known by various names: *catch-or-declare rule, handle-or-declare rule, catch-or-specify requirement*):

- Either use a try block and catch the checked exception in a catch block and deal with it
- Or explicitly allow propagation of the checked exception to its caller by declaring it in the throws clause

Note that catching and dealing with a checked exception does not necessarily imply resumption of normal execution. A catch clause can catch the checked exception and choose to throw some other exception or even the same exception that is either unchecked or declared in the throws clause (p. 401). This rule ensures that a checked exception will be dealt with, regardless of the path of execution. This aids development of robust programs, as allowance can be made for many contingencies.

In Example 7.8, a new checked exception is defined, where the checked exception class IntegerDivisionByZero extends the Exception class. The method call at (2) in the try block at (1) results in the printAverage() method at (6) to be executed. The method call at (7) results in the computeAverage() method at (8) to be executed.

In the if statement at (9), the method computeAverage() throws the checked exception IntegerDivisionByZero. Neither the computeAverage() method nor the printAverage() method catches the exception, but instead throws it to the caller, as declared in the throws clauses in their method headers at (6) and (8). The exception propagates to the main() method. Since the printAverage() method was called from the context of the try block at (1) in the main() method, the exception is successfully caught by its catch clause at (3). The exception is handled and the finally clause at (4) is executed, with normal execution resuming from (5). If the method main() did not catch the exception, it would have to declare this exception in a throws clause. In that case, the exception would end up being handled by the default exception handler.

Example 7.8   *The* throws *Clause*

```
// File: IntegerDivisionByZero.java
public class IntegerDivisionByZero extends Exception {
  IntegerDivisionByZero() { super("Integer Division by Zero"); }
}
```

```
// File: Average8.java
public class Average8 {
  public static void main(String[] args) {
    try {                                                    // (1)
      printAverage(100, 0);                                  // (2)
    } catch (IntegerDivisionByZero idbz) {                   // (3)
      idbz.printStackTrace();
      System.out.println("Exception handled in main().");
    } finally {                                              // (4)
      System.out.println("Finally done in main().");
    }
    System.out.println("Exit main().");                      // (5)
  }

  public static void printAverage(int totalSum, int totalCount)
      throws IntegerDivisionByZero {                         // (6)
    int average = computeAverage(totalSum, totalCount);      // (7)
    System.out.println("Average = " +
        totalSum + " / " + totalCount + " = " + average);
    System.out.println("Exit printAverage().");
  }

  public static int computeAverage(int sum, int count)
      throws IntegerDivisionByZero {                         // (8)
    System.out.println("Computing average.");
    if (count == 0)                                          // (9)
      throw new IntegerDivisionByZero();
    return sum/count;                                        // (10)
  }
}
```

Output from the program:

```
Computing average.
IntegerDivisionByZero: Integer Division By Zero
        at Average8.computeAverage(Average8.java:27)
        at Average8.printAverage(Average8.java:17)
        at Average8.main(Average8.java:5)
Exception handled in main().
Finally done in main().
Exit main().
```

As mentioned earlier, the exception type specified in the throws clause can be a superclass of the actual exceptions thrown—that is, the exceptions thrown must be assignable to the type of the exceptions specified in the throws clause. If a method or a constructor can throw a checked exception, then the throws clause must declare its exception type or a supertype of its exception type; otherwise, a compile-time error will occur. In the printAverage() method, the superclass Exception of the subclass IntegerDivisionByZero could be specified in the throws clause of the method. This would also entail that the main() method either catch an Exception or declare it in a throws clause.

```
public static void main(String[] args) throws Exception {
  /* ... */
}

public static void printAverage(int totalSum, int totalCount) throws Exception {
  /* ... */
}
```

It is generally considered bad programming style to specify exception superclasses in the throws clause when the actual exceptions thrown are instances of their subclasses. It is also recommended to use the @throws tag in a Javadoc comment to document the checked exceptions that a method or a constructor can throw, together with any unchecked exceptions that might also be relevant to catch.

Overriding the throws Clause

A subclass can *override* a method defined in its superclass by providing a new implementation (§5.1, p. 196). What happens when a superclass method with a list of exceptions in its throws clause is overridden in a subclass? The method declaration in the subclass need not specify a throws clause if it does not throw any checked exceptions, and if it does, it can specify only *checked* exception classes that are already in the throws clause of the superclass method, or that are subclasses of the checked exceptions in the throws clause of the superclass method. As a consequence, an overriding method can have more number of exceptions, but it *cannot* allow *broader* checked exceptions in its throws clause than the superclass method does. Allowing broader checked exceptions in the overriding method would create problems for clients who already deal with the exceptions specified in the superclass method. Such clients would be ill prepared if an object of the subclass threw a checked exception they were not prepared for. However, there are no restrictions on specifying *unchecked* exceptions in the throws clause of the overriding method. The preceding discussion also applies to overriding methods from an interface that a class implements.

In the code below, the method compute() at (1) in superclass A is overridden correctly at (2) in subclass B. The throws clause of the method at (2) in subclass B specifies only one checked exception (ThirdException) from the throws clause at (1) and adds the more specific subclass exception (SubFirstException) of the superclass exception (FirstException) that is specified in the throws clause at (1). An unchecked exception (NumberFormatException) is also specified in the throws clause at (2). The checked exceptions in the throws clause at (2) are covered by the checked exceptions specified in the throws clause at (1). Unchecked exceptions are inconsequential in this regard. The subclass C does not override the compute() method from class A correctly, as the throws clause at (3) specifies an exception (FourthException) that the overridden method at (1) in class A cannot handle.

```
// New exception classes:
class FirstException    extends Exception { }
class SecondException   extends Exception { }
class ThirdException    extends Exception { }
class FourthException   extends Exception { }
class SubFirstException extends FirstException { }

// Superclass
class A {
  protected void compute()
      throws FirstException, SecondException, ThirdException { /* ... */ }  // (1)
}
// Subclass
class B extends A {
  @Override
  protected void compute()
      throws ThirdException, SubFirstException, NumberFormatException {     // (2)
    /* ... */
  }
}

//Subclass
class C extends A {
  @Override
  protected void compute()                                // Compile-time error at (3)
      throws FirstException, ThirdException, FourthException { /* ... */ }  // (3)
}
```

Usage of checked and unchecked exceptions in different contexts is compared in Table 7.1.

Table 7.1 *Comparing Checked and Unchecked Exceptions*

Context	Checked exceptions	Unchecked exceptions
The throws clause	Can include any checked exception, but when overridden it cannot specify new checked exceptions.	Can include any unchecked exception, whether it is overridden or not.
The try block	Can throw any checked exception.	Can throw any unchecked exception.
The catch clause	Can only catch a checked exception that is thrown by the try block. A catch clause can always be used to catch an Exception.	Can catch any unchecked exception, whether or not it is thrown by the try block.
The throw statement	Can throw any checked exception.	Can throw any unchecked exception.
The *catch-or-declare* rule	Applies only to checked exceptions.	Does not apply to unchecked exceptions.

 Review Questions

7.1   Which digits, and in which order, will be printed when the following program is run?

```java
public class DemoClass {
  public static void main(String[] args) {
    int k=0;
    try {
      int i = 5/k;
    } catch (ArithmeticException e) {
      System.out.println("1");
    } catch (RuntimeException e) {
      System.out.println("2");
      return;
    } catch (Exception e) {
      System.out.println("3");
    } finally {
      System.out.println("4");
    }
    System.out.println("5");
  }
}
```

Select the one correct answer.

(a) The program will only print 5.

(b) The program will only print 1 and 4, in that order.

(c) The program will only print 1, 2, and 4, in that order.

(d) The program will only print 1, 4, and 5, in that order.

(e) The program will only print 1, 2, 4, and 5, in that order.

(f) The program will only print 3 and 5, in that order.

7.2 Which of the following statements are true about the following program?

```java
public class Exceptions {
  public static void main(String[] args) {
    try {
      if (args.length == 0) return;
      System.out.println(args[0]);
    } finally {
      System.out.println("The end");
    }
  }
}
```

Select the two correct answers.

(a) If run with no program arguments, the program will produce no output.

(b) If run with no program arguments, the program will print The end.

(c) The program will throw an ArrayIndexOutOfBoundsException.

(d) If run with one program argument, the program will simply print the specified argument.

(e) If run with one program argument, the program will print the specified argument followed by The end.

7.3 Which of the following statements are true?
Select the two correct answers.

(a) If an exception is not caught in a method, the method will terminate and normal execution will resume.

(b) An overriding method must declare that it throws the same exception classes as the method it overrides.

(c) The main() method of a program can declare that it throws checked exceptions.

(d) A method declaring that it throws an exception of a certain class may throw instances of any subclass of that exception class.

(e) The finally clause is executed if, and only if, an exception is thrown in the corresponding try block.

7.4 Which statement is true about the following code?

```java
class A extends Throwable {}

class B extends A {}

public class RQ6A20 {
  public static void main(String[] args) throws A {
    try {
      action();
    } finally {
      System.out.println("Done.");
    } catch (A e) {
```

```
        throw e;
      }
    }
    public static void action() throws B {
      throw new B();
    }
  }
```

Select the one correct answer.

(a) The `main()` method must declare that it throws B.

(b) The `finally` clause must follow the catch clause in the `main()` method.

(c) The catch clause in the `main()` method must declare that it catches B rather than A.

(d) A single try block cannot be followed by both catch and `finally` clauses.

(e) The declaration of class A is not valid.

7.5   Which statement is true about the following code?

```
        public class Calculator {
          public static int average(int... values) {
            int result = 0;
            for (int i = 0; i < values.length; i++) {
              result += values[i];
            }
            return result/values.length;
          }
          public static void main(String[] args) {
            int value = 1;
            try {
              value = average();
            } catch (ArithmeticException e) {
              System.out.print("error");
            }
            System.out.print(value);
          }
        }
```

Select the one correct answer.

(a) The program will print error0.

(b) The program will print error1.

(c) The program will print error.

(d) The program will print 0.

(e) The program will print 1.

(f) The program will terminate by throwing an exception.

(g) The program will fail to compile.

7.6   What will be the output of the following program?

```
        public class PlayerException extends Exception {
          public PlayerException(String message) { super(message); }
        }
```

```
public class Player {
  public static String reaction (String action)  throws PlayerException {
    if (action == null || action.isEmpty()) {
      throw new PlayerException("Invalid action");
    }
    return ">" + action;
  }
  public static void main(String[] args) {
    String message = null;
    try {
      message = reaction(message);
    } catch (PlayerException e) {
      message = e.getMessage();
    }
    System.out.print(message);
  }
}
```

Select the one correct answer.

(a) message
(b) >message
(c) >null
(d) >
(e) Invalid action
(f) >Invalid action

7.7   What will be the output of the following program?

```
import java.io.*;
public class FileReader {
  public static void readFile(String name) throws Exception {
    if (name == null) throw new FileNotFoundException("invalid file name");
  }
  public static void main(String[] args) {
    String file = null;
    try {
      readFile(file);
    } catch (IOException e) {
      System.out.print("IO error: " + e.getMessage());
    } catch (Exception e) {
      System.out.print("Other error: " + e.getMessage());
    } finally {
      System.out.print(" finally");
    }
    System.out.print(" the end");
  }
}
```

Select the one correct answer.

(a) IO error: invalid file name finally
(b) IO error: invalid file name the end
(c) IO error: invalid file name finally the end
(d) Other error: invalid file name finally

(e) Other error: invalid file name the end

(f) Other error; invalid file name finally the end

(g) finally the end

(h) the end

(i) Nothing will be printed.

(j) An uncaught exception stack trace will be printed.

7.8   What will be the output of the following program?

```java
import java.io.*;
public class FileReader {
  public static void readFile(String name)  throws Exception {
    if (name != null) throw new FileNotFoundException("invalid file name");
  }
  public static void main(String[] args) {
    String file = null;
    try {
      readFile(file);
    } catch (IOException e) {
      System.out.print("IO error: " + e.getMessage()+" ");
    } catch (Exception e) {
      System.out.print("Other error: " + e.getMessage()+" ");
    } finally {
      System.out.print("finally");
    }
    System.out.print(" the end");
  }
}
```

Select the one correct answer.

(a) IO error: invalid file name finally

(b) IO error: invalid file name the end

(c) IO error: invalid file name finally the end

(d) Other error: invalid file name finally

(e) Other error: invalid file name the end

(f) Other error: invalid file name finally the end

(g) finally the end

(h) the end

(i) Nothing will be printed.

(j) An uncaught exception stack trace will be printed.

7.9   What will be the output of the following program?

```java
import java.io.*;
public class FileReader {
  public static void readFile(String name) throws IOException {
    if (name == null) {
      throw new NullPointerException("invalid file name");
    } else {
      throw new IOException("file read not implemented");
    }
  }
}
```

```
        public static void main(String[] args) {
          String file = null;
          try {
            readFile(file);
          } catch (IOException e) {
            System.out.print("IO error: " + e.getMessage());
          } catch (Exception e) {
            System.out.print("Other error: " + e.getMessage());
            return;
          } finally {
            System.out.print(" finally");
          }
          System.out.print(" the end");
        }
      }
```

Select the one correct answer.

(a) `IO error: file read not implemented finally`
(b) `IO error: file read not implemented the end`
(c) `IO error: file read not implemented finally the end`
(d) `Other error: invalid file name finally`
(e) `Other error: invalid file name the end`
(f) `Other error: invalid file name finally the end`
(g) `finally the end`
(h) `the end`
(i) Nothing will be printed.
(j) An uncaught exception stack trace will be printed.

7.6 The Multi-catch Clause

Example 7.9 uses a try block that has multiple uni-catch clauses. This example is based on Example 7.8. The sum of the values and the number of values needed to calculate the average are now read as program arguments from the command line at (2) and (3), respectively. The example shows a try statement at (1) that uses three uni-catch clauses: at (5), (6), and (7). In a *uni*-catch clause, a *single* exception type is specified for the catch parameter.

In Example 7.9, the method `printAverage()` is only called at (4) if there are at least two consecutive integers specified on the command line. An unchecked `ArrayIndexOutOfBoundsException` is thrown if there are not enough program arguments, and an unchecked `NumberFormatException` is thrown if an argument cannot be converted to an `int` value. The astute reader will notice that the code for handling these two exceptions is the same in the body of the respective catch clauses. In order to avoid such code duplication, one might be tempted to replace the two catch clauses with a single catch clause that catches a more *general* exception, for example:

```
  catch (RuntimeException rte) { // NOT RECOMMENDED!
    System.out.println(rte);
    System.out.println("Usage: java Average9 <sum of values> <no. of values>");
  }
```

This is certainly not recommended, as specific exceptions are to be preferred over general exceptions, not the least because a more general exception type might unintentionally catch more exceptions than intended.

Example 7.9   *Using Multiple* catch *Clauses*

```java
// File: IntegerDivisionByZero.java
public class IntegerDivisionByZero extends Exception {
  IntegerDivisionByZero() { super("Integer Division by Zero"); }
}
```

```java
// File: Average9.java
public class Average9 {
  public static void main(String[] args) {
    try {                                               // (1)
      int sum        = Integer.parseInt(args[0]);       // (2)
      int numOfValues = Integer.parseInt(args[1]);      // (3)
      printAverage(sum, numOfValues);                   // (4)
    } catch (ArrayIndexOutOfBoundsException aioob) {    // (5) uni-catch
      System.out.println(aioob);
      System.out.println("Usage: java Average9 <sum of values> <no. of values>");
    } catch (NumberFormatException nfe) {               // (6) uni-catch
      System.out.println(nfe);
      System.out.println("Usage: java Average9 <sum of values> <no. of values>");
    } catch (IntegerDivisionByZero idbz) {              // (7) uni-catch
      idbz.printStackTrace();
      System.out.println("Exception handled in main().");
    } finally {                                         // (8)
      System.out.println("Finally done in main().");
    }
    System.out.println("Exit main().");                 // (9)
  }

  public static void printAverage(int totalSum, int totalCount)
      throws IntegerDivisionByZero {
    int average = computeAverage(totalSum, totalCount);
    System.out.println("Average = " +
        totalSum + " / " + totalCount + " = " + average);
    System.out.println("Exit printAverage().");
  }

  public static int computeAverage(int sum, int count)
      throws IntegerDivisionByZero {
    System.out.println("Computing average.");
    if (count == 0)
      throw new IntegerDivisionByZero();
    return sum/count;
  }
}
```

Running the program:

```
>java Average9 100 twenty
java.lang.NumberFormatException: For input string: "twenty"
Usage: java Average9 <sum of values> <no. of values>
Finally done in main().
Exit main().
```

Running the program:

```
>java Average9 100
java.lang.ArrayIndexOutOfBoundsException: 1
Usage: java Average9 <sum of values> <no. of values>
Finally done in main().
Exit main().
```

The *multi*-catch clause provides the solution, allowing specific exceptions to be declared and avoiding duplicating the same code for the body of the catch clauses. The syntax of the multi-catch clause is as follows:

catch (*exception_type*$_1$|*exception_type*$_2$| ... |*exception_type*$_k$ *parameter*) {
   statements
}

The multi-catch clause still has a single *parameter*, but now a list of exception types, delimited by the vertical bar (|), can be specified as the types for this parameter. This list defines a *union of alternatives* that are the exception types which the multi-catch clause can handle. The *statements* in the body of the multi-catch clause will be executed when an object of any of the specified exception types is caught by the multi-catch clause.

The multiple catch clauses at (5) and (6) in Example 7.9 have been replaced with a multi-catch clause at (5) in Example 7.10:

```
catch (ArrayIndexOutOfBoundsException |                    // (5) multi-catch
       NumberFormatException ep) {
  System.out.println(ep);
  System.out.println("Usage: java Average10 <sum of values> <no. of values>");
}
```

The multi-catch clause in Example 7.10 is semantically equivalent to the two uni-catch clauses in Example 7.9, and we can expect the same program behavior in both examples.

Example 7.10 *Using the Multi-catch Clause*

```
// File: Average10.java
public class Average10 {
  public static void main(String[] args) {
    try {                                                  // (1)
      int sum = Integer.parseInt(args[0]);                 // (2)
      int numOfValues = Integer.parseInt(args[1]);         // (3)
```

```
      printAverage(sum, numOfValues);                        // (4)
    } catch (ArrayIndexOutOfBoundsException |                // (5) multi-catch
            NumberFormatException ep) {
      System.out.println(ep);
      System.out.println("Usage: java Average10 <sum of values> <no. of values>");
    } catch (IntegerDivisionByZero idbz) {                   // (6) uni-catch
      idbz.printStackTrace();
      System.out.println("Exception handled in main().");
    } finally {                                              // (7)
      System.out.println("Finally done in main().");
    }
    System.out.println("Exit main().");                      // (8)
  }

  public static void printAverage(int totalSum, int totalCount)
      throws IntegerDivisionByZero {
    // See Example 7.9.
  }

  public static int computeAverage(int sum, int count)
      throws IntegerDivisionByZero {
    // See Example 7.9.
  }
}
```

A few remarks are in order regarding the alternatives of a multi-catch clause. There should be no subtype–supertype relationship between any of the specified exception types in the alternatives of a multi-catch clause. The following multi-catch clause will not compile, as ArrayIndexOutOfBoundsException is a subtype of IndexOutOfBoundsException:

```
catch (IndexOutOfBoundsException |                 // Compile-time error!
       ArrayIndexOutOfBoundsException e) {
  // ...
}
```

The parameter of a multi-catch clause is also considered to be *implicitly* final, and therefore cannot be assigned to in the body of the multi-catch clause. In a uni-catch clause, the parameter is considered to be *effectively* final if it does not occur on the left-hand side of an assignment in the body of the uni-catch clause.

```
try {
  // Assume appropriate code to throw the right exceptions.
} catch (NumberFormatException |
         IndexOutOfBoundsException e) {    // Parameter is final.
  e = new ArrayIndexOutOfBoundsException();// Compile-time error!
                                           // Cannot assign to final parameter e.
} catch (IntegerDivisionByZero idbz) {     // Parameter is effectively final.
  idbz.printStackTrace();
} catch (IOException ioe) {                 // Parameter is not effectively final.
  ioe = new FileNotFoundException("No file.");
}
```

Disallowing any subtype–supertype relationship between alternatives and the parameter being final in a multi-catch clause or effectively final in a uni-catch clause allows the compiler to perform precise exception handling analysis.

The compiler also generates effective bytecode for a *single* exception handler corresponding to all the alternatives in a multi-catch clause, in contrast to generating bytecode for *multiple* exception handlers for uni-catch clauses that correspond to the multi-catch clause.

Rethrowing Exceptions

Rethrowing an exception refers to throwing an exception in the body of a catch clause. The catch clause catches an exception, but then throws this exception or another exception in its body. This allows an exception to be partially handled when it is caught the first time, and then again when the rethrown exception is caught later. Typically, the first exception handler is a common handler for the situation and the later exception handler is a more specific one.

Exception parameters that are explicitly, implicitly, or effectively final in catch clauses allow the compiler to perform improved analysis of exception handling in the code, especially when it comes to rethrowing exceptions.

For the examples in this section, it is important to keep in mind that the exception type IOException is the supertype of both EOFException and FileNotFoundException.

Example 7.11 illustrates how the compiler is able to identify unreachable code by precise analysis of rethrown exceptions that are either final or effectively final. The body of the try statement at (1) can only throw a FileNotFoundException that is caught by the catch clause at (3). This exception is effectively final in the catch clause at (3), as no assignment is made to it in the body of the catch clause. This exception is rethrown in the nested try statement at (4), but the catch clause at (6) of this try statement can only catch an EOFException. Since parameter ex is effectively final, it can only denote a FileNotFoundException, never an EOFException. The catch clause at (6) is unreachable, and the compiler flags an error.

Example 7.11 *Precise Rethrowing of Exceptions*

```
import java.io.EOFException;
import java.io.FileNotFoundException;
import java.io.IOException;

public class ExceptionAnalysis {
  public static void main(String[] args) throws IOException {
    try {                                   // (1)
      throw new FileNotFoundException();    // (2)
    } catch (IOException ex) {              // (3)
      try {                                 // (4) Nested try statement
        throw ex;                           // (5) Can only rethrow FileNotFoundException
      } catch (EOFException se) {  // (6) Compile-time error: clause unreachable
        System.out.println("I am unreachable.");
      }
    }
```

```
      }
    }
  }
```

Example 7.12 illustrates how final or effectively final catch parameters allow more precise exceptions to be specified in the throws clause of a method. The thing to note is that the parameter e in the catch clause at (5) is not effectively final, as an assignment is made to the parameter at (6). All bets are off when the parameter is not final and the exception is rethrown. The throws clause must specify the same type as the type of the catch parameter, as shown at (3a). This has consequences for the caller method main(). Its try statement at (1) must include the catch clause at (2) to catch an IOException as well, or the compiler will flag an error about an uncaught checked exception. The contract of the checkIt() method allows for all exceptions that are either IOException or its subtypes.

If the assignment statement at (6) is commented out, the catch parameter e is effectively final in the catch body. The compiler can deduce that the rethrown exception can only be of type FileNotFoundException or EOFException. The throws clause of the checkIt() method can be made more specific, as at (3b). Note that the type of the catch parameter is the supertype IOException of the subtypes specified in the throws clause at (3b). Commenting out the assignment statement at (6) and uncommenting the more precise throws clause at (3b) has consequences for the caller method main() as well. The catch clause at (2) becomes unreachable, and the compiler issues a *warning*. Note also that the type of the exception parameter e at (5) is IOException, which is the supertype of the exception types specified in the throws clause. However, static analysis by the compiler is able to confirm that the exception parameter e can only denote objects of either FileNotFoundException or EOFException, but not of supertype IOException.

Example 7.12   *Precise* throws *Clause*

```
      import java.io.EOFException;
      import java.io.FileNotFoundException;
      import java.io.IOException;

      public class MorePreciseRethrow {
        public static void main(String[] args) {                          // (1)
          try {
            checkIt(1);
          } catch (FileNotFoundException fnfe) {
            System.out.println("Check that the file exits.");
          } catch (EOFException eofe) {
            System.out.println("Check the contents of the file.");
          } catch (IOException ioe) { // (2) mandatory with (3a), but compiler warning
                                      //      that clause is unreachable with (3b).
            System.out.println("This should never occur.");
          }
        }
```

```
    public static void checkIt(int value) throws IOException {      // (3a)
    //public static void checkIt(int value)                         // (3b)
    //     throws FileNotFoundException, EOFException {
        try {                                                       // (4)
            switch (value) {
                case 1:
                    throw new FileNotFoundException("File not found");
                case 2:
                    throw new EOFException("End of file");
                default:
                    System.out.println("OK");
            }
        } catch (IOException e) {                                   // (5)
            System.out.println(e.getMessage());
            e = new EOFException("End of file");        // (6) not effectively final,
            //                                               requires (3a).
            //                                               When commented out,
            //                                               can use (3b).

            throw e;
        }
    }
}
```

Program output with (3a) and (6) uncommented, and (3b) commented out:

```
File not found
Check the contents of the file.
```

Program output with (3a) and (6) commented out, and (3b) is uncommented:

```
File not found
Check that the file exits.
```

In summary, a throw statement in the body of a catch clause can throw a final or an effectively final exception parameter that has exception type E if *all* of the following conditions are satisfied:

- Exception type E can be thrown in the body of the try statement with which the catch clause is associated.

- Exception type E is assignment compatible with any of the exception types declared for the parameter in the catch clause.

- Exception type E is not assignment compatible with any of the exception types declared for the parameters in any preceding catch clause in the same try statement.

In Example 7.13, the throw statements at (1), (2), and (3) all try to rethrow an exception that is effectively final in the body of the catch clause.

- The throw statement at (1) in the main() method satisfies all the conditions. The try block throws an exception of the right type (EOFException). The exception thrown (EOFException) is assignment compatible with the type declared for the parameter in the catch clause (IOException). There is no preceding catch clause that handles the exception (EOFException).

- The throw statement at (2) in the rethrowA() method cannot throw the exception, as the first condition is not satisfied: The try block does not throw an exception of the right type (EOFException). The compiler flags an *error* for the catch clause that is unreachable.

- The throw statement at (3) in the rethrowB() method cannot throw the exception, as the third condition is not satisfied: A preceding catch clause can handle the exception (EOFException). The compiler flags a *warning* for the catch clause which is unreachable.

Example 7.13 *Conditions for Rethrowing Final Exceptions*

```java
import java.io.EOFException;
import java.io.FileNotFoundException;
import java.io.IOException;

public class RethrowMe {
  public static void main(String[] args) throws EOFException {
    try {
      switch (1) {
        case 1: throw new FileNotFoundException("File not found");
        case 2: throw new EOFException("End of file");
        default: System.out.println("OK");
      }
    } catch (FileNotFoundException fnfe) {
      System.out.println(fnfe);
    } catch (IOException ioe) {
      throw ioe;                                                    // (1)
    }
  }

  public static void rethrowA() throws EOFException {
    try {
      // Empty try block.
    } catch (EOFException eofe) { // Compile-time error: exception not thrown
                              //                         in try block.
      throw eofe;                                                   // (2)
    }
  }

  public static void rethrowB() throws EOFException {
    try {
      throw new EOFException("End of file");
    } catch (EOFException eofe) {
      System.out.println(eofe);
    } catch (IOException ioe) {   // Compile-time warning: unreachable clause
      throw ioe;                                                    // (3)
    }
  }
}
```

Chaining Exceptions

It is common that the handling of an exception leads to the throwing of another exception. In fact, the first exception is the cause of the second exception being thrown. Knowing the *cause* of an exception can be useful, for example, when debugging the application. The Java API provides a mechanism for *chaining* exceptions for this purpose.

The class Throwable provides the following constructors and methods to handle chained exceptions:

Throwable(Throwable cause)
Throwable(String msg, Throwable cause)

Sets the throwable to have the specified cause, and also specifies a detail message if the second constructor is used. Most exception types provide analogous constructors.

Throwable initCause(Throwable cause)

Sets the cause of this throwable. Typically called on exception types that do not provide a constructor to set the cause.

Throwable getCause()

Returns the cause of this throwable, if any; otherwise, it returns null.

Example 7.14 illustrates how a chain of cause-and-effect exceptions, referred to as the *backtrace*, associated with an exception can be created and manipulated. In the method chainIt(), declared at (2), an exception is successively caught and associated as a *cause* with a new exception before the new exception is thrown, resulting in a chain of exceptions. This association is made at (3) and (4). The catch clause at (1) catches the exception thrown by the method checkIt(). The causes in the chain are successively retrieved by calling the getCause() method. Program output shows the resulting backtrace: which exception was the cause of which exception, and the order shown being reverse to the order in which they were thrown, the first one in the chain being thrown last.

Example 7.14 *Chaining Exceptions*

```
import java.io.EOFException;
import java.io.FileNotFoundException;
import java.io.IOException;

public class ExceptionsInChain {
  public static void main(String[] args) {
    try {
      chainIt();
    } catch (Exception e) {                                      // (1)
      System.out.println("Exception chain: " + e);
      Throwable t = e.getCause();
      while (t != null) {
        System.out.println("Cause: " + t);
```

```
        t = t.getCause();
      }
    }
  }

  public static void chainIt() throws Exception {          // (2)
    try {
      throw new FileNotFoundException("File not found");
    } catch (FileNotFoundException e) {
      try {
        IOException ioe = new IOException("File error");
        ioe.initCause(e);                                  // (3)
        throw ioe;
      } catch (IOException ioe) {
        Exception ee = new Exception("I/O error", ioe);    // (4)
        throw ee;
      }
    }
  }
}
```

Output from the program:

```
Exception chain: java.lang.Exception: I/O error
Cause: java.io.IOException: File error
Cause: java.io.FileNotFoundException: File not found
```

- -

A convenient way to print the backtrace associated with an exception is to invoke the printStackTrace() method on the exception. The catch clause at (1) in Example 7.14 can be replaced with the catch clause at (1') below that calls the print-StackTrace() method on the exception.

```
...
try {
  chainIt();
} catch (Exception e) {                                   // (1')
  e.printStackTrace();                                    // Print backtrace.
}
...
```

The refactoring of Example 7.14 will result in the following analogous printout of the backtrace, showing as before the exceptions and their causes in the reverse order to the order in which they were thrown:

```
java.lang.Exception: I/O error
    at ExceptionsInChain.chainIt(ExceptionsInChain.java:23)
    at ExceptionsInChain.main(ExceptionsInChain.java:8)
Caused by: java.io.IOException: File error
    at ExceptionsInChain.chainIt(ExceptionsInChain.java:19)
    ... 1 more
Caused by: java.io.FileNotFoundException: File not found
    at ExceptionsInChain.chainIt(ExceptionsInChain.java:16)
    ... 1 more
```

7.7 The try-with-resources Statement

Normally, objects in Java are automatically garbage collected at the discretion of the JVM when they are no longer in use. However, *resources* are objects that need to be explicitly closed when they are no longer needed. Files, streams, and database connections are all examples that fall into this category of objects. Such resources also rely on underlying system resources for their use. By closing such resources, any underlying system resources are also freed, and can therefore be recycled. Resource leakage (i.e., failure to close resources properly) can lead to performance degradation as resources get depleted.

Best practices recommend the following idiom for using a resource:

- Open the resource—that is, allocate or assign the resource.
- Use the resource—that is, call the necessary operations on the resource.
- Close the resource—that is, free the resource.

Typically, all three steps above can throw exceptions, and to ensure that a resource is always closed after use, the recommended practice is to employ a combination of try-catch-finally blocks. The first two steps are usually nested in a try block, with any associated catch clauses, and the third step is executed in a finally clause to ensure that the resource, if it was opened, is always closed regardless of the path of execution through the try-catch blocks.

Example 7.15 shows a naive approach to resource management, that can result in resource leakage. It uses a BufferedReader associated with a FileReader to read a line from a text file (§20.3, p. 1251). The example follows the idiom for resource usage. As we can see, an exception can be thrown from each of the steps. If any of the first two steps throw an exception, the call to the close() method at (4) will never be executed to close the resource and thereby any underlying resources, as execution of the method will be terminated and the exception propagated.

Example 7.15 *Naive Resource Management*

```
import java.io.EOFException;
import java.io.FileReader;
import java.io.BufferedReader;
import java.io.FileNotFoundException;
import java.io.IOException;

public class NaiveResourceUse {
  public static void main(String[] args)
      throws FileNotFoundException, EOFException, IOException {

    // Open the resource:
    var fis = new FileReader(args[0]);              // (1) FileNotFoundException
    var br = new BufferedReader(fis);

    // Use the resource:
    String textLine = br.readLine();                // (2) IOException
```

```
      if (textLine != null) {
        System.out.println(textLine);
      } else {
        throw new EOFException("Empty file.");          // (3) EOFException
      }

      // Close the resource:
      System.out.println("Closing the resource.");
      br.close();                                       // (4) IOException
    }
  }
```

Running the program:

```
>java NaiveResourceUse EmptyFile.txt
Exception in thread "main" java.io.EOFException: Empty file.
        at NaiveResourceUse.main(NaiveResourceUse.java:20)
```

Running the program:

```
>java NaiveResourceUse Slogan.txt
Code Compile Compute
Closing the resource.
```

Example 7.16 improves on Example 7.15 by explicitly using try-catch-finally blocks to manage the resources. No matter how the try-catch blocks execute, the finally block at (4) will always be executed. If the resource was opened, the close() method will be called at (5). The close() method is only called on the BufferedReader object, and not on the FileReader object. The reason is that the close() method of the BufferedReader object implicitly calls the close() method of the FileReader object associated with it. This is typical of how the close() method of such resources works. Also, calling the close() method on a resource that has already been closed normally has no effect; the close() method is said to be *idempotent*.

Example 7.16 *Explicit Resource Management*

```
import java.io.EOFException;
import java.io.FileReader;
import java.io.BufferedReader;
import java.io.FileNotFoundException;
import java.io.IOException;

public class TryWithoutARM {
  public static void main(String[] args) {
    BufferedReader br = null;
    try {
      // Open the resource:
      var fis = new FileReader(args[0]);                // (1) FileNotFoundException
      br = new BufferedReader(fis);

      // Use the resource:
      String textLine = br.readLine();                  // (2) IOException
```

```
            if (textLine != null) {
              System.out.println(textLine);
            } else {
              throw new EOFException("Empty file.");         // (3) EOFException
            }
        } catch (FileNotFoundException | EOFException e) {
            e.printStackTrace();
        } catch (IOException ioe) {
            ioe.printStackTrace();
        } finally {                                          // (4)
            if (br != null) {
              try {
                System.out.println("Closing the resource.");
                br.close();                                  // (5) IOException
              } catch(IOException ioe) {
                ioe.printStackTrace();
              }
            }
        }
      }
    }
```

Running the program:

```
>java TryWithoutARM EmptyFile.txt
java.io.EOFException: Empty file.
      at TryWithoutARM.main(TryWithoutARM.java:20)
Closing the resource.
```

Running the program:

```
>java TryWithoutARM Slogan.txt
Code Compile Compute
Closing the resource.
```

A lot of boilerplate code is required in explicit resource management using try-catch-finally blocks, and the code can get tedious and complex, especially if there are several resources that are open and they all need to be closed explicitly. The try-with-resources statement takes the drudgery out of associating try blocks with corresponding finally blocks to ensure proper resource management. Any resource declared in the header of the try-with-resources statement will be automatically closed, regardless of how execution proceeds in the try block. The compiler expands the try-with-resources statement (and any associated catch or finally clauses) into basic try-catch-finally blocks to guarantee this behavior. It implicitly generates a finally block that calls the close() method of each resource declared in the header of the try-with-resources statement. There is no need to call the close() method of the resource, let alone provide any explicit finally clause for this purpose.

The close() method provided by the resources declared in a try-with-resources statement is the implementation of the sole abstract method declared in the java.lang.AutoCloseable interface. In other words, these resources must implement the AutoCloseable interface (p. 412).

The syntax of the try-with-resources statement augments the try statement with a try *header* that comprises a list of *resource declaration statements* separated by a semi-colon (;).

```
try ( resource_declaration_statement₁; ... ; resource_declaration_statementₘ ) {
  statements
} catch (exception_type₁ |...| exception_typeₖ parameter₁) { // multi-catch
  statements
}
...
  catch (exception_typeₙ parameterₙ) {                       // uni-catch
  statements
} finally {                                                  // finally
  statements
}
```

The syntax shown above is for the *extended* try-with-resources statement, which has explicit catch and/or finally clauses associated with it. The *basic* try-with-resources statement has no explicit catch or finally clauses associated with it.

We will use Example 7.17 to illustrate the salient features of the try-with-resources statement. The extended try-with-resources statement at (1) declares and initial-izes two resources in its try header:

```
try (var fis = new FileReader(args[0]);        // (1) FileNotFoundException
     var br = new BufferedReader(fis)) {
  // ...
}
```

Note that no calls should be made to the close() method of a resource variable that is declared and initialized in the try header. Any catch clause or finally clauses associated with an extended try-with-resources statement will be executed *after* all the declared resources have been closed. When running Example 7.17 with an empty file, the EOFException is caught and handled *after* the two resources denoted by the references br and fis have been closed.

The scope of a resource variable is the try block—that is, it is a local variable in the try block. Local variable type inference with var can be used with advantage in declaring resources in this context (§3.13, p. 142). Also, the resource variables are implicitly final, guaranteeing that they cannot be assigned to in the try block, thus ensuring that the right resources will be closed when the close() method is called after the execution of the try block. The closing order of the resources is the reverse order in which they are declared in the try header—that is, the resource declared first in the try header is closed last after the execution of the try block. In Example 7.17, the close() method is first called on the BufferedReader object denoted by the reference br as it is declared last, followed by a call to the close() method of the FileReader object denoted by the reference fis. Note how the idem-potent behavior of the close() method in the FileReader object comes into play: It is first called implicitly by the close() method of the BufferedReader object, and then again by virtue of the resource declaration statement in the try header. The try-with-resources statement at (1) can be easily rewritten to avoid this redundant call, where now only the `BufferedReader` resource is declared, ensuring that the `close()` method of the `FileReader` resource will be called only once when the `BufferedReader` resource is closed:

```
try (var br = new BufferedReader(new FileReader(args[0]))) {
  // ...
}
```

Example 7.17 *Using* try *with Automatic Resource Management (ARM)*

```
import java.io.EOFException;
import java.io.FileReader;
import java.io.BufferedReader;
import java.io.FileNotFoundException;
import java.io.IOException;
import java.util.stream.Stream;

public class TryWithARM {
  public static void main(String[] args) {
    try (var fis = new FileReader(args[0]);        // (1) FileNotFoundExeception
         var br = new BufferedReader(fis)) {
      String textLine = br.readLine();             // (2) IOException
      if (textLine != null) {
        System.out.println(textLine);
      } else {
        throw new EOFException("Empty file.");      // (3) EOFException
      }
    } catch (FileNotFoundException | EOFException e) {
      e.printStackTrace();
    } catch (IOException ioe) {
      ioe.printStackTrace();
    }
  }
}
```

Running the program:

```
>java TryWithARM EmptyFile.txt
java.io.EOFException: Empty file.
        at TryWithARM.main(TryWithARM.java:15)
```

Running the program:

```
>java TryWithARM Slogan.txt
Code Compile Compute
```

Concise try-with-resources Statement

The header of the try-with-resources statement can be made less verbose by factoring out the resource declarations from the header. This refactoring involves *declaring the resources preceding* the try statement and specifying instead the *resource variables* in the header. The resources must be `AutoCloseable` (to provide the `close()`

method) as before, but in addition must also be *either* final *or effectively* final to
ensure that the right resource is closed.

```
final ACResource1 acr1 = new ACResource1();      // (1)
ACResource2 acr2 = new ACResource2();            // (2) Effectively final at (3)
// ...
try (acr1; acr2) {                               // (3) Resource variables.
  // Use the resources.
} // Both resources closed on exit.
```

The variable names of the AutoCloseable resources declared at (1) and (2) are specified in the header of the try-with-resources statement at (3). Apart from the syn-
tactic difference, the semantics of the try-with-resources statement are not changed
in any way. The resources acr1 and acr2 are guaranteed to be closed no matter how
the execution of the try statement at (3) proceeds.

However, care must be taken if any resource declarations proceeding the try-with-
resources statement can throw exceptions. For example, if the declaration of acr2
at (2) above throws an exception, the execution will be interrupted and the
resource acr1 created at (1) will not be closed—leading to resource leakage. One
solution is to move the declaration of acr2 into the header of the try-with-resources
statement as shown below at (3). The list in the header can be a mix of resource
variables and resource declarations. This setup will ensure that both resources will
be closed regardless of how the execution in the try statement proceeds. The try-
with-resources statement can be augmented with the necessary catch blocks to
catch any exceptions thrown during its execution, as shown at (4).

```
final ACResource1 acr1 = new ACResource1();         // (1)
// ...
try (acr1; ACResource2 acr2 = new ACResource2()) {  // (3)
  // Use the resources.
} catch (Exception ex) {                            // (4)
  ex.printStackTrace();
} // Both resources closed on exit.
```

Implementing the AutoCloseable **Interface**

A declared resource must provide the close() method that will be called when the
resource is to be closed. This is guaranteed by the fact that the resource must implement the java.lang.AutoCloseable interface which specifies the close() method. The
compiler only allows resource declarations or resource variables in the try header
that are AutoCloseable. Many classes in the Java API implement the AutoCloseable
interface: byte input streams, byte output streams, readers and writers in the
java.io package (Chapter 20, p. 1231), and database connections, query statements, and data result sets in the java.sql package (Chapter 24, p. 1511).

The abstract void method close() in the java.lang.AutoCloseable interface is
declared to throw an Exception. Files and streams implement the java.io.Closeable
interface which extends the AutoCloseable interface, but the abstract method close()
in the Closeable interface is specified to throw an IOException, a subtype of Exception.

```
interface AutoCloseable {                          // java.lang package
  void close() throws Exception;
}

interface Closeable extends AutoCloseable {        // java.io package
  void close() throws IOException;                 // Mandatory idempotent
}
```

What is important is that any class implementing the AutoCloseable interface can override the throws clause of the abstract close() method. The implementation of the close() method can choose to throw any Exception, meaning either an Exception or subtypes of Exception, but also throw no exception at all if the method cannot fail.

An implementation of the close() method of the Closeable interface must be idempotent. There is no such requirement for implementations of the close() method of the AutoCloseable interface, but it is highly recommended that they are idempotent.

In Example 7.18, the class Gizmo implements the AutoCloseable interface. The class uses the field closed to keep track of whether the gizmo is closed or not. The close() method at (2) reports whether the gizmo is already closed; if not, it sets the closed flag to true and throws an unchecked IllegalArgumentException. The close() method is idempotent, as it will only report that the gizmo is already closed once it has been called. The class Gizmo also has the method compute() at (3), that throws an unchecked ArithmeticException.

The class GizmoTest uses the Gizmo class. It declares and initializes a Gizmo in a try-with-resources statement at (4), and calls its compute() method. The output shows that the unchecked ArithmeticException thrown by the compute() method is caught by the catch clause at (5), after the close() method has been called on the resource—any catch clauses and finally clause explicitly specified with an extended try-with-resources statement are executed *after* the declared resources have been closed.

Example 7.18 *Implementing the* AutoCloseable *Interface*

```
// File: Gizmo.java
public class Gizmo implements AutoCloseable {
  private boolean closed = false;                  // (1) Closed if true
  @Override
  public void close() {                            // (2) Idempotent
    System.out.println("Enter: close()");
    if (closed) {
      System.out.println("Already closed");
    } else {
      closed = true;
      System.out.println("Gizmo closed");
      System.out.println("Throwing IllegalArgumentException in close()");
      throw new IllegalArgumentException("thrown in close()"); // Suppressed
    }
    System.out.println("Exit: close()");      // Only executed if already closed.
  }
```

```java
        public void compute() {                              // (3)
            System.out.println("Enter: compute()");
            System.out.println("Throwing ArithmeticException in compute()");
            throw new ArithmeticException("thrown in compute()");
        }
    }
```

```java
// File: GizmoTest.java
public class GizmoTest {
    public static void main(String[] args) {
        try (var myGizmo = new Gizmo()) {                    // (4)
            myGizmo.compute();
        } catch (Exception ex) {                             // (5)
            System.out.println("Printing stack trace in catch clause of main():");
            ex.printStackTrace();
        } finally {
            System.out.println("Finally: Done in main()");
        }
    }
}
```

```java
// File: GizmoTest2.java
public class GizmoTest2 {
    public static void main(String[] args) {
        try (var myGizmo = new Gizmo()) {
            myGizmo.compute();
        } catch (Exception ex) {                             // (6)
            System.out.println("Exception caught in the catch clause of main():\n\t"
                    + ex);
            System.out.println("Printing suppressed exceptions "
                    + "in the catch clause of main():");
            Throwable[] supressedEx = ex.getSuppressed();    // (7)
            for (Throwable t : supressedEx) {
                System.out.println("\t" + t);
            }
        } finally {
            System.out.println("Finally: Done in main()");
        }
    }
}
```

Output from running GizmoTest:

```
Enter: compute()
Throwing ArithmeticException in compute()
Enter: close()
Gizmo closed
Throwing IllegalArgumentException in close()
Printing stack trace in catch clause of main():
java.lang.ArithmeticException: thrown in compute()
        at Gizmo.compute(Gizmo.java:21)
        at GizmoTest.main(GizmoTest.java:5)
        Suppressed: java.lang.IllegalArgumentException: thrown in close()
            at Gizmo.close(Gizmo.java:13)
```

```
              at GizmoTest.main(GizmoTest.java:6)
     Finally: Done in main()
```

Output from running GizmoTest2:

```
Enter: compute()
Throwing ArithmeticException in compute()
Enter: close()
Gizmo closed
Throwing IllegalArgumentException in close()
Exception caught in the catch clause of main():
        java.lang.ArithmeticException: thrown in compute()
Printing suppressed exceptions in the catch clause of main():
        java.lang.IllegalArgumentException: thrown in close()
Finally: Done in main()
```

Suppressed Exceptions

The program output from GizmoTest in Example 7.18 shows that the Arithmetic-Exception was thrown in the compute() method called in the try block at (4) *before* the IllegalArgumentException was thrown by the implicit call to the close() method. Since only one exception can be propagated, the IllegalArgumentException thrown last would mask the ArithmeticException and the IllegalArgumentException would be propagated. However, the stack trace shows that this is not the case.

Exceptions thrown from the body of a try-with-resources statement are given preferential treatment over exceptions thrown by the close() method when called implicitly to close a declared resource. Exceptions thrown in the try block pertain to the program logic and should not be masked, but at the same time any exceptions thrown in the close() method should not be ignored. A solution is provided through *suppressed exceptions*. The class Throwable provides the following methods to handle such exceptions:

void addSuppressed(Throwable exception)

Appends the specified exception to the exceptions that were suppressed in order to deliver this exception.

Throwable[] getSuppressed()

Returns an array containing all of the exceptions that were suppressed in order to deliver this exception.

An exception s that is associated with an exception e through the method call e.addSuppressed(s) is called a *suppressed exception*. The idea is that if exception s was thrown during the propagation of exception e, then exception s is suppressed and the propagation of exception e continues. When exception e is caught, it is possible to retrieve all its suppressed exceptions by the method call e.getSuppressed().

From the stack trace printed by GizmoTest in Example 7.18, we see that the Illegal-ArgumentException was thrown in the close() method and is implicitly associated with the ArithmeticException that was thrown earlier in the compute() method—that is, the IllegalArgumentException was suppressed and the ArithmeticException was propagated.

In the catch clause at (6) of GizmoTest2 in Example 7.18, the exception thrown and the suppressed exception are printed explicitly. The method call ex.getSuppressed() at (7) returns an array of Throwable containing the suppressed IllegalArgument-Exception. Of course, suppressing any exception from the close() method is only warranted if an exception is thrown in the body of the try-with-resources statement.

The compiler expands the try-with-resources statement into code (essentially a combination of basic try-catch-finally blocks with the necessary control flow) that ensures proper closing of the declared resources, and handling of suppressed exceptions.

7.8 Advantages of Exception Handling

Robustness refers to the ability of a software system to respond to errors during execution. A system should respond to unexpected situations at runtime in a responsible way. Applications that provide the user with frequent cryptic messages with error codes or that repeatedly give the user the silent treatment when something goes wrong can hardly be considered robust.

The exception handling mechanism in Java offers the following advantages that facilitate developing robust applications in Java:

- *Separation of exception handling code*

  The code for handling error situations can be separated from the code for the program logic by using the exception handling constructs provided by the language. Code that can result in error situations is confined in the try block, and their handling in the catch clause.

- *Transparent exception propagation*

  Propagation of a checked exception in the JVM stack cannot be ignored by an active method. The method must comply with the catch-or-declare requirement: Either catch and handle the exception, or propagate it by declaring it in the method's throws clause. Error situations causing exception propagation are thus always detected, and can be caught and remedied.

- *Exception categorization and specialization*

  The exception and error classes in the Java SE Platform API are organized in an inheritance hierarchy (Figure 7.3, p. 369). Classes higher in this hierarchy represent *categories* of exceptions and errors (Exception, RuntimeException, IOException, Error), whereas classes lower in this hierarchy represent more *specific* exceptions and errors (NullPointerException, FileNotFoundException, AssertionError). The try-catch construct allows flexibility in catching and handling exceptions.

A catch clause can specify an exception category for coarse-grained exception handling, as the exception category class will subsume its more specific exception subclasses, or it can specify a more specific exception class for fine-grained exception handling. Best practice dictates that fine-grained exception handling be used.

 Review Questions

7.10   Which of these methods in the class will compile?

```
import java.io.BufferedReader;
import java.io.FileNotFoundException;
import java.io.FileReader;
import java.io.IOException;

public class ARMy {

  public static void methodA(String filename) throws FileNotFoundException {// (1)
    var fis = new FileReader(filename);
    try (var br = new BufferedReader(fis)) { }
  }

  public static void methodB(String filename)throws IOException {        // (2)
    var fis = new FileReader(filename);
    try (var br = new BufferedReader(fis)) { }
  }

  public static void methodC(String filename)throws FileNotFoundException { // (3)
    var fis = new FileReader(filename);
    try (var br = new BufferedReader(fis)) { }
    catch (IOException ioe) { }
  }

  public static void methodD(String filename) throws FileNotFoundException {// (4)
    try (var fis = new FileReader(filename);
         var br = new BufferedReader(fis)) { }
  }

  public static void methodE(String filename) throws IOException {        // (5)
    try (FileReader fis = null; BufferedReader br = null) {
    }
  }

  public static void methodF(String filename) {                          // (6)
    try (FileReader fis = null; BufferedReader br = null) {
    }
  }

  public static void methodG(String filename)
                        throws IOException {                             // (7)
    try (FileReader fis = null; BufferedReader br = null) {
      fis = new FileReader(filename);
      br = new BufferedReader(fis);
    }
  }
}
```

Select the three correct answers.

(a) The method at (1).
(b) The method at (2).
(c) The method at (3).
(d) The method at (4).
(e) The method at (5).
(f) The method at (6).
(g) The method at (7).

7.11 What will the following program print when run?

```java
import java.io.EOFException;
import java.io.IOException;

public class TryTwisting {
  public static void main(String[] args) {
    try {
      justDoIt();
    } catch (Exception t1) {
      System.out.println(t1);
      for (Throwable t : t1.getSuppressed())
        System.out.println("Suppressed: " + t);
    }
  }

  public static void justDoIt() throws Exception {
    IOException t2 = null;
    try {
      t2 = new IOException();
      throw t2;
    } finally {
      try {
        throw new EOFException();
      } catch (Exception t3) {
        t2.addSuppressed(t3);
      }
    }
  }
}
```

Select the one correct answer.

(a) java.io.EOFException

(b) java.io.IOException

(c) java.io.Exception

(d) java.io.EOFException
    Suppressed: java.io.IOException

(e) java.io.EOFException
    Suppressed: java.io.Exception

(f) java.io.Exception
    Suppressed: java.io.IOException

(g) java.io.Exception
    Suppressed: java.io.EOFException
(h) java.io.IOException
    Suppressed: java.io.EOFException
(i) java.io.IOException
    Suppressed: java.io.Exception

7.12 What will make the following program compile and run without throwing an exception?

```java
public class Truck implements AutoCloseable {
  public void close() {
    throw new Exception("Cannot close.");
  }

  public void load() {
    System.out.println("Loading truck.");
  }

  public static void main(String[] args) {
    try (var t1 = new Truck()) {
      t1.load();
    }
  }
}
```

Select the one correct answer.

(a) The program will compile and run without reporting any exception.
(b) Add a throws Exception clause to the close() method.
(c) Add a throws Exception clause to the main() method.
(d) Add a throws Exception clause to both the close() and the main() methods.
(e) Add a catch (Exception e) {} clause to the try statement in the main() method.
(f) Add a throws Exception clause to the close() method and add a catch (Exception e) {} clause to the try statement in the main() method.
(g) None of the above

7.13 Which one of these methods will fail to compile?
Select the three correct answers.

(a) ```java
    void task1(int value) throws IOException {
      try {
        switch (value) {
          case 1: throw new EOFException();
          case 2: throw new FileNotFoundException();
        }
      } catch (EOFException | FileNotFoundException e) {
        e = new IOException();
        throw e;
      }
    }
    ```
    ```

```
(b)  void task2(int value) throws IOException {
       try {
         switch (value) {
           case 1: throw new EOFException();
           case 2: throw new FileNotFoundException();
         }
       } catch (EOFException e) {
         e = new IOException();
         throw e;
       } catch (FileNotFoundException e) {
         e = new IOException();
         throw e;
       }
     }

(c)  void task3() throws IOException {
       try {
         throw new FileNotFoundException();
       } catch (Exception e) {
         e = new IOException();
         throw e;
       }
     }

(d)  void task4() throws FileNotFoundException {
       try {
         throw new FileNotFoundException();
       } catch (Exception e) {
         throw e;
       }
     }

(e)  void task5() throws Exception {
       try {
         throw new FileNotFoundException();
       } catch (IOException e) {
         throw e;
       }
     }
```

7.14   What will be the output of the following program?

```
public class Resource implements AutoCloseable {
  public void action() { System.out.print("action "); }
  public void close() throws Exception { System.out.print("closure "); }
}
```
- -
```
public class Test {
  public static void main(String[] args) {
    try (Resource r  = new Resource()) {
      r.action();
    } catch (Exception ex) {
```

```
          System.out.print("error ");
        }
        System.out.print("the end ");
      }
    }
```

Select the one correct answer.

(a) action closure the end
(b) action the end
(c) action error the end
(d) action closure error the end

7.15   What will be the output of the following program?

```
import java.io.IOException;
public class Resource implements AutoCloseable {
  public void action() throws IOException {
    throw new IOException("action error ");
  }
  public void close() throws Exception {
    throw new Exception("closure error ");
  }
}
```

- -

```
import java.io.IOException;
public class Test {
  public static void main(String[] args) {
    try (Resource r  = new Resource()) {
      r.action();
    } catch (IOException ex) {
      System.out.print("IO ");
      System.out.print(ex.getMessage());
    } catch (Exception ex) {
      System.out.print("Other ");
      System.out.print(ex.getSuppressed()[0].getMessage());
    }
    System.out.print("the end ");
  }
}
```

Select the one correct answer.

(a) IO action error Other closure error the end
(b) IO action error the end
(c) Other closure error IO action error the end
(d) IO action error
(e) IO action error Other closure error

7.16   Which of the following statements is true?
        Select the one correct answer.

(a) Implicit and explicit finally blocks cannot coexist with the same try-with-resources statement.

(b) The implicit `finally` block is executed before any explicit `finally` block.

(c) Any explicit `finally` block is executed before the implicit `finally` block.

(d) The execution order of the implicit and any explicit `finally` blocks is undetermined.

Selected API Classes 8

 Chapter Topics

- An overview of the java.lang package

- Understanding the importance of the Object class and its API

- Handling primitive values as objects with the wrapper classes

- Converting between primitive values and wrapper classes that represent them, and their text representation

- Creating and manipulating immutable strings with the String class, including text blocks

- Creating and manipulating mutable strings with the StringBuilder class

- Comparing the String and StringBuilder classes

- Using common mathematical functions provided by the Math class

- Generating pseudorandom numbers using the Math and Random classes

- Using big numbers for arbitrary-precision arithmetic operations

Java SE 17 Developer Exam Objectives	
[1.1] Use primitives and wrapper classes including Math API, parentheses, type promotion, and casting to evaluate arithmetic and boolean expressions ○ *Only wrapper classes and the Math API are covered in this chapter.* ○ *For primitive data types, operators, conversions, and evaluation of expressions, see Chapter 2, p. 29.*	§8.3, p. 429 §8.6, p. 478
[1.2] Manipulate text, including text blocks, using String and StringBuilder classes	§8.4, p. 439 §8.5, p. 464

Java SE 11 Developer Exam Objectives	

[1.1] Use primitives and wrapper classes, including, operators, the use of parentheses, type promotion and casting
    o *Only wrapper classes are covered in this chapter.*
    o *For primitive data types, operators, and conversions, see Chapter 2, p. 29.*
	§8.3, p. 429

[1.2] Handle text using String and StringBuilder classes	§8.4, p. 439 §8.5, p. 464

The Object class, being the superclass of all classes, defines general functionality for all classes. The wrapper classes provide the support to treat primitive values as objects. The classes String and StringBuilder provide the support to create and manipulate strings. In addition, the Math, Random, and BigDecimal classes are introduced to leverage mathematical functions, pseudorandom number generators, and arbitrary-precision arithmetic operations, respectively. The APIs of these classes are the main subject of this chapter.

8.1 Overview of the java.lang Package

The java.lang package is indispensable when programming in Java. It is automatically imported into every source file at compile time. The package contains the Object class that is the superclass of all classes, and the wrapper classes (Boolean, Character, Byte, Short, Integer, Long, Float, Double) that are used to handle primitive values as objects. It provides classes essential for interacting with the JVM (Runtime), for security (SecurityManager), for loading classes (ClassLoader), for dealing with threads (Thread), and for handling exceptions (Throwable, Error, Exception, Runtime-Exception). The java.lang package also contains classes that provide the standard input, output, and error streams (System), string handling (String, StringBuilder), and mathematical functions (Math).

Figure 8.1 shows the important classes whose API is discussed in subsequent sections.

Figure 8.1 *Partial Inheritance Hierarchy in the* java.lang *Package*

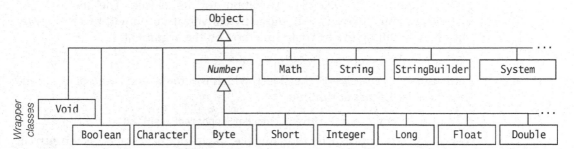

8.2 The Object Class

All classes extend the Object class, either directly or indirectly. A class declaration, without the extends clause, implicitly extends the Object class (§5.1, p. 191). Thus the Object class is always at the root of any inheritance hierarchy. The Object class defines the basic functionality that all objects exhibit and all classes inherit. This relationship also applies to arrays, since these are genuine objects in Java.

The Object class defines common functionality for all objects through the following methods (see Example 8.1 for usage of these methods):

`public boolean equals(Object obj)`

The general contract of the `equals()` method is discussed in connection with object comparison (§14.2, p. 744). Object reference and value equality are discussed together with the `==` and `!=` operators (§2.13, p. 75). The `equals()` method in the Object class returns true only if the two references compared denote the same object—that is, they are aliases. The `equals()` method is normally overridden to provide the semantics of object value equality, as is the case for the wrapper classes (p. 432) and the String class (p. 439).

`public int hashCode()`

Returns an int value as the *hash value* of the object. The general contract of the `hashCode()` method is discussed in connection with object comparison (§14.3, p. 753). In *hash tables*, the hash value can be used to store and retrieve objects efficiently (§15.8, p. 830). The `hashCode()` method is normally overridden by a class, as is the case for the wrapper classes (p. 432) and the String class (p. 439).

`public String toString()`

The general contract of the method is to return a text representation of the object. If a subclass does not override this method, it returns a text representation of the object, which has the following format:

   `"<class_name>@<hash_code>"`

Since the hash value of an object is an int value, this value is printed as a hexadecimal number (e.g., 3e25a5). This method is usually overridden by a class to provide appropriate text representation for its object. The method call `System.out.println(objRef)` will implicitly convert its argument to a text representation by calling the `toString()` method on the argument.

`public final Class<?> getClass()`

Returns the *runtime class* of the object, which is represented by an object of the class `java.lang.Class` at runtime.

`protected Object clone() throws CloneNotSupportedException`

New objects that are exactly the same (i.e., have identical states) as the current object can be created by using the `clone()` method; that is, primitive values and reference values are copied. This is called *shallow copying*. A class can override this method to provide its own notion of cloning. For example, cloning a composite object by recursively cloning the constituent objects is called *deep copying*.

When overridden, the method in the subclass is usually declared as public to allow any client to clone objects of the class. Not declaring the overriding method as public or protected violates the contract for overriding, as it narrows the accessibility of the method, and will be flagged as a compile-time error.

If the overriding clone() method in the subclass relies on the clone() method in the Object class (i.e., a shallow copy), the subclass must implement the Cloneable marker interface to indicate that its objects can be safely cloned. Otherwise, the clone() method in the Object class will throw a checked CloneNotSupported-Exception.

@Deprecated(since="9") protected void finalize() throws Throwable

This method is called on an object just before it is garbage collected so that any clean-up can be done. However, the finalize() method in the Object class has been deprecated since Java 9—it should no longer be used and it may be removed in the future. The method is deemed problematic, and better solutions exist for implementing the same functionality.

In addition, the following final methods in the Object class provide support for thread communication in synchronized code (§22.4, p. 1400).

```
public final void wait(long timeout) throws InterruptedException
public final void wait(long timeout, int nanos) throws InterruptedException
public final void wait() throws InterruptedException
public final void notify()
public final void notifyAll()
```

A thread invokes these methods on the object whose lock it holds. A thread waits for notification by another thread.

Example 8.1 *Methods in the* Object *Class*

```
// File: ObjectMethods.java
class MyClass implements Cloneable {
  @Override
  public MyClass clone() {
    MyClass obj = null;
    try { obj = (MyClass) super.clone(); }  // Calls overridden method.
    catch (CloneNotSupportedException e) { System.out.println(e);}
    return obj;
  }
}
//_____
public class ObjectMethods {
  public static void main(String[] args) {
    // Two objects of MyClass.
    MyClass obj1 = new MyClass();
    MyClass obj2 = new MyClass();

    // Two strings.
    String str1 = new String("WhoAmI");
    String str2 = new String("WhoAmI");

    System.out.println("str1: " + str1.toString());
    System.out.println("str2: " + str2.toString() + "\n");
```

```
      // Method hashCode() overridden in String class.
      // Strings that are equal have the same hash code.
      System.out.println("hash code for str1: " + str1.hashCode());
      System.out.println("hash code for str2: " + str2.hashCode() + "\n");

      // Hash codes are different for different MyClass objects.
      System.out.println("hash code for MyClass obj1: " + obj1.hashCode());
      System.out.println("hash code for MyClass obj2: " + obj2.hashCode()+"\n");

      // Method equals() overridden in the String class.
      System.out.println("str1.equals(str2): " + str1.equals(str2));
      System.out.println("str1 == str2:      " + (str1 == str2) + "\n");

      // Method equals() from the Object class called.
      System.out.println("obj1.equals(obj2): " + obj1.equals(obj2));
      System.out.println("obj1 == obj2:      " + (obj1 == obj2) + "\n");

      // The runtime object that represents the class of an object.
      Class<? extends String> rtStringClass  = str1.getClass();
      Class<? extends MyClass> rtMyClassClass = obj1.getClass();
      // The name of the class represented by the runtime object.
      System.out.println("Class for str1: " + rtStringClass);
      System.out.println("Class for obj1: " + rtMyClassClass + "\n");

      // The toString() method is overridden in the String class.
      String textRepStr = str1.toString();
      String textRepObj = obj1.toString();
      System.out.println("Text representation of str1: " + textRepStr);
      System.out.println("Text representation of obj1: " + textRepObj + "\n");

      // Shallow copying of arrays.
      MyClass[] array1 = {new MyClass(), new MyClass(), new MyClass()};
      MyClass[] array2 = array1.clone();
      // Array objects are different, but share the element objects.
      System.out.println("array1 == array2:          " + (array1 == array2));
      for(int i = 0; i < array1.length; i++) {
        System.out.println("array1[" + i + "] == array2[" + i + "] : " +
                           (array1[i] == array2[i]));
      }
      System.out.println();

      // Clone an object of MyClass.
      MyClass obj3 = obj1.clone();
      System.out.println("hash code for cloned MyClass obj3: " + obj3.hashCode());
      System.out.println("obj1 == obj3: " + (obj1 == obj3));
    }
}
```

Probable output from the program:

```
str1: WhoAmI
str2: WhoAmI

hash code for str1: -1704812257
hash code for str2: -1704812257
```

```
hash code for MyClass obj1: 2036368507
hash code for MyClass obj2: 1785210046

str1.equals(str2): true
str1 == str2:      false

obj1.equals(obj2): false
obj1 == obj2:      false

Class for str1: class java.lang.String
Class for obj1: class MyClass

Text representation of str1: WhoAmI
Text representation of obj1: MyClass@7960847b

array1 == array2:        false
array1[0] == array2[0] : true
array1[1] == array2[1] : true
array1[2] == array2[2] : true

hash code for cloned MyClass obj3: 1552787810
obj1 == obj3: false
```

8.3 The Wrapper Classes

Wrapper classes were introduced with the discussion of the primitive data types (Table 2.16, p. 43), and also in connection with boxing and unboxing of primitive values (§2.3, p. 45). Primitive values in Java are not objects. To manipulate these values as objects, the java.lang package provides a *wrapper* class for each of the primitive data types (shown in the bottom left of Figure 8.2). The name of the wrapper class is the name of the primitive data type with an uppercase letter, except for int (Integer) and char (Character). All wrapper classes are final, meaning that they cannot be extended. The objects of all wrapper classes that can be instantiated are *immutable*; in other words, the value in the wrapper object cannot be changed.

Although the Void class is considered a wrapper class, it does not wrap any primitive value and is not instantiable (i.e., has no public constructors). It just denotes the Class object representing the keyword void. The Void class will not be discussed further in this section.

In addition to the methods defined for constructing and manipulating objects of primitive values, the wrapper classes define useful constants, fields, and conversion methods.

A very important thing to note about the wrapper classes is that their constructors are now *deprecated*. So these constructors should not be used to create wrapper objects, as these constructors will be removed from the API in the future. As we shall see later in this section, the APIs include methods for this purpose that provide significantly improved space and time performance.

Figure 8.2   *Converting Values among Primitive, Wrapper, and* String *Types*

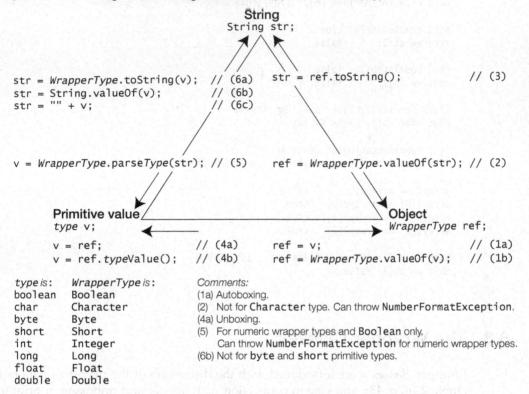

type is:	*WrapperType is:*	*Comments:*
boolean	Boolean	(1a) Autoboxing.
char	Character	(2) Not for Character type. Can throw NumberFormatException.
byte	Byte	(4a) Unboxing.
short	Short	(5) For numeric wrapper types and Boolean only.
int	Integer	Can throw NumberFormatException for numeric wrapper types.
long	Long	(6b) Not for byte and short primitive types.
float	Float	
double	Double	

Common Wrapper Class Utility Methods

Converting Primitive Values to Wrapper Objects

Autoboxing is a convenient way to wrap a primitive value in an object ((1a) in Figure 8.2 and §2.3, p. 45).

```
Character charObj1  = '\n';
Boolean   boolObj1  = true;
Integer   intObj1   = 2020;
Double    doubleObj1 = 3.14;
```

We can also use the following valueOf(*type* v) method that takes the primitive value of *type* to convert as an argument ((1b) in Figure 8.2).

```
static WrapperType valueOf(type v)
```

```
Character charObj1  = Character.valueOf('\n');
Boolean   boolObj1  = Boolean.valueOf(true);
Integer   intObj1   = Integer.valueOf(2020);
Double    doubleObj1 = Double.valueOf(3.14);
```

Converting Strings to Wrapper Objects

Each wrapper class (except `Character`) defines the static method `valueOf(String str)` that returns the wrapper object corresponding to the primitive value represented by the `String` object passed as an argument ((2) in Figure 8.2). This method for the numeric wrapper types also throws a `NumberFormatException` if the `String` parameter is not a valid number.

```
static WrapperType valueOf(String str)

Boolean boolObj4  = Boolean.valueOf("false");
Integer intObj3   = Integer.valueOf("1949");
Double  doubleObj2 = Double.valueOf("3.14");
Double  doubleObj3 = Double.valueOf("Infinity");
```

In addition to the one-argument `valueOf()` method, the integer wrapper classes define an overloaded `static valueOf()` method that can take a second argument. This argument specifies the base (or *radix*) in which to interpret the string representing the signed integer in the first argument. Note that the string argument does not specify the prefix for the number system notation.

```
static IntegerWrapperType valueOf(String str, int base)
                          throws NumberFormatException

Byte    byteObj1  = Byte.valueOf("1010", 2);      // Decimal value 10
Short   shortObj2 = Short.valueOf("12", 8);       // Decimal value 10
Short   shortObj3 = Short.valueOf("012", 8);      // Decimal value 10
Short   shortObj4 = Short.valueOf("\012", 8);     // NumberFormatException
Integer intObj4   = Integer.valueOf("-a", 16);    // Decimal value -10
Integer intObj6   = Integer.valueOf("-0xa", 16);  // NumberFormatException
Long    longObj2  = Long.valueOf("-a", 16);       // Decimal value -10L
```

Converting Wrapper Objects to Strings

Each wrapper class overrides the `toString()` method from the `Object` class. The overriding method returns a `String` object containing the text representation of the primitive value in the wrapper object ((3) in Figure 8.2).

```
String toString()

String charStr   = charObj1.toString();    // "\n"
String boolStr   = boolObj2.toString();    // "true"
String intStr    = intObj1.toString();     // "2020"
String doubleStr = doubleObj1.toString();  // "3.14"
```

Converting Primitive Values to Strings

Each wrapper class defines a `static` method `toString(type v)` that returns the string corresponding to the primitive value of *type*, which is passed as an argument ((6a) in Figure 8.2).

```
static String toString(type v)
```

```
String charStr2   = Character.toString('\n');  // "\n"
String boolStr2   = Boolean.toString(true);    // "true"
String intStr2    = Integer.toString(2020);    // "2020"
String doubleStr2 = Double.toString(3.14);     // "3.14"
```

For integer primitive types, the base is assumed to be 10. For floating-point numbers, the text representation (decimal form or scientific notation) depends on the sign and the magnitude (absolute value) of the number. The NaN value, positive infinity, and negative infinity will result in the strings "NaN", "Infinity", and "-Infinity", respectively.

In addition, the wrapper classes Integer and Long define methods for converting integers to text representations in decimal, binary, octal, and hexadecimal notation (p. 435).

Converting Wrapper Objects to Primitive Values

Unboxing is a convenient way to unwrap the primitive value in a wrapper object ((4a) in Figure 8.2 and §2.3, p. 45).

```
char    c = charObj1;        // '\n'
boolean b = boolObj2;        // true
int     i = intObj1;         // 2020
double  d = doubleObj1;      // 3.14
```

Each wrapper class defines a *type*Value() method that returns the primitive value in the wrapper object ((4b) in Figure 8.2).

```
type typeValue()
```

```
char    c = charObj1.charValue();        // '\n'
boolean b = boolObj2.booleanValue();     // true
int     i = intObj1.intValue();          // 2020
double  d = doubleObj1.doubleValue();    // 3.14
```

In addition, each numeric wrapper class defines *type*Value() methods for converting the wrapper object to a value of any numeric primitive data type. These methods are discussed later.

Wrapper Comparison, Equality, and Hash Code

Each wrapper class implements the Comparable<*Type*> interface, which defines the following method:

```
int compareTo(Type obj2)
```

This method returns a value that is less than, equal to, or greater than zero, depending on whether the primitive value in the current wrapper *Type* object is less than, equal to, or greater than the primitive value in the wrapper *Type* object denoted by argument obj2, respectively.

```
// Comparisons based on objects created earlier
Character charObj2    = 'a';
int result1 = charObj1.compareTo(charObj2);      // result1 < 0
int result2 = intObj1.compareTo(intObj3);        // result2 > 0
int result3 = doubleObj1.compareTo(doubleObj2);  // result3 == 0
int result4 = doubleObj1.compareTo(intObj1);     // Compile-time error!
```

Each wrapper class overrides the equals() method from the Object class. The overriding method compares two wrapper objects for object value equality.

```
boolean equals(Object obj2)
```

```
// Comparisons based on objects created earlier
boolean charTest   = charObj1.equals(charObj2);      // false
boolean boolTest   = boolObj2.equals(Boolean.FALSE); // false
boolean intTest    = intObj1.equals(intObj3);        // true
boolean doubleTest = doubleObj1.equals(doubleObj2);  // true
boolean test       = intObj1.equals(Long.valueOf(2020L)); // false. Not same type.
```

The following values are *interned* when they are wrapped during boxing. That is, only *one* wrapper object exists in the program for these primitive values when boxing is applied:

- The boolean value true or false
- A byte
- A char with a Unicode value in the interval [\u0000, \u007f] (i.e., decimal interval [0, 127])
- An int or short value in the interval [-128, 127]

If references w1 and w2 refer to two wrapper objects that box the *same* value, which fulfills any of the conditions mentioned above, then w1 == w2 is always true. In other words, for the values listed previously, object equality and reference equality give the same result.

```
// Reference and object equality
Byte bRef1 = 10;
Byte bRef2 = 10;
System.out.println(bRef1 == bRef2);              // true
System.out.println(bRef1.equals(bRef2));         // true

Integer iRef1 = 1000;
Integer iRef2 = 1000;
System.out.println(iRef1 == iRef2);              // false, values not in [-128, 127]
System.out.println(iRef1.equals(iRef2));         // true
```

Each wrapper class also overrides the hashCode() method in the Object class. The overriding method returns a hash value based on the primitive value in the wrapper object.

```
int hashCode()
```

```
int index = charObj1.hashCode();                 // 10 ('\n')
```

Numeric Wrapper Classes

The numeric wrapper classes Byte, Short, Integer, Long, Float, and Double are all subclasses of the abstract class Number (Figure 8.1, p. 425).

Each numeric wrapper class defines an assortment of constants, including the minimum and maximum values of the corresponding primitive data type:

```
NumericWrapperType.MIN_VALUE
NumericWrapperType.MAX_VALUE
```

The following code retrieves the minimum and maximum values of various numeric types:

```
byte   minByte    = Byte.MIN_VALUE;      // -128
int    maxInt     = Integer.MAX_VALUE;   // 2147483647
double maxDouble  = Double.MAX_VALUE;    // 1.7976931348623157e+308
```

Converting Numeric Wrapper Objects to Numeric Primitive Types

Each numeric wrapper class defines the following set of *type*Value() methods for converting the primitive value in the wrapper object to a value of any numeric primitive type:

```
byte   byteValue()
short  shortValue()
int    intValue()
long   longValue()
float  floatValue()
double doubleValue()
```

See also (4b) in Figure 8.2.

The following code shows conversion of values in numeric wrapper objects to any numeric primitive type:

```
Byte    byteObj2   = (byte)16;           // Cast mandatory
Integer intObj5    = 42030;
Double  doubleObj4 = Math.PI;

short  shortVal  = intObj5.shortValue();     // (1)
long   longVal   = byteObj2.longValue();
int    intVal    = doubleObj4.intValue();    // (2) Truncation
double doubleVal = intObj5.doubleValue();
```

Notice the potential for loss of information at (1) and (2), when the primitive value in a wrapper object is converted to a narrower primitive data type.

Converting Strings to Numeric Values

Each numeric wrapper class defines a static method parse*Type*(String str), which returns the primitive numeric value represented by the String object passed as an argument. The *Type* in the method name parse*Type* stands for the name of a numeric wrapper class, except for the name of the Integer class, which is abbreviated to Int.

These methods throw a NumberFormatException if the String parameter is not a valid argument ((5) in Figure 8.2).

```
static type parseType(String str) throws NumberFormatException
```

```
byte   value1 = Byte.parseByte("16");
int    value2 = Integer.parseInt("2020");      // parseInt, not parseInteger
int    value3 = Integer.parseInt("7UP");       // NumberFormatException.
double value4 = Double.parseDouble("3.14");
double value5 = Double.parseDouble("Infinity");
```

For the integer wrapper types, the overloaded static method parse*Type*() can additionally take a second argument, which can specify the base in which to interpret the string representing the signed integer in the first argument. Note that the string argument does not specify the prefix for the number system notation.

```
type parseType(String str, int base) throws NumberFormatException
```

```
byte  value6  = Byte.parseByte("1010", 2);     // Decimal value 10
short value7  = Short.parseShort("12", 8);     // Decimal value 10
short value8  = Short.parseShort("012", 8);    // Decimal value 10
short value9  = Short.parseShort("\012", 8);   // NumberFormatException
int   value10 = Integer.parseInt("-a", 16);    // Decimal value -10
int   value11 = Integer.parseInt("-0xa", 16);  // NumberFormatException
long  value12 = Long.parseLong("-a", 16);      // Decimal value -10L
```

Converting Integer Values to Strings in Different Notations

The wrapper classes Integer and Long provide static methods for converting integers to text representations in decimal, binary, octal, and hexadecimal notation. Some of these methods from the Integer class are listed here, but analogous methods are also defined in the Long class. Example 8.2 demonstrates the use of these methods.

```
static String toBinaryString(int i)
static String toHexString(int i)
static String toOctalString(int i)
```

These three methods return a text representation of the integer argument as an *unsigned* integer in base 2, 16, and 8, respectively, with no extra leading zeroes.

```
static String toString(int i, int base)
static String toString(int i)
```

The first method returns the minus sign (-) as the first character if the integer i is negative. In all cases, it returns the text representation of the *magnitude* of the integer i in the specified base.

The second method is equivalent to the method toString(int i, int base), where the base has the value 10, and which returns the text representation as a signed decimal ((6a) in Figure 8.2).

Example 8.2 *Text Representation of Integers*

```
public class IntegerRepresentation {
  public static void main(String[] args) {
    int positiveInt = +41;     // 0b101001, 051, 0x29
    int negativeInt = -41;     // 0b11111111111111111111111111010111, -0b101001,
                               // 037777777727, -051, 0xffffffd7, -0x29
    System.out.println("Text representation for decimal value: " + positiveInt);
    integerStringRepresentation(positiveInt);
    System.out.println("Text representation for decimal value: " + negativeInt);
    integerStringRepresentation(negativeInt);
  }

  public static void integerStringRepresentation(int i) {
    System.out.println("    Binary:     " + Integer.toBinaryString(i));
    System.out.println("    Octal:      " + Integer.toOctalString(i));
    System.out.println("    Hex:        " + Integer.toHexString(i));
    System.out.println("    Decimal:    " + Integer.toString(i));

    System.out.println("    Using toString(int i, int base) method:");
    System.out.println("    Base 2:     " + Integer.toString(i, 2));
    System.out.println("    Base 8:     " + Integer.toString(i, 8));
    System.out.println("    Base 16:    " + Integer.toString(i, 16));
    System.out.println("    Base 10:    " + Integer.toString(i, 10));
  }
}
```

Output from the program:

```
Text representation for decimal value: 41
    Binary:    101001
    Octal:     51
    Hex:       29
    Decimal:   41
    Using toString(int i, int base) method:
    Base 2:    101001
    Base 8:    51
    Base 16:   29
    Base 10:   41
Text representation for decimal value: -41
    Binary:    11111111111111111111111111010111
    Octal:     37777777727
    Hex:       ffffffd7
    Decimal:   -41
    Using toString(int i, int base) method:
    Base 2:    -101001
    Base 8:    -51
    Base 16:   -29
    Base 10:   -41
```

The Character **Class**

The Character class defines a myriad of constants, including the following, which represent the minimum and the maximum values of the char type (§2.2, p. 42):

```
Character.MIN_VALUE
Character.MAX_VALUE
```

The Character class also defines a plethora of static methods for handling various attributes of a character, and case issues relating to characters, as defined by the Unicode standard:

```
static int     getNumericValue(char ch)
static boolean isLowerCase(char ch)
static boolean isUpperCase(char ch)
static boolean isTitleCase(char ch)
static boolean isDigit(char ch)
static boolean isLetter(char ch)
static boolean isLetterOrDigit(char ch)
static char    toUpperCase(char ch)
static char    toLowerCase(char ch)
static char    toTitleCase(char ch)
```

The following code converts a lowercase character to an uppercase character:

```
char ch = 'a';
if (Character.isLowerCase(ch)) ch = Character.toUpperCase(ch); // A
```

The Boolean **Class**

In addition to the common utility methods for wrapper classes discussed earlier in this section, the Boolean class defines the following wrapper objects to represent the primitive values true and false, respectively:

```
Boolean.TRUE
Boolean.FALSE
```

Converting Strings to Boolean Values

The wrapper class Boolean defines the following static method, which returns the boolean value true only if the String argument is equal to the string "true", ignoring the case; otherwise, it returns the boolean value false. Note that this method does not throw any exceptions, as its numeric counterparts do.

```
static boolean parseBoolean(String str)
```

```
boolean b1 = Boolean.parseBoolean("TRUE");      // true.
boolean b2 = Boolean.parseBoolean("true");      // true.
boolean b3 = Boolean.parseBoolean("false");     // false.
boolean b4 = Boolean.parseBoolean("FALSE");     // false.
boolean b5 = Boolean.parseBoolean("not true");  // false.
boolean b6 = Boolean.parseBoolean("null");      // false.
boolean b7 = Boolean.parseBoolean(null);        // false.
```

Review Questions

8.1   Which of the following statements is true?
Select the one correct answer.

(a) If the references x and y denote two different objects, the expression
x.equals(y) is always false.

(b) If the references x and y denote two different objects, the expression
(x.hashCode() == y.hashCode()) is always false.

(c) The hashCode() method in the Object class is declared as final.

(d) The equals() method in the Object class is declared as final.

(e) All arrays have a method named clone.

8.2   What will be the result of compiling and running the following program?

```
public class RQ200A70 {
  public static void main(String[] args) {
    Integer i = Integer.valueOf(-10);
    Integer j = Integer.valueOf(-10);
    Integer k = -10;
    System.out.print((i==j) + "|");
    System.out.print(i.equals(j) + "|");
    System.out.print((i==k) + "|");
    System.out.print(i.equals(k));
  }
}
```

Select the one correct answer.

(a) false|true|false|true

(b) true|true|true|true

(c) false|true|true|true

(d) true|true|false|true

(e) None of the above

8.3   Which statement is true about primitives and wrapper classes?
Select the one correct answer.

(a) Java automatically converts primitives to wrapper objects with no performance penalty.

(b) Java automatically converts wrapper objects to primitives with no performance penalty.

(c) Wrapper references can be assigned the null value.

(d) A variable of a primitive type can be assigned the null value.

(e) Auto-unboxing of an uninitialized numeric wrapper reference results in a primitive value of zero.

8.4 Given the following code:

```
public class Test {
    public static void main(String[] args) {
        Integer i1 = 10;
        Integer i2 = 10;
        int i3 = 10;
        Integer x1 = i1*i2*i3;
        Integer x2 = i1*i2*i3;
        int x3 = i1*i2*i3;
        String result = (i1 == i2) ? "A" : "";
        result += (i1 == i3) ? "B" : "";
        result += (x1 == x2) ? "C" : "";
        result += (x1 == x3) ? "D" : "";
        System.out.print(result);
    }
}
```

What is the result?
Select the one correct answer.

(a) ABCD

(b) ABD

(c) AC

(d) BD

(e) The program will fail to compile.

8.4 The String Class

Handling character sequences is supported primarily by the String and String-Builder classes. This section discusses the String class that provides support for creating, initializing, and manipulating immutable character strings. The next section discusses support for mutable strings provided by the StringBuilder class (p. 464).

Internal Representation of Strings

The following character encoding schemes are commonly used for encoding character data on computers:

- LATIN-1: Also known as ISO 8859-1. LATIN-1 is a fixed-length encoding that uses 1 byte to represent a character in the range 00 to FF—that is, characters that can be represented by 8 bits. This encoding suffices for most Western European languages.

- UTF-16: This encoding scheme is a variable-length scheme that uses either 2 bytes or 4 bytes to represent a character in the range 0000 to 10FFFF. This encoding suffices for most languages in the world. However, the char type in Java only represents values in the UTF-16 range 0000 to FFFF—that is, characters that can be represented by 2 bytes.

Internally, the character sequence in a String object is stored as *an array of* byte. If *all* characters in the string can be stored as a *single* byte per character, they are all encoded in the array with the LATIN-1 encoding scheme—1 byte per character. If any character in the sequence requires more than 1 byte, they are all encoded in the array with the UTF-16 encoding scheme—2 bytes per character. To keep track of which encoding is used for the characters in the internal byte array, the String class has a private final encoding-flag field named coder which the string methods can consult to correctly interpret the bytes in the internal array. What encoding to use is detected when the string is created. With this strategy of *compact strings*, storage is not wasted as would be the case if all strings were to be encoded in the UTF-16 encoding scheme.

Creating and Initializing Strings

Immutability

The String class implements *immutable* character strings, which are read-only once the string has been created and initialized. Objects of the String class are thus *thread-safe*, as the state of a String object cannot be corrupted through concurrent access by multiple threads. Operations on a String object that modify the characters return a new String object. The StringBuilder class implements mutable strings (p. 464).

String Internment

The easiest way to create a String object is to use a string literal:

```
String str1 = "You cannot change me!";
```

A string literal is a *reference* to a String object. The value in the String object is the character sequence that is enclosed in the double quotes of the string literal. Since a string literal is a reference, it can be manipulated like any other String reference. The reference value of a string literal can be assigned to another String reference: The reference str1 will denote the String object with the value "You cannot change me!" after the preceding assignment. A string literal can be used to invoke methods on its String object:

```
int strLength = "You cannot change me!".length(); // 21
```

The compiler optimizes handling of string literals (and compile-time constant expressions that evaluate to strings): Only one String object is shared by all string-valued constant expressions with the same character sequence. Such strings are said to be *interned*, meaning that they share a unique String object if they have the same character sequence. The String class maintains a private *string pool* where such strings are interned.

```
String str2 = "You cannot change me!";      // Interned string assigned.
```

Both String references str1 and str2 denote the same interned String object initialized with the character string: "You cannot change me!". So does the reference str3 in the following code. The compile-time evaluation of the constant expression involving the two string literals results in a string that is already interned:

```
String str3 = "You cannot" + " change me!"; // Compile-time constant expression
```

In the following code, both the references can1 and can2 denote the same interned String object, which contains the string "7Up":

```
String can1 = 7 + "Up";       // Value of compile-time constant expression: "7Up"
String can2 = "7Up";          // "7Up"
boolean r = can1 == can2;     // true
```

However, in the following code, the reference can4 denotes a *new* String object that will have the value "7Up" at runtime:

```
String word = "Up";
String can4 = 7 + word;  // Not a compile-time constant expression.
```

The sharing of String objects between string-valued constant expressions poses no problem, since the String objects are immutable. Any operation performed on one String reference will never have any effect on the usage of other references denoting the same object. The String class is also declared as final so that no subclass can override this behavior. Internally using both compact strings and string internment optimizes memory allocation and performance for strings, which is fully transparent for programmers.

String Constructors

The String class has numerous constructors to create and initialize String objects based on various types of arguments. Here we present a few selected constructors:

String()

Creates a new String object, whose content is the *empty string*, "".

String(String str)

Creates a new String object, whose contents are the same as those of the String object passed as the argument.

String(char[] value)
String(char[] value, int offset, int count)

Create a new String object, whose contents are copied from a char array. The second constructor allows extraction of a certain number of characters (count) from a given offset in the specified array.

String(StringBuilder builder)

This constructor allows interoperability with the StringBuilder class.

Note that using a constructor creates a brand-new String object; using a constructor does *not* intern the string. In the following code, the String object denoted by
str4 is different from the interned String object passed as an argument:

```
String str4 = new String("You cannot change me!");
```

Constructing String objects can also be done from arrays of bytes, arrays of characters, and string builders:

```
byte[] bytes = {97, 98, 98, 97};
char[] characters = {'a', 'b', 'b', 'a'};
StringBuilder strBuilder = new StringBuilder("abba");
//...
String byteStr  = new String(bytes);       // Using array of bytes: "abba"
String charStr  = new String(characters);  // Using array of chars: "abba"
String buildStr = new String(strBuilder);  // Using string builder: "abba"
```

In Example 8.3, note that the reference str1 does not denote the same String object
as the references str4 and str5. Using the new operator with a String constructor
always creates a new String object. The expression "You cannot" + words is not a constant expression, and therefore, results in the creation of a new String object. The
local references str2 and str3 in the main() method and the static reference str1 in
the Auxiliary class all denote the same interned string. Object value equality is
hardly surprising between these references.

The String method intern() allows the contents of a String object to be interned. If
a string with the same contents is not already in the string pool, it is added; otherwise, the already interned string is returned. The following relationship holds
between any two strings strX and strY:

strX.intern() == strY.intern() *is true* *if and only if* strX.equals(strY) *is* true.

In Example 8.3, as the local references str2 and str3 in the main() method and the
static reference str1 in the Auxiliary class all denote the same interned string, the
call to the intern() method on any of these String objects will return the same
canonical string from the pool. The method call str4.intern() will find that a string
with its contents ("You cannot change me") already exists in the string pool, and will
also return this string from the pool. Thus the object reference comparison
str1.intern() == str4.intern() will return true, but str4 == str4.intern() is still false,
as the String object denoted by str4 is not interned and therefore does not denote
the same String object as the one that is interned.

String intern()

> If the string pool already contains a string that is equal to this String object
> (determined by the equals(Object) method), then the string from the pool is
> returned. Otherwise, this String object is added to the pool and a reference to
> this String object is returned.

Example 8.3   *String Construction and Internment*

```java
// File: StringConstruction.java
class Auxiliary {
  static String str1 = "You cannot change me!";          // Interned
}
//_____
public class StringConstruction {

  static String str1 = "You cannot change me!";          // Interned

  public static void main(String[] args) {
    String emptyStr = new String();                      // ""
    System.out.println("emptyStr: \"" + emptyStr + "\"");

    String str2 = "You cannot change me!";               // Interned
    String str3 = "You cannot" + " change me!";          // Interned
    String str4 = new String("You cannot change me!");   // New String object

    String words = " change me!";
    String str5 = "You cannot" + words;                  // New String object

    System.out.println("str1 == str2:      " + (str1 == str2));       // (1) true
    System.out.println("str1.equals(str2): " + str1.equals(str2));    // (2) true

    System.out.println("str1 == str3:      " + (str1 == str3));       // (3) true
    System.out.println("str1.equals(str3): " + str1.equals(str3));    // (4) true

    System.out.println("str1 == str4:      " + (str1 == str4));       // (5) false
    System.out.println("str1.equals(str4): " + str1.equals(str4));    // (6) true

    System.out.println("str1 == str5:      " + (str1 == str5));       // (7) false
    System.out.println("str1.equals(str5): " + str1.equals(str5));    // (8) true

    System.out.println("str1 == Auxiliary.str1:      " +
                       (str1 == Auxiliary.str1));        // (9) true
    System.out.println("str1.equals(Auxiliary.str1): " +
                         str1.equals(Auxiliary.str1));   // (10) true

    System.out.println("\"You cannot change me!\".length(): " +
                       "You cannot change me!".length());// (11) 21

    System.out.println("str1.intern() == str4.intern(): " +
                       (str1.intern() == str4.intern()));// (12) true
    System.out.println("str4 == str4.intern(): " +
                       (str4 == str4.intern()));         // (13) false
  }
}
```

Output from the program:

```
emptyStr: ""
str1 == str2:      true
str1.equals(str2): true
str1 == str3:      true
```

```
str1.equals(str3): true
str1 == str4;       false
str1.equals(str4): true
str1 == str5:       false
str1.equals(str5): true
str1 == Auxiliary.str1:       true
str1.equals(Auxiliary.str1): true
"You cannot change me!".length(): 21
str1.intern() == str4.intern(): true
str4 == str4.intern(): false
```

The CharSequence Interface

This interface defines a readable sequence of char values. It is implemented by the String and StringBuilder classes. Many methods in these classes accept arguments of this interface type, and specify it as their return type. This interface facilitates interoperability between these classes. It defines the following methods:

int length()

Returns the number of char values in this sequence.

default boolean isEmpty()

Returns true if this character sequence is empty. The default implementation returns the result of this.length() == 0. See also the String.isBlank() method (p. 453).

char charAt(int index)

A character at a particular index in a sequence can be read using the charAt() method. The first character is at index 0 and the last one at index 1 less than the number of characters in the string. If the index value is not valid, an IndexOutOfBoundsException is thrown.

CharSequence subSequence(int start, int end)

Returns a new CharSequence that is a subsequence of this sequence. Characters from the current sequence are read from the index start to the index end-1, inclusive.

String toString()

Returns a string containing the characters in this sequence in the same order as this sequence.

static int compare(CharSequence cs1, CharSequence cs2)

Compares two CharSequence instances lexicographically. It returns a negative value, 0, or a positive value if the first sequence is lexicographically less than, equal to, or greater than the second, respectively.

default IntStream chars()

This default method returns an IntStream of char values from this sequence (§16.4, p. 901).

Reading Characters from a String

The following methods can be used for character-related operations on a string:

char charAt(int index)   From the CharSequence interface (p. 444).

char[] toCharArray()

Returns a new character array, with length equal to the length of this string, that contains the characters in this string.

void getChars(int srcBegin, int srcEnd, char[] dst, int dstBegin)

Copies characters from the current string into the destination character array. Characters from the current string are read from index srcBegin to the index srcEnd-1, inclusive. They are copied into the destination array (dst), starting at index dstBegin and ending at index dstbegin+(srcEnd-srcBegin)-1. The number of characters copied is (srcEnd-srcBegin). An IndexOutOfBoundsException is thrown if the indices do not meet the criteria for the operation.

IntStream chars()   From the CharSequence interface (p. 444).

int length()   From the CharSequence interface (p. 444).

boolean isEmpty()   From the CharSequence interface (p. 444).

Reading Lines from a String

The following method can be used to extract lines from a string:

Stream<String> lines()

Returns a stream of lines extracted from this string, separated by a *line terminator* (§16.4, p. 902). A line is defined as a sequence of characters terminated by a line terminator.

A line terminator is one of the following: a line feed character "\n", a carriage return character "\r", or a carriage return followed immediately by a line feed "\r\n".

Example 8.4 uses some of these methods for reading characters from strings at (3), (4), (5), and (6). The program prints the frequency of a character in a string and illustrates copying from a string into a character array.

- -

Example 8.4   *Reading Characters from a* String

```
public class ReadingCharsFromString {
  public static void main(String[] args) {
    int[] frequencyData = new int [Character.MAX_VALUE];    // (1)
    String str = "You cannot change me!";                   // (2)

    // Count the frequency of each character in the string.
    for (int i = 0; i < str.length(); i++) {                // (3)
```

```
            try {
              frequencyData[str.charAt(i)]++;                    // (4)
            } catch(StringIndexOutOfBoundsException e) {
              System.out.println("Index error detected: "+ i +" not in range.");
            }
        }

        // Print the character frequency.
        System.out.println("Character frequency for string: \"" + str + "\"");
        for (int i = 0; i < frequencyData.length; i++) {
          if (frequencyData[i] != 0)
            System.out.println((char)i + " (code "+ i +"): " + frequencyData[i]);
        }

        System.out.println("Copying into a char array:");
        char[] destination = new char [str.length() - 3];       // 3 characters less.
        str.getChars( 0,               7, destination, 0);       // (5) "You can"
        str.getChars(10, str.length(), destination, 7);         // (6) " change me!"
                                                                // "not" not copied.

        // Print the character array.
        for (int i = 0; i < destination.length; i++) {
          System.out.print(destination[i]);
        }
        System.out.println();
      }
    }
```

Output from the program:

```
Character Frequency for string: "You cannot change me!"
  (code 32): 3
! (code 33): 1
Y (code 89): 1
a (code 97): 2
c (code 99): 2
e (code 101): 2
g (code 103): 1
h (code 104): 1
m (code 109): 1
n (code 110): 3
o (code 111): 2
t (code 116): 1
u (code 117): 1
Copying into a char array:
You can change me!
```

In Example 8.4, the frequencyData array at (1) stores the frequency of each character that can occur in a string. The string in question is declared at (2). Since a char value is promoted to an int value in arithmetic expressions, it can be used as an index in an array. Each element in the frequencyData array functions as a frequency counter for the character corresponding to the index value of the element:

```
frequencyData[str.charAt(i)]++;                    // (4)
```

The calls to the getChars() method at (5) and (6) copy particular substrings from the string into designated places in the destination array, before printing the whole character array.

Comparing Strings

Characters are compared based on their Unicode values.

```
boolean test = 'a' < 'b';     // true since 0x61 < 0x62
```

Two strings are compared *lexicographically,* as in a dictionary or telephone directory, by successively comparing their corresponding characters at each position in the two strings, starting with the characters in the first position. The string "abba" is less than "aha", since the second character 'b' in the string "abba" is less than the second character 'h' in the string "aha". The characters in the first position in each of these strings are equal.

The following public methods can be used for comparing strings:

```
boolean equals(Object obj)
boolean equalsIgnoreCase(String str2)
```

The String class overrides the equals() method from the Object class. The String class equals() method implements String object value equality as two String objects having the same sequence of characters. The equalsIgnoreCase() method does the same, but ignores the case of the characters.

```
int compareTo(String str2)
```

The String class implements the Comparable<String> interface (§14.4, p. 761). The compareTo() method compares the two strings, and returns a value based on the outcome of the comparison:

- The value 0, if this string is equal to the string argument
- A value less than 0, if this string is lexicographically less than the string argument
- A value greater than 0, if this string is lexicographically greater than the string argument

Here are some examples of string comparisons:

```
String strA = new String("The Case was thrown out of Court");
String strB = new String("the case was thrown out of court");

boolean b1 = strA.equals(strB);               // false
boolean b2 = strA.equalsIgnoreCase(strB);     // true

String str1 = "abba";
String str2 = "aha";

int compVal1 = str1.compareTo(str2);          // negative value => str1 < str2
```

Character Case in a String

```
String toUpperCase()
String toUpperCase(Locale locale)
String toLowerCase()
String toLowerCase(Locale locale)
```

Note that the original string is returned if none of the characters needs its case changed, but a new String object is returned if any of the characters need their case changed. These methods delegate the character-by-character case conversion to corresponding methods from the Character class.

These methods use the rules of the (default) *locale* (returned by the method Locale.getDefault(), §18.1, p. 1096), which embodies the idiosyncrasies of a specific geographical, political, or cultural region regarding number/date/ currency formats, character classification, alphabet (including case idiosyncrasies), and other localizations.

Examples of case in strings:

```
String strA = new String("The Case was thrown out of Court");
String strB = new String("the case was thrown out of court");

String strC = strA.toLowerCase();  // Case conversion => New String object:
                                   // "the case was thrown out of court"
String strD = strB.toLowerCase();  // No case conversion => Same String object
String strE = strA.toUpperCase();  // Case conversion => New String object:
                                   // "THE CASE WAS THROWN OUT OF COURT"

boolean test1 = strC == strA;      // false
boolean test2 = strD == strB;      // true
boolean test3 = strE == strA;      // false
```

Concatenation of Strings

Concatenation of two strings results in a new string that consists of the characters of the first string followed by the characters of the second string. The overloaded operator + for string concatenation is discussed in §2.8, p. 63. In addition, the following method can be used to concatenate two strings:

```
String concat(String str)
```

The concat() method does not modify the String object on which it is invoked, as String objects are immutable. Instead, the concat() method returns a reference to a brand-new String object:

```
String billboard = "Just";
billboard.concat(" lost in space."); // (1) Returned reference value not stored.
System.out.println(billboard);       // (2) "Just"
billboard = billboard.concat(" advertise").concat(" here.");  // (3) Chaining.
System.out.println(billboard);       // (4) "Just advertise here."
```

At (1), the reference value of the String object returned by the method concat() is not stored. This String object becomes inaccessible after (1). We see that the reference billboard still denotes the string literal "Just" at (2).

At (3), two method calls to the concat() method are *chained*. The first call returns a reference value to a new String object, whose content is "Just advertise". The second method call is invoked on this String object using the reference value that was returned in the first method call. The second call results in yet another new String object, whose content is "Just advertise here." The reference value of this String object is assigned to the reference billboard. Because String objects are immutable, the creation of the temporary String object with the content "Just advertise" is inevitable at (3).

Some more examples of string concatenation follow:

```
String motto = new String("Program once");      // (1)
motto += ", execute everywhere.";               // (2)
motto  = motto.concat(" Don't bet on it!");     // (3)
```

Note that a new String object is assigned to the reference motto each time in the assignments at (1), (2), and (3). The String object with the contents "Program once" becomes inaccessible after the assignment at (2). The String object with the contents "Program once, execute everywhere." becomes inaccessible after (3). The reference motto denotes the String object with the following contents after execution of the assignment at (3):

```
"Program once, execute everywhere. Don't bet on it!"
```

Repeating Strings

The String class provides the repeat() method that creates a string which is the result of concatenating the current string with itself a specified number of times. The code below illustrates the operation with the String banner, which is repeated three times. The method returns a new string, and the original string is intact.

```
String banner = "Let's ace that Exam! ";
String bigBanner = banner.repeat(3);
System.out.println("|" + bigBanner + "|");
```

The code prints:

```
|Let's ace that Exam! Let's ace that Exam! Let's ace that Exam! |
```

```
String repeat(int count)
```
Returns a string whose value is the concatenation of this string repeated count number of times. If this string is empty (i.e., its length is zero) then the empty string is returned.

Joining of CharSequence Objects

One operation commonly performed on a sequence of strings is to format them so that each string is separated from the next one by a delimiter. For example, given the following sequence of strings:

```
"2014"
"January"
"11"
```

we wish to format them so that individual strings are separated by the delimiter "/":

```
"2014/January/11"
```

The following static methods in the String class can be used for this purpose:

```
static String join(CharSequence delimiter, CharSequence... elements)
static String join(CharSequence delimiter,
                    Iterable<? extends CharSequence> elements)
```

Both static methods return a new String composed of copies of the CharSequence elements joined together with a copy of the specified CharSequence delimiter. Thus the resulting string is composed of text representations of the elements separated by the text representation of the specified delimiter.

If either delimiter is null or elements is null, a NullPointerException is thrown. If both are null, the method call is ambiguous.

If an element in elements is null, the string "null" is added as its text representation.

Note that both the individual strings and the delimiter string are of type CharSequence. The examples in this section use String and StringBuilder objects that implement the CharSequence interface (p. 444).

An Iterable provides an iterator to iterate over its elements. The following examples use an ArrayList (§12.5, p. 657) that implements the Iterable interface. The second join() method is then able to iterate over the Iterable using the iterator. This method will accept only an Iterable whose elements are of type CharSequence or are subtypes of CharSequence.

The first example shows joining of String objects. The first join() method is called in this case.

```
// (1) Joining individual String objects:
String dateStr = String.join("/", "2014", "January", "11");
System.out.println(dateStr);                    // 2014/January/11
```

The second example shows joining of elements in a StringBuilder array. Again the first join() method is called, with the array being passed as the second parameter.

```
// (2) Joining elements in a StringBuilder array:
StringBuilder left          = new StringBuilder("Left");
StringBuilder right         = new StringBuilder("Right");
StringBuilder[] strBuilders = { left, right, left };
```

```
String march = String.join("-->", strBuilders);
System.out.println(march);                              // Left-->Right-->Left
```

The third example shows joining of elements in an ArrayList of StringBuilder. The second join() method is called, with the ArrayList being passed as the second parameter. Note that some of the elements of the ArrayList are null.

```
// (3) Joining elements in a StringBuilder list:
ArrayList<StringBuilder> sbList = new ArrayList<>();
sbList.add(right); sbList.add(null); sbList.add(left); sbList.add(null);
String resultStr = "[" + String.join(", ", sbList) + "]";
System.out.println(resultStr);                          // [Right, null, Left, null]
```

The last example shows joining of elements in an ArrayList of CharSequence. Again the second join() method is called, with the ArrayList being passed as the second parameter. Note that elements of the ArrayList are String and StringBuilder objects that are also of type CharSequence.

```
// (4) Joining elements in a CharSequence list:
ArrayList<CharSequence> charSeqList = new ArrayList<>();
charSeqList.add(right); charSeqList.add(left);       // Add StringBuilder objects.
charSeqList.add("Right"); charSeqList.add("Left"); // Add String objects.
String resultStr2 = "<" + String.join("; ", charSeqList) + ">";
System.out.println(resultStr2);                         // <Right; Left; Right; Left>
```

Searching for Characters and Substrings in Strings

The following overloaded methods can be used to find the index of a character or the start index of a substring in a string. These methods search *forward* toward the end of the string. In other words, the index of the *first* occurrence of the character or substring is found. If the search is unsuccessful, the value -1 is returned.

```
int indexOf(int ch)
int indexOf(int ch, int fromIndex)
```

The first method finds the index of the first occurrence of the argument character in a string. The second method finds the index of the first occurrence of the argument character in a string, starting at the index specified in the second argument. If the index argument is negative, the index is assumed to be 0. If the index argument is greater than the length of the string, it is effectively considered to be equal to the length of the string, resulting in the value -1 being returned.

```
int indexOf(String str)
int indexOf(String str, int fromIndex)
```

The first method finds the start index of the first occurrence of the substring argument in a string. The second method finds the start index of the first occurrence of the substring argument in a string, starting at the index specified in the second argument.

The `String` class also defines a set of methods that search for a character or a substring, but the search is *backward* toward the start of the string. In other words, the index of the *last* occurrence of the character or substring is found.

```
int lastIndexOf(int ch)
int lastIndexOf(int ch, int fromIndex)
int lastIndexOf(String str)
int lastIndexOf(String str, int fromIndex)
```

The following methods can be used to create a string in which all occurrences of a character or a subsequence in a string have been replaced with another character or subsequence:

```
String replace(char oldChar, char newChar)
String replace(CharSequence target, CharSequence replacement)
```

The first method returns a new `String` object that is the result of replacing all occurrences of the `oldChar` in the current string with the `newChar`. The current string is returned if no occurrences of the `oldChar` can be found.

The second method returns a new `String` object that is the result of replacing all occurrences of the character sequence `target` in the current string with the character sequence `replacement`. The current string is returned if no occurrences of the `target` can be found.

The following methods can be used to test whether a string satisfies a given criterion:

```
boolean contains(CharSequence cs)
```

Returns `true` if the current string contains the specified character sequence, and `false` otherwise.

```
boolean startsWith(String prefix)
```

Returns `true` if the current string starts with the character sequence specified by parameter `prefix`, and `false` otherwise.

```
boolean startsWith(String prefix, int index)
```

Returns `true` if the substring of the current string at the specified `index` starts with the character sequence specified by parameter `prefix`, and `false` otherwise.

```
boolean endsWith(String suffix)
```

Returns `true` if the current string ends with the character sequence specified by parameter `suffix`, and `false` otherwise.

Examples of search and replace methods in the `String` class:

```
String funStr = "Java Jives";
//               0123456789

int jInd1a = funStr.indexOf('J');          // 0
int jInd1b = funStr.indexOf('J', 1);       // 5
```

```
int jInd2a = funStr.lastIndexOf('J');          // 5
int jInd2b = funStr.lastIndexOf('J', 4);       // 0

String banner = "One man, One vote";
//               01234567890123456

int subInd1a = banner.indexOf("One");          // 0
int subInd1b = banner.indexOf("One", 3);       // 9
int subInd2a = banner.lastIndexOf("One");      // 9
int subInd2b = banner.lastIndexOf("One", 10);  // 9
int subInd2c = banner.lastIndexOf("One", 8);   // 0
int subInd2d = banner.lastIndexOf("One", 2);   // 0

String newStr    = funStr.replace('J', 'W');        // "Wava Wives"
String newBanner = banner.replace("One", "No");     // "No man, No vote"
boolean found1   = banner.contains("One");          // true
boolean found2   = newBanner.contains("One");       // false

String song = "Start me up!";
//             012345677890
boolean found3    = song.startsWith("Start");       // true
boolean notFound1 = song.startsWith("start");       // false
boolean found4    = song.startsWith("me", 6);       // true
boolean found5    = song.endsWith("up!");           // true
boolean notFound2 = song.endsWith("up");            // false
```

Extracting Substrings from Strings

The String class provides methods to trim and strip strings, and also extract substrings.

```
boolean isBlank()
```

Returns true if the string is empty or contains only *whitespace*; otherwise, it returns false. See also the method isEmpty() in the CharSequence interface (p. 444).

```
String strip()
String stripLeading()
String stripTrailing()
```

Return a string whose value is this string, with all leading and trailing *whitespace* removed, or with all leading whitespace removed, or with all trailing whitespace removed, respectively. If this String object represents an empty string, or if all characters in this string are whitespace, then an empty string is returned. See also the method stripIndent() (p. 444).

```
String trim()
```

This method can be used to create a string where all characters with values less than or equal to the space character '\u0020' have been removed from the front (leading) and the end (trailing) of a string. It is recommended to use the strip methods to remove leading and trailing whitespace in a string.

```
String substring(int startIndex)
String substring(int startIndex, int endIndex)
```

The String class provides these overloaded methods to extract substrings from a string. A new String object containing the substring is created and returned. The first method extracts the string that starts at the given index startIndex and extends to the end of the string. The end of the substring can be specified by using a second argument endIndex that is the index of the first character *after* the substring—that is, the last character in the substring is at index endIndex-1. If the index value is not valid, an IndexOutOfBoundsException is thrown.

CharSequence subSequence(int start, int end) From the CharSequence interface (p. 444)

This method behaves the same way as the substring(int start, int end) method.

The Character.isWhitespace() method can be used to determine whether a character is whitespace.

```
System.out.println(Character.isWhitespace('\t'));  // true
System.out.println(Character.isWhitespace('\n'));  // true
System.out.println(Character.isWhitespace('a'));   // false
```

Examples of blank strings:

```
System.out.println("".isBlank());       // true
System.out.println(" \t ".isBlank());   // true
```

Examples of stripping a string:

```
String utopia = "\t\n  Java Nation \n\t  ";
System.out.println(utopia.strip().equals("Java Nation"));                  // true
System.out.println(utopia.stripLeading().equals("Java Nation \n\t  ")); // true
System.out.println(utopia.stripTrailing().equals("\t\n  Java Nation")); // true
```

Examples of extracting substrings:

```
String utopia2 = "\t\n  Java Nation \n\t  ";
utopia2 = utopia2.trim();                   // "Java Nation"
utopia2 = utopia2.substring(5);             // "Nation"
String radioactive = utopia2.substring(3,6);  // "ion"
```

Converting Primitive Values and Objects to Strings

The String class overrides the toString() method in the Object class and returns the String object itself:

String toString()   From the CharSequence interface (p. 444).

The String class also defines a set of static overloaded valueOf() methods to convert objects and primitive values into strings:

```
static String valueOf(Object obj)
static String valueOf(char[] charArray)
static String valueOf(boolean b)
static String valueOf(char c)
```

All of these methods return a string representing the given parameter value. A call to the method with the parameter obj is equivalent to obj.toString() when obj is not null; otherwise, the "null" string is returned. The boolean values true and false are converted into the strings "true" and "false". The char parameter is converted to a string consisting of a single character.

```
static String valueOf(int i)
static String valueOf(long l)
static String valueOf(float f)
static String valueOf(double d)
```

The static valueOf() method, which accepts a primitive value as an argument, is equivalent to the static toString() method in the corresponding wrapper class for each of the primitive data types ((6a) and (6b) in §8.3, p. 430). Note that there are no valueOf() methods that accept a byte or a short.

Examples of string conversions:

```
String anonStr   = String.valueOf("Make me a string.");      // "Make me a string."
String charStr   = String.valueOf(new char[] {'a', 'h', 'a'});// "aha"
String boolTrue  = String.valueOf(true);                     // "true"
String doubleStr = String.valueOf(Math.PI);                  // "3.141592653589793"
```

Transforming a String

The transform() method allows a function to be applied to a string to compute a result. The built-in functional interface Function<T, R>, and writing lambda expressions to implement such functions, are covered in the following sections: §13.8, p. 712, and §13.2, p. 679, respectively.

```
<R> R transform(Function<? super String,? extends R> f)
```

The specified function f is applied to this string to produce a result of type R.

The example below illustrates using the transform() method to reverse the characters in a string via a StringBuilder (p. 464). Its versatility becomes apparent when the string contains lines of text or a text block that needs to be processed (p. 458).

```
String message = "Take me to your leader!";
String tongueSpeake = message.transform(s ->
    new StringBuilder(s).reverse().toString().toUpperCase());
System.out.println(tongueSpeake); // !REDAEL RUOY OT EM EKAT
```

Indenting Lines in a String

The indent() method allows indentation of lines in a string to be adjusted.

```
String indent(int n)
```

Adjusts the indentation of each line of this string based on the value of n, and normalizes line termination characters.

This string is conceptually separated into lines using the String.lines() method (p. 445). Each line is then adjusted depending on the value of n, and then terminated with a line feed ("\n"). The resulting lines are then concatenated and the final string returned.

If n > 0 then n spaces are inserted at the beginning of each line. This also applies to an empty line.

If n == 0 then the line remains unchanged. However, line terminators are still normalized.

If n < 0 then at most n whitespace characters are removed from the beginning of each line, depending on the number of leading whitespace characters in the line. Each whitespace character is treated as a single character; specifically, the tab character "\t" is considered a single character and is not expanded.

The example below illustrates how indentation is adjusted depending on the value passed to the indent() method. The string cmds constructed at (0) has four lines, where the third line is an empty line. The first, second, and last lines are indented by one, two, and three spaces, respectively. The first line is terminated with the return character (\r), and the last line is not terminated at all. The other lines are terminated normally with a newline character (\n). Keep also in mind that the string cmds is immutable.

```
String cmds = " Attention!\r  Quick march!\n\n   Eyes left!"; // (0)
String str1 = cmds.indent(0);                                // (1)
String str2 = cmds.indent(3);                                // (2)
String str3 = cmds.indent(-1);                               // (3)
String str4 = cmds.indent(-2);                               // (4)
String str5 = cmds.indent(-3);                               // (5)
```

The lines numbered (1) to (5) below show the resulting string from the method calls above from (1) to (5), respectively, applied to the string cmds at (0) above. The jshell tool can readily be used to execute the method calls above to examine the resulting strings. Note that termination of all lines is normalized with the newline character (\n).

```
(0) cmds ==> " Attention!\r  Quick march!\n\n   Eyes left!"
(1) str1 ==> " Attention!\n  Quick march!\n\n   Eyes left!\n"
(2) str2 ==> "    Attention!\n     Quick march!\n   \n      Eyes left!\n"
(3) str3 ==> "Attention!\n Quick march!\n\n  Eyes left!\n"
(4) str4 ==> "Attention!\nQuick march!\n\n Eyes left!\n"
(5) str5 ==> "Attention!\nQuick march!\n\nEyes left!\n"
```

In Table 8.1, the columns correspond to the resulting strings from (1) to (5) above. The last row in Table 8.1 shows the output when the resulting strings are printed.

The underscore (_) in each cell in the last row is a visual marker that indicates the position after printing the resulting string. Note that the empty line at (0) above is indented (marked visually as *sss*), as shown in column (2). A value less than -3 does not change the result shown in column (5).

Table 8.1 *Indenting Lines in a String*

(1)	(2)	(3)	(4)	(5)
n = 0	n = 3	n = -1	n = -2	n = -3
123456789	123456789	123456789	123456789	123456789
Attention! Quick march! Eyes left! _	Attention! Quick march! sss Eyes left! _	Attention! Quick march! Eyes left! _	Attention! Quick march! Eyes left! _	Attention! Quick march! Eyes left! _

Formatted Strings

We have used the System.out.printf() method to format values and print them to the terminal window (§1.9, p. 24). To just create the string with the formatted values, but not print the formatted result, we can use the following static method from the String class. It accepts the same arguments as the printf() method, and uses the same format specifications (Table 1.2, p. 26).

> static String format(String format, Object... args)
> Returns a string with the result of formatting the values in the variable arity parameter args according to the String parameter format. The format string contains format specifications that determine how each subsequent value in the variable arity parameter args will be formatted.
>
> Any error in the format string will result in a runtime exception.
>
> String formatted(Object... args)
> Formats the supplied arguments using this string as the format string. It is equivalent to String.format(this, args).

The following call to the format() method creates a formatted string with the three values formatted according to the specified format string:

```
String formattedStr = String.format("Formatted values|%5d|%8.3f|%5s|",
                          2020, Math.PI, "Hi");
System.out.println(formattedStr);  // Formatted values| 2020|   3.142|   Hi|
formattedStr = formattedStr.toUpperCase();
System.out.println(formattedStr);  // FORMATTED VALUES| 2020|   3.142|   HI|
```

Alternatively, we can use the formatted() method:

```
String formattedStr1 = "Formatted values|%5d|%8.3f|%5s|"
                     .formatted(2020, Math.PI, "Hi");
System.out.println(formattedStr1); // Formatted values| 2020|   3.142|   Hi|
```

For formatting strings in a language-neutral way, the MessageFormat class can be considered (§18.7, p. 1139). Other miscellaneous methods exist in the String class for pattern matching (matches()), splitting strings (split()), and converting a string to an array of bytes (getBytes()). The method hashCode() can be used to compute a hash value based on the characters in the string. Please consult the Java SE Platform API documentation for more details.

Text Blocks

Constructing string literals that span multiple lines can be tedious using string concatenation and line terminators. Text blocks provide a better solution—avoiding having to escape tab, newline, and double-quote characters in the text, and in addition preserving indentation of a multiline string.

Basic Text Blocks

The string sql1 below represents a three-line SQL query. It is constructed using a *text block*, resulting in an object of type String. We will use it as an example to illustrate constructing text blocks.

```
String sql1 = """
SELECT *
FROM Programmers
WHERE Language = 'Java';
""";
```

The string literal resulting from entering the text block in the jshell tool:

```
sql1 ==> "SELECT *\nFROM Programmers\nWHERE Language = 'Java';\n";
```

Printing the text block sql1 above will give the following result, where the underscore (_) is used as a visual marker to indicate the position after printing the resulting string:

```
SELECT *
FROM Programmers
WHERE Language = 'Java';
_
```

A text block starts with three double quotes (""") and ends with three double quotes ("""). The *opening delimiter* of a text block consists of the opening three double quotes (followed by any spaces, tabs, or form feed characters) that must be terminated by a line terminator. The *closing delimiter* of a text block consists of three double quotes.

The *content of a text block* begins with the sequence of characters that immediately *begins after the line terminator* of the opening delimiter and *ends with the first double quote* of the closing delimiter. Note that the line terminator of the opening delimiter is *not* part of the text block's content.

The following attempt to construct a text block will result in a compile-time error because of erroneous characters (i.e., the // comment) that follow the opening three double quotes of the text block.

```
String badBlock = """        // (1) Compile-time error!
Not a good start.
""";
```

The text block below results in an empty string (""):

```
String emptyBlock = """
""";
```

Using Escape Sequences in Text Blocks

We do not need to end each text line with the \n escape sequence, as the text block retains the line terminators entered directly into the text. However, using the \n escape sequence will be interpreted as literally inserting a newline character in the text. The query sql2 below is equivalent to the query sql1 above, and will result in the same string. (For escape sequences, see Table 2.10, p. 38.)

```
String sql2 = """
SELECT *
FROM Programmers\nWHERE Language = 'Java';
""";
```

The string literal resulting from entering the text block in the jshell tool:

```
sql2 ==> "SELECT *\nFROM Programmers\nWHERE Language = 'Java';\n"
```

However, ending a line explicitly in the text block with a newline character will result in an empty line being inserted into the resulting string, as can be seen in the code below:

```
String sql3 = """
SELECT *
FROM Programmers\n
WHERE Language = 'Java';
""";
```

The string literal resulting from entering the text block in the jshell tool:

```
sql3 ==> "SELECT *\nFROM Programmers\n\nWHERE Language = 'Java';\n"
```

Printing the text block sql3 above will give the following result, where the underscore (_) is used as a visual marker to indicate the position after printing the resulting string:

```
SELECT *
FROM Programmers

WHERE Language = 'Java';

_
```

In the examples so far, the closing delimiter of a text block was specified on the last line by itself, resulting in the *last line of text* in the text block being terminated by the line terminator that was entered directly. If the last line of text should not be terminated, the closing delimiter can be used at the end of this line as shown below.

```
String sql14 = """
SELECT *
FROM Programmers
WHERE Language = 'Java';"""; // No line terminator. Closing delimiter ends block.
```

The string literal resulting from entering the text block in the jshell tool shows no line terminator for the last line of the query:

```
sql14 ==> "SELECT *\nFROM Programmers\nWHERE Language = 'Java';"
```

The print statement below does not print a newline after the last line:

```
System.out.print(sql14);

SELECT *
FROM Programmers
WHERE Language = 'Java';
```

Other escape sequences (Table 2.10, p. 38) can also be used in a text block. In contrast to the \n escape sequence, the \Line terminator escape sequence, allowed only in a text block, escapes the line terminator, thus preventing the termination of the current line so that it is joined with the next line.

```
String sql15 = """
SELECT * \
FROM Programmers \
WHERE Language = 'Java';
""";
```

The string literal resulting from entering the text block in the jshell tool shows that the three lines were joined and no characters were substituted for the \Line terminator escape sequence:

```
sql15 ==> "SELECT * FROM Programmers WHERE Language = 'Java';\n"
```

The result from printing the string sql15 is shown below, where the underscore (_) is used as a visual marker to indicate the position after printing the resulting string.

```
SELECT * FROM Programmers WHERE Language = 'Java';
_
```

To include a backslash (\) in any context other than line continuation will require escaping the backslash, analogous to using it in a string literal.

By default, any trailing whitespace on a line is removed and line termination normalized. In some cases, it might be necessary to retain trailing whitespace. This can be achieved by using the \s escape sequence. Replacing the last trailing space that should be retained with this escape sequence will preserve any trailing whitespace *before* the \s escape sequence, including the space replaced by the escape sequence. At (1) below, *four* trailing spaces are retained.

```
String sql16 = """
SELECT *
```

```
              FROM Programmers   \s       """;                              // (1) No line termination.
              // sql6 ==> "SELECT *\nFROM Programmers     "

              String sql7 = "WHERE Language = 'Java';\n";
              System.out.print(sql6 + sql7);
```

Output from the code, showing the retained spaces, where the underscore (_) is used as a visual marker to indicate the position after printing the resulting string:

```
SELECT *
FROM Programmers    WHERE Language = 'Java';
_
```

Double quotes (") are treated like any other character and can be used without escaping them in a text block, except when a three double quote sequence is used in the text. It is enough to escape the first double quote in a three double quote sequence, but all three double quotes can also be escaped individually in the sequence. It is also not required that double quotes should be balanced. The code below illustrates using double quotes in a text block.

```
String fact = """
The sequence \""""
has "special" meaning in a text block.
""";
// fact ==> "The sequence \"\"\"\nhas \"special\" meaning in a text block.\n"
System.out.print(fact);
```

Output from the code, where the underscore (_) is used as a visual marker to indicate the position after printing the resulting string:

```
The sequence """
has "special" meaning in a text block.
_
```

A text block can be used to define the *format string* for value substitution in formatted text (p. 457). Below, the text block defines the format string used by the formatted() method for substituting values of its arguments.

```
String query = """
SELECT *
FROM %s
WHERE %s = '%s';
""".formatted("Customers", "Country", "Norway");
System.out.print(query);
```

Output from the print statement, where the underscore (_) is used as a visual marker to indicate the position after printing the resulting string:

```
SELECT *
FROM Customers
WHERE Country = 'Norway';
_
```

Incidental Whitespace

So far the lines in the text blocks have all been left-justified. This need not be the case. Indentation can be used if desired. However, one needs to be careful as *incidental whitespace* from *each* line is removed by the compiler. Incidental whitespace is indentation that is common to all lines in the text block. It is equal to the number of leading whitespace characters in the *least indented* lines in the text block. The least indented lines end up with no indentation. The line containing the closing delimiter also plays a part in determining the incidental whitespace to be removed from all lines. Regardless of how much incidental whitespace is removed from the other lines in the text box, *all* leading whitespace preceding the closing delimiter is always removed, resulting in an empty line.

Whitespace that is not incidental is referred to as *essential whitespace*.

Figure 8.3   *Incidental Whitespace in Text Blocks*

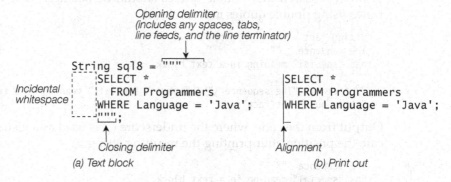

sql8 ==> "SELECT *\n   FROM Programmers\nWHERE Language = 'Java';\n"

(c) The string literal resulting from entering the text block in the jshell *tool*

In Figure 8.3a, we see that the first and third lines, and the line with the closing delimiter, are the ones that are least indented in the text block. The number of leading whitespace characters in each of these lines is four. The indentation in the second line is six positions. The least number (i.e., four) of leading whitespace characters common to all lines is the incidental whitespace that is removed from *each* line. Figure 8.3b shows how the contents of the text block will be printed. The underscore (_) is a visual marker that indicates the position after printing the text block, showing that a newline is printed for the last line of the text block. Removing the incidental whitespace preserves the relative indentation of the lines in the text block. Figure 8.3c shows the string literal resulting from entering the text block in the jshell tool.

As stated earlier, the whitespace preceding the closing delimiter is significant in determining incidental whitespace. Table 8.2 shows a few more examples to illustrate how incidental whitespace is calculated and removed in a text block. The last two rows show the text block declaration and the result of printing the text block, respectively. The underscore (_) in each cell in the last row is a visual marker that indicates the position after printing the text block, showing that no newline is printed for the last line of the text blocks in columns (4) and (5). The numbered remarks below refer to the column numbers in Table 8.2. The string literal resulting from entering each text block in the jshell tool is also shown.

(1) The least indentation (0) is determined by the last line with the closing delimiter. No incidental whitespace is removed.

    tb1 ==> "   KEEP\n   IT\n   SIMPLE\n"

(2) The least indentation (2) is determined by the last line with the closing delimiter.

    tb2 ==> " KEEP\n   IT\n   SIMPLE\n"

(3) The least indentation (1) is determined by the line containing the word IT. However, *all* leading whitespace in the *last* line is removed, not just four spaces as in the other lines—we can see the result in the string literal below:

    tb3 ==> "   KEEP\nIT\n SIMPLE\n"

(4) The least indentation (2) is determined by the last line containing the word SIMPLE and the closing delimiter. Note that the last line is not terminated.

    tb4 ==> " KEEP\n   IT\nSIMPLE"

(5) The least indentation (4) is determined by the lines containing the words KEEP and IT, respectively. Note that in the last line only incidental whitespace is removed, and the line is not terminated.

    tb5 ==> "KEEP\nIT\n SIMPLE"

Table 8.2 *Incidental Whitespace in Text Blocks*

(1)	(2)	(3)	(4)	(5)
Least indent is 0	**Least indent is 2**	**Least indent is 4**	**Least indent is 2**	**Least indent is 4**
123456789012345	123456789012345	123456789012345	123456789012345	123456789012345

String tb1 =
"""
    KEEP
      IT
         SIMPLE
""";
	String tb2 =
	"""
	    KEEP
	      IT
	         SIMPLE
	  """;
		String tb3 =
		"""
		    KEEP
		      IT
		         SIMPLE
		    """;
			String tb4 =
			"""
			    KEEP
			      IT
			SIMPLE""";
				String tb5 =
				"""
				    KEEP
				      IT
				      SIMPLE""";

KEEP
    IT
       SIMPLE
_
	KEEP
	    IT
	       SIMPLE
	_
		KEEP
		IT
		  SIMPLE
		_
			KEEP
			    IT
			SIMPLE_
				KEEP
				IT
				  SIMPLE_

A blank line (i.e., one that is empty or contains only whitespace) in a text block is replaced by an empty line—that is, any whitespace it contains is removed.

Incidental whitespace in a text block is processed internally as if by the execution of the String.stripIndent() method. Calling this method on a text block with one or more lines has *no* effect on the content of the text block, but it will strip any whitespace from a text block that has *no line structure*.

The reader is encouraged to use the jshell tool to examine the string literal result-ing from entering the text blocks presented in this section.

String stripIndent()
Returns a string whose value is this string, with incidental whitespace removed from the beginning and end of every line.

8.5 The StringBuilder Class

Although there is a close relationship between objects of the String and StringBuilder classes, these are two independent final classes, both directly extending the Object class. Hence, String references cannot be stored (or cast) to StringBuilder references, and vice versa. However, both classes implement the CharSequence interface (p. 444) and the Comparable interface (§14.4, p. 761).

Since the StringBuilder class does not override the equals() and hashCode() methods from the Object class, the contents of string builders should be converted to String objects for equality comparison and to compute a hash value.

The StringBuilder class has many operations analogous to the ones in the String class. In addition, it provides support for manipulating *mutable* strings (p. 467).

Constructing String Builders

Mutability

In contrast to the String class, which implements immutable character sequences, the StringBuilder class implements *mutable* character sequences. Not only can the character sequences in a string builder be changed, but the capacity of the string builder can also change dynamically. The *capacity* of a string builder is the maxi-mum number of characters that a string builder can accommodate before its size is automatically augmented.

The legacy class StringBuffer (Figure 8.1, p. 425) also implements *mutable* sequences of characters. It support the same operations as the StringBuilder class, but the StringBuffer class is *thread-safe*. Certain operations on a string buffer are synchronized so that when accessed concurrently by multiple threads, these oper-ations are safe to perform without corrupting the state of the string buffer (§22.4, p. 1387). Note that a String object is also thread-safe—because it is immutable, a thread cannot change its state. String builders are preferred when heavy modifica-tion of character sequences is involved and synchronization of operations, which also carries a performance penalty, is not important. Although the rest of this sec-tion focuses on string builders, it is equally applicable to string buffers.

String Builder Constructors

The final class StringBuilder provides four constructors that create and initialize StringBuilder objects and set their initial capacity.

```
StringBuilder(String str)
StringBuilder(CharSequence charSeq)
```

The contents of the new StringBuilder object are the same as the contents of the String object or the character sequence passed as an argument. The initial capacity of the string builder is set to the length of the argument sequence, plus room for 16 more characters.

```
StringBuilder(int initialCapacity)
```

The new StringBuilder object has no content. The initial capacity of the string builder is set to the value of the argument, which cannot be less than 0.

```
StringBuilder()
```

This constructor also creates a new StringBuilder object with no content. The initial capacity of the string builder is set to 16 characters.

Examples of StringBuilder object creation and initialization:

```
StringBuilder strBuilder1 = new StringBuilder("Phew!");   // "Phew!", capacity 21
StringBuilder strBuilder2 = new StringBuilder(10);        // "", capacity 10
StringBuilder strBuilder3 = new StringBuilder();          // "", capacity 16
```

Reading Characters from String Builders

The following methods can be used for reading characters in a string builder:

```
char charAt(int index)
```
From the CharSequence interface (p. 444).

```
void getChars(int srcBegin, int srcEnd, char[] dst, int dstBegin)
```

Copies characters from the current string builder into the destination character array. Characters from the current string builder are read from index srcBegin to index srcEnd-1, inclusive. They are copied into the destination array (dst), starting at index dstBegin and ending at index dstbegin+(srcEnd-srcBegin)-1. The number of characters copied is (srcEnd-srcBegin). An IndexOutOfBoundsException is thrown if the indices do not meet the criteria for the operation.

```
IntStream chars()
```
From the CharSequence interface (p. 444).

```
int length()
```
From the CharSequence interface (p. 444).

The following is an example of reading the contents of a string builder:

```
StringBuilder strBuilder = new StringBuilder("Java");      // "Java", capacity 20
char charFirst = strBuilder.charAt(0);                     // 'J'
char charLast  = strBuilder.charAt(strBuilder.length()-1); // 'a'
```

Searching for Substrings in String Builders

The methods for searching substrings in string builders are analogous to the ones in the String class (p. 451).

```
int indexOf(String substr)
int indexOf(String substr, int fromIndex)

int lastIndexOf(String str)
int lastIndexOf(String str, int fromIndex)
```

Examples of searching for substrings in a StringBuilder:

```
StringBuilder banner2 = new StringBuilder("One man, One vote");
//                                         01234567890123456

int subInd1a = banner2.indexOf("One");          // 0
int subInd1b = banner2.indexOf("One", 3);       // 9
int subInd2a = banner2.lastIndexOf("One");      // 9
int subInd2b = banner2.lastIndexOf("One", 10);  // 9
int subInd2c = banner2.lastIndexOf("One", 8);   // 0
int subInd2d = banner2.lastIndexOf("One", 2);   // 0
```

Extracting Substrings from String Builders

The StringBuilder class provides the following methods to extract substrings, which are also provided by the String class (p. 453).

```
String substring(int startIndex)
String substring(int startIndex, int endIndex)
```

CharSequence subSequence(int start, int end) From the CharSequence interface (p. 444).

Examples of extracting substrings:

```
StringBuilder bookName = new StringBuilder("Java Gems by Anonymous");
//                                          01234567890123456789012
String title  = bookName.substring(0,9);   // "Java Gems"
String author = bookName.substring(13);    // "Anonymous"
```

Constructing Strings from String Builders

The StringBuilder class overrides the toString() method from the Object class (see also the CharSequence interface, p. 444). It returns the contents of a string builder as a String object.

```
String toString()                          From the CharSequence interface (p. 444).
```

```
StringBuilder strBuilder = new StringBuilder("Build or not to build.");
String fromBuilder = strBuilder.toString();    // "Build or not to build."
```

Comparing String Builders

String builders implement the Comparable<StringBuilder> interface and can be compared lexicographically, analogous to String objects (p. 447).

```
int compareTo(StringBuilder anotherSB)
```

Here are some examples of string builder comparisons:

```
StringBuilder sb1 = new StringBuilder("abba");
StringBuilder sb2 = new StringBuilder("aha");

int compValue1 = sb1.compareTo(sb2);              // negative value => sb1 < sb2
int compValue2 = sb2.compareTo(sb1);              // positive value => sb2 > sb1
boolean isEqual = sb1.compareTo(sb2) == 0;                   // false
boolean flag    = sb1.toString().equals(sb2.toString()); // false
```

Modifying String Builders

Appending, inserting, replacing, and deleting characters automatically results in adjustment of the string builder's structure and capacity, if necessary. The indices passed as arguments in the methods must be equal to or greater than 0. An IndexOutOfBoundsException is thrown if an index is not valid.

Note that the methods in this subsection return the reference value of the modified string builder, making it convenient to chain calls to these methods.

Appending Characters to a String Builder

The overloaded method append() can be used to *append* characters at the *end* of a string builder.

```
StringBuilder append(Object obj)
```

The obj argument is converted to a string as if by the static method call String.valueOf(obj), and this string is appended to the current string builder.

```
StringBuilder append(String str)
StringBuilder append(CharSequence charSeq)
StringBuilder append(CharSequence charSeq, int start, int end)
StringBuilder append(char[] charArray)
StringBuilder append(char[] charArray, int offset, int length)
StringBuilder append(char c)
```

Allow characters from various sources to be appended to the end of the current string builder.

```
StringBuilder append(boolean b)
StringBuilder append(int i)
StringBuilder append(long l)
StringBuilder append(float f)
StringBuilder append(double d)
```

Convert the primitive value of the argument to a string by applying the static method String.valueOf() to the argument, before appending the result to the string builder.

Inserting Characters in a String Builder

The overloaded method insert() can be used to *insert* characters at a *given offset* in a string builder.

```
StringBuilder insert(int offset, Object obj)
StringBuilder insert(int dstOffset, CharSequence seq)
StringBuilder insert(int dstOffset, CharSequence seq, int start, int end)
StringBuilder insert(int offset, String str)
StringBuilder insert(int offset, char[] charArray)
StringBuilder insert(int offset, type c)
```

In the methods above, *type* can be char, boolean, int, long, float, or double. The second argument is converted to a string, if necessary, by applying the static method String.valueOf(). The offset argument specifies where the characters are to be inserted in the string builder, and must be greater than or equal to 0. Note that the offset specifies the number of characters from the start of the string builder.

Replacing Characters in a String Builder

The following methods can be used to replace characters in a string builder:

```
void setCharAt(int index, char ch)
```

Changes the character at a specified index in the string builder. An IndexOutOf-BoundsException is thrown if the index is not valid. This method does not change the length of the string builder, and does *not* return a value.

```
StringBuilder replace(int start, int end, String replacement)
```

Replaces the characters in a subsequence of the string builder with the characters in the specified String. The subsequence is defined by the start index (inclusive) and the end index (exclusive). It returns the modified string builder. If the start index is not valid (i.e., start index is negative, greater than length(), or greater than end index.), a StringIndexOutOfBoundsException is thrown.

Deleting Characters in a String Builder

The following methods can be used to delete characters from *specific positions* in a string builder:

```
StringBuilder deleteCharAt(int index)
StringBuilder delete(int start, int end)
```

The first method deletes a character at a specified index in the string builder, contracting the string builder by one character. The second method deletes a substring, which is specified by the start index (inclusive) and the end index (exclusive), contracting the string builder accordingly. If start index is equal to end index, no changes are made.

Reversing Characters in a String Builder

The following method in the class `StringBuilder` reverses the contents of a string builder:

```
StringBuilder reverse()
```

Examples of using methods that modify string builders:

```
StringBuilder builder = new StringBuilder("banana split");   // "banana split"
builder.delete(4,12);                                        // "bana"
builder.append(42);                                          // "bana42"
builder.insert(4,"na");                                      // "banana42"
builder.reverse();                                           // "24ananab"
builder.deleteCharAt(builder.length()-1);                    // "24anana"
builder.replace(0, 2, "b");                                  // "banana"
builder.append('s');                                         // "bananas"
```

All of the previously mentioned methods modify the contents of the string builder and return a reference value denoting the current string builder. This allows *chaining* of method calls. The method calls invoked on the string builder denoted by the reference `builder` can be chained as follows, giving the same result:

```
builder.delete(4,12).append(42).insert(4,"na").reverse()
       .deleteCharAt(builder.length()-1).replace(0, 2, "b")
       .append('s');                                         // "bananas"
```

The method calls in the chain are evaluated from left to right, so the previous chain of calls is interpreted as follows:

```
(((((builder.delete(4,12)).append(42)).insert(4,"na")).reverse())
      .deleteCharAt(builder.length()-1)).replace(0, 2, "b"))
      .append('s');                                          // "bananas"
```

Each method call returns the reference value of the modified string builder, which is then used to invoke the next method. The string builder remains denoted by the reference `builder`.

The compiler uses string builders to implement string concatenation with the + operator in `String`-valued non-constant expressions. The following code illustrates this optimization:

```
String theChosen = "U";
String str1 = 4 + theChosen + "Only";            // (1) Non-constant expression.
```

The assignment statement at (1) is equivalent to the following code using a string builder:

```
String str2 = new StringBuilder().
                append(4).append(theChosen).append("Only").toString(); // (2)
```

The code at (2) does not create any temporary `String` objects when concatenating several strings, since a single `StringBuilder` object is modified and finally converted to a `String` object having the string content "4UOnly".

Controlling String Builder Capacity

The following methods are exclusive to the `StringBuilder` class and can be used to control various capacity-related aspects of a string builder:

`int capacity()`

Returns the current capacity of the string builder, meaning the number of characters the current builder can accommodate without allocating a new, larger array to hold characters.

`void ensureCapacity(int minCapacity)`

Ensures that there is room for at least a `minCapacity` number of characters. It expands the string builder, depending on the current capacity of the builder.

`void trimToSize()`

Attempts to reduce the storage used for the character sequence. It may affect the capacity of the string builder.

`void setLength(int newLength)`

Ensures that the actual number of characters—that is, the length of the string builder—is exactly equal to the value of the `newLength` argument, which must be greater than or equal to 0. This operation can result in the string being truncated or padded with null characters (`'\u0000'`). This method affects the capacity of the string builder only if the value of the parameter `newLength` is greater than the current capacity.

Example 8.5 illustrates the various capacity-related methods of the `StringBuilder` class. It is instructive to go through the output to see how these methods affect the length and the capacity of a string builder.

- -

Example 8.5 *Controlling String Builder Capacity*

```java
public class StringBuilderCapacity {
  public static void main(String[] args) {
    StringBuilder builder = new StringBuilder("No strings attached!");
    System.out.println("Builder contents: " + builder);
    System.out.println("Builder length:    " + builder.length());
    System.out.println("Builder capacity: " + builder.capacity());
    System.out.println("Ensure capacity of 40");
    builder.ensureCapacity(40);
    System.out.println("Builder capacity: " + builder.capacity());

    System.out.println("Trim to size");
    builder.trimToSize();
    System.out.println("Builder length:    " + builder.length());
    System.out.println("Builder capacity: " + builder.capacity());

    System.out.println("Set length to 10");
    builder.setLength(10);
    System.out.println("Builder length:    " + builder.length());
```

```
        System.out.println("Builder contents: " + builder);
        System.out.println("Set length to 0");
        builder.setLength(0);
        System.out.println("Builder is empty: " + (builder.length() == 0));
    }
}
```

Probable output from the program:

```
Builder contents: No strings attached!
Builder length:    20
Builder capacity: 36
Ensure capacity of 40
Builder capacity: 74
Trim to size
Builder length:    20
Builder capacity: 20
Set length to 10
Builder length:    10
Builder contents: No strings
Set length to 0
Builder is empty: true
```

Review Questions

8.5 Which expression will extract the substring "kap", given the following declaration?

```
String str = "kakapo";
```

Select the one correct answer.

(a) `str.substring(2, 2)`
(b) `str.substring(2, 3)`
(c) `str.substring(2, 4)`
(d) `str.substring(2, 5)`
(e) `str.substring(3, 3)`

8.6 What will be the result of attempting to compile and run the following code?

```
class MyClass {
    public static void main(String[] args) {
        String str1 = "str1";
        String str2 = "str2";
        String str3 = "str3";

        str1.concat(str2);
        System.out.println(str3.concat(str1));
    }
}
```

Select the one correct answer.

(a) The code will fail to compile.
(b) The program will print str3str1str2 at runtime.

(c) The program will print str3 at runtime.

(d) The program will print str3str1 at runtime.

(e) The program will print str3str2 at runtime.

8.7 What will be the result of attempting to compile and run the following program?

```
public class RefEq {
  public static void main(String[] args) {
    String s = "ab" + "12";
    String t = "ab" + 12;
    String u = new String("ab12");
    System.out.println((s==t) + " " + (s==u));
  }
}
```

Select the one correct answer.

(a) The program will fail to compile.

(b) The program will print false false at runtime.

(c) The program will print false true at runtime.

(d) The program will print true false at runtime.

(e) The program will print true true at runtime.

8.8 What will be the result of attempting to compile and run the following program?

```
public class Uppity {
  public static void main(String[] args) {
    String str1 = "lower", str2 = "LOWER", str3 = "UPPER";
    str1.toUpperCase();
    str1.replace("LOWER","UPPER");
    System.out.println((str1.equals(str2)) + " " + (str1.equals(str3)));
  }
}
```

Select the one correct answer.

(a) The program will print false true.

(b) The program will print false false.

(c) The program will print true false.

(d) The program will print true true.

(e) The program will fail to compile.

(f) The program will compile, but it will throw an exception at runtime.

8.9 What will be the result of attempting to compile and run the following program?

```
public class FunCharSeq {
  private static void putO(String s1) {
    s1 = s1.trim();
    s1 += "O";
  }

  public static void main(String[] args) {
    String s1 = " W ";
    putO(s1);
```

```
        s1.concat("W");
        System.out.println("|" + s1 + "|");
    }
}
```

Select the one correct answer.

(a) |WOW|
(b) | W W|
(c) |WO|
(d) | W |
(e) The program will fail to compile.
(f) The program will compile, but it will throw an exception at runtime.

8.10   What will be the result of attempting to compile and run the following program?

```
public class Uppity {
    public static void main(String[] args) {
        String str1 = "lower", str2 = "LOWER", str3 = "UPPER";
        str1.toUpperCase();
        str1.replace("LOWER","UPPER");
        System.out.println((str1.equals(str2)) + " " + (str1.equals(str3)));
    }
}
```

Select the one correct answer.

(a) The program will print false true.
(b) The program will print false false.
(c) The program will print true false.
(d) The program will print true true.
(e) The program will fail to compile.
(f) The program will compile, but it will throw an exception at runtime.

8.11   What will the following code print when run?

```
String s = "This is hard";
s = "-" + s.substring(s.indexOf(' '), s.indexOf(' ', s.indexOf(' ') + 1) + 1)
    .strip() + "-";
System.out.println(s);
```

Select the one correct answer.

(a) - is -
(b) -is-
(c) -is -
(d) - is-
(e) -s is h-
(f) -sish-

8.12   Given the following code:

```
String txt = """
    a
```

```
      b
    c
""";
int from = 0;
int to = txt.indexOf('\n');
String line = null;
while(to < txt.length()-1) {
  to = txt.indexOf('\n', from);
  line = txt.substring(from, to);
  System.out.print(line.length());
  from = to+1;
}
```

The first line of the text block has two leading spaces, the second line has four leading spaces, and the third line has two leading spaces. There are no leading spaces on the line with the closing delimiter of the text block.

What is the result?
Select the one correct answer.

(a) 353
(b) 3530
(c) 1510
(d) 131

8.13 Which text block produces a single line of text with the following exact characters when printed?

    "a""b"

Select the one correct answer.

(a) `String txt = """"a""b\"""";`

(b) `String txt = """"a""b`
    `""";`

(c) `String txt = """`
    `"a""b""""";`

(d) `String txt = """`
    `"a""b\""""";`

(e) `String txt = """`
    `"a""b"`
    `""";`

(f) `String txt = """`
    `"a\""b"\""";`

8.14 Which of the following statements are true about text blocks?
Select the two correct answers.

(a) Content of a text block starts immediately after the line terminator of the opening delimiter.

(b) Content of a text block ends immediately after the line terminator of the closing delimiter.

(c) A text block is a subtype of the String class.

(d) All leading whitespace is removed from each line in the text block.

(e) All trailing whitespace is removed from each line in the text block.

(f) Incidental whitespace is not removed from each line in the text block.

8.15 What will be the result of attempting to compile and run the following program?

```
public class MyClass {
  public static void main(String[] args) {
    String str = "hello";
    StringBuilder sb = new StringBuilder(str);
    sb.reverse();
    if (str == sb) System.out.println("a");
    if (str.equals(sb)) System.out.println("b");
    if (sb.equals(str)) System.out.println("c");
  }
}
```

Select the one correct answer.

(a) The program will fail to compile.

(b) The program will compile, but it will throw an exception at runtime.

(c) The program will compile, but it will not print anything.

(d) The program will compile, and will print abc.

(e) The program will compile, and will print bc.

(f) The program will compile, and will print a.

(g) The program will compile, and will print b.

(h) The program will compile, and will print c.

8.16 What will be the result of attempting to compile and run the following program?

```
public class MyClass {
  public static void main(String[] args) {
    StringBuilder sb = new StringBuilder("Have a nice day");
    sb.setLength(6);
    System.out.println(sb);
  }
}
```

Select the one correct answer.

(a) The code will fail to compile because there is no method named setLength in the StringBuilder class.

(b) The code will fail to compile because the StringBuilder reference sb is not a legal argument to the println() method.

(c) The program will throw a StringIndexOutOfBoundsException at runtime.

(d) The program will print Have a nice day at runtime.

(e) The program will print Have a at runtime.

(f) The program will print ce day at runtime.

8.17 Which statement is true about the following code, where the argument string
" 1234 " has two leading and two trailing spaces?

```java
public class RQ_8_24 {
  public static void main(String[] args) {
    StringBuilder sb = new StringBuilder("  1234  ");
    sb.trimToSize();
    sb.append("!");
    sb.reverse();
    sb.setLength(5);
    System.out.println("|" + sb + "|");
  }
}
```

Select the one correct answer.

(a) The program will print |4321!|.
(b) The program will print |!1234|.
(c) The program will print |! 43|.
(d) The program will print |1234!|.
(e) The program will print |!4321|.
(f) The program will fail to compile.

8.18 What will be the result of attempting to compile and run the following program?

```java
public class PeskyCharSeq {
  public static void main (String[] args) {
    StringBuilder sb1 = new StringBuilder("WOW");
    StringBuilder sb2 = new StringBuilder(sb1);
    System.out.println((sb1==sb2) + " " + sb1.equals(sb2));
  }
}
```

Select the one correct answer.

(a) The program will print false true.
(b) The program will print false false.
(c) The program will print true false.
(d) The program will print true true.
(e) The program will fail to compile.
(f) The program will compile, but it will throw an exception at runtime.

8.19 What will be the result of attempting to compile and run the following program?

```java
public class MoreCharSeq {
  public static void main (String[] args) {
    String s1 = "WOW";
    StringBuilder s2 = new StringBuilder(s1);
    String s3 = new String(s2);
    System.out.println((s1.hashCode() == s2.hashCode()) + " " +
                       (s1.hashCode() == s3.hashCode()));
  }
}
```

Select the one correct answer.

(a) The program will print false true.
(b) The program will print false false.
(c) The program will print true false.
(d) The program will print true true.
(e) The program will fail to compile.
(f) The program will compile, but it will throw an exception at runtime.

8.20 What will be the result of attempting to compile and run the following program?

```java
public class Appendage {
  private static void putO(StringBuilder s1) {
    s1.append("O"),
  }

  public static void main(String[] args) {
    StringBuilder s1 = new StringBuilder("W");
    putO(s1);
    s1.append("W!");
    System.out.println(s1);
  }
}
```

Select the one correct answer.

(a) The program will print WW!.
(b) The program will print WOW!.
(c) The program will print W.
(d) The program will print WO.
(e) The program will fail to compile.
(f) The program will compile, but it will throw an exception at runtime.

8.21 What will the following code print when run?

```java
StringBuilder text = new StringBuilder();
text.append("12");
text.insert(1, "34");
text.delete(1, 1);
text.replace(0, 1, "");
System.out.println(text);
```

Select the one correct answer.

(a) 2
(b) 12
(c) 32
(d) 34
(e) 42
(f) 134
(g) 234
(h) 312
(i) 342
(j) 412

8.22   What will the following code print when run?

```
StringBuilder text = new StringBuilder();
text.append("42");
text.delete(1,2);
System.out.println(text.toString() + (text.capacity() + text.length()));
```

Select the one correct answer.
(a) 416
(b) 417
(c) 4161
(d) 4171
(e) 410
(f) 411
(g) 4101
(h) 4111

8.6 The Math Class

The final class java.lang.Math defines a set of static methods to support common mathematical functions, including functions for rounding numbers, finding the maximum and minimum of two numbers, calculating logarithms and exponentiation, performing exact arithmetic, generating pseudorandom numbers, and much more. The Math class is a utility class and cannot be instantiated.

The final class Math provides constants to represent the value of e, the base of the natural logarithms, and the value π (*pi*), the ratio of the circumference of a circle to its diameter:

```
Math.E
Math.PI
```

Miscellaneous Rounding Functions

```
static int    abs(int i)
static long   abs(long l)
static float  abs(float f)
static double abs(double d)
```

The overloaded method abs() returns the absolute value of the argument. For a non-negative argument, the argument is returned. For a negative argument, the negation of the argument is returned.

```
static int    min(int a, int b)
static long   min(long a, long b)
static float  min(float a, float b)
static double min(double a, double b)
```

The overloaded method min() returns the smaller of the two values a and b for any numeric type.

```
static int    max(int a, int b)
static long   max(long a, long b)
static float  max(float a, float b)
static double max(double a, double b)
```

The overloaded method max() returns the greater of the two values a and b for any numeric type.

The following code illustrates the use of these methods from the Math class:

```
long   l1 = Math.abs(2022L);          // 2022L
double dd = Math.abs(-Math.PI);       // 3.141592653589793

double d1 = Math.min(Math.PI, Math.E);  // 2.718281828459045
long   m1 = Math.max(1984L, 2022L);     // 2022L
int    i1 = (int) Math.max(3.0, 4);     // Cast required.
```

Note the cast required in the last example. The method with the signature max(double, double) is executed, with implicit conversion of the int argument to a double. Since this method returns a double, it must be explicitly cast to an int in order to assign it to an int variable.

```
static double ceil(double d)
```

Returns the *smallest (closest to negative infinity)* double value that is *greater than or equal to* the argument d, and is equal to a mathematical integer.

```
static double floor(double d)
```

Returns the *largest (closest to positive infinity)* double value that is *less than or equal to* the argument d, and is equal to a mathematical integer. Note that Math.ceil(d) is exactly the value of -Math.floor(-d).

```
static int  round(float f)
static long round(double d)
```

The overloaded method round() returns the integer closest to the argument. This is equivalent to adding 0.5 to the argument, taking the floor of the result, and casting it to the return type. This is not the same as rounding to a specific number of decimal places, as the name of the method might suggest.

If the fractional part of a *positive* argument is *less than* 0.5, then the result returned is the same as Math.floor(). If the fractional part of a positive argument is *greater than or equal to* 0.5, then the result returned is the same as Math.ceil().

If the fractional part of a *negative* argument is *less than or equal to* 0.5, then the result returned is the same as Math.ceil(). If the fractional part of a negative argument is *greater than* 0.5, then the result returned is the same as Math.floor().

It is important to note the result obtained on negative arguments, keeping in mind that a negative number whose absolute value is less than that of another negative number is actually greater than the other number (e.g., –3.2 is greater than –4.7). Compare also the results returned by these methods, shown in Table 8.3, p. 480.

```
double upPI    = Math.ceil(3.14);       // 4.0
double downPI  = Math.floor(3.14);      // 3.0
long   roundPI = Math.round(3.14);      // 3L

double upNegPI    = Math.ceil(-3.14);   // -3.0
double downNegPI  = Math.floor(-3.14);  // -4.0
long   roundNegPI = Math.round(-3.14);  // -3L
```

Table 8.3 *Applying Rounding Functions*

Argument:	7.0	7.1	7.2	7.3	7.4	7.5	7.6	7.7	7.8	7.9	8.0
ceil:	7.0	8.0	8.0	8.0	8.0	8.0	8.0	8.0	8.0	8.0	8.0
floor:	7.0	7.0	7.0	7.0	7.0	7.0	7.0	7.0	7.0	7.0	8.0
round:	7	7	7	7	7	8	8	8	8	8	8
Argument:	-7.0	-7.1	-7.2	-7.3	-7.4	-7.5	-7.6	-7.7	-7.8	-7.9	-8.0
ceil:	-7.0	-7.0	-7.0	-7.0	-7.0	-7.0	-7.0	-7.0	-7.0	-7.0	-8.0
floor:	-7.0	-8.0	-8.0	-8.0	-8.0	-8.0	-8.0	-8.0	-8.0	-8.0	-8.0
round:	-7	-7	-7	-7	-7	-7	-8	-8	-8	-8	-8

Exponential Functions

`static double pow(double d1, double d2)`
Returns the value of d1 raised to the power of d2 (i.e., $d1^{d2}$).

`static double exp(double d)`
Returns the exponential number e raised to the power of d (i.e., e^d).

`static double log(double d)`
Returns the natural logarithm (base e) of d (i.e., $\log_e d$).

`static double sqrt(double d)`
Returns the square root of d (i.e., $d^{0.5}$). For a NaN or a negative argument, the result is a NaN.

Some examples of exponential functions:

```
double r = Math.pow(2.0, 4.0);   // 16.0
double v = Math.exp(2.0);        // 7.38905609893065
double l = Math.log(Math.E);     // 0.9999999999999981
double c = Math.sqrt(25.0);      // 5.0
```

Exact Integer Arithmetic Functions

Integer arithmetic operators (like +, -, *) do not report *overflow errors*—that is, the integer values *wrap around* (§2.8, p. 59). However, if it is important to detect overflow errors, the Math class provides methods that report overflow errors by throwing an ArithmeticException when performing integer arithmetic operations. The relevant methods have the postfix "Exact" in their name, and are shown below.

The code snippets below illustrate exact integer arithmetic operations provided by the Math class, where we assume the field System.out is statically imported. The results computed at (1a), (2a), and (3a) are incorrect due to overflow, but the standard arithmetic operators do not report overflow errors. (1b), (2b), and (3b) use exact arithmetic operations and throw an ArithmeticException when an overflow is detected. (1c), (2c), and (3c) compute correct results as there is no overflow in performing the operation.

```
out.println(Integer.MAX_VALUE + 1);                      // (1a) -2147483648
out.println(Math.addExact(Integer.MAX_VALUE, 1));        // (1b) ArithmeticException
out.println(Math.addExact(1_000_000, 1_000));            // (1c) 1001000

out.println(Integer.MAX_VALUE * 100);                    // (2a) -100
out.println(
    Math.multiplyExact(Integer.MAX_VALUE, 100)           // (2b) ArithmeticException
);
out.println(Math.multiplyExact(1_000_000, 1_000));       // (2c) 1000000000

out.println((int)Long.MAX_VALUE);                        // (3a) -1
out.println(Math.toIntExact(Long.MAX_VALUE));            // (3b) ArithmeticException
out.println(Math.toIntExact(1_000_000));                 // (3c) 1000000
```

Selected exact integer arithmetic methods in the Math class are shown below.

```
static int  absExact(int a)
static long absExact(long a)
```

Return the mathematical absolute value of an int or a long value if it is exactly representable as an int or a long, throwing ArithmeticException if the argument is Integer.MIN_VALUE or Long.MIN_VALUE, as these argument values would overflow the positive int or long range, respectively.

```
static int  addExact(int x, int y)
static long addExact(long x, long y)
static int  subtractExact(int x, int y)
static long subtractExact(long x, long y)
```

Return the sum or difference of the given arguments, throwing Arithmetic-Exception if the result overflows an int or a long, respectively.

```
static int  multiplyExact(int x, int y)
static long multiplyExact(long x, int y)
static long multiplyExact(long x, long y)
```

Return the product of the arguments, throwing ArithmeticException if the result overflows an int in the first method or a long in the last two methods.

```
static int  incrementExact(int a)
static long incrementExact(long a)
static int  decrementExact(int a)
static long decrementExact(long a)
```

Return the argument incremented or decremented by 1, throwing Arithmetic-Exception if the result overflows an int or a long, respectively.

```
static int  negateExact(int a)
static long negateExact(long a)
```

Return the negation of the argument, throwing ArithmeticException if the result overflows an int or a long, respectively.

```
static int toIntExact(long value)
```

Returns the value of the long argument as an int, throwing ArithmeticException if the value overflows an int.

Pseudorandom Number Generator

The class Math provides the random() method for generating pseudorandom numbers of type double that are in the open interval [0.0, 1.0). The Random class (p. 482) should also be considered, as it is more versatile and easier to use.

```
static double random()
```

Returns a random number greater than or equal to 0.0 and less than 1.0, where the value is selected randomly from the range according to a uniform distribution.

We can simulate a dice roll as follows:

```
int diceValue = 1 + (int)(Math.random() * 6.0);  // A dice roll in range [1 .. 6]
```

The dice value will always be in the interval [1, 6], depending on the pseudorandom number returned by the Math.random() method, as we can see from the sample dice rolls below.

```
Math.random():   {0.0, 0.1, 0.2, 0.3, 0.4, 0.5, 0.6, 0.7, 0.8, 0.9}
Multiply by 6:   {0.0, 0.6, 1.2, 1.8, 2.4, 3.0, 3,6, 4.2, 4.8, 5.4}
Convert to int:  {0,   0,   1,   1,   2,   3,   3,   4,   4,   5}
Add offset 1:    {1,   1,   2,   2,   3,   4,   4,   5,   5,   6}
```

8.7 The Random Class

In computer games and simulations we often need to generate a sequence of random numbers. For a dice game it is necessary to simulate rolling the dice—that is, generating a dice roll value between 1 and 6. Ideally, the probability of a given value is the same (one-sixth) for each value on a die. The numbers generated this way are called *random numbers*. To generate random numbers with the help of a program is not possible, as a program can only compute values, not pick them randomly. To guarantee equal probability for all cases is very difficult, so we have to settle for *pseudorandom numbers*—that is, a sequence of numbers that closely approximates a sequence of random numbers. A lot of research has gone into finding mathematical formulae that compute good approximations to random numbers.

The java.util.Random class implements the java.util.random.RandomGenerator interface that defines the common protocol for pseudorandom number generators (PRNGs) in Java.

Generating *numeric streams of pseudorandom values* using the Random class is covered with the discussion on creating streams (§16.4, p. 900).

The following constructors can be used to create a new random number generator, optionally specifying a *seed* value (p. 484).

```
Random()
Random(long seed)
```

The Random class implements PRNGs for different primitive data types. The appropriate *next* method can be called on a Random object to obtain the next pseudorandom value.

```
int     nextInt()
int     nextInt(int bound)
long    nextLong()
float   nextFloat()
double  nextDouble()
boolean nextBoolean()
```

Return the next pseudorandom, uniformly distributed value that is either int, int between 0 and bound (exclusive), long, float between 0.0f and 1.0f (exclusive), double between 0.0d and 1.0d (exclusive), or true/false, respectively.

Here we will concentrate on a pseudorandom generator for int values, but first we need to create an object of the Random class:

```
Random generator = new Random();
```

We can then call the method nextInt() repeatedly on this object every time we need a new random int value:

```
int number = generator.nextInt();
```

Each call to the method will return a random integer in the interval $[-2^{31}, 2^{31} - 1]$, which is the range of the int data type.

Determining the Range

We are often interested in generating random numbers in a particular range. For example, the following code will return a random number in the interval [0, 10]:

```
number = generator.nextInt(11);      // Random integer in the interval [0, 10]
```

If the bound value is n, the integer returned is in the interval [0, n-1]. By supplying a new bound value to the nextInt() method, we can change the upper bound of the original interval.

If we want to shift the interval, we can add (or subtract) an offset from the value returned by the nextInt() method. In the code below, values generated in the original interval [0, 10] will now lie in the interval [2, 12]—that is, the offset 2 maps the interval [0, 10] onto the interval [2, 12]:

```
number = 2 + generator.nextInt(11);  // Random integer in the interval [2, 12]
```

If we want the values in the interval to have a distance greater than 1, we can multiply the value generated by a distance value:

```
number = 2 + 3*generator.nextInt(5); // Random integer in the set {2, 5, 8, 11, 14}
```

With a distance value of 3, the expression 3*generator.nextInt(5) always returns a value in the set {0, 3, 6, 9, 12}, and an offset of 2 ensures that the variable number is assigned a value from the set {2, 5, 8, 11, 14}.

We can simulate a dice roll as follows:

```
int diceValue = 1 + generator.nextInt(6);  // A dice value in the interval [1, 6]
```

The expression generator.nextInt(6) always returns a value in the set {0, 1, 2, 3, 4, 5}, and an offset of 1 ensures that the variable diceValue is assigned a value from the set {1, 2, 3, 4, 5, 6}.

Generating the Same Sequence of Pseudorandom Numbers

The way in which we have used the pseudorandom number generator up to now cannot guarantee the same sequence of pseudorandom numbers each time the program is run. This is because the pseudorandom number generator is based on the time of the system clock. This is obviously different each time the program is run. If we want to generate the same sequence of pseudorandom numbers each time the program is run, we can specify a *seed* in the call to the Random constructor:

```
Random persistentGenerator = new Random(31);
```

In the declaration above, the seed is the prime number 31. The seed is usually a prime number (i.e., a number that is only divisible by itself or one), as such numbers are highly suitable for implementing good, viable pseudorandom number generators.

8.8 Using Big Numbers

There is a need for greater precision in arithmetic calculations than the precision offered by arithmetic operators performing calculations on finite-precision values of numeric primitive types. This is especially true for calculations involving financial or monetary values, where accumulation of rounding errors and precision is paramount. The classes `BigInteger` and `BigDecimal` in the `java.math` package support arbitrary-precision integers and arbitrary-precision decimal numbers, respectively, and provide methods for arbitrary-precision computations (Table 8.4). Both classes extend the `java.lang.Number` abstract class (Figure 8.1).

Table 8.4 *Big Number Classes*

Big number classes in the java.math package	Description
BigDecimal extends Number	A class that represents immutable, arbitrary-precision, signed decimal numbers
BigInteger extends Number	A class that represents immutable, arbitrary-precision signed integers

A `BigDecimal` is represented as an arbitrary-precision *unscaled integer value* and a 32-bit *integer scale*. For a non-negative unscaled value, the scale represents the number of digits to the right of the decimal point. For a negative unscaled value, the number represented is (unscaled value * 10^{-scale}). For example:

```
The BigDecimal  3.14   has unscaled value =  314   and scale = 2.
The BigDecimal -3.1415 has unscaled value = -31415 and scale = 4.
```

The `BigDecimal` class can represent very large and very small decimal numbers with very high precision. The class provides methods that allow control over scale and rounding behavior for arithmetic operations. In addition, the class provides support for converting to different representations and comparing `BigDecimal` values.

Formatting, parsing, and rounding of `BigDecimal` values is covered with formatting of numbers and currency (§18.5, p. 1116).

A `BigInteger` represents an arbitrary-precision signed integer value in base 10 and two's-complement notation, which is internally implemented by an arbitrary-size int array. The `BigInteger` class has methods analogous to the `BigDecimal` class for arithmetic calculations, conversions, and comparison.

Here we will only provide a few examples of using the `BigDecimal` class. The API for the `BigDecimal` and `BigInteger` classes in the java.math package should be consulted, both for details on features presented here and additional features provided for high-precision manipulation of big numbers.

BigDecimal **Constants**

The class `BigDecimal` provides the following ready-made constants corresponding to the decimal values 0, 1, and 10, that are represented with a scale of 0:

```
BigDecimal.ZERO
BigDecimal.ONE
BigDecimal.TEN
```

Constructing BigDecimal Numbers

Selected constructors of the BigDecimal class are shown below.

```
BigDecimal(int value)
BigDecimal(long value)
BigDecimal(double value)
```

Create a BigDecimal with the decimal number representation of the specified value. Note that these constructors can result in a loss of precision if the specified numerical value does not have an exact representation.

```
BigDecimal(String strValue)
```

Creates a BigDecimal from the string representation of a numerical value. Recommended as the preferred way of creating BigDecimal numbers.

The following valueOf() methods also create BigDecimal numbers:

```
static BigDecimal valueOf(long value)
static BigDecimal valueOf(double value)
```

Create a BigDecimal from the specified numerical value. The second method uses the string representation of the double value obtained from the Double.toString(double) method to create a BigDecimal.

The following code creates BigDecimal values and also shows the string representation of the BigDecimal numbers created. It shows that the constructor BigDecimal(String) or the static valueOf() methods are preferable when creating BigDecimal values, especially for decimal values that cannot be represented as exact double values.

```
BigDecimal dTobd   = new BigDecimal(0.7);        // 0.6999999999999999555910...
BigDecimal strTobd = new BigDecimal("0.7");      // 0.7
BigDecimal valTobd = BigDecimal.valueOf(0.7);    // 0.7
```

Computing with BigDecimal Numbers

Selected methods that perform common arithmetic operations with BigDecimal numbers are given below.

The limitations of arithmetic operators on decimal values are shown by the code below. An incorrect result may be computed if the representation of a decimal value is inexact in the format of the double primitive type.

```
double d1 = 0.70;
double d2 = 0.10;
System.out.println(d1 + d2);
```

Output: 0.7999999999999999

However, using BigDecimal values gives the correct result:

```
BigDecimal bd1b = new BigDecimal("0.70");
BigDecimal bd2b = new BigDecimal("0.10");
System.out.println(bd1b.add(bd2b));
```

Output: 0.80

Finally, here is a simple arithmetic calculation using BigDecimal numbers to compute the total cost of 10^3 items, priced at \$2.99 each and 25% sales tax.

```
BigDecimal price     = new BigDecimal("2.99");
BigDecimal tax       = new BigDecimal("0.25");
BigDecimal quantity  = BigDecimal.TEN.pow(3);
BigDecimal totalCost = price.add(price.multiply(tax)).multiply(quantity);
System.out.println(totalCost);
```

Output: 3737.5000

It is worth keeping in mind that BigDecimal numbers are immutable, and not to fall into the pitfall shown in the code below:

```
BigDecimal sum = BigDecimal.ZERO;
sum.add(BigDecimal.ONE);            // sum is not updated! Returns new BigDecimal.
```

Selected methods for computing with BigDecimal numbers:

```
BigDecimal add(BigDecimal val)
BigDecimal subtract(BigDecimal val)
BigDecimal multiply(BigDecimal val)
BigDecimal divide(BigDecimal val)
BigDecimal remainder(BigDecimal val)
```

Return a BigDecimal whose value represents the result of performing the operation (this + val), (this - val), (this * val), (this / val), or (this % val), respectively.

```
BigDecimal abs()
```

Returns a BigDecimal whose value is the absolute value of this BigDecimal.

```
BigDecimal negate()
```

Returns a BigDecimal whose value is (-this).

```
BigDecimal pow(int n)
```

Returns a BigDecimal whose value is (this^n).

 ## Review Questions

8.23 Given the following program, which lines will print 11 exactly?

```
class MyClass {
    public static void main(String[] args) {
        double v = 10.5;
```

```
System.out.println(Math.ceil(v));        // (1)
System.out.println(Math.round(v));       // (2)
System.out.println(Math.floor(v));       // (3)
System.out.println((int) Math.ceil(v));  // (4)
System.out.println((int) Math.floor(v)); // (5)
    }
}
```

Select the two correct answers.

(a) The line at (1).
(b) The line at (2).
(c) The line at (3).
(d) The line at (4).
(e) The line at (5).

8.24 What will be the result of attempting to compile and run the following program?

```
public class Round {
    public static void main(String[] args) {
        System.out.println(Math.round(-0.5) + " " + Math.round(0.5));
    }
};
```

Select the one correct answer.

(a) 0 0
(b) 0 1
(c) -1 0
(d) -1 1
(e) None of the above

8.25 Which of the following statements are true about the expression ((int)(Math.random()*4))?
Select the three correct answers.

(a) It may evaluate to a negative number.
(b) It may evaluate to the number 0.
(c) The probability of it evaluating to the number 1 or the number 2 is the same.
(d) It may evaluate to the number 3.
(e) It may evaluate to the number 4.

Nested Type Declarations

 Chapter Topics

- Categorizing nested classes:
    - Static member type which can be a class, an enum type, a record class, or an interface
    - Inner class which can be a non-static member class, a local class, or an anonymous class
    - Static local type which can be an interface, an enum type, or a record class

- Understanding the salient aspects of nested types:
    - The context in which they can be defined
    - Which accessibility modifiers are valid for nested types
    - Whether an instance of the enclosing context is associated with an instance of the nested class
    - Which entities a nested type can access in its enclosing context and in its inheritance hierarchy
    - Whether both static and non-static members can be defined in a nested type

- Importing and using nested types

- Instantiating non-static member classes using the *enclosing_object_reference*.new syntax

- Accessing members in the enclosing context of inner classes using the *enclosing_class_name*.this syntax

- Implementing anonymous classes by extending an existing class or by implementing an interface

Java SE 17 Developer Exam Objectives	
[3.1] Declare and instantiate Java objects including nested class objects, and explain the object life-cycle including creation, reassigning references, and garbage collection ○ *Only nested types are covered in this chapter.* ○ *For object lifecycle and garbage collection, see Chapter 10, p. 531.*	*§9.1, p. 491* *to* *§9.6, p. 521*

Java SE 11 Developer Exam Objectives	
[3.1] Declare and instantiate Java objects including nested class objects, and explain objects' lifecycles (including creation, dereferencing by reassignment, and garbage collection) ○ Only nested types are covered in this chapter. ○ For object lifecycle and garbage collection, see Chapter 10, p. 531.	§9.1, p. 191 to §9.6, p. 521

This chapter covers the different kinds of nested type declarations—that is, type declarations that can be declared inside a language construct such as a class, an interface, or even a method. In particular, we look at declaring, instantiating, and using such types. Since they are nested, we consider the rules for accessing entities in their enclosing context and in their inheritance hierarchy. Please hold on, as we first introduce the terminology for these nested types.

9.1 Overview of Nested Type Declarations

A *type declaration* allows a *new reference type* to be defined. A type declaration can either be a *top-level type declaration* or a *nested type declaration*. Figure 9.1 gives an overview of the different kinds of type declarations that can be defined in Java.

Figure 9.1 *Overview of Type Declarations*

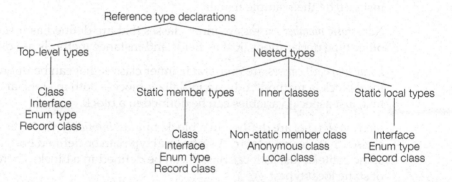

A *top-level type declaration* is a type declaration that is *not* defined inside another type declaration. A top-level type declaration can be any one of the following: a *top-level class*, a *top-level interface*, a *top-level enum type*, or a *top-level record class*. We invariably use the shorter names *class*, *interface*, *enum type*, and *record class* when it is clear we are not referring to their nested counterparts.

A *nested type declaration* is a type declaration that is defined inside another declaration. There are three categories of nested types:

- Static member types (a.k.a. *static nested types*)
- Inner classes (a.k.a. *non-static nested classes*)
- Static local types (a.k.a. *static local nested types*)

As the name implies, *static member types* can be declared as a static *member* of either a top-level type or a nested type declaration. There are four kinds of static member types:

- Static member class (a.k.a. *static nested class*)
- Static member interface (a.k.a. *nested interface*)

- Static member enum type (a.k.a. *nested enum type*)
- Static member record class (a.k.a. *nested record class*)

A static member class or record class can be instantiated like any ordinary top-level class or record class, using its *qualified name* when calling the constructor with the new operator. It is not possible to instantiate an enum type or an interface.

Inner classes are non-static nested classes. There are three kinds of inner classes:

- Non-static member class
- Local class
- Anonymous class

Inner classes differ from static member classes in one important aspect: An instance of an inner class has an instance of the enclosing class (called the *immediately enclosing instance*) associated with it when the inner class is declared in a non-static context. An instance of an inner class can access the members of its enclosing instance by their simple names.

Non-static member classes are inner classes that are defined as instance members of other type declarations, just as fields and instance methods are defined in a class.

Local (normal) classes are non-static inner classes that can be defined in a block—a local block, a method body, an initializer block—both in static and non-static context, just as local variables can be defined in a block.

Static local types are defined in a block, but are *implicitly* static as opposed to local classes that are non-static. A static local type can be defined both in static and non-static context, just as local classes can be defined in a block. There are three kinds of static local types:

- Static local interface
- Static local enum type
- Static local record class

Anonymous classes are inner classes that can be defined as expressions and in expression statements, both in static and non-static context, and instantiated *on the fly*.

In Figure 9.1 we see that there are four kinds of *nested classes* (static member classes, non-static member classes, local classes, anonymous classes), two kinds of *nested interfaces* (static member interfaces, static local interfaces), two kinds of *nested enum types* (static member enum types, static local enum types), and two kinds of *nested record classes* (static member record classes, static local record classes)—all defined by the context in which these nested types are declared.

Given the terminology introduced for nested types in Figure 9.1, a *member type declaration* can be any one of the following nested types: a static member type (class, interface, enum type, record class) or a non-static member class. Note that local classes, anonymous classes, local interfaces, local enum types, and local record classes are *not* member type declarations, as they *cannot* be declared as a *member* of a type declaration.

Example 9.1 *Overview of Type Declarations*

```
class TLC {                           // (1) Top-level class

  // Static member types:
  static class    SMC {}              // (2) Static member class
         interface SMI {}             // (3) Static member interface
         enum     SME {}              // (4) Static member enum
         record   SMR() {}            // (5) Static member record

  // Non-static member class:
  class NSMC {}                       // (6) Inner class

  // Local types in non-static context (analogous for static context).
  void nsm() {                        // Non-static method
    class     LC {}                   // (7) Local class (inner class)
    interface SLI {}                  // (8) Static local interface
    enum      SLE {}                  // (9) Static local enum
    record    SLR() {}                // (10) Static local record
  }

  // Anonymous classes (here defined as initializer expressions):
         SMC nsf = new SMC() {};  // (11) Inner class in non-static context
  static SMI  sf = new SMI() {};  // (12) Inner class in static context
}
```

Skeletal code for nested types is shown in Example 9.1. Table 9.1 presents a summary of various aspects relating to nested types. Subsequent sections on each nested type elaborate on the summary presented in this table. (*N/A* in the table means *"not applicable"*.)

- The *Type* column lists the different kinds of types that can be declared.
- The *Declaration context* column lists the lexical context in which a type can be declared.
- The *Access modifiers* column indicates what access can be specified for the type.
- The *Enclosing instance* column specifies whether an enclosing instance is associated with an instance of the type.
- The *Direct access to enclosing context* column lists what is directly accessible in the enclosing context from within the type.

Generic nested classes and interfaces are discussed in §11.13, p. 633. It is not possible to declare a generic enum type (§11.13, p. 635).

Locks on nested classes are discussed in §22.4, p. 1391.

Nested types can be regarded as a form of encapsulation, enforcing relationships between types by greater proximity. They allow structuring of types and a special binding relationship between a nested object and its enclosing instance. Used judiciously, they can be beneficial, but unrestrained use of nested types can easily result in unreadable code.

A word about the examples in this chapter: They are concocted to illustrate various aspects of nested types, and are not solutions to any well-defined or meaningful problems.

Table 9.1 *Various Aspects of Type Declarations*

Type	Declaration context	Access modifiers	Enclosing instance	Direct access to enclosing context
Top-level class, interface, enum type, or record class *(Top-level types)*	Package	public or package access	No	N/A
Static member class, interface, enum type, or record class *(Static member types)*	As static member of a top-level type or a nested type	All, except when declared in interfaces whose member type declarations are implicitly public	No	Static members in enclosing context
Non-static member class *(Inner class)*	As non-static member of a top-level type or a nested type	All	Yes	All members in enclosing context
Local class *(Inner class)*	In block with non-static context	None	Yes	All members in enclosing context plus final or effectively final local variables
	In block with static context	None	No	Static members in enclosing context plus final or effectively final local variables
Anonymous class *(Inner class)*	As expression in non-static context	None	Yes	All members in enclosing context plus final or effectively final local variables
	As expression in static context	None	No	Static members in enclosing context plus final or effectively final local variables
Local interface, enum type, or record class *(Static local types)*	In block with static and non-static context	None	No	Static members in enclosing context

9.2 Static Member Types

Declaring Static Member Types

Static member types can be declared in top-level type declarations, or within other nested types. For all intents and purposes, a static member type is very much like a top-level type.

A static member class, enum type, record class, or *interface* has the same declarations as those allowed in a top-level class, enum type, record class, or interface type, respectively. A static member class is declared with the keyword static, except when declared in an interface where a static member class is considered implicitly static. Static member enum types, record classes and interfaces are considered implicitly static, and the keyword static can be omitted.

Any access level (public, protected, package, private) can be specified for a static member type, except when declared in interfaces, where public access is implied for member type declarations.

Although the discussion in this section is primarily about static member classes and interfaces, it is also applicable to static member enum types and record classes.

In Example 9.2, the top-level class ListPool at (1) declares the static member class MyLinkedList at (2), which in turn defines a static member interface ILink at (3) and a static member class BiNode at (4). The static member class BiNode at (4) implements the static member interface IBiLink declared at (7). Note that each static member class is defined as static, just like static variables and methods in a top-level class.

In Example 9.2, an attempt to declare the static member class Traversal with private access at (8) in the interface IBiLink results in a compile-time error, as only public access is permitted for interface members. Since the class BiTraversal at (9) is defined in an interface; it is implicitly public and static, and *not* a non-static member class with package access.

The static member class SortCriteria at (11) in the non-static member class SortedList is allowed, as a static member type can be declared in non-static context.

Example 9.2 *Static Member Types*

```
// File: ListPool.java
package smc;

public class ListPool {                       // (1) Top-level class

    public static class MyLinkedList {        // (2) Static member class

        private interface ILink { }           // (3) Static member interface

        public static class BiNode            // (4) Static member class
                    implements IBiLink {
```

```
        public static void printSimpleName() {        // (5) Static method
          System.out.println(BiNode.class.getSimpleName());
        }

        public void printName() {                     // (6) Instance method
          System.out.println(this.getClass().getName());
        }
      } // end BiNode
    } // end MyLinkedList

    interface IBiLink
            extends MyLinkedList.ILink {           // (7) Static member interface
//    private static class Traversal { }           // (8) Compile-time error!
                                                   //     Can only be public.
      class BiTraversal { }                        // (9) Class is public and static
    } // end IBiLink

    public class SortedList {                      // (10) Non-static member class
      private static class SortCriteria {}         // (11) Static member class
    }
  }
```

```
// File: MyBiLinkedList.java
package smc;

public class MyBiLinkedList implements ListPool.IBiLink {        // (12)

  public static void main(String[] args) {
    ListPool.MyLinkedList.BiNode.printSimpleName();              // (13)
    ListPool.MyLinkedList.BiNode node1
            = new ListPool.MyLinkedList.BiNode();                // (14)
    node1.printName();                                           // (15)

//  ListPool.MyLinkedList.ILink ref;                             // (16) Compile-time error!
  }
}
```

Output from the program:

```
BiNode
smc.ListPool$MyLinkedList$BiNode
```

Using Qualified Name of Nested Types

The *qualified name* of a (static or non-static) member type includes the names of the enclosing types it is lexically nested in—that is, it associates the member type with its enclosing types. In Example 9.2, the qualified name of the static member class BiNode at (4) is ListPool.MyLinkedList.BiNode. The qualified name of the nested interface IBiLink at (7) is ListPool.IBiLink, determined by the lexical nesting of the types. Each member class or interface is uniquely identified by this naming syntax, which is a generalization of the naming scheme for packages. The qualified name can be used in exactly the same way as any other top-level class or interface name, as shown at (12) and (13). Such a member's *fully qualified name* is its qualified name prefixed by the name of its package. For example, the fully qualified name of the static member class at (4) is smc.ListPool.MyLinkedList.BiNode. Note that a nested member type cannot have the same name as an enclosing type.

If the source file ListPool.java containing the declarations in Example 9.2 is compiled, it will result in the generation of the following class files in the package smc, where each class file corresponds to either a class or an interface declaration in the source file:

```
ListPool$IBiLink$BiTraversal.class
ListPool$IBiLink.class
ListPool$MyLinkedList$BiNode.class
ListPool$MyLinkedList$ILink.class
ListPool$MyLinkedList.class
ListPool$SortedList.class
ListPool.class
```

Note how the full class name corresponds to the class file name (minus the extension), with the dollar symbol ($) replaced by the dot (.).

Within the scope of its top-level type, a static member type can be referenced regardless of its access modifier and lexical nesting, as shown at (7) in Example 9.2. Although the interface MyLinkedList.ILink has private access, it is accessible at (7), outside its enclosing class. Its access modifier (and that of the types making up its qualified name) comes into play when it is referenced by an external client. The declaration at (16) in Example 9.2 will not compile because the member interface ListPool.MyLinkedList.ILink has private access.

Instantiating Static Member Classes

A static member class can be instantiated without first creating an instance of the enclosing class. Example 9.2 shows a client creating an instance of a static member class at (14) using the new operator and the qualified name of the class. Not surprisingly, the compiler will flag an error if any of the types in the qualified name are not accessible by an external client.

```
ListPool.MyLinkedList.BiNode objRef1
        = new ListPool.MyLinkedList.BiNode();                    // (14)
```

External clients must use the (fully) qualified name of a static member class in order to access such a class.

A static member class is loaded and initialized when the types in its enclosing context are loaded at runtime. Analogous to top-level classes, nested static members can always be accessed by the qualified name of the class, and no instance of the enclosing type is required, as shown at (13) where the full class name is used to invoke the static method printSimpleName() at (5) in the static member class BiNode. At (15), the reference node1 is used to invoke the instance method print-Name() at (6) in an instance of the static member class BiNode. An instance of a static member class can exist independently of any instance of its enclosing class.

Importing Static Member Types

There is seldom any reason to import nested types from packages. It would undermine the encapsulation achieved by such types. However, a compilation unit can use the import facility to provide a shortcut for the names of member types. Note that type import and static import of static member types are equivalent. Type import can be used to import the static member type as a type name, and static import can be used to import the static member type as the name of a static member.

Usage of the (static) import declaration for static member classes is illustrated in Example 9.3. In the file Client1.java, the import statement at (1) allows the static member class BiNode to be referenced as MyLinkedList.BiNode at (2), whereas in the file Client2.java, the static import at (3) allows the same class to be referenced using its simple name, as at (4). At (5), the fully qualified name of the static member interface is used in an implements clause. However, in Example 9.2 at (5), the interface smc.ListPool.IBiLink is declared with package access in its enclosing class ListPool in the package smc, and therefore is not visible in other packages, including the default package.

Example 9.3 *Importing Static Member Types*

```
// File: Client1.java
import smc.ListPool.MyLinkedList;                           // (1) Type import

public class Client1 {
  MyLinkedList.BiNode objRef1 = new MyLinkedList.BiNode(); // (2)
}
```

```
// File: Client2.java
import static smc.ListPool.MyLinkedList.BiNode;            // (3) Static import

public class Client2 {
  BiNode objRef2 = new BiNode();                          // (4)
}

//class BiListPool implements smc.ListPool.IBiLink { }    // (5) Compile-time error!
                                                          // Not accessible!
```

Accessing Members in Enclosing Context

Static member classes do not have a this reference, as they do not have any notion of an enclosing instance. This means that *any* code in a static member class can *only* directly access static members in its enclosing context. Trying to access any instance members directly in its enclosing context results in a compile-time error.

Figure 9.2 is a class diagram that illustrates static member classes and interfaces. These are shown as members of the enclosing context, with the {static} tag to indicate that they are static members. Since they are members of a class or an interface, their accessibility can be specified exactly like that of any other member of a class or interface: Class members can be declared with any of the four access levels (public, protected, package, private), but interface members are always implicitly public. The classes from the diagram are implemented in Example 9.4.

Figure 9.2   *Static Member Classes and Interfaces*

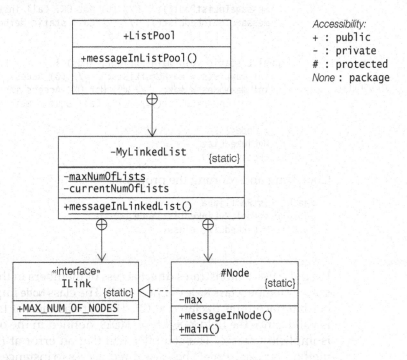

Accessibility:
+ : public
- : private
: protected
None : package

......

Example 9.4   *Accessing Members in Enclosing Context (Static Member Classes)*

```
// File: ListPool.java
public class ListPool {                                 // Top-level class

  public void messageInListPool() {                     // Instance method
    System.out.println("This is a ListPool object.");
  }

  private static class MyLinkedList {                   // (1) Static member class
    private static int maxNumOfLists = 100;             // Static field
    private int currentNumOfLists;                      // Instance field

    public static void messageInLinkedList() {          // Static method
      System.out.println("This is MyLinkedList class.");
    }

    interface ILink { int MAX_NUM_OF_NODES = 2000; }// (2) Static member interface

    protected static class Node implements ILink {  // (3) Static member class
```

```
       private int max = MAX_NUM_OF_NODES;               // (4) Instance field

       public void messageInNode() {                    // Instance method
//        int currentLists = currentNumOfLists;// (5) Not OK. Access instance field
                                              //              in outer class
          int maxLists = maxNumOfLists;      // Access static field in outer class
          int maxNodes = max;                // Access instance field in member class

//        messageInListPool();     // (6) Not OK. Call instance method in outer class
          messageInLinkedList();   // (7) Call static method in outer class
       }

       public static void main(String[] args) {
          int maxLists = maxNumOfLists;     // (8) Access static field in outer class
//        int maxNodes = max;     // (9) Not OK. Access instance field in member class
          messageInLinkedList();// (10) Call static method in outer class
       }
    }  // Node
  } // MyLinkedList
} // ListPool
```

Compiling and running the program:

```
>javac ListPool.java
>java ListPool$MyLinkedList$Node
This is MyLinkedList class.
```

Example 9.4 demonstrates direct access of members in the enclosing context of the static member class Node defined at (3). The class Node implements the static member interface ILink declared at (2). The initialization of the instance field max at (4) is valid, since the field MAX_NUM_OF_NODES, defined in the outer interface ILink at (2), is implicitly static. The compiler will flag an error at (5) and (6) in the instance method messageInNode() because direct access to instance members in the enclosing context is not permitted by *any* method in a static member class. It will also flag an error at (9) in the method main() because a static method cannot directly access instance fields in its own class. The statements at (8) and (10) can directly access static members in the enclosing context. The references in these two statements can also be specified using qualified names.

```
int maxLists = ListPool.MyLinkedList.maxNumOfLists;           // (8')
ListPool.MyLinkedList.messageInLinkedList();                  // (10')
```

Note that a static member class can define both static and instance members, like any other top-level class. However, its code can only directly access static members in its enclosing context.

Example 9.4 also illustrates that static member types when declared as class members can have any access level. In the class ListPool, the static member class MyLinkedList at (1) has private access, whereas its static member interface ILink at (2) has package access and its static member class Node at (3) has protected access.

The class Node defines the method main() which can be executed by the following command:

```
>java ListPool$MyLinkedList$Node
```

Note that the class Node in the command line is specified using the qualified name of the class file minus the extension.

9.3　Non-Static Member Classes

Declaring Non-Static Member Classes

Non-static member classes are *inner classes*—that is, non-static nested classes—that are defined without the keyword static as instance members of either a class, an enum type, or a record class. Non-static member classes cannot be declared as an instance member in an interface, as a class member in an interface is implicitly static. Non-static member classes are on par with other non-static members defined in a reference type.

Since a non-static member class can be an instance member of a class, an enum type, or a record class, it can have any accessibility: public, package, protected, or private.

The compiler generates separate class files for the non-static member classes defined in a top-level type declaration, as it does for static member classes.

A typical application of non-static member classes is implementing data structures. For example, a class for linked lists could define the nodes in the list with the help of a non-static member class which could be declared private so that it was not accessible outside the top-level class, but also nodes could not exist without the list object of the enclosing class. Nesting promotes encapsulation, and the close proximity allows classes to exploit each other's capabilities.

Example 9.5 illustrates nesting and use of non-static member classes, and is in no way meant to be a complete implementation for linked lists. The class MyLinkedList at (1) defines a non-static member class Node at (5). The class Node has public access.

Example 9.5　*Defining and Instantiating Non-Static Member Classes*

```
// File: ListClient.java
class MyLinkedList {                              // (1)
  private String message = "Shine the light";     // (2)

  public Node makeNode(String info, Node next) {  // (3)
    return new Node(info, next);                  // (4)
  }

  public class Node {                             // (5) Non-static member class
    // Static field:
    static int maxNumOfNodes = 100;               // (6)
```

```
      // Instance fields:
      private String nodeInfo;                          // (7)
      private Node next;

      // Non-zero argument constructor:
      public Node(String nodeInfo, Node next) {         // (8)
        this.nodeInfo = nodeInfo;
        this.next = next;
      }

      // Instance methods:
      public Node getNext() { return next; }
      @Override
      public String toString() {
        return message + " in " + nodeInfo + " (" + maxNumOfNodes + ")"; // (9)
      }
    }
  }
}
//_____
public class ListClient {                                 // (10)
  public static void main(String[] args) {                // (11)
    MyLinkedList list = new MyLinkedList();               // (12)
    MyLinkedList.Node node1 = list.makeNode("node1", null); // (13)
    MyLinkedList.Node node2 = list.new Node("node2", node1);// (14)
    for (MyLinkedList.Node node = node2;
        node!=null;
        node = node.getNext()) {                          // (15)
      System.out.println(node);
    }

    // MyLinkedList.Node nodeX
    //             = new MyLinkedList.Node("nodeX", node1);   // (16) Not OK.

  }
}
```

Output from the program:

```
Shine the light in node1 (100)
Shine the light in node2 (100)
```

Instantiating Non-Static Member Classes

An instance of a non-static member class can only exist when associated with an instance of its enclosing class. This means that an instance of a non-static member class must be created in the context of an instance of the enclosing class. In other words, the non-static member class does not provide any services; only instances of the class do.

A special form of the new operator (called the *qualified class instance creation expression*) is used to instantiate a non-static member class and associate it with the immediately enclosing object:

enclosing_object_reference.new *non_static_member_class_constructor_call*

The *enclosing object reference* in the instance creation expression evaluates to an instance of the immediately enclosing class in which the designated non-static member class is defined. A new instance of the non-static member class is created and associated with the indicated instance of the enclosing class. Note that the expression returns a reference value that denotes a new instance of the non-static member class. It is illegal to specify the qualified name of the non-static member class in the constructor call, as the enclosing context is already given by the *enclosing object reference*.

In Example 9.5, the non-static method makeNode() at (3) in the class MyLinkedList illustrates how to instantiate a non-static member class in non-static context within the enclosing class. The non-static method makeNode() creates an instance of the non-static member class Node using the new operator, as shown at (4):

```
return new Node(info, next);                    // (4)
```

This creates an instance of the non-static member class Node in the context of the current instance of the enclosing class on which the makeNode() method is invoked. The new operator in the statement at (4) has an implicit this reference as the *enclosing object reference* that denotes this outer object. In the qualified class instance creation expression at (4') below, the this reference is explicitly specified to indicate the enclosing object:

```
return this.new Node(info, next);               // (4')
```

The makeNode() method is called at (13). This method call associates an inner object of the Node class with the MyLinkedList object denoted by the reference list. This inner object is denoted by the reference node1. This reference can now be used in the normal way to access members of the inner object.

In Example 9.5, the declaration statement at (14) in the main() method illustrates how external clients can instantiate a non-static member class using the qualified class instance creation expression. The reference list at (12) denotes an object of the enclosing class MyLinkedList. This reference is specified in the qualified class instance creation expression, as shown at (14).

```
MyLinkedList.Node node2 = list.new Node("node2", node1);     // (14)
```

After the execution of the statement at (14), the MyLinkedList object denoted by the list reference has two instances of the non-static member class Node associated with it. This is depicted in Figure 9.3, where the outer object (denoted by list) of the class MyLinkedList is shown with its two associated inner objects (denoted by the references node1 and node2, respectively) right after the execution of the statement at (14). In other words, multiple objects of the non-static member classes can be associated with an object of the enclosing class at runtime.

Figure 9.3 *Outer Object with Associated Inner Objects*

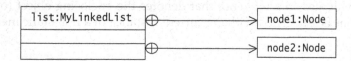

In Example 9.5, if the non-static method makeNode() at (3) in the class MyLinkedList is made static, the constructor call to the Node class at (4) will *not* compile. Static code in a class can only refer to other static members, and not to non-static members. A static method would have to provide an instance of the outer object, as would any other external client, seen here in the static version of the makeNode() method:

```
public static Node makeNode(String info, Node next) {        // (3') Static method
    return new MyLinkedList().new Node(info, next);   // (4') Explicit outer object
}
```

An example of using the inner objects is shown at (15) in the for loop. The print statement in the loop body calls the toString() method implicitly on each inner object to print its text representation.

An attempt to create an instance of the non-static member class using the new operator with the qualified name of the inner class, as shown at (16), results in a compile-time error. The full class name creation expression at (16) applies to creating instances of static member classes.

Accessing Members in Enclosing Context

An implicit reference to the enclosing object is always available in every method and constructor of a non-static member class. A method or constructor can explicitly specify this reference using a special form of the this construct and access its enclosing object, as explained in the next example.

From within a non-static member class, it is possible to refer to all members in the enclosing class directly, unless they are hidden. An example is shown at (9) in Example 9.5, where the instance field message in an object of the enclosing class is accessed by its simple name in the non-static member class. It is also possible to explicitly refer to members in the enclosing class, but this requires special usage of the this reference. One might be tempted to write the statement at (9) as follows:

```
return this.message + " in " + this.nodeInfo +
                    " (" + this.maxNumOfNodes + ")";            // (9a) Not ok.
```

The reference this.nodeInfo is correct because the field nodeInfo certainly belongs to the current object (denoted by this) of the Node class, but this.message *cannot* possibly work, as the current object (indicated by this) of the Node class has no field named message. The correct syntax is the following:

```
return MyLinkedList.this.message + " in " + this.nodeInfo +
                    " (" + this.maxNumOfNodes + ")"; // (9b)
```

The expression (called the *qualified* this)

    enclosing_class_name.this

evaluates to a reference that denotes the enclosing object (of the specified class) that is associated with the current instance of a non-static member class.

Accessing Hidden Members

Fields and methods in the enclosing context can be *hidden* by fields and methods
with the same names in the non-static member class. The qualified this can be used
to access members in the enclosing context, somewhat analogous to using the keyword super in subclasses to access hidden superclass members.

Example 9.6 *Qualified* this *and Qualified Class Instance Creation Expression*

```
// File: OuterInstances.java
class TLClass {                                        // (1)  TLC
  private String id = "TLClass ";                      // (2)
  public TLClass(String objId) { id = id + objId; }    // (3)
  public void printId() {                              // (4)
    System.out.println(id);
  }

  class InnerB {                                        // (5)  NSMC
    private String id = "InnerB ";                     // (6)
    public InnerB(String objId) { id = id + objId; }   // (7)
    public void printId() {                            // (8)
      System.out.print(TLClass.this.id + " : ");       // (9)  Refers to (2)
      System.out.println(id);                          // (10) Refers to (6)
    }

    class InnerC {                                      // (11) NSMC
      private String id = "InnerC ";                   // (12)
      public InnerC(String objId) { id = id + objId; } // (13)
      public void printId() {                          // (14)
        System.out.print(TLClass.this.id + " : ");     // (15) Refers to (2)
        System.out.print(InnerB.this.id + " : ");      // (16) Refers to (6)
        System.out.println(id);                        // (17) Refers to (12)
      }
      public void printIndividualIds() {               // (18)
        TLClass.this.printId();                        // (19) Calls (4)
        InnerB.this.printId();                         // (20) Calls (8)
        printId();                                     // (21) Calls (14)
      }
    } // InnerC
  } // InnerB
} // TLClass
//_____
public class OuterInstances {                          // (22)
  public static void main(String[] args) {             // (23)
    TLClass a = new TLClass("a");                      // (24)
    TLClass.InnerB b = a.new InnerB("b");              // (25) b  --> a
    TLClass.InnerB.InnerC c1 = b.new InnerC("c1");     // (26) c1 --> b
    TLClass.InnerB.InnerC c2 = b.new InnerC("c2");     // (27) c2 --> b
    b.printId();                                       // (28)
    c1.printId();                                      // (29)
    c2.printId();                                      // (30)
    System.out.println("------------");
```

```
      TLClass.InnerB bb = new TLClass("aa").new InnerB("bb");  // (31)
      TLClass.InnerB.InnerC cc = bb.new InnerC("cc");          // (32)
      bb.printId();                                            // (33)
      cc.printId();                                            // (34)
      System.out.println("------------");

      TLClass.InnerB.InnerC ccc =
        new TLClass("aaa").new InnerB("bbb").new InnerC("ccc");// (35)
      ccc.printId();                                           // (36)
      System.out.println("------------");

      ccc.printIndividualIds();                                // (37)
    }
}
```

Output from the program:

```
TLClass a : InnerB b
TLClass a : InnerB b : InnerC c1
TLClass a : InnerB b : InnerC c2
------------
TLClass aa : InnerB bb
TLClass aa : InnerB bb : InnerC cc
------------
TLClass aaa : InnerB bbb : InnerC ccc
------------
TLClass aaa
TLClass aaa : InnerB bbb
TLClass aaa : InnerB bbb : InnerC ccc
```

Example 9.6 illustrates the qualified this employed to access members in the enclosing context, and also demonstrates the qualified class instance creation expression employed to create instances of non-static member classes. The example shows the non-static member class InnerC at (11), which is nested in the non-static member class InnerB at (5), which in turn is nested in the top-level class TLClass at (1). All three classes have a private non-static String field named id and a non-static method named printId. The member name in the nested class *hides* the name in the enclosing context. These members are *not* overridden in the nested classes because no inheritance is involved. In order to refer to the hidden members, the nested class can use the qualified this, as shown at (9), (15), (16), (19), and (20).

Within the nested class InnerC, the three forms used in the following statements to access its field id are equivalent:

```
System.out.println(id);            // (17)
System.out.println(this.id);       // (17a)
System.out.println(InnerC.this.id);// (17b)
```

The main() method at (23) uses the special syntax of the new operator to create objects of non-static member classes and associate them with enclosing objects. An instance of class InnerC (denoted by c1) is created at (26) in the context of an instance of class InnerB (denoted by b), which was created at (25) in the context of an instance of class TLClass (denoted by a), which in turn was created at (24).

```
TLClass a = new TLClass("a");                         // (24)
TLClass.InnerB b = a.new InnerB("b");                 // (25) b  --> a
TLClass.InnerB.InnerC c1 = b.new InnerC("c1");        // (26) c1 --> b
```

The reference c1 is used at (29) to invoke the method printId() declared at (14) in
the nested class InnerC. This method prints the field id from all the objects associated with an instance of the nested class InnerC.

```
TLClass a : InnerB b : InnerC c1
```

When the intervening references to an instance of a non-static member class are of
no interest—that is, if the reference values need not be stored in variables—the new
operator can be chained as shown at (31) and (35).

```
TLClass.InnerB bb = new TLClass("aa").new InnerB("bb");   // (31)
...
TLClass.InnerB.InnerC ccc =
  new TLClass("aaa").new InnerB("bbb").new InnerC("ccc");// (35)
```

Note that the (outer) objects associated with the instances denoted by the references c1, cc, and ccc (at (26), (32), and 35), respectively) are distinct, as evident from
the program output. However, the instances denoted by references c1 and c2 (at
(26) and (27), respectively) have the same outer objects associated with them.

Inheritance Hierarchy and Enclosing Context

A non-static member class can extend another class and implement interfaces, as
any normal class. An inherited field (or method) in a non-static member subclass
can *hide* a field (or method) with the same name in the enclosing context. Using the
simple name to access this member will access the inherited member, not the one
in the enclosing context.

Example 9.7 illustrates the situation. In the inner subclass at (4), the field name
value at (1) in the superclass hides the field with the same name in the enclosing
class at (3). In Example 9.7, the standard form of the this reference is used to access
the inherited field value, as shown at (6). The simple name of the field would also
work in this case, as would the keyword super with the simple name. The super
keyword would be mandatory to access the superclass field if the inner subclass
also declared a field with the same name. However, to access the member from the
enclosing context, the qualified this must be used, as shown at (7).

- -

Example 9.7   *Inheritance Hierarchy and Enclosing Context*

```
// File: HiddenAndInheritedAccess.java
class Superclass {
  protected int value = 3;              // (1) Instance field in superclass
}
//_____
class TopLevelClass {                   // (2) Top-level Class
  private double value = 3.14;          // (3) Hidden by the instance field
                                        //     at (1) in the inner subclass
```

```
        class InnerSubclass extends Superclass {  // (4) Non-static member subclass
          public void printHidden() {              // (5)
            // (6) value from superclass:
            System.out.println("this.value: " + this.value);

            // (7) value from enclosing context:
            System.out.println("TopLevelClass.this.value: "
                               + TopLevelClass.this.value);
          }
        } // InnerSubclass
      } // TopLevelClass
      //_____
      public class HiddenAndInheritedAccess {
        public static void main(String[] args) {
          TopLevelClass.InnerSubclass ref = new TopLevelClass().new InnerSubclass();
          ref.printHidden();
        }
      }
```

Output from the program:

```
this.value: 3
TopLevelClass.this.value: 3.14
```

Some caution should be exercised when extending an inner class. Some of the subtleties involved are illustrated by Example 9.8. The nesting and the inheritance hierarchy of the classes involved are shown in Figure 9.4. The question that arises is how do we provide an *outer instance* when creating a *subclass instance* of a non-static member class—for example, when creating objects of the subclasses SubInnerA and InnerB in Figure 9.4.

Figure 9.4 *Non-Static Member Classes and Inheritance*

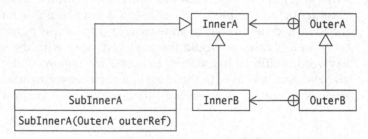

Example 9.8 *Extending Inner Classes*

```
      // File: Extending.java
      class OuterA {                           // (1)
        class InnerA { }                       // (2)
      }
      //_____
      class SubInnerA extends OuterA.InnerA {  // (3) Extends NSMC at (2)
```

```
                  // (4) Mandatory non-zero argument constructor:
                  SubInnerA(OuterA outerRef) {
                    outerRef.super();                            // (5) Explicit super() call
                  }
                }
                //_____
                class OuterB extends OuterA {                    // (6) Extends class at (1)
                  class InnerB extends OuterA.InnerA { }          // (7) Extends NSMC at (2)
                }
                //_____
                public class Extending {
                  public static void main(String[] args) {

                    // (8) Outer instance passed explicitly in constructor call:
                    SubInnerA obj1 = new SubInnerA(new OuterA());
                    System.out.println(obj1.getClass());

                    // (9) No outer instance passed explicitly in constructor call to InnerB:
                    OuterB.InnerB obj2 = new OuterB().new InnerB();
                    System.out.println(obj2.getClass());
                  }
                }
```

Output from the program:

```
class SubInnerA
class OuterB$InnerB
```

In Example 9.8, the non-static member class InnerA, declared at (2) in the class OuterA at (1), is extended by SubInnerA at (3). Note that SubInnerA and the class OuterA are not related in any way, and that the subclass OuterB inherits the class InnerA from its superclass OuterA. An instance of SubInnerA is created at (8). An instance of the class OuterA is explicitly passed as an argument in the constructor call to SubInnerA. The constructor at (4) for SubInnerA has a special super() call in its body at (5), called a *qualified superclass constructor invocation*. This call ensures that the constructor of the superclass InnerA has an outer object (denoted by the reference outerRef) to bind to. Using the standard super() call in the subclass constructor is not adequate because it does not provide an outer instance for the superclass constructor to bind to. The non-zero argument constructor at (4) and the outer-Ref.super() expression at (5) are mandatory to set up the relationships correctly between the objects involved.

The outer object problem mentioned above does not arise if the subclass that extends an inner class is also declared within an outer class that extends the outer class of the superclass. This situation is illustrated at (6) and (7): The classes InnerB and OuterB extend the classes InnerA and OuterA, respectively. The member class InnerA is inherited by the class OuterB from its superclass OuterA—and can be regarded as being nested in the class OuterB. Thus an object of class OuterB can act as an outer object for both an instance of class InnerA and that of class InnerB. The object creation expression new OuterB().new InnerB() at (9) creates an OuterB object and implicitly passes its reference to the default constructor of class InnerB. The default constructor of class InnerB invokes the default constructor of its superclass InnerA by calling super() and passing it the reference of the OuterB object, which the constructor of class InnerA can readily bind to.

It goes without saying that such convoluted inheritance and nesting relationships as those in Example 9.8 hardly qualify as best coding practices.

 ## Review Questions

9.1 Which statement is true about the following program?

```java
public class MyClass {
  public static void main(String[] args) {
    Outer objRef = new Outer();
    System.out.println(objRef.createInner().getSecret());
  }
}

class Outer {
  private int secret;
  Outer() { secret = 123; }

  class Inner {
    int getSecret() { return secret; }
  }

  Inner createInner() { return new Inner(); }
}
```

Select the one correct answer.

(a) The program will fail to compile because the class Inner cannot be declared within the class Outer.

(b) The program will fail to compile because the method createInner() cannot be allowed to pass objects of the class Inner to methods outside the class Outer.

(c) The program will fail to compile because the field secret is not accessible from the method getSecret().

(d) The program will fail to compile because the method getSecret() is not accessible from the main() method in the class MyClass.

(e) The code will compile and print 123 at runtime.

9.2 Which of the following statements are true about nested classes?
Select the two correct answers.

(a) An instance of a static member class has an implicit outer instance.

(b) A static member class can contain non-static fields.

(c) A static member interface can contain non-static fields.

(d) A static member interface has an implicit outer instance.

(e) An instance of the outer class can be associated with many instances of a non-static member class.

9.3 Which statement is true about the following program?

```java
public class Nesting {
  public static void main(String[] args) {
    B.C obj = new B().new C();
  }
}

class A {
  int val;
  A(int v) { val = v; }
}

class B extends A {
  int val = 1;
  B() { super(2); }

  class C extends A {
    int val = 3;
    C() {
      super(4);
      System.out.println(B.this.val);
      System.out.println(C.this.val);
      System.out.println(super.val);
    }
  }
}
```

Select the one correct answer.

(a) The program will fail to compile.

(b) The program will compile and print 2, 3, and 4, in that order at runtime.

(c) The program will compile and print 1, 4, and 2, in that order at runtime.

(d) The program will compile and print 1, 3, and 4, in that order at runtime.

(e) The program will compile and print 3, 2, and 1, in that order at runtime.

9.4 Which of the following statements are true about the following program?

```java
public class Outer {
  public void doIt() {}
  public class Inner {
    public void doIt() {}
  }

  public static void main(String[] args) {
    new Outer().new Inner().doIt();
  }
}
```

Select the two correct answers.

(a) The doIt() method in the Inner class overrides the doIt() method in the Outer class.

(b) The doIt() method in the Inner class overloads the doIt() method in the Outer class.

(c) The doIt() method in the Inner class hides the doIt() method in the Outer class.

(d) The qualified name of the Inner class is Outer.Inner.

(e) The program will fail to compile.

9.4 Local Classes

Declaring Local Classes

A local class is an inner class that is defined in a block. This can be essentially any context where a local block or block body is allowed: a method, a constructor, an initializer block, a try-catch-finally construct, loop bodies, or an if-else statement. Example 9.9 shows declaration of the local class StaticLocal at (5) that is defined in the static context of the method staticMethod() at (1).

A local class cannot have any access modifier and cannot be declared static, as shown at (4) in Example 9.9. However, it can be declared abstract or final, as shown at (5). The declaration of the class is only accessible in the context of the block in which it is defined, subject to the same scope rules as for local variable declarations. In particular, it must be declared before use in the block. In Example 9.9, an attempt to create an object of class StaticLocal at (2) and use the class Static-Local at (3) fails, as the class has not been defined before use, but this is not a problem at (11), (12), (13), and (14).

A local class can declare members and constructors, shown from (6) to (10), as in a normal class. The members of the local class can have any access level, and are accessible in the enclosing block regardless of their access level. Even though the field if1 at (7) is private, it is accessible in the enclosing method at (12).

Blocks in non-static context have a this reference available, which refers to an instance of the class containing the block. An instance of a local class, which is declared in such a non-static block, has an instance of the enclosing class associated with it. This gives such a non-static local class much of the same capability as a non-static member class.

However, if the block containing a local class declaration is defined in static context (i.e., a static method or a static initializer block), the local class is implicitly static in the sense that its instantiation does not require any outer object. This aspect of local classes is reminiscent of static member classes. However, note that a local class cannot be specified with the keyword static. The static method at (1) is called at (15). The local class StaticLocal can only be instantiated, as shown at (11), in the enclosing method staticMethod() and does not require any outer object of the enclosing class. Analogous to the value of a local variable, the object of the local class is not available to the caller of the method after the method completes execution, unless measures are taken to store it externally or if its reference value is returned by the call.

Example 9.9   *Declaring Local Classes*

```
// File: LocalClient1.java
class TLCWithSLClass {                                  // Top-level Class

    static void staticMethod(final int fp) {            // (1) Static Method
//  StaticLocal slRef = new StaticLocal(10);            // (2) Class cannot be resolved
//  System.out.println(StaticLocal.staticValue());      // (3) Class cannot be resolved


//  public static class StaticLocal { // (4) Not OK. Cannot be static,
//                                 //                and no access modifier
        final class StaticLocal {                       // (5) Static local class
          public static final int sf1 = 10;             // (6) Static field
          private int if1;                              // (7) Instance field
          public StaticLocal(int val) {                 // (8) Constructor
            this.if1 = val;
          }
          public int getValue() { return if1; }         // (9) Instance method
          public static int staticValue() { return sf1; }// (10) Static method
        } // end StaticLocal

        StaticLocal slRef2 = new StaticLocal(100);                      // (11)
        System.out.println("Instance field: " + slRef2.if1);           // (12)
        System.out.println("Instance method call: " + slRef2.getValue());    // (13)
        System.out.println("Static method call: " + StaticLocal.staticValue());// (14)
    } // end staticMethod
}

public class LocalClient1 {
  public static void main(String[] args) {
    TLCWithSLClass.staticMethod(100);                                   // (15)
  }
}
```

Output from the program:

```
Instance field: 100
Instance method call: 100
Static method call: 10
```

Accessing Declarations in Enclosing Context

Declaring a local class in a static or a non-static block influences what the class can access in the enclosing context.

Accessing Local Declarations in the Enclosing Block

Example 9.10 illustrates how a local class can access declarations in its enclosing block. Example 9.10 shows declaration of the local class NonStaticLocal at (7) that is defined in the non-static context of the method nonStaticMethod() at (1).

A local class can access variables (local variables, method parameters, and catch-block parameters) that are declared final or *effectively* final in the scope of its local context. A variable whose value does not change after it is initialized is said to be *effectively* final. This situation is shown at (8) and (9) in the NonStaticLocal class, where the final parameter fp and the effectively final local variable flv of the method nonStaticMethod() are accessed. Access to local variables that are not final or effectively final is not permitted from local classes. The local variable nfv1 at (4) is accessed at (10) in the local class, but this local variable is not effectively final as it is reassigned a new value at (6).

Accessing a local variable from the local context that has not been declared or has not been *definitely assigned* (§5.5, p. 232) results in a compile-time error, as shown at (11) and (12). The local variable nflv2 accessed at (11) is not declared before use, as it is declared at (16). The local variable nflv3 accessed at (12) is not initialized before use, as it is initialized at (17)—which means it is not definitely assigned at (12).

Declarations in the local class can *shadow* declarations in the enclosing block. The field hlv at (13) shadows the local variable by the same name at (3) in the enclosing method. There is no way for the local class to refer to shadowed declarations in the enclosing block.

The non-static method at (1) is called at (19) on an instance of its enclosing class. When the constructor at (15) in the non-static method is executed, the reference to this instance is passed implicitly to the constructor, thus this instance acts as the enclosing object of the local class instance.

Example 9.10 *Accessing Local Declarations in the Enclosing Block (Local Classes)*

```java
// File: LocalClient2.java
class TLCWithNSLClass {                    // Top-level Class

  void nonStaticMethod(final int fp) { // (1) Non-static Method
    // Local variables:
    int flv = 10;              // (2) Effectively final local variable
    final int hlv = 20;        // (3) Final local variable (constant variable)
    int nflv1 = 30;            // (4) Non-final local variable
    int nflv3;                 // (5) Non-final local variable declaration

    nflv1 = 40;                // (6) Not effectively final local variable

    // Non-static local class
    class NonStaticLocal {// (7)
       int f1 = fp;         // (8) Final param from enclosing method
       int f2 = flv;        // (9) Effectively final variable from enclosing method
//     int f3 = nflv1;      // (10) Not effectively final from enclosing method
//     int f4 = nflv2;      // (11) Name nflv2 cannot be resolved: use-before-decl
//     int f5 = nflv3;      // (12) Not definitely assigned
       int hlv;             // (13) Shadows local variable at (3)
       NonStaticLocal (int value) {
         hlv = value;
         System.out.println("Instance field: " + hlv);// (14) Prints value from (13)
```

```
        }
    } // end NonStaticLocal

    NonStaticLocal nslRef = new NonStaticLocal(200);// (15) Implicit outer object
    int nflv2 = 50;                                  // (16) Attempted use in (11)
    nflv3 = 60;                                       // (17) Initializes (4)
    System.out.println("Local variable: " + hlv);   // (18) Prints value from (3)
    } // end nonStaticMethod
}

public class LocalClient2 {
    public static void main(String[] args) {
        new TLCWithNSLClass().nonStaticMethod(1000);    // (19)
    }
}
```

Output from the program:

```
Instance field: 200
Local variable: 20
```

Accessing Members in the Enclosing Class

Example 9.11 illustrates how a local class can access members in its enclosing class. The top-level class TLCWith2LCS declares two methods: nonStaticMethod() and staticMethod(). Both methods define a local class each: NonStaticLocal at (1) in non-static context and StaticLocal at (8) in static context, both of which are subclasses of the superclass Base.

A local class can access members inherited from its superclass in the usual way. The field nsf1 in the superclass Base is inherited by the local subclass NonStatic-Local. This inherited field is accessed in the NonStaticLocal class, as shown at (2), (3), and (4), by using the field's simple name, the standard this reference, and the super keyword, respectively. This also applies for static local classes, as shown at (9), (10), and (11).

Fields and methods in the enclosing class can be *hidden* by member declarations in the local class. The non-static field nsf1, inherited by the local classes, hides the field by the same name in the enclosing class TLCWith2LCS. The qualified this can be used in non-static local classes for *explicit* referencing of members in the enclosing class, regardless of whether these members are hidden or not.

```
double f4 = TLCWith2LCS.this.nsf1;       // (5) In enclosing object.
```

However, the special form of the this construct *cannot* be used in a local class that is declared in static context, as shown at (12), since it does not have any notion of an outer object. A local class in static context cannot refer to non-static members in the enclosing context.

A non-static local class can access both static and non-static members defined in the enclosing class. The non-static field nsf2 and static field sf are defined in the enclosing class TLCWith2LCS. They are accessed in the NonStaticLocal class at (6) and (7), respectively. The special form of the this construct can also be used in non-static local classes, as previously mentioned.

However, a local class that is declared in static context can only directly access static members defined in the enclosing class. The static field sf in the class TLCWith2LCS is accessed in the StaticLocal class at (14), but the non-static field nsf1 cannot be accessed, as shown at (13).

Example 9.11 *Accessing Members in the Enclosing Class (Local Classes)*

```
// File: LocalClient3.java
class Base { protected int nsf1; }      // Superclass
//_____
class TLCWith2LCS {                     // Top-level Class
  private int nsf1;                     // Non-static field
  private int nsf2;                     // Non-static field
  private static int sf;                // Static field

  void nonStaticMethod( int fp) {       // Non-static Method

    class NonStaticLocal extends Base {// (1) Non-static local subclass
      int f1 = nsf1;                    // (2) Inherited from superclass.
      int f2 = this.nsf1;               // (3) Inherited from superclass.
      int f3 = super.nsf1;              // (4) Inherited from superclass.
      int f4 = TLCWith2LCS.this.nsf1;   // (5) In enclosing object.
      int f5 = nsf2;                    // (6) Instance field in enclosing object.
      int f6 = sf;                      // (7) static field from enclosing class.
    } // NonStaticLocal

  } // nonStaticMethod

  static void staticMethod(final int fp) { // Static Method

    class StaticLocal extends Base {    // (8) Static local subclass
      int f1 = nsf1;                    // (9) Inherited from superclass.
      int f2 = this.nsf1;               // (10) Inherited from superclass.
      int f3 = super.nsf1;              // (11) Inherited from superclass.
//    int f4 = TLCWith2LCS.this.nsf1;   // (12) No enclosing object.
//    int f5 = nsf2;                    // (13) No enclosing object.
      int f6 = sf;                      // (14) static field from enclosing class.
    } // StaticLocal

  } // staticMethod
}

public class LocalClient3 {
  public static void main(String[] args) {
    TLCWith2LCS.staticMethod(200);            // (15)
    new TLCWith2LCS().nonStaticMethod(100);   // (16)
  }
}
```

Instantiating Local Classes

Clients outside the scope of a local class cannot instantiate the class directly because such classes are, after all, local. A local class can be instantiated in the block in which it is defined. Like a local variable, a local class must be declared before being used in the block.

A method can return instances of any local class it declares. The local class type must then be assignable to the return type of the method. The return type cannot be the same as the local class type, since this type is not accessible outside the method. A supertype of the local class must be specified as the return type. This also means that, in order for the objects of the local class to be useful outside the method, a local class should implement an interface or override the behavior of its supertypes.

Example 9.12 illustrates how clients can instantiate local classes. The nesting and the inheritance hierarchy of the classes involved are shown in Figure 9.5. The non-static local class Circle at (5) is defined in the non-static method createCircle() at (4), which has the return type Shape. The static local class Graph at (9) is defined in the static method createGraph() at (8), which has the return type IDrawable.

Figure 9.5 *Local Classes and Inheritance Hierarchy*

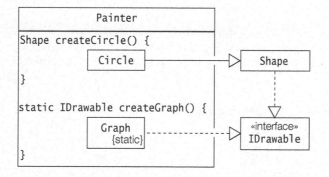

Example 9.12 *Instantiating Local Classes*

```
// File: LocalClassClient.java
interface IDrawable {                       // (1)
  void draw();
}
//_____
class Shape implements IDrawable {          // (2)
  @Override
  public void draw() { System.out.println("Drawing a Shape."); }
}
//_____
class Painter {                             // (3) Top-level Class
  public Shape createCircle(final double radius) { // (4) Non-static Method
    class Circle extends Shape {            // (5) Non-static local class
```

```java
      @Override
      public void draw() {
        System.out.println("Drawing a Circle of radius: " + radius); // (6)
      }
    }
    return new Circle();                    // (7) Passed enclosing object reference
  }

  public static IDrawable createGraph() { // (8) Static Method
    class Graph implements IDrawable {     // (9) Static local class
      @Override
      public void draw() { System.out.println("Drawing a Graph."); }
    }
    return new Graph();                     // (10) Object of static local class
  }
}
//_____
public class LocalClassClient {
  public static void main(String[] args) {
    IDrawable[] drawables = {               // (11)
        new Painter().createCircle(5),      // (12) Object of non-static local class
        Painter.createGraph(),              // (13) Object of static local class
        new Painter().createGraph()         // (14) Object of static local class
    };
    for (IDrawable aDrawable : drawables) // (15)
      aDrawable.draw();

    System.out.println("Local Class Names:");
    System.out.println(drawables[0].getClass().getName());   // (16)
    System.out.println(drawables[1].getClass().getName());   // (17)
  }
}
```

Output from the program:

```
Drawing a Circle of radius: 5.0
Drawing a Graph.
Drawing a Graph.
Local Class Names:
Painter$1$Circle
Painter$1$Graph
```

The main() method in Example 9.12 creates a polymorphic array drawables of type IDrawable[] at (11), which is initialized at (12) through (14) with instances of the local classes.

Creating an instance of a non-static local class requires an instance of the enclosing class. In Example 9.12, the non-static method createCircle() is invoked on the instance of the enclosing class Painter to create an instance of the non-static local class Circle in the non-static method, as shown at (12). The reference to the instance of the enclosing class is passed implicitly in the constructor call at (7) to the non-static local class.

A static method can be invoked either through the class name or through a reference of the class type. An instance of a static local class can be created either way by calling the createGraph() method, as shown at (13) and (14). As might be expected in static context, no outer object is involved.

As references to a local class cannot be declared outside the local context, the functionality of the class is only available through supertype references. The method draw() is invoked on objects in the array IDrawable at (15). The program output indicates which objects were created. In particular, note that the final parameter radius of the method createCircle() at (4) is accessed in the draw() method of the local class Circle at (6). An instance of the local class Circle is created at (12) by a call to the method createCircle(). The draw() method is invoked on this instance of the local class Circle in the loop at (15). The value of the final parameter radius is still accessible to the draw() method invoked on this instance, although the call to the method createCircle(), which created the instance in the first place, has completed. Values of (effectively) final local variables continue to be available to instances of local classes whenever these values are needed.

The output in Example 9.12 also shows the actual names of the local classes. In fact, the local class names are reflected in the generated class file names. Because multiple local class declarations with the same name can be defined in the methods of the enclosing class, a numbering scheme ($i) is used to generate distinct class file names.

9.5 Static Local Types

It is possible to declare local interfaces, local enum types, and local record classes. However, these local nested types are implicitly static—as opposed to local classes that are never static. A local class declared in a static context is *not* the same as a static local type, and they are compared next.

Since these local nested types are implicitly static, this has implications for these types, as listed below. We illustrate these implications for a static local record class in Example 9.13, but they apply equally to local interfaces and local enum types as well.

- A local record class can be instantiated with the new operator without specifying an immediately enclosing instance. Interfaces and enum types cannot be instantiated with the new operator.

  At (10) in Example 9.13, an instance of the static local record class is created without passing a reference to the enclosing object.

- Static local types can only access static members in the enclosing context—this is the same as local classes declared in static context, whereas local classes declared in non-static context can access all members in the enclosing context.

  In Example 9.13, it is possible to access the static field in the enclosing class in the declaration of the local record class at (7) and (9), but it is not possible to access non-static fields as shown at (8).

- Static local types cannot access any local variables in the enclosing method—in contrast to local classes that can access (effectively) final local variables in the enclosing method.

  In Example 9.13, it is not possible to access any local variables, as shown at (5) and (6), in the enclosing method.

Example 9.13 *Defining Static Local Record Classes*

```java
// File: LocalTypesClient.java
class LocalTypes {                          // Top-level Class
  private int nsf;                          // (1) Non-static field
  private static int sf;                    // (2) Static field

  void nonStaticMethod(final int fp) {      // (3) Non-static Method. Final parameter.
    int lv = 20;                            // (4) Local variable

    record StaticLocalRecord(int val) {     // Static local record
      // Cannot access local variables:
//    static int f1 = fp;  // (5) Cannot access final param from enclosing method.
//    static int f2 = lv;  // (6) Cannot access effectively final local variable
                           //     from enclosing method.

      // Can only access static fields in enclosing context:
      static int f3 = sf;          // (7) Access static field in enclosing context.

      void printFieldsFromEnclosingContext() {
//      System.out.println(nsf);   // (8) Cannot access non-static field
                                   //     in enclosing context.
        System.out.println(sf);    // (9) Access static field in enclosing context.
      }
    }

    // (10) Create local record. No enclosing instance passed to the constructor.
    StaticLocalRecord lrRef = new StaticLocalRecord(100);
    System.out.println("Value: " + lrRef.val());
  } // nonStaticMethod
}

public class LocalTypesClient {
  public static void main(String[] args) {
    new LocalTypes().nonStaticMethod(1000);     // (10)
  }
}
```

Output from the program:

```
Value: 100
```

9.6 Anonymous Classes

Declaring Anonymous Classes

Classes are usually first defined and then instantiated using the new operator. Anonymous classes combine the process of definition and instantiation into a single step. Anonymous classes are defined at the location they are instantiated, using additional syntax with the new operator. As these classes do not have a name, an instance of the class can only be created together with the definition. Like local classes, anonymous classes are inner classes that can be defined in static and non-static context.

An anonymous class can be defined and instantiated in contexts where a reference value can be used—that is, as expressions that evaluate to a reference value denoting an object of the anonymous class. Anonymous classes are typically used for creating objects *on the fly* in contexts such as the value in a return statement, an argument in a method call, or in initialization of variables. The reference value of an anonymous class object can be assigned to any kind of variable (fields and local variables) whose type is a supertype of the anonymous class.

An anonymous class cannot be declared with an access modifier, nor can it be declared static, final, or abstract.

Typical uses of anonymous classes are to implement *event listeners* in GUI-based applications, threads for simple tasks (see examples in Chapter 22, p. 1365), and comparators for providing a total ordering for objects (see Example 14.11, p. 772).

Extending an Existing Class

The following syntax can be used for defining and instantiating an anonymous class that extends an existing class specified by *superclass name*:

```
new superclass_name<optional_type_arguments> (optional_constructor_arguments)
{
  member_declarations
}
```

Optional type arguments and constructor arguments can be specified, which are passed to the superclass constructor. Thus the superclass must provide a constructor corresponding to the arguments passed. No extends clause is used in the construct. Since an anonymous class cannot define constructors (as it does not have a name), an instance initializer can be used to achieve the same effect as a no-arg constructor.

Both static and non-static members can be declared in the class body. An anonymous class can override any instance methods accessible by their simple name from the superclass, but if it extends an abstract class, then it must provide implementation for all abstract methods from the superclass. The declaration is terminated by a semicolon (;), unless the reference value of the resulting object is immediately used to access a member of this object.

Example 9.14 *Defining Anonymous Classes*

```java
// File: AnonClassClient.java
interface IDrawable {                          // (1)
  void draw();
}
//_____
class Shape implements IDrawable {             // (2)
  @Override
  public void draw() { System.out.println("Drawing a Shape."); }
}
//_____
class Painter {                                // (3) Top-level Class

  public Shape createShape() {                 // (4) Non-static Method
    return new Shape() {                        // (5) Extends superclass at (2)
      @Override
      public void draw() { System.out.println("Drawing a new Shape."); }
    };
  }
  public static IDrawable createIDrawable() {  // (7) Static Method
    return new IDrawable() {                    // (8) Implements interface at (1)
      @Override
      public void draw() {
        System.out.println("Drawing a new IDrawable.");
      }
    };
  }
}
//_____
public class AnonClassClient {
  public static void main(String[] args) {     // (9)
    IDrawable[] drawables = {                   // (10)
      new Painter().createShape(),             // (11) Non-static anonymous class
      Painter.createIDrawable(),               // (12) Static anonymous class
      new Painter().createIDrawable()          // (13) Static anonymous class
    };
    for (IDrawable aDrawable : drawables)      // (14)
      aDrawable.draw();

    System.out.println("Anonymous Class Names:");
    System.out.println(drawables[0].getClass().getName());// (15)
    System.out.println(drawables[1].getClass().getName());// (16)
  }
}
```

Output from the program:

```
Drawing a new Shape.
Drawing a new IDrawable.
Drawing a new IDrawable.
Anonymous Class Names:
Painter$1
Painter$2
```

Class declarations from Example 9.12 are adapted to use anonymous classes in Example 9.14. The non-static method createShape() at (4) defines a non-static anonymous class at (5), which extends the superclass Shape. The anonymous class at (5) overrides the inherited method draw() from the superclass Shape at (2).

```
// ...
class Shape implements IDrawable {                    // (2)
  @Override public void draw() { System.out.println("Drawing a Shape."); }
}

class Painter {                                       // (3) Top-level Class

  public Shape createShape() {                        // (4) Non-static Method
    return new Shape() {                              // (5) Extends superclass at (2)
      @Override public void draw() { System.out.println("Drawing a new Shape."); }
    };
  }
  // ...

}
// ...
```

Implementing an Interface

The following syntax can be used for defining and instantiating an anonymous class that implements an interface specified by the *interface name*:

```
new interface_name<optional_parameterized_types>() { member_declarations }
```

An anonymous class provides a *single* interface implementation. No arguments are passed, as an interface does not define a constructor. The anonymous class implicitly extends the Object class. Note that no implements clause is used in the construct. The class body must provide implementation for all abstract methods declared in the interface.

An anonymous class implementing an interface is shown below. Details can be found in Example 9.14. The static method createIDrawable() at (7) defines a static anonymous class at (8), which implements the interface IDrawable, by providing an implementation of the method draw(). The functionality of objects of an anonymous class that implements an interface is available through references of the interface type and the Object type—that is, its supertypes.

```
interface IDrawable {                                 // (1) Interface
  void draw();
}
// ...
class Painter {                                       // (3) Top-level Class
  // ...
  public static IDrawable createIDrawable() {  // (7) Static Method
    return new IDrawable() {                          // (8) Implements interface at (1)
      @Override public void draw() {
        System.out.println("Drawing a new IDrawable.");
      }
```

```
    };
  }
 }
 // ...
```

The following code is an example of a typical use of anonymous classes in building GUI applications. The anonymous class at (1) implements the java.awt.event.- ActionListener interface that has the method actionPerformed(). When the add- ActionListener() method is called on the GUI button denoted by the reference quitButton, the anonymous class is instantiated and the reference value of the object is passed as a parameter to the method. The method addActionListener() of the GUI button registers the reference value, and when the user clicks the GUI button, it can invoke the actionPerformed() method on the ActionListener object.

```
quitButton.addActionListener(
    new ActionListener() {     // (1) Anonymous class implements an interface
      // Invoked when the user clicks the quit button.
      @Override public void actionPerformed(ActionEvent evt) {
        System.exit(0);        // (2) Terminates the program
      }
    }
);
```

Instantiating Anonymous Classes

The discussion on instantiating local classes (see Example 9.12) is also valid for instantiating anonymous classes. The class AnonClassClient in Example 9.14 creates one instance at (11) of the non-static anonymous class defined at (5) by calling the non-static method createShape() on an instance of the class Painter, and two instances at (12) and (13) of the anonymous class that is defined in static context at (8) by calling the static method createDrawable() in the class Painter. The program output shows the polymorphic behavior and the runtime types of the objects. Similar to a non-static local class, an instance of a non-static anonymous class has an instance of its enclosing class associated with it. An enclosing instance is not mandatory for creating objects of a static anonymous class.

The names of the anonymous classes at runtime are also shown in the program output in Example 9.14. A numbering scheme ($i) is used to designate the anonymous classes according to their declaration order inside the enclosing class. They are also the names used to designate their respective class files. Anonymous classes are not so anonymous after all.

Referencing Instances of an Anonymous Class

Each time an anonymous class declaration is executed it returns a reference value of a new instance of the anonymous class. Either an anonymous class extends an existing class or it implements an interface. Usually it makes sense to override (and implement) methods from its supertype. References of its supertype can refer to objects of the anonymous subclass. As we cannot declare references of an anonymous class, an instance of an anonymous class can only be manipulated by a supertype reference. Any subclass-specific members in an anonymous class cannot be accessed directly by external clients—the only functionality available is that provided by inherited methods and overridden methods which can be invoked by a supertype reference denoting an anonymous subclass instance.

Accessing Declarations in Enclosing Context

Member declarations and access rules for local classes (p. 512) also apply to anonymous classes. Example 9.15 is an adaptation of Example 9.9, Example 9.10, and Example 9.11. It illustrates what members can be declared in an anonymous class and what can be accessed in its enclosing context. The local classes from previous examples have been adapted to anonymous classes in Example 9.15.

The TLCWithAnonClasses class declares a non-static method at (3) in which a local variable (baseRef) is initialized with an instance of a non-static anonymous class at (9). The baseRef variable is used to invoke the printValue() method on this instance at (28).

The TLCWithAnonClasses class declares a static field baseField at (29) that is initialized with an instance of a static anonymous class. The field baseField is used to invoke the printValue() method on this instance at (36).

Accessing Local Declarations in the Enclosing Block

Being inner classes, there are many similarities between local classes and anonymous classes. An anonymous class can only access (effectively) final variables in its enclosing local context, shown both for static fields at (10), (11), and (12), and for instance fields at (13), (14), and (15). Local variables accessed in the anonymous class must be declared before use, and definitely assigned, as shown at (16) and (17), respectively. A field name in the anonymous class can shadow a local variable with the same name in the local context, as shown at (18). Note that the anonymous class declared at (29) does *not* have an enclosing local context, only an enclosing class, as it is defined in non-static context.

Accessing Members in the Enclosing Class

A member (either inherited or declared) in an anonymous class can hide a member with the same name in the enclosing object or class. The inherited field nsf1 hides the field by the same name in the enclosing class, as shown at (19), (20), and (21).

Non-static anonymous classes can access any non-hidden members in the enclosing class by their simple names and the qualified this, as shown at (22), (23), and (24). Static anonymous classes can only access non-hidden static members in the enclosing class by their simple names, as shown at (30), (31), and (32).

Example 9.15 *Accessing Declarations in Enclosing Context (Anonymous Classes)*

```java
// File: AnonClient.java
abstract class Base {              // (1) Superclass
  protected int nsf1;
  abstract void printValue();
}
//_____
class TLCWithAnonClasses {         // (2) Top level Class
  private int nsf1;                // Non-static field
  private int nsf2;                // Non-static field
  private static int sf = 5;       // Static field

  public void nonStaticMethod(final int fp) { // (3) Non-static Method
    // Local variables:
    int flv = 10;                  // (4) Effectively final local variable
    final int hlv = 20;            // (5) Final local variable (constant variable)
    int nflv1 = 30;                // (6) Non-final local variable
    int nflv3;                     // (7) Non-final local variable declaration

    nflv1 = 40;                    // (8) Not effectively final local variable

    Base baseRef = new Base() { // (9) Non-static anonymous class
      // Static fields: Accessing local declarations in the enclosing block:
      static int sff1 = fp;   // (10) Final param from enclosing method
      static int sff2 = flv;  // (11) Effect. final variable from enclosing method
//    static int sf1 = nflv1; // (12) Not effect. final from enclosing method

      // Instance fields: Accessing local declarations in the enclosing block:
      int f1 = fp;        // (13) Final param from enclosing method
      int f2 = flv;       // (14) Effectively final variable from enclosing method
//    int f3 = nflv1;     // (15) Not effectively final from enclosing method

//    int f4 = nflv2;     // (16) nflv2 cannot be resolved: not decl-before-use
//    int f5 = nflv3;     // (17) Not definitely assigned: not initialized
      int hlv;            // (18) Shadows local variable at (5)

      // Accessing member declarations inherited from superclass:
      int f6 = nsf1;                 // (19) Inherited from superclass
      int f7 = this.nsf1;            // (20) Inherited from superclass
      int f8 = super.nsf1;           // (21) Inherited from superclass

      // Accessing (hidden) member declarations in the enclosing class:
      int f9 = TLCWithAnonClasses.this.nsf1;        // (22) In enclosing object
      int f10 = nsf2;                // (23) Instance field in enclosing object
      int f11 = sf;                  // (24) Static field from enclosing class

      { nsf1 = fp; }                 // (25) Non-static initializer block

      @Override void printValue() {                 // (26) Instance method
        System.out.println("Instance field nsf1: " + nsf1);// (27)
      }
    };
```

```
              int nflv2 = 70;
              nflv3 = 80;
              baseRef.printValue();              // (28) Invoke method on anonymous object
          }

      public static final Base baseField = new Base() { // (29) Static anonymous class
          // Accessing (hidden) member declarations in the enclosing class:
      //   int f1 = TLCWithAnonClasses.this.nsf1; // (30) Not OK. No enclosing object
      //   int f2 = nsf2;                         // (31) Not OK. No enclosing object
          { nsf1 = sf; }                          // (32) Non-static initializer block

          @Override void printValue() {                     // (33) Instance method
            System.out.println("Instance field nsf1: " + nsf1);// (34)
          }
      };
   }
//_____
public class AnonClient {
  public static void main(String[] args) {
    new TLCWithAnonClasses().nonStaticMethod(100);           // (35)
    TLCWithAnonClasses.baseField.printValue();               // (36)
  }
}
```

Output from the program:

```
Instance field nsf1: 100
Instance field nsf1: 5
```

Review Questions

9.5 Which statement is true about nested classes?
Select the one correct answer.

(a) Non-static member classes must have either package or public access.
(b) All nested classes cannot declare static member classes.
(c) Methods in all nested classes cannot be declared static.
(d) All nested classes can be declared static.
(e) Static member classes can declare non-static methods.

9.6 Given the declaration:

```
interface IntHolder { int getInt(); }
```

Which of the following methods are valid?

```
//----(1)----
IntHolder makeIntHolder(int i) {
  i = 10;
  return new IntHolder() {
    public int getInt() { return i; }
  };
}
```

```
//----(2)----
  IntHolder makeIntHolder(final int i) {
    return new IntHolder {
      public int getInt() { return i; }
    };
  }
//----(3)----
  IntHolder makeIntHolder(int i) {
    class MyIH implements IntHolder {
      public int getInt() { return i; }
    }
    return new MyIH();
  }
//----(4)----
  IntHolder makeIntHolder(final int i) {
    class MyIH implements IntHolder {
      public int getInt() { return i; }
    }
    return new MyIH();
  }
//----(5)----
  IntHolder makeIntHolder(int i) {
    return new MyIH(i);
  }
  static class MyIH implements IntHolder {
    final int j;
    MyIH(int i) { j = i; }
    public int getInt() { return j; }
  }
```

Select the three correct answers.

(a) The method at (1).
(b) The method at (2).
(c) The method at (3).
(d) The method at (4).
(e) The method at (5).

9.7   Which statement is true about nested classes?
       Select the one correct answer.

(a) No other static members, except static final fields declared as constant variables, can be declared within a non-static member class.
(b) If a non-static member class is nested within a class named Outer, methods within the non-static member class must use the prefix Outer.this to access the members of the class Outer.
(c) All fields in any nested class must be declared final.
(d) Anonymous classes cannot have constructors.
(e) If the reference objRef denotes an instance of any nested class within the class Outer, the expression (objRef instanceof Outer) will evaluate to true.

9.8 Which expression can be inserted independently at (1) so that compiling and running the program will print LocalVar.str1?

```
public class Access {
  final String str1 = "Access.str1";

  public static void main(final String args[]) {
    final String str1 = "LocalVar.str1";

    class Helper { String getStr1() { return str1; } }
    class Inner {
      String str1 = "Inner.str1";
      Inner() {
        System.out.println( /* (1) INSERT EXPRESSION HERE */ );
      }
    }
    Inner inner = new Inner();
  }
}
```

Select the one correct answer.

(a) str1
(b) this.str1
(c) Access.this.str1
(d) new Helper().getStr1()
(e) this.new Helper().getStr1()
(f) Access.new Helper().getStr1()
(g) new Access.Helper().getStr1()
(h) new Access().new Helper().getStr1()

9.9 Which statement is true about the following program?

```
public class Test {
  private char x = '=';
  public static void main(String[] args) {
    char x = '<';
    Test t = new Test() {
      private char x = '>';
      public String toString() {
        return this.x + super.toString() + x;
      }
    };
    System.out.println(t);
  }
  public String toString() {
    return x + "42";
  }
}
```

Select the one correct answer.

(a) The program will print <=42>.
(b) The program will print <=42<.

(c) The program will print >=42>.
(d) The program will print >=42<.
(e) The program will compile, but it will throw an exception at runtime.
(f) The program will fail to compile.

9.10   Which statement is true about the following program?

```java
public class Test {
  public static void main(String[] args) {
    int x = 42;
    String s = new String() {
      int x = 24;
      public int hashCode() {
        return this.x;
      }
    };
    System.out.println(s.hashCode());
  }
}
```

Select the one correct answer.

(a) The program will print 42.
(b) The program will print 24.
(c) The program will compile, but it will throw an exception at runtime.
(d) The program will fail to compile.

Object Lifetime 10

Chapter Topics

- Understanding automatic garbage collection and guidelines for facilitating garbage collection
- Using static and instance initializers, in particular declaration order, forward references, and exception handling
- Understanding the role played by initializers and constructors in initializing objects, classes, and interfaces

Java SE 11 Developer Exam Objectives *(Continued)*	
[3.3] Initialize objects and their members using instance and static initialiser statements and constructors ○ *Initializers and object construction are covered in this chapter.* ○ *For initializing objects using initialization statements and constructors, see Chapter 3, p. 97.*	*§10.5, p. 540* *to* *§10.9, p. 555*

One of the most important features of Java is its *automatic memory management*, also know as *automatic garbage collection*. This chapter provides a non-technical discussion of this important topic about reclaiming storage of unused objects in a program at runtime. In addition, we look at the role of initializer expressions, initializer blocks, and constructors to initialize the state of an object when it is created with the new operator, and which includes the construction of the state from its superclasses.

10.1 Garbage Collection

Efficient memory management is essential in a runtime system. Storage for objects is allocated in a designated part of the memory called the *heap*, which has a finite size. Garbage collection (GC) is a process of managing the heap efficiently, by reclaiming memory occupied by objects that are no longer needed and making it available for new objects. Java provides automatic garbage collection, meaning that the runtime environment can take care of memory management without the program having to take any special action. Objects allocated on the heap (through the new operator) are administered by the automatic garbage collector. The automatic garbage collection scheme guarantees that a reference to an object is always valid while the object is needed by the program. Specifically, the object will not be reclaimed if it will result in a *dangling reference*—that is, a reference to an object that no longer exists.

Having an automatic garbage collector frees the programmer from the responsibility of writing code for deleting objects. By relying on the automatic garbage collector, a Java program also forfeits any significant influence on the garbage collection of its objects (p. 537). However, this price is insignificant when compared to the cost of putting the code for object management in place and plugging all the memory leaks. Time-critical applications should recognize that the automatic garbage collector runs as a background task and may have a negative impact on their performance.

10.2 Reachable Objects

An automatic garbage collector essentially performs two tasks:

- Decides if and when memory needs to be reclaimed
- Finds objects that are no longer needed by the program and reclaims their storage

A program has no guarantees that the automatic garbage collector will be run during its execution. Consequently, a program should not rely on the scheduling of the automatic garbage collector for its behavior (p. 537).

To understand how the automatic garbage collector finds objects whose storage should be reclaimed, we need to look at the activity happening in the JVM. Java provides *thread-based multitasking*, meaning that several threads can be executing concurrently in the JVM, each doing its own task. A *thread* is an independent path of execution through the program code. A thread is alive if it has not completed its execution. Each live thread has its own JVM stack (§7.1, p. 365). The JVM stack contains activation frames of methods that are currently active. Local references declared in a method can always be found in the method's activation frame, stored on the JVM stack associated with the thread in which the method is called. Objects, in contrast, are always created on the heap. If an object has a field reference, the field will be found inside the object in the heap, and the object denoted by the field reference will also be found in the heap.

An example of how memory is organized during execution is depicted in Figure 10.1, which shows two live threads (t_1 and t_2) and their respective JVM stacks with the activation frames. The diagram indicates which objects in the heap are referenced by local references in the method activation frames. It also identifies field references in objects, which refer to other objects in the heap. Some objects have several aliases.

An object in the heap is said to be *reachable* if it is referenced by any *local* reference in a JVM stack. Likewise, any object that is denoted by a reference in a reachable object is said to be reachable. Reachability is a transitive relationship. Thus a reachable object has at least one chain of reachable references from the JVM stack. Any reference that makes an object reachable is called a *reachable reference*. An object that is not reachable is said to be *unreachable*.

A reachable object is *alive*, and is *accessible* by a live thread. Note that an object can be accessible by more than one thread. Any object that is *not* accessible by a live thread is a candidate for garbage collection. When an object becomes unreachable and is waiting for its memory to be reclaimed, it is said to be *eligible* for garbage collection. An object is eligible for garbage collection if all references denoting it are in eligible objects. Eligible objects do not affect the future course of program execution. When the garbage collector runs, it finds and reclaims the storage of eligible objects, although garbage collection does not necessarily occur as soon as an object becomes unreachable.

In Figure 10.1, the objects o4, o5, o11, o12, o14, and o15 all have reachable references. Objects o13 and o16 have no reachable references, and therefore, are eligible for garbage collection.

From the preceding discussion we can conclude that if a compound object becomes unreachable, its constituent objects also become unreachable, barring any reachable references to the constituent objects. Although the objects o1, o2, and o3 in Figure 10.1 form a circular list, they do not have any reachable references. Thus these objects are all eligible for garbage collection. Conversely, the objects o5, o6, and o7 form a linear list, but they are all reachable, as the first object in the list, o5, is reachable. The objects o8, o10, o11, and o9 also form a linear list (in that order), but not all objects in the list are reachable. Only the objects o9 and o11 are reachable, as object o11 has a reachable reference. The objects o8 and o10 are eligible for garbage collection.

The *lifetime* of an object is the time from its creation to the time it is garbage collected. Under normal circumstances, an object is accessible from the time when it is created to the time when it becomes unreachable. The lifetime of an object can also include a period when it is eligible for garbage collection, waiting for its storage to be reclaimed.

Figure 10.1   *Memory Organization at Runtime*

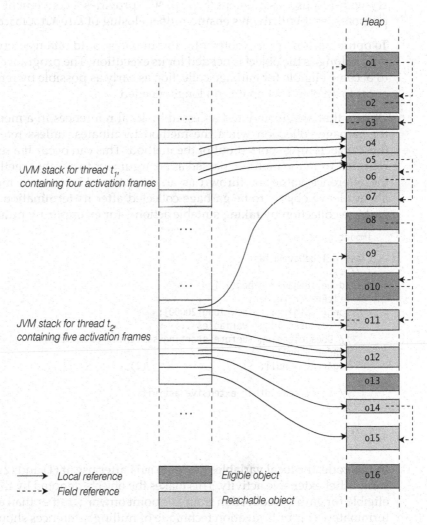

10.3 Facilitating Garbage Collection

The automatic garbage collector determines which objects are not reachable, and therefore, are eligible for garbage collection. It will certainly go to work if there is an imminent memory shortage. Even so, automatic garbage collection should not be perceived as a license for creating a plethora of objects and then forgetting about them. Nevertheless, certain programming practices can help in minimizing the overhead associated with garbage collection during program execution.

Certain objects, such as files and network connections, can tie up resources and should be disposed of properly when they are no longer needed. In most cases, the try-with-resources statement (§7.7, p. 407) provides a convenient facility for such purposes, as it will always ensure proper closing of any AutoCloseable resources.

To optimize its memory footprint, a live thread should retain access to an object for only as long as the object is needed for its execution. The program can allow objects to become eligible for garbage collection as early as possible by removing all references to an object when it is no longer needed.

Objects that are created and accessed by local references in a method are eligible for garbage collection when the method terminates, unless reference values to these objects are exported out of the method. This can occur if a reference value is returned from the method, passed as an argument to another method that records the reference value, or thrown as an exception. However, a method need not always leave objects to be garbage collected after its termination. It can facilitate garbage collection by taking suitable action—for example, by nulling references.

```
import java.io.*;

class WellBehavedClass {
  // ...
  void wellBehavedMethod() {
    FileReader reader;
    long[] bigArray = new long[20000];
    // ... uses local variables ...
    // Does clean-up (before starting something extensive)
    reader = null;                  // (1)
    bigArray = null;                // (2)

    // Start some other extensive activity
    // ...
  }
  // ...
}
```

In this code, the local variables are set to null after use at (1) and (2), before starting some other extensive activity. This makes the objects denoted by the local variables eligible for garbage collection from this point onward, rather than after the method terminates. This optimization technique of nulling references should be used only as a last resort when resources are scarce.

Here are some other techniques to facilitate garbage collection:

- When a method returns a reference value and the object denoted by the value is not needed, not assigning this value to a reference facilitates garbage collection.
- If a reference is assigned a new value, the object that was previously denoted by the reference can become eligible for garbage collection.
- Removing reachable references to a compound object can make the constituent objects become eligible for garbage collection, as explained earlier.

10.4 Invoking Garbage Collection Programmatically

Although Java provides facilities to invoke the garbage collector explicitly, there are no guarantees that it will be run. The program can request that garbage collection be performed, but there is no way to force garbage collection to be activated.

The `System.gc()` method can be used to request garbage collection.

```
static void gc()
```

Requests that garbage collection be run.

Alternatively, corresponding methods in the `Runtime` class can be used. A Java application has a unique `Runtime` object that can be used by the application to interact with the JVM. An application can obtain this object by calling the method `Runtime.getRuntime()`. The `Runtime` class provides several methods related to memory issues:

```
static Runtime getRuntime()
```

Returns the `Runtime` object associated with the current application.

```
void gc()
```

Requests that garbage collection be run. There are no guarantees that it will be run. It is recommended to use the more convenient static method `System.gc()`.

```
long freeMemory()
```

Returns the amount of free memory (bytes) in the JVM that is available for new objects.

```
long totalMemory()
```

Returns the total amount of memory (bytes) available in the JVM, including both memory occupied by current objects and memory available for new objects.

The following points regarding automatic garbage collection should be noted:

- Trying to initiate garbage collection programmatically does not guarantee that it will actually be run.

- Garbage collection might not even be run if the program execution does not warrant it. Thus any memory allocated during program execution might remain allocated after program termination, but will eventually be reclaimed by the operating system.
- There are also no guarantees about the order in which the objects will be garbage collected. Therefore, the program should not make any assumptions based on this criteria.
- Garbage collection does not guarantee that there will be enough memory for the program to run. A program can rely on the garbage collector to run when memory gets very low, and it can expect an OutOfMemoryError to be thrown if its memory demands cannot be met.

 Review Questions

10.1 Which of the following statements is true?
Select the one correct answer.

(a) Objects can be explicitly destroyed using the keyword delete.
(b) An object will be garbage collected immediately after it becomes unreachable.
(c) If object obj1 is accessible from object obj2, and object obj2 is accessible from obj1, then obj1 and obj2 are not eligible for garbage collection.
(d) If object obj1 can access object obj2 that is eligible for garbage collection, then obj1 is also eligible for garbage collection.

10.2 Identify the location in the following program where the object, initially referenced by arg1, is eligible for garbage collection.

```
public class MyClass {
  public static void main(String[] args) {
    String msg;
    String pre = "This program was called with ";
    String post = " as first argument.";
    String arg1 = new String((args.length > 0) ? "'" + args[0] + "'" :
                             "<no argument>");
    msg = arg1;
    arg1 = null;          // (1)
    msg = pre + msg + post;  // (2)
    pre = null;           // (3)
    System.out.println(msg);
    msg = null;           // (4)
    post = null;          // (5)
    args = null;          // (6)
  }
}
```

Select the one correct answer.

(a) After the line at (1).
(b) After the line at (2).
(c) After the line at (3).

(d) After the line at (4).

(e) After the line at (5).

(f) After the line at (6).

10.3   How many objects are eligible for garbage collection when control reaches (1)?

```
public class Elements {
  public static void main(String[] args) {
    int[] array = new int[4];
    for (int i = 0; i < 4; i++) {
      array[i] = i;
    }
    array[0] = array[1] = array[2] = array[3] = 0;
    System.gc();                            // (1);
  }
}
```

Select the one correct answer.

(a) 0

(b) 1

(c) 4

(d) It's hard to say.

10.4   How many objects are eligible for garbage collection when control reaches (1)?

```
public class Link {
  private Link next;
  Link(Link next) { this.next = next; }

  public static void main(String[] args) {
    Link p = null;
    for (int i = 0; i < 5; i++) {
      p = new Link(p);
    }
    System.gc();                            // (1)
  }
}
```

Select the one correct answer.

(a) 0

(b) 5

(c) 10

(d) It's hard to say.

10.5   How many objects are eligible for garbage collection when control reaches (1)?

```
public class Song { }
```

```
public class Album {
  private Song[] songs = { new Song(), new Song() };
  public Song[] getSongs() {
    return songs;
  }
}
```

```
    public void removeAll() {
      songs = null;
    }
  }
```

```
  public class Test {
    public static void main(String[] args) {
      Album album = new Album();
      Song[] songs = album.getSongs();
      album.removeAll();
      System.out.println(album.getSongs());
      // Line (1)
    }
  }
```

Select the one correct answer.

(a) 0
(b) 1
(c) 2
(d) 3
(e) 4

10.5 Initializers

Initializers can be used to set initial values for fields in objects and classes. There are three kinds of initializers:

- *Field initializer expressions*
- *Static initializer blocks*
- *Instance initializer blocks*

Subsequent sections in this chapter provide details on these initializers, concluding with a discussion of the procedure involved in constructing the state of an object when the object is created using the new operator.

For brevity, we have dispensed with the access modifier for fields in most class declarations in the rest of this chapter, as field accessibility by clients is not of primary concern here.

10.6 Field Initializer Expressions

Initialization of fields can be specified in field declaration statements using initializer expressions. The value of the initializer expression must be assignment compatible with the declared field. We distinguish between static and non-static field initializers.

```
  class ConstantInitializers {
      int minAge = 12;                // (1) Non-static
```

```
    static double pensionPoints = 10.5; // (2) Static
    // ...
}
```

The fields of an object are initialized with the values of initializer expressions when the object is created by using the new operator. In the previous example, the declaration at (1) will result in the field minAge being initialized to 12 in every object of the class ConstantInitializers created with the new operator. If no explicit initializer expressions are specified, default values are assigned to the fields.

When a class is loaded, it is initialized, meaning its static fields are initialized with the values of the initializer expressions. The declaration at (2) will result in the static field pensionPoints being initialized to 10.5 when the class is loaded by the JVM. Again, if no explicit initializers are specified, default values are assigned to the static fields.

An initializer expression for a static field cannot refer to non-static members by their simple names. The keywords this and super cannot occur in a static initializer expression.

Since a class is always initialized before it can be instantiated, an instance initializer expression can always refer to any static member of a class, regardless of the member declaration order. In the following code, the instance initializer expression at (1) refers to the static field NO_OF_WEEKS declared and initialized at (2). Such a *forward reference* is legal. More examples of forward references are given in the next subsection.

```
    class MoreInitializers {
            int noOfDays   = 7 * NO_OF_WEEKS;   // (1) Non-static
    static int NO_OF_WEEKS = 52;                // (2) Static
        // ...
    }
```

Initializer expressions can also be used to define constants in interfaces (§5.6, p.254). Such initializer expressions are implicitly static, as they define values of static final fields in an interface.

Initializer expressions are used to initialize local variables as well (§3.4, p.102). A local variable is initialized with the value of the initializer expression every time the local variable declaration is executed.

Declaration Order of Initializer Expressions

When an object is created using the new operator, instance initializer expressions are executed in the order in which the instance fields are declared in the class.

Java requires that the declaration of a field must occur *before its usage* in any initializer expression if the field is *used on the right-hand side of an assignment* in the initializer expression. This essentially means that the declaration of a field must occur before the value of the field is *read* in an initializer expression. Using the field on the left-hand side of an assignment in the initializer expression does not violate the *declaration-before-reading rule*, as this constitutes a *write* operation. This rule applies when the usage of the field is by its *simple name*.

There is one caveat to the declaration-before-reading rule: It does not apply if the initializer expression defines an anonymous class, as the usage then occurs in a different class that has its own accessibility rules in the enclosing context. The restrictions outlined earlier help to detect initialization anomalies at compile time.

In the next code example, the initialization at (2) generates a compile-time error because the field width in the initializer expression violates the declaration-before-reading rule. Because the usage of the field width in the initializer expression at (2) does not occur on the left-hand side of the assignment, this is an illegal forward reference. To remedy the error, the declaration of the field width at (4) can be moved in front of the declaration at (2). In any case, we can use the keyword this as shown at (3), but it will read the default value 0 in the field width.

```
class NonStaticInitializers {
  int length   = 10;               // (1)
//double area = length * width;    // (2) Not OK. Illegal forward reference.
  double area = length * this.width; // (3) OK, but width has default value 0.
  int width    = 10;               // (4)

  int sqSide = height = 20;         // (5) OK. Legal forward reference.
  int height;                       // (6)
}
```

The forward reference at (5) is legal. The usage of the field height in the initializer expression at (5) occurs on the left-hand side of the assignment. The initializer expression at (5) is evaluated as (sqSide = (height = 20)). Every object of the class NonStaticInitializers will have the fields height and sqSide set to the value 20.

The declaration-before-reading rule is equally applicable to static initializer expressions when static fields are referenced by their simple names.

Example 10.1 shows why the order of field initializer expressions can be important. The initializer expressions in this example are calls to methods defined in the class, and methods are not subject to the same access rules as initializer expressions. The call at (2) to the method initMaxGuests() defined at (4) is expected to return the maximum number of guests, but the field occupancyPerRoom at (3) will not have been explicitly initialized at this point; therefore, its default value 0 will be used in the method initMaxGuests(), which will return a logically incorrect value. The program output shows that after object creation, the occupancy per room is correct, but the maximum number of guests is wrong.

- -

Example 10.1   *Initializer Expression Order and Method Calls*

```
// File: TestOrder.java
class Hotel {
  private int noOfRooms       = 12;              // (1)
  private int maxNoOfGuests   = initMaxGuests(); // (2) Bug
  private int occupancyPerRoom = 2;              // (3)
```

```
    public int initMaxGuests() {                                          // (4)
        System.out.println("occupancyPerRoom: " + occupancyPerRoom);
        System.out.println("maxNoOfGuests:    " + noOfRooms * occupancyPerRoom);
        return noOfRooms * occupancyPerRoom;
    }

    public int getMaxGuests() { return maxNoOfGuests; }                   // (5)

    public int getOccupancy() { return occupancyPerRoom; }                // (6)
}
//_____
public class TestOrder {
    public static void main(String[] args) {
        Hotel hotel = new Hotel();                                        // (7)
        System.out.println("AFTER OBJECT CREATION");
        System.out.println("occupancyPerRoom: " + hotel.getOccupancy());  // (8)
        System.out.println("maxNoOfGuests:    " + hotel.getMaxGuests());  // (9)
    }
}
```

Output from the program:

```
occupancyPerRoom: 0
maxNoOfGuests:    0
AFTER OBJECT CREATION
occupancyPerRoom: 2
maxNoOfGuests:    0
```

Exception Handling and Initializer Expressions

Initializer expressions in named classes and interfaces must not result in any uncaught checked exception (§7.2, p.374). If any checked exception is thrown during execution of an initializer expression, it must be caught and handled by code called from the initializer expression. This restriction does not apply to instance initializer expressions in anonymous classes.

Example 10.2 illustrates exception handling for initializer expressions in named classes. The static initializer expression at (3) calls the static method createHotel-Pool() at (4), which catches and handles the checked TooManyHotelsException defined at (2). If the method createHotelPool() were to use the throws clause to specify the checked exception, instead of catching and handling it within a try-catch block, the initializer expression at (3), which called the method, would have to handle the exception. However, the initializer expression cannot specify any exception handling, as the compiler would complain.

The instance initializer expression at (5) calls the method initMaxGuests() at (6), which can throw the unchecked RoomOccupancyTooHighException. If thrown, this exception will be caught and handled in the main() method. Program output confirms that an unchecked RoomOccupancyTooHighException was thrown during program execution.

Example 10.2 *Exceptions in Initializer Expressions*

```java
// File: ExceptionsInInitializers.java
class RoomOccupancyTooHighException
    extends RuntimeException {}                    // (1) Unchecked Exception
class TooManyHotelsException
    extends Exception {}                           // (2) Checked Exception
//_____
class Hotel {
  // Static Members
  private static int noOfHotels = 12;
  private static Hotel[] hotelPool = createHotelPool();    // (3)

  private static Hotel[] createHotelPool() {               // (4)
    try {
      if (noOfHotels > 10)
        throw new TooManyHotelsException();
    } catch (TooManyHotelsException e) {
      noOfHotels = 10;
      System.out.println("No. of hotels adjusted to " + noOfHotels);
    }
    return new Hotel[noOfHotels];
  }
  // Instance Members
  private int noOfRooms      = 215;
  private int occupancyPerRoom = 5;
  private int maxNoOfGuests   = initMaxGuests();            // (5)

  private int initMaxGuests() {                             // (6)
    if (occupancyPerRoom > 4)
      throw new RoomOccupancyTooHighException();
    return noOfRooms * occupancyPerRoom;
  }
}
//_____
public class ExceptionsInInitializers {
  public static void main(String[] args) {
    try { new Hotel(); }
    catch (RoomOccupancyTooHighException exception) {
      exception.printStackTrace();
    }
  }
}
```

Output from the program:

```
No. of hotels adjusted to 10
RoomOccupancyTooHighException
        at Hotel.initMaxGuests(ExceptionsInInitializers.java:29)
        at Hotel.<init>(ExceptionsInInitializers.java:25)
        at ExceptionsInInitializers.main(ExceptionsInInitializers.java:36)
```

10.7 Static Initializer Blocks

Java allows static initializer blocks to be defined in a class. Although such blocks can include arbitrary code, they are primarily used for initializing static fields. The code in a static initializer block is executed only once, when the class is loaded and initialized.

Local variables in static and instance initializer blocks can be declared with the reserved type name var—that is, local variable type inference using var is permitted for local variable declarations in initializer blocks. Code in the rest of this chapter shows many examples of such declarations.

The syntax of a static initializer block comprises the keyword static followed by a local block that can contain arbitrary code, as shown at (3) in the declaration of the following class:

```
class MatrixData {
  static final int ROWS = 12, COLUMNS = 10;        // (1)
  static long[][] matrix = new long[ROWS][COLUMNS]; // (2)
  // ...
  static {                                          // (3) Static initializer
    for (int i = 0; i < matrix.length; i++)
      for (int j = 0; j < matrix[i].length; j++)
        matrix[i][j] = 2*i + j;
  }
  // ...
}
```

When the class MatrixData is first loaded, the static final fields at (1) are initialized. Then the array of arrays matrix of specified size is created at (2), followed by the execution of the static block at (3).

Note that the static initializer block is not contained in any method. A class can have more than one static initializer block. Initializer blocks are *not* members of a class, and they cannot have a return statement because they cannot be called directly.

When a class is initialized, the initializer expressions in static field declarations and static initializer blocks are executed in the order in which they are specified in the class. In the class MatrixData, the initializer expressions at (1) and (2) are executed before the static initializer block at (3).

Similar restrictions apply to static initializer blocks as for static initializer expressions: The keywords this and super cannot occur in a static initializer block, as such a block defines a static context.

Declaration Order of Static Initializers

In the class ScheduleV1 below, the static field declaration at (1) has a *forward reference* to the static field numOfWeeks which has not been declared yet. The simple name of the static field numOfWeeks cannot be used in the initializer expression at (1) before its declaration.

```
public class ScheduleV1 {
//static int numOfDays  = 7 * numOfWeeks; // (1) Compile-time error! Simple name.
  static int numOfWeeks = 52;            // (2)
}
```

The code will compile if we change the order of the declarations, and the static fields numOfWeeks and numOfDays will be initialized correctly with the values 52 and 364, respectively.

```
public class ScheduleV2 {
  static int numOfWeeks = 52;                     // (2) 52
  static int numOfDays  = 7 * numOfWeeks;         // (1) 364
}
```

The code will also compile if the *class name* is used to access the field, but the static field numOfDays will *not* be initialized correctly.

```
public class ScheduleV3 {
  static int numOfDays  = 7 * ScheduleV3.numOfWeeks;  // (1) 0
  static int numOfWeeks = 52;                         // (2) 52
}
```

The code above is actually executed as follows, with the default value 0 of the static field numOfWeeks being used in the initializer expression at (1):

```
public class ScheduleV3 {
  static int numOfDays;                           // Default value: 0
  static int numOfWeeks;                          // Default value: 0
  static {
    numOfDays  = 7 * numOfWeeks;                  // (1) 0
    numOfWeeks = 52;                              // (2) 52
  }
}
```

However, the static field numOfDays will be initialized correctly if the static field numOfWeeks is declared final.

```
public class ScheduleV4 {
  static int numOfDays  = 7 * ScheduleV4.numOfWeeks;  // (1) 364
  static final int numOfWeeks = 52;                   // (2) final: 52
}
```

The initializer expression 52 for the static field numOfWeeks at (2) is a *constant expression* of type int, which is an int literal. The compiler is able to compute the value of a constant expression. A final variable of either a primitive type or type String that is initialized with a constant expression is called a *constant variable*—that is, once initialized, the value of a final variable cannot be changed (§5.5, p. 230). At (2), the final static field numOfWeeks is a constant variable. During class initialization, such final static fields are always initialized first, before any other initializers are executed. Such a constant field never gets initialized with the default value of its type at runtime. Rearrangement of code done by the compiler in this case is equivalent to the following code:

```
public class ScheduleV4 {
  static final int numOfWeeks = 52;          // Constant variable: 52
  static int numOfDays;                      // Default value: 0
  static {
    numOfDays  = 7 * numOfWeeks;             // (1) 364
  }
}
```

Static fields should be accessed statically—that is, using the class name—which is the best policy, but care should be exercised in the order of their declaration and initialization.

When making forward references using *simple names*, code in a static initializer is subject to the declaration-before-reading rule. Note that this rule applies only when the use of the field is by its simple name. Using the class name to access a static field is never a problem.

Example 10.3 illustrates forward references and the order of execution for static initializer expressions in field declarations and code in static initializer blocks. An illegal forward reference occurs at (4), where an attempt is made to read the value of the field sf1 before its declaration. At (11) the read operation is after the declaration, and therefore, allowed. Forward reference made on the left-hand side of the assignment is always allowed, as shown at (2), (5), and (7). The initializers are executed in their declaration order. A static field has the value it was last assigned in an initializer. If there is no explicit assignment, the static field has the default value of its type. Referring to a static field using the class name is always allowed.

Declaring local variables using the reserved word var in static initializer blocks can be found at (5) and (12) in Example 10.3.

- -

Example 10.3 *Static Initializers and Forward References*

```
package refs1;

public class ForwardRefs {

  static {                          // (1) Static initializer block
    System.out.printf("Enter static block 1: sf1=%s, sf2=%s%n",
        ForwardRefs.sf1, ForwardRefs.sf2); // Enter static block 1: sf1=0, sf2=0

    sf1 = 10;                       // (2) OK. Assignment to sf1 allowed
//  sf1 = if1;                      // (3) Not OK. Non-static field access in static context
//  int a = 2 * sf1;                // (4) Not OK. Read operation before declaration
    var b = sf1 = 20;               // (5) OK. Assignment to sf1 allowed
    int c = ForwardRefs.sf1;        // (6) OK. Not accessed by simple name

    System.out.printf("Exit static block 1:  sf1=%s, sf2=%s%n",
        ForwardRefs.sf1, ForwardRefs.sf2); // Exit static block 1:  sf1=20, sf2=0
  }

  // Field declarations:
  static int sf1 = sf2 = 30;  // (7) Static field. Assignment to sf2 allowed
```

```
    static int sf2;              // (8) Static field
    int if1 = 5;                 // (9) Non-static field

    static {                     // (10) Static initializer block
      System.out.printf("Enter static block 2: sf1=%s, sf2=%s%n",
          ForwardRefs.sf1, ForwardRefs.sf2); // Enter static block 2: sf1=30, sf2=30

      int d = 2 * sf1;           // (11) OK. Read operation after declaration
      var e = sf1 = 50;          // (12) OK. Assignment to sf1 allowed

      System.out.printf("Exit static block 2:  sf1=%s, sf2=%s%n",
          ForwardRefs.sf1, ForwardRefs.sf2); // Exit static block 2:  sf1=50, sf2=30
    }

    public static void main(String[] args) {
    }
  }
```

Output from the program:

```
Enter static block 1: sf1=0, sf2=0
Exit static block 1:  sf1=20, sf2=0
Enter static block 2: sf1=30, sf2=30
Exit static block 2:  sf1=50, sf2=30
```

Example 10.4 gives an idea of the code rearrangement that the compiler does to facilitate the initialization for the class in Example 10.3. Field declarations from Example 10.3 are arranged first at (1) and (2) in Example 10.4, followed by a single static initializer block at (3). The static initializer block in Example 10.4 contains the code for the first static initializer block, followed by the initializer expression from the first static field declaration statement, and lastly the code from the second static initializer block in the order these initializers are declared in Example 10.3.

During class initialization, first the declarations of the static fields sf1 and sf2 at (1) and (2), respectively, result in them being created and initialized to their default value 0. Not surprisingly, execution of the code in the static initializer block at (3) gives the same result as in Example 10.3.

Example 10.4 *Static Initializers and Order of Execution*

```
    package refs2;

    public class ForwardRefsSimulated {

    // Declaration of static fields:
    static int sf1;              // (1) Initialized to default value: 0
    static int sf2;              // (2) Initialized to default value: 0

    static {                     // (3) Static initializer block
      // Code from static block 1:
```

```
        System.out.printf("Enter static block 1: sf1=%s, sf2=%s%n",
            sf1, sf2);                  // Enter static block 1: sf1=0, sf2=0

        sf1 = 10;                       // (4) sf1 gets the value 10
        var b = sf1 = 20;               // (5) b and sf1 get the value 20
        int c = sf1;                    // (6) c gets the value 20

        System.out.printf("Exit static block 1:  sf1=%s, sf2=%s%n",
            sf1, sf2);                  // Exit static block 1:  sf1=20, sf2=0

        // Initializer expressions for field declaration:
        sf1 = sf2 = 30;                 // (7) sf1 and sf2 get the value 30

        // Code from static block 2:
        System.out.printf("Enter static block 2: sf1=%s, sf2=%s%n",
            sf1, sf2);                  // Enter static block 2: sf1=30, sf2=30

        int d = 2 * sf1;                // (8) d gets the value 60
        var e = sf1 = 50;               // (9) e and sf1 get the value 50

        System.out.printf("Exit static block 2:  sf1=%s, sf2=%s%n",
            sf1, sf2);                  // Exit static block 2:  sf1=50, sf2=30
    }

    public static void main(String[] args) {
    }
}
```

Output from the program:

```
Enter static block 1: sf1=0, sf2=0
Exit static block 1:  sf1=20, sf2=0
Enter static block 2: sf1=30, sf2=30
Exit static block 2:  sf1=50, sf2=30
```

Exception Handling in Static Initializer Blocks

Exception handling in static initializer blocks is no different from that in static initializer expressions: Uncaught checked exceptions cannot be thrown. Code in initializers cannot throw *checked* exceptions. A static initializer block cannot be called directly. Therefore, any checked exceptions must be caught and handled in the body of the static initializer block; otherwise, the compiler will issue an error. Example 10.5 shows a static initializer block at (3) that catches and handles a checked exception in the try-catch block at (4).

Example 10.5 *Static Initializer Blocks and Exceptions*

```
// File: ExceptionInStaticInitBlocks.java
package version1;

class TooManyCellsException extends Exception {        // (1) Checked Exception
    TooManyCellsException(String number) { super(number); }
}
```

```
//_____
class Prison {
  // Static Members
  private static int   noOfCells = 365;
  private static int[] cells;                    // (2) No initializer expression

  static {                                       // (3) Static block
    try {                                        // (4) Handles checked exception
      if (noOfCells > 300)
        throw new TooManyCellsException(String.valueOf(noOfCells));
    } catch (TooManyCellsException e) {
      System.out.println("Exception handled: " + e);
      noOfCells = 300;
      System.out.println("No. of cells adjusted to " + noOfCells);
    }
    cells = new int[noOfCells];
  }
}
//_____
public class ExceptionInStaticInitBlocks {
  public static void main(String[] args) {
    new Prison();
  }
}
```

Output from the program:

```
Exception handled: version1.TooManyCellsException: 365
No. of cells adjusted to 300
```

Static initializer blocks do not exactly aid code readability, and should be used sparingly, if at all. The code in the static initializer block at (3) in Example 10.5 can easily be refactored to instantiate the static array field cells at (2) using the private static method at (3) that handles the checked exception TooManyCellsException:

```
class Prison {
  // Static Members
  private static int   noOfCells = 365;
  private static int[] cells = initPrison();  // (2) Initializer expression

  //
  private static int[] initPrison() {         // (3) Private static method
    try {                                     // (4) Handles checked exception
      if (noOfCells > 300)
        throw new TooManyCellsException(String.valueOf(noOfCells));
    } catch (TooManyCellsException e) {
      System.out.println("Exception handled: " + e);
      noOfCells = 300;
      System.out.println("No. of cells adjusted to " + noOfCells);
    }
    return new int[noOfCells];
  }
}
```

10.8 Instance Initializer Blocks

Just as static initializer blocks can be used to initialize static fields in a named class, Java provides the ability to initialize fields during object creation using instance initializer blocks. In this respect, such blocks serve the same purpose as constructors during object creation. The syntax of an instance initializer block is the same as that of a local block, as shown at (2) in the following code. The code in the local block is executed every time an instance of the class is created.

```
class InstanceInitializers {

  long[] squares = new long[10];     // (1)
  // ...
  {                                  // (2) Instance Initializer
    for (int i = 0; i < squares.length; i++)
      squares[i] = i*i;
  }
  // ...
}
```

The array squares of specified length is first created at (1); its creation is followed by the execution of the instance initializer block at (2) every time an instance of the class InstanceInitializers is created. Note that the instance initializer block is not contained in any method. A class can have more than one instance initializer block, and these (and any instance initializer expressions in instance field declarations) are executed in the order they are specified in the class.

Declaration Order of Instance Initializers

Analogous to the other initializers discussed earlier, an instance initializer block cannot make a forward reference to a field by its simple name in a read operation as that would violate the declaration-before-reading rule. However, using the this keyword to access a field is not a problem.

The class below has an instance initializer block at (1) with forward references to the fields i, j, and k that are declared at (7), (8), and (9), respectively. These fields are accessed using the this reference in *read* operations at (3), (4), (5), and (6). Using the simple name of these fields at (3), (4), (5), and (6) to access their values will violate the declare-before-use rule, resulting in compile-time errors—regardless of whether the fields are declared with initializer expressions or not, or whether they are final or not. The fields i and j are accessed at (2) in *write* operations, which are permitted using the simple name. However, care must be exercised to ensure that the fields are initialized correctly. At (3), (4), and (5), the fields i and j have the value 10. However, when the initializer expressions are evaluated in the instance field declarations, the value of j will be set to 100.

```
public class InstanceInitializersII {

  { //Instance initializer with forward references.   (1)
    i = j = 10;                              // (2) Permitted.
    int result = this.i * this.j;            // (3) i is 10, j is 10.
```

```
        System.out.println(this.i);          // (4) 10
        System.out.println(this.j);          // (5) 10
        System.out.println(this.k);          // (6) 50
    }
    // Instance field declarations.
    int i;                      // (7) Field declaration without initializer expression.
    int j = 100;                // (8) Field declaration with initializer expression.
    final int k = 50;           // (9) Final instance field with constant expression.


}
```

Example 10.6 illustrates some additional subtle points regarding instance initializer blocks. In Example 10.6, an illegal forward reference occurs in the code at (4), which attempts to read the value of the field nsf1 before it is declared. The read operation at (11) occurs after the declaration, and therefore, is allowed. Forward reference made on the left-hand side of the assignment is always allowed, as shown at (2), (3), (5), and (7).

Declaring local variables using the reserved word var in instance initializer blocks is shown at (5) and (12) in Example 10.6.

Example 10.6 *Instance Initializers and Forward References*

```
        public class NonStaticForwardReferences {

            {                           // (1) Instance initializer block.
              nsf1 = 10;                // (2) OK. Assignment to nsf1 allowed.
              nsf1 = sf1;               // (3) OK. Static field access in non-static context.
              // int a = 2 * nsf1;      // (4) Not OK. Read operation before declaration.
              var b = nsf1 = 20;        // (5) OK. Assignment to nsf1 allowed.
              int c = this.nsf1;        // (6) OK. Not accessed by simple name.
            }

            int nsf1 = nsf2 = 30;       // (7) Non-static field. Assignment to nsf2 allowed.
            int nsf2;                   // (8) Non-static field.
            static int sf1 = 5;         // (9) Static field.

            {                           // (10) Instance initializer block.
              int d = 2 * nsf1;         // (11) OK. Read operation after declaration.
              var e = nsf1 = 50;        // (12) OK. Assignment to nsf1 allowed.
            }

            public static void main(String[] args) {
                NonStaticForwardReferences objRef = new NonStaticForwardReferences();
                System.out.println("nsf1: " + objRef.nsf1);
                System.out.println("nsf2: " + objRef.nsf2);
            }
        }
```

Output from the program:

```
    nsf1: 50
    nsf2: 30
```

As in an instance initializer expression, the keywords this and super can be used to refer to the current object in an instance initializer block.

As in a static initializer block, the return statement is also not allowed in instance initializer blocks.

An instance initializer block can be used to factor out common initialization code that will be executed regardless of which constructor is invoked. A typical usage of an instance initializer block is in anonymous classes (§9.6, p.521), which cannot declare constructors, but can instead use instance initializer blocks to initialize fields. In Example 10.7, the anonymous class defined at (1) uses an instance initializer block at (2) to initialize its fields.

Example 10.7 *Instance Initializer Block in Anonymous Class*

```java
// File: InstanceInitBlock.java
class Base {
  protected int a;
  protected int b;
  void print() { System.out.println("a: " + a); }
}
//_____
class AnonymousClassMaker {
  Base createAnonymous() {
    return new Base() {          // (1) Anonymous class
      {                          // (2) Instance initializer
        a = 5; b = 10;
      }

      @Override
      void print() {
        super.print();
        System.out.println("b: " + b);
      }
    };  // end anonymous class
  }
}
//_____
public class InstanceInitBlock {
  public static void main(String[] args) {
    new AnonymousClassMaker().createAnonymous().print();
  }
}
```

Output from the program:

```
a: 5
b: 10
```

Exception Handling and Instance Initializer Blocks

Exception handling in instance initializer blocks is similar to that in static initializer blocks. Example 10.8 shows an instance initializer block at (3) that catches and handles a checked exception in the try-catch block at (4). Another instance initializer block at (5) throws an unchecked exception at (6). The runtime system handles the runtime exception, printing the stack trace and terminating the program.

Exception handling in instance initializer blocks differs from that in static initializer blocks in the following aspect: The execution of an instance initializer block can result in an uncaught checked exception, provided the exception is declared in the throws clause of *every* constructor in the class. Static initializer blocks cannot allow this, since no constructors are involved in class initialization. Instance initializer blocks in anonymous classes have even greater freedom: They can throw any exception.

Example 10.8 *Exception Handling in Instance Initializer Blocks*

```java
// File: ExceptionsInInstBlocks.java
class RoomOccupancyTooHighException
      extends Exception {}                        // (1) Checked exception
class BankruptcyException
      extends RuntimeException {}                 // (2) Unchecked exception
//_____
class Hotel {
  // Instance Members
  private boolean bankrupt      = true;
  private int     noOfRooms     = 215;
  private int     occupancyPerRoom = 5;
  private int     maxNoOfGuests;

  {                                               // (3) Instance initializer block
    try {                                         // (4) Handles checked exception
      if (occupancyPerRoom > 4)
        throw new RoomOccupancyTooHighException();
    } catch (RoomOccupancyTooHighException exception) {
      System.out.println("ROOM OCCUPANCY TOO HIGH: " + occupancyPerRoom);
      occupancyPerRoom = 4;
    }
    maxNoOfGuests = noOfRooms * occupancyPerRoom;
  }

  {                                               // (5) Instance initializer block
    if (bankrupt)
      throw new BankruptcyException();            // (6) Throws unchecked exception
  }  // ...
}
//_____
public class ExceptionsInInstBlocks {
  public static void main(String[] args) {
```

```
        new Hotel();
    }
}
```

Output from the program:

```
ROOM OCCUPANCY TOO HIGH: 5
Exception in thread "main" BankruptcyException
        at Hotel.<init>(ExceptionsInInstBlocks.java:27)
        at ExceptionsInInstBlocks.main(ExceptionsInInstBlocks.java:33)
```

10.9 Constructing Initial Object State

Object initialization involves constructing the initial state of an object when it is created by the new operator. First the fields are initialized to their default values (§3.4, p.103)—whether they are subsequently given non-default initial values or not—and then the constructor is invoked. This can lead to *local* chaining of constructors. The invocation of the constructor at the end of the local chain of constructor invocations results in the following actions, before the constructor's execution resumes:

- Implicit or explicit invocation of the superclass constructor. Constructor chaining ensures that the state from the object's superclasses is constructed first (§5.3, p.209).
- Initialization of the instance fields by executing their instance initializer expressions and any instance initializer blocks, in the order they are specified in the class declaration.

Example 10.9 illustrates object initialization. The new operator is used at (8) to create an object of SubclassB. The no-argument constructor SubclassB() at (2) uses the this() construct to locally chain to the non-zero argument constructor at (3). This constructor then leads to an implicit call of the superclass constructor. As can be seen from the program output, the execution of the superclass's constructor at (1) reaches completion first. This is followed by the execution of the instance initializer block at (4) and the instance initializer expression at (6). Then the execution of the body of the non-zero argument constructor at (3) resumes. Finally, the no-argument constructor completes its execution, thereby completing the construction of the object state.

Note that the instance initializers are executed in the order they are specified in the class declaration. The forward reference to the field value at (5) is legal because the usage of the field value is on the left-hand side of the assignment (it does not violate the declaration-before-reading rule). The default value of the field value is overwritten by the instance initializer block at (5). The field value is again overwritten by the instance initializer expression at (6), and finally by the non-zero argument constructor at (3).

Example 10.9   *Object State Construction*

```java
// File: ObjectConstruction.java
class SuperclassA {
  public SuperclassA() {                      // (1) Superclass constructor
    System.out.println("Constructor in SuperclassA");
  }
}
//_____
class SubclassB extends SuperclassA {

  SubclassB() {                               // (2) No-argument constructor
    this(3);
    System.out.println("No-argument constructor in SubclassB");
  }

  SubclassB(int i) {                          // (3) Non-zero argument constructor
    System.out.println("Non-zero argument constructor in SubclassB");
    value = i;
  }

  {                                           // (4) Instance initializer block
    System.out.println("Instance initializer block in SubclassB");
    value = 2;                                // (5)
  }

  int value = initializerExpression();        // (6) Instance field declaration

  private int initializerExpression() {       // (7)
    System.out.println("Instance initializer expression in SubclassB");
    return 1;
  }
}
//_____
public class ObjectConstruction {
  public static void main(String[] args) {
    SubclassB objRef = new SubclassB();          // (8)
    System.out.println("value: " + objRef.value);
  }
}
```

Output from the program:

```
Constructor in SuperclassA
Instance initializer block in SubclassB
Instance initializer expression in SubclassB
Non-zero argument constructor in SubclassB
No-argument constructor in SubclassB
value: 3
```

Some care should be exercised when writing constructors for non-final classes, since the object that is constructed might be a subclass instance. Example 10.10 shows a situation where use of overridden methods in *superclass* initializers and constructors can give unexpected results. The example intentionally uses the this reference to underline that the instance methods and constructors are invoked on the current object, and that the constructor call results in the initialization of the object state, as expected.

The program output from Example 10.10 shows that the field superValue at (1) in SuperclassA never gets initialized explicitly when an object of SubclassB is created at (8). The SuperclassA constructor at (2) does have a call to a method that has the name doValue at (3). A method with such a name is defined in SuperclassA at (4), but is also overridden in SubclassB at (7). The program output indicates that the method doValue() from SubclassB is called at (3) in the SuperclassA constructor. The implementation of the method doValue() at (4) never gets executed when an object of SubclassB is created. Method invocation always determines the implementation of the method to be executed, based on the *actual* type of the object. Keeping in mind that it is an object of SubclassB that is being initialized, the call to the method named doValue at (3) results in the method from SubclassB being executed. This can lead to unintended results. The overriding method doValue() at (7) in SubclassB can access the field value declared at (5) before its initializer expression has been executed; thus the method invoked can access the state of the object *before* this has been completely initialized. The value 0 is then printed, as the field value has not yet been initialized with the value 800 when the superclass constructor is executed.

Class initialization takes place before any instance of the class can be created or a static method of the class can be invoked. A superclass is initialized before its subclasses are initialized. Initializing a class involves initialization of the static fields by executing their static initializer expressions and any static initializer blocks.

Initialization of an interface involves execution of any static initializer expressions for the public static final fields declared in the interface. An interface cannot specify instance initializer expressions because it has no instance fields, nor can it specify any initializer blocks because it cannot be instantiated.

Example 10.10 *Initialization Anomaly under Object State Construction*

```java
// File: ObjectInitialization.java
class SuperclassA {
  protected int superValue;                          // (1)
  SuperclassA() {                                    // (2)
    System.out.println("Constructor in SuperclassA");
    this.doValue();                                  // (3)
  }
  void doValue() {                                   // (4)
    this.superValue = 911;
    System.out.println("superValue (from SuperclassA): " + this.superValue);
  }
}
//_____
class SubclassB extends SuperclassA {
  private int value = 800;                           // (5)
  SubclassB() {                                      // (6)
    System.out.println("Constructor in SubclassB");
```

```
        this.doValue();
        System.out.println("superValue (from SuperclassA): " + this.superValue);
    }
    @Override
    void doValue() {                                              // (7)
        System.out.println("value (from SubclassB): " + this.value);
    }
}
//_____
public class ObjectInitialization {
    public static void main(String[] args) {
        System.out.println("Creating an object of SubclassB.");
        new SubclassB();                                          // (8)
    }
}
```

Output from the program:

```
Creating an object of SubclassB.
Constructor in SuperclassA
value (from SubclassB): 0
Constructor in SubclassB
value (from SubclassB): 800
superValue (from SuperclassA): 0
```

 ## Review Questions

10.6 Given the following class, which of these static initializer blocks can be independently inserted at (1)?

```
public class MyClass {
    private static int count = 5;
    static final int STEP = 10;
    boolean alive;

    // (1) INSERT STATIC INITIALIZER BLOCK HERE
}
```

Select the three correct answers.

(a) static { alive = true; count = 0; }
(b) static { STEP = count; }
(c) static { count += STEP; }
(d) static ;
(e) static { }
(f) static { count = 1; }

10.7 What will be the result of compiling and running the following program?

```
public class MyClass {
    public static void main(String[] args) {
        MyClass obj = new MyClass(n);
    }
```

```
        static int i = 5;
        static int n;
        int j = 7;
        int k;

        public MyClass(int m) {
            System.out.println(i + ", " + j + ", " + k + ", " + n + ", " + m);
        }

        { j = 70; n = 20; } // Instance initializer block

        static { i = 50; }  // Static initializer block
    }
```

Select the one correct answer.

(a) The code will fail to compile because of the instance initializer block.
(b) The code will fail to compile because of the static initializer block.
(c) The code will compile and print 50, 70, 0, 20, 0 at runtime.
(d) The code will compile and print 50, 70, 0, 20, 20 at runtime.
(e) The code will compile and print 5, 70, 0, 20, 0 at runtime.
(f) The code will compile and print 5, 70, 0, 20, 20 at runtime.
(g) The code will compile and print 5, 7, 0, 20, 0 at runtime.
(h) The code will compile and print 5, 7, 0, 20, 20 at runtime.

10.8 Given the following class, which instance initializer block inserted independently at (1) will allow the class to be compiled?

```
    public class FirstClass {
        static int gap = 10;
        double length;
        final boolean active;

        // (1) INSERT CODE HERE
    }
```

Select the one correct answer.

(a) instance { active = true; }
(b) FirstClass { gap += 5; }
(c) { gap = 5; length = (active ? 100 : 200) + gap; }
(d) { }
(e) { length = 4.2; }
(f) { active = (gap > 5); length = 5.5 + gap;}

10.9 What will be the result of compiling and running the following program?

```
    public class Initialization {
        private static String msg(String msg) {
            System.out.println(msg);
            return msg;
        }

        public Initialization() { m = msg("1"); }

        { m = msg("2"); }
```

```
      String m = msg("3");
      public static void main(String[] args) {
        Object obj = new Initialization();
      }
    }
```

Select the one correct answer.

(a) The program will fail to compile.
(b) The program will compile and print 1, 2, and 3 at runtime.
(c) The program will compile and print 2, 3, and 1 at runtime.
(d) The program will compile and print 3, 1, and 2 at runtime.
(e) The program will compile and print 1, 3, and 2 at runtime.

10.10   What is the result of executing the following program?

```
      public class Music {
        static {
          System.out.print("-C-");
        }
        {
          System.out.print("-D-");
        }
        public Music(){
          System.out.print("-E-");
        }
      }
```

```
      public class Song extends Music {
        static {
          System.out.print("-F-");
        }
        {
          System.out.print("-G-");
        }
        public Song(){
          System.out.print("-A-");
        }
      }
```

```
      public class Test {
        public static void main(String[] args) {
          Music x1 = new Song();
          Song x2 = new Song();
        }
      }
```

Select the one correct answer.

(a) -C--D--E--F--G--A--G--A--G--A-
(b) -C--D--E--F--G--A--D--E--G--A-
(c) -C--F--D--E--G--A--D--E--G--A-

(d) -C--F--D--G--E--A--D--G--E--A-
(e) -C--F--E--D--A--G--E--D--A--G-

10.11 Which labeled lines in the following code can be independently *uncommented* by removing the // characters at the beginning of a line, such that the code will still compile?

```
class GeomInit {
//int width = 14;              // (1)

  {
//  area = width * height;     // (2)
  }

  int width = 37;

  {
//  height = 11;               // (3)
  }

  int height, area;
//area = width * height;       // (4)

  {
//  int width = 15;            // (5)
    area = 100;
  }
}
```

Select the two correct answers.

(a) Line (1)
(b) Line (2)
(c) Line (3)
(d) Line (4)
(e) Line (5)

Generics 11

Chapter Topics

- Understanding the relationship between generic types, parameterized types, and raw types
- Declaring generic types (normal classes, record classes, enum types and interfaces) and parameterized types
- Use of the diamond operator (<>) when creating objects of generic classes
- Using the restricted keyword var to declare local generic type references
- Extending generic types
- Understanding the folly of mixing generic code and legacy code
- Understanding the significance of unchecked warnings on type-safety
- Understanding subtype relationships for wildcards
- Understanding type hierarchy for wildcard parameterized types
- Understanding widening and narrowing reference conversions in type hierarchy of wildcard parameterized types
- Understanding restrictions on set and get operations when using references of wildcard parameterized types
- Using bounded type parameters
- Understanding how to implement a generic class that is also Iterable
- Understanding wildcard capture
- Programming with wildcard parameterized types
- Writing generic methods and constructors
- Understanding the implications of type erasure
- Understanding how overloading and overriding work with generics

- Understanding reifiable and non-reifiable types, and their role in generics
- Understanding the limitations and restrictions that generics place on instance tests, casting, arrays, varargs, and exception handling

Java SE 17 Developer Supplementary Topics	
[12.3] Use generics, including wildcards. ○ *Note that this is a supplementary objective in the description of the Java SE 17 Developer exam.*	*§11.1, p. 565* *to* *§11.4, p. 579*
Java SE 11 Developer Exam Objectives	
[5.1] Use generics, including wildcards	*§11.1, p. 565* *to* *§11.13, p. 623*

Introduction of generics in Java was a major step in the evolution of the language. Extending the language with generics provides even stronger type checking at compile time and allows implementing generic algorithms, especially for managing *containers* of data, like the collections discussed in Chapter 15.

Generics in Java is a large topic with some subtle details. Extending the language with generics has consequences for many aspects of the language. Familiarity with topics covered in this chapter will be beneficial in both using and implementing generic types.

The basics of generics are covered in §11.1, §11.2, and §11.3, which introduce the terminology, the underlying concepts, and the motivation for using generics for implementing collections.

On a first reading, §11.4 to §11.8 should be read to become familiar with wildcards and the flexibility they provide in defining parameterized types, and with generic methods and constructors. The reader should come back to these topics for an in-depth study when the need arises.

For an even deeper dive into generics, we suggest studying the topics from §11.9 onward: wildcard capture and wildcard parameterized types, implications of type erasure, and restrictions on generic types.

11.1 Introducing Generics

Generics allow classes and interfaces, as well as methods and constructors, to be *parameterized* with *type information*. An *abstract data type* (ADT) defines both the *types* of objects and the *operations* that can be performed on these objects. Generics allow us to specify the types used by the ADT so that the *same* definition of an ADT can be used on *different* types of objects.

Generics in Java are a way of providing type information in ADTs so that the compiler can guarantee type-safety of operations at runtime. Generics are implemented as compile-time transformations, with negligible impact on the JVM. The generic type declaration is compiled once into a single Java class file, and the use of the generic type is checked against this file. Also, no extraneous Java class files are generated for each use of the generic type.

The primary benefits of generics are increased language expressiveness with improved type-safety, resulting in improved robustness and reliability of code. Generics avoid verbosity of using casts in many contexts, thus improving code clarity. Since the compiler guarantees type-safety, this eliminates the necessity of explicit type checking and casting at runtime.

One major goal when introducing generics in Java has been backward compatibility with legacy code (i.e., non-generic code). Interoperability with legacy code and the lack of generic type information at runtime largely determine how generics work in Java. Many of the restrictions on generics in Java can be attributed to these two factors.

Generics are used extensively in implementing the Java Collections Framework. An overview of Chapter 15 on collections and maps is therefore recommended as many of the examples in this chapter make use of generic types from this framework.

Before the introduction of generics in Java, a general implementation of a collection maintained its objects by using references of the type Object. The bookkeeping of the actual type of the objects fell on the client code. Example 11.1 illustrates this approach. It implements a *self-referential data structure* called a *node*. Each node holds a data value and a reference to another node. Such data structures form the basis for building *linked data structures*.

Example 11.1 *A Legacy Class*

```java
class LegacyNode {
  private Object    data;   // The value in the node
  private LegacyNode next;   // The reference to the next node.
  LegacyNode(Object data, LegacyNode next) {
    this.data = data;
    this.next = next;
  }
  public void       setData(Object obj)     { this.data = obj; }
  public Object     getData()               { return this.data; }
  public void       setNext(LegacyNode next) { this.next = next; }
  public LegacyNode getNext()               { return this.next; }
  @Override public String toString() {
    return this.data + (this.next == null? "" : ", " + this.next);
  }
}
```

The class LegacyNode can be used to create a linked list with arbitrary objects:

```java
LegacyNode node1 = new LegacyNode(4, null);       // 4 --> null
LegacyNode node2 = new LegacyNode("July", node1); // "July" --> 4 --> null
```

Primitive values are encapsulated in corresponding wrapper objects. If we want to retrieve the data from a node, the data is returned via an Object reference:

```java
Object obj = node2.getData();
```

In order to access type-specific properties or behavior of the fetched object, the reference value in the Object reference must be converted to the right type. To avoid a ClassCastException at runtime when applying the cast, we must make sure that the object referred to by the Object reference is of the right type. All that can be accomplished by using the instanceof pattern match operator:

```java
if (obj instanceof String str) {
  System.out.println(str.toUpperCase()); // Method specified in the String class.
}
```

The approach outlined above places certain demands on how to use the class
LegacyNode to create and maintain linked structures. For example, it is the responsibility of the client code to ensure that the objects being put in nodes are of the same
type. Implementing classes for specific types of objects is not a good solution. First,
it can result in code duplication, and second, it is not always known in advance
what types of objects will be put in the nodes. Generic types offer a better solution,
where one generic class is defined and specific reference types are supplied each
time we want to instantiate the class.

11.2 Generic Types and Parameterized Types

We first introduce the basic terminology and concepts relating to generics in Java.
Note that the discussion here on generic and parameterized types also applies to
enum types (§5.13, p. 287) and record classes (§5.14, p. 299).

Generic Types

A *generic type* is a reference type that defines a *list of formal type parameters* or *type
variables* that must be provided before it can be used as a type. Example 11.2
declares a generic type which, in this case, is a *generic class* called Node<E> that
allows nodes of specific types to be maintained. It has only one formal type parameter, E, that represents the type of the data in a node.

```
class Node<E> {
...
}
```

The formal type parameter E does not explicitly specify a type, but serves as a
placeholder for a type to be defined in an invocation of the generic type. The formal
type parameters of a generic type are specified within angle brackets, <>, immediately after the class name. A type parameter is an unqualified identifier. If a generic
class has several formal type parameters, these are specified as a comma-separated
list, <T1, T2, ..., Tn>. It is quite common to use one-letter names for formal type
parameters; a convention that we will follow in this book. For example, E is used
for the type of elements in a collection, K and V are used for the type of the keys and
the type of the values in a map, and T is used to represent an arbitrary type.

As a starting point for declaring a generic class, we can begin with a class where
the Object type is utilized to generalize the use of the class. In Example 11.2, the
declaration of the generic class Node<E> uses E in all the places where the type Object
was used in the declaration of the class LegacyNode in Example 11.1. From the declaration of the class Node<E>, we can see that the formal type E is used like a reference type in the class body: as a field type at (1), as a return type at (5), and as a
parameter type in the methods at (4) to (8). Use of the class name in the generic
class declaration is parameterized by the type parameter ((2), (6), (7)), with one
notable exception: The formal type parameter is *not* specified after the class name
in the constructor declaration at (3). Which actual reference type the formal type

parameter E represents is not known in the generic class Node<E>. Therefore, we can only call methods that are inherited from the Object class on the field data, as these methods are inherited by all objects, regardless of their object type. One such example is the call to the toString() method in the method declaration at (8).

The scope of the type parameter E of the generic type includes any non-static inner classes, but excludes any static member types—the parameter E cannot be accessed in static context. It also excludes any nested generic declarations where the same name is redeclared as a formal type parameter. Shadowing of type parameter names should be avoided.

Example 11.2 *A Generic Class for Nodes*

```
class Node<E> {
  private E          data;    // Data                              (1)
  private Node<E>    next;    // Reference to next node            (2)
  Node(E data, Node<E> next) {                                  // (3)
    this.data = data;
    this.next = next;
  }
  public void    setData(E data)        { this.data = data; }   // (4)
  public E       getData()              { return this.data; }   // (5)
  public void    setNext(Node<E> next) { this.next = next; }   // (6)
  public Node<E> getNext()              { return this.next; }   // (7)
  @Override public String toString() {                          // (8)
    return this.data.toString() +
          (this.next == null ? "" : ", " + this.next.toString());
  }
}
```

Some Restrictions on the Use of Type Parameters in a Generic Type

A constructor declaration in a generic class cannot specify the formal type parameters of the generic class in its constructor header after the class name:

```
class Node<E> {
  ...
  Node<E>() { ... }                          // Compile-time error!
  ...
}
```

A formal type parameter cannot be used to create a new instance, as it is not known which concrete type it represents. The following code in the declaration of the Node<E> class would be illegal:

```
E ref = new E();                           // Compile-time error!
```

A formal type parameter is a *non-static type*. It cannot be used in a static context, for much the same reason as an instance variable cannot be used in a static context: It is associated with objects. The compiler will report errors at (1), (2), and (3) in the code below:

```
class Node<E> {
  private static E e1;                     // (1) Compile-time error!
  public  static E oneStaticMethod(E e2) { // (2) Compile-time error!
    E e3;                                  // (3) Compile-time error!
    System.out.println(e3);
  }
  // ...
}
```

Parameterized Types

A *parameterized type* (also called a *type instance*) is an *invocation* or *instantiation* of a generic type that is a specific usage of the generic type where the formal type parameters are replaced by *actual type parameters*. Analogy with method declarations and method invocations can be helpful in understanding the relationship between generic types and parameterized types. We pass actual parameters in a method invocation to execute a method. In the case of a generic type invocation, we pass actual *type* parameters in order to instantiate a generic type.

We can declare references and create objects of parameterized types, and call methods on these objects, in much the same way as we use non-generic classes.

```
Node<Integer> intNode = new Node<Integer>(2020, null);
```

The actual type parameter Integer, explicitly specified in the declaration statement above, binds to the formal type parameter E in Example 11.2. The compiler treats the parameterized type Node<Integer> as a *new type*. The parameterized type Node<Integer> constrains the generic type Node<E> to Integer objects, thus implementing homogenous nodes with Integers. The reference intNode can only refer to a Node of Integer. The node created can only be used to store an object of this concrete type.

Methods can be called on objects of parameterized types:

```
Integer iRef = intNode.getData();           // Integer object with int value 2020
```

In the method call above, the actual type parameter is determined from the type of the reference used to make the call. The type of the intNode reference is Node<Integer>; therefore, the actual type parameter is Integer. The method header is Integer getData(), meaning that the method will return a value of type Integer. The compiler checks that the return value can be assigned. As the compiler guarantees that the return value will be an Integer and can be assigned, no explicit cast or runtime check is necessary. The compiler actually inserts the necessary cast. Here are some more examples of calling methods of parameterized types:

```
intNode.setData(2020);                       // Ok.
intNode.setData("TwentyTwenty");             // (1) Compile-time error!
intNode.setNext(new Node<Integer>(2019, null)); // (2020, (2019, null))
intNode.setNext(new Node<String>("Hi", null));  // (2) Compile-time error!
```

In the method calls shown above, the compiler determines that the actual type parameter is Integer. The method signatures are setData(Integer) and setNext(Node<Integer>). As expected, we get a compile-time error when we try to pass an argument that is not compatible with the parameter type in the method declarations; for example, at (1) and (2). The parameterized types Node<Integer> and Node<String> are two *unrelated* types. The compiler reports any inconsistent use of a parameterized type so that errors can be caught earlier at compile time and the use of explicit casts in the source code is minimized, as evident from (3) and (4), respectively.

```
Node<String> strNode = new Node<String>("Hi", null);
intNode = strNode;                      // (3) Compile-time error!
String str = strNode.getData();         // (4) No explicit cast necessary.
```

The Diamond Operator (<>)

In the object creation expression of the new operator, the actual type parameter was explicitly specified after the class name—in contrast to the constructor declaration.

```
Node<String> 1st = new Node<String>("Hi", null); // Explicit actual type parameter
```

The actual type parameters can be omitted, but not the angle brackets (<>), if the compiler can infer the actual type parameters from the context of the object creation expression. The angle brackets with no actual parameters (<>) are commonly referred to as the *diamond operator*.

```
Node<String> 1st = new Node<>("Hi", null); // Actual type parameter inferred.
```

In the object creation expression above, the compiler performs automatic type inference to infer that the actual type parameter in the expression must be String. The compiler is able to infer the actual type parameter from the type information of the constructor call arguments.

```
new Node<>(null, null);  // Actual type parameter: Object.
```

In the code below, the compiler uses the type information of the variable on the left-hand side to infer the actual type parameter of the object creation expression, thereby ensuring compatibility with the *target type* on the left-hand side of the assignment.

```
Node<String>  strNode = new Node<>(null, null); // Actual type parameter: String.
Node<Integer> intNode = new Node<>(null, null); // Actual type parameter: Integer.
Node<Number>  numNode = new Node<>(null, null); // Actual type parameter: Number.
Node<Number>  1stNode = new Node<>(2021, null); // Actual type parameter: Number.
```

In the last declaration, the int value 2021 is boxed into an Integer object that can be assigned to a reference of its superclass Number. In other words, the signature of the constructor call is Node<Number>(Number, Node<Number>).

Given the following scenario:

```
// (1) Method declaration with parameterized type as formal parameter.
void find(Node<String> node) { /* ... */ }
...
// (2) Method call where actual argument uses diamond operator.
find(new Node<>(null,null)); // Actual type parameter: Object or String?
```

The compiler takes the target type (Node<String>) in the method declaration into consideration, correctly inferring the actual type parameter to be String, in order for the actual and the formal parameters in the call to be assignment compatible.

A single diamond operator must replace the entire actual type parameter list in the object creation expression. In the first declaration below, the compiler infers that the actual type parameter list is <String, List<Integer>>.

```
HashMap<String, List<Integer>> map = new HashMap<>();
HashMap<String, List<Integer>> map = new HashMap<String,<>>(); // Error!
```

If the actual type parameters are not specified and the diamond operator is omitted, the compiler issues an *unchecked conversion warning*—that is, the code will compile, but all bets are off at runtime. Below, the reference type Node in the object creation expression is interpreted as a *raw type*. Implications of interoperability between generic types and raw types are discussed on p. 575.

```
Node<String> rawNode = new Node("Hi", null); // Unchecked conversion warning!
```

The diamond operator can be used to instantiate an anonymous class (see p. 633).

```
new Node<>("Hi", null) {/* ... */}; // Parameterized type: Node<String>
new Node("Hi", null)   {/* ... */}; // Raw type: Node
```

Parameterized Local Variable Type Inference

Consider the four local variable declarations shown below. The first three declarations are equivalent, as they create a Node<String> object whose data and next fields are null. In declaration (1), since the type String is explicitly specified in the object creation expression, the actual type parameter is deduced to be String. In declaration (2), the diamond operator is specified in the object creation expression, but the compiler is able to infer that the actual type parameter is String from the left-hand side of the declaration—that is, the compiler considers the context of the whole declaration. In the case of the parameterized local variable declarations with var, both the actual type parameters and the parameterized type denoted by var are inferred from the object creation expression.

```
// Parameterized local variable declarations:
Node<String> node1 = new Node<String>(null, null); // (1) Node of String
Node<String> node2 = new Node<>(null, null);        // (2) Node of String
var node3 = new Node<String>(null, null);           // (3) Node of String
var node4 = new Node<>(null, null);                 // (4) Node of Object
```

In declaration (3), as String is explicitly specified in the object creation expression, the actual type parameter is inferred to be String and the parameterized type of node3 denoted by var is inferred to be Node<String>.

However, in declaration (4), the diamond operator is used in the object creation expression. In this case, the actual type parameter is inferred to be Object and the parameterized type of node4 denoted by var is inferred to be Node<Object>. Adequate type information should be provided in the object creation expression when declaring parameterized local variables with var in order to avoid unexpected types being inferred for the actual parameter types and the parameterized type denoted by var.

Generic Interfaces

Generic types also include generic interfaces, which are declared analogous to generic classes. The specification of formal type parameters in a generic interface is the same as in a generic class. Example 11.3 declares a generic interface that defines the reference type IMonoLink<E> for objects that store a data value of type E.

Example 11.3   *A Generic Interface and Its Implementation*

```
interface IMonoLink<E> {
  void         setData(E data);
  E            getData();
  void         setNext(IMonoLink<E> next);
  IMonoLink<E> getNext();
}

class MonoNode<E> implements IMonoLink<E> {
  private E           data;    // Data
  private IMonoLink<E> next;    // Reference to next node                    (1)

  MonoNode(E data, IMonoLink<E> next) {                                      // (2)
    this.data = data;
    this.next = next;
  }

  @Override public void setData(E data) { this.data = data; }
  @Override public E    getData()        { return this.data; }
  @Override public void setNext(IMonoLink<E> next) { this.next = next; } // (3)
  @Override public IMonoLink<E> getNext()            { return this.next; } // (4)
  @Override public String toString() {
    return this.data.toString() + (this.next == null? "" : ", " + this.next);
  }
}
```

A generic interface can be implemented by a generic (or a non-generic) class:

```
class MonoNode<E> implements IMonoLink<E> {
  // ...
}
```

Note that the construct <E> is used in two different ways in the class header. The first occurrence of <E> *declares* E to be a type parameter, and the second occurrence of <E> *parameterizes* the generic interface with this type parameter. The declare-before-use rule also applies to type parameters. The version of the MonoNode class in Example 11.3 differs from the Node class in Example 11.2 at (1), (2), (3), and (4). These changes were necessary to make the MonoNode<E> class compliant with the IMonoLink<E> interface.

A generic interface can be parameterized in the same way as a generic class. In the code below, the reference strNode has the parameterized type IMonoLink<String>. It is assigned the reference value of a node of inferred type MonoNode<String>. The assignment is legal, since the parameterized type MonoNode<String> is a subtype of the parameterized type IMonoLink<String>:

```
IMonoLink<String> strNode2 = new MonoNode<>("Bye", null);
System.out.println(strNode2.getData());                    // Prints: Bye
```

As with non-generic interfaces, generic interfaces cannot be instantiated either:

```
IMonoLink<String> strNode3 = new IMonoLink<>("Bye", null); // Compile-time error!
```

Example 11.4 shows a non-generic class implementing a generic interface. The generic interface IMonoLink<E> is parameterized by a *concrete type*, namely, Lymph. The type LymphNode is a subtype of the parameterized type IMonoLink<Lymph>, as it implements the methods of the generic interface IMonoLink<E> in accordance with the concrete type parameter Lymph.

The Java standard library contains many examples of generic interfaces. The two interfaces java.lang.Comparable<E> and java.util.Comparator<E> are discussed in detail in §14.4, p. 761, and §14.5, p. 769, respectively. The Java Collections Framework also includes many examples of generic interfaces, such as Collection<E>, List<E>, Set<E>, and Map<K,V> (Chapter 15, p. 781).

Example 11.4 *A Non-Generic Class Implementing a Generic Interface*

```
// File: LymphNode.java
class Lymph { /*... */ }

public class LymphNode implements IMonoLink<Lymph> {
  private Lymph            body;
  private IMonoLink<Lymph> location;
  @Override public void  setData(Lymph obj) { body = obj; }
  @Override public Lymph getData()          { return body; }
  @Override public void  setNext(IMonoLink<Lymph> loc) { this.location = loc; }
  @Override public IMonoLink<Lymph> getNext()          { return this.location; }
}
```

Extending Generic Types

A non-final generic type can be extended. Example 11.5 shows that the generic interface IBiLink<E> extends the generic interface IMonoLink<E>, and that the generic class BiNode<E> extends the generic class MonoNode<E> and implements the generic interface IBiLink<E> (see Figure 11.1).

```
interface IBiLink<E> extends IMonoLink<E> {
  // ...
}
```

```
class BiNode<E> extends MonoNode<E> implements IBiLink<E> {
  // ...
}
```

The compiler checks that the formal type parameters of the superclass in the extends clause can be resolved. In the case above, the formal type parameter E, which is specified for the subclass, is also used as the type parameter for the superclass and is used to constrain the interface to the same type parameter. This dependency ensures that an invocation of the subclass will result in the same actual type parameter being used by the superclass and for the interface.

```
BiNode<Integer> intBiNode = new BiNode<>(2020, null, null);
MonoNode<Integer> intMonoNode = intBiNode;        // (1)
Integer iRef = intMonoNode.getData();             // Integer with int value 2020
MonoNode<Number> numMonoNode = intBiNode;         // (2) Compile-time error!
```

The assignment at (1) is type-safe, as the parameterized class BiNode<Integer> is a subtype of the parameterized class MonoNode<Integer>. It is important to note that the superclass and the subclass are parameterized with the *same* type parameter; otherwise, the subtype relationship between the superclass and the subclass does not hold. We get a compile-time error at (2) because the parameterized class BiNode<Integer> is *not* a subtype of the parameterized class MonoNode<Number>. Subtype relationships for generic types are discussed in a later section (p. 579).

Figure 11.1 *Extending Generic Types*

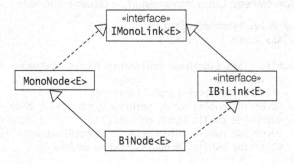

. . . .

Example 11.5 *Extending Generic Types*

```
interface IBiLink<T> extends IMonoLink<T> {
  void       setPrevious(IBiLink<T> previous);
  IBiLink<T> getPrevious();
}

class BiNode<E> extends MonoNode<E> implements IBiLink<E> {
  private IBiLink<E> previous;    // Reference to previous node

  BiNode(E data, IBiLink<E> next, IBiLink<E> previous) {
    super(data, next);
    this.previous = previous;
  }
```

```
            @Override public void setPrevious(IBiLink<E> previous) {
              this.previous = previous;
            }
            @Override public IBiLink<E> getPrevious() { return this.previous; }
            @Override public String toString() {
              return (this.previous == null? "" : this.previous + ", ") +
                      this.getData() +
                      (this.getNext() == null? "" : ", " + this.getNext());
            }
          }
```

Example 11.5 showed examples of generic types being extended to create new generic subtypes. We can extend a non-generic type to a generic subtype as well:

```
class AbstractNode { /* ... */ }                    // A non-generic supertype
class SimpleNode<E> extends AbstractNode { /* ... */ }// A generic subtype
```

We can also extend concrete parameterized types to specialized non-generic subtypes:

```
class IntegerBiNode extends BiNode<Integer> {        // A non-generic subtype
  IntegerBiNode(Integer data, IntegerBiNode next, IntegerBiNode previous) {
    super(data, next, previous);
  }
  //...
}
```

Note that a subtype can inherit only one parameterization of the same generic interface supertype. Implementing or extending a parameterized type fixes the parameterization for the subtype and its supertypes. In the declaration below, the subtype WeirdNode<E> tries to implement the interface IMonoLink<Integer>, but at the same time, it is a subtype of the interface IMonoLink<E> which the superclass Mono-Node<E> implements:

```
class WeirdNode<E> extends MonoNode<E> implements IMonoLink<Integer> { // Error!
  //...
}
```

There is great flexibility in extending reference types, but care must be exercised to achieve the desired result.

Raw Types and Unchecked Warnings

A generic type without its formal type parameters is called a *raw type*. The raw type is the supertype of all parameterized types of the generic type. For example, the raw type Node is the supertype of the parameterized types Node<String>, Node<Integer>, and Node<Node<String>>. The last parameterized type is an example of a *nested parameterization*. It means that a node of this type has a node of type Node<String> as data.

A parameterized type (e.g., Node<String>) is *not* a class. Parameterized types are used by the compiler to check that objects created are used correctly in the program. The parameterized types `Node<String>`, `Node<Integer>`, and `Node<Node<String>>` are all represented at runtime by their raw type `Node`. In other words, the compiler does *not* create a new class for each parameterized type. Only one class (`Node`) exists that has the name of the generic class (`Node<E>`), and the compiler generates only one class file (`Node.class`) with the Java bytecode for the generic class.

Only reference types (excluding array creation and enumerations) can be used in invocations of generic types. A primitive type is not permitted as an actual type parameter, the reason being that values of primitive types have different sizes. This would require different code being generated for each primitive type used as an actual type parameter, but there is only one implementation of a generic class in Java.

Generics are implemented in the compiler only. The JVM is oblivious about the use of generic types. It does not differentiate between `Node<String>` and `Node<Integer>`, and just knows about the class `Node`. The compiler translates the generic class by a process known as *type erasure*; meaning that information about type parameters is erased and casts are inserted to make the program type-safe at runtime. The compiler guarantees that casts added at compile time never fail at runtime, when the program compiles without any *unchecked warnings*.

It is possible to use a generic class by its raw type only, like a non-generic class, without specifying actual type parameters for its usage. Example 11.6 illustrates mixing generic and non-generic code. The compiler will issue an unchecked warning if such a use can be a potential problem at runtime. Such usage is permitted for backward compatibility with legacy code, but is strongly advised against when writing new code.

The assignment at (5) in Example 11.6 shows that it is always possible to assign the reference value of a parameterized type to a reference of the raw type, as the latter is the supertype of the former. However, the raw type reference can be used to violate the type-safety of the node at runtime, as shown at (6). Calling a method on a node using the raw type reference results in an *unchecked call warning* by the compiler. In this particular case, a `String` is set as the data of an `Integer` node.

```
    ...
    Node<Integer> intNode = new Node<>(2020, null);
    Integer iRef = intNode.getData();        // Integer object with int value 2020
    ...
    Node rawNode = intNode;             // (5) Assigning to raw type always possible.
    rawNode.setData("BOOM");            // (6) Unchecked call warning!
    intNode = rawNode;                  // (7) Unchecked conversion warning!
    iRef = intNode.getData();           // (8) ClassCastException!
    iRef = rawNode.getData();           // (9) Compile-time error!
```

Assigning the reference value of a raw type to a reference of the parameterized type results in an *unchecked conversion warning* from the compiler, as shown at (7). If the node referred to by the raw type reference is not of type `Integer`, using it as a node of type `Integer` can lead to problems at runtime, as shown at (8). The assignment at (8) is only type compatible, not type-safe, as its type-safety is compromised at (6) as explained above. A ClassCastException is thrown at runtime, since an Integer was expected, but a String was returned by the getData() method.

The assignment at (9) does not compile because of type mismatch: Without the generic type information, the compiler infers that the call on the getData() method using the raw type reference rawNode can only return an Object, whereas the type of the variable on the left-hand side is Integer.

The class Preliminaries in Example 11.6 is shown compiled with the non-standard option -Xlint:unchecked. The compiler recommends using this option when non-generic and generic code are mixed in this way. The program compiles in spite of the unchecked warnings, and can be executed. But all guarantees of type-safety are off in the face of unchecked warnings. See also §11.11, p. 613, which provides details on translation of generic code by type erasure.

- -

Example 11.6 *Unchecked Warnings*

```java
// A client for the generic class Node<E> in Example 11.2, p. 568.
public class Preliminaries {
  public static void main(String[] args) {
    Node<Integer> intNode = new Node<>(2018, null);
    Integer iRef = intNode.getData();          // Integer object with int value 2018
    intNode.setData(2020);                     // Ok.
//  intNode.setData("TwentyTwenty");           // (1) Compile-time error!
    intNode.setNext(new Node<>(2019, null));   // (2020, (2019, null))
//  intNode.setNext(new Node<>("Hi", null));   // (2) Compile-time error!

    Node<String> strNode = new Node<>("Hi", null);
//  intNode = strNode;                         // (3) Compile-time error!
    String str = strNode.getData();            // (4) No explicit cast necessary.

    Node rawNode = intNode;                    // (5) Assigning to raw type always possible.
    rawNode.setData("BOOM");                   // (6) Unchecked call warning!
    intNode = rawNode;                         // (7) Unchecked conversion warning!
    iRef = intNode.getData();                  // (8) ClassCastException!
//  iRef = rawNode.getData();                  // (9) Compile-time error!
  }
}
```

Compiling the program:

```
>javac -Xlint:unchecked Preliminaries.java
Preliminaries.java:16: warning: [unchecked] unchecked call to setData(E) as a
member of the raw type Node
    rawNode.setData("BOOM");                   // (6) Unchecked call warning!
            ^
  where E is a type-variable:
    E extends Object declared in class Node
Preliminaries.java:17: warning: [unchecked] unchecked conversion
    intNode = rawNode;                         // (7) Unchecked conversion warning!
              ^
  required: Node<Integer>
  found:    Node
2 warnings
```

Running the program:

```
>java Preliminaries
Exception in thread "main" java.lang.ClassCastException: java.lang.String cannot
  be cast to java.lang.Integer
          at Preliminaries.main(Preliminaries.java:18)
```

11.3 Collections and Generics

Before the introduction of generics in Java 1.5, a collection in the Java Collections Framework could hold references to objects of any type. For example, any object which is an instance of the java.lang.Object class or its subclasses could be maintained in an instance of the java.util.ArrayList class, which implements the java.util.List interface.

```
List wordList = new ArrayList();        // Using non-generic types.
wordList.add("two zero two zero");      // Can add any object.
wordList.add(2020);
//...
Object element = wordList.get(0);       // Always returns an Object.
//...
if (element instanceof String str) {    // Runtime check to avoid ClassCastException.
    // Use reference str.
}
```

The client of a collection has to do most of the bookkeeping with regard to using the collection in a type-safe manner: which objects are put in the collection and how objects retrieved are used. Using the Object class as the element type allows the implementation of the collection class to be specific, but its use to be generic. An ArrayList is a specific implementation of the List interface, but usage of the class ArrayList is generic with regard to any object.

Using a generic collection, the compiler provides the type-safety, and the resulting code is less verbose.

```
List<String> wordList = new ArrayList<>();        // Using a specific type.
wordList.add("two zero two zero");                // Can add strings only.
wordList.add(2020);                               // Compile-time error!
//...
String element = wordList.get(0);                 // Always returns a String.
//...
```

Runtime checks or explicit casts are not necessary now. Generic types allow the implementation of the collection class to be generic, but its use to be specific. The generic type ArrayList<E> is a generic implementation of the List<E> interface, but now the usage of the parameterized type ArrayList<String> is specific, as it constrains the generic type ArrayList<E> to strings.

11.4 Wildcards

In this section, we discuss how using wildcards can increase the expressive power of generic types. But first we examine one major difference between array types and parameterized types. The generic class Node<E> used in this subsection is defined in Example 11.2, p. 568.

The Subtype Covariance Problem with Parameterized Types

The following three declarations create three nodes of Integer, Double, and Number type, respectively.

```
Node<Integer> intNode    = new Node<>(2020,null);        // (1)
Node<Double>  doubleNode = new Node<>(3.14,null);        // (2)
Node<Number>  numNode    = new Node<>(2021, null);       // (3)
```

In the declaration at (3), the signature of the constructor call is Node(Integer, null). The formal type parameter E of the generic class Node<E> is bound to the actual type parameter Number—that is, the signature of the constructor is Node(Number, Node<Number>). Since the type Integer is a subtype of the type Number, and null can be assigned to any reference, the constructor call succeeds.

In the method calls at (4) and (5) below, the method signature in both cases is setData(Number). The method calls again succeed, since the actual parameters are of types Double and Integer, which are subtypes of Number:

```
numNode.setData(10.5);                          // (4)
numNode.setData(2022);                          // (5)
```

However, the following calls do *not* succeed:

```
numNode.setNext(intNode);                       // (6) Compile-time error!
numNode = new Node<Number>(2030, doubleNode);   // (7) Compile-time error!
```

The actual type parameter at (6) is determined to be Number. The generic class Node<E> is thus parameterized with the class Number. The compiler complains that the method setNext(Node<Number>) in the parameterized class Node<Number> is *not* applicable for the actual argument (Node<Integer>) at (6)—that is, the method signature setNext(Node<Number>) is *not* compatible with the method call signature setNext(Node<Integer>). The compiler also complains at (7): The constructor signature Node(Number, Node<Number>) is *not* applicable for the arguments (int, Node<Double>). The problem is with the second argument at (7). We cannot pass an argument of type Node<Integer> or Node<Double> where a parameter of type Node<Number> is expected. The following assignments will also not compile:

```
numNode = intNode;                              // (8) Compile-time error!
numNode = doubleNode;                           // (9) Compile-time error!
```

The reason for the compile-time errors is that Node<Integer> and Node<Double> are *not* subtypes of Node<Number>, although Integer and Double are subtypes of Number. In the case of arrays, the array types Integer[] and Double[] *are* subtypes of the array type Number[]. The subtyping relationship between the individual types carries over to corresponding array types. This type relationship is called *subtype covariance* (see Figure 11.2). This relationship holds for arrays because the element type is available at runtime, and can be checked. If the subtype covariance were allowed for parameterized type, it could lead to problems at runtime, as the element type would not be known and cannot be checked, since it has been erased by the compiler.

```
numNode = intNode;                    // If this assignment was allowed,
numNode.setData(25.5);                // the data could be corrupted,
Integer iRef = intNode.getData();     // resulting in a ClassCastException!
```

Therefore, the *subtype covariance* relationship does *not* hold for parameterized types that are instantiations of the same generic type with different actual type parameters, regardless of any subtyping relationship between the actual type parameters. The actual type parameters are *concrete* types (e.g., Integer, Number), and therefore, the parameterized types are called *concrete parameterized types*. Such parameterized types are totally unrelated. As an example from the Java Collections Framework, the parameterized type Map<Integer, String> is not a subtype of the parameterized type Map<Number, String>.

Figure 11.2   *No Subtype Covariance for Parameterized Types*

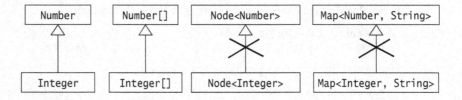

Wildcard Types

Wildcard types are type parameters defined using the *wildcard* symbol ?. The wildcard ? by itself represents *all* types. The parameterized type List<?> represents a list of all types, whereas the concrete parameterized type List<Integer> only represents a list of Integer. In other words, a *wildcard type* can represent *many types*. Therefore, a parameterized type that has wildcard types as actual type parameters can represent a family of types, in contrast to a concrete parameterized type that only represents itself. The wildcard types provided in Java represent four subtype relationships that are summarized in Table 11.1.

Wildcard types provide the solution for increased expressive power to overcome the limitations discussed earlier when using generics in Java, but introduce limitations of their own as to what operations can be carried out on an object using references of wildcard types. We will use the class Node<E> in Example 11.2, p. 568, as a running example to discuss the use of wildcard types.

Table 11.1 *Summary of Subtyping Relationships for Generic Types*

Name	Syntax	Semantics	Description
Subtype covariance	? extends Type	Any subtype of Type (including Type)	*Bounded wildcard with upper bound*
Subtype contravariance	? super Type	Any supertype of Type (including Type)	*Bounded wildcard with lower bound*
Subtype bivariance	?	All types	*Unbounded wildcard*
Subtype invariance	Type	Only type Type	*Type parameter/argument*

Subtype Covariance: ? extends Type

The wildcard type ? extends Type represents all *subtypes* of Type (including Type itself). The wildcard type ? extends Type is called an *upper bounded wildcard* with Type representing its *upper bound*.

Figure 11.3 *Partial Type Hierarchy for* Node<? extends Number>

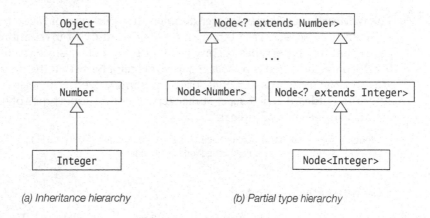

(a) Inheritance hierarchy   (b) Partial type hierarchy

The wildcard type ? extends Number denotes all subtypes of Number, and the parameterized type Node<? extends Number> denotes the family of invocations of Node<E> for types that are subtypes of Number. Figure 11.3 shows a partial type hierarchy for the parameterized type Node<? extends Number>. Note that the parameterized type Node<? extends Integer> is a subtype of the parameterized type Node<? extends Number>, since the wildcard type ? extends Integer represents all subtypes of Integer, and these are also subtypes of Number.

```
Node<? extends Integer> intSubNode = new Node<Integer>(100, null);
Node<? extends Number> numSupNode = intSubNode;
```

Subtype Contravariance: ? super Type

The wildcard type ? super Type represents all *supertypes* of Type (including Type itself). The wildcard type ? super Type is called a *lower bounded wildcard* with Type representing its *lower bound*.

Figure 11.4 *Partial Type Hierarchy for* Node<? super Integer>

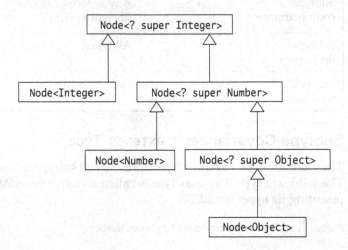

The wildcard type ? super Integer denotes all supertypes of Integer, and the parameterized type Node<? super Integer> denotes a family of invocations of Node<E> for types that are supertypes of Integer. Figure 11.4 shows a partial type hierarchy for the parameterized type Node<? super Integer>. Note that the parameterized type Node<? super Number> is a *subtype* of the parameterized type Node<? super Integer>, since the wildcard type ? super Number represents all supertypes of Number, and these are also supertypes of Integer.

```
Node<? super Number> numSupNode = new Node<Number>(100, null);
Node<? super Integer> numIntSupNode = numSupNode;
```

Subtype Bivariance: ?

As mentioned earlier, the wildcard type ? represents *all* types. The wildcard type ? is called the *unbounded wildcard*, since it has no bounds as do the other two wildcard types. By definition, it represents both the upper and the lower bounded wildcards for any bound.

The parameterized type Node<?> denotes the family of invocations of Node<E> for any type—that is, denotes a Node of any kind, and is therefore the supertype of all invocations of Node<E> (see also Figure 11.5, p. 583, and §11.5, p. 584).

Figure 11.5 *Partial Type Hierarchy for Selected Parameterized Types of* Node<E>

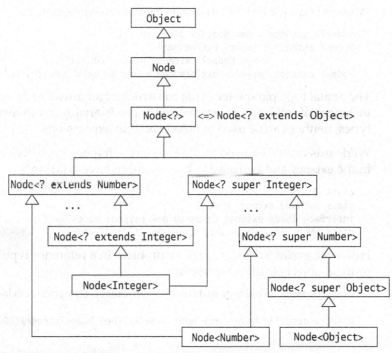

All widening reference conversions are type-safe.
All narrowing reference conversions require an explicit cast, except for the following:
- Narrowing reference conversion from Node to Node<?>,
  or from Node<?> to Node<? extends Object>, is safe.
- Narrowing reference conversion from Node to Node<? extends Object>,
  or to any subtype below Node<?>, results in an unchecked conversion warning.

Subtype Invariance: Type

When a concrete type Type is used as an actual type parameter in a parameterized type, it represents Type itself. Since Type can be *any* concrete type, it is called an *unbounded type parameter*. The concrete parameterized type Node<Integer> represents the invocation of Node<E> for the concrete actual type parameter Integer. As we have seen earlier, there is no subtype covariance relationship between concrete parameterized types, but there is such a relationship between bounded parameterized types and concrete parameterized types (see also Figure 11.3 and Figure 11.4).

Let us recapitulate the basic terminology before proceeding further. A generic type can specify one or more formal type parameters. A parameterized type is an invocation of a generic type, supplying the required actual type parameters. An actual type parameter can be a wildcard type (possibly bounded) or a concrete type. A concrete type is either a non-generic type or a parameterized type that has concrete types as parameters.

Some Restrictions on Wildcard Types

Wildcards *cannot* be used in instance creation expressions:

```
Node<?> anyNode = new Node<?>(2020, null);                    // Compile-time error!
Node<? extends Integer> extIntNodeA
            = new Node<? extends Integer>(0, null);     // Compile-time error!
Node<? extends Integer> extIntNodeB = new Node<Integer>(0, null);  // OK
```

The actual type parameter in the constructor call must be a concrete type. Creating instances of wildcard parameterized types is analogous to instantiating interface types; neither can be used in object creation expressions.

Wildcards *cannot* be used in the *header* of reference type declarations. Supertypes in the extends and implements clauses cannot have wildcards.

```
class QuestionableNode<?>  { /* ... */ }                      // Not OK.
class SubNode extends Node<?> { /* ... */ }                   // Not OK.
interface INode extends Comparable<? extends Node<?>> { /* ... */ }  // Not OK.
class XNode implements Comparable<?>  { /* ... */ }           // Not OK.
```

However, *nested wildcards* are not a problem in a reference type declaration header or in an object creation expression:

```
class OddNode extends Node<Node<?>> implements Comparable<Node<?>> { /* ... */ }
...
Node<?> nodeOfAnyNode = new Node<Node<?>>(new Node<Integer>(2020, null), null);
```

11.5 Using References of Wildcard Parameterized Types

A wildcard type can be used to declare parameterized references—that is, references whose type is a wildcard parameterized type. In this section, we look at how such references are used in the following contexts:

- Assignment between such references
- Calling methods of generic types using such references

The generic class Node<E> used in this subsection is defined in Example 11.2, p. 568.

Generic Reference Assignment

A reference of a supertype can refer to an object of a subtype, and this substitution principle applies to parameterized types as well. Assignment compatibility is according to the type hierarchy of the parameterized types. Figure 11.5 shows partial type hierarchy for selected parameterized types of the generic class Node<E>. It combines the type hierarchies from Figure 11.3 and Figure 11.4. As we would expect, *widening reference conversions* according to the type hierarchy are always type-safe. All but the last assignment statement in the code below are legal. The types Node<Number> and Node<Integer> are unrelated. (The notation B <: A means B is a subtype of A.)

```
Node<Object>  objNode = new Node<Object>(100, null);
Node<Number>  numNode = new Node<Number>(200, null);
Node<Integer> intNode = new Node<Integer>(300, null);
Node<? extends Number> extNumNode
                     = intNode; // Node<Integer> <: Node<? extends Number>
Node<? super Integer>  supIntNode
                     = numNode; // Node<Number> <: Node<? super Integer>
supIntNode = objNode;          // Node<Object> <: Node<? super Integer>
numNode    = intNode;          // Compile-time error! Types unrelated.
```

In the code below, we get an error at (1) because the types Node<? extends Number> and Node<? super Number> are unrelated, but that is not the case for the types Node<? extends Object> and Node<? super Object> at (2). The family of types denoted by the type Node<? super Object> has the subtype Node<Object> only, which is also a subtype of the type Node<? extends Object>. In the assignment at (3), the type Node<? extends Object> is not a subtype of the type Node<? super Object>, but the converse is true as established at (2).

```
Node<? super Number>  supNumNode;
Node<? extends Object> extObjNode;
Node<? super Object>  supObjNode;
extNumNode = supNumNode;  // (1) Compile-time error! Types unrelated.
extObjNode = supObjNode;  // (2) Node<? super Object> <: Node<? extends Object>
supObjNode = extObjNode;  // (3) Compile-time error!
```

Narrowing reference conversion requires an explicit cast, except for the cases noted below (see also Figure 11.5). The raw type Node and the unbounded wildcard parameterized type Node<?> are essentially equivalent in this regard. Conversion between the two is type-safe:

```
Node     rawNode;
Node<?> anyNode;
rawNode = anyNode; // Node <-- Node<?> is type-safe.
anyNode = rawNode; // Node<?> <-- Node is type-safe.
```

The unbounded wildcard parameterized type Node<?> and the upper bounded wildcard parameterized type Node<? extends Object> are also essentially equivalent (see (4)), except when assigned a value of the raw type Node (see (5)).

```
// (4):
anyNode = extObjNode;  // Node<?> <-- Node<? extends Object> is type-safe.
extObjNode = anyNode;  // Node<? extends Object> <-- Node<?> is type-safe.

// (5):
anyNode    = rawNode;  // Node<?> <-- Node is type-safe.
extObjNode = rawNode;  // Node<? extends Object> <-- Node: Unchecked Conversion
```

Assigning a value of the raw type Node to a reference of the type Node<? extends Object> results in an *unchecked conversion warning*—which conforms to the general rule when mixing legacy and generic code: Assigning the value of a raw type to a reference of a bounded wildcard parameterized type or a concrete parameterized type results in an unchecked conversion warning, as illustrated by the examples below.

```
extNumNode = rawNode; // Node<? extends Number> <-- Node: Unchecked Conversion
intNode    = rawNode; // Node<Integer> <-- Node: Unchecked Conversion
```

For a discussion of explicit casting of parameterized references, see §11.13, p. 625. Suppressing different kinds of unchecked warnings with the @SuppressWarnings("unchecked") annotation is discussed in §11.13, p. 623, and §25.5, p. 1582.

Using Parameterized References to Call Set and Get Methods

Generic classes are suitable for implementing ADTs called *collections* (also called *containers*) where the element type is usually specified by a type parameter. The Java Collections Framework is a prime example of such collections. A collection usually provides two basic operations: a *set* operation (also called a *write* or *put* operation) to add an element to the collection, and a *get* operation (also called a *read* operation) to retrieve an element from the collection. The *set* operation takes a parameter of the type T, where T is a type parameter of the generic class. The *get* operation returns a value of the type parameter T. The class Node<E> provides these two basic operations to manipulate the data in a node:

```
class Node<E> {
  private E data;
  // ...
  public void setData(E obj) { data = obj; }        // (1) Set operation.
  public E    getData()      { return data; }        // (2) Get operation.
  // ...
}
```

So far we have called these two methods using references of concrete parameterized types:

```
Node<Number> numNode = new Node<>(2020, null);
numNode.setData(2021);                    // (3) Can only set a Number.
Number data = numNode.getData();          // (4) Can only get a Number.
```

The actual type parameter in the above method calls is a *concrete type*, but what happens when we use a reference of a wildcard parameterized type that represents a family of types? For example, what if the type of the reference numNode is Node<? extends Number>? Is the method call at (3) type-safe? Is the assignment at (4) type-safe? Operations that can potentially break the type-safety are flagged as either compile-time errors or warnings. If there are warnings but no errors, the program still compiles. However, type-safety at runtime is not guaranteed.

The key to using generics in Java is understanding the implications of wildcard parameterized types in the language—and why the compiler will not permit certain operations involving wildcards, since these might break the type-safety of the program. To illustrate some of the subtleties, we compile the class in Example 11.7 successively with different headers for the method checkIt(). The parameter type is different in each method header, from (h1) to (h5). The method uses three local variables object, number, and integer of type Object, Number, and Integer, respectively ((v1) to (v3)). There are three calls to the setData() method of the generic class Node<E> to set an Object, a Number, and an Integer as the data in the node referenced by the reference s0 ((s1) to (s3)). There are also three calls to the getData() method of the generic class Node<E>, assigning the return value to each of the local variables ((s4) to (s6)). And finally, the last statement, (s7), tests whether the data retrieved can be put back in again.

Example 11.7 *Illustrating Get and Set Operations Using Parameterized References*

```
class WildcardAccessRestrictions {

    static void checkIt(Node s0) {                          // (h1)
//static void checkIt(Node<?> s0) {                         // (h2)
//static void checkIt(Node<? extends Number> s0) {          // (h3)
//static void checkIt(Node<? super Number> s0) {            // (h4)
//static void checkIt(Node<Number> s0) {                    // (h5)
        // Local variables
        Object  object  = new Object();                     // (v1)
        Number  number  = 1.5;                              // (v2)
        Integer integer = 10;                               // (v3)
        // Method calls
        s0.setData(object);                                 // (s1)
        s0.setData(number);                                 // (s2)
        s0.setData(integer);                                // (s3)
        object  = s0.getData();                             // (s4)
        number  = s0.getData();                             // (s5)
        integer = s0.getData();                             // (s6)
        s0.setData(s0.getData());                           // (s7)
    }
}
```

Attempts to compile the method in Example 11.7 with different headers are shown in Table 11.2. The rows are statements from (s1) to (s7) from Example 11.7. The columns indicate the type of the parameter s0 in the method headers (h1) to (h5). The reference s0 is used to call the methods. The entry **ok** means the compiler did not report any errors or any unchecked warnings. The entry **!** means the compiler did not report any errors but issued an unchecked call warning. The entry × means the compiler reported an error. In other words, we cannot carry out the operations that are marked with the entry ×.

Table 11.2 *Get and Set Operations Using Parameterized References*

Type of s0 / Operation	Node	Node<?>	Node <? extends Number>	Node <? super Number>	Node<Number>
s0.setData(object);	!	×	×	×	×
s0.setData(number);	!	×	×	ok	ok
s0.setData(integer);	!	×	×	ok	ok

Table 11.2 *Get and Set Operations Using Parameterized References (Continued)*

Operation \ Type of s0	Node	Node<?>	Node <? extends Number>	Node <? super Number>	Node<Number>
`object = s0.getData();`	ok	ok	ok	ok	ok
`number = s0.getData();`	×	×	ok	×	ok
`integer = s0.getData();`	×	×	×	×	×
`s0.setData(s0.get-Data());`	!	×	×	×	ok

Raw Type References

The type of the reference s0 is the raw type Node. This case illustrates the non-generic paradigm of using a collection: We can put any object, but we can only get an Object. From Table 11.2, we see that we can put any object as data in a node of the raw type Node, but the compiler issues *unchecked call warnings*, as we are putting an object into a raw type node whose element type is not known. We can only get an Object, as we cannot be more specific about the data type.

Unbounded Wildcard References: <?>

The type of the reference s0 is Node<?>. The compiler determines that the actual type parameter for each method call is the wildcard ?—that is, any type. Obviously, we cannot set any data in a node whose element type cannot be determined. It might not be type-safe. And we cannot guarantee the type of its data either because the data type can be of any type, but we can safely read it as an Object. Note that we can always write a null, as the null value can be assigned to any reference.

Typical use of unbounded wildcard reference is in writing methods that treat the objects in a container as of type Object and make use of Object methods for their operation. The method below can print the data in *any* sequence of nodes, given the start node. The specific type of the data in the node is immaterial. Note also that the method is not dependent on any type parameter.

```
void printNodeDataSequence(Node<?> s0) {          // Unbounded parameterized type
  Node<?> next = s0.getNext();                    // Returns node as Node<Object>
  while (next != null) {
    Object obj = next.getData();                  // Object reference.
    System.out.println(obj.toString());           // Call Object method
    next = next.getNext();
  }
}
```

Upper Bounded Wildcard References: `<? extends Type>`

The type of the reference s0 is `Node<? extends Number>`, where `Type` is `Number`. This means that the reference s0 refers to a node containing an object whose type is either `Number` or a subtype of `Number`, but the specific (sub)type of the object cannot always be determined at compile time. Putting *any* object, except a `null`, into such a node might not be type-safe.

The code below shows what would happen if any object was allowed to be set as data in a `Long` node via its alias s0. If (1), (2), or (3) were allowed, we would get a `ClassCastException` at (4) because the data could not be assigned to a `Long` reference, as the type-safety of the node `longNode` will have been compromised, either with a supertype object or an object of an unrelated type.

```
Long longInt = 20L;
Node<Long> longNode = new Node<>(longInt, null);  // Node of Long, that is
Node<? extends Number> s0 = longNode;// referenced by a Node<? extends Number> ref.
s0.setData(object);                   // If this was allowed, or            (1)
s0.setData(number);                   // if this was allowed, or            (2)
s0.setData(integer);                  // if this was allowed,               (3)
longInt = longNode.getData();         // we would get an exception here.    (4)
```

The following method call will also not compile, as the compiler cannot give any guarantees at compile time that the reference s0 will refer to a node of `Long` at runtime:

```
s0.setData(longInt);                    // Compile-time error!
```

The upper bound in the wildcard type `? extends Number` is `Number`. Therefore, the data of the node with the wildcard type `? extends Number` must be a `Number` (i.e., either an object of type `Number` or an object of a subtype of `Number`). Thus we can only safely assign the reference value returned by the *get* operation to a reference of type `Number` or a supertype of `Number`.

Lower Bounded Wildcard References: `<? super Type>`

Using a reference of type `Node<? super Number>`, where `Type` is `Number`, we can only put a `Number` or a subtype object of `Number` into the node, as such a number would also be a subtype object of any supertype of `Number`. Since we cannot guarantee which specific supertype of `Number` the node actually has, we cannot put any supertype object of `Number` in the node. The code below shows what would happen if an unrelated supertype object was put in as data in a `Node<? super Number>`. If (1) were allowed, we would get a `ClassCastException` at (2) because the data value (of a supertype) cannot be assigned to a `Number` reference (which is a subtype).

```
Node<Number> numNode = new Node<>(2020, null);
Node<? super Number> s0 = numNode;
s0.setData(object);            // (1) If this set operation was allowed,
number = numNode.getData();    // (2) we would get an exception here.
```

Since the type of the reference s0 is Node<? super Number>, the reference s0 can refer to a node containing an object whose type is either Number or some supertype of Number. When we *get* the data from such a node, we can only safely assume that it is an Object. Keeping in mind that a reference of a supertype of Number can refer to objects that are unrelated to Number (e.g., an Object reference that can refer to a String), if (3) were allowed in the code below, we would get a ClassCastException at (3):

```
Node<Object> objNode = new Node<>("Hi", null);  // String as data.
Node<? super Number> s0 = objNode;
number = s0.getData();          // (3) If allowed, we would get an exception here.
object = s0.getData();          // This is always ok.
```

Unbounded Type References: <Type>

The type of the reference s0 is Node<Number>, where Type is Number. The actual type parameter for each method call is determined to be Number. Thus the type of the parameter in the setData() method and the return value of the getData() method is Number. Therefore, we can pass the reference value of a Number or a subclass object of Number to the setData() method, and can assign the reference value returned by the getData() method to a reference of the type Number or a supertype of Number. In this case, we can put a Number, and get a Number.

Table 11.3 gives a summary of using parameterized references for *set* and *get* operations on a container. Here are some general guidelines for choosing a wildcard parameterized type:

- If we only want to *get* an element of type E from a container, we can use the upper bounded wildcard ? extends E for the reference.
- If we only want to *put* an element of type E into a container, we can use the lower bounded wildcard ? super E for the reference.
- If we want to both *get* and *set* elements of type E in a container, we can use the unbounded type E for the reference.

The following acronym might help to remember which parameterized references should be used to invoke *get* and *set* methods of a container: GESS (*Get-extends-Set-super*), meaning for a *get* method use reference of type <? extends T> and for a *set* method use reference of type <? super T>.

Table 11.3 *Summary of Get and Set Operations Using Parameterized References*

Type of s0 / Operation	Node	Node<?>	Node <? extends Number>	Node <? super Number>	Node<Number>
set/put/write	*Any object*	*Cannot put anything except* nulls.	*Cannot put anything except* nulls.	Number *or subtype*	Number *or subtype*
get/read	Object *only*	Object *only*	Number	Object *only*	Number

11.6 Bounded Type Parameters

In the declaration of the generic class Node<E>, the type parameter E is *unbounded*—that is, it can be any reference type. However, sometimes it may be necessary to restrict what type the type parameter E can represent. The canonical example is restricting that the type parameter E is Comparable<E> so that objects can be compared.

Wildcard types *cannot* be used in the header of a generic class to restrict the type parameter:

```
class CmpNode<? extends Comparable> { ... }          // Compile-time error!
```

However, the type parameter can be bounded by a *constraint* as follows:

```
class CmpNode<E extends Comparable<E>> {              // E is bounded.
  // ...
}
```

In the constraint <E extends Comparable<E>>, E is *bounded* and Comparable<E> is the *upper bound*. This is an example of a *recursive type bound*. The declaration above states that the actual type parameter when we parameterize the generic class CmpNode must implement the Comparable interface, and that the objects of the actual type parameter must be comparable to each other. This implies that the type, say A, that we can use to parameterize the generic class, must implement the parameterized interface Comparable<A>.

If we base the implementation of the CmpNode class on the generic class Node<E>, we can write the declaration as follows:

```
class CmpNode<E extends Comparable<E>> extends Node<E> {
  // ...
}
```

The extends clause is used in two different ways: for the generic class CmpNode to extend the class Node<E>, and to constrain the type parameter E of the generic class CmpNode to the Comparable<E> interface. Although the type parameter E must implement the interface Comparable<E>, we do *not* use the keyword implements in a constraint. Neither can we use the super clause to constrain the type parameter of a generic class.

If we want CmpNodes to have a natural ordering based on the natural ordering of their data values, we can declare the generic class CmpNode as shown in Example 11.8:

```
class CmpNode<E extends Comparable<E>> extends Node<E>
                            implements Comparable<CmpNode<E>> {
  // ...
}
```

Note how the Comparable interface is parameterized in the implements clause. The constraint <E extends Comparable<E>> specifies that the type parameter E is Comparable, and the clause implements Comparable<CmpNode<E>> specifies that the generic class CmpNode is Comparable.

Example 11.8 *Implementing the* Comparable<E> *Interface*

```
class CmpNode<E extends Comparable<E>> extends Node<E>
                                    implements Comparable<CmpNode<E>> {

  CmpNode(E data, CmpNode<E> next) { super(data, next); }

  @Override public int compareTo(CmpNode<E> node2) {
    return this.getData().compareTo(node2.getData());
  }
}
```

Here are some examples of how the generic class CmpNode in Example 11.8 can be parameterized:

```
CmpNode<Integer> intCmpNode  = new CmpNode<>(2020, null);       // (1)
CmpNode<Number>  numCmpNode  = new CmpNode<Number>(2020, null);  // (2) Error!
CmpNode<Integer> intCmpNode2 = new CmpNode<>(2021, null);
int result = intCmpNode.compareTo(intCmpNode2);
```

The actual type parameter Integer at (1) implements Comparable<Integer>, but the actual type parameter Number at (2) is not Comparable. In the declaration CmpNode<A>, the compiler ensures that A implements Comparable<A>.

Multiple Bounds

A bounded type parameter can have *multiple bounds*, B_1 & B_2 & ... & B_n, which must be satisfied by the *actual* type parameter:

```
class CmpNode<E extends Number & Serializable> ...
```

An extra bound, the Serializable interface, has been added using the ampersand (&). The formal type parameter E is a subtype of *both* Number and Serializable, and represents both of these concrete types in the body of the generic class. The constraint above will only allow the generic type to be parameterized by an actual type parameter which is a subtype of *both* Number and Serializable.

We can add as many bounds as necessary. A type parameter E having multiple bounds is a *subtype* of all of the types denoted by the individual bounds. A bound can be a parameterized type, as in the following generic class header:

```
class CmpNode<E extends Comparable<E> & Serializable> ...
```

If the raw type of a bound is a (non-final) superclass of the bounded type parameter, it can only be specified as the first bound, and there can only be one such bound (as a subclass can only extend one immediate superclass). The raw type of an individual bound cannot be used with different type arguments, since a type parameter cannot be the subtype of more than one bound having the same raw type. In the class header below, whatever E is, it cannot be a subtype of two parameterizations of the same interface type (i.e., Comparable) at the same time:

```
class CmpNode<E extends Comparable<E> & Serializable & Comparable<String>> //Error
```

If the type parameter has a bound, methods of the bound can be invoked on instances of the type parameter in the generic class. Otherwise, only methods from the Object class can be invoked on instances of the type parameter. In the declaration of the generic class Node<E> in Example 11.2, p. 568, we cannot call any methods on instances of the type parameter except for those in the Object class because the type parameter is unbounded. Since the instances of the type parameter E are guaranteed to be Comparable<E> in the generic class CmpNode, we can call the method compareTo() of the Comparable interface on these instances.

11.7 Generic Methods and Constructors

We first look at how generic methods and constructors are declared, and then at how they can be called—both with and without explicit actual type parameters.

Declaring Generic Methods

A generic method (also called *polymorphic method*) is implemented like an ordinary method, except that one or more formal type parameters are specified immediately preceding the return type. In the case of a generic constructor, the formal parameters are specified before the class name in the constructor header. Much of what applies to generic methods in this regard also applies to generic constructors.

Example 11.9 *Declaring Generic Methods*

```
public class Utilities {

  // The key type and the array element type can be any type.
  static boolean containsV1(Object key, Object[] array) { // (1) Non-generic
                                                    //      version
    for (Object element : array)
      if (key.equals(element)) return true;
    return false;
  }

  // The key type and the array element type are the same.
  static <E> boolean containsV2(E key, E[] array) {      // (2) Generic version
    for (E element : array)
      if (key.equals(element)) return true;
    return false;
  }

  // The key type is a subtype of the array element type.
  static <K extends E, E> boolean containsV3(K key, E[] array) {  // (3)
    for (E element : array)
      if (key.equals(element)) return true;
    return false;
  }
}
```

In Example 11.9, the method containsV1() at (1) is a non-generic method to determine the membership of an arbitrary key in an arbitrary array of objects.

```
static boolean containsV1(Object key, Object[] array) { // (1) Non-generic version
    // ...
}
```

The method declaration at (1) is too general, in the sense that it does not express any relationship between the key and the array. This kind of type dependency between parameters can be achieved by using generic methods. In Example 11.9, the method containsV2() at (2) is a generic method to determine the membership of a key of type E in an array of type E. The type Object at (1) has been replaced by the type parameter E at (2), with the formal type parameter E being specified before the return type, in the same way as for a generic type.

```
static <E> boolean containsV2(E key, E[] array) {        // (2) Generic version
    // ...
}
```

As with the generic types, a formal type parameter can have a bound, which is a type (i.e., not a type parameter). A formal type parameter can be used in the return type, in the formal parameter list, and in the method body. It can also be used to specify *bounds* in the formal type parameter list.

A generic method need not be declared in a generic type. If declared in a generic type, a *generic instance method* can also use the type parameters of the generic type as any other non-generic instance methods of the generic type. In contrast, a *generic static method* can only use the type parameters declared in its method header.

Calling Generic Methods

Consider the following class declaration:

```
public class ClassDecl {
    static <E_1,..., E_k> void genericMethod(P_1 p_1,..., P_m p_m) { ... }
    // ...
}
```

Note that in the method declaration above, a type P_i may or may not be from the list of type parameters E_1, ..., E_k. We can call the method in various ways. One main difference from calling a non-generic method is that the actual type parameters can be specified before the method name in the call to a generic method. In the method calls shown below, <A_1,..., A_k> are the actual type parameters and (a_1,..., a_m) are the actual arguments. The specification <A_1,..., A_k> of the actual type parameters is known as a *type witness*, as it corroborates the types to use in the method call. If included, it must be specified in its entirety. If there is not type witness, then the compiler *infers* the actual type parameters.

The following method calls can occur in any static or non-static context where the class CallDecl is accessible:

```
CallDecl ref;
ref.<A_1,..., A_k>genericMethod(a_1,..., a_m);
CallDecl.<A 1,..., A_k>genericMethod(a_1,..., a_m);
```

The following method calls can only occur in a non-static context of the class
CallDecl:

```
this.<A_1,..., A_k>genericMethod(a_1,..., a_m);            // Non-static context
super.<A_1,..., A_k>genericMethod(a_1,..., a_m);           // Non-static context
CallDecl.super.<A_1,..., A_k>genericMethod(a_1,..., a_m);  // Non-static context
```

Another difference from calling non-generic methods is that, if the type witness is
explicitly specified, the syntax of a generic *static* method call requires an explicit
reference or the raw type. When the type witness is not explicitly specified, the syntax of a generic method call is similar to that of a non-generic method call.

```
<A_1,..., A_k>genericMethod(a_1,..., a_m);    // Compile-time error!
genericMethod(a_1,..., a_m);                  // Ok.
```

Here are some examples of calls to the containsV2() method at (2) in the class
Utilities in Example 11.9, where the type witness is specified. We can see from the
method signature and the method call signature that the method can be applied to
the arguments at (1), (2), and (3), but not at (4). At (5), we must specify a reference
or the class name because a type witness with the actual type parameter is
specified.

```
Integer[] intArray = {10, 20, 30};

boolean f1 = Utilities.<Integer>containsV2(20, intArray);            // (1) true
// E is Integer.
// Method signature:       containsV2(Integer, Integer[])
// Method call signature: containsV2(Integer, Integer[])

boolean f2 = Utilities.<Number>containsV2(30.5, intArray);           // (2) false
// E is Number.
// Method signature:       containsV2(Number, Number[])
// Method call signature: containsV2(Double, Integer[])

boolean f3 = Utilities.<Comparable<Integer>> containsV2(20, intArray); // (3) true
// E is Comparable<Integer>.
// Method signature:       containsV2(Comparable<Integer>, Comparable<Integer>[])
// Method call signature: containsV2(Integer,              Integer[])

boolean f4 = Utilities.<Integer>containsV2(30.5, intArray);          // (4) Error!
// E is Integer.
// Method signature:       containsV2(Integer, Integer[])
// Method call signature: containsV2(Double,  Integer[])

// Requires explicit reference or raw type.
boolean f5 = <Integer>containsV2(20, intArray);              // (5) Syntax error!
```

Here are some examples of method calls where the compiler infers the actual type
parameters from the method call. At (6), both the key and the element type are
Integer, the compiler infers that the actual type parameter is Integer. At (7), where

the key type is Double and the element type is Integer, the compiler infers the actual type parameter to be Number—that is, the first common supertype of Double and Integer. At (8), the compiler infers the actual type parameter to be Serializable—that is, the first common supertype of String and Integer. In all the cases below, the method is applicable to the arguments.

```
boolean f6 = Utilities.containsV2(20, intArray);                        // (6) true
// E is inferred to be Integer.
// Method signature:      containsV2(Integer, Integer[])
// Method call signature: containsV2(Integer, Integer[])

boolean f7 = Utilities.containsV2(30.5, intArray);                      // (7) false;
// E is inferred to be Number.
// Method signature:      containsV2(Number, Number[])
// Method call signature: containsV2(Double, Integer[])

boolean f8 = Utilities.containsV2("Hi", intArray);                      // (8) false;
// E is inferred to be Serializable.
// Method signature:      containsV2(Serializable, Serializable[])
// Method call signature: containsV2(String, Integer[])
```

At (8), if we had specified the actual type parameter explicitly to be Integer, the compiler would flag an error, as shown at (9), since the method signature is not applicable to the arguments:

```
boolean f9 = Utilities.<Integer>containsV2("Hi", intArray);            // (9) Error!
// E is Integer.
// Method signature:      containsV2(Integer, Integer[])
// Method call signature: containsV2(String, Integer[])
```

We can explicitly specify the key type to be a subtype of the element type by introducing a new formal parameter and a bound on the key type, as for the method containsV3() at (3) in Example 11.9:

```
static <K extends E, E> boolean containsV3(K key, E[] array) {
    // ...
}
```

The following calls at (10) and (11) illustrates inferring of actual type parameters from the method call when no type witness is specified. At (10), the compiler infers the K type parameter to be Double and the type parameter E to be Number—that is, the first common supertype of Double and the array element type Integer. The constraint is satisfied and the method signature is applicable to the arguments.

```
boolean f10 = Utilities.containsV3(30.5, intArray);                    // (10) false
// K is inferred to be Double. E is inferred to be Number.
// The constraint (K extends E) is satisfied.
// Method signature:      containsV3(Double, Number[])
// Method call signature: containsV2(Double, Integer[])

boolean f11 = Utilities.containsV3("Hi", intArray);                    // (11) false
// K is inferred to be String. E is inferred to be Serializable.
// The constraint (K extends E) is satisfied.
```

```
// Method signature:       containsV3(String, Serializable[])
// Method call signature: containsV2(String, Integer[])
```

At (11), the compiler infers the K type parameter to be String and the type parameter E to be Serializable—that is, the first common supertype of String and the array element type Integer. The constraint is satisfied and the method signature is applicable to the arguments, as both String and Integer are Serializable.

The examples below illustrate how constraints come into play in method calls. At (12), the constraint is satisfied and the method signature is applicable to the arguments. At (13), the constraint is not satisfied; therefore, the call is rejected. At (14), the constraint is satisfied, but the method signature is not applicable to the arguments. The call at (15) is rejected because the number of actual type parameters specified in the call is incorrect.

```
boolean f12 = Utilities.<Number, Number>containsV3(30.0, intArray); // (12) false
// K is Number. E is Number.
// The constraint (K extends E) is satisfied.
// Method signature:       containsV3(Number, Number[])
// Method call signature: containsV3(Double, Integer[])

boolean f13 = Utilities.<Number, Integer>
                        containsV3(30.5, intArray);                 // (13) Error!
// K is Number. E is Integer.
// The constraint (K extends E) is not satisfied.

boolean f14 = Utilities.<Integer, Number>
                        containsV3(30.5, intArray);                 // (14) Error!
// K is Integer. E is Number.
// The constraint (K extends E) is satisfied.
// Method signature:       containsV3(Integer, Number[])
// Method call signature: containsV3(Double, Integer[])

boolean f15 = Utilities.<Number>containsV3(30.5, intArray);         // (15) Error!
// Incorrect no. of type parameters.
```

Typically, the dependencies among the parameters of a method and its return type are expressed by formal type parameters. Here are some examples:

```
public static <K,V> Map<V,List<K>> toMultiMap(Map<K,V> origMap) { ... } // (16)
public static <N> Set<N> findVerticesOnPath(Map<N,Collection<N>> graph,
                                    N startVertex)        { ... } // (17)
```

The method header at (16) expresses the dependency that the map returned by the method has the values of the original map as keys, and its values are lists of keys of the original map—that is, the method creates a *multimap*. In the method header at (17), the type parameter N specifies the element type of the set of vertices to be returned, the type of the keys in the map, the element type of the collections that are values of the map, and the type of the start vertex.

11.8 Implementing a Simplified Generic Stack

The Node<E> class from Example 11.2, p. 568, can be used to implement linked data structures. Example 11.10 is an implementation of a simplified generic stack using the Node<E> class. The emphasis is not on how to develop a full-blown, industrial-strength implementation, but on how to present a simple example in the context of this book in order to become familiar with code that utilizes generics. For thread-safety issues concerning a stack, see §22.4, p. 1396.

The class MyStack<E> implements the interface IStack<E> shown in Example 11.10, and uses the class Node<E> from Example 11.2. The class NodeIterator<E> in Example 11.10 provides an iterator to iterate over linked nodes. The class MyStack<E> is Iterable<E>, meaning we can use the for(:) loop to iterate over a stack of this class (see (9) and (12)). It is instructive to study the code to see how type parameters are used in various contexts, how the iterator is implemented, and how we can use the for(:) loop to iterate over a stack. For details on the Iterable<E> and Iterator<E> interfaces, see §15.2, p. 791.

Example 11.10 *Implementing a Simplified Generic Stack*

```java
/** Interface of a generic stack */
public interface IStack<E> extends Iterable<E> {
  void push(E element);              // Add the element to the top of the stack
  E pop();                           // Remove the element at the top of the stack.
  E peek();                          // Get the element at the top of the stack.
  int size();                        // No. of elements on the stack.
  boolean isEmpty();                 // Determine if the stack is empty.
  boolean isMember(E element);       // Determine if the element is in the stack.
  E[] toArray(E[] toArray);          // Copy elements from stack to array
  @Override
  String toString();                 // Return suitable text representation of
                                     // elements on the stack: (e1, e2, ..., en)
}
```

```java
import java.util.Iterator;
import java.util.NoSuchElementException;

/** Simplified implementation of a generic stack */
public class MyStack<E> implements IStack<E> {          // (1)
  // Top of stack.
  private Node<E> tos;                                   // (2)
  // Size of stack
  private int numOfElements;                             // (3)

  @Override public boolean isEmpty() { return tos == null; }    // (4)
  @Override public int size()        { return numOfElements; }  // (5)

  @Override public void push(E element) {               // (6)
    tos = new Node<>(element, tos);
    ++numOfElements;
  }
```

```java
@Override public E pop() {                                    // (7)
  if (!isEmpty()) {
    E data = tos.getData();
    tos = tos.getNext();
    --numOfElements;
    return data;
  }
  throw new NoSuchElementException("No elements.");
}

@Override public E peek()  {                                  // (8)
  if (!isEmpty()) return tos.getData();
  throw new NoSuchElementException("No elements.");
}

// Membership
@Override public boolean isMember(E element) {                // (9)
  for (E data : this)
    if (data.equals(element))
      return true;       // Found.
  return false;          // Not found.
}

// Get iterator.
@Override public Iterator<E> iterator() {                     // (10)
  return new NodeIterator<>(this.tos);
}

// Copy to array as many elements as possible.
@Override public E[] toArray(E[] toArray) {                   // (11)
  Node<E> thisNode = tos;
  for (int i = 0; thisNode != null && i < toArray.length; i++) {
    toArray[i] = thisNode.getData();
    thisNode = thisNode.getNext();
  }
  return toArray;
}

// Text representation of stack: (e1, e2, ..., en).
@Override public String toString() {                          // (12)
  StringBuilder rep = new StringBuilder("(");
  for (E data : this) {
    rep.append(data + ", ");
  }
  if (!isEmpty()) {
    int len = rep.length();
    rep.delete(len - 2, len);                    // Delete the last ", ".
  }
  rep.append(")");
  return rep.toString();
}
}
```

```java
import java.util.Iterator;

/** Iterator for nodes */
public class NodeIterator<E> implements Iterator<E> {
  private Node<E> thisNode;

  public NodeIterator(Node<E> first) { thisNode = first;  }

  @Override public boolean hasNext() { return thisNode != null; }

  @Override public E next() {
    E data = thisNode.getData();
    thisNode = thisNode.getNext();
    return data;
  }

  @Override public void remove() { throw new UnsupportedOperationException(); }
}
```

 ## Review Questions

11.1   Which statement is true about the following program?

```java
import java.util.*;

public class RQ100_50 {
  public static void main(String[] args) {
    List<Integer> intList = new ArrayList<>();      // (1)
    intList.add(2020);
    intList.add(2021);
    List<Number> numList = intList;                 // (2)
    for (Number n : numList)                        // (3)
      System.out.println(n + " ");
  }
}
```

Select the one correct answer.

(a)   The code will fail to compile because of an error at (1).
(b)   The code will fail to compile because of an error at (2).
(c)   The code will fail to compile because of an error at (3).
(d)   The code will compile. When run, it will throw a ClassCastException at (2).
(e)   The code will compile. When run, it will print "2020 2021 ".

11.2   Which statement is true about the following program?

```java
import java.util.*;

public class RQ100_40 {
  public static void main(String[] args) {
    List <? super Integer> sList = new ArrayList<Number>(); //(1)
    int i = 2020;
```

```
        sList.add(i);
        sList.add(++i);                              //(2)
        Number num = sList.get(0);                   //(3)
    }
}
```

Select the one correct answer.

(a) The code will fail to compile because of an error at (1).
(b) The code will fail to compile because of an error at (2).
(c) The code will fail to compile because of an error at (3).
(d) The code will compile. When run, it will throw a ClassCastException at (3).
(e) The code will compile and execute normally.

11.3 Which statement is true about the following program?

```
import java.util.*;

public class RQ100_70 {
    public static void main(String[] args) {
        List<Integer> glst1 = new ArrayList();     //(1)
        List nglst1 = glst1;                        //(2)
        List nglst2 = nglst1;                       //(3)
        List<Integer> glst2 = glst1;                //(4)
    }
}
```

Select the one correct answer.

(a) The code will compile without any warnings.
(b) The code will compile with an unchecked warning at (1).
(c) The code will compile with an unchecked warning at (2).
(d) The code will compile with an unchecked warning at (3).
(e) The code will compile with an unchecked warning at (4).
(f) The code will fail to compile.

11.4 Which occurrences of the type parameter T are illegal in the following class?

```
public class Box<T> {
    private T item;                                 // (1)

    private static T[] storage = new T[100];        // (2)

    public Box(T item) { this.item = item; }        // (3)

    public T getItem() { return item; }             // (4)

    public void setItem(T newItem) { item = newItem; }  // (5)

    public static void getAllItems(T newItem) {     // (6)
        T temp;                                     // (7)
    }
}
```

Select the three correct answers.

(a) The occurrence of the type parameter T at (1)
(b) The occurrence of the type parameter T at (2)
(c) The occurrence of the type parameter T at (3)
(d) The occurrence of the type parameter T at (4)
(e) The occurrence of the type parameter T at (5)
(f) The occurrence of the type parameter T at (6)
(g) The occurrence of the type parameter T at (7)

11.5 Which of the following declarations will not result in compile-time errors?
Select the four correct answers.

(a) `Map<Integer, Map<Integer, String>> map1`
`          = new HashMap<Integer, HashMap<Integer, String>>();`
(b) `Map<Integer, HashMap<Integer, String>> map2 = new HashMap<>();`
(c) `Map<Integer, Integer> map3 = new HashMap<Integer, Integer>();`
(d) `Map<? super Integer, ? super Integer> map4`
`          = new HashMap<? super Integer, ? super Integer>();`
(e) `Map<? super Integer, ? super Integer> map5 = new HashMap<Number, Number>();`
(f) `Map<? extends Number, ? extends Number> map6`
`          = new HashMap<Number, Number>();`
(g) `Map <?,?> map7 = new HashMap<?,?>();`

11.6 Which statement is true about the following program?

```
import java.util.*;

class Fruit {}
class Apple extends Fruit {}

public class RQ100_15 {
  public static void main(String[] args) {
    List<? extends Apple> lst1 = new ArrayList<Fruit>(); // (1)
    List<? extends Fruit> lst2 = new ArrayList<Apple>(); // (2)
    List<? super Apple> lst3 = new ArrayList<Fruit>();   // (3)
    List<? super Fruit> lst4 = new ArrayList<Apple>();   // (4)
    List<?> lst5 = lst1;                                 // (5)
    List<?> lst6 = lst3;                                 // (6)
    List lst7 = lst6;                                    // (7)
    List<?> lst8 = lst7;                                 // (8)
  }
}
```

Select the one correct answer.

(a) (1) will compile, but (2) will not.
(b) (3) will compile, but (4) will not.
(c) (5) will compile, but (6) will not.
(d) (7) will compile, but (8) will not.
(e) None of the above

11.7 Which statement is true about the following program?

```java
import java.util.*;

public class RQ100_11 {
  public static void main(String[] args) {
    Set set = new TreeSet<String>();
    set.add("one");
    set.add(2);
    set.add("three");
    System.out.println(set);
  }
}
```

Select the one correct answer.

(a) The program will fail to compile.

(b) The program will compile with unchecked warnings, and will print the elements in the set.

(c) The program will compile without unchecked warnings, and will print the elements in the set.

(d) The program will compile with unchecked warnings, and will throw an exception at runtime.

(e) The program will compile without unchecked warnings, and will throw an exception at runtime.

11.8 Which of the following statements are true about the following program?

```java
class Vehicle {}
class Car extends Vehicle {}
class Sedan extends Car {}

class Garage<V> {
  private V v;
  public V get() { return this.v; }
  public void put(V v) { this.v = v; }
}

public class GarageAdmin {

  private Object object = new Object();
  private Vehicle vehicle = new Vehicle();
  private Car car = new Car();
  private Sedan sedan = new Sedan();

  public void doA(Garage g) {
    g.put(object);          // (1)
    g.put(vehicle);         // (2)
    g.put(car);             // (3)
    g.put(sedan);           // (4)
    object  = g.get();      // (5)
    vehicle = g.get();      // (6)
    car     = g.get();      // (7)
    sedan   = g.get();      // (8)
  }
}
```

Select the two correct answers.

(a) The call to the put() method in statements (1) through (4) will compile.

(b) The assignment statement (5) will compile.

(c) The assignment statements (6), (7), and (8) will compile.

11.9   Which method calls can be inserted individually at (1) so that the program will compile without warnings?

```
import java.util.*;

public class GenParam {
  public static void main(String[] args) {
    List<Number> numList = new ArrayList<>();
    List<Integer> intList = new ArrayList<>();
    // (1) INSERT CODE HERE
  }

  static <T> void move(List<? extends T> lst1, List<? super T> lst2) {}
}
```

Select the three correct answers.

(a) GenParam.move(numList, intList);

(b) GenParam.<Number>move(numList, intList);

(c) GenParam.<Integer>move(numList, intList);

(d) GenParam.move(intList, numList);

(e) GenParam.<Number>move(intList, numList);

(f) GenParam.<Integer>move(intList, numList);

11.10   Given the class below, which declaration statement is not valid?

```
class Box<T> {
      Box()            {System.out.println(this);}          // (1)
  <V> Box(V v)         {System.out.println(v);}             // (2)
  <V> Box(T t, V v)    {System.out.println(t + ", " + v);}  // (3)
}
```

Select the one correct answer.

(a) Box<String> ref1 = new Box<>();

(b) Box<String> ref2 = new Box<>("one");

(c) Box<String> ref3 = new Box<>(2020);

(d) Box<Integer> ref4 = new Box<>(2020, "one");

(e) Box<String> ref5 = new Box<>("one", 2020);

(f) Box<Integer> ref6 = new Box<>("one", 2020);

11.9 Wildcard Capture

As we have seen, a wildcard can represent a family of types. However, the compiler needs to have a more concrete notion of a type than a wildcard in order to do the necessary type checking. Internally, the compiler represents the wildcard by some anonymous but specific type. Although this type is unknown, it belongs to the family of types represented by the wildcard. This specific but unknown type is called the *capture of* the wildcard.

Compiler messages about erroneous usage of wildcards often refer to the capture of a wildcard. Here are some examples of such error messages, based on compiling the following code:

```
// File: WildcardCapture.java
...
Node<?>                 anyNode;
Node<? super Number>    supNumNode;

Node<Integer> intNode = anyNode;                        // (1) Compile-time error!
Node<? extends Number> extNumNode = supNumNode; // (2) Compile-time error!
anyNode.setData("Trash");                               // (3) Compile-time error!
```

The assignment at (1) results in the following rather cryptic error message:

```
WildcardCapture.java:10: error: incompatible types: Node<CAP#1> cannot be
converted to Node<Integer>
    Node<Integer> intNode = anyNode;                    // (1) Compile-time error!
                            ^
  where CAP#1 is a fresh type-variable:
    CAP#1 extends Object from capture of ?
```

The type of the reference anyNode is Node<CAP#1>. The name CAP#1 is used by the compiler to designate the *type capture* of the wildcard ("capture of ?") at (1). The type of the reference intNode is Node<Integer>. The reference value of a Node<CAP#1> cannot be assigned to a Node<Integer> reference. Whatever the type capture of the wildcard is, it cannot be guaranteed to be Integer, and the assignment is rejected. To put it another way, the assignment involves a narrowing reference conversion, requiring an explicit cast which is not provided: Node<?> is the supertype of all invocations of the generic class Node<E>.

The error message below for the assignment at (2) shows the type capture CAP#1 of the lower bounded wildcard at (2) to be "capture of ? super Number". Figure 11.5, p. 583, also shows that the Node<capture of ? super Number> and Node<? extends Number> types are unrelated.

```
WildcardCapture.java:11: error: incompatible types: Node<CAP#1> cannot be
converted to Node<? extends Number>
    Node<? extends Number> extNumNode = supNumNode; // (2) Compile-time error!
                                        ^
  where CAP#1 is a fresh type-variable:
    CAP#1 extends Object super: Number from capture of ? super Number
```

The method call at (3) results in the following error message:

```
WildcardCapture.java:12: error: incompatible types: String cannot be converted to
CAP#1
    anyNode.setData("Trash");                           // (3) Compile-time error!
                    ^
  where CAP#1 is a fresh type-variable:
    CAP#1 extends Object from capture of ?
```

The type of the reference anyNode is Node<?> and the type of the formal parameter in the method declaration is CAP#1, where CAP#1 is "capture of ?". The type of the actual parameter in the method call is String, which is not compatible with CAP#1. The call is not allowed. As we have seen earlier, with a <?> reference we cannot put anything into a data structure, except nulls.

If we have the following method in the class MyStack:

```
public static <T> void move(MyStack<? extends T> srcStack,
                            MyStack<? super T> dstStack) {
  while (!srcStack.isEmpty())
    dstStack.push(srcStack.pop());
}
```

and we try to compile the following client code in the source file MyStackUser.java:

```
MyStack<?> anyStack;
MyStack.move(anyStack, anyStack);   // Compile-time error!
```

the compiler issues the following error message:

```
MyStackUser.java:68: error: method move in class MyStack<E#2> cannot be applied to
given types;
      MyStack.move(anyStack, anyStack);       // Compile-time error!
      ^
  required: MyStack<? extends E#1>,MyStack<? super E#1>
  found: MyStack<CAP#1>,MyStack<CAP#2>
  reason: cannot infer type-variable(s) E#1
    (argument mismatch; MyStack<CAP#2> cannot be converted to MyStack<? super E#1>)
  where E#1,E#2 are type-variables:
    E#1 extends Object declared in method <E#1>move(MyStack<? extends E#1>,My-
Stack<? super E#1>)
    E#2 extends Object declared in class MyStack
  where CAP#1,CAP#2 are fresh type-variables:
    CAP#1 extends Object from capture of ?
    CAP#2 extends Object from capture of ?
```

The error message shows that each occurrence of a wildcard in a statement is represented by a distinct type capture, namely CAP#1 and CAP#2. We see that the signature of the move() method is move(MyStack<? extends E#1>, MyStack<? super E#1>). The type of the reference anyStack is MyStack<?>. The static types of the two arguments in the method call are MyStack<CAP#1> and MyStack<CAP#2>, where CAP#1 and CAP#1 designate two distinct type captures (capture of ?). The signature of the argument list is (MyStack<CAP#1>, MyStack<CAP#2>). The type parameter T cannot be inferred from the types of the arguments, as the stacks are considered to be of two different types, and therefore, the call is rejected.

Capture Conversion

Consider the following non-generic method which does not compile:

```
static void fillWithFirstV1(List<?> list) {
  Object firstElement = list.get(0);       // (1)
```

```
    for (int i = 1; i < list.size(); i++)
        list.set(i, firstElement);              // (2) Compile-time error
}
```

The method should fill any list passed as an argument with the element in its first position. The call to the set() method at (2) is not permitted, as a *set* operation is not possible with a <?> reference (see Table 11.3, p. 590). Using the unbounded wildcard ? to parameterize the list does not work. We can replace the wildcard with a type parameter of a *generic method*, as follows:

```
static <E> void fillWithFirstV2(List<E> list) {
    E firstElement = list.get(0);           // (3)
    for (int i = 1; i < list.size(); i++)
        list.set(i, firstElement);          // (4)
}
```

Since the type of the argument is List<E>, we can set and get objects of type E from the list. We have also changed the type of the reference firstElement from Object to E in order to set the first element in the list.

It turns out that if the first method fillWithFirstV1() is reimplemented with a call to the generic method fillWithFirstV2(), it all works well:

```
static void fillWithFirstV3(List<?> list) {
    fillWithFirstV2(list);                  // (5) Type conversion
}
```

The wildcard in the argument of the fillWithFirstV3() method has a type capture. In the call to the fillWithFirstV2() method at (5), this type capture is converted to the type E. This conversion is called *capture conversion*, and it comes into play under certain conditions, which are beyond the scope of this book.

11.10 Flexibility with Wildcard Parameterized Types

Nested Wildcards

In this subsection, the examples make use of type parameters that are specified for the interfaces Collection<E>, Set<E>, and Map<K,V> in the java.util package (Chapter 15, p. 781). In the discussion below, the important fact to keep in mind is that the interface Set<E> is a subinterface of Collection<E>.

We have seen that the subtype relationship is invariant for the unbounded type parameter <T>:

```
Collection<Number> colNum;
Set<Number> setNum;
Set<Integer> setInt;
colNum = setNum; // (1) Set<Number> <: Collection<Number>
colNum = setInt; // (2) Compile-time error!
```

The same is true when concrete parameterized types are used as actual type parameters, implementing what are called *nested parameterized types*—that is, using parameterized types as type parameters.

```
Collection<Collection<Number>> colColNum; // Collection of Collections of Number
Set<Collection<Number>>        setColNum; // Set of Collections of Number
Set<Set<Integer>>              setSetInt; // Set of Sets of Integer
colColNum = setColNum;                    // (3) Set<Collection<Number>> <:
                                          //     Collection<Collection<Number>>
colColNum = setSetInt;                    // (4) Compile-time error!
setColNum = setSetInt;                    // (5) Compile-time error!
```

Again, we can use the upper bounded wildcard to induce subtype covariance. The upper bounded wildcard is applied at the *top level* in the code below. The assignment below at (8) is not compatible because Set<Set<Integer>> is *not* a subtype of Collection<? extends Collection<Number>>.

```
Collection<? extends Collection<Number>> colExtColNum;
colExtColNum = colColNum;        // (6) Collection<Collection<Number>> <:
                                 //     Collection<? extends Collection<Number>>
colExtColNum = setColNum;        // (7) Set<Collection<Number>> <:
                                 //     Collection<? extends Collection<Number>>
colExtColNum = setSetInt;        // (8) Compile-time error!
```

In the code below, the wildcard is applied at the *innermost* level:

```
Collection<Collection<? extends Number>> colColExtNum;
colColExtNum = colColNum;        // (9)  Compile-time error!
colColExtNum = setColNum;        // (10) Compile-time error!
colColExtNum = setSetInt;        // (11) Compile-time error!
```

The assignments above show that the upper bounded wildcard induces subtype covariance *only* at the top level. At (9), type A (=Collection<Number>) is a subtype of type B (=Collection<? extends Number>), but because a subtype covariance relationship does not hold between parameterized types, the type Collection<A> (=Collection<Collection<Number>>) is *not* a subtype of Collection<B> (= Collection<Collection<? extends Number>>).

The above discussion also applies when a parameterized type has more than one type parameter:

```
Map<Number, String>  mapNumStr;
Map<Integer, String> mapIntStr;
mapNumStr = mapIntStr;                // (12) Compile-time error!
```

Again, the upper bounded wildcard can only be used at the top level to induce subtype covariance:

```
Map<Integer, ? extends Collection<String>> mapIntExtColStr;
Map<Integer, Collection<? extends String>> mapIntColExtStr;
Map<Integer, Collection<String>>           mapIntColStr;
Map<Integer, Set<String>>                  mapIntSetStr;
mapIntExtColStr = mapIntColStr;// (13) Map<Integer, Collection<String>> <:
                               //      Map<Integer, ? extends Collection<String>>
mapIntExtColStr = mapIntSetStr;// (14) Map<Integer, Set<String>> <:
                               //      Map<Integer, ? extends Collection<String>>
```

```
mapIntColStr    = mapIntSetStr;    // (15) Compile-time error!
mapIntColExtStr = mapIntColStr;    // (16) Compile-time error!
mapIntColExtStr = mapIntSetStr;    // (17) Compile-time error!
```

Wildcard Parameterized Types as Formal Parameters

We now examine the implications of using wildcard parameterized types to declare formal parameters of a method.

We want to add a method in the class MyStack<E> (Example 11.10, p. 598) for moving the elements of a source stack to the current stack. Here are three attempts at implementing such a method for the class MyStack<E>:

```
public void moveFromV1(MyStack<F> srcStack) {            // (1)
  while (!srcStack.isEmpty())
    this.push(srcStack.pop());
}

public void moveFromV2(MyStack<? extends E> srcStack) {  // (2)
  while (!srcStack.isEmpty())
    this.push(srcStack.pop());
}

public void moveFromV3(MyStack<? super E> srcStack) {    // (3)
  while (!srcStack.isEmpty())
    this.push(srcStack.pop());                           // Compile-time error!
}
```

Given the following three stacks:

```
MyStack<Number> numStack    = new MyStack<>();                     // Stack of Number
numStack.push(5.5); numStack.push(10.5); numStack.push(20.5);
MyStack<Integer> intStack1 = new MyStack<>();                      // Stack of Integer
intStack1.push(5); intStack1.push(10); intStack1.push(20);
MyStack<Integer> intStack2 = new MyStack<>();                      // Stack of Integer
intStack2.push(15); intStack2.push(25); intStack2.push(35);
```

We can only move elements between stacks of the same concrete type with the method at (1). The compile-time error below is due to the fact that MyStack<Integer> is not a subtype of MyStack<Number>.

```
intStack1.moveFromV1(intStack2); // Ok.
numStack.moveFromV1(intStack2);  // Compile-time error!
```

We can also move elements from a stack of type MyStack<? extends E> to the current stack, using the method at (2). This is possible because a reference of a type MyStack<? extends E> can refer to a stack with objects of type E or its subclass, and the *get* operation (i.e., the pop() method) is permissible, returning an object which has an actual type bounded by the upper bound E. The returned object can always be put into a stack of type E or its supertype.

```
intStack1.moveFromV2(intStack2); // Pop from intStack2. Push on intStack1.
numStack.moveFromV2(intStack2);  // Pop from intStack2. Push on numStack.
```

The method at (3) will only allow Objects to be popped from a stack of type
MyStack<? super E>, which could only be pushed onto a stack of type Object. Since E
cannot be determined at compile time, the push() operation on the current stack is
not permitted. Of the first two methods, the method at (2) is more flexible in permitting the widest range of calls for copying from the source stack to the current
stack.

Similarly, we can add a method in the class MyStack<E> for moving the elements of
the current stack to a destination stack:

```
public void moveToV1(MyStack<E> dstStack) {                    // (4)
  while (!this.isEmpty())
    dstStack.push(this.pop());
}

public void moveToV2(MyStack<? extends E> dstStack) {     // (5)
  while (!this.isEmpty())
    dstStack.push(this.pop());                              // Compile-time error!
}

public void moveToV3(MyStack<? super E> dstStack) {         // (6)
  while (!this.isEmpty())
    dstStack.push(this.pop());
}
```

In the method at (5), the reference of type MyStack<? extends E> does not allow any
set operations (in this case, the push() method) on the destination stack. The
method at (6) provides the most flexible solution, as a reference of type MyStack<?
super E> permits *set* operations for objects of type E or its subtypes:

```
intStack1.moveToV1(intStack2);     // Pop from intStack1. Push on intStack2.
intStack1.moveToV1(numStack);      // Compile-time error!

intStack1.moveToV3(intStack2);     // Pop from intStack1. Push on intStack2.
intStack1.moveToV3(numStack);      // Pop from intStack1. Push on numStack.
```

Evidently, the method at (6) is more flexible in permitting the widest range of calls
for copying from the current stack to the destination stack.

Based on the discussion above, we can write a *generic method* for moving elements
from a source stack to a destination stack. The following method signature is preferable, where objects of type E or its subtypes can be popped from the source stack
and pushed onto a destination stack of type E or its supertype:

```
public static <E> void move(MyStack<? extends E> srcStack,  // (7)
                            MyStack<? super E> dstStack) {
  while (!srcStack.isEmpty())
    dstStack.push(srcStack.pop());
}

// Client code
MyStack.move(intStack1, intStack2);
MyStack.move(intStack1, numStack);
MyStack.move(numStack, intStack2);       // Compile-time error!
```

It is a common idiom to use wildcards as shown above in the method at (7), as the upper bounded wildcard (? extends Type) can be used to *get* objects from a data structure, and the lower bounded wildcard (? super Type) can be used to *set* objects in a data structure. Using wildcards in the method signature can increase the utility of a method, especially when explicit type parameters are specified in the method call.

Recursive Type Bounds Revisited

The class MonoNode and the interface IMonoLink<E> are declared in Example 11.3, p. 572, and the class BiNode and the interface IBilink<E> are declared in Example 11.5, p. 574. See also Figure 11.1, p. 574.

```
class MonoNode<E> implements IMonoLink<E> {
  private E              data;   // Data
  private IMonoLink<E>   next;   // Reference to next node       (1)
  // ...
}

class BiNode<E> extends MonoNode<E> implements IBiLink<E> {
  private IBiLink<E> previous;   // Reference to previous node   (2)
  // ...
}
```

Note that the next field has the type IMonoLink<E>, but the previous field has the type IBiLink<E>, and that the type IBiLink<E> is a subtype of the type IMonoLink<E>. This means that when iterating over a linked structure constructed from nodes that implement the IBiLink<E> interface, we have to be careful. The method traverseBinTree() below traverses a binary tree constructed from such nodes. The method prints the data in the nodes. Note that it is necessary to cast the reference value returned by the getNext() method, as shown at (3), from the supertype IMonoLink<E> to the subtype IBiLink<E>.

```
public static <E> void traverseBinTree(IBiLink<E> root) {
  if (root.getPrevious() != null)
    traverseBinTree(root.getPrevious());
  System.out.print(root.getData() + ", ");
  if (root.getNext() != null)
    traverseBinTree((IBiLink<E>)root.getNext());  // (3) Cast necessary.
}
```

Example 11.11 declares a class called RecNode. The header of this class at (1) is declared as follows:

```
abstract class RecNode<E, T extends RecNode<E, T>>
```

The class specifies two type parameters: E and T. The type parameter E stands for the type of the data in the node, (2). The type parameter T stands for the type of the next field in the node, (3). It has the upper bound RecNode<E, T>, meaning that T must be a subtype of the bound—that is, of RecNode<E, T>. In other words, the class RecNode can only be parameterized by itself or its subclasses. The two parameters E and T are used in the class for their respective purposes.

Example 11.11 *Using Recursive Bounds*

```
abstract class RecNode<E, T extends RecNode<E, T>> {        // (1)
  private E data;                                           // (2)
  private T next;                                           // (3)

  RecNode(E data, T next) {
    this.data = data;
    this.next = next;
  }
  public void setData(E obj)  { data = obj; }
  public E    getData()       { return data; }
  public void setNext(T next) { this.next = next; }
  public T    getNext()       { return next; }
  @Override public String toString() {
    return this.data + (this.next == null ? "" : ", " + this.next);
  }
}
```

```
final class RecBiNode<E> extends RecNode<E, RecBiNode<E>> {          // (4)

  private RecBiNode<E>  previous;    // Reference to previous node   // (5)

  RecBiNode(E data, RecBiNode<E> next, RecBiNode<E> previous) {
    super(data, next);
    this.previous = previous;
  }
  public void setPrevious(RecBiNode<E> previous) { this.previous = previous; }
  public RecBiNode<E> getPrevious()              { return this.previous; }
  @Override public String toString() {
    return (this.previous == null? "" : this.previous + ", ") +
      this.getData() + (this.getNext() == null? "" : ", " + this.getNext());
  }
}
```

Example 11.11 declares another class, called RecBiNode. The header of this class at
(4) is declared as follows:

```
final class RecBiNode<E> extends RecNode<E, RecBiNode<E>>
```

Note that the class has only one type parameter, E, that represents the data type in
the node. The class extends the RecNode class, which is parameterized with the data
type E and the type RecBiNode<E> to represent the type of the next field in the superclass RecNode. The class RecBiNode also declares a previous field of type RecBiNode<E>
at (5), and the corresponding getter and setter methods. The upshot of this class
declaration is that, for a node of type RecBiNode<E>, both the next and the previous
fields have the same type as a node of this class. The traversal method can now be
written without using any casts, passing it a node of the subtype RecBiNode<E>:

```
public static <E> void traverseBinTree(RecBiNode<E> root) {     // (2)
  if (root.getPrevious() != null)
    traverseBinTree(root.getPrevious());
```

```
        System.out.print(root.getData() + ", ");
        if (root.getNext() != null)
            traverseBinTree(root.getNext());              // No cast necessary!
    }
```

The class declaration at (1) in Example 11.11 uses what is called a *recursive type bound* in its constraint T extends RecNode<E,T>. New subtypes of the class RecNode can be implemented using this idiom, and the type of the next field will be the same as the subtype, as in the case of the subtype RecBiNode<E>. Recursive type bounds allow subclasses to use their own type, avoiding explicit casts to convert from the superclass.

Earlier in this chapter we saw an example of a recursive type bound defined by the constraint T extends Comparable<T>. Another example of a recursive type bound is the declaration of the Enum<E extends Enum<E>> class in the Java standard library.

11.11 Type Erasure

Understanding translation by type erasure aids in understanding the restrictions and limitations that arise when using generics in Java. Although the compiler generates generic-free bytecode, we can view the process as a source-to-source translation that generates non-generic code from generic code.

The translated code has no information about type parameter. That is, the type parameters have been *erased*—hence the term *type erasure*. This involves replacing the usage of the type parameters with concrete types, and inserting suitable type conversions to ensure type correctness. In certain situations, *bridge methods* are also inserted for backward compatibility.

Translation by Type Erasure

The process of determining the *erasure* of a type—that is, what a type in the source code should be replaced with—uses the following rules:

1. Drop all type parameter specifications from parameterized types.
2. Replace any type parameter as follows:

    a. Replace it with the erasure of its bound, if it has one.

    b. Replace it with Object, if it has none.

    c. Replace it with the erasure of the *first* bound, if it has multiple bounds.

Table 11.4 shows examples of translation by erasure for some representative types, and the rules that are applied.

Table 11.4 *Examples of Type Erasure*

Type	Erasure	Rule no.
List<E> List<Integer> List<String> List<List<String>> List<? super Integer> List<? extends Number>	List	1
List<Integer>[]	List[]	1
List	List	1
int	int	For any primitive type
Integer	Integer	For any non-generic type

class Subclass
  extends Superclass
  implements
  Comparable<Subclass> {...}
	class Subclass
	  extends Superclass
	  implements
	  Comparable {...}
		1

public static
  <T extends Comparable<? super T>>
  T
  max(T obj1,
    T obj2)
  { ... }
	public static
	
	  Comparable
	  max(Comparable obj1,
	    Comparable obj2)
	  { ... }
		2a. The first bound is Comparable.

public static <T> T
  doIt(T t)
  { T lv = t; }
	public static Object
	  doIt(Object t)
	  { Object lv = t; }
		2b

T extends MyClass & Comparable<T> & Serializable	MyClass	2c. The first bound is MyClass.

The following code mixes legacy and generic code. Note that a ClassCastException
is expected at (5) because the type-safety of the stack of String has been compromised.

```
// Pre-erasure code
List<String> strList = new ArrayList<>(); // (0)
List list = strList;        // (1) Assignment to non-generic reference is ok.
strList = list;             // (2) warning: unchecked conversion
strList.add("aha");         // (3) Method call type-safe.
list.add(23);               // (4) warning: [unchecked] unchecked call to add(E)
                            //     as a member of the raw type java.util.List
System.out.println(strList.get(1).length()); // (5) ClassCastException
```

It is instructive to compare the corresponding lines of code in the pre-erasure code
above and the post-erasure results shown below. A cast is inserted to convert from
Object type to String type at (5'). This is necessary because post-erasure code can

only get an `Object` from the list, and in order to call the `length()` method, the reference value of this object must be converted to `String`. It is this cast that is the cause of the exception at runtime.

```
// Post-erasure code
List strList = new ArrayList();                          // (0')
List list = strList;                                     // (1')
strList = list;                                          // (2')
strList.add("aha");                                      // (3')
list.add(Integer.valueOf(23));                           // (4')
System.out.println(((String)strList.get(1)).length());  // (5') Cast inserted.
```

Bridge Methods

Bridge methods are inserted in subclasses by the compiler to ensure that overriding of methods works correctly. The canonical example is the implementation of the `Comparable` interface. The post-erasure code of the class `CmpNode<E>` from Example 11.8 is shown below. A second `compareTo()` method has been inserted by the compiler at (2), whose method signature is `compareTo(Object)`. This is necessary because, without this method, the class would not implement the `Comparable` interface, as the post-erasure `compareTo(Object)` method of the interface would not be overridden correctly in the erasure code.

```
class CmpNode extends Node implements Comparable {
  CmpNode(Object data, CmpNode next) {
    super(data, next);
  }
  public int compareTo(CmpNode node2) {         // (1) Implemented method erasure
    return this.getData().compareTo(node2.getData());
  }
  public int compareTo(Object node2) {          // (2) Inserted bridge method.
    return this.compareTo((CmpNode)node2);      // Calls the method at (1).
  }
}
```

Such a bridge method cannot be invoked in the source code, and is provided for backward compatibility with legacy code. There are Java decompilers readily available that can be used to examine the code generated by the compiler.

11.12 Implications for Overloading and Overriding

Before discussing the implications generics have for overloading and overriding, we need a few definitions regarding method signatures.

Method Signatures Revisited

Method signatures play a crucial role in overloading and overriding of methods. The method signature comprises the method name and the formal parameter list.

Two methods (or constructors) have the *same signature* if both of the following conditions are fulfilled:

- They have the *same name.*
- They have the *same formal parameter types.*

Two methods (or constructors) have the *same formal parameter types* if both of the following conditions are fulfilled:

- They have the *same number* of *formal parameters* and *type parameters.*
- The formal parameters and the bounds of the type parameters are the same after the occurrences of formal parameters in one are substituted with the corresponding types from the second.

The signature of a method m() is a *subsignature* of the signature of another method n(), if either one of these two conditions hold:

- Method n() has the *same* signature as method m(), or
- The signature of method m() is the same as the *erasure* of the signature of method n().

The signatures of the two methods m() and n() are *override-equivalent* if either one of these two conditions hold:

- The signature of method m() is a *subsignature* of the signature of method n(), or
- The signature of method n() is a *subsignature* of the signature of method m().

Implications for Overloading

Given the definitions above, we can now state that two methods are *overloaded* if they have the same name, but their signatures are *not override-equivalent*. Given the following three generic method declarations in a class:

```
static <T> void merge(MyStack<T> s1, MyStack<T> s2) { /*...*/ }
static <T> void merge(MyStack<T> s1, MyStack<? extends T> s2) { /*...*/ }
static <T> void merge(MyStack<T> s1, MyStack<? super T> s2) { /*...*/ }
```

After erasure, the signature of all three methods is:

```
merge(MyStack, MyStack)
```

That is, the signatures of the methods are override-equivalent, hence these methods are *not* overloaded. A class cannot contain two methods with override-equivalent signatures, and the compiler will report an error.

These three methods:

```
static <T> void merge(Node<T> s1, MyStack<T> s2)                { /*...*/ }
static <T> void merge(MyStack<T> s1, MyStack<? extends T> s2) { /*...*/ }
static <T> void merge(MyStack<T> s1, Node<? super T> s2)        { /*...*/ }
```

have the following signatures after erasure, respectively:

```
merge(Node, MyStack)
merge(MyStack, MyStack)
merge(MyStack, Node)
```

We can see that no two signatures are override-equivalent. Therefore, the three methods are overloaded.

The declaration of the class `MethodSGN` below shows some variations on the method signature. The resulting signature of the method header (which includes the method signature) is shown after erasure in the comment corresponding to the method.

```
class MethodSGN<T> {
  void doIt(boolean b) {}                      // (1) void doIt(boolean)

  void doIt(T t) {}                            // (2) void doIt(Object)

  List<StringBuilder> doIt(StringBuilder sb) { // (3) List doIt(StringBuilder)
    return null;
  }

  <E extends Comparable<E>> void doIt(E element) // (4) void doIt(Comparable)
    {}

  <E> E doIt(MyStack<? extends E> stack) {     // (5) Object doIt(MyStack)
    return null;
  }
}
```

Adding any of the method declarations given below to the class `MethodSGN` would be an error, as each one of these method declarations has a method signature that is the same as one of the methods already in the class—that is, the signatures are override-equivalent.

```
void doIt(Object obj) {}                      // (2') void doIt(Object)

<E extends StringBuilder> List<E> doIt(E sb) { // (3') List doIt(StringBuilder)
  return null;
}

void doIt(Comparable<T> element) {}           // (4') void doIt(Comparable)

<E> E doIt(MyStack<? super E> stack) {        // (5') Object doIt(MyStack)
  return null;
}
```

Implications for Overriding

The following conditions (referred to as *override criteria*) should be satisfied in order for a subtype method to override a supertype method:

- The signature of the subtype method is a *subsignature* of the signature of the supertype method (which is discussed in this subsection).
- Their *return types* should be compatible.
- Their throws *clauses* should be compatible (§7.5, p. 388).

Here we discuss the implication of method signatures for overriding.

The @Override *Annotation*

We can solicit the aid of the compiler to ensure that a method declaration in a subtype correctly overrides a method from its supertype. If a method declaration is preceded by the annotation @Override (§25.5, p. 1578), the compiler will issue an error if the method in the subtype does not override a method from its supertype. The examples in this book make heavy use of this annotation.

Example 11.12 illustrates the use of this annotation. The intention in the class CmpNode is to override the equals() method from the Object class and the compareTo() method from the Comparable interface. The error messages alert us to the fact that the annotated methods do not override any methods. The method signatures are not subsignatures of any methods that are inherited. The formal parameters are not correct for overriding at (1) and (2). Correct method headers are shown at (1') and (2').

Example 11.12 *Using the @Override Annotation*

```
class CmpNode<E extends Comparable<E>> extends Node<E>
                                    implements Comparable<CmpNode<E>> {

    CmpNode(E data, CmpNode<E> next) { super(data, next); }

    @Override
    public boolean equals(CmpNode node2) {         // (1) Compile-time error.
//public boolean equals(Object node2) {            // (1') Correct header.
        return this.compareTo(node2) == 0;
    }

    @Override
    public int compareTo(Object node2) {           // (2) Compile-time error.
//public int compareTo(CmpNode<E> node2) {         // (2') Correct header
        return this.getData().compareTo(node2.getData());
    }
}
```

Compiling the class CmpNode:

>javac CmpNode.java
```
...
CmpNode.java:8: method does not override or implement a method from a supertype
    @Override
    ^
...
CmpNode.java:14: method does not override or implement a method from a supertype
    @Override
    ^
```

Overriding Methods from Non-Generic Supertype

In Example 11.13, the signature at (1') is the same as the signature at (1): set(Integer). The signature at (2') is the same as the *erasure* of the signature at (2): set(List). The method at (2') shows a non-generic subtype method overriding a supertype method that uses generics. This is needed for legacy code: *Legacy supertypes* can be generified without it having consequences for any subtypes, as the signature of a subtype method that overrides a supertype method will be the same as the erasure of the signature of this supertype method.

Example 11.13 *Subsignatures*

```
import java.util.List;

class SupA {
  public void set(Integer ref)        {/*...*/}    // (1)
  public void set(List<Integer> list) {/*...*/}    // (2)
}

class SubA extends SupA {
  @Override public void set(Integer ref) {/*...*/} // (1') same as at (1)
  @Override public void set(List list) {/*...*/}// (2') same as the erasure at (2)
}
```

Overriding Methods from Generic Supertype

In Example 11.14, both the subclasses SubB1 and SubB2 are subtypes of the parameterized supertype SupB<Number>—that is, T is Number in SupB<T>. At compile time, the signatures of the methods in SubB1 are the same as the signatures of the methods in SupB; therefore, the methods are overridden. After erasure, the methods in SupB are equivalent to:

```
public void set(Object t) {/*...*/}             // (1)
public Object get()       {return null;}        // (2)
```

The compiler adds the following bridge method in SubB1 in order for overriding to work properly at runtime:

```
public void set(Object t) {set((Number)t);}     // (1')
```

It does not add a bridge method for the get() method in SubB1 because of covariant return: The return type Number for the method get() in SubB1 is a subtype of the return type Object of the method get() in SupB.

Example 11.14 *Overriding from Generic Supertype*

```
class SupB<T> {
  public void set(T t) {/*...*/}                 // (1)
  public T get()       {return null;}            // (2)
}
```

```
class SubB1 extends SupB<Number> {
  @Override public void set(Number num) {/*...*/} // (1a) Overrides
  @Override public Number get()       {return 0;} // (2a) Overrides
}

class SubB2 extends SupB<Number> {
  @Override public void set(Object obj) {/*...*/} // (1b) Error: same erasure
  @Override public void set(Long l)     {/*...*/} // (1c) Error: overloads

  @Override public Object get() {               // (2b) Error: incompatible return type
    return null;
  }
}
```

We now examine the methods in SubB2. The set() method at (1b) has the *same sig-nature* as *the erasure* of the signature of the set() method at (1) in the supertype SupB. If overriding were allowed, the bridge method added would result in *two* methods with the same signature set(Object) in SubB2. Two methods with the same signature are not permitted in the same class—called a *name clash*—therefore, (1b) is not allowed.

The method set() at (1c) is overloaded because its signature is different from the other set() methods in SubB2 and SupB. It would compile if the @Override annotation was removed. The method get() at (2b) has the return type Object, while the get() method in SupB<Number> has the return type Number. The return types are not covariant, and (2b) is rejected.

Example 11.15 shows a typical error where a generic supertype is extended, but its parameterization is missing in the extends clause of the subtype, as shown at (2). The set() method in SubZ neither overrides nor overloads the method at (1). Both methods have the same signature after erasure: set(Object). Adding a bridge method in SubZ to make the overriding work properly would result in a name clash. (1a) is rejected.

Example 11.15 *Missing Supertype Parameterization*

```
class SupZ<T> {
  public void set(T t) {/*...*/}               // (1)
}

class SubZ<E> extends SupZ {                    // Superclass not parameterized
  @Override public void set(E e) {/*...*/}      // (1a) Error: same erasure
}
```

Genericity and Inherited Methods

The subsignature requirement for overriding means that the signature of the sub-type method must be the *same* as that of the supertype method, or it must be the same as the *erasure* of the signature of the supertype method. Note the implication of the last sentence: The signature of the subtype method must be the same as the *erasure of the supertype method, not* the other way around. The converse is neither overloading nor overriding, but a *name clash* and is reported as an error.

The subsignature requirement also implies that a *generic subtype method cannot override a non-generic supertype method.* In other words, genericity cannot be added to an inherited method. This case is illustrated in Example 11.16. It is the erasures of the signatures of the generic methods in the subtype that are the same as the signatures of the non-generic methods in the supertype. Overriding requires the converse. A name clash is generally the reason why neither overriding nor overloading is permitted.

Example 11.16 *Genericity Cannot be Added to Inherited Methods*

```
class SupJ {
  public void set(Object obj) {/*...*/}     // (1)
  public Object get()     {return null;}    // (2)
}

class SubJ extends SupJ {
  @Override public <T> void set(T t) {/*...*/}   // (1a) Error: same erasure
  @Override public <S> S get() {return null;}    // (2a) Error: same erasure
}
```

Overriding Abstract Methods from Multiple Superinterfaces

The code below illustrates the simple case where the subinterface TaskAB at (3) extends the two superinterfaces, TaskA and TaskB, whose abstract methods are *override-equivalent*—that is, they have the same signature. The abstract method declared at (4) in the subinterface TaskAB *overrides* the two abstract method declarations from the superinterfaces. This method represents the two abstract method declarations from the superinterfaces. The compiler can also infer it from the inherited methods, and its declaration at (4) can be omitted.

```
interface TaskA { Object compute(Integer iRef1); }   // (1)
interface TaskB { Object compute(Integer iRef2); }   // (2)
interface TaskAB extends TaskA, TaskB {              // (3)
  @Override Object compute(Integer iRef3);           // (4) Can be omitted.
}

interface TaskC { String compute(Integer iRef4); }   // (5)
interface TaskABC extends TaskA, TaskB, TaskC {      // (6)
  @Override String compute(Integer iRef5);           // (7a) Can be omitted.
//@Override Object compute(Integer iRef6);           // (7b) Compile-time error!
}
```

The subinterface TaskABC at (6) extends the superinterfaces TaskA, TaskB, and TaskC. The abstract methods of the three superinterfaces are override-equivalent, since they have the same method signature: compute(Integer). The abstract method at (5) in TaskC can *override* the other two methods with its *covariant* return, as String type is a subtype of Object type. The compiler infers that the abstract method at (5) can represent the methods from the superinterfaces in the subinterface TaskABC. Again we can omit the abstract method declaration at (7a), as the compiler can infer it. A client of course must make sure that it implements the correct abstract method when implementing the interface TaskABC.

If the abstract method declaration at (7a) is replaced with the abstract method declaration at (7b) where the return type is Object, the code will not compile, as this method cannot override the abstract method declaration at (5) declared with the return type String. This is an example of a *name clash*—that is, the inherited methods from the superinterfaces are override-equivalent, but the method at (7b) cannot override them all, thus resulting in a compile-time error.

The next example shows that the multiple abstract methods inherited by the ContractZ are not override-equivalent—in fact they are overloaded, and both are inherited from their respective interfaces by the subinterface.

```
interface ContractX { void doIt(int i); }
interface ContractY { void doIt(double d); }
interface ContractZ extends ContractX, ContractY {
  @Override void doIt(int d);                     // Can be omitted.
  @Override void doIt(double d);                  // Can be omitted.
}
```

So far all examples have involved methods without generics, where a subtype method could override a supertype method that had the same signature.

A subtype method *without generics* can *override* supertype methods *with generics* that have the same signature *after type erasure*. After type erasure of the bake() methods at (1) and (2) in the code below, all three bake() methods at (1), (2), and (3) are override-equivalent with the signature bake(List). However, it is the bake() method at (3) that *overrides* the bake() methods at (1) and (2). This bake() method *without generics* at (3) logically represents all the inherited bake() methods in the Bakeable subinterface. The implementation of the Bakeable subinterface thus requires implementation of the bake() method without generics declared at (3).

```
class Ingredient { }

interface PizzaBakeable {
  void bake(List<Ingredient> ingredients);  // (1) After type erasure: bake(List)
}

interface CalzoneBakeable {
  void bake(List<Ingredient> ingredients);  // (2) After type erasure: bake(List)
}

interface SimplyBakeable {
  void bake(List ingredients);              // (3) Signature: bake(List)
}
```

```
interface Bakeable extends SimplyBakeable, PizzaBakeable, CalzoneBakeable {
  @Override void bake(List ingredients);    // Can be omitted.
}
```

In the code above, the bake() method without generics at (3) that *overrides* the other two inherited bake() methods, and thus represents all the inherited bake() methods in the subinterface, can be inferred by *type erasure of any of the inherited* bake() *methods with generics*, since they are all override-equivalent.

From the examples in this subsection, we see that override-equivalent methods in superinterfaces can be legally inherited by a subinterface, if a method can be inferred that *overrides* all inherited override-equivalent methods (after any type erasure), and which then represents these methods in the subinterface. In the case of override-equivalent methods *with generics* from multiple superinterfaces, the type erasure of *any* of the override-equivalent methods is always a candidate that can override and represent these methods in the subinterface.

11.13 Limitations and Restrictions on Generic Types

In this section we take a look at implications and restrictions on generic types for instance tests, casting, arrays, variable arity parameters, exception handling, nested classes, and enum types.

Reifiable Types

Concrete parameterized types are used by the compiler and then translated by erasure to their raw types, losing information about the parameterization in the process. In other words, only the raw types of these concrete parameterized types are available at runtime. For example, List<Integer> and List<String> are both erased to the raw type List. The same applies to unbounded parameterized types: List<E> is erased to List.

Non-generic types are not affected by type erasure, and therefore, have *not* lost any information and are, therefore, available fully at runtime. For example, the types Integer and String remain intact and are present unchanged at runtime.

Types that are completely available at runtime are known as *reifiable types*—that is, type erasure has *not* removed any important information about them (see Table 11.5). Types whose information has been affected by erasure are called *non-reifiable types* (see Table 11.6).

Note that unbounded wildcard parameterized types (Node<?>, MyStack<?>) are reifiable, whereas concrete parameterized types (Node<Number>, MyStack<String>) and bounded wildcard parameterized types (Node<? extends Number>, MyStack<? super String>) are non-reifiable.

As we shall see in the rest of this section, certain operations in Java are only permitted on reifiable types (as their type information is fully intact and available at runtime), and not on non-reifiable types (as their type information is not fully available at runtime, since it has been affected by type erasure).

Table 11.5 *Examples of Reifiable Types*

Reifiable type	Example
A primitive type	`int, double, boolean`
A non-generic type	`Exception, System, Math, Number`
A raw type	`List, ArrayList, Map, HashMap`
A parameterized type in which all type arguments are *unbounded wildcards* (unbounded wildcard parameterized type)	`List<?>, ArrayList<?>, Map<?,?>, HashMap<?,?>`
An *array type* whose component type is reifiable	`double[], Number[], List[], HashMap<?,?>[], Number[][]`

Table 11.6 *Examples of Non-Reifiable Types*

Non-Reifiable type	Example
A type parameter	`E, T, K, V`
A parameterized type with *concrete or unbounded type parameters* (concrete or unbounded parameterized type)	`List<E>, List<String>, ArrayList<Integer>, HashMap<String, Number> Map<K, V>`
A parameterized type with a *bound* (bounded wildcard parameterized type)	`List<? extends Object>, ArrayList<? extends Number>, Comparable<? super Integer>`
An *array type* whose component type is non-reifiable	`List<E>[], ArrayList<Number>[], Comparable<? super Integer>[], HashMap<K, V>[]`

Implications for the `instanceof` operator

Although the discussion here is about the `instanceof` type comparison operator, it applies equally to the `instanceof` pattern match operator.

At (1) below, we want to determine whether the object referenced by `obj` is an instance of the concrete parameterized type `MyStack<Integer>`—that is, whether it is a stack of `Integer`.

```
Object obj;
...
boolean isIntStack = obj instanceof MyStack<Integer>; // (1) Compile-time error!
```

The post-erasure code for (1) is equivalent to the following statement:

```
boolean isIntStack = obj instanceof MyStack;          // (1')
```

The statement at (1') cannot perform the instanceof type comparison as expected at (1), since the type erasure has removed the information about the concrete type parameter Integer—that is, the type MyStack<Integer> is non-reifiable. The compiler issues an error because the type Object cannot be *safely cast* to the type MyStack at runtime.

In the following code, the fact that IStack<Integer> is a supertype of MyStack<Integer> can be checked at compile time —that is, the type MyStack<Integer> can be considered a *refinement* of the type IStack<Integer>. Such refinement of a generic type can be checked with the instanceof type comparison operator as it is deemed safe at runtime.

```
IStack<Integer> iStack;
...
boolean isIntegerStack = iStack instanceof MyStack<Integer>;   // (2) OK.
```

The post-erasure code for (2) is equivalent to the following statement, where MyStack is a subtype of IStack (i.e., the type of iStack), making the cast from IStack to MyStack safe.

```
boolean isIntegerStack = iStack instanceof MyStack;   // (2')
```

Given that T is a formal type parameter, the following code will not compile, as the arguments of the instanceof type comparison operator are non-reifiable types.

```
boolean isT     = obj instanceof T;            // (3) Compile-time error!
boolean isTStack = obj instanceof MyStack<T>;  // (4) Compile-time error!
```

The post-erasure code for (2) and (3) is equivalent to the following statements. Again, casting the type Object to the types Object and MyStack, respectively, is not deemed safe at runtime.

```
boolean isT     = obj instanceof Object;       // (3')
boolean isTStack = obj instanceof MyStack;     // (4')
```

If we just wanted to determine that an instance was some stack, the instance test can be performed against the raw type or the unbounded wildcard parameterized type, as these types are reifiable:

```
boolean isRawStack = obj instanceof MyStack;
boolean isAnyStack = obj instanceof MyStack<?>;       // Preferable.
```

Implications for Casting

A non-reifiable type can lose important type information during erasure and the cast may not have the desired effect at runtime. A cast to a non-reifiable type is *generally* flagged as an *unchecked cast warning*, and the cast is *replaced by a cast to its erasure*. Again, the compiler permits casts to allow interoperability between legacy code and generic code—usually with a warning.

The following code shows why a warning is necessary. The reference value of a Number node, declared at (1), is assigned to a reference of type Node<?> at (2). This reference is cast to a Node<String> and its reference value is assigned to a reference of type Node<String> at (3). A String is set as data in the node at (4). The data is retrieved from the node via the numNode reference and assigned to a Number reference at (5).

```
Node<Number> numNode = new Node<>(20, null);         // (1)
Node<?> anyNode = numNode;                           // (2)
Node<String> strNode = (Node<String>) anyNode;       // (3) Unchecked cast warning
strNode.setData("Peekaboo");                         // (4)
Number num = numNode.getData();                      // (5) ClassCastException
```

The erasure of the assignment at (3) is equivalent to the following assignment, with the cast succeeding at runtime:

```
Node strNode = (Node) anyNode;                       // (3')
```

However, a ClassCastException occurs at (5) because a String cannot be assigned to a Number. The compiler warns of potential problems by issuing an unchecked cast warning at (3).

The types Node<String> and Node<Number> are unrelated. That is the reason why the Number node in the above example was compromised by going through a node of type Node<?>. As we would expect, a cast between unrelated types results in a compile-time error:

```
strNode = (Node<String>) numNode;                    // Compile-time error
```

If we are casting a generic supertype to a generic subtype, where the parameterization is identical, the cast is safe and no warning is issued:

```
// BiNode<E> is a subtype of MonoNode<E>.
MonoNode<String> monoStrNode = new BiNode<>("Hi", null, null);
BiNode<String> biStrNode = (BiNode<String>) monoStrNode; // Ok. No warning.
```

The method castaway() below shows examples of casting an Object reference that refers to a node of type String, declared at (2).

```
//@SuppressWarnings("unchecked")              // (1) Suppress warnings at (4),(6),(7).
public static void castaway() {
  Object obj = new Node<>("one", null);                // (2)
  Node<String> node1 = obj;                            // (3) Compile-time error!
  Node<String> node2 = (Node<String>) obj;             // (4) Unchecked cast
  Node<String> node3 = (Node<?>) obj;                  // (5) Compile-time error!
  Node<String> node4 = (Node<String>)(Node<?>) obj;    // (6) Unchecked cast
  Node<String> node5 = (Node) obj;                     // (7) Unchecked conversion
  Node<?> node6 = (Node) obj;                          // (8) OK.
  Node<?> node7 = (Node<?>)obj;                        // (9) OK.
}
```

It is instructive to see what warnings and errors are issued by the compiler. The compile-time error at (3) is due to incompatible types: An Object cannot be assigned to a Node<String> reference. The compiler issues an *unchecked cast warning* at (4) because of the cast from an Object to the concrete parameterized type Node<String>. The compile-time error at (5) is due to incompatible types: A Node<?> cannot be assigned to a Node<String> reference. There are two casts at (6): An Object is cast to Node<?>, which in turn is cast to Node<String>. The cast to Node<?> is permitted, but the second cast results in an unchecked cast warning. The compiler issues an *unchecked conversion warning* at (7), since a raw type (Node) is being assigned to a parameterized type (Node<String>). (8) and (9) show that casting to the raw type or to the unbounded wildcard is always permitted, since both types are reifiable.

If the annotation @SuppressWarnings("unchecked") at (1) is uncommented, the unchecked warnings at (4), (6), and (7) in the method castaway() will be suppressed (§25.5, p. 1582). Use of this annotation is recommended when we *know* that unchecked cast warnings are inevitable in a language construct (a type declaration, a field, a method, a parameter, a constructor, a local variable). Any unchecked warnings reported by the compiler are those that were *not* documented using this annotation. The use of an unbounded wildcard is recommended in casts, rather than using raw types, as it provides for stricter type checking.

Implications for Arrays

Array store checks are based on the element type being a reifiable type, in order to ensure that subtype covariance between array types is not violated at runtime. In the code below, the element type of the array is String and the array store check at (1) disallows the assignment, resulting in an ArrayStoreException because the reference value of a Double cannot be stored in a String reference.

```
String[] strArray = new String[] {"Hi", "Hello", "Howdy"};
Object[] objArray = strArray; // String[] is a subtype of Object[]
objArray[0] = 2020.5;          // (1) ArrayStoreException
```

We cannot instantiate a formal type parameter, nor can we create an array of such a type:

```
// T is a formal type parameter.
T t = new T();            // Compile-time error!
T[] anArray = new T[10];  // Compile-time error!
```

It is also not possible to create an array whose element type is a concrete or a bounded wildcard parameterized type:

```
// An array of Lists of String
List<String>[] list1 = {                      // Compile-time error
  Arrays.asList("one", "two"), Arrays.asList("three", "four")
};

List<String>[] list2 = new List<String>[] {   // Compile-time error
  Arrays.asList("one", "two"), Arrays.asList("three", "four")
};
```

```
// An array of Lists of any subtype of Number
List<? extends Number>[] list3
                = new List<? extends Number>[] {     // Compile-time error
   Arrays.asList(20.20, 60.60), Arrays.asList(1948, 1949)
};
```

Unbounded wildcard parameterized types are allowed as element types because these types are essentially equivalent to the raw types (p. 584):

```
List<?>[] list4 = {
   Arrays.asList("one", "two"), Arrays.asList("three", "four")
};

List<?>[] list5 = new List<?>[] {
   Arrays.asList(20.20, 60.60), Arrays.asList(1978, 1981)
};
List[] list6 = list5;
```

Note that we can always declare a *reference* of a non-reifiable type. It is creating arrays of these types that is not permitted.

```
class MyIntList extends ArrayList<Integer> {}      // A reifiable subclass.

// Client code
List<Integer>[] arrayOfLists = new MyIntList[5];  // Array of Lists of Integer
List<Integer[]> listOfArrays = new ArrayList<>(); // List of Arrays of Integer
```

The class MyStack<E> in Example 11.10, p. 598, implements a method to convert a stack to an array:

```
// Copy to array as many elements as possible.
public E[] toArray(E[] toArray) {                              // (11)
   Node<E> thisNode = tos;
   for (int i = 0; thisNode != null && i < toArray.length; i++) {
      toArray[i] = thisNode.getData();
      thisNode = thisNode.getNext();
   }
   return toArray;
}
```

Note that the array is passed as a parameter because we cannot create an array of the parameter type, as the following version of the method shows:

```
public E[] toArray2() {
   E[] toArray = new E[numOfElements];           // Compile-time error
   int i = 0;
   for (E data : this) { toArray[i++] = data; }
   return toArray;
}
```

The third version below uses an array of Object. The cast is necessary in order to be compatible with the return type. However, the cast is to a non-reifiable type, resulting in an unchecked cast warning:

```
public E[] toArray3() {
   E[] toArray = (E[])new Object[numOfElements];  // (1) Unchecked cast warning
   int i = 0;
```

```
    for (E data : this) { toArray[i++] = data; }
    return toArray;
  }
```

The method implementation above has a serious problem, even though the code compiles. We get a ClassCastException at (2) below because we cannot assign the reference value of an Object[] to an Integer[] reference:

```
MyStack<Integer> intStack = new MyStack<>();
intStack.push(9); intStack.push(1); intStack.push(1);
Integer[] intArray = intStack.toArray3();        // (2) ClassCastException
```

The final and correct version of this method uses *reflection* to create an array of the right element type:

```
@SuppressWarnings("unchecked")
public E[] toArray4(E[] toArray) {
  if (toArray.length != numOfElements) {
    toArray = (E[])java.lang.reflect.Array.newInstance(           // (3)
                    toArray.getClass().getComponentType(),
                    numOfElements);            // Suppressed unchecked warning
  }
  int i = 0;
  for (E data : this) { toArray[i++] = data; }
  return toArray;
}
```

The method is passed an array whose element type is determined through reflection, and an array of this element type (and right size) is created at (3). The method newInstance() of the Array class creates an array of specified element type and size. The element type is looked up through the class literal of the array supplied as an argument. The unchecked cast warning is suppressed because we know it is unavoidable. We will not go into the nitty-gritty details of using reflection here.

The client code now works as expected. We pass an array of zero length, and let the method create the array.

```
MyStack<Integer> intStack = new MyStack<>();
intStack.push(9); intStack.push(1); intStack.push(1);
Integer[] intArray = intStack.toArray4(new Integer[0]);          // OK.
```

The next example demonstrates the danger of casting an array of a reifiable type to an array of a non-reifiable type. An array of the raw type List (reifiable type) is created at (1), and cast to an array of List<Double> (non-reifiable type). The cast results in an unchecked cast warning. The first element of the array of List<Double> is initialized with a list of Double at (2). The reference value of this array is assigned to a reference of type List<? extends Number> at (3). Using this reference, the list of Double in the first element of the array is replaced with a list of Integer at (4). Using the alias arrayOfListsOfDouble of type List<Double>[], the first element in the first list of the array (an Integer) is assigned to a Double reference. Since the types are incompatible, a ClassCastException is thrown at (5). Note that the array store check at (4) succeeds because the check is against the reified element type of the array, List, and not List<Double>.

```
List<Double>[] arrayOfListsOfDouble
               = (List<Double>[]) new List[1];    // (1) Unchecked cast warning!
arrayOfListsOfDouble[0] = Arrays.asList(10.10);   // (2) Initialize
List<? extends Number>[] arrayOfListsOfExtNums = arrayOfListsOfDouble; // (3)
arrayOfListsOfExtNums[0] = Arrays.asList(10);     // (4) Array storage check ok
Double firstOne = arrayOfListsOfDouble[0].get(0); // (5) ClassCastException!
```

Implications for Non-Reifiable Variable Arity Parameter

Because variable arity parameters are treated as arrays, generics have implications for non-reifiable variable arity parameters (T ... varargs). Most of the workarounds for arrays are not applicable, as array creation is implicit for variable arity parameters. In a method declaration with a non-reifiable variable arity parameter, the compiler flags a warning about possible *heap pollution* from using a non-reifiable variable arity type. Heap pollution occurs when a reference of a parameterized type refers to an object that is not of the parameterized type. This can only occur when both the compiler and the JVM cannot guarantee the validity of an operation involving parameterized types. The compiler issues a warning about potential heap pollution, and the JVM normally throws an appropriate exception.

The method asStack() below has a variable arity parameter at (1) whose type is a non-reifiable type T. The method pushes the specified elements on to the specified stack. The compiler issues a possible heap pollution warning at (1).

```
public static <T> void
  asStack(MyStack<T> stack, T...elements) { // (1) Possible heap pollution warning
    for (T element : elements) { stack.push(element); }
}
```

In a method call, implicit creation of a *generic array with the variable arity parameter* results in an *unchecked generic array creation warning*—and type-safety is no longer guaranteed. The method above is called by the client code below at (4). The idea is to initialize a stack of stacks of Integer with a stack of Integer. An implicit generic array (new MyStack[] { intStack }) is created by the compiler, which is passed in the method call at (4). The compiler also issues an *unchecked array creation warning*, but the code compiles and runs without any problems.

```
/* Client code */
// (2) Create a stack of stacks of Integer:
MyStack<MyStack<Integer>> stackOfIntStacks = new MyStack<>();

// (3) Create a stack of Integer:
MyStack<Integer> intStack = new MyStack<>();
intStack.push(2019); intStack.push(2020);

// Initializes the stack of stacks with the stack of Integer.
MyStack.asStack(stackOfIntStacks, intStack); // (4) Unchecked array creation!
intStack = stackOfIntStacks.pop();         // (5) Pop the stack of stacks of Integer.
int tos = intStack.pop();                   // (6) Pop the stack of Integer.
assert tos == 2020;
```

The implicit array passed as an argument is available as an array of a *non-reifiable type* in the body of the method asStack(). The integrity of this array can be compromised by making the array store check report a false positive at runtime—that is, succeed when the store operation should normally fail, thereby resulting in heap pollution. This is demonstrated by the method declaration below, in the assignment statement at (1a), where the contents of the elements array are changed before they are copied to the specified stack. The compiler issues a possible heap pollution warning at (1) and an unchecked cast warning at (1a).

```
public static <T> void asStackMalicious(
          MyStack<T> stack, T... elements) { // (1) Possible heap pollution warning
    // Compromise the elements array:
    MyStack<Double> doubleStack = new MyStack<>();
    doubleStack.push(20.20);
    elements[0] = (T) doubleStack;              // (1a) Unchecked cast warning!

    // Copy from elements array:
    for (T element : elements) { stack.push(element); }
}
```

A partial erasure for the method asStackMalicious() is shown below.

```
public static void asStackMalicious(MyStack stack, Object...elements) {
    // Compromise the elements array:
    MyStack doubleStack = new MyStack();
    doubleStack.push(Double.valueOf(20.20));
    elements[0] = (Object) doubleStack;                     // (1b)
    for (Object element : elements) { stack.push(element); } // (1c)
    ...
}
```

Note that the *cast* at (1b) succeeds for *any* object at runtime, as any object can be cast to Object. The assignment at (1b) succeeds if the array store check succeeds.

If we now call the method asStackMalicious(), instead of the method asStack() at (4) in the client code above, the code compiles with a generic array creation warning as before.

```
MyStack.asStackMalicious(stackOfIntStacks, intStack); // (4') Unchecked warning!
```

At runtime, the reference elements in the method asStackMalicious() refers to the implicit array created in the call—that is, new MyStack[] { intStack }. The signature of the method call at runtime is equivalent to:

```
asStackMalicious(MyStack, MyStack[])
```

At runtime, the actual type of the stack parameter is MyStack and the actual type of the elements array parameter is MyStack[]. The element type of a stack has been erased. The references doubleStack and elements[0] both have the runtime type MyStack. When the code is run, the array store check succeeds at (1b), and element[0] now refers to a stack of Double. In the loop at (1c), this stack of Double is pushed on the stack of stacks of Integer referred to by the formal parameter stack. Heap pollution is now a fact.

After return from the call at (4) in the client code, the assignment at (5) also succeeds, as this is an assignment of a `MyStack` to a reference of the same type after erasure. The reference `intStack` now refers to a stack of `Double`. The error is only discovered after a `ClassCastException` is thrown at (6) because the `Double` that is popped from the stack of `Integer` cannot be converted and assigned to an `Integer`.

The general rule is to avoid the variable arity parameter in methods where the parameter is of a non-reifiable type. No matter what, it is the responsibility of the method declaration to ensure that the non-reifiable variable arity parameter is handled in a type-safe manner, and then to use one of the two annotations below to suppress unchecked warnings:

```
@SuppressWarnings("unchecked")                           // (1)
public static <T> void asStack(MyStack<T> stack, T...elements) { ... }

@SafeVarargs                                             // (2)
public static <T> void asStack(MyStack<T> stack, T...elements) { ... }
```

The method `asStack()` handles the non-reifiable variable arity parameter `elements` in a type-safe way, so suppressing the unchecked warning is justified. The annotation at (1) suppresses *all* unchecked warnings in the method declaration, but it does *not* suppress the unchecked generic array creation warning at the call sites. The annotation at (2) suppresses all unchecked warnings in the method declaration, as well as the unchecked generic array creation warning at the call sites. However, the `@SafeVarargs` annotation (§25.5, p. 1582) is only applicable to a variable arity method or constructor, and the method cannot be overridden—that is, the method must be either `static`, `private`, or `final`.

Implications for Exception Handling

When an exception is thrown in a `try` block, it is matched against the parameter of each `catch` block that is associated with the `try` block. This test is similar to the instance test, requiring reifiable types. The following restrictions apply, and are illustrated in Example 11.17:

- A generic type cannot extend the `Throwable` class.
- A parameterized type cannot be specified in a `throws` clause.
- The type of the parameter of a `catch` block must be a reifiable type, and it must also be a subtype of `Throwable`.

- -

Example 11.17 *Restrictions on Exception Handling*

```
// File: ExceptionErrors.java

// (1) A generic class cannot extend Exception:
class MyGenericException<T> extends Exception { }         // Compile-time error!

public class ExceptionErrors {
```

```
        // (2) Cannot specify parameterized types in throws clause:
        public static void main(String[] args)
                          throws MyGenericException<String> { // Compile-time error!
          try {
            throw new MyGenericException<String>();
          } // (3) Cannot use parameterized type in catch block:
            catch (MyGenericException<String> e) {          // Compile-time error!
            e.printStackTrace();
          }
        }
      }
```

However, *type parameters* are allowed in the throws clause, as shown in Example
11.18. In the declaration of the MyActionListener interface, the method doAction()
can throw an exception of type E. The interface is implemented by the class
FileAction, that provides the actual type parameter (FileNotFoundException) and
implements the doAction() method with this actual type parameter. All is aboveboard,
as only reifiable types are used for exception handling in the class FileAction.

Example 11.18 *Type Parameter in* throws *Clause*

```
        public interface MyActionListener<E extends Exception> {
          public void doAction() throws E;      // Type parameter in throws clause
        }
```

```
        import java.io.FileNotFoundException;

        public class FileAction implements MyActionListener<FileNotFoundException> {

          @Override public void doAction() throws FileNotFoundException {
            throw new FileNotFoundException("Does not exist");
          }

          public static void main(String[] args) {
            FileAction fileAction = new FileAction();
            try {
              fileAction.doAction();
            } catch (FileNotFoundException e) {
              e.printStackTrace();
            }
          }
        }
```

Implications for Nested Classes

Nested classes and interfaces can be declared as generic types, as shown in Example 11.19. All nested generic classes, except anonymous classes, can specify formal
type parameters in their declaration, as at (2) through (6). Anonymous classes do
not have a name, and a class name is required to declare a generic class and specify

its formal type parameters. Thus an anonymous class can only be declared as a parameterized type, where the actual type parameters are either specified in the anonymous class expression, as at (7) through (9), or can be inferred from the context when the diamond operator is used, as at (10).

Example 11.19 *Generic Nested Types*

```
class GenericTLC<A> {                    // (1) Top-level class

    static class SMC<B> {/*...*/}         // (2) Static member class

    interface SMI<C> {/*...*/}            // (3) Static member interface

    class NSMC<D> {/*...*/}               // (4) Non-static member (inner) class

    void nsm() {
        class NSLC<E> {/*...*/}           // (5) Local (inner) class in non-static context
    }

    static void sm() {
        class SLC<F> {/*...*/}            // (6) Local (inner) class in static context
    }

    // Anonymous classes as parameterized types:
    SMC<A> xsf = new SMC<A>() {     // (7) In non-static context.
        /*...*/                     //      A is type parameter in top-level class.
    };
    SMC<Integer> nsf = new SMC<Integer>() {        // (8) In non-static context
        /*...*/
    };
    static SMI<String> sf = new SMI<String>() {    // (9) In static context
        /*...*/
    };
    SMC<String> nsf1 = new SMC<>() {               // (10) Using diamond operator
        /*...*/
    };
}
```

The type parameter names of a generic nested class can hide type parameter names in the enclosing context (see (2) in Example 11.20). Only a non-static nested class can use the type parameters in its enclosing context, as type parameters cannot be referenced in a static context.

Example 11.20 also illustrates instantiating generic nested classes. As a static member class does not have an outer instance, only its simple name is parameterized, and not the enclosing types, as shown by the code at (6). As a non-static member class requires an outer instance, any generic enclosing types must also be parameterized and instantiated, as shown by the code at (7). See §9.3, p. 502, for the syntax used in instantiating nested classes.

Example 11.20 *Instantiating Generic Nested Classes*

```
public class ListPool<T> {         // (1) Top-level class

    static class MyLinkedList<T> { // (2) Hiding type parameter in enclosing context
        T t;                       // T refers to (2)
    }

    class Node<E> {                // (4) Non-static member (inner) class
        T t;                       // T refers to (1)
        E e;
    }

    public static void main(String[] args) {
        // (5) Instantiating a generic top-level class:
        ListPool<String> lp = new ListPool<>();

        // (6) Instantiating a generic static member class:
        ListPool.MyLinkedList<String> list = new ListPool.MyLinkedList<>();

        // (7) Instantiating a generic non-static member class:
        ListPool<String>.Node<Integer> node1 = lp.new Node<>();
        ListPool<String>.Node<Double> node2 = lp.new Node<>();
        ListPool<Integer>.Node<String> node3
                        = new ListPool<Integer>().new Node<>();
    }
}
```

Other Implications

Enum Types

Because of the way enum types are implemented using the java.lang.Enum class, we cannot declare a generic enum type:

```
enum CoinToss<C> { HEAD, TAIL; }                    // Compile-time error!
```

An enum type can implement a parameterized interface, just like a non-generic class can. Example 11.21 shows the enum type TripleJump that implements the Comparator<TripleJump> interface.

Example 11.21 *Enum Implements Parameterized Generic Interface*

```
enum TripleJump implements java.util.Comparator<TripleJump> {
    HOP, STEP, JUMP;

    @Override public int compare(TripleJump a1, TripleJump a2) {
        return a1.compareTo(a2);
    }
}
```

Class Literals

Objects of the class Class<T> represent classes and interfaces at runtime. For example, an instance of the Class<String> represents the type String at runtime.

A class literal expression (using .class notation) can only use reifiable types as type parameters, as there is only one class object created for each reifiable type.

```
Class<Node> class0 = Node<Integer>.class;// Non-reifiable type. Compile-time error!
Class<Node> class1 = Node.class;         // Reifiable type. Ok.
```

The getClass() method of the Object class also returns a Class object. The actual result type of this object is Class<? extends |T|> where |T| is the erasure of the static type of the expression on which the getClass() method is called. The following code shows that all invocations of the generic type Node<T> are represented by a single class literal:

```
Node<Integer> intNode = new Node<>(2019, null);
Node<String> strNode = new Node<>("Hi", null);
Class<?> class2 = strNode.getClass();
Class<?> class3 = intNode.getClass();
assert class1 == class2;
assert class2 == class3;
```

 Review Questions

11.11   What will be the result of compiling and running the following program?

```
import java.util.*;

public class RQ100_00 {
  public static void main(String[] args) {
    List<String> lst1 = new ArrayList<>();
    List<Integer> lst2 = new ArrayList<>();
    List<List<Integer>> lst3 = new ArrayList<>();
    System.out.print(lst1.getClass() + ", ");
    System.out.print(lst2.getClass() + ", ");
    System.out.println(lst3.getClass());
  }
}
```

Select the one correct answer.

(a) class java.util.ArrayList<String>, class java.util.ArrayList<Integer>, class java.util.ArrayList<List<Integer>>

(b) class java.util.ArrayList, class java.util.ArrayList, class java.util.ArrayList

(c) class java.util.List, class java.util.List, class java.util.List

(d) class java.util.List<String>, class java.util.List<Integer>, class java.util.List<List<Integer>>

(e) The program will fail to compile.

(f) The program will compile, but it will throw an exception at runtime.

11.12 Which method header can be inserted at (1) so that the program will compile and runs without errors?

```java
import java.util.*;

public class RQ100_02 {
  public static void main(String[] args) {
    List<String> lst = Arrays.asList("Java", "only", "promotes", "fun");
    Collection<String> resultList = delete4LetterWords(lst);
  }

  // (1) INSERT METHOD HEADER HERE
  {
    Collection<E> permittedWords = new ArrayList<>();
    for (E word : words) {
      if (word.length() != 4) permittedWords.add(word);
    }
    return permittedWords;
  }
}
```

Select the one correct answer.

(a) static <E extends CharSequence>
    Collection<? extends CharSequence> delete4LetterWords(Collection<E> words)
(b) static <E extends CharSequence>
    List<E> delete4LetterWords(Collection<E> words)
(c) static <E extends CharSequence>
    Collection<E> delete4LetterWords(Collection<? extends CharSequence> words)
(d) static <E extends CharSequence>
    List<E> delete4LetterWords(Collection<? extends CharSequence> words)
(e) static <E extends CharSequence>
    Collection<E> delete4LetterWords(Collection<E> words)
(f) static <E super CharSequence>
    Collection<E> delete4LetterWords(Collection<E> words)

11.13 Which method declarations cannot be inserted independently at (2) to overload the method at (1)?

```java
import java.util.*;

public class RQ_Overloading {

  static <T> void overloadMe(List<T> s1, List<T> s2) {} // (1)
  // (2) INSERT METHOD DECLARATIONS HERE
}
```

Select the two correct answers.

(a) static <T> void overloadMe(Collection<T> s1, List<T> s2) {}
(b) static <T> void overloadMe(List<T> s1, List<? extends T> s2) {}
(c) static <T> void overloadMe(List<T> s1, Collection<? super T> s2) {}
(d) static <T> void overloadMe(Collection<T> s1, Collection<? super T> s2) {}
(e) static <T> void overloadMe(Collection<T> s1, List<? super T> s2) {}
(f) static <T> void overloadMe(List<? extends T> s1, List<? super T> s2) {}

11.14 Which method declaration can be inserted at (1) so that the program will compile without warnings?

```
import java.util.*;

public class RQ100_87 {
  public static void main(String[] args) {
    List raw = new ArrayList();
    raw.add("2020");
    raw.add(2021);
    raw.add("2022");
    justDoIt(raw);
  }
  // (1) INSERT METHOD DECLARATION HERE
}
```

Select the one correct answer.

(a) static void justDoIt(List<Integer> lst) {}

(b) static void justDoIt(List<?> lst) {}

(c) static <T> void justDoIt(List<T> lst) {}

(d) None of the above

11.15 Which of the following statements are true about the following code?

```
class SupC<T> {
  public void set(T t) {/*...*/}      // (1)
  public T get() {return null;}       // (2)
}

class SubC1<M,N> extends SupC<M> {
  public void set(N n) {/*...*/}      // (3)
  public N get() {return null;}       // (4)
}

class SubC2<M,N extends M> extends SupC<M> {
  public void set(N n) {/*...*/}      // (5)
  public N get() {return null;}       // (6)
}
```

Select the four correct answers.

(a) The method at (3) overloads the method at (1).

(b) The method at (3) overrides the method at (1).

(c) The method at (3) will fail to compile.

(d) The method at (4) overloads the method at (2).

(e) The method at (4) overrides the method at (2).

(f) The method at (4) will fail to compile.

(g) The method at (5) overloads the method at (1).

(h) The method at (5) overrides the method at (1).

(i) The method at (5) will fail to compile.

(j) The method at (6) overloads the method at (2).

(k) The method at (6) overrides the method at (2).

(l) The method at (6) will fail to compile.

11.16 Which types cannot be declared as generic types?
Select the three correct answers.

(a) Enum types
(b) Static member classes
(c) Any subclass of Throwable
(d) Nested interfaces
(e) Anonymous classes
(f) Non-static member classes
(g) Local classes

11.17 Which statement is true about the following code?

```java
import java.util.*;

public class CastAway {
  public static void main(String[] args) {
    Object obj = new ArrayList<Integer>();     // (1)
    List<?>       list1 = (List<?>) obj;        // (2)
    List<?>       list2 = (List) obj;           // (3)
    List          list3 = (List<?>) obj;        // (4)
    List<Integer> list4 = (List) obj;           // (5)
    List<Integer> list5 = (List<Integer>) obj;  // (6)
  }
}
```

Select the one correct answer.

(a) The program will fail to compile.
(b) The program will compile without any unchecked warnings. It will run with no output and terminate normally.
(c) The program will compile without any unchecked warnings. When run, it will throw an exception.
(d) The program will compile, but with unchecked warnings. It will run with no output and terminate normally.
(e) The program will compile, but with unchecked warnings. When run, it will throw an exception.

11.18 Which statement is true about the following code?

```java
import java.util.*;

public class InstanceTest2 {
  public static void main(String[] args) {
    List<Integer> intList = new ArrayList<>();
    Set<Double> doubleSet = new HashSet<>();
    List<?>       list = intList;
    Set<?>        set = doubleSet;

    scuddle(intList);
    scuddle(doubleSet);
    scuddle(list);
    scuddle(set);
  }
```

```
    private static void scuddle(Collection<?> col) {
      if (col instanceof List<?>) {
        System.out.println("I am a list.");
      } else if (col instanceof Set<?>) {
        System.out.println("I am a set.");
      }
    }
  }
}
```

Select the one correct answer.

(a) The method scuddle() will fail to compile.

(b) The method main() will fail to compile.

(c) The program will compile, but with an unchecked warning in method scuddle(). It will run and terminate normally with the following output:
```
I am a list.
I am a set.
I am a list.
I am a set.
```

(d) The program will compile, but with an unchecked warning in the method main(). When run, it will throw an exception.

(e) The program will compile without any unchecked warnings. It will run and terminate normally, with the following output:
```
I am a list.
I am a set.
I am a list.
I am a set.
```

(f) The program will compile without any unchecked warnings. It will run and terminate normally, with the following output:
```
I am a list.
I am a set.
```

(g) None of the above

11.19 Which statement is true about the following code?

```
public class GenArrays {
  public static <E> E[] copy(E[] srcArray) {
    E[] destArray = (E[]) new Object[srcArray.length];
    int i = 0;
    for (E element : srcArray) {
      destArray[i++] = element;
    }
    return destArray;
  }

  public static void main(String[] args) {
    String[] sa = {"9", "1", "1" };
    String[] da = GenArrays.copy(sa);
    System.out.println(da[0]);
  }
}
```

Select the one correct answer.

(a) The program will fail to compile.
(b) The program will compile, but with an unchecked warning. When run, it will print 9.
(c) The program will compile, but with an unchecked warning. When run, it will throw an exception.
(d) The program will compile without any unchecked warnings. When run, it will print 9.
(e) The program will compile without any unchecked warnings. When run, it will throw an exception.

11.20   Which statement is true about the following code?

```java
import java.util.*;

public class GenVarArgs {
  public static <T> void doIt(List<T>... aols) {              // (1)
    for (int i = 0; i < aols.length; i++) {
      System.out.print(aols[i] + " ");
    }
  }

  public static void main(String... args) {                  // (2)
    List<String> ls1 = Arrays.asList("one", "two");
    List<String> ls2 = Arrays.asList("three", "four");
    List<String>[] aols = new List[] {ls1, ls2};             // (3)
    doIt(aols);                                              // (4)
  }
}
```

Select the one correct answer.

(a) The program will fail to compile because of errors at (1).
(b) The program will fail to compile because of errors at (2).
(c) The program will fail to compile because of errors at (3).
(d) The program will fail to compile because of errors at (4).
(e) The program will compile with unchecked warnings. When run, it will print [one, two] [three, four].

Collections, Part I: ArrayList<E>

12

Chapter Topics

- Understanding the concept of a list as a collection
- The inheritance relationship between the `ArrayList<E>` class, the `List<E>` interface, and the `Collection<E>` interface in the Java Collections Framework
- Declaring and using references of the `ArrayList<E>` type
- Creating unmodifiable lists
- Creating, modifying, querying, and traversing `ArrayLists`
- Interoperability between arrays and `ArrayLists`
- Comparison of arrays and `ArrayLists`

Java SE 17 Developer Exam Objectives	
[5.1] Create Java arrays, List, Set, Map and Deque collections, and add, remove, update, retrieve and sort their elements	§12.1, p. 644, to §12.8, p. 662.
○ Only `ArrayList` *is covered in this chapter.*	
○ *For arrays, see §3.9, p. 117.*	
○ *For comparing elements, see §14.4, p. 761, and §14.5, p. 769.*	
○ *For list, set, map, and deque collections, see Chapter 15, p. 781.*	

Java SE 11 Developer Exam Objectives	
[5.2] Use a Java array and List, Set, Map and Deque collections, including convenience methods	§12.1, p. 644, to §12.8, p. 662.
○ Only `ArrayList` *is covered in this chapter.*	
○ *For arrays, see §3.9, p. 117.*	
○ *For list, set, map, and deque collections, see Chapter 15, p. 781.*	

A program manipulates data, so naturally, organizing and using data efficiently is important in a program. *Data structures* allow data to be organized in an efficient way. Java uses the term *collection* to mean a data structure that can maintain a group of objects so that the objects can be manipulated as a *single entity* or *unit*. Objects can be stored, retrieved, and manipulated as *elements* of a collection. The term *container* is also used in the literature for such data structures. Arrays are one example of such collections. Other examples include lists, sets, queues, and stacks, among many others.

The Java Collections Framework provides the support for collections in Java. This chapter only covers the core API of the ArrayList<E> class that implements dynamic lists. We will have more to say about the ArrayList<E> class when we discuss the other collections in the Java Collections Framework in Chapter 15, p. 781. Diving deep into the Java Collections Framework is a beneficial exercise that is highly recommended for all Java programmers.

As the collections in the Java Collections Framework are implemented as generic types, knowledge of at least the basics of generics in Java is essential to utilize these collections effectively (Chapter 11, p. 563).

12.1 Lists

Once an array is created, its length cannot be changed. This inflexibility can be a significant drawback when the amount of data to be stored in an array is not known a priori. In Java, the structures known as lists alleviate this shortcoming. Lists are collections that maintain their elements *in order* and can contain duplicates. The order of elements in a list is *positional order*, and individual elements can be accessed according to their position in the list. Each element, therefore, has a position in the list. A zero-based index can be used to access the element at the position designated by the index value, analogous to accessing elements in an array. However, unlike in an array, the position of an element in a list can change as elements are inserted or deleted from the list—that is, as the list changes dynamically.

Sorting implies ordering the elements in a collection according to some *ranking criteria*, usually based on the *values* of the elements. However, elements is an ArrayList are maintained in the order they are inserted in the list, known as the *insertion order*. The elements in such a list are therefore *ordered*, but they are *not* sorted, as it is not the values of the elements that determine their ranking in the list. Thus ordering does *not* necessarily imply sorting.

Overview of the Java Collections Framework

The Collection<E> interface in the java.util package (also known as the Java Collections Framework) defines the general operations that a collection should provide (see Figure 12.1). Note that the Collection<E> interface extends the Iterable<E> interface, so all collections in this framework can be traversed using the for(:)

loop. Other subinterfaces in the Java Collections Framework augment this interface to provide specific operations for particular kinds of collections. The java.util.List<E> interface extends the java.util.Collection<E> interface with the operations necessary to maintain the collection as a list. In addition to the operations inherited from the java.util.Collection<E> interface, the java.util.List<E> interface defines operations that work specifically on lists: position-based access of the list elements, searching in a list, operations on parts of a list (called *open range-view* operations), and creation of customized iterators to iterate over a list. For methods used in this chapter, we will indicate which interface they are defined in. The impatient reader can refer to Chapter 15, p. 781, at any time for more details on these interfaces.

Figure 12.1 *Partial* ArrayList *Inheritance Hierarchy*

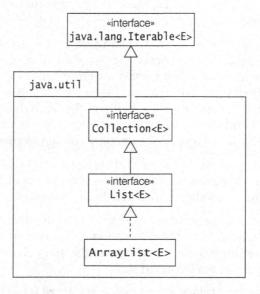

The *generic* class java.util.ArrayList<E> implements the java.util.List<E> interface. The type parameter E represents the type of the element in the list. Use of a generic type requires a *concrete* reference type to be substituted for the type parameter E. For example, the parameterized class ArrayList<String> is an ArrayList of String, where the type parameter T is substituted with the concrete class String.

The ArrayList<E> class is a dynamically resizable implementation of the List<E> interface using arrays (also known as *dynamic arrays*), providing fast random access (i.e., position-based access in constant time) and fast list traversal—very much like using an ordinary array. The ArrayList<E> class is not *thread-safe*; that is, its integrity can be jeopardized by concurrent access. The Java Collections Framework provides other implementations of the List<E> interface, but in most cases the ArrayList<E> implementation is the overall best choice for implementing lists.

12.2 Declaring References and Constructing ArrayLists

In the discussion that follows, we assume that any class or interface used from the java.util package has been imported with an appropriate import statement.

The code below illustrates how we can create an empty ArrayList of a specific element type, and assign its reference value to a reference:

```
ArrayList<String> palindromes = new ArrayList<String>(); // (1)
```

The element type is specified using angle brackets (<>). The reference palindromes can refer to any ArrayList whose element type is String. The type parameter E of the class ArrayList in Figure 12.1 is replaced by the concrete class String. The compiler ensures that the reference palindromes can only refer to an ArrayList whose elements are of type String, and any operations on this list via this reference are type-safe.

The simplest way to construct an ArrayList is to use the zero-argument constructor to create an empty ArrayList, as shown in the declaration above. The zero-argument constructor creates an empty list with the initial capacity of 10. The *capacity* of a list refers to how many elements it can contain at any given time, not how many elements are actually in the list (which is called the *size*). The capacity of a list and its size can change dynamically as the list is manipulated. The ArrayList<String> created at (1) can only contain elements of type String.

The assignment in the declaration statement (1) is valid because the types on both sides are assignment compatible—an ArrayList of String. The reference palindromes can now be used to manipulate the ArrayList<String> that it denotes.

We can use the *diamond operator* (<>) in the ArrayList creation expression on the right-hand side of the declaration statement. In this particular context, the compiler can infer the element type of the ArrayList from the declaration of the reference type on the left-hand side.

```
ArrayList<String> palindromes = new ArrayList<>(); // Using the diamond operator
```

However, if the diamond operator is omitted, the compiler will issue an *unchecked conversion warning*, as shown at (2) in the next code snippet. A new ArrayList is created based on an ArrayList of Integer that is passed as an argument to the constructor. The ArrayList of Integer is created at (1). The reference newList1 of type ArrayList<String> refers to an ArrayList whose element type is Integer, not String. The code at (2) compiles, but we get a ClassCastException at runtime at (3) when we retrieve an element from this list. The get() method call at (3) expects a String in the ArrayList, but gets an Integer. If the diamond operator is used, as shown at (4), the compiler reports a compile-time error, and the problem described at (3) cannot occur at runtime. By issuing an unchecked conversion warning at (2), the compiler alerts us to the fact that it cannot guarantee type-safety of the list created at (2).

```
ArrayList<Integer> intList = new ArrayList<>();        // (1) ArrayList of Integer
intList.add(10); intList.add(100); intList.add(1000);
```

```
ArrayList<String> newList1 = new ArrayList(intList);   // (2) Unchecked conversion
                                                       //     warning
System.out.println(newList1.get(0));                   // (3) ClassCastException!

ArrayList<String> newList2 = new ArrayList<>(intList); // (4) Compile-time error!
```

Best practices advocate *programming to an interface*. In practical terms, this means using references of an interface type to manipulate objects of a concrete class that implement this interface. Since the class java.util.ArrayList<E> implements the java.util.List<E> interface, the declaration at (1) can be written as shown in the next code snippet. This declaration is valid, since the reference value of a subtype object (ArrayList<String>) can be assigned to a reference of its supertype (List<String>).

```
List<String> palindromes = new ArrayList<>();   // (2) List<String> reference
```

This best practice provides great flexibility in substituting other objects for a task when necessary. The current concrete class can easily be replaced by another concrete class that implements the same interface. Only code creating objects needs to be changed. As it happens, the Java Collections Framework provides another implementation of lists: the java.util.LinkedList<E> class, which also implements the List<E> interface. If this class is found to be more conducive for maintaining palindromes in a list, we need simply change the name of the class in declaration (2), and continue using the reference palindromes in the program:

```
List<String> palindromes = new LinkedList<>(); // Changing implementation.
```

The ArrayList<E> class also provides a constructor that allows an empty ArrayList to be created with a specific initial capacity.

```
List<String> palindromes = new ArrayList<>(20); // Initial capacity is 20.
```

The ArrayList class provides the add(E) method to append an element to the end of the list. The new element is added after the last element in the list, thereby increasing the list size by 1.

```
palindromes.add("level"); palindromes.add("Ada"); palindromes.add("kayak");
System.out.println(palindromes);
```

The print statement calls the toString() method in the ArrayList<E> class to print the elements in the list. This toString() method applies the toString() method of the individual elements to create a text representation in the following default format:

```
[level, Ada, kayak]
```

A third constructor allows an ArrayList to be constructed from another collection. The following code creates a list of words from a list of palindromes. The order of the elements in the new ArrayList<String> is the same as that in the ArrayList<String> that was passed as an argument in the constructor.

```
List<String> wordList = new ArrayList<>(palindromes);
System.out.println(wordList); // [level, Ada, kayak]
wordList.add("Naan");
System.out.println(wordList); // [level, Ada, kayak, Naan]
```

The next examples illustrate the creation of empty lists of different types of elements. The compiler ensures that operations on the ArrayList are type-safe with respect to the element type. Declaration (3) shows how we can create nested list structures (i.e., a list of lists), analogous to an array of arrays. Note that the diamond operator is not nested at (3). Declaration (4) shows that the element type cannot be a primitive type; rather, it must be a reference type.

```
List<StringBuilder> synonyms    = new ArrayList<>(); // List of StringBuilder
List<Integer> attendance        = new ArrayList<>(); // List of Integer
List<List<String>> listOfLists  = new ArrayList<>(); // (3) List of List of String
List<int> frequencies           = new ArrayList<>(); // (4) Compile-time error!
```

When comparing arrays and ArrayLists, there is one other significant difference that concerns the subtype relationship.

```
Object[] objArray = new String[10];                      // (5) OK!
```

In declaration (5), since String is a subtype of Object, String[] is a subtype of Object[]. Thus we can manipulate the array of String using the objArray reference.

```
objArray[2] = "Green";                                   // (6) OK!
objArray[1] = Integer.valueOf(2016);                     // ArrayStoreException!
```

The preceding assignment requires a runtime check to guarantee that the assignment is type compatible. Otherwise, an ArrayStoreException is thrown at runtime.

For the ArrayList<E>, the following declarations will not compile:

```
ArrayList<Object> objList1 = new ArrayList<String>();// (7) Compile-time error!
List<Object> objList2 = new ArrayList<String>();     // (8) Compile-time error!
```

Although String is a subtype of Object, it is not the case that an ArrayList<String> is a subtype of ArrayList<Object>. If this were the case, we could use the objList1 reference to add other types of objects to the ArrayList of String, thereby jeopardizing its type-safety. Since there is no information about the element type E available at runtime to carry out a type compatibility check, as in the case of arrays, the subtype relationship is not allowed at (7). For the same reason, (8) will also not compile: ArrayList<String> is not a subtype of List<Object>. In general, the *subtype covariant relationship* does not hold for generic types. The Java language provides *wildcards* to overcome this restriction (§11.4, p. 579).

The ArrayList<E> constructors are summarized here:

```
ArrayList()
ArrayList(int initialCapacity)
ArrayList(Collection<? extends E> c)
```

The zero-argument constructor creates a new, empty ArrayList with an initial capacity of 10.

The second constructor creates a new, empty ArrayList with the specified initial capacity.

The third constructor creates a new ArrayList containing the elements in the specified collection. The declaration of the parameter c essentially means that parameter c can refer to any collection whose element type is E or a subtype of E. The new ArrayList<E> will retain any duplicates. The ordering in the ArrayList<E> will be determined by the traversal order of the iterator for the collection passed as an argument.

In a constructor call, the element type of the list is specified enclosed in angle brackets or by the diamond operator after the class name if it is to be inferred by the compiler. A raw ArrayList is created if the angle brackets are omitted, and the compiler will issue an unchecked warning.

Creating Unmodifiable Lists

Unmodifiable collections are useful to prevent a collection from accidently being modified, as doing so might cause the program to behave incorrectly. Such collections are also stored efficiently, as no bookkeeping is required to support any further modifications and data in the collection can be packed more densely since it can never change.

Here we look at how to create unmodifiable lists. Later we will discuss unmodifiable sets (§15.4, p. 804) and unmodifiable maps (§15.8, p. 832), and we will also contrast *unmodifiable collections* with *unmodifiable views of collections* (§15.11, p. 856).

The List<E> interface provides generic static methods to create *unmodifiable* lists that have the following characteristics:

- An unmodifiable list cannot be modified *structurally*; for example, elements cannot be added, removed, replaced, or sorted in such a list. Any such attempt will result in an UnsupportedOperationException to be thrown. However, if the elements themselves are mutable, the elements may appear modified.

- Although duplicates are allowed, unmodifiable lists do not allow null elements, and will result in a NullPointerException if an attempt is made to create them with the null elements.

- The order of the elements in an unmodifiable list is the same as the order of the arguments or the order of the elements in the array of the variable arity argument of the static method.

- An unmodifiable list can be serialized if its elements are serializable (§20.5, p. 1261).

```
static <E> List<E> of(E e1, E e2, E e3, E e4, E e5,
                      E e6, E e7, E e8, E e9, E e10)
```

The of() method is overloaded. The 11 overloaded methods are fixed-argument methods for accepting 0 to 10 arguments. They return an unmodifiable list containing the number of elements specified. They throw a NullPointerException, if an element is null. These overloaded methods are convenient for creating short lists.

```
@SafeVarargs static <E> List<E> of(E... elements)
```

This variable arity method returns an unmodifiable list containing an arbitrary number of elements specified by its variable arity argument. It throws a Null-PointerException, if an element is null or if the array of the variable arity parameter is null.

The @SafeVarargs annotation suppresses the heap pollution warning in the method declaration and also the unchecked generic array creation warning at the call sites (§25.5, p. 1585).

```
static <E> List<E> copyOf(Collection<? extends E> collection)
```

This generic method returns an unmodifiable list containing the elements of the specified collection, in its iteration order. The specified collection must not be null, and it must not contain any null elements—otherwise, a NullPointer-Exception is thrown. If the specified collection is subsequently modified, the returned list will not reflect such modifications.

The code below shows that a list created by the List.of() method cannot be modified. The list returned is also not an instance of ArrayList.

```
List<String> list = List.of("Tom", "Dick", "Harriet");
// list.add("Harry");                      // UnsupportedOperationException
// list.remove(2);                         // UnsupportedOperationException
// list.set(0, "Tommy");                   // UnsupportedOperationException
System.out.println(list);                  // [Tom, Dick, Harriet]
System.out.println(list instanceof ArrayList); // false
```

The List.of() method does not allow null elements:

```
List<String> coinList = List.of("nickel", "dime", null); // NullPointerException
```

For arguments up to 10, an appropriate fixed-arity List.of() method is called. For more than 10 arguments, the variable arity List.of(E...) method is called, passing an implicitly created array that contains the arguments.

```
List<Integer> intList1 = List.of(1, 2, 3, 4, 5, 6, 7, 8, 9, 10);   // Fixed-arity
List<Integer> intList2 = List.of(1, 2, 3, 4, 5, 6, 7, 8, 9, 10, 11); // Varargs
System.out.println(intList1);       // [1, 2, 3, 4, 5, 6, 7, 8, 9, 10]
System.out.println(intList2);       // [1, 2, 3, 4, 5, 6, 7, 8, 9, 10, 11]
```

At (1) below, an explicit array is passed as an argument, resulting in the variable arity List.of(E...) method being called, creating a list of String. At (2), the method call explicitly specifies the type of its argument as String[]. In this case the one-argument List.of(E) method is called, creating a list of length 1 and whose element type is String[].

```
String[] strArray = {"Tom", "Dick", "Harriet"};
List<String> strList = List.of(strArray);                  // (1) List of String
List<String[]> strArrayList = List.<String[]>of(strArray); // (2) List of String[]
System.out.println(strList);         // [Tom, Dick, Harriet]
System.out.println(strArrayList);    // [[Ljava.lang.String;@3b22cdd0]
```

The code below shows how we can make a copy of a collection, in this case, a list. The copyOf() method creates a copy of the list passed as an argument at (1). The list created is unmodifiable analogous to the lists created with the List.of() methods.

The code also shows that modifying the original list does *not* reflect in the copy of the list.

```
List<String> fab4 = new ArrayList<>();
fab4.add("John"); fab4.add("Paul"); fab4.add("George"); fab4.add("Ringo");
System.out.println(fab4);                 // [John, Paul, George, Ringo]
List<String> fabAlways = List.copyOf(fab4);   // (1)
fab4.remove("John"); fab4.remove("George");   // Modify original list
System.out.println(fab4);                 // [Paul, Ringo]
System.out.println(fabAlways);            // [John, Paul, George, Ringo]
```

12.3 Modifying an ArrayList<E>

The ArrayList<E> class provides methods to append, insert, replace, and remove elements from a list. In addition, it has methods to modify the capacity of a list.

Adding Elements

The various add methods allow elements to be *appended at the end of a list* and also *inserted at a specified index* in the list.

```
boolean add(E element)                          From List<E> interface.
void add(int index, E element)                  From List<E> interface.
```

The first method will append the specified element to the *end* of the list. It returns true if the collection was modified as a result of the operation.

The second method inserts the specified element at the specified index. If necessary, it shifts the element previously at this index and any subsequent elements one position toward the end of the list. The method will throw an IndexOutOfBoundsException if the index is out of range (index < 0 || index > size()).

The type parameter E represents the element type of the list.

```
boolean addAll(Collection<? extends E> c)       From List<E> interface.
boolean addAll(int index,                       From List<E> interface.
               Collection<? extends E> c)
```

The first method inserts the elements from the specified collection at the end of the list. The second method inserts the elements from the specified collection at the specified index; that is, the method splices the elements of the specified collection into the list at the specified index. These methods return true if any elements were added. Elements are inserted using an iterator of the specified collection (§15.2, p. 791). The second method will throw an IndexOutOf-BoundsException if the index is out of range (index < 0 || index > size()).

The declaration of the parameter c essentially means that parameter c can refer to any collection whose element type is E or whose element type is a subtype of E.

Replacing Elements

The following methods replace elements in a list with new elements.

`E set(int index, E element)`   From `List<E>` interface.

Replaces the element at the specified index with the specified element. It returns the previous element at the specified index. The method throws an `IndexOutOfBoundsException` if the index is out of range (`index < 0 || index >= size()`).

`default void replaceAll(UnaryOperator<E> operator)`   From `List<E>` interface.

Replaces each element of this list with the result of applying the unary operator (§13.10, p. 720) to that element. See also the `List<E>` interface (§15.3, p. 801).

Removing Elements

A summary of selected methods that can remove elements of a list is given here:

`void clear()`   From `List<E>` interface.

Deletes all elements from the list. The list is empty after the call, so it has size 0.

`E remove(int index)`   From `List<E>` interface.
`boolean remove(Object element)`   From `List<E>` interface.

The first method deletes and returns the element at the specified index. The method throws an `IndexOutOfBoundsException` if the index is out of range (`index < 0 || index >= size()`).

The second method removes the *first* occurrence of the element from the list, using object value equality. The method returns `true` if the call was successful. This method does not throw an exception if an element value is `null`, or if it is passed a `null` value.

Both methods will contract the list accordingly if any elements are removed.

`boolean removeAll(Collection<?> c)`   From `List<E>` interface.
`boolean removeIf(Predicate<? super E> filter)`   From `Collection<E>` interface.

The first method removes from this list all elements that are contained in the specified collection.

The second method removes from this list all elements that satisfy the filtering criteria defined by a lambda expression that implements the `Predicate<T>` functional interface (§13.6, p. 703). See also filtering a list (§15.2, p. 797).

Both methods return `true` if the call was successful. The list is contracted accordingly if any elements are removed.

Modifying Capacity

The following two methods can be used to modify the capacity of a list. There is no method that returns the current capacity of an ArrayList<E>.

```
void trimToSize()
```

Trims the capacity of this list to its current size.

```
void ensureCapacity(int minCapacity)                    From List<E> interface.
```

Ensures that the capacity of this list is large enough to hold at least the number of elements specified by the minimum capacity.

All the code snippets in this section can be found in Example 12.1, p. 663. The method printListWithIndex() at (16) in Example 12.1 prints the elements prefixed with their index in the list, making it easier to see how the list changes structurally:

```
[0:level, 1:Ada, 2:Java, 3:kayak, 4:Bob, 5:Rotator, 6:Bob]
```

We have seen that the add(E) method appends an element to the end of the list. The following code adds the strings from an array of String to an ArrayList of String. The output from Example 12.1 at (2) shows how the elements are added at the end of the list.

```java
System.out.println("\n(2) Add elements to list:");
for (String str : wordArray) {
  strList.add(str);
  printListWithIndex(strList);
}
```

We can insert a new element at a specific index using the overloaded method add(int, E). The output from the following code shows how inserting an element at index 2 shifted the elements structurally in the list.

```java
                                // [0:level, 1:Ada, 2:kayak, 3:Bob, 4:Rotator, 5:Bob]
strList.add(2, "Java");         // Insert an element at index 2 in the list.
printListWithIndex(strList);    // [0:level, 1:Ada, 2:Java, 3:kayak, 4:Bob,
                                // 5:Rotator, 6:Bob]
```

Note that an index value equal to 0 or the size of the list is always allowed for the method add(int, E).

```java
List<String> list1 = new ArrayList<>();    // []
list1.add(0, "First");                      // [First]
list1.add(list1.size(), "Last");            // [First, Last]
```

We can replace an element at a specified index using the set(int, E) method. The method returns the element that was replaced.

```java
System.out.println("(3) Replace the element at index 1:");
String oldElement = strList.set(1, "Naan");
System.out.println("Element that was replaced: " + oldElement);    // "Ada"
printListWithIndex(strList); // [0:level, 1:Naan, 2:Java, 3:kayak, 4:Bob,
                             // 5:Rotator, 6:Bob]
```

We can remove or empty a list of all its elements using the `clear()` method:

```
// list1 is [First, Last].
list1.clear();                                      // []
```

We can also remove elements from a list, with the list being contracted accordingly.

```
System.out.println("(4) Remove the element at index 0:");
System.out.println("Element removed: " + strList.remove(0));        // "level"
printListWithIndex(strList); // [0:Naan, 1:Java, 2:kayak, 3:Bob, 4:Rotator, 5:Bob]

System.out.println("(5) Remove the first occurrence of \"Java\":");
System.out.println("Element removed: " + strList.remove("Java")); // true
printListWithIndex(strList); // [0:Naan, 1:kayak, 2:Bob, 3:Rotator, 4:Bob]
```

The `remove(int)` removes the element at the specified index. The method `remove(Object)` needs to search the list and compare the argument object with elements in the list for object value equality. This test requires that the argument object override the `equals()` method from the `Object` class, which merely determines reference value equality. The `String` class provides the appropriate `equals()` method. However, the following code will not give the expected result because the `StringBuilder` class does not provide its own `equals()` method.

```
List<StringBuilder> sbList = new ArrayList<>();
for (String str : wordArray)
  strList.add(str);
System.out.println(sbList); // [level, Ada, kayak, Bob, Rotator, Bob]
StringBuilder element = new StringBuilder("Ada");
System.out.println("Element to be removed: " + element);           // "Ada"
System.out.println("Element removed: " + sbList.remove(element)); // false
System.out.println(sbList); // [level, Ada, kayak, Bob, Rotator, Bob]
```

Once it is known that an `ArrayList<E>` will not grow in size, it might be a good idea to trim its capacity down to its size by calling the `trimToSize()` method, thereby minimizing the storage used by the `ArrayList<E>`. To reduce the number of times the capacity is increased when adding a large number of elements to the list, appropriate capacity can be set via the `ensureCapacity()` method before the operation.

```
sbList.trimToSize();              // Capacity is now same as size-that is, 6.
sbList.ensureCapacity(10000);     // Capacity is now large enough for 10000 elements.
                                  // Size is still 6.
```

Primitive Values and `ArrayLists`

Since primitive values cannot be stored in an `ArrayList<E>`, we can use the wrapper classes to box such values first. In the following code, we create a list of `Integer` in which the `int` values are autoboxed in `Integer` objects and then added to the list. We try to delete the element with value 1, but end up deleting the element at index 1 instead (i.e, the value 20).

```
List<Integer> intList = new ArrayList<>();
intList.add(10); intList.add(20); intList.add(1);
System.out.println(intList);                        // [10, 20, 1]
System.out.println("Element to be removed: " + 1);  // 1
```

```
System.out.println("Element removed: " + intList.remove(1));   // 20
System.out.println(intList);                                    // [10, 1]
```

The method call

```
intList.remove(1)
```

has the signature

```
intList.remove(int)
```

This signature matches the overloaded method that removes the element at a specified index, so it is this method that is called at runtime. We say that this method is the *most specific* in this case. For the code to work as intended, the primitive value must be explicitly boxed.

```
System.out.println(intList);                          // [10, 20, 1]
System.out.println("Element to be removed: " + 1);                    // 1
System.out.println("Element removed: " +
                intList.remove(Integer.valueOf(1)));  // true
System.out.println(intList);                          // [10, 20]
```

The method call

```
intList.remove(Integer.valueOf(1))
```

has the signature

```
intList.remove(Integer)
```

This call matches the overloaded remove(Object) method, since an Integer object can be passed to an Object parameter. This method is the most specific in this case, and is executed.

12.4 Querying an ArrayList<E>

A summary of useful methods that can be used to query a list is provided below.

int size()   From List<E> interface.

Returns the number of elements currently in the list. In a non-empty list, the first element is at index 0 and the last element is at index size()-1.

boolean isEmpty()   From List<E> interface.

Determines whether the list is empty (i.e., whether its size is 0).

E get(int index)   From List<E> interface.

Returns the element at the specified *positional index*. The method throws an IndexOutOfBoundsException if the index is out of range (index < 0 || index >= size()).

boolean contains(Object element)   From List<E> interface.

Determines whether the argument object is contained in the collection, using object value equality. This is called the *membership test*.

```
int indexOf(Object o)                              From List<E> interface.
int lastIndexOf(Object o)                          From List<E> interface.
```

Return the indices of the first and last occurrences of the element that are equal (using object value equality) to the specified argument, respectively, if such an element exists in the list; otherwise, the value -1 is returned. These methods provide *element search* in the list.

```
List<E> subList(int fromIndex, int toIndex)        From List<E> interface.
```

Returns a *view* of the list, which consists of the sublist of the elements from the index fromIndex to the index toIndex-1 (i.e., a half-open interval). A view allows the range it represents in the underlying list to be manipulated. Any changes in the view are reflected in the underlying list, and vice versa. Views can be used to perform operations on specific ranges of a list.

```
boolean equals(Object o)                           From List<E> interface.
```

Compares the specified object with this list for object value equality. It returns true if and only if the specified object is also a list, both lists have the same size, and all corresponding pairs of elements in the two lists are equal according to object value equality.

The method size() returns the number of elements in the list, and the method empty() determines whether the list is empty.

```
// [Naan, kayak, Bob, Rotator, Bob]
System.out.println("The size of the list is " + strList.size());        // 5
boolean result = strList.isEmpty();
System.out.println("The list " + (result ? "is" : "is not") + " empty."); // false
```

The method get(int) retrieves the element at the specified index.

```
// [Naan, kayak, Bob, Rotator, Bob]
System.out.println("First element: " + strList.get(0);                  // Naan
System.out.println("Last element: " + strList.get(strList.size()-1));   // Bob
```

The equals() method of the ArrayList class can be used to compare two lists for equality with regard to size and corresponding elements being equal in each list.

```
List<String> strList2 = new ArrayList<>(strList);
boolean trueOrFalse = strList.equals(strList2);                         // true
```

The method subList() returns a *view* of a list—that is, a sublist of the list. As the view is backed by the underlying list, operations on the sublist will be reflected in the underlying list, as demonstrated by the following code:

```
out.println("Underlying list: " + strList); // [Naan, kayak, Bob, Rotator, Bob]
List<String> strList3 = strList.subList(1, 4);
out.println("Sublist before remove: " + strList3);     // [kayak, Bob, Rotator]
out.println("Remove: " + strList3.get(0));  // "kayak"
strList3.remove(0);                                    // Remove element at index 0
out.println("Sublist after remove: " + strList3);      // [Bob, Rotator]
out.println("Underlying list: " + strList); // [Naan, Bob, Rotator, Bob]
```

The membership test is carried out by the contains(Object) method. We can find the index of a specified element in the list by using the indexOf() and lastIndexOf() methods.

```
boolean found = strList.contains("Naan");      // true
int index = strList.indexOf("Bob");            // 2
index = strList.indexOf("BOB");                // -1 (Not found)
index = strList.lastIndexOf("Bob");            // 4 (Last occurrence)
```

Again, these methods require that the element type provide a meaningful equals() method for object value equality testing.

12.5 Iterating Over an ArrayList<E>

Various methods for iterating over collections are discussed in §15.2, p. 791. Here we look at a very common task of iterating over a list to perform some operation on each element of the list.

We can use positional access to iterate over a list with the for(;;) loop. The generic method printListWithIndex() in Example 12.1 uses the for(;;) loop to create a new ArrayList of String that contains each element of the argument list prefixed with the index of the element.

```
public static <E> void printListWithIndex(List<E> list) {
  List<String> newList = new ArrayList<>();
  for (int i = 0; i < list.size(); i++) {
    newList.add(i + ":" + list.get(i));
  }
  System.out.println(newList);
}
```

Sample output from the method call printListWithIndex(strList) is shown here:

```
[0:level, 1:Ada, 2:kayak, 3:Bob, 4:Rotator, 5:Bob]
```

The method printListWithIndex() in Example 12.1 can print *any* list in this format. Its header declaration says that it accepts a list of element type E. The element type E is determined from the method call. In the preceding example, E is determined to be String, as a List of String is passed in the method call.

Since the ArrayList<E> class implements the Iterable<E> interface (i.e., the class provides an iterator), we can use the for(:) loop to iterate over a list.

```
for (String str : strList) {
  System.out.print(str + " ");
}
```

The ArrayList<E> also provides specialized iterators to iterate over a list (§15.3, p. 801).

For performing a given action on each element of a list, the forEach() method can be used (§15.2, p. 796), where the action is specified by a consumer (§13.7, p. 709).

One pertinent question to ask is how to remove elements from the list when iterating over the list. The for(:) loop does not allow the list structure to be modified:

```
for (String str : strList) {
  if (str.length() <= 3) {
    strList.remove(str);                    // Throws ConcurrentModificationException
  }
}
```

We can use positional access in a loop to iterate over the list, but we must be careful in updating the loop variable, as the list contracts when an element is removed. Better solutions for this purpose are discussed in §15.2, p. 796.

12.6 Converting an ArrayList<E> to an Array

The following methods are specified by the Collection<E> interface and can be used to convert a collection to an array. List and set implementations in the java.util package provide customized versions of the first two methods for this purpose. In this section we consider how to convert lists to arrays.

Object[] toArray()   From Collection<E> interface.
<T> T[] toArray(T[] a)   From Collection<E> interface.

The first method returns an array of type Object filled with all the elements of a collection. The returned array can be modified independently of the list from which it was created.

The second method is a generic method that stores the elements of a collection in an array of type T. If the specified array is big enough, the elements are stored in this array. If there is room to spare in the array—that is, if the length of the array is greater than the number of elements in the collection—the element found immediately after storing the elements of the collection is set to the null value before the array is returned. If the array is too small, a new array of type T and appropriate size is created. If T is not a supertype of the runtime type of every element in the collection, an ArrayStoreException is thrown.

default <T> T[]
        toArray(IntFunction<T[]> generator)   From Collection<E> interface.

Allows creation of an array of a particular runtime type given by the parameterization of the type parameter T[], using the specified generator function (§13.8, p. 717) to allocate the array of the desired type and the specified length.

The default implementation calls the generator function with 0 and then passes the resulting array of length 0 to the toArray(T[]) generic method.

See also array operations in the Collection<E> interface (§15.2, p. 798).

The actual element type of the elements in the Object array returned by the first toArray() method can be any subtype of Object. It may be necessary to cast the Object reference of an element to the appropriate type, as in the following code:

```
System.out.println("(15) Convert list to array:");
Object[] objArray = strList.toArray();                        // Object[]
System.out.println("Object[] length: " + objArray.length); // 5
System.out.print("Length of each string in the Object array: ");
for (Object obj : objArray) {
  String str = (String) obj;                                  // Cast required.
  System.out.print(str.length() + " ");
}
System.out.println();
```

The generic `toArray()` method returns an array of type T, when it is passed an array of type T as an argument. In the following code, the array of `String` that is returned has the same length as the size of the list of `String`, even though a `String` array of length 0 was passed as an argument:

```
String[] strArray = strList.toArray(new String[0]);          // String[]
System.out.println("String[] length: " + strArray.length);  // 5
System.out.print("Length of each string in the String array: ");
for (String str : strArray) {
  System.out.print(str.length() + " ");
}
System.out.println();
```

12.7 Creating List Views

The `asList()` method in the `Arrays` class and the `toArray()` methods in the `Collection<E>` interface provide the bidirectional bridge between arrays and collections. The `asList()` method of the `Arrays` class creates `List<E>` views of arrays.

> @SafeVarargs <E> List<E> asList(E... elements)   From Arrays class.
>
> Returns a *fixed-size list view* that is backed by the *array* corresponding to the variable arity parameter `elements`. The method is annotated with @SafeVarargs because of the variable arity parameter. The annotation suppresses the heap pollution warning in its declaration and also unchecked generic array creation warning at the call sites (§25.5, p. 1585).

Changes to the elements of the list view are reflected in the array, and vice versa. The list view is said to be *backed* by the array. The size of the list view is equal to the array length and *cannot* be changed. The iterator for a list view does not support the `remove()` method.

The code below illustrates use of the `asList()` method. The `list1` at (1) is backed by the `array1`. The `list2` is backed by an implicit array of `Integer` at (2). An array of a primitive type cannot be passed as an argument to this method, as evident by the compile-time error at (3). However, the `Collections.addAll()` method provides better performance when adding a few elements to an *existing* collection.

```
Integer[] array1 = new Integer[] {9, 1, 1};
List<Integer> list1 = Arrays.asList(array1);                  // (1) A list of Integer
```

```
List<Integer> list2 = Arrays.asList(9, 1, 1);          // (2) Varargs

int[] array2 = new int[] {9, 1, 1};                    // An array of int
// List<Integer> intList3 = Arrays.asList(array2);     // (3) Compile-time error!
```

Various operations on the list1 show how changes are reflected in the backing array1. Elements cannot be added to the list view (shown at (4)), and elements cannot be removed from the list view (shown at (9)). An UnsupportedOperationException is thrown in both cases. An element at a given position can be changed, as shown at (5). The change is reflected in the list1 and the array1, as shown at (6) and (7), respectively. A sublist view is created from the list1 at (8), and sorted at (10). The changes in the sublist1 are reflected in the list1 and the backing array1.

```
System.out.println(list1);                        // [9, 1, 1]
// list1.add(10);                                 // (4) UnsupportedOperationException
list1.set(0, 10);                                 // (5)
System.out.println(list1);                        // (6) [10, 1, 1]
System.out.println(Arrays.toString(array1));      // (7) [10, 1, 1]

List<Integer> sublist1 = list1.subList(0, 2);     // (8)
System.out.println(sublist1);                     // [10, 1]
// sublist1.clear();                              // (9) UnsupportedOperationException
Collections.sort(sublist1);                       // (10)
System.out.println(sublist1);                     // [1, 10]
System.out.println(list1);                        // [1, 10, 1]
System.out.println(Arrays.toString(array1));      // [1, 10, 1]
```

The code below shows how duplicates can be eliminated from an array:

```
String[] jiveArray     = new String[] {"java", "jive", "java", "jive"};
Set<String> jiveSet    = new HashSet<>(Arrays.asList(jiveArray));// (1)
String[] uniqueJiveArray = jiveSet.toArray(new String[0]);    // (2)
System.out.println(Arrays.toString(uniqueJiveArray));         // (3) [java, jive]
```

At (1), the jiveArray is used to create a List, which in turn is used to create a Set. At (2), the argument to the toArray() method specifies the type of the array to be created from the set. The final array uniqueJiveArray does not contain duplicates, as can be seen at (3).

Comparing Unmodifiable Lists and List Views

There are subtle differences to be aware of between unmodifiable lists and list views.

• *Backing an array*

The Arrays.asList() method returns a *fixed-size list view* that is backed by the array passed as an argument so that any changes made to the array are reflected in the view list as well. This is not true of the List.of() and List.ofCopy() methods, as they create *unmodifiable lists* which are *not backed* by any argument array that is passed either explicitly or implicitly as a variable arity parameter.

In the code below, we see that the list view returned by the `Arrays.asList()` method reflects the change at (1) in its backing array, but not the unmodifiable list returned by the `List.of()` method at (2) when its argument array is modified.

```
Integer[] yrArray1 = {2020, 2021, 2022};
List<Integer> yrlist1 = Arrays.asList(yrArray1);
yrArray1[0] = 2019;                                      // Modify the array
out.println("yrArray1: " + Arrays.toString(yrArray1)); //    [2019, 2021, 2022]
out.println("yrlist1: " + yrlist1);                    // (1) [2019, 2021, 2022]

Integer[] yrArray2 = {2020, 2021, 2022};
List<Integer> yrlist2 = List.of(yrArray2);
yrArray2[0] = 2019;                                      // Modify the array
out.println("yrArray2: " + Arrays.toString(yrArray2)); //    [2019, 2021, 2022]
out.println("yrlist2: " + yrlist2);                    // (2) [2020, 2021, 2022]
```

- *Mutability*

The list view returned by the `Arrays.asList()` method is *mutable*, but it cannot be structurally modified. In contrast, the unmodifiable list returned by the `List.of()` method is *immutable*.

In the code below, only the list view returned by the `Arrays.asList()` method can be modified as shown at (1), but an attempt to modify the unmodifiable list returned by the `List.of()` method at (2) throws an exception.

```
List<Integer> yrList3 = Arrays.asList(2020, 2021, 2022);
yrList3.set(2, 2023);                  // (1) OK
out.println(yrList3);                  // [2020, 2021, 2023]

List<Integer> yrlist4 = List.of(2020, 2021, 2022);
yrlist4.set(2, 2023);                          // (2) UnsupportedOperationException
```

However, both lists will throw an exception if an attempt is made to change them *structurally*—that is, add or remove elements from the list:

```
yrList3.add(2050);                     // UnsupportedOperationException
yrlist4.remove(0);                     // UnsupportedOperationException
```

- *The* `null` *value*

The `Arrays.asList()` method allows `null` elements, whereas the `List.of()` and `List.ofCopy()` methods do not.

```
List<Integer> yrList5 = Arrays.asList(2020, 2021, null); // OK.
List<Integer> yrlist6 = List.of(2020, 2021, null);       // NullPointerException
```

The behavior of the `List.contains()` method when passed the `null` value is dependent on which method created the list.

```
boolean flag1 = Arrays.asList(2021, 2022).contains(null); // OK.
boolean flag2 = List.of(2021, 2022).contains(null);       // NullPointerException
```

12.8 Arrays versus ArrayLists

Table 12.1 summarizes the differences between arrays and ArrayLists.

Table 12.1   *Summary of Arrays versus* ArrayLists

	Arrays	ArrayLists
Construct support	Built into the language.	Provided by the generic class ArrayList<E>.
Initial length/ size specification	Length is specified in the array construction expression directly or indirectly by the initialization block.	Cannot specify the size at construction time. However, initial capacity can be specified.
Length/size	The length of an array is static (fixed) once it is created. Each array has a public final int field called length. (The String and the StringBuilder class provide the method length() for this purpose.)	Both size and capacity can change dynamically. ArrayList<E> provides the method size() to obtain the current size of the list.
Element type	Primitive and reference types.	Only reference types.
Operations on elements	An element in the array is designated by the array name and an index using the [] operator, and can be used as a simple variable.	The ArrayList<E> class provides various methods to add, insert, replace, retrieve, and remove elements from a list.
Iterator	Arrays do not provide an iterator, apart from using the for(:) loop for traversal.	The ArrayList<E> class provides customized iterators for lists, in addition to the for(:) loop for iterating over the elements (§15.2, p. 791).
Generics	Cannot create arrays of generic types using the new operator. Runtime check required for storage at runtime.	ArrayList<E> is a generic type. Can create parameterized ArrayLists of reference types using the new operator. No runtime check required for storage at runtime, as type-safety is checked at compile time.

Table 12.1 *Summary of Arrays versus* ArrayLists *(Continued)*

	Arrays	ArrayLists
Subtype relationship	Subtype relationship between two reference types implies subtype relationship between arrays of the two types—that is, element subtype relationship implies array subtype relationship.	Subtype relationship between two reference types does not imply covariance relationship between ArrayLists of the two types—that is, element subtype relationship does not imply list subtype relationship.
Sorting	`java.util.Arrays.sort(array)` `java.util.Arrays.sort(array, comparator)` (§15.12, p. 864)	`java.util.Collections.sort(list)` `java.util.Collections.sort(list, comparator)` `java.util.List.sort(comparator)` (§15.11, p. 856)
Text representation	`java.util.Arrays.toString(array)`	`list.toString()`

Example 12.1 is a collection of code snippets used throughout this chapter to illustrate the various methods of the ArrayList<E> class.

Example 12.1 *Using an* ArrayList

```java
import java.util.ArrayList;
import java.util.List;

import static java.lang.System.out;

public class ArrayListMethods {

  public static void main(String[] args) {

    String[] wordArray = { "level", "Ada", "kayak", "Bob", "Rotator", "Bob" };

    out.println("(1) Create an empty list of strings:");
    List<String> strList = new ArrayList<>();
    printListWithIndex(strList);

    out.println("\n(2) Add elements to list:");
    for (String str : wordArray) {
      strList.add(str);
      printListWithIndex(strList);
    }
    out.println("Insert an element at index 2 in the list:");
    strList.add(2, "Java");
    printListWithIndex(strList);

    out.println("\n(3) Replace the element at index 1:");
    String oldElement = strList.set(1, "Naan");
    out.println("Element that was replaced: " + oldElement);
    printListWithIndex(strList);
```

```java
out.println("\n(4) Remove the element at index 0:");
out.println("Element removed: " + strList.remove(0));
printListWithIndex(strList);

out.println("\n(5) Remove the first occurrence of \"Java\":");
out.println("Element removed: " + strList.remove("Java"));
printListWithIndex(strList);

out.println("\n(6) Determine the size of the list:");
out.println("The size of the list is " + strList.size());

out.println("\n(7) Determine if the list is empty:");
boolean result = strList.isEmpty();
out.println("The list " + (result ? "is" : "is not") + " empty.");

out.println("\n(8) Get the element at specific index:");
out.println("First element: " + strList.get(0));
out.println("Last element: " + strList.get(strList.size() - 1));

out.println("\n(9) Compare two lists:");
List<String> strList2 = new ArrayList<>(strList);
boolean trueOrFalse = strList.equals(strList2);
out.println("The lists strList and strList2 are"
    + (trueOrFalse ? "" : " not") + " equal.");
strList2.add(null);
printListWithIndex(strList2);
trueOrFalse = strList.equals(strList2);
out.println("The lists strList and strList2 are"
    + (trueOrFalse ? "" : " not") + " equal.");

out.println("\n(10) Sublists as views:");
out.println("Underlying list: " + strList); // [Naan, kayak, Bob, Rotator, Bob]
List<String> strList3 = strList.subList(1, 4);
out.println("Sublist before remove: " + strList3);    // [kayak, Bob, Rotator]
out.println("Remove: " + strList3.get(0));  // "kayak"
strList3.remove(0);                           // Remove element at index 0
out.println("Sublist after remove: " + strList3);     // [Bob, Rotator]
out.println("Underlying list: " + strList); // [Naan, Bob, Rotator, Bob]

out.println("\n(11) Membership test:");
boolean found = strList.contains("Naan");
String msg = found ? "contains" : "does not contain";
out.println("The list " + msg + " the string \"Naan\".");

out.println("\n(12) Find the index of an element:");
int pos = strList.indexOf("Bob");
out.println("The index of string \"Bob\" is: " + pos);
pos = strList.indexOf("BOB");
out.println("The index of string \"BOB\" is: " + pos);
pos = strList.lastIndexOf("Bob");
out.println("The last index of string \"Bob\" is: " + pos);
printListWithIndex(strList);

out.println("\n(13) Iterating over the list using the for(;;) loop:");
for (int i = 0; i < strList.size(); i++) {
  out.print(i + ":" + strList.get(i) + " ");
```

```
      }
      out.println();

      out.println("\n(14) Iterating over the list using the for(:) loop:");
      for (String str : strList) {
        out.print(str +   " ");
        // strList.remove(str);          // Throws ConcurrentModificationException.
      }
      out.println();

      out.println("\n(15) Convert list to array:");
      Object[] objArray = strList.toArray();
      out.println("Object[] length: " + objArray.length);
      out.print("Length of each string in the Object array: ");
      for (Object obj : objArray) {
        String str = (String) obj; // Cast required.
        out.print(str.length() + " ");
      }
      out.println();
      String[] strArray = strList.toArray(new String[0]);
      out.println("String[] length: " + strArray.length);
      out.print("Length of each string in the String array: ");
      for (String str : strArray) {
        out.print(str.length() + " ");
      }
    }

    /**
     * Print the elements of a list, together with their index:
     * [0:value0, 1:value1, ...]
     * @param list    List to print with index
     */
    public static <E> void printListWithIndex(List<E> list) {              // (16)
      List<String> newList = new ArrayList<>();
      for (int i = 0; i < list.size(); i++) {
        newList.add(i + ":" + list.get(i));
      }
      out.println(newList);
    }
  }
```

Output from the program:

```
(1) Create an empty list of strings:
[]

(2) Add elements to list:
[0:level]
[0:level, 1:Ada]
[0:level, 1:Ada, 2:kayak]
[0:level, 1:Ada, 2:kayak, 3:Bob]
[0:level, 1:Ada, 2:kayak, 3:Bob, 4:Rotator]
[0:level, 1:Ada, 2:kayak, 3:Bob, 4:Rotator, 5:Bob]
Insert an element at index 2 in the list:
[0:level, 1:Ada, 2:Java, 3:kayak, 4:Bob, 5:Rotator, 6:Bob]
```

(3) Replace the element at index 1:
Element that was replaced: Ada
[0:level, 1:Naan, 2:Java, 3:kayak, 4:Bob, 5:Rotator, 6:Bob]

(4) Remove the element at index 0:
Element removed: level
[0:Naan, 1:Java, 2:kayak, 3:Bob, 4:Rotator, 5:Bob]

(5) Remove the first occurrence of "Java":
Element removed: true
[0:Naan, 1:kayak, 2:Bob, 3:Rotator, 4:Bob]

(6) Determine the size of the list:
The size of the list is 5

(7) Determine if the list is empty:
The list is not empty.

(8) Get the element at specific index:
First element: Naan
Last element: Bob

(9) Compare two lists:
The lists strList and strList2 are equal.
[0:Naan, 1:kayak, 2:Bob, 3:Rotator, 4:Bob, 5:null]
The lists strList and strList2 are not equal.

(10) Sublists as views:
Underlying list: [Naan, kayak, Bob, Rotator, Bob]
Sublist before remove: [kayak, Bob, Rotator]
Remove: kayak
Sublist after remove: [Bob, Rotator]
Underlying list: [Naan, Bob, Rotator, Bob]

(11) Membership test:
The list contains the string "Naan".

(12) Find the index of an element:
The index of string "Bob" is: 1
The index of string "BOB" is: -1
The last index of string "Bob" is: 3
[0:Naan, 1:Bob, 2:Rotator, 3:Bob]

(13) Iterating over the list using the for(;;) loop:
0:Naan 1:Bob 2:Rotator 3:Bob

(14) Iterating over the list using the for(:) loop:
Naan Bob Rotator Bob

(15) Convert list to array:
Object[] length: 4
Length of each string in the Object array: 4 3 7 3
String[] length: 4
Length of each string in the String array: 4 3 7 3

Review Questions

12.1 Which statement is true about the following program?

```java
import java.util.ArrayList;
import java.util.List;

public class RQ12A10 {
  public static void main(String[] args) {
    List<String> strList = new ArrayList<>();
    strList.add("Anna"); strList.add("Ada"); strList.add("Ada");
    strList.add("Bob"); strList.add("Bob"); strList.add("Adda");
    for (int i = 0; i < strList.size(); /* empty */) {
      if (strList.get(i).length() <= 3) {
        strList.remove(i);
      } else {
        ++i;
      }
    }
    System.out.println(strList);
  }
}
```

Select the one correct answer.

(a) The program will fail to compile.

(b) The program will throw an IndexOutOfBoundsException at runtime.

(c) The program will throw a ConcurrentModificationException at runtime.

(d) The program will not terminate when run.

(e) The program will print [Anna, Adda].

(f) The program will print [Anna, Ada, Bob, Adda].

12.2 Which of the following statements are true about the following program?

```java
import java.util.ArrayList;
import java.util.List;

public class RQ12A15 {
  public static void main(String[] args) {
    doIt1(); doIt2();
  }

  public static void doIt1() {
    List<StringBuilder> sbListOne = new ArrayList<>();
    sbListOne.add(new StringBuilder("Anna"));
    sbListOne.add(new StringBuilder("Ada"));
    sbListOne.add(new StringBuilder("Bob"));
    List<StringBuilder> sbListTwo = new ArrayList<>(sbListOne);
    sbListOne.add(null);
    sbListTwo.get(1).reverse();
    System.out.println(sbListOne);                              // (1)
  }

  public static void doIt2() {
    List<String> listOne = new ArrayList<>();
```

```
    listOne.add("Anna"); listOne.add("Ada"); listOne.add("Bob");
    List<String> listTwo = new ArrayList<>(listOne);
    String strTemp = listOne.get(0);
    listOne.set(0, listOne.get(listOne.size()-1));
    listOne.set(listOne.size()-1, strTemp);
    System.out.println(listTwo);                                    // (2)
  }
}
```

Select the two correct answers.

(a) (1) will print [Anna, Ada, Bob, null].
(b) (1) will print [Anna, adA, Bob, null].
(c) (2) will print [Anna, Ada, Bob].
(d) (2) will print [Bob, Ada, Anna].
(e) The program will throw an IndexOutOfBoundsException at runtime.

12.3 Which statement is true about the following program?

```
import java.util.ArrayList;
import java.util.List;

public class RQ12A20 {
  public static void main(String[] args) {
    List<String> strList = new ArrayList<>();
    strList.add("Anna"); strList.add("Ada"); strList.add(null);
    strList.add("Bob"); strList.add("Bob"); strList.add("Adda");
    for (int i = 0; i < strList.size(); ++i) {
      if (strList.get(i).equals("Bob")) {
        System.out.print(i);
      }
    }
    System.out.println();
  }
}
```

Select the one correct answer.

(a) The program will fail to compile.
(b) The program will throw an IndexOutOfBoundsException at runtime.
(c) The program will throw a NullPointerException at runtime.
(d) The program will print 34.

12.4 Which statement is true about the following program?

```
import java.util.ArrayList;
import java.util.List;

public class RQ12A30 {
  public static void main(String[] args) {
    List<String> strList = new ArrayList<>();
    strList.add("Anna"); strList.add("Ada");
    strList.add("Bob"); strList.add("Bob");
    for (int i = 0; i < strList.size(); ++i) {
      if (strList.get(i).equals("Bob")) {
        strList.remove(i);
      }
    }
  }
}
```

```
      System.out.println(strList);
  }
}
```

Select the one correct answer.

(a) The program will fail to compile.
(b) The program will throw an IndexOutOfBoundsException at runtime.
(c) The program will throw a NullPointerException at runtime.
(d) The program will throw a ConcurrentModificationException at runtime.
(e) The program will not terminate when run.
(f) The program will print [Anna, Ada, Bob].
(g) The program will print [Anna, Ada].

12.5 Which statement is true about the following program?

```
import java.util.ArrayList;
import java.util.List;

public class RQ12A40 {
  public static void main(String[] args) {
    List<String> strList = new ArrayList<>();
    strList.add("Anna"); strList.add("Ada"); strList.add(null);
    strList.add("Bob"); strList.add("Bob"); strList.add("Adda");
    while (strList.remove("Bob"));
    System.out.println(strList);
  }
}
```

Select the one correct answer.

(a) The program will fail to compile.
(b) The program will throw a NullPointerException at runtime.
(c) The program will not terminate when run.
(d) The program will print [Anna, Ada, Adda].
(e) The program will print [Anna, Ada, Bob, Adda].
(f) The program will print [Anna, Ada, null, Adda].
(g) The program will print [Anna, Ada, null, Bob, Adda].

12.6 What will be the result of running the following program?

```
import java.util.*;
public class Test12_01 {
  public static void main(String[] args) {
    String[] data1 = {"A","B","B","A"};
    List<String> data2 = new ArrayList<>();
    for (String s : data1) {
      data2.add(s);
    }
    data2.set(1, "X");
    data2.add(1, "X");
    data2.remove(2);
    System.out.println(data2);
  }
}
```

Select the one correct answer.

(a) [X, B, B, A]

(b) [A, X, B, A]

(c) [A, X, A]

(d) [A, X, X]

(e) The program will throw an exception at runtime.

(f) The program will fail to compile.

12.7   What will be the result of running the following program?

```java
import java.util.*;
public class Test12_02 {
  public static void main(String[] args) {
    String[] data1 = {"A","B","B","A"};
    List<String> data2 = Arrays.asList(data1);
    data2.set(1, "X");
    data2.set(2, "X");
    System.out.println(data2);
  }
}
```

Select the one correct answer.

(a) [A, X, X, A]

(b) [X, X, B, A]

(c) [A, X, X, B, B, A]

(d) [X, X, A, B, B, A]

(e) The program will throw an exception at runtime.

(f) The program will fail to compile.

12.8   What will be the result of running the following program?

```java
public class Song {
  private String name;
  public Song(String name) {
    this.name = name;
  }
  public void update() {
    name = name.toUpperCase();
  }
  public String toString() {
    return name;
  }
}
```

```java
import java.util.*;
public class Test12_04 {
  public static void main(String[] args) {
    Song[] playArray1 = {new Song("a"), new Song("b")};
    List<Song> playlist = Arrays.asList(playArray1);
    Song[] playArray2 = playlist.toArray(new Song[]{});
    playArray1[1].update();
    System.out.print(playArray1[1]);
```

```
        System.out.print(playlist.get(1));
        System.out.print(playArray2[1]);
    }
}
```

Select the one correct answer.

(a) Bbb
(b) BBb
(c) BBB
(d) bbb
(e) The program will throw an exception at runtime.
(f) The program will fail to compile.

12.9 What will be the result of running the following program?

```
public class MySong {
    private String name;
    public MySong(String name) {
        this.name = name;
    }
    public String toString() {
        return name;
    }
}
```

```
import java.util.*;
public class Test12_05 {
    public static void main(String[] args) {
        MySong[] playArray1 = {new MySong("A"), new MySong("B")};
        List<MySong> playlist = List.of(playArray1);
        MySong[] playlist2 = playlist.toArray(new MySong[]{});
        playArray1[0] = new MySong("C");
        System.out.print(playArray1[0]);
        System.out.print(playlist.get(0));
        System.out.print(playlist2[0]);
    }
}
```

Select the one correct answer.

(a) CCA
(b) CAA
(c) CCC
(d) AAA
(e) The program will throw an exception at runtime.
(f) The program will fail to compile.

12.10 What will be the result of running the following program?

```
import java.util.*;
public class Test12_06 {
    public static void main(String[] args) {
        List<String> data1 = List.of("A","B","C");
```

```
        String[] data2 = data1.toArray(new String[]{"X","Y","Z"});
        data2[1] = data1.get(0).toLowerCase();
        for (String s: data2) {
          System.out.print(s);
        }
      }
    }
  }
```

Select the one correct answer.

(a) AaC

(b) AbC

(c) XaZ

(d) XbZ

(e) The program will throw an exception at runtime.

(f) The program will fail to compile.

12.11   What will be the result of running the following program?

```
    import java.util.*;
    public class Test12_07 {
      public static void main(String[] args) {
        List<Character> text = new ArrayList<>(3);
        for (char a = 'a'; a <= 'e'; a++) {
          text.add(a);
        }
        System.out.println(text);
      }
    }
```

Select the one correct answer.

(a) [a, b, c]

(b) [a, b, c, d, e]

(c) [a, b, c, d]

(d) The program will throw an exception at runtime.

(e) The program will fail to compile.

Functional-Style Programming

13

 Chapter Topics

- Declaring functional interfaces
- Defining lambda expressions
- Implementing functional interfaces using lambda expressions
- Defining and type checking lambda expressions in the context of a functional interface
- Understanding deferred execution of a lambda expression
- Understanding the implications of using class members from the enclosing class, and of using local variables from the enclosing method in a lambda expression
- Comparing lambda expressions and anonymous classes
- Understanding behavior parameterization in functional-style programing
- Using built-in functional interfaces in the `java.util.function` package: suppliers, predicates, consumers, and functions
- Composing compound operators with built-in functional interfaces
- Using specializations of built-in functional interfaces
- Using primitive type specializations of built-in functional interfaces
- Using method and constructor references
- Understanding the contexts in which lambda expressions can be defined

Java SE 17 Developer Exam Objectives	
[6.1] Use Java object and primitive Streams, including lambda expressions implementing functional interfaces, to supply, filter, map, consume, and sort data	*§13.1, p. 675 to §13.14, p. 733*
o *Lambda expressions to implement functional interfaces are covered in this chapter.*	
o *For streams, see Chapter 16, p. 879.*	
Java SE 11 Developer Exam Objectives	
[6.1] Implement functional interfaces using lambda expressions, including interfaces from the java.util.function package	*§13.1, p. 675 to §13.14, p. 733*

In many ways, Java 8 represented a watershed in the history of the language. Before Java 8, the language supported only object-oriented programming. Packing state and behavior into objects that communicate in a procedural manner was the order of the day. Java 8 brought *functional-style programming* into the language, where code representing *functionality* could be passed as values to tailor the *behavior* of methods.

We first look at the two language features that are the basis for functional-style programming in Java—functional interfaces and lambda expressions—before diving into a comparison of lambda expressions and anonymous classes, method and constructor references, and coverage of the built-in general-purpose generic functional interfaces provided by the java.util.function package. Subsequent chapters provide ample examples of this functional-style programming paradigm.

13.1 Functional Interfaces

Functional interfaces and lambda expressions together facilitate *behavior parameterization* (p. 691), a powerful programming paradigm that allows code representing behavior to be passed around as values, and executed when the abstract method of the functional interface is invoked. This approach is scalable, requiring only a lambda expression to implement the functional interface.

Declaring a Functional Interface

A functional interface has exactly one abstract method. This abstract method is called the *functional method* of that interface. Like any other interface, a functional interface can declare other interface members, including static, default, and private methods (§5.6, p. 237). Here we concentrate on the single abstract method of a functional interface. This single abstract method, like all abstract methods in an interface, is implicitly abstract and public.

The StrPredicate interface shown below has only one abstract method and is, by definition, a functional interface.

```
@FunctionalInterface                         // Annotation.
interface StrPredicate {
  boolean test(String str);                  // Sole public abstract method.
}
```

The annotation @FunctionalInterface (§25.5, p. 1579) is optional when defining functional interfaces. If the annotation is specified, the compiler will issue an error if the declaration violates the definition of a functional interface, and the Javadoc tool will also automatically generate an explanation about the functional nature of the interface. In the absence of this annotation, there is no clue from the compiler to assert that an interface is a functional interface.

The CharSeqPredicate interface declaration below has two abstract methods, albeit they are overloaded, but it is not a functional interface.

```
@FunctionalInterface
interface CharSeqPredicate {                     // Compile-time error!
  boolean test(String str);                      // Abstract method.
  boolean test(StringBuilder sb);                // Abstract method.
}
```

The functional interface NewStrPredicate below declares only one abstract method at (1). In addition, it provides the implementations of one default and one static method at (2) and (3), respectively.

```
@FunctionalInterface
interface NewStrPredicate {
  boolean test(String str);                                // (1) Abstract method
  default void msg(String str) { System.out.println(str); } // (2) Default method
  static void info() { System.out.println("Testing!"); }    // (3) Static method
}
```

An interface can provide *explicit* public abstract method declarations for any of the three *non*-final public instance methods in the Object class (equals(), hashCode(), toString()). Including these methods explicitly in an interface should not be attempted, unless there are compelling reasons for doing so. These methods are automatically implemented by every class that implements an interface, since every class directly or indirectly inherits from the Object class. Therefore, such method declarations are not considered abstract in the definition of a functional interface.

In the Funky interface below, the first three abstract method declarations are those of the non-final public methods from the Object class. As explained above, these methods do not count toward the definition of a functional interface. Effectively, the Funky interface declares only one abstract method given by the last abstract method declaration.

```
@FunctionalInterface
interface Funky {
  @Override int hashCode();                      // From Object class
  @Override boolean equals(Object obj);          // From Object class
  @Override String toString();                   // From Object class
  boolean doTheFunk(Object obj);                 // Abstract method
}
```

The Java SE 17 platform API provides general-purpose functional interfaces in the java.util.function package that are discussed later (p. 695). Partial declaration of one such functional interface is shown below. It is the generic version of the StrPredicate functional interface defined earlier. The test() method of the Predicate<T> functional interface defines a boolean-valued predicate and evaluates it on the given object.

```
@FunctionalInterface
interface Predicate<T> {
  boolean test(T element);                       // Functional method.
  // ...
}
```

Just like any other interface, a functional interface can be implemented by a class. The following generic method takes an object of type T and a Predicate<T> and determines whether the object satisfies the predicate.

```
public static <T> boolean testPredicate(T object, Predicate<T> predicate) {
    return predicate.test(object);
}
```

Below are two implementations of the parameterized functional interface Predicate<String> using a concrete class and an anonymous class, respectively.

```
// Class implementation of Predicate<String>.
class PredicateTest implements Predicate<String> {
    public boolean test(String str) {
        return str.startsWith("A");              // (1)
    }
}

// An anonymous class implementation of Predicate<String>.
static Predicate<String> testLength = new Predicate<>() {
    public boolean test(String str) {
        return str.length() < 4;                 // (2)
    }
};

// Client code:
System.out.println(testPredicate("Anna", new PredicateTest()));   // true
System.out.println(testPredicate("Anna", testLength));            // false
```

Note that for any combination of an object type and a predicate criteria, the Predicate<T> interface has to be implemented by a *new* class (or a *new* anonymous class) in order to utilize the testPredicate() method. Looking at the two implementations of the Predicate<String> above, it is essentially the expressions in the respective return statements at (1) and (2) that are different. This is where lambda expressions come in, allowing more concise implementation of the abstract method of a functional interface, without requiring all the boilerplate code.

Overriding Abstract Methods from Multiple Interfaces, Revisited

A general discussion on overriding abstract methods from multiple superinterfaces can be found in §11.12, p. 621. In general, an interface can inherit multiple abstract methods from its superinterfaces, but a functional interface can only have a single abstract method. Note that superinterfaces need not be functional interfaces. It is even more imperative to use the @FunctionalInterface annotation to catch any inadvertent errors when a functional interface inherits abstract methods from multiple superinterfaces.

In the code below, the compiler does not flag any error in the declaration of the subinterface ContractZ. It is perfectly valid for the subinterface to inherit the doIt() method from each of its superinterfaces, as the two method declarations will be overloaded.

```
interface ContractX { void doIt(int i); }
interface ContractY { void doIt(double d); }
interface ContractZ extends ContractX, ContractY {
  @Override void doIt(int d);                                 // Can be omitted.
  @Override void doIt(double d);                              // Can be omitted.
}
```

Trying to declare the subinterface ContractZ as a functional interface, however, does not work. The multiple abstract methods inherited by the ContractZ are not override-equivalent—their signatures are different—and there is no single method that can override these methods, thus disqualifying ContractZ as a functional interface.

```
interface ContractX { void doIt(int i); }
interface ContractY { void doIt(double d); }
@FunctionalInterface interface ContractZ                     // Compile-time error!
                 extends ContractX, ContractY {
  @Override void doIt(int d);                                // Compile-time error!
  @Override void doIt(double d);                             // Compile-time error!
}
```

In the code below, the subinterface Features<T> at (1) is a functional interface, as the declarations of the abstract method flatten() in its superinterfaces are override-equivalent. Any declaration of the abstract method flatten() can represent the abstract methods from the superinterfaces in the subinterface.

```
interface Feature1<R> { void flatten(List<R> plist); }
interface Feature2<S> { void flatten(List<S> plist); }
@FunctionalInterface
interface Features<T> extends Feature1<T>, Feature2<T> {    // (1)
  @Override void flatten(List<T> plist);                    // Can be omitted.
}
```

Selected Interfaces in the Java SE Platform API

A functional interface, like any other interface, can always be implemented by a class. The @FunctionalInterface annotation on a functional interface in the Java SE Platform API documentation indicates that the implementation of the functional interface is meant to be implemented by lambda expressions.

In the Java SE Platform API, not all interfaces with one abstract method declaration are marked with the @FunctionalInterface annotation. Such single-abstract-method (*SAM*) interfaces usually elicit specific behavior in objects which is best provided by the class of an object, and not by users of the class. Examples of single-abstract-method interfaces that should be implemented by classes include the following interfaces from the java.lang package:

- Comparable<T> for creating an object that can be compared with another object according to their natural ordering (§14.4, p. 761)
- Iterable<T> for creating an object that represents a collection in a for(:) loop to iterate over its elements (§15.2, p. 791)

- `AutoCloseable` for creating an object that represents a resource that is automatically closed when exiting a try-with-resources statement (§7.7, p. 412)

- `Readable` for creating an object that is a source for reading characters (§20.3, p. 1249)

The Java SE Platform API also has ample examples of functional interfaces that are intended to be implemented by lambda expressions. Built-in general-purpose functional interfaces provided in the `java.util.function` package are discussed in §13.4, p. 695. In addition, the following specialized functional interfaces are worth noting:

- `java.util.Comparator<T>` with the method `compare()` for defining criteria for comparing two objects according to their total ordering (§14.5, p. 769)

- `java.lang.Runnable` with the method `run()` for defining code to be executed in threads (§22.3, p. 1370)

- `java.util.concurrent.Callable<V>` with the method `call()` for defining code to be executed in threads, that can return a result and throw an exception (§23.2, p. 1423)

13.2 Lambda Expressions

Lambda expressions *implement* functional interfaces, and thereby define *anonymous functions*—that is, functions that do not have a name. They can be used as a *value* in a program, without the excess baggage of first being packaged into objects. As we shall see, these two features together facilitate *behavior parameterization*— that is, customizing method behavior by passing code as values.

A lambda expression has the following syntax:

formal_parameter_list -> *lambda_body*

The parameter list and the body are separated by the -> operator (a.k.a. the *function arrow*). The arrow operator has the penultimate level of precedence, only higher than the assignment operators which have the lowest precedence, and is right-associative.

The lambda expression syntax resembles a simplified declaration of a method, without many of the bells and whistles of a method declaration—omitting, in particular, any modifiers, return type, or throws clause specification. That is important, as it avoids verbosity and provides a simple and succinct notation to write lambda expressions on the fly.

A lambda expression can only occur in specific contexts: for example, as the value on the right-hand side of an assignment, as an argument passed in a method or constructor call, or as the value to cast with the cast operator (p. 733). Such an occurrence *defines* a lambda expression, which is *evaluated* at runtime to produce a new kind of value: *an instance of a functional interface*. The *(deferred) execution* of the lambda body only occurs at a later time when the sole abstract method of this functional interface instance is invoked.

In the rest of this section, we take a closer look at the parameter list, the lambda body, the type checking, and evaluation of lambda expressions.

Lambda Parameters

The parameter list of a lambda expression is a comma-separated list of formal parameters that is enclosed in parentheses, (), analogous to the parameter list in a method declaration. There is one special case where the parentheses can be omitted, which we shall get to shortly. The lambda body in the code examples in this subsection is intentionally kept simple—an empty code block, {}, that does nothing.

The formal parameters of a lambda expression can be declared as one of the following forms for parameter declarations:

- *Declared-type parameters*

  If the types of the parameters are explicitly specified, they are known as *declared-type parameters*. The syntax of declared-type parameters is analogous to the formal parameters in a method declaration.

  ```
  (Integer a, String y) -> {};            // Multiple declared-type parameters
  ```
- *Inferred-type parameters*

  If the types of the parameters are not explicitly specified, they are known as *inferred-type parameters*. Types of the inferred-type parameters are derived from the context, and if necessary, from the functional type that is the target type of the lambda expression, as explained later in this section.

  ```
  (a, b) -> {};                            // Multiple inferred-type parameters
  ```

  If the types of the parameters are explicitly specified with the reserved type name var, their type is inferred by local variable type inference (§3.13, p. 142). Thus the syntax of such a parameter is consistent with the syntax of a local variable declaration. We will refer to such parameters as var-*type inferred parameters*.

  ```
  (var a, var b) -> {};                    // Multiple var-type inferred parameters
  ```

A lambda expression with inferred parameters is called an *implicitly typed lambda expression*.

All parameters in the parameter list must conform to the same form of parameter declaration—mixing of different forms of parameter declaration is not allowed. Parentheses are mandatory with multiple parameters, whether they are declared-type or inferred-type. For a parameter list with a single inferred-type parameter, the parentheses can be omitted—but not for a declared-type or a var-type inferred parameter. Also, only declared-type parameters and var-type inferred parameters can have modifiers or annotations, like the final modifier or an annotation.

The code examples below illustrate the different forms of formal parameter declarations in a lambda expression.

```
() -> {};                            // Empty parameter list

// Single formal parameter:
(String str) -> {};                  // Single declared-type parameter
(str)        -> {};                  // Single inferred-type parameter
str          -> {};                  // Single inferred-type parameter
(var str)    -> {};                  // Single var-type inferred parameter

// Multiple formal parameters:
(Integer x, Integer y) -> {};        // Multiple declared-type parameters
(x, y)                 -> {};        // Multiple inferred-type parameters
(var x, var y)         -> {};        // Multiple var-type inferred parameters

// Modifiers and annotations with formal parameters:
(final int i, int j) -> {};          // Modifier with declared-type parameters
(final var i, var j) -> {};          // Modifier with var-type inferred parameters
(@NonNull int i, int j) -> {};       // Annotation with declared-type parameter
(var i, @Nullable var j)-> {};       // Annotation with var-type inferred parameter

// Parentheses are mandatory with multiple formal parameters:
String str           -> {};          // Illegal: Missing parentheses
var str              -> {};          // Illegal: Missing parentheses
Integer x, Integer y -> {};          // Illegal: Missing parentheses
x, y                 -> {};          // Illegal: Missing parentheses
var x, var y         -> {};          // Illegal: Missing parentheses

// All formal parameters must be either declared-type, inferred-type, or
// var-type inferred parameters.
(String str, j)      -> {};          // Cannot mix declared-type and inferred-type
(String str, var j)  -> {};          // Cannot mix declared-type and var-type inferred
(var str, j)         -> {};          // Cannot mix var-type inferred and inferred-type

// Modifiers and annotations cannot be used with inferred-type parameters.
(final str, j)       -> {};          // No modifiers with inferred-type parameters
(str, @NonNull j)    -> {};          // No annotations with inferred-type parameters
```

Lambda Body

A lambda body is either a *single expression* or a *statement block*. Execution of a lambda body either has a non-void return (i.e., its evaluation returns a value), or has a void return (i.e., its evaluation does not return a value), or its evaluation throws an exception.

A single-expression lambda body is used for short and succinct lambda expressions. A single-expression lambda body with a void return type is commonly used to achieve side effects. The return keyword is not allowed in a single-expression lambda body.

In the examples below, the body of the lambda expressions is an *expression* whose execution returns a value—that is, has a non-void return.

```
() -> 2021                              // Expression body, non-void return
() -> null                             // Expression body, non-void return
(i, j) -> i + j                        // Expression body, non-void return
(i, j) -> i <= j ? i : j               // Expression body, non-void return
str -> str.length() > 3                // Expression body, non-void return
str -> str != null                     // Expression body, non-void return
        && !str.equals("") && str.length() > 3
        && str.equals(new StringBuilder(str).reverse().toString())
```

In the following examples, the lambda body is an *expression statement* that can have a void or a non-void return. However, if the abstract method of the functional interface does not return a value, the non-void return of an expression statement body can be interpreted as a void return—that is, the return value is ignored.

```
val -> System.out.println(val)         // Method invocation statement, void return
sb -> sb.trimToSize()                  // Method invocation statement, void return
sb -> sb.append("!")                   // Method invocation statement, non-void return
() -> new StringBuilder("?")           // Object creation statement, non-void return
value -> value++                       // Increment statement, non-void return
value -> value *= 2                    // Assignment statement, non-void return
```

The following examples are not legal lambda expressions:

```
(int i) -> while (i < 10) ++i          // Illegal: not an expression but statement
(x, y) -> return x + y                 // Illegal: return not allowed in expression
```

The statement block comprises declarations and statements enclosed in curly brackets ({}). The return statement is only allowed in a block lambda body, and the rules are the same as those in a method body: A return statement with an argument can only be used for a non-void return and its use is mandatory, whereas a return statement with no argument can only be used for a void return, but its use is optional. The return statement terminates the execution of the lambda body immediately.

```
() -> {}                               // Block body, void return
() -> { return 2021; }                 // Block body, non-void return
() -> { return 2021 }       // Illegal: statement terminator (;) in block missing
() -> { new StringBuilder("Go nuts."); }        // Block body, void return
() -> { return new StringBuilder("Go nuts!"); } // Block body, non-void return
(int i) -> { while (i < 10) ++i; }              // Block body, void return
(i, j) -> { if (i <= j) return i; else return j; } // Block body, non-void return
(done) -> {                            // Multiple statements in block body, void return
  if (done) {
    System.out.println("You deserve a break!");
    return;
  }
  System.out.println("Stay right here!");
}
```

Type Checking and Execution of Lambda Expressions

A lambda expression can only be defined in a context where a functional interface can be used: for example, in an assignment context, a method call context, or a cast context (p. 733). The compiler determines the *target type* that is required in the context where the lambda expression is defined. This target type is always a functional interface type. In the assignment context below, the target type is `Predicate<Integer>`, as it is the target of the assignment statement. Note that the type parameter T of the functional interface is `Integer`.

```
Predicate<Integer> p1 = i -> i % 2 == 0;  // (1) Target type: Predicate<Integer>
```

The *method type* of a method declaration comprises its type parameters, formal parameter types, return type, and any exceptions the method throws.

The *function type* of a functional interface is the method type of its functional method. The target type `Predicate<Integer>` has the following method, where type parameter T is `Integer`:

```
public boolean test(Integer t);            // Method type: Integer -> boolean
```

The function type of the target type `Predicate<Integer>` is the method type of the this `test()` method:

```
Integer -> boolean
```

The type of the lambda expression defined in a given context must be compatible with the function type of the target type. If the lambda expression has inferred-type parameters, their type is inferred from the context, and if necessary, from the function type. From the lambda body at (1), it is possible to infer that the type of i is int (from the expression i % 2), and the lambda body evaluates to a boolean value (from the evaluation of the == operator). Just from the context, it is thus possible to infer that the type of the lambda expression at (1) is:

```
int -> boolean
```

From the function type of the target type `Predicate<Integer>`, the compiler is able to determine that if the inferred int type of the parameter i in the lambda expression at (1) is promoted to `Integer`, the type of the lambda expression at (1) would then be compatible with the function type of the target type `Predicate<Integer>`, that is:

```
Integer -> boolean
```

The lambda expression defined at (1) above is equivalent to the following implementation using an anonymous class.

```
Predicate<Integer> p1 = new Predicate<>() { // Anonymous class
  public boolean test(Integer i) {
    return i % 2 == 0;
  }
};
```

It is possible to determine that the type of the lambda expression at (1) is compatible with the method type of the only abstract method `test()` defined by the `Predicate<T>` functional interface because it is not ambiguous which method the lambda expression should implement in the functional interface. However, this would not work for an interface that had more than one abstract method, as it would not be clear which abstract method to implement.

In the following assignment, the target type is java.util.function.IntPredicate:

```
IntPredicate p2 = i -> i % 2 == 0;          // (2) Target type: IntPredicate
```

The IntPredicate functional interface has the following abstract method:

```
public boolean test(int i);                 // Method type: int -> boolean
```

The function type of the target type IntPredicate is the method type of its abstract method:

```
int -> boolean
```

The compiler infers that the type of the inferred-type parameter i in the lambda expression at (2) should be int. As the lambda body returns a boolean value, the type of the lambda expression at (2) is

```
int -> boolean
```

The type of the lambda expression is compatible with the function type of the target type IntPredicate.

Note that in both examples, the lambda expression is the same, but their types are different in the two contexts. They represent two different values. The type of a lambda expression is determined by the context in which it is defined.

```
System.out.println(p1 == p2);               // false
```

The process of type checking a lambda expression in a given context is called *target typing*. The presentation here is simplified, but suffices for our purpose to give an idea of what is involved.

The compiler does the type checking for using lambda expressions. The runtime environment provides the rest of the magic to make it all work. At runtime, the lambda expression is executed when the sole abstract method of the functional interface is invoked.

```
boolean result1 = p1.test(2021);            // false
boolean result2 = p2.test(2020);            // true
```

As mentioned earlier, this is an example of deferred execution. Lambda execution is similar to invoking a method on an object. We define a lambda expression as a *function* and use it like a *method*, letting the compiler and the runtime environment put it all together.

Accessing Members in an Enclosing Class

Just like nested blocks, a lambda expression has *lexical or block scope*—that is, names used in a lambda expression are resolved *lexically* in the local context in which the lambda expression is defined.

A lambda expression does *not* inherit names of members declared in the functional interface it implements, which obviously then cannot be accessed in the lambda body.

Since a lambda expression is not a class, there is no notion of the this reference. If the this reference is used in a lambda expression in a non-static context, it refers to the *enclosing object*, and can be used to access members of this object. The name of a member in the enclosing object has the same meaning when used in a lambda expression. In other words, there are no restrictions to accessing members declared in the enclosing object. In the case of shadowing member names by local variables, the keyword this can be explicitly used, and also the keyword super to access any members inherited by the enclosing object.

In Example 13.1, the getPredicate() method at (7) defines a lambda expression at (8). This lambda expression is defined in a non-static context (i.e., an instance method). This lambda expression accesses the static field strList and the instance field banner in the enclosing class at (1) and (2), respectively.

In the main() method in Example 13.1, an ArrayList<String> is assigned to the static field strList at (3) and is initialized. The ArrayList<String> referred to by the static field strList has the following content:

```
[Tom, Dick, Harriet]
```

A MembersOnly object is created at (4). Its StringBuilder field banner is initialized with the string "love ". The local variable obj declared at (4) refers to this MembersOnly object. At (5), a Predicate<String> instance is instantiated by calling the getPredicate() method on the MembersOnly object referred to by the local variable obj. This predicate is first executed when the test() method is called at (6) on the Predicate<String> instance, with the argument string "never dies!". Calling the test() method results in the lambda expression created at (5) by the getPredicate() method to be executed in the context of the enclosing MembersOnly object referred to by the local variable obj.

The parameter str of the lambda expression is initialized with the string "never dies!"—that is, the argument to the test() method. In the body of the lambda expression, the ArrayList<String> referred to by the static field strList in the MembersOnly class is first printed at (9):

```
List: [Tom, Dick, Harriet]
```

At (10), the parameter str (with contents "never dies!") is appended to the StringBuilder (with contents "love ") referred to by the instance field banner in the enclosing object, resulting in the following contents in this StringBuilder:

```
"love never dies!"
```

Since the length of the string "never dies!", referred to by the parameter str, is greater than 5, the lambda expression returns true at (11). This is the value returned by the test() method call at (6).

In the call to the println() method at (6), the argument

```
p.test("never dies!") + " " + obj.banner
```

now evaluates as

```
true + " " + "love never dies!"
```

Example 13.1 *Accessing Members in the Enclosing Object*

```java
import java.util.ArrayList;
import java.util.List;
import java.util.function.Predicate;

public class MembersOnly {

  // Instance variable
  private StringBuilder banner;                                    // (1)

  // Static variable
  private static List<String> strList;                             // (2)

  // Constructor
  public MembersOnly(String str) {
    banner = new StringBuilder(str);
  }

  // Static method
  public static void main(String[] args) {
    strList = new ArrayList<>();                                   // (3)
    strList.add("Tom"); strList.add("Dick"); strList.add("Harriet");

    MembersOnly obj = new MembersOnly("love ");                    // (4)
    Predicate<String> p = obj.getPredicate();                      // (5)
    System.out.println(p.test("never dies!") + " " + obj.banner);  // (6)
  }

  // Instance method
  public Predicate<String> getPredicate() {                // (7)
    return str -> {                                        // (8)  Lambda expression
      System.out.println("List: " + MembersOnly.strList);// (9)  Static field
      this.banner.append(str);                             // (10) Instance field
      return str.length() > 5;                             // (11) boolean value
    };
  }
}
```

Output from the program:

```
List: [Tom, Dick, Harriet]
true love never dies!
```

Accessing Local Variables in the Enclosing Context

All variable declarations in a lambda expression follow the rules of *block scope*. They are not accessible outside the lambda expression. It also means that we cannot *redeclare* local variables already declared in the enclosing scope. In Example 13.2, redeclaring the parameter banner and the local variable words at (6) and (7), respectively, in the body of the lambda expression results in a compile-time error.

Local variables declared in the enclosing method, including its formal parameters, can be accessed in a lambda expression provided they are *effectively final*. This means that once a local variable has been assigned a value to the time when it is used, its value has not changed during that time. Using the final modifier in the declaration of a local variable explicitly instructs the compiler to ensure that this is the case. The final modifier implies effectively final. If the final modifier is omitted and a local variable is used in a lambda expression, the compiler effectively performs the same analysis as if the final modifier had been specified.

A lambda expression may be executed at a later time, after the method in which it is defined has finished execution. At that point, the local variables in its enclosing context that are used in the lambda expression are no longer accessible. To ensure their availability, *copies of their values* are maintained with the lambda expression. This is called *variable capture*, although in essence it is the values that are captured. Note that it is not the object that is copied in the case of a local reference variable, but the reference value. Objects reside on the heap and are accessible via a copy of the reference value. Correct execution of the lambda expression is guaranteed, since these effectively final values cannot change. Note that the state of an object referred to by a final or an effectively final reference can change, but not the reference value stored in the reference—that is, such a reference will continue to refer to the same object once it is initialized.

In Example 13.2, the method getPredicate() at (1) has one formal parameter (banner), and a local variable (words) declared at (2). Although the state of the Array-List<String> object, referred to by the reference words, is changed in the method (we add elements to it), the reference value in the reference does not—that is, it continues to refer to the same object whose reference value it was assigned at (2). The parameter banner is assigned the reference value of the argument object when the method is invoked, and continues to refer to this object throughout the method. Both local variables are effectively final. Their values are captured by the lambda expression, and used when the lambda expression is executed at a later time after the call to the getPredicate() method in the main() method has completed.

However, if we uncomment (3) and (4) in Example 13.2, then both local variables are not effectively final. Their reference values are changed at (3) and (4), respectively. The compiler now flags an error at (8) and (9), respectively because these non-final local variables are used in the lambda expression.

The vigilant reader no doubt will have noticed that no requirement of effectively final was imposed on the field members of the enclosing class or object, when accessed in the lambda body. Reference to the enclosing object or class is captured by the lambda expression, and when the expression is executed at a later time, the reference can readily be used to access values of any fields referenced in the lambda body—no copies of such values need be made, thereby making the effectively final rule unnecessary for accessing fields in the enclosing context.

Example 13.2 *Accessing Local Variables in the Enclosing Method*

```java
import java.util.ArrayList;
import java.util.List;
import java.util.function.Predicate;

public class LocalsOnly {

  public static void main(String[] args) {
    StringBuilder banner = new StringBuilder("love ");
    LocalsOnly instance = new LocalsOnly();
    Predicate<String> p = instance.getPredicate(banner);
    System.out.println(p.test("never dies!") + " " + banner);
  }

  public Predicate<String> getPredicate(StringBuilder banner) {   // (1)
    List<String> words = new ArrayList<>();                       // (2)
    words.add("Tom"); words.add("Dick"); words.add("Harriet");

//  banner = new StringBuilder();        // (3) Illegal: Not effectively final
//  words = new ArrayList<>();           // (4) Illegal: Not effectively final

    return str -> {                          // (5) Lambda expression
//    String banner = "Don't redeclare me!";   // (6) Illegal: Redeclared
//    String[] words = new String[6];          // (7) Illegal: Redeclared
      System.out.println("List: " + words);    // (8) Local variable
      banner.append(str);                      // (9) Parameter
      return str.length() > 5;
    };
  }
}
```

Output from the program:

```
List: [Tom, Dick, Harriet]
true love never dies!
```

13.3 Lambda Expressions and Anonymous Classes

As we have seen in this chapter so far, both anonymous classes and lambda expressions can be used to provide implementation of functional interfaces. Example 13.3 illustrates using both anonymous classes and lambda expressions for this purpose.

A common operation on elements in a collection is to select those elements that satisfy certain criteria. This operation is called *filtering*. Given a list of words, we would like to filter this list for one-word *palindromes*—that is, words spelled the same forward and backward. For example, "anana" is a palindrome, but "banana" is not.

Example 13.3 defines the generic method filterList() at (7) for filtering a list. Its first parameter is a list of type T to filter, and the filtering criteria is given by the second parameter which is a generic functional interface. This functional interface, Predicate<T>, specifies the boolean abstract method test(T t). The argument passed to the method must implement the Predicate<T> interface, supplying the implementation of the boolean method test() that actually determines if an element satisfies the criteria. The test() method is an example of a *predicate*—that is, a function that takes an argument and returns a boolean value.

The following boolean expressions are used to determine whether a word (given by the reference str) is a case-sensitive or case-insensitive palindrome, respectively:

```
str.equals(new StringBuilder(str).reverse().toString())
str.equalsIgnoreCase(new StringBuilder(str).reverse().toString())
```

Whether a string is a palindrome is determined by comparing the string for equality with the result of reversing the string using a StringBuilder.

Example 13.3   *Filtering an* ArrayList<E>

```java
import java.util.ArrayList;
import java.util.List;
import java.util.function.Predicate;

public class FunWithPalindromes {

  public static void main(String[] args) {

    List<String> words = new ArrayList<>();
    words.add("Otto"); words.add("ADA"); words.add("Alyla");
    words.add("Bob"); words.add("HannaH"); words.add("Java");
    System.out.println("List of words:                  " + words);

    System.out.println("-----------Using Anonymous Classes--------------------");
    // Use an anonymous class to filter for palindromes (case sensitive).  (1)
    List<String> palindromesA = filterList(words,
        new Predicate<String>() {
          @Override public boolean test(String str) {
            return str.equals(new StringBuilder(str).reverse().toString());
          }
        }
    );
    System.out.println("Case-sensitive palindromes:   " + palindromesA);

    // Use an anonymous class to filter for palindromes (case insensitive). (2)
    List<String> palindromesB = filterList(words,
        new Predicate<String>() {
          @Override public boolean test(String str) {
            return str.equalsIgnoreCase(
                        new StringBuilder(str).reverse().toString());
          }
        }
    );
    System.out.println("Case-insensitive palindromes: " + palindromesB);
```

```
    System.out.println("-----------Using Lambda Expressions--------------------");
    Predicate<String> predicate1 = str ->
        str.equals(new StringBuilder(str).reverse().toString());        // (3)
    List<String> palindromes1 = filterList(words, predicate1);          // (4)
    System.out.println("Case-sensitive palindromes:   " + palindromes1);

    Predicate<String> predicate2 = str ->
        str.equalsIgnoreCase(new StringBuilder(str).reverse().toString());// (5)
    List<String> palindromes2 = filterList(words, predicate2);          // (6)
    System.out.println("Case-insensitive palindromes: " + palindromes2);
  }

  /**
   * Filters a list according to the criteria of the predicate.
   * @param list       List to filter
   * @param predicate  Provides the criteria for filtering the list
   * @return           List of elements that match the criteria
   */
  public static <E> List<E> filterList(List<E> list,                    // (7)
                                  Predicate<E> predicate) {
    List<E> result = new ArrayList<>();
    for (E element : list) {
      if (predicate.test(element)) {                                    // (8)
        result.add(element);
      }
    }
    return result;
  }
}
```

Output from the program:

```
List of words:              [Otto, ADA, Alyla, Bob, HannaH, Java]
-----------Using Anonymous Classes--------------------
Case-sensitive palindromes:   [ADA, HannaH]
Case-insensitive palindromes: [Otto, ADA, Alyla, Bob, HannaH]
-----------Using Lambda Expressions--------------------
Case-sensitive palindromes:   [ADA, HannaH]
Case-insensitive palindromes: [Otto, ADA, Alyla, Bob, HannaH]
```

Filtering Criteria Defined by Anonymous Classes

Example 13.3 uses anonymous classes to instantiate the criteria object, as shown at
(1) and (2). The basic idea is that we can both declare and instantiate the class at the
same time, where it is needed in the code, and in our case, as an argument in the
call to the filterList() method. The type parameter E in this case is String. The
anonymous classes at (1) and (2) provide implementations of the test() method for
strings. The method is called at (8) to determine whether a String fulfills the selection criteria.

By using anonymous classes, we have avoided creating separate concrete classes,
but the verbosity of declaring anonymous classes to encapsulate a single method

is inescapable. And we still have to declare a new anonymous class for each selection criterion, duplicating a lot of boilerplate code.

Filtering Criteria Defined by Lambda Expressions

Ideally we would like to pass the code for the selection criteria as an argument to the filterList() method so that the method can apply the criteria to the elements in the list—that is, be able to change the behavior of the filterList() method depending on the selection criteria. This is an example of *behavior parameterization*.

Knowing that something is a Predicate<T>, all the information about the abstract method it implements can be inferred, as it is the only abstract method in the interface: its name, its parameters, any value it returns, and whether it throws any exceptions.

The assignment at (3) in Example 13.3 uses a lambda expression to provide an implementation for the parameterized Predicate<String> functional interface:

```
Predicate<String> predicate1 = str ->
        str.equals(new StringBuilder(str).reverse().toString());          // (3)
```

The reference predicate1 on the left-hand side is of type Predicate<String>, and it is assigned the value of the lambda expression on the right-hand side.

The lambda expression at (3) defines an anonymous function that takes a String as the only parameter, and returns a boolean value. Its type is String -> boolean. Recall that the test() method of the Predicate<String> functional interface type does exactly that. The function type of the Predicate<String> functional interface is also String -> boolean. The compiler can type check that the lambda expression is assignable to the reference on the left-hand side, since the expression represents an anonymous function that is compatible with the sole abstract method test() of the parameterized Predicate<String> interface.

The lambda expression at (3) is passed as an argument to the filterList() method via the reference predicate1 at (4). It is only executed when the test() method is called with a String argument in the filterList() method at (8).

The anonymous class declaration at (1):

```
new Predicate<String>() {
  @Override public boolean test(String str) {
    return str.equals(new StringBuilder(str).reverse().toString());
  }
}
```

is implemented by the lambda expression at (3):

```
str -> str.equals(new StringBuilder(str).reverse().toString())
```

Now we need only pass a new lambda expression to the filterList() method to filter a list based on selection criteria. Using lambda expressions is more precise, concise, and readable than using anonymous classes.

Later, when we discuss *streams* (Chapter 16, p. 879), we will also do away with the filterList() method for filtering lists.

Lambda Expressions versus Anonymous Classes

Implementation

A lambda expression can only be used to provide implementation of exactly one functional interface. It represents an anonymous function. Unlike an object, it has only behavior and no state.

An anonymous class is restricted to either implementing one interface or extending one class, but it is not restricted to implementing only one abstract method from its supertype.

No separate class file with Java bytecode is created for a lambda expression, in contrast to a separate class file for each anonymous class declared in a source file.

Scope

Lambda expressions do not introduce a new naming scope, and follow the lexical scope rules for nested blocks. Names in a lambda expression are resolved lexically in its enclosing block and enclosing class.

An anonymous class introduces a new naming scope, where names are resolved according to the inheritance hierarchy of the anonymous class, its local enclosing block, and its enclosing class.

Accessing Inherited Members from the Inheritance Hierarchy

Members in the functional interface implemented by a lambda expression are not accessible in the lambda body.

Since an anonymous class can declare and inherit members from its supertype, instances of anonymous classes can have *state*. The this and super references can be used to access members in the current instance of the anonymous class and its superclass object, respectively.

Accessing Local Declarations in the Enclosing Block

An anonymous class and a lambda expression can only access effectively final local variables in their enclosing local context.

A local variable in a lambda expression cannot shadow a local variable with the same name in the local context because local variables cannot be redeclared. A field name in the anonymous class can shadow a local variable with the same name in the local context.

Accessing Members in the Enclosing Class

A local variable in a lambda expression and a member (either inherited or declared) in an anonymous class can hide a member with the same name in the enclosing class.

A lambda expression and an anonymous class can access any non-hidden members in the enclosing class by their simple names.

In a non-static context, a lambda expression and an anonymous class can access any hidden members in the enclosing class by the this reference and the *qualified* this reference, respectively.

In a static context, a lambda expression and an anonymous class can access any hidden members in the enclosing class by their qualified names.

Best Practices

Defining an anonymous class can be verbose. Even an implementation of a single method requires a lot of boilerplate code to encapsulate the method in a class definition, with the added risk of making the code hard to read and understand.

The obvious choice for implementing functional interfaces is lambda expressions. Anything beyond that, and there is little choice but to bring in the anonymous classes.

 Review Questions

13.1 Which statement is true about functional interfaces and lambda expressions? Select the one correct answer.

(a) A functional interface can only be implemented by lambda expressions.
(b) A functional interface declaration can have only one method declaration.
(c) In the body of a lambda expression, only public members in the enclosing class can be accessed.
(d) In the body of a lambda expression, all local variables in the enclosing scope can be accessed.
(e) None of the above

13.2 Which of the following statements are true about the following code?

```
interface Funky1    { void    absMethod1(String s); }
interface Funky2    { String  absMethod2(String s); }

public class RQ12A99 {
  public static void main(String[] args) {

    Funky1 p1;
    p1 = s -> System.out.println(s);        // (1)
    p1 = s -> s.length();                   // (2)
```

```
        p1 = s -> s.toUpperCase();                 // (3)
        p1 = s -> { s.toUpperCase(); };            // (4)
        p1 = s -> { return s.toUpperCase(); };     // (5)

        Funky2 p2;
        p2 = s -> System.out.println(s);           // (6)
        p2 = s -> s.length();                      // (7)
        p2 = s -> s.toUpperCase();                 // (8)
        p2 = s -> { s.toUpperCase(); };            // (9)
        p2 = s -> { return s.toUpperCase(); };     // (10)
    }
}
```

Select the four correct answers.

(a) (1) will fail to compile.
(b) (2) will fail to compile.
(c) (3) will fail to compile.
(d) (4) will fail to compile.
(e) (5) will fail to compile.
(f) (6) will fail to compile.
(g) (7) will fail to compile.
(h) (8) will fail to compile.
(i) (9) will fail to compile.
(j) (10) will fail to compile.

13.3   Which statement is true about the following code?

```
interface AgreementA { void doIt(); }
interface AgreementB extends AgreementA {}
interface AgreementC extends AgreementB {
  void doIt();
  boolean equals(Object obj);
}

class Beta implements AgreementB {
  public void doIt() {
    System.out.print("Jazz|");
  }
}

public class RQ12A999 {
  public static void main(String[] args) {
    AgreementA a = () -> System.out.print("Java|");     // (1)
    AgreementB b = () -> System.out.print("Jive|");     // (2)
    AgreementC c = () -> System.out.print("Jingle|");   // (3)
    Object o = a = c;                                   // (4)
    b = new Beta();                                     // (5)
    a.doIt();                                           // (6)
    b.doIt();                                           // (7)
    c.doIt();                                           // (8)
    ((AgreementA) o).doIt();                            // (9)
  }
}
```

Select the one correct answer.

(a) The program will fail to compile.

(b) The program will throw a ClassCastException.

(c) The program will print Jingle|Jingle|Jazz|Jingle|.

(d) The program will print Jingle|Jazz|Jingle|Jingle|.

(e) The program will print Jingle|Jingle|Jingle|Jazz|.

13.4 Overview of Built-In Functional Interfaces

Earlier in this chapter, specialized interfaces (including some functional ones) were mentioned that are readily available in the Java SE Platform API (p. 678). To facilitate defining common functions with lambda expressions, the Java SE Platform API also provides a versatile set of functional interfaces for this purpose.

The main support for functional interfaces is found in the java.util.function package. The general-purpose generic functional interfaces shown in Table 13.1 represent the four basic operations that are commonly implemented by functions: to *get* a value (Supplier<T>), to *test* a predicate (Predicate<T>), to *accept* a value but not return a result (Consumer<T>), and to *apply* a function to a value in order to compute a new result (Function<T, R>).

The term *arity* refers to the number of arguments that a method requires as its input. A method is called *zero-arity, one-arity,* or *two-arity,* depending on whether the method has *zero, one,* or *two* arguments, respectively. Depending on whether the functional method is zero-arity, one-arity, or two-arity, its functional interface is likewise referred to as zero-arity, one-arity, or two-arity, respectively. Note that the arity of the functional interface reflects the arity of its functional method. Particularly for a generic functional interface, the arity should *not* be confused with the number of type parameters specified for the generic functional interface.

In Table 13.1, except for the Supplier<T> functional interface which has a zero-arity functional method, the functional methods for the other three basic functional interfaces are one-arity methods. Accordingly, the Supplier<T> functional interface is a zero-arity functional interface, whereas the other functional interfaces are one-arity functional interfaces.

Table 13.1 *Basic Functional Interfaces in the* java.util.function *Package*

Functional interface (T and R are type parameters)	Functional method	Function	Arity of function type
Supplier<T>	get: () -> T	Provide an instance of a T.	Zero-arity
Predicate<T>	test: T -> boolean	Evaluate a predicate on a T.	One-arity
Consumer<T>	accept: T -> void	Perform action on a T.	One-arity
Function<T, R>	apply: T -> R	Transform a T to an R.	One-arity

It is important to understand the abstract operations that the basic functional interfaces provide before tackling the specialized versions of these functional interfaces in the java.util.function package. Since the package provides a wide range of functional interfaces for various purposes, defining new ones should hardly be necessary.

The complete list of all built-in functional interfaces in the java.util.function package is given in Table 13.2. The table also shows any default methods that a built-in functional interface defines. The idea is not to memorize them all, but to understand how they are categorized according to the four basic functional interfaces in Table 13.1. The specialized versions of the basic functional interfaces are derived by combining one or more of the following three forms:

- *Two-arity specializations of the basic functional interfaces*

  These functional interfaces (BiPredicate<T,U>, BiConsumer<T,U>, BiFunction<T,U,R>) are two-arity specialized counterparts to the corresponding basic functional interface, except for the Supplier<T> interface which does not have a two-arity specialization.

- *Extended versions of the* Function<T,R> *and* BiFunction<T,U,R> *interfaces*

  The functional interfaces UnaryOperator<T> and BinaryOperator<T> *extend* the Function<T,T> and BiFunction<T,T,T> interfaces, respectively. As their names imply, the two specialized functional interfaces UnaryOperator<T> and BinaryOperator<T> are one-arity and two-arity functional interfaces as their superinterfaces, respectively, *where the parameters and the result in each have the same type.*

- *Primitive type specializations of generic functional interfaces*

  The primitive type specializations avoid excessive boxing and unboxing of primitive values when such values are used as objects.

  The primitive type counterparts are specializations of each generic functional interface where one or more type parameters are replaced by a primitive type. Primitive type specializations primarily involve one or more of the primitive types int, long, or double.

  The naming scheme uses one or more prefixes in front of the name of a primitive type functional interface to indicate its function type—that is, the type of the parameters and that of the result. For example, IntPredicate has the function type int -> boolean, whereas IntToDoubleFunction has the function type int -> double, and LongBinaryOperator has the function type (long, long) -> long.

Table 13.2 *Built-In Functional Interfaces in the* java.util.function *Package*

Functional interface (T, U, and R are type parameters)	Functional method		Default methods unless otherwise indicated
Supplier<T>	get:	() -> T	–
IntSupplier	getAsInt:	() -> int	–
LongSupplier	getAsLong:	() -> long	–

Table 13.2 *Built-In Functional Interfaces in the* `java.util.function` *Package (Continued)*

Functional interface (T, U, and R are type parameters)	Functional method	Default methods unless otherwise indicated
DoubleSupplier	getAsDouble: () -> double	–
BooleanSupplier	getAsBoolean: () -> boolean	–
Predicate<T>	test: T -> boolean	and(), or(), negate(), static isEqual(), static not()
IntPredicate	test: int -> boolean	and(), or(), negate()
LongPredicate	test: long -> boolean	and(), or(), negate()
DoublePredicate	test: double -> boolean	and(), or(), negate()
BiPredicate<T, U>	test: (T, U) -> boolean	and(), or(), negate()
Consumer<T>	accept: T -> void	andThen()
IntConsumer	accept: int -> void	andThen()
LongConsumer	accept: long -> void	andThen()
DoubleConsumer	accept: double -> void	andThen()
BiConsumer<T, U>	accept: (T, U) -> void	andThen()
ObjIntConsumer<T>	accept: (T, int) -> void	–
ObjLongConsumer<T>	accept: (T, long) -> void	–
ObjDoubleConsumer<T>	accept: (T, double) -> void	–
Function<T, R>	apply: T -> R	compose(), andThen(), static identity()
IntFunction<R>	apply: int -> R	–
LongFunction<R>	apply: long -> R	–
DoubleFunction<R>	apply: double -> R	–
ToIntFunction<T>	applyAsInt: T -> int	–
ToLongFunction<T>	applyAsLong: T -> long	–
ToDoubleFunction<T>	applyAsDouble: T -> double	–
IntToLongFunction	applyAsLong: int -> long	–
IntToDoubleFunction	applyAsDouble: int -> double	–
LongToIntFunction	applyAsInt: long -> int	–
LongToDoubleFunction	applyAsDouble: long -> double	–
DoubleToIntFunction	applyAsInt: double -> int	–
DoubleToLongFunction	applyAsLong: double -> long	–

Table 13.2　*Built-In Functional Interfaces in the* `java.util.function` *Package (Continued)*

Functional interface (T, U, and R are type parameters)	Functional method	Default methods unless otherwise indicated
`BiFunction<T, U, R>`	`apply: (T, U) -> R`	`andThen()`
`ToIntBiFunction<T, U>`	`applyAsInt:　(T, U) -> int`	–
`ToLongBiFunction<T, U>`	`applyAsLong:　(T, U) -> long`	–
`ToDoubleBiFunction<T, U>`	`applyAsDouble: (T, U) -> double`	–
`UnaryOperator<T> extends Function<T,T>`	`apply: T -> T`	`compose(), andThen(), static identity()`
`IntUnaryOperator`	`applyAsInt:　int -> int`	`compose(), andThen()`
`LongUnaryOperator`	`applyAsLong:　long -> long`	`compose(), andThen()`
`DoubleUnaryOperator`	`applyAsDouble: double -> double`	`compose(), andThen()`
`BinaryOperator<T> extends BiFunction<T,T,T>`	`apply: (T, T) -> T`	`andThen(), static maxBy(), static minBy()`
`IntBinaryOperator`	`applyAsInt:　(int, int) -> int`	–
`LongBinaryOperator`	`applyAsLong:　(long, long) -> long`	–
`DoubleBinaryOperator`	`applyAsDouble: (double, double) -> double`	–

The columns in Table 13.3 list the built-in functional interfaces in the `java.util.function` package according to each category of basic functional interface.

Table 13.3　*Summary of Built-In Functional Interfaces*

Supplier<T>	Predicate<T>	Consumer<T>	Function<T, R>	UnaryOperator<T>
`IntSupplier`	`IntPredicate`	`IntConsumer`	`IntFunction<R>`	`IntUnaryOperator`
`LongSupplier`	`LongPredicate`	`LongConsumer`	`LongFunction<R>`	`LongUnaryOperator`
`DoubleSupplier`	`DoublePredicate`	`DoubleConsumer`	`DoubleFunction<R>`	`DoubleUnaryOperator`
`BooleanSupplier`			`ToIntFunction<T>`	
			`ToLongFunction<T>`	
			`ToDouble-Function<T>`	
			`IntToLong-Function`	

Table 13.3   *Summary of Built-In Functional Interfaces (Continued)*

Supplier<T>	Predicate<T>	Consumer<T>	Function<T, R>	UnaryOperator<T>
			IntToDouble-Function	
			LongToInt-Function	
			LongToDouble-Function	
			DoubleToInt-Function	
			DoubleToLong-Function	
	BiPredicate<T,U>	BiConsumer<T,U>	BiFunction<T,U,R>	BinaryOperator<T>
		ObjInt-Consumer<T>	ToInt-BiFunction<T,U>	IntBinaryOperator
		ObjLong-Consumer<T>	ToLong-BiFunction<T,U>	LongBinaryOperator
		ObjDouble-Consumer<T>	ToDouble-BiFunction<T,U>	DoubleBinaryOperator

13.5   Suppliers

As the name suggests, the Supplier<T> functional interface represents a supplier of
values. From Table 13.4, we see that its functional method get() has the type () ->
T—that is, it takes no argument and returns a value of type T.

Table 13.4 shows all supplier functional interfaces provided in the java.util.function
package. Apart from the functional method shown in Table 13.4, these functional
interfaces do not define any additional methods.

Table 13.4   *Suppliers*

Functional interface (T, U, and R are type parameters)	Functional method		Default methods
Supplier<T>	get:	() -> T	–
IntSupplier	getAsInt:	() -> int	–
LongSupplier	getAsLong:	() -> long	–
DoubleSupplier	getAsDouble:	() -> double	–
BooleanSupplier	getAsBoolean:	() -> boolean	–

A supplier typically generates, creates, or produces values. Example 13.4 illustrates defining and using suppliers.

The supplier at (1) in Example 13.4 will always create a StringBuilder from the string "Howdy". The StringBuilder is not created until the get() method of the supplier is called.

```
Supplier<StringBuilder> createSB = () -> new StringBuilder("Howdy!");   // (1)
System.out.println(createSB.get());                        // Prints: Howdy!

String str = "uppercase me!";
Supplier<String> makeUppercase = () -> str.toUpperCase();              // (2)
System.out.println(makeUppercase.get());          // Prints: UPPERCASE ME!
```

The supplier at (2) returns a string that is an uppercase version of the string on which the method toUppercase() is invoked. Note that the value of the reference str is captured at (2) when the lambda expression is defined and the reference str is effectively final. Calling the get() method of the supplier results in the toUppercase() method being invoked on the String instance referenced by the reference str.

In the examples below, we use a pseudorandom number generator to define a supplier that can return integers between different ranges. The intSupplier below generates a number between 0 (inclusive) and 100 (exclusive).

```
Random numGen = new Random();

Supplier<Integer> intSupplier = () -> numGen.nextInt(100); // numGen effect. final
System.out.println(intSupplier.get());                 // Prints a number in [0, 100).
```

The generic method listBuilder() at (12) can be used to build a list of specified length, where the specified supplier generates a value every time the get() method is called at (13).

The code below builds a list of Integer with five values between 0 (inclusive) and 100 (exclusive) by calling the listBuilder() method.

```
List<Integer> intRefList = listBuilder(5, () -> numGen.nextInt(100));
```

Primitive Type Specializations of Supplier<T>

The primitive type versions of the generic supplier interface are appropriately named with a prefix to indicate the type of primitive value returned by their functional methods. For example, the integer supplier is named IntSupplier. Their functional methods are also appropriately named with a postfix to indicate the type of value they return. For example, the functional method of the IntSupplier interface is named getAsInt. These primitive type versions are *not* subinterfaces of the generic Supplier<T> interface. BooleanSupplier is the only specialization with a primitive type other than int, long, or double in the java.util.function package.

Example 13.4 also illustrates defining and using suppliers that return primitive values. Non-generic int suppliers are used in the following examples, without the overhead of boxing and unboxing int values. Calling the getAsInt() method results in the lambda expression to be executed.

```
IntSupplier intSupplier2 = () -> numGen.nextInt(100);
System.out.println(intSupplier2.getAsInt());   // Prints a number in [0, 100).
```

The method roleDice() at (14) prints statistics of rolling a many-sided dice a specified number of times using an IntSupplier as a dice roller. In the call below, a six-sided dice is rolled 100,000 times using the specified int supplier that generates numbers from 1 to 6.

```
roleDice(6, 100_000, () -> 1 + numGen.nextInt(6));
```

The reader is encouraged to work through Example 13.4, as it provides additional examples of defining and using suppliers.

Example 13.4 *Implementing Suppliers*

```
import java.time.LocalTime;
import java.util.ArrayList;
import java.util.Arrays;
import java.util.List;
import java.util.Random;
import java.util.function.DoubleSupplier;
import java.util.function.IntSupplier;
import java.util.function.Supplier;

public class SupplierClient {
  public static void main(String[] args) {

    Supplier<StringBuilder> createSB = () -> new StringBuilder("Howdy!");   // (1)
    System.out.println(createSB.get());                          // Prints: Howdy!

    String str = "uppercase me!";
    Supplier<String> makeUppercase = () -> str.toUpperCase();          // (2)
    System.out.println(makeUppercase.get());              // Prints: UPPERCASE ME!

    // Pseudorandom number generator captured and used in lambda expressions: (3)
    Random numGen = new Random();

    // Generate a number between 0 (inclusive) and 100 (exclusive):          (4)
    Supplier<Integer> intSupplier = () -> numGen.nextInt(100);
    System.out.println(intSupplier.get());          // Prints a number in [0, 100).

    // Build a list of Integers with values between 0 (incl.) and 100 (excl.): (5)
    List<Integer> intRefList = listBuilder(5, () -> numGen.nextInt(100));
    System.out.println(intRefList);

    // Build a list of StringBuilders:                                       (6)
    List<StringBuilder> stringbuilderList = listBuilder(6,
        () -> new StringBuilder("str" + numGen.nextInt(10)));         // [0, 10)
    System.out.println(stringbuilderList);

    // Build a list that has the same string:                               (7)
    List<String> stringList2 = listBuilder(4, () -> "Mini me");
    System.out.println(stringList2);
```

```java
    // Build a list of LocalTime:                                         (8)
    List<LocalTime> dateList1 = listBuilder(3, () -> LocalTime.now());
    System.out.println(dateList1);

    // Generate a number between 0 (inclusive) and 100 (exclusive):       (9)
    IntSupplier intSupplier2 = () -> numGen.nextInt(100);
    System.out.println(intSupplier2.getAsInt());   // Prints a number in [0, 100).

    // Role many-sided dice:                                             (10)
    roleDice(6, 100_000, () -> 1 + numGen.nextInt(6));
    roleDice(8, 1_000_000, () -> 1 + (int) (Math.random() * 8));

    // Build an array of doubles with values
    // between 0.0 (incl.) and 5.0 (excl.):                              (11)
    DoubleSupplier ds = () -> Math.random() * 5;                    // [0.0, 5.0)
    double[] dArray = new double[4];
    for (int i = 0; i < dArray.length; i++) {
      dArray[i] = ds.getAsDouble();
    }
    System.out.println(Arrays.toString(dArray));
  }

  /**
   * Creates a list whose elements are supplied by a Supplier<T>.
   * @param num       Number of elements to put in the list.
   * @param supplier  Supplier that supplies a value to put in the list
   * @return          List created by the method
   */
  public static <T> List<T> listBuilder(int num, Supplier<T> supplier) {   // (12)
    List<T> list = new ArrayList<>();
    for (int i = 0; i < num; ++i) {
      list.add(supplier.get());                                         // (13)
    }
    return list;
  }

  /**
   * Print statistics of rolling a many-sided dice the specified        (14)
   * number of times using an IntSupplier as dice roller.
   */
  public static void roleDice(int numOfSides, int numOfTimes,
                              IntSupplier diceRoller) {
    int[] frequency = new int[numOfSides + 1];          // frequency[0] is ignored.
    for (int i = 0; i < numOfTimes; i++) {
      ++frequency[diceRoller.getAsInt()];                               // (15)
    }
    System.out.println(Arrays.toString(frequency));
  }
}
```

Probable output from the program:

```
Howdy!
UPPERCASE ME!
83
[15, 24, 48, 3, 16]
```

```
[str8, str0, str6, str8, str6, str7]
[Mini me, Mini me, Mini me, Mini me]
[15:32:05.707, 15:32:05.707, 15:32:05.707]
54
[0, 16747, 16723, 16701, 16607, 16637, 16585]
[0, 124918, 124385, 125038, 125451, 124618, 124600, 125230, 125760]
[0.2129971975975531, 0.6933477140020566, 1.3559818256541756, 1.183773498854187]
```

13.6 Predicates

The Predicate<T> interface should be familiar by now, having been used earlier in
Example 13.1, Example 13.2, and Example 13.3.

The Predicate<T> interface defines a boolean-valued function in terms of an instance
of its type parameter T. From Table 13.5, we see that its functional method test()
has the type T -> boolean—that is, it takes an argument of type T and returns a value
of type boolean.

Table 13.5 shows all the predicate functional interfaces provided in the
java.util.function package. In addition to the three primitive type predicates recognized by their characteristic prefixes, there is also a generic two-arity specialization (BiPredicate<T,U>). Apart from the functional method test() shown for each
predicate in Table 13.5, these functional interfaces also define default methods.
Neither the primitive type predicates nor the two-arity predicate are subinterfaces
of the Predicate<T> interface.

Table 13.5 *Predicates*

Functional interface (T, U, and R are type parameters)	Functional method	Default methods unless otherwise indicated
Predicate<T>	test: T -> boolean	and(), or(), negate(), static isEqual(), static not()
IntPredicate	test: int -> boolean	and(), or(), negate()
LongPredicate	test: long -> boolean	and(), or(), negate()
DoublePredicate	test: double -> boolean	and(), or(), negate()
BiPredicate<T, U>	test: (T, U) -> boolean	and(), or(), negate()

The code below illustrates the removeIf() method from the ArrayList<E> class that
requires a predicate and removes all elements from the list that satisfy the predicate. All palindromes are removed from the list denoted by the reference words. The
method call element.test(isPalindrome) is invoked on each element of the list by
the removeIf() method.

```
Predicate<String> isPalindrome
    = str -> new StringBuilder(str).reverse().toString().equalsIgnoreCase(str);
// Before: [Otto, ADA, Alyah, Bob, HannaH, Java]
words.removeIf(isPalindrome);          // Remove all palindromes.
// After:  [Alyah, Java]
```

We can equally implement the Predicate<T> functional interface passed as an argument to the ArrayList.removeIf() method using an anonymous class:

```
// Before: [Otto, ADA, Alyah, Bob, HannaH, Java]
words.removeIf(new Predicate<String>() {
  public boolean test(String str) {
    return new StringBuilder(str).reverse().toString().equalsIgnoreCase(str);
  }
});
// After:  [Alyah, Java]
```

Similarly, the code below removes all words with even length from the list.

```
Predicate<String> isEvenLen = str -> str.length() % 2 == 0;
// Before: [Otto, ADA, Alyah, Bob, HannaH, Java]
words.removeIf(isEvenLen);             // Remove all even length words.
// After:  [ADA, Alyah, Bob]
```

And in this example, all words starting with "A" are removed from the list.

```
Predicate<String> startsWithA = str -> str.startsWith("A");
// Before: [Otto, ADA, Alyah, Bob, HannaH, Java]
words.removeIf(startsWithA);           // Remove all words that start with "A".
// After:  [Otto, Bob, HannaH, Java]
```

Composing Predicates

The predicate interfaces define default methods to compose *compound* predicates—that is, to chain together predicates with logical AND and OR operations.

```
default Predicate<T> negate()
```

Returns a predicate that represents the logical negation of this predicate.

```
default Predicate<T> and(Predicate<? super T> other)
```

Returns a composed predicate that represents a short-circuiting logical AND of this predicate and the predicate specified by the other parameter.

The other predicate is only evaluated if this predicate is true. Any exceptions thrown during the evaluation of either predicate are conveyed to the caller.

```
default Predicate<T> or(Predicate<? super T> other)
```

Returns a composed predicate that represents a short-circuiting logical OR of this predicate and the predicate specified by the other parameter.

The other predicate is only evaluated if this predicate is false. Any exceptions thrown during the evaluation of either predicate are conveyed to the caller.

```
static <T> Predicate<T> not(Predicate<? super T> target)
```
This static method returns a predicate that is the negation of the specified predicate.

```
static <T> Predicate<T> isEqual(Object targetRef)
```
This static method returns a predicate that tests if the argument in the call to the test() method and the targetRef object are equal—for example, Predicate.isEqual("Aha").test("aha"). In contrast to the Object.equals() method, this method returns true if both the argument and the targetRef object are null.

At (1) below, the isPalindrome predicate is negated to define a predicate that tests if a string is *not* a palindrome.

The method calls in a compound predicate are executed from *left to right* with *short-circuit* evaluation of the predicates. The compound predicate x.or(y).and(z) at (2) is evaluated as ((x.or(y)).and(z)), where x, y, and z are constituent predicates isEvenLen, startsWithA, and isNotPalindrome, respectively. The or() method is executed first, followed by the and() method. However, the startsWithA predicate is only evaluated if the isEvenLen predicate was false—that is, the or() method tests the isEvenLen predicate first, but not the startsWithA predicate unless the first one is false. Analogously, the isNotPalindrome predicate is only evaluated if the predicate on which the and() method is invoked is true. Note that the *same* argument is passed to all the constituent predicates that comprise a compound predicate. Schematically, the evaluation of the method call composedPredicate.test("Adda") at (3) proceeds as follows:

```
  ((x.or(y)).and(z))
= ((true.or(y)).and(z))
= (true.and(z))
= (true.and(false))
= false

// A string that is not a palindrome.
Predicate<String> isNotPalindrome = isPalindrome.negate();        // (1)

// A string with even length or starts with an 'A', and is not a palindrome.
Predicate<String> composedPredicate
    = isEvenLen.or(startsWithA).and(isNotPalindrome);             // (2)
System.out.println("Using composed predicate on \"Adda\": "
        + composedPredicate.test("Adda"));                       // (3) false.

// A string with even length, or it starts with an 'A' and is not a palindrome.
Predicate<String> conditionalOperators
    = str -> str.length() % 2 == 0 || str.startsWith("A")         // (4)
          && !(new StringBuilder(str).reverse().toString().equalsIgnoreCase(str));
System.out.println("Using conditional operators on \"Adda\": "
        + conditionalOperators.test("Adda"));                    // (5) true.
```

The evaluation should be contrasted with the predicate at (4) that is defined with the negation operator ! and the short-circuit conditional operators || and &&. Note that the evaluation order is different for the conditional operators because of the precedence rules: a || b && !c is evaluated as (a || (b && (!c))), where a, b, and c are boolean expressions `str.length() % 2 == 0`, `str.startsWith("A")`, and `(new String-Builder(str).reverse().toString().equalsIgnoreCase(str))`, respectively. Schematically, the evaluation of the method call `conditionalOperators.test("Adda")` at (5) proceeds as follows:

```
  (a || (b && (!c)))
= (a || (b && (!true)))
= (a || (b && false))
= (a || (false))
= (true || false)
= true
```

Using equality predicates is illustrated by the following examples:

```
Predicate<String> isEqualToTarget = Predicate.isEqual("Ada");
System.out.println(isEqualToTarget.test("Adda"));          // false.
System.out.println(Predicate.isEqual("Ada").test("Ada"));  // true.
System.out.println(Predicate.isEqual("null").test("null")); // true.
```

Primitive Type Specializations of Predicate<T>

The functional interfaces `IntPredicate`, `LongPredicate`, and `DoublePredicate` evaluate predicates with `int`, `long`, and `double` arguments, respectively, avoiding the overhead of boxing and unboxing of primitive values (see Table 13.5). The primitive type versions are *not* subinterfaces of the `Predicate<T>` interface.

```
Predicate<Integer> isEven = i -> i % 2 == 0;      // Operand unboxed.
System.out.println("2021 is an even number: "
              + isEven.test(2021));                // Argument boxed. false.

IntPredicate isEvenInt = i -> i % 2 == 0;          // No unboxing.
System.out.println("2021 is an even number: "
              + isEvenInt.test(2021));             // No boxing. false.
```

Each primitive type version also provides methods for negating a predicate and composing predicates using the methods for short-circuiting logical AND and OR operations.

```
IntPredicate isOddInt = isEvenInt.negate();        // Negating a predicate.
System.out.println("2020 is an odd number: "
              + isOddInt.test(2020));              // false.

IntPredicate isInRange = i -> -100 <= i && i <= 100; // Range: [-100, 100]
System.out.println("21 is in range and odd: "
              + isInRange.and(isOddInt).test(21));// true.
```

Two-Arity Specialization of Predicate<T>: BiPredicate<T, U>

The `BiPredicate<T, U>` interface is a two-arity specialization of the `Predicate<T>` interface. From Table 13.5, we see that its functional method `test()` has the type `(T, U) -> boolean`—that is, it takes two arguments of type `T` and `U`, and returns a `boolean` value. There are no primitive type specializations of the `BiPredicate<T, U>` interface.

Example 13.5 illustrates defining and using two-arity predicates. The following two-arity predicate tests if an element is a member (or is contained) in a list. The reference `filenames` refers to a list of file names.

```
BiPredicate<String, List<String>> isMember
    = (element, list) -> list.contains(element);
System.out.println(isMember.test("X-File4.doc", filenames));  // true.
```

The two-arity predicate below determines if a file name has an extension from a specified set of file extensions.

```
BiPredicate<String, Set<String>> selector = (filename, extensions) ->
    extensions.contains(filename.substring(filename.lastIndexOf('.')));
System.out.println(selector.test("Y-File.pdf", extSet));       // true.
```

Determining the file extension is generalized in Example 13.5 to a list of file names using the generic method `filterList()` which takes three parameters: a list of file names, a set of file extensions, and a two-arity predicate to do the selection. In the method `filterList()`, for each element in the list, the following method call is executed: `selector.test(element, extSet)`.

The `BiPredicate<T, U>` interface also defines default methods to compose compound two-arity predicates. As expected, the `or()` and the `and()` methods require a two-arity predicate as an argument. A simple example is given in Example 13.5 to check if the product or the sum of two numbers is equal to a given number:

```
int number = 21;
BiPredicate<Integer, Integer> isProduct = (i, j) -> i * j == number;
BiPredicate<Integer, Integer> isSum    = (i, j) -> i + j == number;
System.out.println(isProduct.or(isSum).test(7, 3));        // true.
```

Example 13.5 *Implementing the* BiPredicate<T, U> *Functional Interface*

```
import java.util.ArrayList;
import java.util.HashSet;
import java.util.List;
import java.util.Set;
import java.util.function.BiPredicate;

public class BiPredicateClient {

  public static void main(String[] args) {

    // List with filenames:
    List<String> filenames = new ArrayList<>();
    filenames.add("X-File1.pdf"); filenames.add("X-File2.exe");
    filenames.add("X-File3.fm"); filenames.add("X-File4.doc");
    filenames.add("X-File5.jpg"); filenames.add("X-File6.jpg");
    System.out.println("Filenames: " + filenames);

    // BiPredicate for membership in a list.
    BiPredicate<String, List<String>> isMember =
        (element, list) -> list.contains(element);
    System.out.println(isMember.test("X-File4.doc", filenames)); // true.
```

```java
        // Set with file extensions:
        Set<String> extSet = new HashSet<>();
        extSet.add(".pdf"); extSet.add(".jpg");
        System.out.println("Required extensions: " + extSet);

        // BiPredicate to determine if a filename has an extension from a specified
        // set of file extensions.
        BiPredicate<String, Set<String>> selector = (filename, extensions) ->
            extensions.contains(filename.substring(filename.lastIndexOf('.')));
        System.out.println(selector.test("Y-File.pdf", extSet));        // true.

        List<String> result = filterList(filenames, extSet, selector);
        System.out.println("Files with required extensions: " + result);

        int number = 21;
        BiPredicate<Integer, Integer> isProduct = (i, j) -> i * j == number;
        BiPredicate<Integer, Integer> isSum    = (i, j) -> i + j == number;
        System.out.println(isProduct.or(isSum).test(7, 3));
    }

    /**
     * Filters a list according to the criteria of the selector.
     * @param list       List to filter
     * @param extSet     Set of file extensions
     * @param selector   BiPredicate that provides the criteria for filtering
     * @return           List of elements that match the criteria
     */
    public static <E, F> List<E> filterList(List<E> list,
                                            Set<F> extSet,
                                            BiPredicate<E, Set<F>> selector) {
        List<E> result = new ArrayList<>();
        for (E element : list)
            if (selector.test(element, extSet))
                result.add(element);
        return result;
    }
}
```

Output from the program:

```
Filenames: [X-File1.pdf, X-File2.exe, X-File3.fm, X-File4.doc, X-File5.jpg, X-
File6.jpg]
true
Required extensions: [.pdf, .jpg]
true
Files with required extensions: [X-File1.pdf, X-File5.jpg, X-File6.jpg]
true
```

13.7 Consumers

The Consumer<T> functional interface represents a consumer of values. From Table 13.6, we see that its functional method accept() has the type T -> void—that is, it takes an argument of type T and returns no value (void). Typically, it performs some operation on its argument object.

Table 13.6 shows all the consumer functional interfaces, together with their functional method accept() and any default methods that are provided by the interface. There are three primitive type one-arity specializations of the Consumer<T> functional interface, recognized by their characteristic prefixes. The generic two-arity specialization (BiConsumer<T,U>) also has three two-arity primitive type specializations. Only the one-arity consumers and the two-arity generic consumer define the default method andThen().

Table 13.6 *Consumers*

Functional interface (T, U, and R are type parameters)	Functional method	Default methods
Consumer<T>	accept: T -> void	andThen()
IntConsumer	accept: int -> void	andThen()
LongConsumer	accept: long -> void	andThen()
DoubleConsumer	accept: double -> void	andThen()
BiConsumer<T, U>	accept: (T, U) -> void	andThen()
ObjIntConsumer<T>	accept: (T, int) -> void	–
ObjLongConsumer<T>	accept: (T, long) -> void	–
ObjDoubleConsumer<T>	accept: (T, double) -> void	–

Generally, a consumer performs an operation on its argument object, but does not return a value. The formatter below prints a double value with two decimal places. The type of the lambda expression is Double -> void, and the lambda expression is executed when the method accept() is invoked.

```
Consumer<Double> formatter = d -> System.out.printf("Value: %.2f%n", d);
formatter.accept(3.145);                     // Value: 3.15
```

In the code below, the resizeSB consumer resizes a StringBuilder to length 4—a more flexible resizer is presented a little later. The reverseSb consumer reverses the contents of a StringBuilder. The printSB consumer prints a StringBuilder. In each case, the type of the lambda expression is StringBuilder -> void.

```
StringBuilder sb1 = new StringBuilder("Banana");
Consumer<StringBuilder> resizeSB = sb -> sb.setLength(4);
resizeSB.accept(sb1);                        // Bana
```

```
Consumer<StringBuilder> reverseSB = sb -> sb.reverse();
reverseSB.accept(sb1);                        // anaB

Consumer<StringBuilder> printSB
    = sb -> System.out.println("StringBuilder: " + sb);
printSB.accept(sb1);                          // StringBuilder: anaB
```

The `ArrayList.forEach()` method requires a consumer that is applied to each element of the list—that is, the method call `consumer.accept(element)` is executed on each element in the list. The consumer below prints an element of the list words in lowercase.

```
// [Otto, ADA, Alya, Bob, HannaH, Java]
words.forEach(s -> System.out.print(s.toLowerCase() + " "));
// otto ada alya bob hannah java
```

The code below implements the `Consumer<String>` interface using an anonymous class which is passed as an argument to the `ArrayList.forEach()` method:

```
// [Otto, ADA, Alya, Bob, HannaH, Java]
words.forEach(new Consumer<String>() {
  public void accept(String s) {
    System.out.print(s.toLowerCase() + " ");
  }
});
// otto ada alya bob hannah java
```

The following consumer prints each element of the list words that has an even length:

```
// [Otto, ADA, Alya, Bob, HannaH, Java]
words.forEach(s -> {if (s.length() % 2 == 0) System.out.print(s + " ");});
// Otto Alya HannaH Java
```

Composing Consumers

The method `andThen()` can be used to chain together consumers to compose compound consumers. The three consumers used earlier to resize, reverse, and print a `StringBuilder` can be chained together as seen here:

```
resizeSB.andThen(reverseSB)
    .andThen(printSB).accept(new StringBuilder("Banana")); // StringBuilder: anaB
```

The constituent consumers are executed one after the other from *left to right*. Note that the reference to the `StringBuilder` instance passed to the `accept()` method is also passed to each constituent consumer.

> `default Consumer<T> andThen(Consumer<? super T> after)`
>
> Returns a composed `Consumer` that evaluates this operation first followed by the specified after operation.
>
> Any exception thrown during the evaluation of either operation aborts the evaluation of the composed operation and the exception is conveyed to the caller.

Primitive Type Specializations of Consumer<T>

From Table 13.6, we see that the non-generic functional interfaces IntConsumer, LongConsumer, and DoubleConsumer define the functional method accept() that takes an int, a long, or a double value as an argument, respectively, but does not return a value (void). The primitive type versions avoid the overhead of boxing and unboxing of primitive values. They are *not* subinterfaces of the Consumer<T> interface, and they all provide the andThen() method to compose compound primitive type consumers.

The two IntConsumers below print the square root and the square of their argument, respectively. They are chained by the andThen() method that requires an IntConsumer.

```
IntConsumer sqrt = i -> System.out.printf("%.2f%n", Math.sqrt(i));
IntConsumer sqr = i -> System.out.printf("%d%n", i * i);
sqrt.andThen(sqr).accept(15);    // 3.87
                                 // 225
```

Two-Arity Specialization of Consumer<T>: BiConsumer<T, U>

The BiConsumer<T, U> interface is a two-arity specialization of the Consumer<T> interface. From Table 13.6, we see that its functional method accept() has the type (T, U) -> void—that is, it takes two arguments of type T and type U, and does not return a value (void). The BiConsumer<T, U> interface provides the andThen() method to create compound two-arity consumers.

The following code illustrates defining and using two-arity consumers.

```
BiConsumer<String, Double> formatPrinter
   = (format, obj) -> System.out.printf(format, obj);
formatPrinter.accept("Math.PI:|%10.3f|%n", Math.PI); // Math.PI:|     3.142|
```

The java.util.Map.forEach() method requires a two-arity consumer that is applied to each entry (key, value) in the map—that is, the method call biconsumer.accept(key, value) is executed for each entry in the map. The two-arity consumer below formats and prints all entries in the map given by the reference strLenMap. The key in this map is of type String and the value is of type Integer—that is, HashMap<String, Integer>. The value is the length of the key string.

```
// Map entries (default format): {Java=4, Bob=3, Otto=4, HannaH=6, Alya=4, ADA=3}
strLenMap.forEach((key, value) -> System.out.printf("(%s:%d) ", key, value));
// (Java:4) (Bob:3) (Otto:4) (HannaH:6) (Alya:4) (ADA:3)
```

Primitive Type Specializations of BiConsumer<T, U>

Table 13.6 shows the generic functional interfaces ObjIntConsumer<T>, ObjLongConsumer<T>, and ObjDoubleConsumer<T> that are specializations of the BiConsumer<T, U> interface. The functional method accept() of these primitive type specializations takes two arguments: One is an object of type T and the other is a primitive value.

These functional interfaces are *not* subinterfaces of the BiConsumer<T, U> interface, and they do not provide default methods to chain consumers.

The code below shows a new version of resizing a StringBuilder written earlier, where the required length was hard-coded in the lambda expression definition and could not be changed. Using an ObjIntConsumer<StringBuilder>, the required length can be passed as a parameter in the definition of the lambda expression, as shown below:

```
ObjIntConsumer<StringBuilder> resizeSB2 = (sb, len) -> sb.setLength(len);
StringBuilder sb2 = new StringBuilder("bananarama");
resizeSB2.accept(sb2, 6);        // The required length passed as a parameter.
System.out.println("StringBuilder resized: " + sb2);
// StringBuilder resized: banana
```

13.8 Functions

The Function<T, R> interface represents a function or an operation that transforms an argument object to a result object, where the object types need not be the same. From Table 13.7, we see that its functional method apply() has the type T -> R—that is, it takes an argument of type T and returns a result of type R.

Table 13.7 also shows specialized functions for primitive types, together with their functional methods. They do not define any default methods.

The BiFunction<T, U, R> interface and its primitive type versions are discussed in §13.9, p. 717. The specialized versions UnaryOperator<T> and BinaryOperator<T>, which provide functions where the arguments and the result are of the same type, are discussed in §13.10, p. 720, and §13.11, p. 721, respectively.

Table 13.7 *Functions*

Functional interface (T, U, and R are type parameters)	Functional method	Default methods unless otherwise indicated
Function<T, R>	apply: T -> R	compose(), andThen(), static identity()
IntFunction<R>	apply: int -> R	–
LongFunction<R>	apply: long -> R	–
DoubleFunction<R>	apply: double -> R	–
ToIntFunction<T>	applyAsInt: T -> int	–
ToLongFunction<T>	applyAsLong: T -> long	–
ToDoubleFunction<T>	applyAsDouble: T -> double	–
IntToLongFunction	applyAsLong: int -> long	–

Table 13.7 *Functions (Continued)*

Functional interface (T, U, and R are type parameters)	Functional method	Default methods unless otherwise indicated
IntToDoubleFunction	applyAsDouble: int -> double	–
LongToIntFunction	applyAsInt: long -> int	–
LongToDoubleFunction	applyAsDouble: long -> double	–
DoubleToIntFunction	applyAsInt: double -> int	–
DoubleToLongFunction	applyAsLong: double -> long	–

Example 13.6 illustrates defining and using functions. The first lambda expression tests whether an integer is in a given range. It has the type Integer -> Boolean, compatible with the function type of the Function<Integer, Boolean> interface. Note that it returns a Boolean, as opposed to a lambda expression which implements a Predicate<T> that always returns a boolean value.

```
Function<Integer, Boolean> boolExpr = i -> 50 <= i && i < 100;
System.out.println("Boolean expression is: " + boolExpr.apply(99));
// Boolean expression is: true

Function<Integer, Double> milesToKms = miles -> 1.6 * miles;
System.out.printf("%dmi = %.2fkm%n", 24, milesToKms.apply(24));
// 24mi = 38.40km
```

The second lambda expression above converts miles to kilometers. It has the type Integer -> Double, compatible with the function type of the Function<Integer, Double> interface.

The method listBuilder() in Example 13.6 creates a list from an array by applying a Function<T, R> to each array element. The Function<T, R> is passed as an argument to the method.

```
String[] strArray = {"One", "Two", "Three", "Four"};
List<StringBuilder> sbList = listBuilder(strArray, s -> new StringBuilder(s));
System.out.println("Build StringBuilder list: " + sbList);
// Build StringBuilder list: [One, Two, Three, Four]
```

The example above creates a list of StringBuilder from an array of String. The signature of the method call can be inferred to be the following:

```
listBuilder(String[], String -> StringBuilder)
```

with the type parameters T and R in the generic type Function<T, R> inferred as String and StringBuilder, respectively, resulting in the parameterized type Function<String, StringBuilder>.

The second example creates a list of Integers from an array of Strings, where the functional interface parameter in the method call is inferred to be Function<String, Integer>.

```java
        List<Integer> intList = listBuilder(strArray, s -> s.length());
        System.out.println("Build Integer list: " + intList);
        // Build Integer list: [3, 3, 5, 4]
```

Example 13.6 *Implementing Functions*

```java
        import java.util.ArrayList;
        import java.util.List;
        import java.util.function.Function;
        import java.util.function.IntFunction;
        import java.util.function.IntToDoubleFunction;
        import java.util.function.ToIntFunction;

        public class FunctionClient {
          public static void main(String[] args) {

            // Examples of Function<T,R>:
            Function<Integer, Boolean> boolExpr = i -> 50 <= i && i < 100;
            System.out.println("Boolean expression is: " + boolExpr.apply(99));
            // Boolean expression is: true

            Function<Integer, Double> milesToKms = miles -> 1.6 * miles;
            System.out.printf("%dmi = %.2fkm%n", 24, milesToKms.apply(24));
            // 24mi = 38.40km

            // Create a list of StringBuilders from an array of Strings.
            String[] strArray = {"One", "Two", "Three", "Four"};
            List<StringBuilder> sbList = listBuilder(strArray, s -> new StringBuilder(s));
            System.out.println("Build StringBuilder list: " + sbList);
            // Build StringBuilder list: [One, Two, Three, Four]

            // Create a list of Integers from an array of Strings.
            List<Integer> intList = listBuilder(strArray, s -> s.length());
            System.out.println("Build Integer list: " + intList);
            // Build Integer list: [3, 3, 5, 4]

            /* Composing unary functions. */
            Function<String, String> f = s -> s + "-One";      // (1)
            Function<String, String> g = s -> s + "-Two";      // (2)

            // Using compose() and andThen() methods.
            System.out.println(f.compose(g).apply("Three")); // (3) Three-Two-One
            System.out.println(g.andThen(f).apply("Three")); // (4) Three-Two-One
            System.out.println(f.apply(g.apply("Three")));   // (5) Three-Two-One
            System.out.println();

            System.out.println(f.andThen(g).apply("Three")); // (6) Three-One-Two
            System.out.println(g.compose(f).apply("Three")); // (7) Three-One-Two
            System.out.println(g.apply(f.apply("Three")));   // (8) Three-One-Two
            System.out.println();

            // Examples of primitive unary functions.
            IntFunction<String> intToStr = i -> Integer.toString(i);
            System.out.println(intToStr.apply(2021));        // 2021
```

```
        ToIntFunction<String> strToInt = str -> Integer.parseInt(str);
        System.out.println(strToInt.applyAsInt("2021")); // 2021

        IntToDoubleFunction celsiusToFahrenheit = celsius -> 1.8 * celsius + 32.0;
        System.out.printf("%d Celsius = %.1f Fahrenheit%n",
                             37, celsiusToFahrenheit.applyAsDouble(37));
        // 37 Celsius = 98.6 Fahrenheit
    }

    /**
     * Create a list from an array by applying a Function to each array element.
     * @param arrayT      Array to use for elements
     * @param func        Function to apply to each array element
     * @return            List that is created
     */
    public static <T, R> List<R> listBuilder(T[] arrayT, Function<T, R> func) {
        List<R> listR = new ArrayList<>();
        for (T t : arrayT) {
            listR.add(func.apply(t));
        }
        return listR;
    }
}
```

Output from the program:

```
Boolean expression is: true
24mi = 38.40km
Build StringBuilder list: [One, Two, Three, Four]
Build Integer list: [3, 3, 5, 4]
Three-Two-One
Three-Two-One
Three-Two-One

Three-One-Two
Three-One-Two
Three-One-Two

2021
2021
37 Celsius = 98.6 Fahrenheit
```

Composing Functions

Both the default methods compose() and andThen() of the Function<T, R> interface return an instance of a Function that is created from the caller function (i.e., the function on which the method is invoked) and the argument function (i.e., the function that is passed as an argument to the method). The two methods differ in the order in which they apply the caller and the argument functions. Given two functions f and g, the compose() and the andThen() methods execute as follows:

`f.compose(g).apply(x)` emulates `f.apply(g.apply(x))` or mathematically $f(g(x))$.

`f.andThen(g).apply(x)` emulates `g.apply(f.apply(x))` or mathematically $g(f(x))$.

`f.compose(g).apply(x)` and `g.andThen(f).apply(x)` are equivalent.

The `compose()` method executes the argument function g first and executes the caller function f last. The `andThen()` method does the converse: It executes the caller function f first and executes the argument function g last. Switching the caller and the argument functions of one method in the other method gives the same result. Since the result of one function is passed as an argument to the other function, the return type of the function executed first must be compatible with the parameter type of the function executed last.

Creating compound functions with the `default` methods `compose()` and `andThen()` is illustrated by the code in Example 13.6. Functions f and g are defined at (1) and (2), respectively. The output from the program shows that the `compose()` method at (3) executes the function g first and the function f last—the same as the `andThen()` method at (4) with the functions switched and the explicit application at (5). The `andThen()` method at (6) executes the function f first and the function g last—the same as the `compose()` method at (7) with the functions switched and the explicit application at (8). The return type of the function executed first is also compatible with the parameter type of the function executed last—which is `String` for the functions f and g.

```
Function<String, String> f = s -> s + "-One";    // (1)
Function<String, String> g = s -> s + "-Two";    // (2)

System.out.println(f.compose(g).apply("Three")); // (3) Three-Two-One
System.out.println(g.andThen(f).apply("Three")); // (4) Three-Two-One
System.out.println(f.apply(g.apply("Three")));   // (5) Three-Two-One

System.out.println(f.andThen(g).apply("Three")); // (6) Three-One-Two
System.out.println(g.compose(f).apply("Three")); // (7) Three-One-Two
System.out.println(g.apply(f.apply("Three")));   // (8) Three-One-Two
```

`default <V> Function<V,R> compose(Function<? super V,? extends T> before)`

This generic method returns a composed function that first applies the `before` function to its input, and then applies this function to the result. (This function refers to the function used to invoke the method.)

Given that the type of this function is T -> R and the type of the argument function `before` is V -> T, the `compose()` method creates a compound function of type V -> R, as the function `before` is executed first and this function last.

`default <V> Function<T,V> andThen(Function<? super R,? extends V> after)`

This generic method returns a composed function that first applies this function to its input, and then applies the `after` function to the result.

Given that the type of this function is T -> R and the type of the argument function `after` is R -> V, the `andThen()` method creates a compound function of type T -> V, as this function is executed first and the function `after` last.

Any exception thrown during the evaluation of either function aborts the evaluation of the composed function and the exception is conveyed to the caller.

Primitive Type Specializations of Function<T, R>

As can be seen in Table 13.7, there are three categories of *primitive type one-arity special-izations* of the Function<T, R> interface, each distinguished by a naming scheme. Also, these primitive type one-arity specializations do not define any default methods.

- *Prim*Function<R>, where *Prim* is either Int, Long, or Double

  These one-arity generic functions have the functional method apply: *primitive* -> R, where *primitive* is an int, long, or double—the function takes an argument of primitive type and returns a result of type R.

  ```
  IntFunction<String> intToStr = i -> Integer.toString(i);
  System.out.println(intToStr.apply(2021));          // "2021"
  ```

- To*Prim*Function<T>, where *Prim* is either Int, Long, or Double

  These one-arity generic functions have the functional method applyAs*Prim*: T -> *primitive*, where *primitive* is an int, long, or double—the function takes an argument of type T and returns a result of primitive type.

  ```
  ToIntFunction<String> strToInt = str -> Integer.parseInt(str);
  System.out.println(strToInt.applyAsInt("2021")); // 2021
  ```

- *Prim₁*To*Prim₂*Function, where *Prim₁* and *Prim₂* are Int, Long, or Double, and *Prim₁* != *Prim₂*

  These one-arity non-generic functions have the functional method applyAs*Prim₂*: *primitive₁* -> *primitive₂*, where *primitive₁* and *primitive₂* are int, long, or double, and *primitive₁* != *primitive₂*—the function takes an argument of type *primitive₁* and returns a result of type *primitive₂*.

  ```
  IntToDoubleFunction celsiusToFahrenheit = celsius -> 1.8 * celsius + 32.0;
  System.out.printf("%d Celsius = %.1f Fahrenheit%n",
                  37, celsiusToFahrenheit.applyAsDouble(37));
  // 37 Celsius = 98.6 Fahrenheit
  ```

13.9 Two-Arity Specialization of Function<T, R>: BiFunction<T, U, R>

The BiFunction<T, U, R> interface is the two-arity specialization of the Function<T, R> interface. In Table 13.8, we see that its functional method apply() has the type (T, U) -> R—that is, it takes two arguments of type T and U, and returns a result of type R.

The following code illustrates defining and using two-arity functions. The two-arity function areaOfRectangle calculates the area of a rectangle.

```
BiFunction<Double, Double, Double> areaOfRectangle
    = (length, width) -> length * width;              // (Double, Double) -> Double
System.out.printf("%.2f x %.2f = %.2f%n",
                25.0, 4.0, areaOfRectangle.apply(25.0, 4.0));
// 25.00 x 4.00 = 100.00
```

Table 13.8 *Two-arity Functions*

Functional interface (T, U, and R are type parameters)	Functional method		Default methods
BiFunction<T, U, R>	apply:	(T, U) -> R	andThen()
ToIntBiFunction<T, U>	applyAsInt:	(T, U) -> int	–
ToLongBiFunction<T, U>	applyAsLong:	(T, U) -> long	–
ToDoubleBiFunction<T, U>	applyAsDouble:	(T, U) -> double	–

The two-arity function concatKeyVal below concatenates two strings and returns a new string as the result. The reference map refers to a HashMap<String, String>. The replaceAll() method called on this map takes the two-arity function concatKeyVal as a parameter, and it replaces the *value* of each entry (key, value) in the map with the result of the two-arity function applied to the entry—that is, the method call concatKeyVal.apply(key, value) is executed for each entry in the map. The apply() method is implemented by the lambda expression below, resulting in the method call key.concat(value) being executed for each entry.

```
BiFunction<String, String, String> concatKeyVal = (key, val) -> key.concat(val);
// {Dick=silver, Harriet=platinum, Tom=gold}
map.replaceAll(concatKeyVal);
// {Dick=Dicksilver, Harriet=Harrietplatinum, Tom=Tomgold}
```

It is instructive to implement and compare the two-arity function above using an anonymous class:

```
// {Dick=silver, Harriet=platinum, Tom=gold}
map.replaceAll(new BiFunction<String, String, String>() {
  public String apply(String key, String val) {
    return key.concat(val);
  }
});
// {Dick=Dicksilver, Harriet=Harrietplatinum, Tom=Tomgold}
```

Composing Two-Arity Functions

The interface BiFunction<T, U, R> provides the andThen() method for creating compound two-arity functions. Given a *two-arity function* f and a *one-arity function* g, the method evaluates the functions as follows:

f.andThen(g).apply(x, y) emulates g.apply(f.apply(x, y))—that is, the two-arity function f is executed first and the one-arity function g last.

In the example below, the functions chained by the andThen() method calls are applied from left to right, first the caller function and then the parameter function.

```
BiFunction<String, String, String> concatStr = (s1, s2) -> s1 + s2;
Function<String, String> postfix1 = s -> s + "nana";
```

```
Function<String, String> postfix2 = s -> s + "s!";
System.out.println(concatStr.andThen(postfix1).andThen(postfix2)
                .apply("I am going", " ba"));          // I am going bananas!
```

In the code below, the concatStr two-arity function is both the caller and the parameter function in the call to the andThen() method. However, the code does not compile. The reason is easy to understand: The two-arity parameter function requires *two* arguments, but the two-arity caller function can only return a *single* value. A *one-arity* function as the parameter function avoids this problem, as it can accept the single-value result of the caller function. Chaining instances of BiFunction<T, U, R> is not as straightforward as chaining instances of Function<T, R>.

```
BiFunction<String, String, String> concatTwice
            = concatStr.andThen(concatStr);           // Compile-time error!
```

```
default <V> BiFunction<T,U,V> andThen(Function<? super R,? extends V> after)
```

This generic method returns a composed two-arity function that first applies this function to its input, and then applies the specified after one-arity function to the result.

Note the type of the parameter: It is Function and not BiFunction. Given that the type of this two-arity function is (T, U) -> R and the type of the one-arity parameter function after is R -> V, the andThen() method creates a compound two-arity function of type (T, U) -> V, as this function is executed first and the one-arity function after last.

Any exception thrown during the evaluation of either function aborts the evaluation of the composed function and the exception is conveyed to the caller.

Primitive Type Specializations of BiFunction<T, U, R>

Table 13.8 shows that the BiFunction<T, U, R> interface has three *primitive type two-arity generic specializations* to int, long, and double, but they do not define any default methods for creating compound functions. The specializations are named To*Prim*BiFunction<T, U>, where *Prim* is either Int, Long, or Double. These two-arity generic functions have the functional method applyAs*Prim*: (T, U) -> *primitive*, where *primitive* is an int, long, or double—the function takes two arguments of type T and U, and returns a result of a primitive type.

In the example below, the addIntStrs two-arity function parses two strings as int values and returns the sum of the values.

```
ToIntBiFunction<String, String> addIntStrs
    = (s1, s2) -> Integer.parseInt(s1) + Integer.parseInt(s2);
System.out.println("10 + 20 = " + addIntStrs.applyAsInt("10", "20"));
// 10 + 20 = 30
```

13.10   Extending Function<T,T>: UnaryOperator<T>

Table 13.9 shows that the UnaryOperator<T> interface *extends* the Function<T, T> interface for the special case where the types of the argument and the result are the same. It inherits the functional method apply() from the Function<T, T> interface. It also inherits the default methods compose() and andThen() from its superinterface Function<T, T>, but note that these methods return a Function<T,T>, and not a UnaryOperator<T>.

Functions where the argument and the result type are the same can easily be refactored to use the UnaryOperator<T> interface.

```
UnaryOperator<Double> area = r -> Math.PI * r * r;
System.out.printf("Area of circle, radius %.2f: %.2f%n", 10.0, area.apply(10.0));
// Area of circle, radius 10.00: 314.16

UnaryOperator<Double> milesToKms = miles -> 1.6 * miles;
System.out.printf("%.2fmi = %.2fkm%n", 24.0, milesToKms.apply(24.0));
// 24.00mi = 38.40km
```

The List.replaceAll(UnaryOperator<E>) method can be used to replace each elements in the list with the result of applying the specified unary operator to that element. The method replaces all strings in the list team with their uppercase versions.

```
List<String> team = Arrays.asList("Tom", "Dick", "Harriet");
UnaryOperator<String> toUpper = str -> str.toUpperCase();
team.replaceAll(toUpper);        // [TOM, DICK, HARRIET]
```

Since the UnaryOperator<T> interface is a subinterface of the Function<T, T> interface and inherits the default methods compose() and andThen(), creating compound unary operators is no different from creating compound functions.

```
UnaryOperator<String> f = s -> s + "-One";
UnaryOperator<String> g = s -> s + "-Two";
System.out.println(f.compose(g).apply("Three")); // Three-Two-One
System.out.println(f.andThen(g).apply("Three")); // Three-One-Two
```

Table 13.9   *Unary Operators*

Functional interface (T, U, and R are type parameters)	Functional method		Default methods unless otherwise indicated
UnaryOperator<T> extends Function<T,T>	apply:	T -> T	compose(), andThen(), static identity()
IntUnaryOperator	applyAsInt:	int -> int	compose(), andThen()
LongUnaryOperator	applyAsLong:	long -> long	compose(), andThen()
DoubleUnaryOperator	applyAsDouble:	double -> double	compose(), andThen()

Primitive Type Specializations of UnaryOperator<T>

The UnaryOperator<T> interface has three *primitive type specializations* to int, long, and double. The specializations are named *Prim*UnaryOperator, where *Prim* is either Int, Long, or Double (Table 13.9). These non-generic unary operators have the functional method applyAs*Prim*: *primitive* -> *primitive*, where *primitive* is an int, long, or double—the operator takes an argument of a primitive type and returns a result of the *same* primitive type.

```
DoubleUnaryOperator celsiusToFahrenheit = celsius -> 1.8 * celsius + 32.0;
System.out.printf("%.1f Celsius = %.1f Fahrenheit%n",
                  25.0, celsiusToFahrenheit.applyAsDouble(25.0));
// 25.0 Celsius = 77.0 Fahrenheit

DoubleUnaryOperator kms = miles -> 1.6 * miles;
System.out.printf("%.2fmi = %.2fkm%n", 25.0, kms.applyAsDouble(25.0));
// 25.00mi = 40.00km
```

The primitive type unary operators define the default methods compose() and andThen() for creating compound primitive type unary operators. The semantics of these default methods are the same as what we saw earlier (p. 715).

```
IntUnaryOperator incrBy1 = i -> i + 1;
IntUnaryOperator multBy2 = i -> i * 2;
System.out.println(incrBy1.compose(multBy2).applyAsInt(4)); // 9
System.out.println(incrBy1.andThen(multBy2).applyAsInt(4)); // 10
```

13.11 Extending BiFunction<T,T,T>: BinaryOperator<T>

In Table 13.10, we see that the BinaryOperator<T> interface *extends* the BiFunction<T, T, T> interface for the special case where the types of the two arguments and the result are the same. It inherits the functional method apply() from the BiFunction<T, T, T> interface, as well as its andThen() method.

```
BinaryOperator<Double> areaOfRectangle = (length, width) -> length * width;
System.out.printf("%.2f x %.2f = %.2f%n",
                  25.0, 4.0, areaOfRectangle.apply(25.0, 4.0));
// 25.00 x 4.00 = 100.00
```

Creating compound binary operators is no different from creating compound two-arity functions using the andThen() method, where the parameter function of the method must be a unary operator or a one-arity function.

```
BinaryOperator<String> concatTwo = (s1, s2) -> s1 + s2;
UnaryOperator<String> postfix1 = s -> s + "nana";
UnaryOperator<String> postfix2 = s -> s + "s!";
System.out.println(concatTwo.andThen(postfix1).andThen(postfix2)
                .apply("I am going", " ba"));      // I am going bananas!
```

The two utility methods maxBy() and minBy() can be used to compare two elements according to a given comparator:

```
String maxStr = BinaryOperator.maxBy(String.CASE_INSENSITIVE_ORDER)
                              .apply("aha", "Madonna");          // Madonna
String minStr = BinaryOperator.minBy(String.CASE_INSENSITIVE_ORDER)
                              .apply("aha", "Madonna");          // aha
```

Table 13.10 *Binary Operators*

Functional interface (T, U, and R are type parameters)	Functional method		Default methods unless otherwise indicated
BinaryOperator<T> extends BiFunction<T,T,T>	apply:	(T, T) -> T	andThen(), static maxBy(), static minBy()
IntBinaryOperator	applyAsInt:	(int, int) -> int	–
LongBinaryOperator	applyAsLong:	(long, long) -> long	–
DoubleBinaryOperator	applyAsDouble:	(double, double) -> double	–

The BinaryOperator<T> interface also provides two utility methods to create binary operators for comparing two elements according to a given comparator:

static <T> BinaryOperator<T> maxBy(Comparator<? super T> comparator)

Returns a BinaryOperator which returns the greater of two elements according to the specified comparator.

static <T> BinaryOperator<T> minBy(Comparator<? super T> comparator)

Returns a BinaryOperator which returns the lesser of two elements according to the specified comparator.

Primitive Type Specializations of BinaryOperator<T>

Table 13.10 shows that the BinaryOperator<T> interface has three *primitive type specializations* to int, long, and double. The specializations are named *Prim*BinaryOperator, where *Prim* is either an Int, Long, or Double (Table 13.10). These primitive type binary operators have the functional method applyAs*Prim*: (*primitive*, *primitive*) -> *primitive*, where *primitive* is an int, long, or double—the operator takes two arguments of a primitive type and returns a result of the same primitive type.

```
DoubleBinaryOperator areaOfRectangle2 = (length, width) -> length * width;
System.out.printf("%.2f x %.2f = %.2f%n",
                  25.0, 4.0, areaOfRectangle2.applyAsDouble(25.0, 4.0));
// 25.00 x 4.00 = 100.00
```

13.12 Currying Functions

The functional interfaces in the `java.util.function` package define functional methods that are either one-arity or two-arity methods. For higher arity functional methods, one recourse is to define functional interfaces whose functional method has the desired arity. The functional interface below defines a three-arity functional method—that is, it takes three arguments.

```
@FunctionalInterface
interface TriFunction<T, U, V, R> {
  R compute(T t, U u, V v);              // (T, U ,V) -> R
}
```

The `TriFunction<T, U, V, R>` interface can be used to define a lambda expression to calculate the volume of a cuboid.

```
// (Double, Double, Double) -> Double
TriFunction<Double, Double, Double, Double> cubeVol = (x, y, z) -> x * y * z;
System.out.println(cubeVol.compute(10.0,  20.0,  30.0)); // 6000.0
```

Another recourse is to apply the technique of *currying* to transform a multi-argument function into a chain of lower arity functions.

The process of currying is illustrated by implementing the three-arity lambda expression above for calculating the volume of a cuboid. Step 1 below derives *a chain of three one-arity functions* that will together compute the volume of a cuboid. At (1), parentheses are used explicitly to show the nested lambdas that *define* each of the one-arity functions—grouping is from right to left. The nesting of the one-arity functions is compatible with the nesting of the types in the parameterized functional interface type. An outer function returns its immediate inner function. Step 2 supplies the x argument. This is called *partial application*, as it returns a function where the remaining arguments y and z are still unknown. Step 3 is also partial application, only the y argument is supplied, returning a function where now only the z argument is unknown. Only at Step 4, when the z argument is supplied at (2), can the final one-arity function be executed. The application of the individual one-arity functions can also be chained as shown at (3), without going through the intermediate steps.

```
// Step 1:
// Partial application: double -> DoubleFunction<DoubleUnaryOperator>
DoubleFunction<DoubleFunction<DoubleUnaryOperator>> uniFuncA
    = (x -> (y -> (z -> x * y * z)));              // (1)

// Step 2:
// Partial application: double -> DoubleUnaryOperator
DoubleFunction<DoubleUnaryOperator> uniFuncB
    = uniFuncA.apply(10.0);                        // 10.0 * y * z

// Step 3:
// Partial application: double -> double
DoubleUnaryOperator uniOpC = uniFuncB.apply(20.0); // 10.0 * 20.0 * z
```

```
// Step 4:
// Application:
double vol1 = uniOpC.applyAsDouble(30.0);         // (2) 10.0 * 20.0 * 30.0 = 6000.0
double vol2 = uniFuncA.apply(10.0).apply(20.0).applyAsDouble(30.0); // (3) 6000.0
```

The sequence in which the arguments are supplied in the currying process is irrelevant, and more than one argument can be supplied in each step in accordance with the target type. Each step is a partial application, except for the last one which executes the final function. The process ensures that the number of unknown arguments decreases in each step.

Here we have provided just a taste of currying, but it is a topic worth exploring further. The technique bears the name of Haskell Curry, a famous mathematician and logician of the twentieth century.

13.13 Method and Constructor References

So far we have seen that a Java program can use primitive values, objects (including arrays), and lambda expressions. In this section, we introduce the fourth kind of value that a Java program can use, called *method references* (and their specializations to constructors and array construction). As we shall see, there is a very tight relationship between method references and lambda expressions.

Quite often the body of a lambda expression is just a call to an existing method. The lambda expression simply supplies the arguments required to call and execute the method. In such cases, method references can provide a more concise notation than a lambda expression, potentially increasing the readability of the code. The following code illustrates the relationship between the two notations.

```
// String -> void
Consumer<String> outLE = obj -> System.out.println(obj); // (1a)
Consumer<String> outMR = System.out::println;            // (1b)
outMR.accept("Save trees!");                             // (2)
// Calls System.out.println("Save trees!") that prints: Save trees!
```

The lambda expression at (1a):

```
obj -> System.out.println(obj)
```

can be replaced by the *method reference* at (1b):

```
System.out::println
```

The method reference above is composed of the *target reference* (System.out) on which the method is invoked and the *name of the method* (println), separated by the double-colon (::) delimiter:

```
targetReference::methodName
```

Note that the target reference precedes the double-colon (::) delimiter, and no arguments are specified after the method name. Table 13.11 summarizes the variations in the definition of a method reference which we will discuss in this section.

Table 13.11 *Method and Constructor References*

Purpose of method reference	Lambda expression/ Method reference syntax	Comment

Designate a static method	`(args) -> RefType.staticMethod(args)`
	
	`RefType::staticMethod`	

Designate an instance method of a *bounded* instance	`(args) -> expr.instanceMethod(args)`
	
	`expr::instanceMethod`
		Target reference provided by the method reference.

Designate an instance method of an *unbounded* instance	`(arg0,rest)->arg0.instanceMethod(rest)`
	
	`RefType::instanceMethod`
		arg0 is of RefType. Target reference provided later when the method is invoked.

Designate a constructor	`(args) -> new ClassType(args)`
	
	`ClassType::new`
		Deferred creation of an instance.

Designate array construction	`arg -> new ElementType[arg][]...[]`
	
	`ElementType[][]...[]::new`
		Deferred creation of an array.

A method reference must have a compatible target type that is a functional interface—a method reference implements an instance of a functional interface, analogous to a lambda expression. The compiler does similar type checking as for lambda expressions to determine whether the method reference is compatible with a given target type.

At (1b) above, the function type of the target type `Consumer<String>` is `String -> void`. The compiler can infer from the target type that the type of the argument passed to the `println()` method must be `String`. The type of the method reference is defined by the type of the method specified in its definition. In this case, the type of the `println()` method is `String -> void`, as it accepts a `String` parameter and does not return a value. Thus the target type `Consumer<String>` is compatible with the method reference `System.out::println`. The reference `outMR` is assigned the value of the method reference at (1b).

Analogous to single-method lambda expressions, method references when executed result in the execution of the method specified in its definition. The instance method `println()` at (1b) accepts a single `String` argument. This argument is passed to the method when the functional method `accept()` of the target type is invoked on the reference `outMR`, as shown at (2). The method `println()` is invoked on the same object (denoted by `System.out`) every time this method reference is executed.

Execution of the lambda expression at (1a) will give the same result. Not surprisingly, a method reference and its corresponding single-method lambda expression are semantically equivalent.

Static Method References

Sometimes the lambda body of a lambda expression is just a call to a static *method*. The lambda expression at (1a) calls the static method now() in the class java.time.LocalDate to obtain the current date from the system clock.

```
Supplier<LocalDate> dateNowLE = () -> LocalDate.now();  // (1a) Lambda expression
```

The lambda expression has the type () -> LocalDate, and not surprisingly, it is also the type of the static method now() which takes no arguments and returns an instance of the LocalDate class. The method type is compatible with the function type of the target type—that is, it is compatible with the type of the functional method get() of the parameterized functional interface Supplier<LocalDate>. The compiler can infer from the context that the type of the static method is compatible with the target type of the functional interface. In such a case, the lambda expression can be replaced by a *static method reference*:

```
Supplier<LocalDate> dateNowMR = LocalDate::now;           // (1b) Method reference
```

The double-colon delimiter (::) separates the reference type name (class LocalDate) from the static method name (now) in the syntax of the static method reference.

Analogous to a lambda expression, a method reference can be used as a value in an assignment, passed as an argument in a method or constructor call, returned in a return statement, or cast with the cast operator (p. 733). Its execution is deferred until the functional method of its target type is invoked, as at (2).

```
LocalDate today = datenowMR.get();     // (2) Method reference at (1b) executed.
System.out.println(today.format(DateTimeFormatter.ISO_DATE)); // 2021-03-01
```

The following rule can be helpful in converting between a lambda expression and a static method reference:

A lambda expression of the form

```
(args) -> RefType.staticMethod(args)
```

is semantically equivalent to the *static method reference*:

```
RefType::staticMethod
```

where RefType is the *name* of a class, an enum type, or an interface that defines the static method whose *name* staticMethod is specified after the double-colon (::) delimiter.

Arguments are generally not specified in the method reference, and any parameters required by the method are determined by the target type of the context.

```
// String -> Integer
Function<String, Integer> strToIntLE = s -> Integer.parseInt(s); // (3a)
Function<String, Integer> strToIntMR = Integer::parseInt;        // (3b)
```

```
System.out.println(strToIntMR.apply("100"));                          // (4)
// Calls Integer.parseInt("100") that returns the int value 100 which is boxed
// into an Integer.
```

The static method `Integer.parseInt()` in the lambda body at (3a) takes one argument. Its type is `String -> Integer`. Using the one-arity `Function<String, Integer>` as the target type is appropriate as its function type is also `String -> Integer`. We can convert the lambda expression at (3a) to the static method reference shown at (3b). Note that no arguments are specified at (3b). The argument is passed to the static method at a later time when the functional method `apply()` of the functional interface is invoked, as demonstrated at (4).

Similarly, we can define static method references whose static method takes two arguments. A two-arity function or a binary operator from the `java.util.function` package can readily serve as the target type, as demonstrated by the following examples. Note that the static method `Math.min()` is overloaded, but the target type of the context determines which method will be executed. The type of the method `min()` at (5) is different than the type at (6). Analogous to lambda expressions, the same method reference can have different target types depending on the context.

```
// (double, double) -> double
DoubleBinaryOperator minDoubleLE = (x, y) -> Math.min(x, y);
DoubleBinaryOperator minDoubleMR = Math::min;            // (5)
System.out.println(minDoubleMR.applyAsDouble(20.0, 30.0));
// Calls Math.min(20.0, 30.0) that returns the double value 20.0.

// (int, int) -> (int)
IntBinaryOperator minIntLE = (x, y) -> Math.min(y, y);
IntBinaryOperator minIntMR = Math::min;                  // (6)
System.out.println(minIntMR.applyAsInt(20, 30));
// Calls Math.min(20, 30) that returns the int value 20.
```

If the static method requires more that than two arguments, we can either define new functional interfaces with the appropriate arity for their functional method, or use the currying technique (p. 723).

Bounded Instance Method References

When the body of a lambda expression is a call to an *instance method*, the method reference specified depends on whether the object on which the instance method is invoked exists or not at the time the method reference is defined.

In the code below, the reference sb is declared and initialized at (1). It is effectively final when accessed in the lambda expression at (2a). The reference value of the reference sb is *captured* by the lambda expression. When the lambda expression is executed at a later time, the `reverse()` method is executed on the object denoted by the reference sb. In this case, the *bounded instance method reference* is simply the reference and the instance method name, separated by the double-colon delimiter, as shown at (2b). The bounded instance method reference at (2b) can replace the lambda expression at (2a). It is executed when the functional method `get()` of the parameterized functional interface `Supplier<StringBuilder>` is called, as shown at (3).

```
StringBuilder sb = new StringBuilder("!em esreveR");        // (1)
// () -> StringBuilder
Supplier<StringBuilder> sbReverserLE = () -> sb.reverse();  // (2a)
Supplier<StringBuilder> sbReverserMR = sb::reverse;         // (2b)
System.out.println(sbReverserMR.get());                     // (3)
// Calls sb.reverse() that returns the StringBuilder with character sequence
// "Reverse me!".
```

The case where the object on which the instance method is executed does not exist when the method reference is defined, but will be supplied when the method reference is executed, requires an *unbounded* instance method reference (p. 729).

The following rule can be used for converting between a lambda expression and a bounded instance method reference:

A lambda expression of the form

```
(args) -> expr.instanceMethod(args)
```

is semantically equal to the *bounded instance method reference*:

```
expr::instanceMethod
```

where expr is an expression that evaluates to a reference value that is captured by the bounded instance method reference and becomes the *target reference* for the bounded instance method reference.

Any reference involved in the evaluation of expr must be effectively final, and is captured by the bounded instance method reference. The target reference represented by expr is separated from the instance method name by the double-colon delimiter. The target reference is fixed when the bounded instance method reference is defined. The instance method is invoked on the object denoted by the target reference when the method reference is executed at a later time, and any arguments required by the instance method are passed at the same time.

Given an ArrayList<String> denoted by the reference words, we can pass the method reference System::println to the forEach() method of the ArrayList<E> class in order to print each element of the list. The method takes a consumer as an argument, and the type of the object to print is inferred from the element type of the list.

```
words.forEach(obj -> System.out.println(obj));
words.forEach(System.out::println);
```

The syntax of the bounded instance method reference where the instance method has more than one argument is no different. In the code below, the replace() method of the String class has two arguments. Its type is (String, String) -> String, the same as the function type of the target type BinaryOperator<String>. The target reference is the reference str that is defined at (4). It is effectively final when accessed in the code, and its reference value is captured at (5b) where the method reference is defined. The method replaces each occurrence of s1 in str with s2. The arguments are passed to the method when the functional method apply() of the target type BinaryOperator<String> is executed, as shown at (6).

```
String str = "Java Jive";                                    // (4)
// (String, String) -> String
```

```java
BinaryOperator<String> replaceOpLE = (s1, s2) -> str.replace(s1, s2);  // (5a)
BinaryOperator<String> replaceOpMR = str::replace;                      // (5b)
System.out.println(replaceOpMR.apply("Jive", "Jam"));                   // (6)
// Calls str.replace("Jive", "Jam") that returns the string "Java Jam".
```

In a *non-static* context, the final references this and super can also be used as the target reference of a bounded instance method reference.

```java
Predicate<String> p1 = s -> this.equals(s);     // String -> boolean
Predicate<String> p2 = this::equals;            // String -> boolean
Supplier<String> s1 = () -> super.toString();   // () -> String
Supplier<String> s2 = super::toString;          // () -> String
```

Unbounded Instance Method References

In the case of an unbounded instance method reference, the target reference is determined when the method reference is executed, as it is the first argument passed to the method reference. This is embodied in the following rule:

A lambda expression of the form

```java
(arg0, rest) -> arg0.instanceMethod(rest)
```

is semantically equivalent to the *unbounded instance method reference*:

```java
RefType::instanceMethod
```

where RefType is the reference type of the target reference arg0. The names of the reference type and the instance method are separated by the double-colon (::) delimiter.

The instance method is invoked on the object denoted by the target reference arg0 (i.e., the first argument) when the method reference is executed, and any remaining arguments are passed to the instance method at the same time.

In the code below, the type of the unbounded instance method reference String::length at (1) is String -> int, the same as the function type of the target type ToIntFunction<String>. Invoking the functional method applyAsInt() on the reference lenMR results in the method length() being invoked on the string "Java" that was passed as a parameter.

```java
// String -> int
ToIntFunction<String> lenLE = s -> s.length();
ToIntFunction<String> lenMR = String::length;          // (1)
System.out.println(lenMR.applyAsInt("Java"));          // 4
// Calls "Java".length() that returns the int value 4.
```

The static method listBuilder() in Example 13.6, p. 714, creates a list from an array by applying a Function<T, R> to each array element. An instance of the Function<T, R> is passed as a parameter to the method. Both lines of code below create a list of Integer from an array of String, where the functional interface parameter in the method call is inferred to be Function<String, Integer>. The method length() is executed on the first argument of the unbounded instance method reference—that is, on each String element of the list.

```
List<Integer> intList1 = listBuilder(strArray, s -> s.length()); // Lambda expr.
List<Integer> intList2 = listBuilder(strArray, String::length);  // Method ref.
```

The code below illustrates the case where the unbounded instance method reference String::concat at (2) requires two arguments. Its target type is BinaryOperator<String> that has the function type (String, String) -> String. The instance method concat() is invoked on the first argument, and the second argument is passed to the method as a parameter.

```
// (String, String) -> String
BinaryOperator<String> concatOpLE = (s1, s2) -> s1.concat(s2);
BinaryOperator<String> concatOpMR = String::concat;            // (2)
System.out.println(concatOpMR.apply("Java", " Jive"));        // Java Jive
// Calls "Java".concat(" Jive") that returns the string "Java Jive".
```

The code below illustrates using parameterized types in method references. At (3), the type of the argument of the generic interface List<T> in the method reference is inferred from the context to be String. At (4), the type of the argument is explicitly specified to be String. This can be necessary if the compiler cannot infer it from the context. The type of the List::contains instance method reference is (List<String>, String) -> boolean, which is compatible with the function type of the parameterized functional interface BiPredicate<List<String>, String>.

```
// (List<String>, String) -> boolean
BiPredicate<List<String>, String> containsLE
    = (list, element) -> list.contains(element);
BiPredicate<List<String>, String> containsMR1 = List::contains;          // (3)
BiPredicate<List<String>, String> containsMR2 = List<String>::contains;  // (4)
System.out.println(containsMR2.test(words, "BOB"));  // words is a List<String>.
// Calls words.contains("BOB") that returns a boolean value.
```

If the method in the unbounded instance method reference requires several arguments, compatible target types can be defined by either defining new functional interfaces with the appropriate arity for their functional method, or applying the currying technique (p. 723).

Constructor References

A constructor reference is similar to a static method reference, but with the keyword new instead of the static method name, signifying that a constructor of the specified class should be executed. Its purpose of course is to instantiate the class.

We can convert between a constructor reference and a lambda expression using the following rule:

A lambda expression of the form

```
(args) -> new ClassType(args)
```

is semantically equivalent to the *constructor reference*:

```
ClassType::new
```

where ClassType is the name of the class that should be instantiated. The class name and the keyword new are separated by the double-colon (::) delimiter.

Which constructor of ClassType is executed depends on the target type of the context, since it determines the arguments that are passed to the constructor.

Execution of the constructor reference sbCR defined at (1) results in the zero-argument constructor of the StringBuilder class to be executed, as evident from the type of the constructor reference.

```java
// () -> StringBuilder
Supplier<StringBuilder> sbLE = () -> new StringBuilder();
Supplier<StringBuilder> sbCR = StringBuilder::new;            // (1)
StringBuilder sbRef = sbCR.get();
// Calls new StringBuilder() to create an empty StringBuilder instance.
```

However, execution of the constructor reference sb4 defined at (2) results in the constructor with the String parameter to be executed, as evident from the type of the constructor reference. The target types at (1) and (2) are different. The target type determines which constructor of the StringBuilder class is executed.

```java
// String -> StringBuilder
Function<String, StringBuilder> sb3 = s -> new StringBuilder(s);
Function<String, StringBuilder> sb4 = StringBuilder::new;     // (2)
System.out.println(sb4.apply("Build me!"));                  // Build me!
// Calls new StringBuilder("Build me!") to create a StringBuilder instance
// based on the string "Build me!".
```

The following code illustrates passing two arguments to a constructor using an appropriate target type—in this case, a two-arity function—that ensures applicable arguments are passed to the constructor.

```java
// (String, String) -> Locale
BiFunction<String, String, Locale> locConsLE
    = (language, country) -> new Locale(language, country);
BiFunction<String, String, Locale> locConsCR = Locale::new;
System.out.println(locConsCR.apply("en","US"));             // en_US
// Calls new Locale("en", "US") to create a Locale instance with the specified
// parameter values.
```

Note that the constructor reference is *defined* first without any instance being created, and its execution is deferred until later when the functional method of its target type is invoked.

Array Constructor References

Array constructor reference is specialization of the constructor reference for creating arrays. We can convert between an array constructor reference and a lambda expression using the following rule:

A lambda expression of the form

```java
arg -> new ElementType[arg][]...[]
```

is semantically equivalent to the *array constructor reference*:

```java
ElementType[][]...[]::new
```

The array type and the keyword new are separated by the double-colon (::) delimiter. The ElementType is designated with the necessary pairs of square brackets ([]) to indicate that it is an array type of a specific number of dimensions. Only the length of the *first* dimension of the array can be created using an array constructor reference. As one would expect, the elements are initialized to the default value for the element type.

The array constructor reference at (1) will create a simple array of element type int. The target type IntFunction<int[]> is compatible with the type of the array constructor reference (int -> int[]). The array of int created at (2) has length 4, where each element has the default value 0.

```
// int -> int[]
IntFunction<int[]> intArrConsLE = n -> new int[n];
IntFunction<int[]> intArrConsCR = int[]::new;                    // (1)
int[] intArr = intArrConsCR.apply(4);                           // (2)
// Creates an int array of length 4.
```

In the code below, we can define a lambda expression to create a two-dimensional array that takes two arguments. However, this is *not* possible using an array constructor reference, as only the length of the first dimension can be passed to an array constructor reference. The line at (3) will not compile, since the target type ((Integer, Integer) -> int[][]) is not compatible with the type of the array constructor reference (int -> int[][]).

```
// (int, int) -> int[][]
BiFunction<Integer, Integer, int[][]> twoDimArrConsLE1 = (n, m) -> new int[n][m];
// BiFunction<Integer, Integer, int[][]> twoDimArrConsCR1
//        = int[][]:: new;                                       // (3) Compile-time error!
```

It is only possible to define an array constructor reference to create the length of the first dimension of an array, regardless of how many dimensions it has. This is illustrated by the array constructor reference at (4), which creates a two-dimensional array where only the first dimension is constructed—keeping in mind that in Java, multidimensional arrays are implemented as arrays of arrays. The code at (5) returns an array with three rows, where each row is initialized to the null value. Individual arrays can be constructed and stored in the two-dimensional array, as shown at (6).

```
// int -> int[][]
IntFunction<int[][]> twoDimArrConsLE = n -> new int[n][];
IntFunction<int[][]> twoDimArrConsCR = int[][]::new;            // (4)
int[][] twoDimIntArr1 = twoDimArrConsCR.apply(3);              // (5)
// [null, null, null]
for (int i = 0; i < twoDimIntArr1.length; ++i)
  twoDimIntArr1[i] = intArrConsCR.apply(i+1);                   // (6) Calls (1).
// [[0], [0, 0], [0, 0, 0]]
```

The example below illustrates constructing an array of objects. The procedure is no different from constructing arrays of primitive values, as explained above. The array returned by the code at (7) has five elements, where each element is initialized to the null value.

```
// int -> StringBuilder[]
IntFunction<StringBuilder[]> sbaConsLE = n -> new StringBuilder[n];
IntFunction<StringBuilder[]> sbaConsCR = StringBuilder[]::new;
StringBuilder[] sbArr2 = sbaConsCR.apply(5);                      // (7)
// [null, null, null, null, null]
```

Java does not allow creation of generic arrays, as demonstrated by the declaration statement at (8), where an attempt is made to construct an array of formal parameter type A (§11.13, p. 627). This can be overcome by using either a lambda expression or an array constructor reference whose target type is a parameterization of IntFunction<A[]>, and which is passed to the generic method createArray() below, together with the required array length, to create an array of a specific type.

```
public static <A> A[] createArray(int length, IntFunction<A[]> creator) {
//A[] arr = new A[length];        // (8) Cannot create generic array!
   return creator.apply(length);  // Lambda expression or
                                   // array constructor reference executed.
}
```

The code below calls the generic method createArray() with a lambda expression and an array constructor reference at (9) and (10), respectively, to create a String array of length 5. The target type in both cases is parameterized functional interface IntFunction<String[]>.

```
// n -> String[]
String[] strArrLE = createArray(5, n -> new String[n]); // (9)
String[] strArrACE = createArray(5, String[]::new);     // (10)
```

13.14 Contexts for Defining Lambda Expressions

In this section, we summarize the main contexts that can provide target types for lambda expressions and method references.

Declaration and Assignment Statements

Ample examples of defining lambda expressions and method references in this context have been presented throughout this chapter. As we have seen earlier, the target type is inferred from the type of the assignment target—that is, the functional interface type being assigned to on the left-hand side of the assignment operator.

```
DoubleFunction cToF = x -> 1.8 * x + 32.0;           // double -> double
ToIntFunction<String> lenFunc1 = s -> s.length();    // String -> int
ToIntFunction<String> lenFunc2 = String::length;     // String -> int
lenFunc1 = s -> Integer.parseInt(s);                 // String -> int
lenFunc2 = Integer::parseInt;                         // String -> int
```

Method and Constructor Calls

We have seen several examples where a lambda expression is passed as an argument in a method or constructor call. The target type is the functional interface type of the corresponding formal parameter.

```
List<Integer> numbers = Arrays.asList(1, 2, 3);
numbers.forEach(i -> System.out.println(i));   // Target type: Consumer<Integer>
numbers.forEach(System.out::println);
```

Expressions in return Statements

The expression in a return statement can define a lambda expression (or a method reference) whose target type is the return type of the method. The method below returns a function of type int -> int:

```
static IntUnaryOperator createLinearFormula(int a, int b) {
    return x -> a * x + b;        // int -> int
}

// Client code:
IntUnaryOperator y = createLinearFormula(10, 5);   // 10 * x + 5
y.applyAsInt(2);                                   // 25
```

Ternary Conditional Expressions

For lambda expressions defined in a ternary conditional expression, the target type is inferred from the context of the ternary conditional expression.

In the first ternary conditional expression below, the target type for the lambda expressions that are operands is inferred from the target of the assignment statement, which happens to be an IntUnaryOperator interface.

```
int ii = 10;
IntUnaryOperator iFunc1 = ii % 2 == 0 ? i -> i * 2 : j -> j + 1;   // int -> int
iFunc1.applyAsInt(4);                                             // 8
//IntUnaryOperator iFunc2 = ii % 2 == 0 ? i -> i * 2
//                        : s -> Integer.parseInt(s);   // Compile-time error!
```

In the second ternary conditional expression above, the code does not compile because the type String -> int of the lambda expression that is the second operand is not compatible with the type int -> int of the assignment target.

Cast Expressions

The context of a cast expression can provide the target type for a lambda expression or a method reference.

In the two statements below, the cast provides the target type of the lambda expression. Note that the textual lambda expressions are identical, but their target types are different.

```
System.out.println(((IntUnaryOperator) i -> i * 2).applyAsInt(10));        // 20
System.out.println(((DoubleUnaryOperator) i -> i * 2).applyAsDouble(10.0));// 20.0
```

The first statement below does not compile, as the Object class is not a functional interface and therefore cannot provide a target type. In the second statement, the cast provides the target type of the constructor expression. The type Function<String, StringBuilder> is a subtype of the supertype Object, and the assignment is allowed.

```
// Object obj1 = StringBuilder::new;                    // Compile-time error!
Object obj2 = (Function<String, StringBuilder>) StringBuilder::new;
```

In the code below, the instanceof operator at (1) is used to guarantee that at runtime the cast will succeed at (2) and the lambda expression can be executed at (3). Without the instanceof operator, the cast at (2) will be allowed at compile time, but a resounding ClassCastException will be thrown at runtime, as DoubleUnaryOperator and IntUnaryOperator are not related types. In the code below, the body of the if statement is not executed.

```
Object uFunc1 = (IntUnaryOperator) i -> i * 2;
if (uFunc1 instanceof DoubleUnaryOperator) {            // (1) false
  DoubleUnaryOperator uFunc2 = (DoubleUnaryOperator) uFunc1;   // (2)
  uFunc2.applyAsDouble(10.0);                           // (3)
}
```

Nested Lambda Expressions

When lambda expressions are nested, the context of the outer lambda expressions can provide the target type for the inner lambda expressions. This typically occurs when currying functions.

```
Supplier<Supplier<String>> f = () -> () -> "Hi";
```

The target type for the nested lambda expressions is inferred from the context, which is an assignment statement to a reference of type Supplier<Supplier<String>>. The inner lambda expression () -> "Hi" is inferred to be of target type Supplier<String>, as its type () -> String is compatible with the function type of this target type. The outer lambda expression is then inferred to have the type () -> Supplier<String> which is compatible with the target type Supplier<Supplier<String>>.

 Review Questions

13.4   Given the following code:

```
import java.util.*;
public class Test13RQ5 {
  public static void main(String[] args) {
    List<String> values = new ArrayList<>(List.of("ONE","TWO","THREE","FOUR"));
    values.removeIf(s -> s.length() == 3);
    int sum = 0;
    for (String value: values) {
      sum += value.length();
    }
    System.out.println(sum);
  }
}
```

What is the result?

Select the one correct answer.

(a) 3

(b) 6

(c) 9

(d) The program will throw an exception at runtime.

(e) The program will fail to compile.

13.5　Given the following code:

```java
import java.util.*;
public class Test13RQ6 {
  public static void main(String[] args) {
    List<String> values
        = new ArrayList<>(List.of("ANNA","JANE","ALICE","JOHN"));
    values.removeIf(s -> s.toLowerCase().startsWith("a"));
    System.out.println(values);
  }
}
```

What is the result?

Select the one correct answer.

(a) [jane, john]

(b) [anna, alice]

(c) [JANE, JOHN]

(d) [ANNA, ALICE]

(e) [ANNA, JANE, ALICE, JOHN]

(f) [anna, jane, alice, john]

(g) The program will compile, but it will not produce any output when run.

(h) The program will throw an exception at runtime.

(i) The program will fail to compile.

13.6　Given the following code:

```java
import java.util.*;
public class Test13RQ8 {
  public static void main(String[] args) {
    List<String> values
        = new ArrayList<>(List.of("ANNA","JANE","ALICE","JOHN"));
    String s = values.get(0).substring(0,1);
    values.removeIf(s -> s.toLowerCase().startsWith(s));
    values.forEach(s -> System.out.print(s + " "));
  }
}
```

What is the result?

Select the one correct answer.

(a) jane john

(b) anna alice

(c) JANE JOHN

(d) ANNA ALICE

(e) ANNA JANE ALICE JOHN
(f) anna jane alice john
(g) The program will compile, but it will not produce any output when run.
(h) The program will throw an exception at runtime.
(i) The program will fail to compile.

13.7   Given the following code:

```
import java.util.*;
import java.util.function.*;
public class Test13RQ9 {
  public static void main(String[] args) {
    List<String> values
        = new ArrayList<>(List.of("PLOT","FLOP","LOOP","LEAP"));
    Predicate<String> filter1 = s -> s.contains("O");
    Predicate<String> filter2 = s -> s.endsWith("P");
    values.removeIf(filter1.and(filter2).negate());
    System.out.println(values);
  }
}
```

What is the result?
Select the one correct answer.

(a) [LEAP]
(b) [PLOT]
(c) [FLOP, LOOP]
(d) [PLOT, FLOP, LOOP]
(e) [PLOT, FLOP, LOOP, LEAP]
(f) The program will compile, but it will not produce any output when run.
(g) The program will throw an exception at runtime.
(h) The program will fail to compile.

13.8   Given the following code:

```
import java.util.*;
import java.util.function.*;
public class Test13RQ10 {
  public static void main(String[] args) {
    List<String> values = Arrays.asList("ALICE","BOB","JOHN","JANE");
    UnaryOperator<String> f1 = v1 -> v1.substring(0,1).toUpperCase();
    UnaryOperator<String> f2 = v2 -> v2.substring(1).toLowerCase();
    UnaryOperator<String> f3 = f1.compose(f2);
    values.replaceAll(f3);
    System.out.println(values);
  }
}
```

What is the result?
Select the one correct answer.

(a) [Alice, Bob, John, Jane]
(b) [aLICE, bOB, jOHN, jANE]

(c) The program will throw an exception at runtime.

(d) The program will fail to compile.

13.9 Given the following code:

```
import java.util.*;
import java.util.function.*;
public class Test13RQ11 {
  public static void main(String[] args) {
    List<String> values = Arrays.asList("ALICE","BOB","JOHN","JANE");
    UnaryOperator<String> f1 = v -> v.toLowerCase();
    values.replaceAll(f1);
    Consumer<String> c1 = s -> s = s.substring(0,1).toUpperCase();
    Consumer<String> c2 = s -> System.out.print(s + " ");
    values.forEach(c1.andThen(c2));
  }
}
```

What is the result?

Select the one correct answer.

(a) `Alice Bob John Jane`

(b) `alice bob john jane`

(c) `A B J J`

(d) The program will throw an exception at runtime.

(e) The program will fail to compile.

13.10 Which method references are equivalent to lambda expressions at (1) and (2) in the following code?

```
import java.util.*;
class Test {
  private List<Integer> values = new ArrayList<>(List.of(1,2,3,4,5));
  public List<Integer> getValues()          { return values; }
  public static boolean isEven(int value) { return value % 2 != 0; }
  public void printValue(int value)        { System.out.print(value + " "); }
}

public class Main {
  public static void main(String[] args) {
    Test test = new Test();
    test.getValues().removeIf(v -> v % 2 != 0);               // (1)
    test.getValues().forEach(v -> System.out.print(v + " ") ); // (2)
  }
}
```

Select the one correct answer.

(a) `test.getValues().removeIf(Test::isEven);`
    `test.getValues().forEach(Test::printValue);`

(b) `test.getValues().removeIf(Test::isEven);`
    `test.getValues().forEach(test::printValue);`

(c) `test.getValues().removeIf(test::isEven);`
    `test.getValues().forEach(test::printValue);`

      (d) `test.getValues().removeIf(test::isEven);`
          `test.getValues().forEach(Test::printValue);`

      (e) None of the above

13.11 Which statement is true about method referencing?

      (a) Unbounded instance method reference determines the target reference as the first argument passed to the method reference.

      (b) Unbounded instance method reference determines the target reference as the last argument passed to the method reference.

      (c) Bounded instance method reference determines the target reference as the first argument passed to the method reference.

      (d) Bounded instance method reference determines the target reference as the last argument passed to the method reference.

13.12 Given the following code:

```java
import java.util.function.BiFunction;
public class Test24RQ6 {
  public static void main(String[] args) {
    BiFunction divide = (x, y) -> x/y;
    System.out.print(divide.apply(0.0,0));
  }
}
```

What is the result?
Select the one correct answer.

      (a) 0

      (b) 0.0

      (c) The program will throw an exception at runtime.

      (d) The program will fail to compile.

13.13 Given the following code:

```java
import java.util.function.Function;
public class Test13RQ19 {
  public static void main(String[] args) {
    Function f1 = (x) -> "<" + x;
    Function f2 = (x) -> x + ">";
    System.out.print(f2.compose(f1).apply(42));
  }
}
```

What is the result?
Select the one correct answer.

      (a) <42>

      (b) >42<

      (c) The program will throw an exception at runtime.

      (d) The program will fail to compile.

Object Comparison 14

Chapter Topics

- Overview of selected convenience methods of the Objects class
- How to correctly override and implement the contract of the equals() method of the Object class
- How to correctly override and implement the contract of the hash-Code() method of the Object class
- Comparing objects whose natural order is defined by the contract of the compareTo() method of the java.lang.Comparable<T> interface
- Comparing objects using a comparator that defines a total order according to the contract of the compare() method of the java.util .Comparator<T> interface

Java SE 11 Developer Exam Objectives	
[5.3] Sort collections and arrays using Comparator and Comparable interfaces	§14.4, p. 761 §14.5, p. 769
o Comparable *and* Comparator *interfaces are covered in this chapter.*	
o *For sorted collections and arrays, see Chapter 15, p. 781.*	

This chapter covers the important topic of comparing objects. Many useful operations require that the objects can be compared for *object value equality* and *ranked* according to some meaningful criteria. Typical examples are searching and sorting algorithms for objects maintained in arrays, collections, and maps. Overriding the methods equals() and hashCode() in the Object class and the methods compareTo() and compare() in the interfaces Comparable<T> and Comparator<T>, respectively, is essential in this regard.

The equals() and hashCode() methods of the Object class provide specific contracts for objects, which the classes overriding the methods should honor. It is important to understand how and why a class should override the equals() and hashCode() methods.

The compareTo() method of the Comparable<E> interface defines the contract for comparing objects which classes can implement. In addition, the compare() method of the Comparator<E> interface allows other criteria to be defined for comparing objects.

Objects of a class that override the equals() method make it possible to search for such objects in arrays and lists. If they override the hashCode() method, they can also be searched for as elements in a set and as keys in a map. Implementing the Comparable<E> interface allows them to be sorted and maintained as elements in sorted collections and as keys in sorted maps. Collections and maps are covered in detail in Chapter 15, p. 781.

14.1 The Objects Class

The following static methods of the java.util.Objects class are convenient to use when comparing objects and computing the hash code for an object. They take away the drudgery of checking references for null values before calling them and never throw a NullPointerException—that is, they are null-safe.

static boolean equals(Object obj1, Object obj2)

Returns true if the arguments are equal to each other; otherwise, it returns false. This means that if both arguments are null, true is returned and if only one argument is null, false is returned. Equality is determined by invoking the equals() method on the first argument: obj1.equals(obj2). It is a convenience method for the Object.equals() method (Example 14.3, p. 748).

static int hash(Object... values)
static int hashCode(Object obj)

The first method generates a hash code for a sequence of specified values. It is useful for computing the hash code for objects containing multiple fields that are passed as arguments (Example 14.6, p. 771).

The second method computes and returns the hash code of a non-null argument; otherwise, it returns 0 for a `null` argument.

Both methods are convenience methods for the `Object.hashCode()` method.

`static <T> int compare(T t1, T t2, Comparator<? super T> cmp)`

Returns 0 if the arguments are identical; otherwise, it calls `cmp.compare(t1, t2)`, which is the abstract method in the `Comparator<T>` interface. It also returns 0 if both arguments are `null` (Example 14.8, p. 777).

14.2   Implementing the `equals()` Method

If every object is to be considered unique, then it is not necessary to override the `equals()` method in the `Object` class. This method implements *object reference equality*. It implements the most discriminating equivalence relation possible on objects. Each instance of the class is only equal to itself.

`public boolean equals(Object obj)`

The `equals()` method in the `Object` class tests for *object reference equality*, the same as the == operator. It returns `true` only if the two references compared denote the same object—that is, if they are aliases. The `equals()` method is usually overridden to provide the semantics of *object value equality*, as in the case of the wrapper classes and the `String` class.

As a running example, we will implement different versions of a class for *version numbers*. A version number (VNO) for a software product comprises three pieces of information:

- A release number
- A revision number
- A patch number

The idea is that releases do not happen very often. Revisions take place more frequently than releases, but less frequently than code patches are issued. We can say that the release number is most *significant*. The revision number is less significant than the release number, and the patch number is the least significant of the three fields. This ranking would also be employed when ordering version numbers chronologically.

Example 14.1   *Not Overriding the `Object.equals()` Method*

```
/** A simple version number class */
public class SimpleVNO {

    private int release;
    private int revision;
    private int patch;
```

```
  public SimpleVNO(int release, int revision, int patch) {
    this.release  = release;
    this.revision = revision;
    this.patch    = patch;
  }

  public int getRelease()  { return this.release;  }
  public int getRevision() { return this.revision; }
  public int getPatch()    { return this.patch;    }

  @Override public String toString() {
    return "(" + release + "." + revision + "." + patch + ")";
  }
}
```

The class SimpleVNO in Example 14.1 does not override the equals() method in the Object class. It only overrides the toString() method to generate a meaningful text representation for a version number.

The class TestSimpleVNO in Example 14.2 creates objects of the class SimpleVNO in Example 14.1 to test for *object reference equality* and *object value equality*. The output from Example 14.2 demonstrates that all SimpleVNO objects are unique because the class SimpleVNO does not override the equals() method to provide any other equivalence relation. The result of the == operator is always false for object reference equality, since all SimpleVNO objects are unique. An attempt is made to compare SimpleVNO objects for object value equality using the Object.equals() method, but the implementation of the Object.equals() method tests for object reference equality, the same as the == operator. Not surprisingly, the equals() method returns false even for SimpleVNO objects that have the same state (svno1 and svno2).

Example 14.2 *Implications of Not Overriding the Object.equals() Method*

```
import static java.lang.System.out;

public class TestSimpleVNO {
  public static void main(String[] args) {
    // Print name of version number class:
    out.println(SimpleVNO.class);

    // Three individual version numbers.
    SimpleVNO svno1 = new SimpleVNO(9,1,1);                            // (1)
    SimpleVNO svno2 = new SimpleVNO(9,1,1);                            // (2)
    SimpleVNO svno3 = new SimpleVNO(6,6,6);                            // (3)

    out.printf (" svno1: %s, svno2: %s, svno3: %s%n", svno1, svno2, svno3);
    out.println("Test object reference equality:");                   // (4)
    out.println(" svno1 == svno2:     " + (svno1 == svno2));          // (5)
    out.println(" svno1 == svno3:     " + (svno1 == svno3));          // (6)
    out.println("Test object value equality:");
```

```
    out.println(" svno1.equals(svno2): " + svno1.equals(svno2));  // (7)
    out.println(" svno1.equals(svno3): " + svno1.equals(svno3));  // (8)
  }
}
```

Output from the program:

```
class SimpleVNO
  svno1: (9.1.1), svno2: (9.1.1), svno3: (6.6.6)
Test object reference equality:
  svno1 == svno2:      false
  svno1 == svno3:      false
Test object value equality:
  svno1.equals(svno2): false
  svno1.equals(svno3): false
```

Equivalence Relation of the equals() Method

An implementation of the equals() method must satisfy the properties of an *equivalence relation*:

- *Reflexive*: For any reference self, self.equals(self) is always true.
- *Symmetric*: For any references x and y, if x.equals(y) is true, then y.equals(x) is true.
- *Transitive*: For any references x, y, and z, if both x.equals(y) and y.equals(z) are true, then x.equals(z) is true.
- *Consistent*: For any references x and y, multiple invocations of x.equals(y) will always return the same result, provided the objects referenced by these references have not been modified to affect the equals comparison.
- null *comparison*: For any non-null reference obj, the call obj.equals(null) always returns false.

The general contract of the equals() method is defined between *objects of arbitrary classes*. Understanding its criteria is important for providing a proper implementation.

Reflexivity

This rule simply states that an object is equal to itself, regardless of how it is modified. It is easy to satisfy: The object passed as an argument and the current object are compared for object reference equality (==), the same as the default behavior of the Object.equals() method. If the references are aliases, the equals() implementation returns true.

```
if (this == argumentObj)
  return true;
// ...
```

The reflexivity test can usually be an operand of the short-circuit conditional-OR operator (||) in a return statement, where if the reflexivity test is true, other criteria for equality comparison are not evaluated:

```
return (this == argumentObj)
       || (/* Other criteria for equality. */);
```

Symmetry

The expression x.equals(y) invokes the equals() method on the object referenced by the reference x, whereas the expression y.equals(x) invokes the equals() method on the object referenced by the reference y. If x.equals(y) is true, then y.equals(x) must be true.

If the equals() methods invoked are in different classes, the classes must bilaterally agree whether their objects are equal or not. In other words, symmetry can be violated if the equals() method of a class makes unilateral decisions about which classes it will interoperate with, while the other classes are not aware of this. Avoiding interoperability with other (non-related) classes when implementing the equals() method is strongly recommended.

Transitivity

If two classes, A and B, have a bilateral agreement on their objects being equal, then this rule guarantees that one of them, say B, does not enter into an agreement with a third class C on its own. All classes involved must multilaterally abide by the terms of the contract.

A typical pitfall resulting in broken transitivity is when the equals() method in a subclass calls the equals() method of its superclass, as part of its equals comparison. The equals() method in the subclass can be implemented by code equivalent to the following line:

```
return super.equals(argumentObj) && compareSubclassSpecificAspects();
```

The idea is to compare only the subclass-specific aspects in the subclass equals() method and to use the superclass equals() method for comparing the superclass-specific aspects. However, this approach should be used with extreme caution. The problem lies in getting the equivalence contract fulfilled bilaterally between the superclass and the subclass equals() methods. Symmetry or transitivity can easily be broken.

If the superclass is abstract, using the superclass equals() method works well. There are no superclass objects for the subclass equals() method to consider. In addition, the superclass equals() method cannot be called directly by any clients other than subclasses. The subclass equals() method then has control of how the superclass equals() method is called. It can safely call the superclass equals() method to compare the superclass-specific aspects of subclass objects.

Consistency

This rule enforces that two objects that are equal (or non-equal) remain equal (or non-equal) as long as they are not modified. For mutable objects, the result of the equals comparison can change if one (or both) are modified between method invocations. However, for immutable objects, the result must always be the same. The equals() method should take into consideration whether the class implements immutable objects, and ensure that the consistency rule is not violated.

null *Comparison*

This rule states that no object is equal to null. The contract calls for the equals() method to return false. The method must not throw an exception; that would be violating the contract. A check for this rule is necessary in the implementation. Typically, the argument object is explicitly compared with the null value:

```
if (argumentObj == null)
  return false;
```

In many cases, it is preferable to use the instanceof pattern match operator. It determines whether the argument object is of the appropriate type and introduces a local variable of the appropriate subtype that denotes the argument object. It is always false if its left operand is null:

```
if (!(argumentObj instanceof MyRefType other))
  return false;
// Local variable other can be used in further implementation.
```

Note that if the instanceof pattern match operator is true, the if condition is false so that the local variable other of MyRefType is introduced into the scope *after* the if statement. In fact, the if statement can often be eliminated if the fields are compared individually:

```
return (this == argumentObj)                              // Reflexivity test
    || (argumentObj instanceof MyRefType other           // null comparison & cast
        && /* Can use variable other to compare individual fields. */);
```

The return statement above will now also return false if the instanceof pattern match operator determines that argumentObj is null or if it is not of MyRefType. If the instanceof pattern match operator returns true, the reference other can be safely used to compare the individual fields by short-circuit evaluation of the && operator (see Example 14.3).

- -

Example 14.3 *Implementing the* equals() *Method*

```
import java.util.Objects;

// Overrides equals(), but not hashCode().
public class UsableVNO {

  private int release;
  private int revision;
  private int patch;
```

```
public UsableVNO(int release, int revision, int patch) {
  this.release  = release;
  this.revision = revision;
  this.patch    = patch;
}

public int getRelease()  { return this.release;  }
public int getRevision() { return this.revision; }
public int getPatch()    { return this.patch;    }

@Override public String toString() {
  return "(" + release + "." + revision + "." + patch + ")";
}

@Override public boolean equals(Object obj) {      // (1)
  return (this == obj)                             // (2)
    || (obj instanceof UsableVNO vno               // (3)
        && this.patch    == vno.patch              // (4)
        && this.revision == vno.revision
        && this.release  == vno.release);
}
}
```

Checklist for Implementing the equals() Method

Example 14.3 shows an implementation of the equals() method for version numbers. Next, we provide a checklist for implementing the equals() method.

Method Overriding Signature

The method header is

```
public boolean equals(Object obj)         // (1)
```

The signature of the method requires that the argument passed is of the type Object. The following header will overload the method, not override it:

```
public boolean equals(MyRefType obj)       // Overloaded.
```

The compiler will not complain. Therefore, it is a good idea to use the @Override annotation. Calls to overloaded methods are resolved at compile time, depending on the type of the argument. Calls to overridden methods are resolved at runtime, depending on the type of the actual object referenced by the argument. Comparing the objects of the class MyRefType that *overloads* the equals() method for equivalence can give inconsistent results:

```
MyRefType ref1 = new MyRefType();
MyRefType ref2 = new MyRefType();
Object    ref3 = ref2;
boolean b1 = ref1.equals(ref2);    // True. Calls equals() in MyRefType.
boolean b2 = ref1.equals(ref3);    // Always false. Calls equals() in Object.
```

However, if the equals() method is overridden correctly, only the overriding method in MyRefType is called. A class can provide both implementations, but the equals() methods must be consistent. However, there must be a legitimate reason to overload the equals() method and this practice is not recommended.

Reflexivity Test

This is usually the first test performed in the equals() method, avoiding further computation if the test is true. The equals() method in Example 14.3 does this test at (2):

```
return (this == obj)                                    // (2)
    || (/* */);
```

Correct Argument Type

The equals() method of the UsableVNO class in Example 14.3 checks the type of the argument object and assigns its reference value to the local variable vno at (3) using the instanceof pattern match operator:

```
return (this == obj)                                    // (2)
    || (obj instanceof UsableVNO vno                    // (3)
        && /* Compare individual fields */);
```

This code also does the null comparison correctly, returning false if the argument obj has the value null.

The instanceof operator will also return true if the argument obj denotes a *subclass object* of the class UsableVNO. If the class is final, this issue does not arise—there are no subclass objects. The following test can be explicitly performed in order to exclude all other objects, including subclass objects:

```
if ((obj == null) || (obj.getClass() != this.getClass()))
    return false;
```

The condition in the if statement first performs the null comparison. The expression (obj.getClass() != this.getClass()) determines whether the classes of the two objects have the same runtime object representing them. If this is the case, the objects are instances of the same class.

Field Comparisons

Equivalence comparison involves comparing relevant fields from both objects to determine if their logical states match. For fields that are of primitive data types, their primitive values can be compared. Instances of the class UsableVNO in Example 14.3 have fields of primitive data types only. Values of corresponding fields can be compared to test for equality between two UsableVNO objects, as shown at (4):

```
return (this == obj)                                    // (2)
    || (obj instanceof UsableVNO vno                    // (3)
        && this.patch    == vno.patch                   // (4)
        && this.revision == vno.revision
        && this.release  == vno.release);
```

If all field comparisons evaluate to true, the equals() method returns true.

For fields that are references, the objects referenced by the references can be compared. For example, if the UsableVNO class declares a field called productInfo, which is a reference, the following expression can be used:

```
(this.productInfo != null && this.productInfo.equals(vno.productInfo)))
```

In order to avoid a NullPointerException being thrown, the equals() method is not invoked if the this.productInfo reference is null. However, the Objects.equals() utility method makes this comparison much simpler, as it provides null-safe object value equality operation, only invoking the equals() method on the first productInfo field, if both arguments are not null:

```
Objects.equals(this.productInfo, vno.productInfo)
```

Exact comparison of floating-point values should not be done directly on the values, but on the integer values obtained from their bit patterns (see static methods Float.floatToIntBits() and Double.doubleToLongBits() in the Java SE Platform API documentation). This technique eliminates certain anomalies in floating-point comparisons that involve a NaN value or a negative zero (see also the equals() method in Float and Double classes).

Only fields that have significance for the equivalence relation should be considered. Derived fields, whose computation is dependent on other field values in the object, might be redundant to include. Including only the significant fields may be prudent. Computing the equivalence relation should be deterministic; therefore, the equals() method should not depend on unreliable resources, such as network access.

The order in which the comparisons of the significant fields are carried out can influence the performance of the equals comparison. Fields that are most likely to differ should be compared as early as possible, in order to short-circuit the computation. In our example, patch numbers evolve faster than revision numbers, which, in turn, evolve faster than release numbers. This order is reflected in the return statement at (4) in Example 14.3.

Above all, an implementation of the equals() method must ensure that the equivalence relation is fulfilled.

Example 14.4 is a client that uses the class UsableVNO from Example 14.3. This client runs the same tests as the client in Example 14.2. The difference is that the class UsableVNO overrides the equals() method.

- -

Example 14.4 *Implications of Implementing the* equals() *Method*

```
import static java.lang.System.out;
import java.util.*;

public class TestUsableVNO {
  public static void main(String[] args) {
    // Print name of version number class:
    out.println(UsableVNO.class);

    // Three individual version numbers.
    UsableVNO svno1 = new UsableVNO(9,1,1);                              // (1)
```

```
    UsableVNO svno2 = new UsableVNO(9,1,1);                              // (2)
    UsableVNO svno3 = new UsableVNO(6,6,6);                              // (3)

    // An array of version numbers.
    UsableVNO[] versions =  new UsableVNO[] {                            // (4)
        new UsableVNO( 3,49, 1), new UsableVNO( 8,19,81),
        new UsableVNO( 2,48,28), new UsableVNO(10,23,78),
        new UsableVNO( 9, 1, 1)};

    out.printf (" svno1: %s, svno2: %s, svno3: %s%n", svno1, svno2, svno3);
    out.println("Test object reference equality:");                     // (5)
    out.println(" svno1 == svno2:     " + (svno1 == svno2));            // (6)
    out.println(" svno1 == svno3:     " + (svno1 == svno3));            // (7)
    out.println("Test object value equality:");
    out.println(" svno1.equals(svno2): " + svno1.equals(svno2));        // (8)
    out.println(" svno1.equals(svno3): " + svno1.equals(svno3));        // (9)
    out.println();

    // Search key:
    UsableVNO searchKey = new UsableVNO(9,1,1);                          // (10)

    // Searching in an array:
    boolean found = false;
    for (UsableVNO version : versions) {
      found = searchKey.equals(version);                                // (11)
      if (found) break;
    }
    out.println("Array: " + Arrays.toString(versions));                 // (12)
    out.printf("  Search key %s found in array:    %s%n%n",             // (13)
               searchKey, found);

    // Searching in a list:
    List<UsableVNO> vnoList = Arrays.asList(versions);                  // (14)
    out.println("List:   " + vnoList);
    out.printf("  Search key %s contained in list: %s%n%n", searchKey,
               vnoList.contains(searchKey));                            // (15)
  }
}
```

Output from the program:

```
class UsableVNO
  svno1: (9.1.1), svno2: (9.1.1), svno3: (6.6.6)
Test object reference equality:
  svno1 == svno2:     false
  svno1 == svno3:     false
Test object value equality:
  svno1.equals(svno2): true
  svno1.equals(svno3): false

Array: [(3.49.1), (8.19.81), (2.48.28), (10.23.78), (9.1.1)]
  Search key (9.1.1) found in array:    true

List:   [(3.49.1), (8.19.81), (2.48.28), (10.23.78), (9.1.1)]
  Search key (9.1.1) contained in list: true
```

The output from the program shows that object value equality is compared correctly. Object value equality is now based on identical states, as defined by the equals() method.

The search for a UsableVNO object in an array or a list of UsableVNO objects is successful, since the equals comparison is based on the states of the objects and not on their reference values.

Next, we look at how to fix the version numbers so that they can be used for searching in sets and maps.

14.3 Implementing the hashCode() Method

Hashing is an efficient technique for storing and retrieving data. A common hashing scheme uses an array where each element is a list of items. The array elements are called *buckets*. Operations in a hashing scheme involve computing an array index from an item. Converting an item to its array index is done by a *hash function*. The array index returned by the hash function is called the *hash code* of the item—it is also called the *hash value* of the item. The hash code identifies a particular bucket.

Storing an item involves the following steps:

1. Hash the item to determine the bucket.
2. If the item does not match an item already in the bucket, it is stored in the bucket.

Note that no duplicate items are stored. A lookup for an item is also a two-step process:

1. Hash the item to determine the bucket.
2. If the item matches an item in the bucket, the item is present; otherwise, it is not.

Different items can hash to the same bucket, meaning that the hash function returns the same hash code for these items. This condition is called a *collision*. The list maintained by a bucket contains the items that hash to the bucket.

The hash code of an item only identifies the bucket. Finding an item in the bucket entails a search, and requires an equality function to compare items. The items maintained in a hash-based storage scheme must, therefore, provide two essential functions: a hash function and an equality function.

The performance of a hashing scheme is largely affected by how well the hash function distributes a collection of items over the available buckets. A hash function should not be biased toward any particular hash codes. An ideal hash function produces a uniform distribution of hash codes for a collection of items across all possible hash codes. Such a hash function is not an easy task to design. Fortunately, heuristics exist for constructing adequate hash functions.

Here we mention two abstract data types that can be implemented using a hashing scheme:

- A *set* is an abstract data type that stores an unordered collection of unique items. Items in a set are called *elements* and the element to search for in a set is referred to as the *search key*. The hashing is used to store and lookup an item in a set, as explained earlier in this section.

- A *map* (also called, a *hash table*) is an abstract data type that maintains its items as *key–value entries*. An *entry* associates a *key* with a *value*. The keys in a hash table are unique. The hashing is done on a search key to provide efficient lookup of the entry with the associated value. Matching the search key with a key in an entry determines the value.

If objects of a class are to be maintained in hash-based collections and maps provided by the java.util package (see Table 15.2, p. 788), the class must provide appropriate implementations of the following methods from the Object class:

- A hashCode() method that produces hash codes for the objects
- An equals() method that tests objects for object value equality

int hashCode()

When storing objects in hash tables, this method can be used to get a hash code for an object. This method tries to return distinct integers for distinct objects as their default hash code. The hashCode() method is usually overridden by a class, as in the case of the wrapper classes and the String class.

As a general rule for implementing these methods, *a class that overrides the* equals() *method must override the* hashCode() *method.* Consequences of not doing so are illustrated in Example 14.5 using the class UsableVNO that does not override the hash-Code() method. Elements of this class are used as elements in a set that uses the hashCode() method of its elements to maintain them in the set. The output from the program shows that a set with the following elements is created:

```
Set: [(8.19.81), (2.48.28), (3.49.1), (9.1.1), (10.23.78)]
```

The hashCode() method from the Object class is not overridden by the UsableVNO class and is, therefore, used to compute the hash codes of the elements. This method returns the memory address of the object as the default hash code. The attempt to find the search key (9.1.1) in the set is unsuccessful:

```
Search key (9.1.1) contained in set:  false
```

The output from the program shows the hash codes assigned by this method to the search key and the elements in the set:

```
Search key (9.1.1) has hash code: 2036368507
Hash codes for the elements:
    (3.49.1): 1705929636
   (8.19.81): 1221555852
   (2.48.28): 1509514333
  (10.23.78): 1556956098
    (9.1.1): 1252585652
```

The hash codes of two objects, which are equal according to the equals() method of the class UsableVNO, are not equal according to the hashCode() method of the Object class. Therefore, the version number (9.1.1) in the set has a different hash code than the search key (9.1.1). These objects hash to different buckets. The lookup for the search key is done in one bucket and does not find the element (9.1.1), which is to be found in a completely different bucket. Just overriding the equals() method is not enough. The class UsableVNO violates the key tenet of the hashCode() contract: *Equal objects must produce equal hash codes.*

Example 14.5 *Implications of Not Overriding the* Object.hashCode() *Method*

```java
import static java.lang.System.out;
import java.util.*;

public class TestUsableVNO2 {
  public static void main(String[] args) {
    // Print name of version number class:
    out.println(UsableVNO.class);

    // An array of version numbers.
    UsableVNO[] versions =  new UsableVNO[] {          // (1)
        new UsableVNO( 3,49, 1), new UsableVNO( 8,19,81),
        new UsableVNO( 2,48,28), new UsableVNO(10,23,78),
        new UsableVNO( 9, 1, 1)};

    // Search key:
    UsableVNO searchKey = new UsableVNO(9,1,1);         // (2)

    // Create a list:
    List<UsableVNO> vnoList = Arrays.asList(versions);   // (3)

    // Searching in a set:
    Set<UsableVNO> vnoSet = new HashSet<>(vnoList);      // (4)
    out.println("Set: " + vnoSet);
    out.printf("Search key %s contained in set:  %s%n", searchKey,
            vnoSet.contains(searchKey));                 // (5)
    out.println();

    // Search key and its hash code:
    out.printf("Search key %s has hash code: %d%n", searchKey,
            searchKey.hashCode());                       // (6)

    // Hash values for elements:
    out.println("Hash codes for the elements:");
    for (UsableVNO element : versions) {                 // (7)
      out.printf(" %10s: %s%n", element, element.hashCode());
    }
  }
}
```

Output from the program:

```
class UsableVNO
Set: [(8.19.81), (2.48.28), (3.49.1), (9.1.1), (10.23.78)]
```

```
Search key (9.1.1) contained in set:  false

Search key (9.1.1) has hash code: 2036368507
Hash codes for the elements:
    (3.49.1): 1705929636
   (8.19.81): 1221555852
   (2.48.28): 1509514333
  (10.23.78): 1556956098
    (9.1.1): 1252585652
```

General Contract of the hashCode() Method

The general contract of the hashCode() method stipulates the following:

- *Consistency during execution is a necessary prerequisite*: Multiple invocations of the hashCode() method on an object must consistently return the same hash code during the execution of an application, provided the object is not modified to affect the result returned by the equals() method. The hash code need not remain consistent across different executions of the application. This means that using a pseudorandom number generator to produce hash codes is not a valid strategy.

- *Object value equality implies hash code equality*: If two objects are equal according to the equals() method, then the hashCode() method must produce the same hash code for these objects. This tenet ties in with the general contract of the equals() method.

- *Object value inequality places no restrictions on the hash code*: If two objects are unequal according to the equals() method, then the hashCode() method need not produce distinct hash codes for these objects. However, it is strongly recommended that the hashCode() method produce unequal hash codes for unequal objects.

Note that the hash code contract does not imply that objects with equal hash codes are equal. Not producing unequal hash codes for unequal objects can have an adverse effect on performance, as unequal objects with the same hash code will hash to the same bucket.

Heuristics for Implementing the hashCode() Method

In Example 14.6, the computation of the hash code in the hashCode() method of the ReliableVNO class embodies heuristics that can produce fairly reasonable hash functions. The hash code is computed according to the following formula:

```
hashValue = 11 * 31³ + release * 31² + revision * 31¹ + patch
```

Only the significant fields that have bearing on the equals() method are included. This ensures that objects that are equal according to the equals() method also have equal hash codes according to the hashCode() method.

Example 14.6 *Implementing the* hashCode() *Method*

```java
import java.util.Objects;

// Overrides both equals() and hashCode().
public class ReliableVNO {

  private int release;
  private int revision;
  private int patch;

  public ReliableVNO(int release, int revision, int patch) {
    this.release  = release;
    this.revision = revision;
    this.patch    = patch;
  }

  public int getRelease()  { return this.release;  }
  public int getRevision() { return this.revision; }
  public int getPatch()    { return this.patch;    }

  @Override public String toString() {
    return "(" + release + "." + revision + "." + patch + ")";
  }

  @Override public boolean equals(Object obj) {              // (1)
    return (this == obj)                                     // (2)
        || (obj instanceof ReliableVNO vno                   // (3)
          && this.patch    == vno.patch                      // (4)
          && this.revision == vno.revision
          && this.release  == vno.release);
  }

  @Override public int hashCode() {                          // (5)
    int hashValue = 11;
    hashValue = 31 * hashValue + release;
    hashValue = 31 * hashValue + revision;
    hashValue = 31 * hashValue + patch;
    return hashValue;

//  return Objects.hash(this.release, this.revision, this.patch); // (6)
  }
}
```

The basic idea is to compute an int hash code sfVal for each significant field sf, and include an assignment of the form shown at (1) in the computation below:

```java
public int hashCode() {
  int sfVal;
  int hashValue = 11;
  ...
  sfVal = ...    // Compute hash code for each significant field sf. See below.
  hashValue = 31 * hashValue + sfVal;    // (1)
```

```
    ...
    return hashValue;
}
```

This setup ensures that the result from incorporating a field value is used to calculate the contribution from the next field value.

Calculating the hash code sfVal for a significant field sf depends on the type of the field:

- Field sf is a boolean:

  ```
  sfVal = sf ? 0 : 1;
  ```

- Field sf is a byte, char, short, or int:

  ```
  sfVal = (int)sf;
  ```

- Field sf is a long:

  ```
  sfVal = (int) (sf ^ (sf >>> 32));
  ```

- Field sf is a float:

  ```
  sfVal = Float.floatToInt(sf);
  ```

- Field sf is a double:

  ```
  long sfValTemp = Double.doubleToLong(sf);
  sfVal = (int) (sfValTemp ^ (sfValTemp >>> 32));
  ```

- Field sf is a reference that denotes an object. Typically, the hashCode() method is invoked recursively if the equals() method is invoked recursively:

  ```
  sfVal = (sf == null ? 0 : sf.hashCode());
  ```

- Field sf is an array. The contribution from each element is calculated similarly to a field.

The order in which the fields are incorporated into the hash code computation will influence the hash code. Fields whose values are derived from other fields can be excluded. There is no point in feeding the hash function with redundant information, since this is unlikely to improve the value distribution. Fields that are not significant for the equals() method must be excluded; otherwise, the hashCode() method might end up contradicting the equals() method. As with the equals() method, data from unreliable resources (e.g., network access) should not be used, and inclusion of transient fields should be avoided.

A legal or correct hash function does not necessarily mean it is appropriate or efficient. The classic example of a legal but inefficient hash function is

```
public int hashCode() {
  return 1949;
}
```

All objects using this method are assigned to the same bucket. The hash table is then no better than a list. For the sake of efficiency, a hash function should strive to produce unequal hash codes for unequal objects.

For numeric wrapper types, the hashCode() implementation returns an int representation of the primitive value, converting the primitive value to an int, if necessary. The Boolean objects for the boolean literals true and false have specific hash codes, which are returned by the hashCode() method.

The hashCode() method of the String class returns a hash code that is the value of a polynomial whose variable has the value 31; the coefficients are the characters in the string, and the degree is the string length minus 1. For example, the hash code of the string "abc" is computed as follows:

hashValue = 'a' * 31^2 + 'b' * 31^1 + 'c' * 31^0 = 97 * 31 * 31 + 98 * 31 + 99 = 96354

For immutable objects, the hash code can be cached—that is, calculated once and returned whenever the hashCode() method is called.

However, the hash() method of the Objects class makes it very convenient to compute the hash code for an object with multiple fields. The procedure outlined above for calculating the hash code for a version number can be replaced by a single statement, as shown at (6) in Example 14.6. Each int field value is autoboxed in an Integer and passed in the call to the Objects.hash() method which returns a hash code based on the field values of the version number.

```
return Objects.hash(this.release, this.revision, this.patch); // (6)
```

The client in Example 14.7 demonstrates searching for objects of the class ReliableVNO in a set and in a map. The ReliableVNO objects in the array versions are used as elements in the set and as keys in the map.

Output from the program in Example 14.7 shows that the search key (9.1.1) and the element (9.1.1) in the set vnoSet have the same hash code. The search is successful. These objects hash to the same bucket. Therefore, the search for the element takes place in the right bucket. It finds the element (9.1.1) using the equals() method by successfully checking for equality between the search key (9.1.1) and the element (9.1.1) of the set.

Each entry in the map versionStatistics represents a version number (the *key*) and the number of downloads (the *value*) for that version number. Output from the program also shows that the key (9.1.1) of the entry (9.1.1)=6000 in the map has the same hash code as the search key (9.1.1). The search is successful.

However, we still cannot use objects of the class ReliableVNO in *sorted* sets and maps, as no criteria for comparing the version numbers have been defined.

Example 14.7 *Implications of Implementing the* hashCode() *Method*

```
import static java.lang.System.out;
import java.util.*;

public class TestReliableVNO {
  public static void main(String[] args) {
    // Print name of version number class:
    out.println(ReliableVNO.class);
```

```java
    // An array of version numbers.
    ReliableVNO[] versions =  new ReliableVNO[] {                          // (1)
        new ReliableVNO( 3,49, 1), new ReliableVNO( 8,19,81),
        new ReliableVNO( 2,48,28), new ReliableVNO(10,23,78),
        new ReliableVNO( 9, 1, 1)};

    // Search key and its hash code:
    ReliableVNO searchKey = new ReliableVNO( 9, 1, 1);                     // (2)
    out.printf("Search key %s has hash code: %d%n", searchKey,
        searchKey.hashCode());                                            // (3)

    // Print hash values:
    out.println("Hash codes:");
    for (ReliableVNO element : versions) {                                // (4)
      out.printf("  %10s: %s%n", element, element.hashCode());
    }
    out.println();

    // Searching in a set:
    Set<ReliableVNO> vnoSet = new HashSet<>(Arrays.asList(versions));     // (5)
    out.println("Set: " + vnoSet);
    out.printf("Search key %s contained in set: %s%n%n", searchKey,
                vnoSet.contains(searchKey));                              // (6)

    // Searching in a map:
    Map<ReliableVNO, Integer> versionStatistics = new HashMap<>();        // (7)
    versionStatistics.put(versions[0], 2000);
    versionStatistics.put(versions[1], 3000);
    versionStatistics.put(versions[2], 4000);
    versionStatistics.put(versions[3], 5000);
    versionStatistics.put(versions[4], 6000);
    out.println("Map: " + versionStatistics);                            // (8)
    out.printf("Search key %s contained in map: %s%n", searchKey,
                versionStatistics.containsKey(searchKey));               // (9)
  }
}
```

Output from the program:

```
class ReliableVNO
Search key (9.1.1) has hash code: 336382
Hash codes:
     (3.49.1): 332104
    (8.19.81): 336059
    (2.48.28): 331139
   (10.23.78): 338102
     (9.1.1): 336382

Set: [(10.23.78), (2.48.28), (9.1.1), (3.49.1), (8.19.81)]
Search key (9.1.1) contained in set: true

Map: {(10.23.78)=5000, (2.48.28)=4000, (9.1.1)=6000, (3.49.1)=2000,
     (8.19.81)=3000}
Search key (9.1.1) contained in map: true
```

14.4   Implementing the `java.lang.Comparable<E>` Interface

In order to sort the objects of a class, it should be possible to *compare* the objects. A *total ordering* allows objects to be compared. The criteria used to do the comparison depend on what is meaningful for the class. For example, comparison of `Integer` objects is based on the `int` value in an `Integer` object, whereas comparison of `String` objects is based on the Unicode value of the characters comprising the string in a `String` object. There can be more than one total ordering to compare the objects of a class. For example, another total ordering for `String` objects can be case insensitive—that is, treats uppercase characters as lowercase when comparing `String` objects.

The total ordering for objects of a class that is designated as the *default* ordering is called the *natural ordering*. A class defines the natural ordering for its object by implementing the `java.lang.Comparable<E>` generic interface. Other total orderings can be defined by providing a *comparator* that implements the `java.util.Comparator<E>` generic interface.

We will look at the two generic interfaces `Comparable<E>` and `Comparator<E>` for comparing objects in the rest of this chapter. The `Comparable<E>` interface is implemented by the objects of the class—in other words, the class provides the implementation for comparing its objects according to its natural ordering. The class usually leaves the implementation of a total ordering to its clients who can decide which total ordering is desirable.

The general contract for the `Comparable<E>` interface is defined by its only abstract method `compareTo()`, making this interface technically a functional interface. However, it is not annotated with the `@FunctionalInterface` annotation, and it is not intended to be implemented by lambda expressions.

> `int compareTo(E other)`
>
> Returns a negative integer, zero, or a positive integer if the current object is less than, equal to, or greater than the specified object, respectively, based on the natural ordering. It throws a `ClassCastException` if the reference value passed in the argument cannot be compared to the current object. It throws a `Null-PointerException` if the argument is `null`.

Many of the standard classes in the Java SE APIs, such as the primitive wrapper classes, enum types, `String`, `LocalDate`, `LocalDateTime`, `LocalTime`, and `File`, implement the `Comparable<E>` interface. Objects implementing this interface can be used as

- Elements in a sorted set
- Keys in a sorted map
- Elements in lists that are sorted using the `Collections.sort()` or `List.sort()` method
- Elements in arrays that are sorted using the overloaded `Arrays.sort()` methods

The natural ordering for String objects (and Character objects) is lexicographical ordering—that is, their comparison is based on the Unicode value of each corresponding character in the strings. Objects of the String and Character classes will be lexicographically maintained as elements in a sorted set, or as keys in a sorted map that uses their natural ordering.

The natural ordering for objects of a numerical wrapper class is in ascending order of the values of the corresponding numerical primitive type. As elements in a sorted set or as keys in a sorted map that uses their natural ordering, the objects will be maintained in ascending order.

According to the natural ordering for objects of the Boolean class, a Boolean object representing the value false is less than a Boolean object representing the value true.

An implementation of the compareTo() method for the objects of a class should meet the following criteria:

- For any two objects of the class, if the first object is *less than, equal to,* or *greater than* the second object, then the second object must be *greater than, equal to,* or *less than* the first object, respectively—that is, the comparison is *anti-symmetric*.

- All three comparison relations (*less than, equal to, greater than*) embodied in the compareTo() method must be *transitive*. For example, for any objects obj1, obj2, and obj3 of a class, if obj1.compareTo(obj2) > 0 and obj2.compareTo(obj3) > 0, then obj1.compareTo(obj3) > 0.

- For any two objects of the class that compare as equal, the compareTo() method must return the same result if these two objects are compared with any other object—that is, the comparison is *congruent*.

- The compareTo() method is strongly recommended (but not required) to be *consistent with equals*—that is, (obj1.compareTo(obj2) == 0) == (obj1.equals(obj2)) is true. This is recommended if the objects will be maintained in sorted sets or sorted maps.

The magnitude of non-zero values returned by the compareTo() method is immaterial; the sign indicates the result of the comparison. The general contract of the compareTo() method augments the general contract of the equals() method, providing a natural ordering of the compared objects. The equality test of the compareTo() method has the same provisions as that of the equals() method.

Implementing the compareTo() method is not much different from implementing the equals() method. In fact, given that the functionality of the equals() method is a subset of the functionality of the compareTo() method, the equals() implementation can call the compareTo() method. This guarantees that the two methods are always consistent with each other.

```
@Override public boolean equals(Object obj) {
    return (this == obj)
        || (obj instanceof Whatever other
            && this.compareTo(other) == 0);
}
```

Example 14.8   *Implementing the* compareTo() *Method of the* Comparable<E> *Interface*

```java
import java.util.Comparator;
import java.util.Objects;

public final class VersionNumber implements Comparable<VersionNumber> {

  private final int release;
  private final int revision;
  private final int patch;

  public VersionNumber(int release, int revision, int patch) {
    this.release  = release;
    this.revision = revision;
    this.patch    = patch;
  }

  public int getRelease()  { return this.release;  }
  public int getRevision() { return this.revision; }
  public int getPatch()    { return this.patch;    }

  @Override public String toString() {
    return "(" + release + "." + revision + "." + patch + ")";
  }

  @Override public boolean equals(Object obj) {                      // (1)
    return (this == obj)                                             // (2)
      || (obj instanceof VersionNumber vno                          // (3)
          && this.patch    == vno.patch
          && this.revision == vno.revision
          && this.release  == vno.release);
  }

  @Override public int hashCode() {
    return Objects.hash(this.release, this.revision, this.patch);    // (4)
  }

  @Override public int compareTo(VersionNumber vno) {                // (5)
    // Compare the release numbers.                                     (6)
    if (this.release != vno.release)
      return Integer.compare(this.release, vno.release);

    // Release numbers are equal,                                       (7)
    // must compare revision numbers.
    if (this.revision != vno.revision)
      return Integer.compare(this.revision, vno.revision);

    // Release and revision numbers are equal,                          (8)
    // patch numbers determine the ordering.
    return Integer.compare(this.patch, vno.patch);
  }

  /*
  @Override public int compareTo(VersionNumber vno) {                // (9a)
```

```
        return Comparator.comparingInt(VersionNumber::getRelease)      // (10a)
                   .thenComparingInt(VersionNumber::getRevision)  // (11a)
                   .thenComparingInt(VersionNumber::getPatch)     // (12a)
                   .compare(this, vno);                           // (13a)
    }
    */
}
```

A compareTo() method is seldom implemented to interoperate with objects of other classes. For example, this is the case for primitive wrapper classes and the String class. The calls to the compareTo() method in the last three statements below all result in a compile-time error.

```
Integer iRef = 10;
Double dRef = 3.14;
String str = "ten";
StringBuilder sb = new StringBuilder("ten");
boolean b1 = iRef.compareTo(str) == 0 ;  // compareTo(Integer) not applicable to
                                         // arguments (String).
boolean b2 = dRef.compareTo(iRef) > 0;   // compareTo(Integer) not applicable to
                                         // arguments (Double).
boolean b3 = sb.compareTo(str) == 0; // compareTo(StringBuilder) not applicable to
                                     // arguments (String).
```

A straightforward implementation of the compareTo() method for version numbers is shown in Example 14.8. Note the specification of the implements clause in the class header. By parameterizing the Comparable<E> interface with the VersionNumber type, the class declaration explicitly excludes comparison with objects of other types. Only VersionNumbers can be compared.

```
public final class VersionNumber implements Comparable<VersionNumber> {
    ...
    @Override public int compareTo(VersionNumber vno) {            // (5)
    ...
    }
    ...
}
```

The signature of the compareTo() method is compareTo(VersionNumber). In order to maintain backward compatibility with non-generic code, the compiler inserts the following *bridge method* with the signature compareTo(Object) into the class (§11.11, p. 615).

```
public int compareTo(Object obj) {   // NOT A GOOD IDEA TO RELY ON THIS METHOD!
    return this.compareTo((VersionNumber) obj);
}
```

In an implementation of the compareTo() method, the fields are compared with the most significant field first and the least significant field last. In the case of the version numbers, the release numbers are compared first, followed by the revision numbers, with the patch numbers being compared last. Note that the next lesser significant fields are only compared if the comparison of the previous higher significant fields yielded equality. Inequality between corresponding significant fields short-circuits the computation. If all significant fields are equal, a zero will be returned. This approach is shown in the implementation of the compareTo() method at (5) through (8) in Example 14.8.

Comparison of integer values in fields can be optimized. In the code for comparing the release numbers at (5) in Example 14.8, we have relied on implicit use of the Integer.compareTo() method called by the Integer.compare() method, and autoboxing of the int field values:

```
if (this.release != vno.release)
  return Integer.compare(this.release, vno.release);
// Next field comparison
```

The code above can be replaced by the following code for doing the comparison, which relies on the difference between int values:

```
int releaseDiff = release - vno.release;
if (releaseDiff != 0)
  return releaseDiff;
// Next field comparison
```

However, this code can break if the difference is a value not in the range of the int type.

Significant fields with non-boolean primitive values are normally compared using the relational operators < and >. For comparing significant fields denoting constituent objects, the main options are to either invoke the compareTo() method on them, or use a comparator.

A more compact and elegant implementation of the compareTo() method for version numbers is shown at (9a) in Example 14.8 that exclusively uses methods of the Comparator<E> interface (p. 769). The compareTo() method implementation below is an equivalent version of the compareTo() method at (9a) in Example 14.8, where the method chaining has been split up and the method references replaced with equivalent lambda expressions.

```
@Override public int compareTo(VersionNumber vno) {           // (9b)
  Comparator<VersionNumber> c1
      = Comparator.comparingInt(vn -> vn.getRelease());        // (10b)
  Comparator<VersionNumber> c2
      = c1.thenComparingInt(vn -> vn.getRevision());           // (11b)
  Comparator<VersionNumber> c3
      = c2.thenComparingInt(vn -> vn.getPatch());              // (12b)
//return c3.compare(this, vno);                                // (13b)
  return Objects.compare(this, vno, c3);                       // (13c)
}
```

The method implementations at (9a) and (9b) essentially use a *conditional comparator* that applies its constituent comparators conditionally in the order in which it is composed. The lambda expressions specified as arguments in the method calls above at (10b), (11b), and (12b) will extract the int value of a particular field in a version number when the expression is executed.

- The call to the static method comparingInt() at (10b) returns a Comparator that compares the version numbers by the int value of their release field.

- The call to the default method thenComparingInt() at (11b) on Comparator c1 returns a composed Comparator that first compares version numbers using Comparator c1, and if the comparison result is 0, compares them by the revision field.

- Analogous to (11b), the call to the default method thenComparingInt() at (12b) on Comparator c2 returns a composed Comparator that first compares version numbers using Comparator c2, and if the comparison result is 0, compares them by the patch field.

- It is the call to the functional method compare() at (13b) on the composed Comparator c3 that does the actual comparison on the current version number (this) and the argument object (vno) according to the natural ordering of the int values of their fields, and where the order of the individual field comparisons is given by the composed Comparator c3.

  Equivalently, the return statement at (13b) can be written as (13c), where the convenience method Objects.compare() takes as arguments the current version number (this), the argument object (vno), and the composed Comparator c3. The Objects.compare() method calls the functional method compare() on the composed Comparator c3, passing it the current version number (this) and the argument object (vno).

What is different about this implementation of version numbers is that the class VersionNumber now overrides both the equals() and the hashCode() methods, and implements the compareTo() method of the parameterized Comparable<VersionNumber> interface. In addition, the compareTo() method is consistent with the equals() method. Following general class design principles, the class has been declared final so that it cannot be extended.

- -

Example 14.9 *Implications of Implementing the* compareTo() *Method*

```java
import static java.lang.System.out;
import java.util.*;

public class TestVersionNumber {
  public static void main(String[] args) {
    // Print name of version number class:
    out.println(VersionNumber.class);

    // Create an unsorted array of version numbers:
    VersionNumber[] versions =  new VersionNumber[] {               // (1)
        new VersionNumber( 3,49, 1), new VersionNumber( 8,19,81),
        new VersionNumber( 2,48,28), new VersionNumber(10,23,78),
        new VersionNumber( 9, 1, 1)};
    out.println("Unsorted array: " + Arrays.toString(versions));

    // Create an unsorted list:
    List<VersionNumber> vnoList = Arrays.asList(versions);          // (2)
    out.println("Unsorted list:  " + vnoList);
```

```
        // Create an unsorted map:
        Map<VersionNumber, Integer> versionStatistics = new HashMap<>();          // (3)
        versionStatistics.put(versions[0], 2000);
        versionStatistics.put(versions[1], 3000);
        versionStatistics.put(versions[2], 4000);
        versionStatistics.put(versions[3], 5000);
        versionStatistics.put(versions[4], 6000);
        out.println("Unsorted map: " + versionStatistics);

        // Sorted set:
        Set<VersionNumber> sortedSet = new TreeSet<>(vnoList);                     // (4)
        out.println("Sorted set: " + sortedSet);

        // Sorted map:
        Map<VersionNumber, Integer> sortedMap = new TreeMap<>(versionStatistics);//(5)
        out.println("Sorted map: " + sortedMap);

        // Sorted list:
        Collections.sort(vnoList);                                                // (6)
        out.println("Sorted list:    " + vnoList);

        // Searching in sorted list:
        VersionNumber searchKey = new VersionNumber( 9, 1, 1);                    // (7)
        int resultIndex = Collections.binarySearch(vnoList, searchKey);          // (8)
        out.printf("Binary search in sorted list found key %s at index: %d%n",
                searchKey, resultIndex);

        // Sorted array:
        Arrays.sort(versions);                                                    // (9)
        out.println("Sorted array:    " + Arrays.toString(versions));

        // Searching in sorted array:
        int resultIndex2 = Arrays.binarySearch(versions, searchKey);             // (10)
        out.printf("Binary search in sorted array found key %s at index: %d%n",
                searchKey, resultIndex2);
    }
}
```

Output from the program:

```
class VersionNumber
Unsorted array: [(3.49.1), (8.19.81), (2.48.28), (10.23.78), (9.1.1)]
Unsorted list:  [(3.49.1), (8.19.81), (2.48.28), (10.23.78), (9.1.1)]
Unsorted map: {(10.23.78)=5000, (3.49.1)=2000, (8.19.81)=3000, (9.1.1)=6000,
              (2.48.28)=4000}
Sorted set: [(2.48.28), (3.49.1), (8.19.81), (9.1.1), (10.23.78)]
Sorted map: {(2.48.28)=4000, (3.49.1)=2000, (8.19.81)=3000, (9.1.1)=6000,
              (10.23.78)=5000}
Sorted list:    [(2.48.28), (3.49.1), (8.19.81), (9.1.1), (10.23.78)]
Binary search in sorted list found key (9.1.1) at index: 3
Sorted array:    [(2.48.28), (3.49.1), (8.19.81), (9.1.1), (10.23.78)]
Binary search in sorted array found key (9.1.1) at index: 3
```

Example 14.9 is a client that uses the class VersionNumber from Example 14.8. Unlike previous attempts, the following code from Example 14.9 demonstrates that VersionNumber objects can now be maintained in sorted sets and maps. A sorted set is created at (4) based on the unsorted list vnoList, and a sorted map is created at (5) based on the unsorted map versionStatistics.

```
Set<VersionNumber> sortedSet = new TreeSet<>(vnoList);                    // (4)
...
Map<VersionNumber, Integer> sortedMap = new TreeMap<>(versionStatistics); // (5)
```

The output from executing this code shows that the elements in the set and the keys of the map are sorted in the natural ordering for version numbers:

```
Sorted set: [(2.48.28), (3.49.1), (8.19.81), (9.1.1), (10.23.78)]
Sorted map: {(2.48.28)=4000, (3.49.1)=2000, (8.19.81)=3000, (9.1.1)=6000,
             (10.23.78)=5000}
```

By default, the class TreeSet<E> relies on its elements to implement the equals() method and the compareTo() method. The output from the program in Example 14.9 shows that the TreeSet<VersionNumber> maintains its elements sorted in the natural ordering dictated by the compareTo() method. Analogously, the output from the program in Example 14.9 shows that the TreeMap<VersionNumber, Integer> maintains its entries sorted on the keys which are in the natural ordering dictated by the compareTo() method.

We can run generic operations on collections of version numbers. Utility methods provided by the Collections and Arrays classes in the java.util package are discussed in §15.11, p. 856, and §15.12, p. 864, respectively.

The following code sorts the elements in the list vnoList created at (2) in Example 14.9 according to their natural order:

```
Collections.sort(vnoList);                                               // (6)
```

The output from executing this code shows that the elements in the list are indeed sorted in ascending order:

```
Unsorted list:  [(3.49.1), (8.19.81), (2.48.28), (10.23.78), (9.1.1)]
...
Sorted list:    [(2.48.28), (3.49.1), (8.19.81), (9.1.1), (10.23.78)]
```

A binary search can be run on this sorted list to find the index of the version number (9.1.1) referenced by the reference searchKey at (7) in Example 14.9:

```
VersionNumber searchKey = new VersionNumber( 9, 1, 1);                   // (7)
int resultIndex = Collections.binarySearch(vnoList, searchKey);         // (8)
```

Natural ordering is assumed for the elements in the list. Executing the code prints the correct index of the search key in the sorted list:

```
Binary search in sorted list found key (9.1.1) at index: 3
```

Finally, the code in Example 14.9 sorts the elements in the array versions created at (1) according to their natural order:

```
Arrays.sort(versions);                                                   // (9)
```

The output from executing this code shows that the elements in the array are sorted as expected in ascending order:

```
Unsorted array: [(3.49.1), (8.19.81), (2.48.28), (10.23.78), (9.1.1)]
...
Sorted array:   [(2.48.28), (3.49.1), (8.19.81), (9.1.1), (10.23.78)]
```

We can run a binary search on this sorted list:

```
int resultIndex2 = Arrays.binarySearch(versions, searchKey);          // (10)
```

Again, natural ordering is assumed for the elements in the array. Executing the code prints the correct index of the search key in the sorted array:

```
Binary search in sorted array found key (9.1.1) at index: 3
```

14.5 Implementing the java.util.Comparator<E> Interface

The java.util.Comparator<E> interface is a *functional interface* and is designated as such with the @FunctionalInterface annotation in the Java SE API documentation—in other words, it is intended to be implemented by lambda expressions. Apart from its sole abstract method compare(), it defines a number of useful static and default methods which are listed at the end of this section. Several of these methods are illustrated throughout this chapter.

Precise control of ordering can be achieved by creating a customized comparator that imposes a specific total ordering on the elements. All comparators implement the Comparator<E> interface, providing implementation for its abstract method:

> int compare(E o1, E o2)
> The compare() method returns a negative integer, zero, or a positive integer if the first object is less than, equal to, or greater than the second object, according to the total ordering—that is, its contract is equivalent to that of the compareTo() method of the Comparable<E> interface. Since this method tests for equality, it is strongly recommended that its implementation does not contradict the semantics of the equals() method for the objects.

An alternative ordering to the default natural ordering can be specified by passing a Comparator to the constructor when the sorted set or map is created. The Collections and Arrays classes provide utility methods for sorting and searching, which also take a Comparator (§15.11, p. 856, and §15.12, p. 864).

Example 14.10 demonstrates the use of different comparators for strings. The program creates several empty sorted sets, using the TreeSet<E> class, where the comparator is passed to the constructor ((1b), (1c), (4)). Elements from the words array are added to each sorted set by the Collections.addAll() method, as at (6). A text representation of each sorted set is then printed, as at (7). The output shows the sort order in which the elements are maintained in the set.

Example 14.10 *Natural Ordering and Total Orderings*

```java
import java.util.*;

public class ComparatorUsage {
  public static void main(String[] args) {

    String[] words = {"court", "Stuart", "report", "Resort",        // (1)
                      "assort", "support", "transport", "distort"};

    // Choice of comparator.
    Set<String> strSet1 = new TreeSet<>();             // (1a) Natural ordering
    Set<String> strSet2 = new TreeSet<>(String.CASE_INSENSITIVE_ORDER); // (1b)
    Set<String> strSet3 = new TreeSet<>(              // (1c) Rhyming ordering
      (String obj1, String obj2) -> {
        // Create reversed versions of the strings:                      (2)
        String reverseStr1 = new StringBuilder(obj1).reverse().toString();
        String reverseStr2 = new StringBuilder(obj2).reverse().toString();
        // Compare the reversed strings lexicographically.
        return reverseStr1.compareTo(reverseStr2);             // (3)
      }
    );
    Set<String> strSet4 = new TreeSet<>(
        Comparator.comparingInt(String::length)        // (4) First length, then by
                .thenComparing(Comparator.naturalOrder()))// (5) natural ordering
    );

    // Add the elements from the words array to a set and print the set:
    Collections.addAll(strSet1, words);                              // (6)
    System.out.println("Natural order:\n" + strSet1);                // (7)
    Collections.addAll(strSet2, words);
    System.out.println("Case insensitive order:\n" + strSet2);
    Collections.addAll(strSet3, words);
    System.out.println("Rhyming order:\n" + strSet3);
    Collections.addAll(strSet4, words);
    System.out.println("Length, then natural order:\n" + strSet4);
  }
}
```

Output from the program:

```
Natural order:
[Resort, Stuart, assort, court, distort, report, support, transport]
Case insensitive order:
[assort, court, distort, report, Resort, Stuart, support, transport]
Rhyming order:
[Stuart, report, support, transport, Resort, assort, distort, court]
Length, then natural order:
[court, Resort, Stuart, assort, report, distort, support, transport]
```

The String class implements the Comparable<E> interface, providing an implementation of the compareTo() method. The compareTo() method defines the natural ordering for strings, which is lexicographical. The natural ordering is used to maintain the elements sorted lexicographically when the sorted set at (1a) is used. If we wish to maintain the strings in a different ordering, we need to provide a customized comparator.

The String class provides a static field (CASE_INSENSITIVE_ORDER) that denotes a comparator object with a compare() method that ignores the case when comparing strings lexicographically. This particular total ordering is used to maintain the elements sorted when the sorted set at (1b) is used. The comparator is passed as an argument to the set constructor. The output shows how the elements are maintained sorted in the set by this total ordering, which is a *case-insensitive ordering*.

We can create a string comparator that enforces *rhyming ordering* on the strings. In rhyming ordering, two strings are compared by examining their corresponding characters at each position in the two strings, starting with the characters in the *last* position. First the characters in the last position are compared, then those in the last but one position, and so on. For example, given the two strings "report" and "court", the last two characters in both strings are the same. Continuing toward the start of the two strings, the character 'o' in the first string is less than the character 'u' in the second string. According to rhyming ordering, the string "report" is less than the string "court".

Comparing two strings according to rhyming ordering is equivalent to reversing the strings and comparing the reversed strings lexicographically. If we reverse the two strings "report" and "court", the reversed string "troper" is lexicographically less than the reversed string "truoc".

A rhyming ordering comparator is implemented by the lambda expression at (1c) in Example 14.10. The lambda expression first creates reversed versions of the strings passed as arguments. A reversed version of a string is created using a string builder, which is first reversed and then converted back to a string, as shown at (2). The compareTo() method call at (3) compares the reversed strings, as the lexicographical ordering for the reversed strings is equivalent to the rhyming ordering for the original strings. This particular total ordering is used to maintain the elements sorted when the sorted set at (1c) is used. The lambda expression is passed as an argument to the set constructor, and is executed when the compare() method of the Comparator<String> interface is called by the sorted set implementation. The output shows how the elements are maintained sorted in the set by this total ordering, which is *rhyming ordering*.

Finally, a conditional comparator is composed at (4) and (5) that first compares the strings by their length, and if the lengths are equal, it employs the natural ordering for strings. The output shows that the strings are first sorted according to their lengths, and strings with equal lengths are sorted according to their natural ordering.

Example 14.11 illustrates using a comparator that orders version numbers (Example 14.8, p. 763) according to their reverse natural ordering. The method Comparator .reversedOrder() readily returns a comparator that imposes the reverse of the natural ordering.

A list of version numbers is initialized at (2). This list is sorted using the reverse natural ordering at (3). A binary search is done in this list at (4). We have used the same comparator for the search as we did for the sorting, in order to obtain predictable results. Searching this list with natural ordering at (5) does not find the key.

Example 14.11 *Using a Comparator for Version Numbers*

```java
import static java.lang.System.out;
import java.util.*;

public class UsingVersionNumberComparator {

    public static void main(String[] args) {
        VersionNumber[] versions = new VersionNumber[] {             // (1)
            new VersionNumber(3, 49, 1), new VersionNumber(8, 19, 81),
            new VersionNumber(2, 48, 28), new VersionNumber(10, 23, 78),
            new VersionNumber(9, 1, 1) };

        List<VersionNumber> vnList = new ArrayList<>();
        Collections.addAll(vnList, versions);                        // (2)
        out.println("List before sorting:\n  " + vnList);
        Collections.sort(vnList, Comparator.reverseOrder());         // (3)
        out.println("List after sorting according to " +
                    "reverse natural ordering:\n  " + vnList);

        VersionNumber searchKey = new VersionNumber(9, 1, 1);
        int resultIndex = Collections.binarySearch(vnList, searchKey,
                                    Comparator.reverseOrder());      // (4)
        out.printf("Binary search in list using reverse natural ordering"
                + " found key %s at index: %d%n", searchKey, resultIndex);

        resultIndex = Collections.binarySearch(vnList, searchKey);   // (5)
        out.printf("Binary search in list using natural ordering"
                + " found key %s at index: %d%n", searchKey, resultIndex);
    }
}
```

Output from the program:

```
List before sorting:
  [(3.49.1), (8.19.81), (2.48.28), (10.23.78), (9.1.1)]
List after sorting according to reverse natural ordering:
  [(10.23.78), (9.1.1), (8.19.81), (3.49.1), (2.48.28)]
Binary search in list using reverse natural ordering found key (9.1.1) at index: 1
Binary search in list using natural ordering found key (9.1.1) at index: -6
```

The Comparator<E> interface also provides many useful static and default methods, including composing conditional comparators that can compare on multiple fields. Reference is given in the description below to where the methods are used.

```
default Comparator<T> reversed()
static <T extends Comparable<? super T>> Comparator<T> naturalOrder()
static <T extends Comparable<? super T>> Comparator<T> reverseOrder()
```

The first method returns a comparator that imposes the reverse ordering of this comparator, equivalent to (a, b) -> this.compare(b, a).

The second method returns a comparator that compares Comparable objects in natural order, equivalent to (a, b) -> a.compareTo(b).

The third method returns a comparator that imposes the reverse of the natural ordering on Comparable objects, equivalent to (a, b) -> b.compareTo(a).

See Example 14.10, p. 770, and Example 14.11, p. 772.

```
static <T> Comparator<T> nullsFirst(Comparator<? super T> cmp)
static <T> Comparator<T> nullsLast(Comparator<? super T> cmp)
```

Return a null-friendly comparator that considers null to be either less than non-null or greater than non-null, respectively. These are useful comparators for sorting or searching in collections and maps when nulls are considered as actual values.

```
static <T, U> Comparator<T>
        comparing(Function<? super T,? extends U> func,
                Comparator<? super U> cmp)
```

Returns a Comparator<T> that applies func to the two given elements and compares the results using the specified Comparator cmp. It is effectively equivalent to (a, b) -> cmp.compare(func.apply(a), func.apply(b)).

```
static <T, U extends Comparable<? super U>> Comparator<T>
        comparing(Function<? super T,? extends U> func)
```

Returns a Comparator<T> that applies func to the two given elements first, before comparing the results by natural ordering. It is effectively equivalent to (a, b) -> func.apply(a).compareTo(func.apply(b)).

```
static <T> Comparator<T>
        comparingPrimType(ToPrimTypeFunction<? super T> func)
```

Returns a Comparator<T> that applies func to the two given elements first, before comparing the primitive-value results.

PrimType is either an Int, Long, or Double.

See Example 14.8, p. 763, and Example 14.10, p. 770.

```
default Comparator<T>
        thenComparing(Comparator<? super T> cmp)
```

Returns a *conditional* comparator that first determines using this Comparator whether two given elements are equal. If they are equal, the elements are compared using the specified Comparator cmp. Effectively, this method first executes this.compare(a, b), and then cmp.compare(a, b) if necessary.

See Example 14.10, p. 770.

```
default <U> Comparator<T>
        thenComparing(Function<? super T,? extends U> func,
                      Comparator<? super U> cmp)
```

Returns a conditional comparator that first determines using this Comparator whether two given elements are equal. If they are equal, it then applies func to the elements and the results are compared using the specified Comparator cmp. Effectively, this method first executes this.compare(a, b), and then cmp.compare (func.apply(a), func.apply(b)) if necessary.

```
default <U extends Comparable<? super U>> Comparator<T>
        thenComparing(Function<? super T,? extends U> func)
```

Returns a conditional comparator that first determines using this Comparator whether two given elements are equal. If they are equal, it then applies func to the elements and the results are compared by natural ordering. Effectively, this method first executes this.compare(a, b), and then func.apply(a).compareTo (func.apply(b)) if necessary.

```
default Comparator<T>
        thenComparingPrimType(ToPrimTypeFunction<? super T> func)
```

PrimType is either an Int, Long, or Double.

These primitive-type specialized methods return a conditional comparator that first determines, using this Comparator, if two given elements are equal. If they are equal, it then applies func to the two elements and the primitive-value results are compared.

See Example 14.8, p. 763, and Example 14.10, p. 770.

 Review Questions

14.1   Which of the following statements are true about the hashCode() and equals() methods?
       Select the two correct answers.
       (a) Two objects that are different according to the equals() method must have different hash codes.
       (b) Two objects that are equal according to the equals() method must have the same hash code.
       (c) Two objects that have the same hash code must be equal according to the equals() method.
       (d) Two objects that have different hash codes must be unequal according to the equals() method.

14.2   Given that the objects referenced by the parameters override the equals() and hashCode() methods appropriately, which return values are possible from the following method?

```
String func(Object x, Object y) {
  return (x == y) + " " + x.equals(y) + " " + (x.hashCode() == y.hashCode());
}
```

Select the four correct answers.

(a) "false false false"
(b) "false false true"
(c) "false true false"
(d) "false true true"
(e) "true false false"
(f) "true false true"
(g) "true true false"
(h) "true true true"

14.3   Which code, when inserted at (1), in the equalsImpl() method will fulfill the contract of the equals() method?

```java
public class Pair {
  private int a, b;
  public Pair(int a, int b) {
    this.a = a;
    this.b = b;
  }

  public boolean equals(Object o) {
    return (this == o) || (o instanceof Pair) && equalsImpl((Pair) o);
  }

  private boolean equalsImpl(Pair o) {
    // (1) INSERT CODE HERE
  }
}
```

Select the three correct answers.

(a) return a == o.a || b == o.b;
(b) return false;
(c) return a >= o.a;
(d) return a == o.a;
(e) return a == o.a && b == o.b;

14.4   Which code, when inserted at (1), will provide a correct implementation of the hashCode() method in the following program?

```java
import java.util.*;
public class Measurement {
  private int count;
  private int accumulated;
  public Measurement() {}
  public void record(int v) {
    count++;
    accumulated += v;
  }
  public int average() {
    return accumulated/count;
  }
```

```java
        public boolean equals(Object other) {
          if (this == other)
            return true;
          if (!(other instanceof Measurement))
            return false;
          Measurement o = (Measurement) other;
          if (count != 0 && o.count != 0)
            return average() == o.average();
          return count == o.count;
        }
        public int hashCode() {
          // (1) INSERT CODE HERE
        }
      }
```

Select the two correct answers.

(a) `return 31337;`
(b) `return accumulated / count;`
(c) `return (count << 16) ^ accumulated;`
(d) `return ~accumulated;`
(e) `return count == 0 ? 0 : average();`

14.5 Which statement is true about the following program?

```java
      import java.util.Comparator;
      import java.util.Comparator;
      class Person  implements Comparable<Person > {
        private String name;
        private int age;
        Person (String name, int age) { this.name = name; this.age = age; }

        public int compareTo(Person  p2) {
          Comparator<String> strCmp = Person.cmp();
          int status = strCmp.compare(this.name, p2.name);
          if (status == 0) {
            Comparator<Integer> intCmp = Person.cmp();
            status = intCmp.compare(this.age, p2.age);
          }
          return status;
        }

        public static <E extends Comparable<E>> Comparator<E> cmp() {
          return  (e1, e2) -> e2.compareTo(e1);
        }
      }

      public class Main {
        public static void main(String[] args) {
          Person  p1 = new Person ("Tom", 20);
          Person  p2 = new Person ("Dick", 30);
          Person  p3 = new Person ("Tom", 40);
          System.out.println((p1.compareTo(p2) < 0) + " " + (p1.compareTo(p3) < 0));
        }
      }
```

Select the one correct answer.

(a) The program will fail to compile.
(b) The program will compile. When run, it will throw an exception.
(c) The program will compile. When run, it will print true false.
(d) The program will compile. When run, it will print true true.
(e) The program will compile. When run, it will print false false.
(f) The program will compile. When run, it will print false true.

14.6 Which method returns a Comparator<E> that is not equivalent to the other six?

```java
import java.util.Comparator;
class CompDecls {

  public static <E extends Comparable<E>> Comparator<E> cmp1() {      // (1)
    return new Comparator<E>() {
      public int compare(E e1, E e2) { return e2.compareTo(e1); }
    };
  }

  public static <E extends Comparable<E>> Comparator<E> cmp2() {      // (2)
    return (e1, e2) -> e2.compareTo(e1);
  }

  public static <E extends Comparable<E>> Comparator<E> cmp3() {      // (3)
    return ((Comparator<E>)(e1, e2) -> e1.compareTo(e2)).reversed();
  }

  public static <E extends Comparable<E>> Comparator<E> cmp4() {      // (4)
    return Comparable::compareTo;
  }

  public static <E extends Comparable<E>> Comparator<E> cmp5() {      // (5)
    return ((Comparator<E>)Comparable::compareTo).reversed();
  }

  public static <E extends Comparable<E>> Comparator<E> cmp6() {      // (6)
    Comparator<E> cmp = Comparable::compareTo;
    return cmp.reversed();
  }

  public static <E extends Comparable<E>> Comparator<E> cmp7() {      // (7)
    return Comparator.reverseOrder();
  }
}
```

Select the one correct answer.

(a) (1)
(b) (2)
(c) (3)
(d) (4)
(e) (5)
(f) (6)
(g) (7)

14.7   Given the following code:

```
import java.util.*;
public class Test14RQ8 {
  public static void main(String[] args) {
    Integer[] values = {-42,15,-23,19,11,71};
    Arrays.sort(values, (v1, v2) -> v1.toString().compareTo(v2.toString()));
    System.out.println(Arrays.toString(values));
  }
}
```

What is the result?

Select the one correct answer.

(a) [71, 19, 15, 11, -23, -42]

(b) [-23, -42, 11, 15, 19, 71]

(c) [-42, -23, 11, 15, 19, 71]

(d) [71, 19, 15, 11, -42, -23]

(e) [-42, 15, -23, 19, 11, 71]

(f) The program will throw an exception at runtime.

(g) The program will fail to compile.

14.8   Given the following code:

```
import java.util.*;
import java.util.function.*;
public class Album {
  private static List<Album> albums = new ArrayList<>();
  private String title;
  private Album(String title) { this.title = title; }
  public String toString() { return title; }
  public static void addAlbum(String title) {
    albums.add(new Album(title));
  }
  public static void sortAlbums(Comparator<Album> c) {
    albums.sort(c);
  }
  public static void processAlbums(Consumer<Album> c) {
    albums.forEach(c);
  }
}
```

and

```
public class Test14RQ11 {
  public static void main(String[] args) {
    Album.addAlbum("New Songs");
    Album.addAlbum("More Songs");
    Album.addAlbum("Greatest Hits");
    Album.addAlbum("Old Songs");
    Album.sortAlbums((a1, a2) -> a1.toString().length() - a2.toString().length());
    Album.processAlbums(a -> {
      System.out.print(a.toString() + " ");
    });
  }
}
```

What is the result?

Select the one correct answer.

(a) New Songs Old Songs More Songs Greatest Hits
(b) New Songs More Songs Greatest Hits Old Songs
(c) Greatest Hits More Songs Old Songs New Songs
(d) Old Songs Greatest Hits More Songs New Songs
(e) The program will throw an exception at runtime.
(f) The program will fail to compile.

14.9 Given the following code:

```java
import java.util.Objects;
public class Album1 {
  private String title;
  public Album1(String title) { this.title = title; }
  public int hashCode() {
    int hash = 7;
    hash = 29 * hash + Objects.hashCode(this.title);
    return hash;
  }
  public boolean equals(Object obj) {
    if (this == obj) { return true; }
    if (obj == null) { return false; }
    if (getClass() != obj.getClass()) { return false; }
    final Album1 other = (Album1) obj;
    return Objects.equals(this.title, other.title);
  }
}
```

and

```java
public class LP extends Album1 {
  public LP(String title) { super(title); }
}
```

and

```java
public class Test14RQ9 {
  public static void main(String[] args) {
    Album1 a1 = new Album1("Some Music");
    Album1 a2 = new LP("Some Music");
    if (a1.equals(a2)) {
      System.out.println("Same album");
    } else {
      System.out.println("These are different albums");
    }
  }
}
```

What is the result?

Select the one correct answer.

(a) Same album
(b) These are different albums
(c) The program will throw an exception at runtime.
(d) The program will fail to compile.

14.10   Which of the following statements are true about object ordering?
Select the two correct answers.

(a) Class A can implement the Comparator<A> interface to compare its instances to other objects.

(b) Class A can implement the Comparable<A> interface to compare its instances to other objects.

(c) The Comparator<A> interface is implemented to establish a natural ordering for objects of class A.

(d) The Comparable<A> interface is implemented to establish a natural ordering for objects of class A.

Collections: Part II 15

 Chapter Topics

- An overview of the Java Collections Framework in the `java.util` package: core interfaces and their implementations

- Understanding the functionality provided by the `Collection<E>` interface, and its role in the Java Collections Framework

- How to create and use lists, and how their functionality is defined by the `List<E>` interface and implemented by the classes `ArrayList<E>`, `Vector<E>`, and `LinkedList<E>`

- How to create and use sets, and how their functionality is defined by the `Set<E>` interface and implemented by the classes `HashSet<E>` and `LinkedHashSet<E>`

- How to create and use sorted and navigable sets, and how their functionality is defined by the `SortedSet<E>` and `NavigableSet<E>` interfaces, respectively, and implemented by the class `TreeSet<E>`

- How to create and use queues and deques, and how their functionality is defined by the `Queue<E>` and `Deque<E>` interfaces, and implemented by the classes `PriorityQueue<E>` and `ArrayDeque<E>`, respectively

- How to create and use maps, and how their functionality is defined by the `Map<K, V>` interface and implemented by the classes `HashMap<K, V>`, `LinkedHashMap<K, V>`, and `Hashtable<K, V>`

- How to create and use sorted and navigable maps, and how their functionality is defined by the `SortedMap<K, V>` and `NavigableMap<K, V>` interfaces, respectively, and implemented by the class `TreeMap<K, V>`

- Using the utility methods found in the `Collections` and `Arrays` classes, with emphasis on sorting and searching in lists and arrays

Java SE 17 Developer Exam Objectives	
[5.1] Create Java arrays, List, Set, Map and Deque collections, and add, remove, update, retrieve and sort their elements ○ *List, set, map, deque, and sorted collections and arrays are covered in this chapter.* ○ *For arrays, see §3.9, p. 117.* ○ *For ArrayList, see Chapter 12, p. 643.* ○ *For comparing elements, see §14.4, p. 761, and §14.5, p. 769, respectively.*	*§15.1, p. 783* *to* *§15.12, p. 865*
Java SE 11 Developer Exam Objectives	
[5.2] Use a Java array and List, Set, Map and Deque collections, including convenience methods ○ *List, set, map, and deque collections are covered in this chapter.* ○ *For arrays, see §3.9, p. 117.* ○ *For ArrayList, see Chapter 12, p. 643.*	*§15.1, p. 783* *to* *§15.9, p. 840*
[5.3] Sort collections and arrays using Comparator and Comparable interfaces ○ *Sorting collections and arrays is covered in this chapter.* ○ *For Comparable and Comparator interfaces, see §14.4, p. 761, and §14.5, p. 769, respectively.*	*§15.5, p. 810* *§15.10, p. 845* *§15.11, p. 858* *§15.12, p. 865*

The topics covered in this chapter can be divided into two main parts:

* In-depth coverage of collections, deques, and maps (§15.1 to §15.10)
* Sorting and searching in collections and arrays using the utility methods from the Collections and the Arrays classes (§15.11 and §15.12)

Some topics related to collections and maps are covered elsewhere in the book:

* The ArrayList<E> class is covered in Chapter 12, p. 643.
* Using streams with collections is covered in Chapter 16, p. 879.
* Thread-safe or concurrent collections and maps are covered in Chapter 22, p. 1365.
* Static methods from the utility class Arrays are used in many examples throughout the book.

15.1 The Java Collections Framework

A *collection* allows a group of objects to be treated as a single entity. Objects can be stored, retrieved, and manipulated as *elements* of a collection. Arrays are an example of one kind of collection.

Program design often requires the handling of collections of objects. The Java Collections Framework provides a set of standard utility classes for managing various kinds of collections. The core framework is provided in the java.util package and comprises three main parts:

* The core *interfaces* that allow collections to be manipulated independently of their implementation (see Figure 15.1 and Table 15.1). These *generic* interfaces define the common functionality exhibited by collections, and facilitate data exchange between collections.
* A set of *implementations* (i.e., concrete classes, listed in Table 15.1) that are specific implementations of the core interfaces, providing data structures that a program can readily use.
* *Algorithms* that are an assortment of static *utility methods* found in the Collections and Arrays *classes* that can be used to perform various operations on collections and arrays, such as sorting and searching, or creating customized collections (§15.11, p. 856, and §15.12, p. 864).

Core Interfaces

The generic Collection<E> interface is a generalized interface for maintaining collections, and is the root of the interface inheritance hierarchy for collections shown in Figure 15.1a. These generic subinterfaces are summarized in Table 15.1. The Collection<E> interface extends the Iterable<E> interface that specifies an *iterator* to sequentially access the elements of an Iterable object (p. 791).

Figure 15.1 *The Core Interfaces*

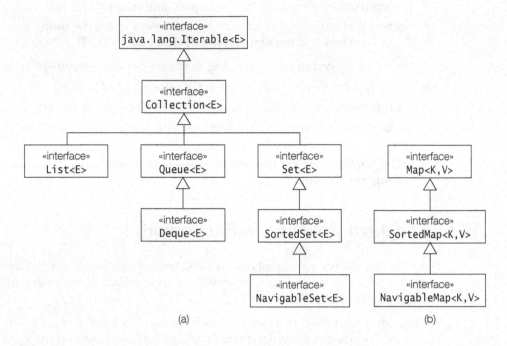

Table 15.1 *Core Interfaces and Concrete Classes in the Collections Framework*

Interface	Description	Concrete classes
Collection<E>	A basic interface that defines the normal operations that allow a collection of objects to be maintained or handled as a single unit.	–
List<E> extends Collection<E>	The List<E> interface extends the Collection<E> interface to maintain a sequence of elements that can contain duplicates.	ArrayList<E>, Vector<E>, LinkedList<E>
Set<E> extends Collection<E>	The Set<E> interface extends the Collection<E> interface to represent its mathematical namesake: a *set* of unique elements.	HashSet<E>, LinkedHashSet<E>
SortedSet<E> extends Set<E>	The SortedSet<E> interface extends the Set<E> interface to provide the required functionality for maintaining a set in which the elements are stored in some sort order.	TreeSet<E>
NavigableSet<E> extends SortedSet<E>	The NavigableSet<E> interface extends and replaces the SortedSet<E> interface to maintain a sorted set, and should be the preferred choice in new code.	TreeSet<E>

Table 15.1 *Core Interfaces and Concrete Classes in the Collections Framework (Continued)*

Interface	Description	Concrete classes
Queue<E> extends Collection<E>	The Queue<E> interface extends the Collection<E> need to be processed according to some policy—that is, insertion at one end and removal at the other, usually as FIFO (first in, first out).	PriorityQueue<E>, LinkedList<E>
Deque<E> extends Queue<E>	The Deque<E> interface extends the Queue<E> interface to maintain a queue whose elements can be processed at both ends: *double-ended queue.*	ArrayDeque<E>, LinkedList<E>
Map<K,V>	A basic interface that defines operations for maintaining mappings of keys to values.	HashMap<K,V>, Hashtable<K,V>, LinkedHashMap<K,V>
SortedMap<K,V> extends Map<K,V>	The SortedMap<K, V> interface extends the Map<K, V> interface for maps that maintain their mappings sorted in key order.	TreeMap<K,V>
NavigableMap<K,V> extends SortedMap<K,V>	The NavigableMap<K, V> interface extends and replaces the SortedMap<K, V> interface for sorted maps.	TreeMap<K,V>

The elements in a Set<E> must be unique—that is, no two elements in the set can be equal. The order of elements in a List<E> is *positional*, and individual elements can be accessed randomly according to their position in the list.

Queues and deques, represented respectively by the Queue<E> and the Deque<E> interfaces, define collections whose elements can be processed according to various policies.

As can be seen in Figure 15.1b, the Map<K, V> interface does not extend the Collection<E> interface because conceptually, a map is not a collection. A map does not contain elements. It contains *mappings* (also called *entries*) from a set of *key* objects to a set of *value* objects. A key can, at most, be associated with one value—that is, it must be unique. As the name implies, the SortedMap<K, V> interface extends the Map<K, V> interface to maintain its mappings sorted in *key order*. It is superseded by the NavigableMap<K, V> interface which should be the preferred choice in new code.

Implementations

The java.util package provides implementations of a selection of well-known abstract data types, based on the core interfaces. Figures 15.2 and 15.3 show the inheritance relationship between the core interfaces and the corresponding implementations. None of the concrete implementations inherit directly from the Collection<E> interface. The abstract classes that provide the basis on which concrete classes are implemented are not shown in Figures 15.2 and 15.3.

Figure 15.2   *The Core Collection Interfaces and Their Implementations*

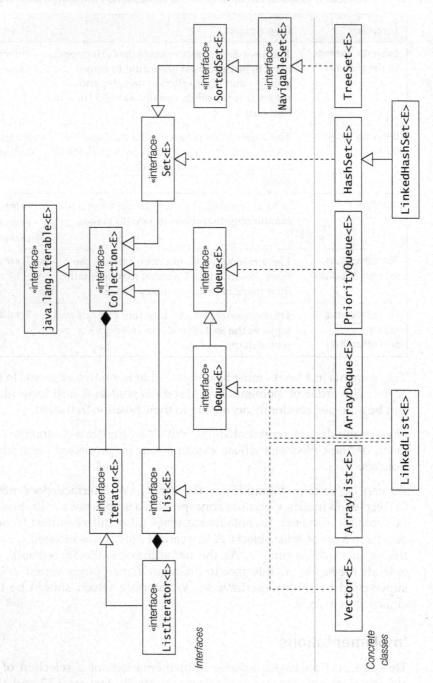

Figure 15.3 *The Core Map Interfaces and Their Implementations*

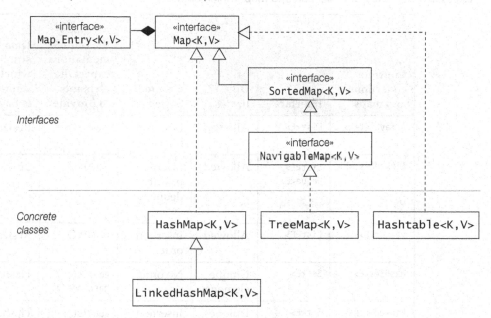

By convention, each of the collection implementation classes provides a constructor for creating a collection based on the elements of another Collection object
passed as an argument. This allows the implementation of a collection to be
changed by merely passing the collection to the constructor of the desired implementation. This interchangeability is also true between Map implementations. But
collections and maps are not interchangeable. Note that a collection (or a map) only
stores reference values of objects, and not the actual objects.

The collections framework is *interface-based*, meaning that collections are manipulated according to their interface types, rather than by the implementation types.
By using these interfaces wherever collections of objects are used, various implementations can be used interchangeably.

All the concrete classes shown in Figures 15.2 and 15.3 implement the Serializable
and the Cloneable interfaces; therefore, the objects of these classes can be serialized
and also cloned.

A summary of collection and map implementations is given in Table 15.2. The contents of this table will be the focus as each core interface and its corresponding
implementations are discussed in the subsequent sections.

In Table 15.2, we see that only lists and queues allow *duplicates*—that is, the same
value can be stored multiple times in the collection. The TreeSet<E> class and the
queue classes PriorityQueue<E> and ArrayDeque<E> do *not* allow the null value to be
stored in the collection. All maps require that the keys are *unique*—that is, no two
keys can be equal, and only the classes Hashtable<K, V> and TreeMap<K, V> disallow
the null value as a key. A Hashtable<K, V>, in addition, does not allow the null value
to be associated with a key.

Table 15.2 *Summary of Collection and Map Implementations*

Concrete collections and maps	Interface	Dup-licates	Ordered/ Sorted	Methods the imple-mentations expect the elements to provide	Data structures on which implementation is based
ArrayList<E>	List<E>	Allowed	Insertion order	equals()	Resizable array
LinkedList<E>	List<E>, Deque<E>	Allowed	Insertion/ priority/ deque order	equals()	Linked list
Vector<E>	List<E>	Allowed	Insertion order	equals()	Resizable array
HashSet<E>	Set<E>	Unique elements	No order	equals(), hashCode()	Hash table
LinkedHash-Set<E>	Set<E>	Unique elements	Insertion order	equals(), hashCode()	Hash table and doubly linked list
TreeSet<E>	Navigable-Set<E>	Unique elements (not null)	Sort order	equals(), hashCode(), compareTo()	Balanced tree
Priority-Queue<E>	Queue<E>	Allowed (not null)	Access according to priority order	equals(), compareTo()	Priority heap (tree-like structure)
ArrayDeque<E>	Deque<E>	Allowed (not null)	Deque order	equals()	Resizable array
HashMap<K,V>	Map<K,V>	Unique keys	No order	equals(), hashCode()	Hash table
LinkedHash-Map<K,V>	Map<K,V>	Unique keys	Key insertion order/ Access order of entries	equals(), hashCode()	Hash table and doubly linked list

Table 15.2 *Summary of Collection and Map Implementations (Continued)*

Concrete collections and maps	Interface	Dup-licates	Ordered/ Sorted	Methods the imple-mentations expect the elements to provide	Data structures on which implementation is based
Hash-table<K,V>	Map<K,V>	Unique keys (no null key and no null values)	No order	equals(), hashCode()	Hash table
TreeMap<K,V>	Navigable-Map<K,V>	Unique keys (no null key)	Sorted in key order	equals(), hashCode(), compareTo()	Balanced tree

From Table 15.2, we also see that elements in a LinkedHashSet<E> are ordered, in a TreeSet<E> they are sorted, and in a HashSet<E> they have no order (i.e., they are *unordered*). *Sorting implies ordering* the elements in a collection according to some ranking criteria, usually based on the *values* of the elements. However, elements in an ArrayList<E> are maintained in the order they are inserted in the list, known as the *insertion order*. The elements in such a list are thus *ordered*, but they are *not* sorted, as it is not the values of the elements that determine their ranking in the list but their position in the list. Thus ordering does *not* necessarily imply sorting. In a HashSet<E>, the elements are unordered. No ranking of elements is implied in such a set. Whether a collection is sorted, ordered, or unordered also has implications when iterating over the collection (p. 791).

In order for sorting and searching to work properly, the collections and maps in Table 15.2 also require that their elements implement the appropriate methods for object comparison. Comparing objects is covered in Chapter 14, p. 741. Sorting and searching in collections is covered in §15.11, p. 856.

Methods defined for collections that specify functional interfaces as a parameter and require lambda expressions as arguments are covered in Chapter 13, p. 673.

Using streams with collections is covered in Chapter 16, p. 879.

The collection and map implementations discussed in this chapter, except for Vector<E> and Hashtable<K, V>, are not *thread-safe*—that is, their integrity can be jeopardized by concurrent access. Concurrent collections and maps are covered in Chapter 22, p. 1365.

The Java Collections Framework provides a plethora of collections and maps for use in single-threaded and concurrent applications, which should eliminate the need to implement one from scratch.

15.2 Collections

The Collection<E> interface specifies the contract that all collections should implement. Some of the operations in the interface are *optional*, meaning that a collection may choose to provide a stub implementation of such an operation that throws an UnsupportedOperationException when invoked—for example, when a collection is unmodifiable. The implementations of collections from the java.util package support all the optional operations in the Collection<E> interface (see Figure 15.2 and Table 15.2).

Many of the methods return a boolean value to indicate whether the collection was modified as a result of the operation.

Basic Operations

The basic operations are used to query a collection about its contents and allow elements to be added to and removed from a collection. Many examples in this chapter make use of these operations.

```
int size()
boolean isEmpty()
boolean contains(Object element)
boolean add(E element)                    Optional
boolean remove(Object element)            Optional
```

The size() method returns the number of elements in the collection, and the isEmpty() method determines whether there are any elements in the collection.

The contains() method checks for membership of the argument object in the collection, using object value equality.

The add() and remove() methods return true if the collection was modified as a result of the operation.

By returning the value false, the add() method indicates that the collection excludes duplicates, and that the collection already contains an object equal to the argument object.

Note that we can only add an object of a specific type (E). However, a collection allows us to determine whether it has an element equal to an arbitrary object, or remove an element that is equal to an arbitrary object.

Bulk Operations

These operations are performed on a collection as a single entity. See §15.4, p. 804, for an example.

```
boolean containsAll(Collection<?> c)
boolean addAll(Collection<? extends E> c)          Optional
boolean removeAll(Collection<?> c)                 Optional
boolean retainAll(Collection<?> c)                 Optional
void    clear()                                    Optional
```

These bulk operations can be used to perform the equivalent of set logic on *arbitrary collections* (i.e., also lists and not just sets). The containsAll() method returns true if all elements of the specified collection are also contained in the current collection.

The addAll(), removeAll(), and retainAll() methods are *destructive* in the sense that the collection on which they are invoked can be modified. The operations performed by these methods are visualized by Venn diagrams in Figure 15.4.

The addAll() method requires that the element type of the other collection is the same as, or a subtype of, the element type of the current collection. The removeAll() and retainAll() operations can be performed with collections of any type.

The clear() method removes all elements in the collection so that the collection is empty.

Figure 15.4   *Bulk Operations on Collections*

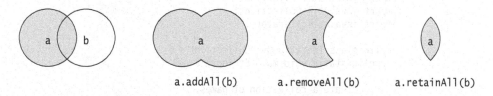

Iterating Over a Collection

A common operation on a collection is to iterate over all elements in a collection in order to perform a particular operation on each individual element. We explore several ways in which this operation can be implemented:

- Using the hasNext() and next() methods of the Iterator<E> interface (p. 793) to access the elements in the underlying collection
- Using the forEachRemaining() default method of the Iterator<E> interface to access the elements in the underlying collection
- Using the enhanced for(:) loop to iterate over an object that implements the Iterable<E> interface (see below)
- Using the forEach() default method of the Iterable<E> interface
- Using a sequential or parallel stream to iterate over a collection (p. 798)

The Iterable<E> interface defines the methods shown below. The enhanced for(:) loop can be used to iterate over objects that implement this interface. The Collection<E> interface extends the Iterable<E> interface, making all collections iterable.

> Iterator<E> iterator()   From Iterable<E> interface.
>
> Returns an iterator that can be used to iterate over the elements in this collection. Any guarantee regarding the order in which the elements are returned is provided by the individual collection.
>
> default void forEach(Consumer<? super T> action)   From Iterable<E> interface.
>
> With this method, the specified action is performed on each of the remaining elements of an Iterable, unless an exception is thrown, which is then relayed to the caller. The functional interface Consumer<T> is covered in §13.7, p. 709.

Example 15.1 illustrates various ways to iterate over a collection that is created at (1). The example uses an ArrayList<E> for a collection of names that are Strings. First an empty ArrayList is created and names are added to the collection. The operation performed on the collection prints each name in uppercase.

Example 15.1 *Iterating Over a Collection*

```java
import java.util.ArrayList;
import java.util.Collection;
import java.util.Collections;
import java.util.Iterator;

public class IterationOverCollections {
  public static void main(String[] args) {

    // Create a collection of names.                                      (1)
    Collection<String> collectionOfNames = new ArrayList<>();
    Collections.addAll(collectionOfNames, "Alice", "Bob", "Tom","Dick","Harriet");
    System.out.println(collectionOfNames);

    // Using an explicit iterator.
    Iterator<String> iterator = collectionOfNames.iterator();        // (2)
    while (iterator.hasNext()) {                                     // (3)
      String name = iterator.next();                                // (4)
      System.out.print(name.toUpperCase() + " ");
    }
    System.out.println();

    // Using the forEachRemaining() method of the Iterator interface.
    iterator = collectionOfNames.iterator();                        // (5)
    iterator.forEachRemaining(name ->                               // (6)
        System.out.print(name.toUpperCase() + " "));
    System.out.println();

    // Using the for(:) loop on an Iterable.
    for (String name : collectionOfNames) {                         // (7)
      System.out.print(name.toUpperCase() + " ");
    }
    System.out.println();
```

```
    // Using the forEach() method of the Collection interface.
    collectionOfNames.forEach(name ->                              // (8)
        System.out.print(name.toUpperCase() + " "));
    System.out.println();

    // Filtering using an explicit iterator.
    iterator = collectionOfNames.iterator();                       // (9)
    while (iterator.hasNext()) {                                   // (10)
      String name = iterator.next();                               // (11)
      if (name.length() == 3)
        iterator.remove();                                         // (12)
    }
    System.out.println(collectionOfNames);

    // Filtering using the removeIf() method of the Collection interface.
    collectionOfNames.removeIf(name -> name.startsWith("A"));       // (13)
        System.out.println(collectionOfNames);

    // Using the stream() method of the Collection interface.
    collectionOfNames.stream()                                      // (14)
                  .forEach(name -> System.out.print(name.toUpperCase() + " "));
    System.out.println();
  }
}
```

Output from the program:

```
[Alice, Bob, Tom, Dick, Harriet]
ALICE BOB TOM DICK HARRIET
ALICE BOB TOM DICK HARRIET
ALICE BOB TOM DICK HARRIET
ALICE BOB TOM DICK HARRIET
[Alice, Dick, Harriet]
[Dick, Harriet]
DICK HARRIET
```

- -

Using an Explicit Iterator on a Collection

A collection provides an iterator which allows sequential access to the elements of a collection. An iterator can be obtained by calling the iterator() method of the Collection<E> interface. An iterator is defined by the generic interface java.util.Iterator<E> that has the following methods:

boolean hasNext()   From Iterator<E> interface.

Returns true if the underlying collection still has elements left to return. A future call to the next() method will return the next element from the collection.

E next()   From Iterator<E> interface.

Moves the iterator to the next element in the underlying collection, and returns the current element. If there are no more elements left to return, it throws a NoSuchElementException.

| void remove() | Optional | From Iterator<E> interface. |

Removes the element that was returned by the last call to the next() method from the underlying collection. Invoking this method results in an Illegal-StateException if the next() method has not yet been called, or when the remove() method has already been called after the last call to the next() method. This method is optional for an iterator—that is, it throws an Unsupported-OperationException if the remove operation is not supported.

```
default void
    forEachRemaining(Consumer<? super E> action) From Iterator<E> interface.
```

The specified action is performed on each of the remaining elements in the collection associated with an iterator, unless an exception is thrown during its execution. The functional interface Consumer<T> is covered in §13.7, p. 709.

After obtaining the iterator for a collection, the methods provided by the Iterator<E> interface can be used systematically to iterate over the elements of the underlying collection one at a time.

In Example 15.1, an explicit iterator is obtained at (2) and used in the loop at (3) to iterate over all elements in the underlying collection. A call to the hasNext() method in the condition of the loop ensures that there is still an element to retrieve from the collection. At (4) the current element is retrieved by the iterator from the collection by calling the next() method. No casts are necessary at (4), as the compiler guarantees that the iterator will return a String object from the underlying collection.

```
Iterator<String> iterator = collectionOfNames.iterator();      // (2)
while (iterator.hasNext()) {                                    // (3)
  String name = iterator.next();                               // (4)
  System.out.print(name.toUpperCase() + " ");
}
```

Note that the methods are invoked on the iterator, not the underlying collection. In Example 15.1, the hasNext() method is called *before* the next() method to ensure that there is still an element remaining to be processed; otherwise, a java.util.NoSuch-ElementException can be raised at runtime. Using an explicit iterator puts this responsibility on the user code.

In Example 15.1, we used an iterator in a while loop at (3) for iterating over the collection. It is quite common to use an iterator in a for(;;) loop for this purpose, where the iterator is obtained in the initialization part, and the increment part is left empty:

```
for (Iterator<String> iterator = collectionOfNames.iterator();
     iterator.hasNext(); /* Empty increment. */) {
  String name = iterator.next();
  System.out.print(name.toUpperCase() + " ");
}
```

The majority of the iterators provided in the java.util package are said to be *fail-fast*. When an iterator has already been obtained, structurally modifying the underlying collection by other means will invalidate the iterator. Subsequent use of this iterator will throw a ConcurrentModificationException, as the iterator checks to see if the collection has been structurally modified every time it accesses the collection. The remove() method of an iterator is the only recommended way to delete elements from the underlying collection during iteration with an iterator (p. 796).

The order in which the iterator will return the elements from an underlying collection depends on the iteration order supported by the collection. For example, an iterator for a list will iterate over the elements in the sequential order they have in the list, whereas the iteration order for the elements in an ordinary set is not predetermined. An iterator for a sorted collection will make the elements available in a given sort order. Iteration order will be discussed together with the individual concrete collection classes.

Using the forEachRemaining() Method

A convenient way to perform a task on each element of a collection is to use the forEachRemaining() method of the Iterator<E> interface. This method requires a consumer as an argument (§13.7, p. 709). The lambda expression defining the consumer is executed for each *remaining* element of the collection. In Example 15.1, a new iterator is obtained at (5) as the previous one was exhausted, before calling the method at (6). The lambda expression passed as an argument prints the name in uppercase (postfixed with a space for readability in the output). Note that the method is invoked on the iterator, and not directly on the collection.

```
iterator = collectionOfNames.iterator();                              // (5)
iterator.forEachRemaining(name ->                                     // (6)
    System.out.print(name.toUpperCase() + " "));
```

In Example 15.1, the toString() method of the collection class is used implicitly in print statements to generate a text representation for the collection. The collection classes override the Object.toString() method to provide a text representation of their contents. The standard text representation generated by the toString() method for a collection is

[*element₁*, *element₂*, ..., *element_n*]

where each *element_i*, where 1 <= i <= n, is the text representation generated by the toString() method of the individual elements in the collection.

Using the for(:) Loop to Iterate Over a Collection

A for(:) loop can be used to iterate over an array or a data structure that implements the java.lang.Iterable<E> interface. This interface requires the implementation of the iterator() method to obtain an iterator that is used behind the scenes to iterate over elements of the data structure in a for(:) loop.

In the for(:) loop construct

for (*type variable* : *expression*) *statement*

the value of *expression* can be a reference value that refers to a collection that implements the Iterable<E> interface. In Figure 15.2 we see that the Collection<E>

interface extends the Iterable<E> interface, and therefore, all collections that implement the Collection<E> interface can be iterated over using the for(:) loop. A collection that implements the Collection<E> interface and thereby the Iterable<E> interface has the element type E. This element type E must be assignable to the *type* of the *variable* in the for(:) loop. The *variable* is assigned the reference value of a new element in the collection each time the body of the loop is executed.

The semantics of the for(:) loop also apply when iterating over a collection. In particular, any structural change to the collection (adding or removing elements) in the for(:) loop will result in a ConcurrentModificationException—in other words, the underlying collection is structurally immutable.

Example 15.1 illustrates using a for(:) loop to iterate over a collection. The collection of names is iterated over in the for(:) loop at (7), printing each name in uppercase.

```
for (String name : collectionOfNames) {                              // (7)
  System.out.print(name.toUpperCase() + " ");
}
```

Behind the scenes, however, an appropriate iterator is used to iterate over the collection, but the for(:) loop simplifies iterating over a collection in the source code.

Note that if the collection is ordered or sorted, the iterator will iterate over the collection in the ordering used to maintain the elements in the collection. For example, in the case of an ArrayList, the iterator will yield the elements in the same order as the insertion order. In the case of a TreeSet<E>, the iterator will yield the elements in the sort order used to maintain the elements in the set. If the collection is unordered, the order in which the iterator will yield the elements is not predictable. Thus we cannot be sure in which order the elements of a HashSet will be iterated by the for(:) loop.

Using the forEach() Method to Iterate Over a Collection

The default method forEach() of the Iterable<E> interface (which the Collection<E> interface implements) allows us to do away with an explicit iterator in order to perform an operation on each element of the collection. The method requires a consumer as the argument (§13.7, p. 709). The lambda expression defining the consumer is executed successively for each element of the collection.

In Example 15.1, the lambda expression passed as the argument at (8) prints each name in uppercase. Note that the method is invoked directly on the collection.

```
collectionOfNames.forEach(name ->
  System.out.print(name.toUpperCase() + " "));                       // (8)
```

Filtering

We illustrate here two ways of filtering a collection—in this case, removing elements from the collection that satisfy certain criteria.

Using the `remove()` Method of an Iterator to Filter a Collection

Example 15.1 shows how an explicit iterator can be used in a loop to *remove* elements from a collection that fulfills certain criteria. As we have seen earlier, an explicit iterator is obtained at (9) and used in the loop at (10). The order of calls to the `hasNext()` and `next()` methods on the iterator at (10) and (11), respectively, ensures that each element in the underlying collection is retrieved in the loop. The call to the `remove()` method in the loop at (12) removes the current element from the underlying collection, if the criteria in the `if` statement is satisfied.

```
// [Alice, Bob, Tom, Dick, Harriet]
iterator = collectionOfNames.iterator();                                // (9)
while (iterator.hasNext()) {                                             // (10)
  String name = iterator.next();                                        // (11)
  if (name.length() == 3)
    iterator.remove();                                                  // (12)
}
// [Alice, Dick, Harriet]
```

Best practices dictate that the three methods of the iterator should be used *in lockstep* inside a loop, as shown in Example 15.1. In particular, the `next()` method *must* be called *before* the `remove()` method for each element in the collection; otherwise, a `java.lang.IllegalStateException` or an `UnsupportedOperationException` is raised at runtime, depending on whether the collection provides this optional operation or not. As noted earlier, using an explicit iterator places the responsibility of bookkeeping on the user code.

Using the `removeIf()` Method to Filter a Collection

The following `default` method of the `Collection<E>` interface makes the task of filtering a collection much easier, as no explicit iteration is necessary:

```
default boolean removeIf(Predicate<? super E> filter)
```

All elements that satisfy the predicate defined by the specified `filter` are removed from this collection. The method returns `true` or `false` depending on whether the collection was modified or not. Predicates are covered in §13.6, p. 703.

In Example 15.1, the call to the `removeIf()` method at (13) takes a `Predicate` to test whether a name starts with the letter A, resulting in those names satisfying the predicate to be removed from the collection.

```
// [Alice, Dick, Harriet]
collectionOfNames.removeIf(name -> name.startsWith("A"));        // (13)
// [Dick, Harriet]
```

Ample examples of filtering can also be found in §13.3, p. 691, and §16.5, p. 910.

Streams

The two methods of the Collections interface shown below allow a collection to be used as the *source of a stream*. A stream makes the elements of a collection available as a *sequence* of elements on which *sequential* and *parallel aggregate operations* can be performed.

```
default Stream<E> stream()
default Stream<E> parallelStream()
```
Return a sequential stream or a possibly parallel stream with this collection as its source, respectively.

Example 15.1 illustrates at (14) how a stream can be used to iterate over the collection of names in order to print them in uppercase.

```
collectionOfNames.stream()                                        // (14)
                .forEach(name -> System.out.print(name.toUpperCase() + " "));
```

Details are revealed in §16.4, p. 897, which is devoted entirely to streams, providing many examples of using streams on collections.

Array Operations

The following operations convert collections to arrays. See also array operations on array lists (§12.6, p. 658).

```
Object[] toArray()
<T>  T[] toArray(T[] a)
```
The first toArray() method returns an array of type Object filled with all the elements of the collection. The second method is a generic method that stores the elements of a collection in an array of type T. The default method uses the generator function to allocate the returned array.

If the given array is big enough, the elements are stored in this array. If there is room to spare in the array; that is, the length of the array is greater than the number of elements in the collection—the spare room is filled with null values before the array is returned. If the array is too small, a new array of type T and appropriate size is created. If T is not a supertype of the runtime type of every element in the collection, an ArrayStoreException is thrown.

```
default <T> T[] toArray(IntFunction<T[]> generator)
```
Allows creation of an array of a particular runtime type given by the parameterization of the type parameter T[], using the specified generator function (§13.8, p. 717) to allocate the array of the desired type and the specified length.

The default implementation calls the generator function with 0 and then passes the resulting array of length 0 to the toArray(T[]) generic method.

Example 15.2 illustrates converting a set to an array. At (1), the call to the non-generic toArray() method returns an array of type Object. Since an array of type

Object is not a subtype of an array of type String, the compiler reports an error at (2).

At (3), the call to the generic toArray() method returns an array of size 3 and type Object[], but element type String, when the method was passed a zero-length array of type Object. In other words, the method created a suitable-size array of type Object, since the array passed in the argument was too small. This array was filled with the elements of the set, which are strings. Although the array returned is of type Object, the objects stored in it are of type String. The output from the program confirms these observations.

At (4), the call to the generic toArray() method returns an array of size 3 and type String[], having element type String, when the method was passed a zero-length array of type String. Now the method creates a new suitable-size array of type String and fills it with the elements of the set, which are strings. The output from the program shows that the array passed in the argument is not the same as the array returned by the method call.

At (5), the call to the generic toArray() method returns the same array it was passed in the argument, since it is of appropriate size and type. In other words, the array passed in the argument is filled with the elements of the list, and returned. This is corroborated by the output from the program.

At (6), the actual type parameter is Integer. The generic toArray() method throws an ArrayStoreException because String objects in the set denoted by strSet cannot be stored in an array of type Integer.

Lastly, Example 15.2 illustrates converting a set to an array using the default toArray(IntFunction<T[]>) generic method, which is a convenience method that actually leverages the toArray(T[]) generic method.

```
IntFunction<String[]> createStrArray = nn -> new String[nn];      // (7)
String[] strArray5 = strSet.toArray(createStrArray);             // (8a)
String[] strArray6 = strSet.toArray(String[]::new);             // (8b)
String[] strArray7 = strSet.toArray(createStrArray.apply(0));    // (8c)
```

The lambda expression at (7) creates an array of length nn and of type String[]. This lambda expression is passed to the toArray(IntFunction<String[]>) method at (8a). Equivalently, we can pass a method reference to the method, as shown at (8b). Of course, the lambda expression at (7) only creates an array when the apply() method of the IntFunction<T[]> interface is called with a value for the length of the array. The default behavior of the toArray(IntFunction<T[]>) generic method is illustrated at (8c): The apply() method of the IntFunction<String[]> interface is explicitly called with the value 0 to create a zero-length String array which is then passed as a parameter to the toArray(String[]) method.

- -

Example 15.2 *Converting Collections to Arrays*

```
import java.util.Arrays;
import java.util.Collection;
```

```java
import java.util.HashSet;
import java.util.function.IntFunction;

public class CollectionToArray {
  public static void main(String[] args) {

    Collection<String> strSet = new HashSet<>();
    strSet.add("2021"); strSet.add("2022"); strSet.add("2023");
    int n = strSet.size();

    Object[] objects = strSet.toArray();                    // (1)
//  String[] string = strSet.toArray();                     // (2) Compile-time error!

    Object[] objArray = strSet.toArray(new Object[0]);                    // (3)
    System.out.println("Array size: " + objArray.length);
    System.out.println("Array type: " + objArray.getClass().getName());
    System.out.println("Actual element type: " +
                       objArray[0].getClass().getName());

    String[] strArray1 = new String[0];
    String[] strArray2 = strSet.toArray(strArray1);                    // (4)
    System.out.println("strArray1 == strArray2: " + (strArray1 == strArray2));

    String[] strArray3 = new String[n];
    String[] strArray4 = strSet.toArray(strArray3);                    // (5)
    System.out.println("strArray3 == strArray4: " + (strArray3 == strArray4));

//  Integer[] intArray = strSet.toArray(new Integer[n]);      // (6) Runtime error!

    IntFunction<String[]> createStrArray = nn -> new String[nn];        // (7)
    String[] strArray5 = strSet.toArray(createStrArray);               // (8a)
    String[] strArray6 = strSet.toArray(String[]::new);               // (8b)
    String[] strArray7 = strSet.toArray(createStrArray.apply(0));      // (8c)
    System.out.println("strArray5: " + Arrays.toString(strArray5));
    System.out.println("strArray6: " + Arrays.toString(strArray6));
    System.out.println("strArray7: " + Arrays.toString(strArray7));
  }
}
```

Output from the program:

```
Array size: 3
Array type: [Ljava.lang.Object;
Actual element type: java.lang.String
strArray1 == strArray2: false
strArray3 == strArray4: true
strArray5: [2023, 2022, 2021]
strArray6: [2023, 2022, 2021]
strArray7: [2023, 2022, 2021]
```

15.3 Lists

Lists are collections that maintain their elements *in order* and can contain duplicates. The elements in a list are *ordered*. Each element, therefore, has a position in the list. A zero-based index can be used to access the element at the position designated by the index value. The position of an element can change as elements are inserted or deleted from the list—that is, as the list is changed structurally.

The List<E> Interface

In addition to the operations inherited from the Collection<E> interface, the List<E> interface also defines operations that work specifically on lists: position-based access of the list elements, searching in a list, operations on parts of a list (called *open range-view* operations), and applying an operator to each element. These list operations are covered in Chapter 12, p. 643.

Sorting and searching in lists is covered in §15.11, p. 856.

The List<E> interface also provides the overloaded static method of() to create *unmodifiable* lists (§12.2, p. 649).

Additionally, the List<E> interface provides two customized list iterators:

```
ListIterator<E> listIterator()
ListIterator<E> listIterator(int index)
```

The iterator from the first method iterates over the elements consecutively, starting with the first element of the list, whereas the iterator from the second method starts iterating over the list from the element designated by the specified index.

The declaration of the ListIterator<E> interface is shown below:

```
interface ListIterator<E> extends Iterator<E> {
  boolean hasNext();
  boolean hasPrevious();
  E next();                  // Element after the cursor
  E previous();              // Element before the cursor
  int nextIndex();           // Index of element after the cursor
  int previousIndex();       // Index of element before the cursor
  void remove();             // Optional
  void set(E o);             // Optional
  void add(E o);             // Optional
}
```

The ListIterator<E> interface is a bidirectional iterator for lists. It extends the Iterator<E> interface and allows the list to be iterated over in either direction. When iterating over lists, it can be helpful to imagine a *cursor* moving forward or backward *between* the elements when calls are made to the next() and the previous() methods, respectively. The element that the cursor passes over is returned. When the remove() method is called, the element last passed over is removed from the list.

The `ArrayList<E>`, `LinkedList<E>`, **and** `Vector<E>` **Classes**

Three implementations of the `List<E>` interface are provided in the `java.util` package: `ArrayList<E>`, `LinkedList<E>`, and `Vector<E>`.

The `ArrayList<E>` class implements the `List<E>` interface (Chapter 12, p. 643). The `Vector<E>` class is a legacy class that has been retrofitted to implement the `List<E>` interface, and will not be discussed in detail. The `Vector<E>` and `ArrayList<E>` classes are implemented using dynamically resizable arrays, providing fast *random access by index* (i.e., position-based access) and fast list iteration—very much like using an ordinary array. Unlike the `ArrayList<E>` class, the `Vector<E>` class is thread-safe, meaning that concurrent calls to the vector will not compromise its integrity. The `LinkedList<E>` implementation uses a doubly linked list. Insertions and deletions in a doubly linked list are very efficient.

The `ArrayList<E>` and `Vector<E>` classes offer comparable performance, but `Vectors` suffer a performance penalty due to synchronization. Position-based access has constant-time performance for the `ArrayList<E>` and `Vector<E>` classes. However, position-based access is in linear time for a `LinkedList<E>`, owing to iteration in a doubly linked list. When frequent insertions and deletions occur inside a list, a `LinkedList<E>` can be worth considering. In most cases, the `ArrayList<E>` implementation is the overall best choice for implementing lists.

In addition to the `List<E>` interface, the `LinkedList<E>` class also implements two other interfaces that allow it to be used for stacks and different kinds of queues (p. 814).

Example 15.3 illustrates some basic operations on lists. The user gets one shot at guessing a five-digit code. The solution is hardwired in the example as a list of five `Integer` objects. The `secretSolution` list is created at (1), and populated using the `Collections.addAll()` static method (p. 862). The guess specified at the command line is placed in a separate list, called `guess`, at (2).

The number of digits that are correctly guessed is determined at (3). The solution is first duplicated, and each digit in the guess is removed from the duplicated solution. The number of deletions corresponds to the number of correct digits in the guess list. A digit at a particular index in the guess list is returned by the `get()` method. The `remove()` method returns `true` if the duplicate list was modified—that is, the digit from the guess was found and removed from the duplicated solution. Of course, one could use the `retainAll()` method, as shown below, but the idea in Example 15.3 is to use positional access on the guess list.

```
// Find the number of digits that were correctly included.          (3)
List<Integer> duplicate = new ArrayList<>(secretSolution);
duplicate.retainAll(guess);
numOfDigitsIncluded = duplicate.size();
```

Finding the number of digits that are correctly placed is achieved by using two list iterators at (4), which allow digits in the same position in the `guess` and the `secretSolution` lists to be compared.

Example 15.3 *Using Lists*

```java
import java.util.ArrayList;
import java.util.Collections;
import java.util.List;
import java.util.ListIterator;

public class TakeAGuess {
  static final int NUM_DIGITS = 5;

  public static void main(String[] args) {

    // Sanity check on the given data.
    try {
      if (args.length != 1 || args[0].length() != NUM_DIGITS)
        throw new IllegalArgumentException();
      Integer.parseInt(args[0]);
    } catch(IllegalArgumentException nfe) {
      System.err.println("Guess should be " + NUM_DIGITS + " digits.");
      return;
    }
    String guessStr = args[0];
    System.out.println("Guess: " + guessStr);

    /* Initialize the solution list. This program has a fixed solution: 53272 */
    List<Integer> secretSolution = new ArrayList<>();                    // (1)
    Collections.addAll(secretSolution, 5, 3, 2, 7, 2);

    // Convert the guess from string to a list of Integers.             (2)
    List<Integer> guess = new ArrayList<>();
    for (int i = 0; i < guessStr.length(); i++)
      guess.add(Character.getNumericValue(guessStr.charAt(i)));

    // Find the number of digits that were correctly included.          (3)
    List<Integer> duplicate = new ArrayList<>(secretSolution);
    int numOfDigitsIncluded = 0;
    for (int i = 0; i < NUM_DIGITS; i++)
      if (duplicate.remove(guess.get(i))) numOfDigitsIncluded++;

    /* Find the number of digits correctly placed by comparing the two
       lists, element by element, counting each correct placement. */
    // Need two iterators to traverse through the guess and solution lists.   (4)
    ListIterator<Integer> correct = secretSolution.listIterator();
    ListIterator<Integer> attempt = guess.listIterator();
    int numOfDigitsPlaced = 0;
    while (correct.hasNext())
      if (correct.next().equals(attempt.next())) numOfDigitsPlaced++;

    // Print the results.
    System.out.println(numOfDigitsIncluded + " digit(s) correctly included.");
    System.out.println(numOfDigitsPlaced +   " digit(s) correctly placed.");
  }
}
```

Running the program with the following command:

```
>java TakeAGuess 32227
```

gives the following output:

```
Guess: 32227
4 digit(s) correctly included.
1 digit(s) correctly placed.
```

15.4 Sets

The Java Collections Framework provides the Set<E> interface to model the mathematical *set* abstraction.

The Set<E> Interface

Unlike other implementations of the Collection<E> interface, implementations of the Set<E> interface do not allow duplicate elements. The Set<E> interface does not define any new methods, and its add() and addAll() methods will not store duplicates. If an element is not currently in the set, two consecutive calls to the add() method to insert the element will first return true, then false. A Set<E> models a mathematical set (see Table 15.3)—that is, it is an unordered collection of distinct objects.

Multisets (also called *bags*) that allow duplicate elements cannot be implemented using the Set<E> interface, since this interface requires that elements are unique in the collection. An implementation of the Set<E> interface can choose to allow the null value, but the concrete class TreeSet<E> does *not*.

Table 15.3   *Bulk Operations and Set Logic*

Set methods (a and b are sets)	Corresponding mathematical operations
a.containsAll(b)	$b \subseteq a$ (subset)
a.addAll(b)	$a = a \cup b$ (union)
a.removeAll(b)	$a = a - b$ (difference)
a.retainAll(b)	$a = a \cap b$ (intersection)
a.clear()	$a = \varnothing$ (empty set)

Creating Unmodifiable Sets

Unmodifiable collections are useful to prevent a collection from accidently being modified, as doing so might cause the program to behave incorrectly.

Creating and using unmodifiable sets is very similar to creating and using unmodifiable lists. Not surprisingly, the discussion here on unmodifiable sets reflects the discussion on unmodifiable lists (§12.2, p. 649). Later we will discuss unmodifiable maps (p. 832) and unmodifiable view collections (p. 856).

The Set<E> interface provides generic static methods to create *unmodifiable* sets that have the following characteristics:

- An unmodifiable set cannot be modified *structurally*; for example, elements cannot be added, removed, or replaced in such a set. Any such attempt will result in an UnsupportedOperationException to be thrown. However, if the elements themselves are mutable, the elements may appear modified.
- Both duplicates and null elements are not allowed, and will result in a NullPointerException if an attempt is made to create them with such elements.
- The order of the elements in such a set is unspecified.
- Such a set can be serialized if its elements are serializable (§20.5, p. 1261).

```
static <E> Set<E> of(E e1, E e2, E e3, E e4, E e5,
                     E e6, E e7, E e8, E e9, E e10)
```
This method is overloaded, accepting any number of elements from 0 to 10. It returns an unmodifiable set containing the number of elements specified. It throws a NullPointerException if an element is null.

```
@SafeVarargs static <E> Set<E> of(E... elements)
```
This variable arity method returns an unmodifiable set containing an arbitrary number of elements. It throws a NullPointerException if an element is null or if the array is null. The annotation suppresses the heap pollution warning in its declaration and unchecked generic array creation warning at the call sites.

```
static <E> Set<E> copyOf(Collection<? extends E> collection)
```
This generic method returns an unmodifiable set containing the elements of the specified collection, in its iteration order. The specified collection must not be null, and it must not contain any null elements—otherwise, a NullPointerException is thrown. If the specified collection is subsequently modified, the returned set will not reflect such modifications.

The code below shows that a set created by the Set.of() method cannot be modified. The set returned is also not an instance of the class HashSet.

```
Set<String> set = Set.of("Tom", "Dick", "Harriet");
//  set.add("Harry");                          // UnsupportedOperationException
//  set.remove(2);                             // UnsupportedOperationException
System.out.println(set);                       // [Harriet, Tom, Dick]
System.out.println(set instanceof HashSet);    // false
```

The Set.of() method does not allow null elements:

```
Set<String> coinSet = Set.of("dime", "nickel", null); // NullPointerException
```

For arguments up to 10, an appropriate fixed-arity Set.of() method is called. Above 10 arguments, the variable arity Set.of(E...) method is called, passing an implicitly created array containing the arguments.

```
Set<Integer> intSet1 = Set.of(1, 2, 3, 4, 5, 6, 7, 8, 9, 10);     // Fixed-arity
Set<Integer> intSet2 = Set.of(1, 2, 3, 4, 5, 6, 7, 8, 9, 10, 11); // Varargs
System.out.println(intSet1);        // [9, 8, 7, 6, 5, 4, 3, 2, 1, 10]
System.out.println(intSet2);        // [7, 6, 5, 4, 3, 2, 1, 11, 10, 9, 8]
```

At (1) below, an explicit array is passed as an argument, resulting in the variable arity Set.of(E...) method being called, creating a set of String. At (2), the method call explicitly specifies the type of its argument as String[]. In this case the one-argument Set.of(E) method is called, creating a set of size 1 and whose element type is String[].

```
String[] strArray = {"Tom", "Dick", "Harriet"};
Set<String> strSet = Set.of(strArray);                  // (1) Set of String
Set<String[]> strArraySet = Set.<String[]>of(strArray); // (2) Set of String[]
System.out.println(strSet);              // [Harriet, Dick, Tom]
System.out.println(strArraySet);         // [[Ljava.lang.String;@3b22cdd0]
```

The code below shows how we can make a copy of a collection, in this case, a set. The copyOf() method creates a copy of the set passed as an argument at (1). The set created is unmodifiable analogous to the sets created with the Set.of() methods. The code also shows that modifying the original set does *not* reflect in the copy of the set.

```
Set<String> fab4 = new HashSet<>();
fab4.add("John"); fab4.add("Paul"); fab4.add("George"); fab4.add("Ringo");
System.out.println(fab4);               // [George, John, Ringo, Paul]
Set<String> fabAlways = Set.copyOf(fab4);   // (1)
fab4.remove("John"); fab4.remove("George"); // Modify original set
System.out.println(fab4);               // [Ringo, Paul]
System.out.println(fabAlways);          // [John, Paul, Ringo, George]
```

The HashSet<E> and LinkedHashSet<E> Classes

The HashSet<E> class implements the Set<E> interface. Since this implementation uses a hash table, it offers near-constant-time performance for most operations. A HashSet<E> does not guarantee any ordering of the elements. However, the LinkedHashSet<E> subclass of HashSet<E> guarantees insertion order. It is also the implementation of choice if frequent iteration is necessary over the set. The sorted counterpart is TreeSet<E>, which implements the SortedSet<E> and the NavigableSet<E> interfaces and has logarithmic time complexity (p. 810).

A HashSet<E> relies on the implementation of the hashCode() and equals() methods of its elements (§14.2, p. 744, and §14.3, p. 753). The hashCode() method is used for hashing the elements, and the equals() method is needed for comparing elements for equality. In fact, the equality and the hash codes of HashSets are defined in terms of the equality and the hash codes of their elements.

HashSet()

Constructs a new, empty set.

HashSet(Collection<? extends E> c)

Constructs a new set containing the elements in the specified collection. The new set will not contain any duplicates. This offers a convenient way to remove duplicates from a collection.

HashSet(int initialCapacity)

Constructs a new, empty set with the specified initial capacity.

HashSet(int initialCapacity, float loadFactor)

Constructs a new, empty set with the specified initial capacity and the specified load factor.

As mentioned earlier, the LinkedHashSet<E> implementation is a subclass of the HashSet<E> class. It works similarly to a HashSet<E> except for one important detail. Unlike a HashSet<E>, a LinkedHashSet<E> guarantees that the iterator will access the elements in *insertion order*—that is, in the order in which the elements were inserted into the LinkedHashSet<E>.

The LinkedHashSet<E> class offers constructors analogous to the ones in the Hash-Set<E> class. The initial *capacity* (i.e., the number of buckets in the hash table) and its *load factor* (i.e., the ratio of number of elements stored to its current capacity) can be tuned when the set is created. The default values for these parameters will, under most circumstances, provide acceptable performance.

Example 15.4 demonstrates iterating over a HashSet<E> and a LinkedHashSet<E> created at (1) and (2), respectively. Regardless of the order in which elements are inserted into a HashSet<E>, we cannot depend on the order in which the for(:) loop will iterate over the elements in the set, as is evident from the program output. A LinkedHashSet<E>, on the other hand, is always iterated over in *insertion order*—that is, the first element inserted is the first element retrieved by the for(:) loop. The program output confirms this behavior, as the meal that was inserted last into the LinkedHashSet<E> is served first. The same behavior will be exhibited if an explicit iterator is used to iterate over the sets.

Example 15.4 *Iterating Over Sets*

```java
import java.util.HashSet;
import java.util.LinkedHashSet;
import java.util.Set;
public class IterationHashSetAndLinkedHashSet {
  public static void main(String[] args) {
    Set<String> set1 = new HashSet<>();                          // (1)
    set1.add("breakfast"); set1.add("lunch"); set1.add("dinner");
    System.out.println("Serving meals from a HashSet (order can vary):");
    for (String meal : set1) {
      System.out.println(meal);
    }
    Set<String> set2 = new LinkedHashSet<>();                    // (2)
    set2.add("breakfast"); set2.add("lunch"); set2.add("dinner");
    System.out.println("Serving meals from a LinkedHashSet" +
                " (always insertion order):");
```

```
        for (String meal : set2) {
            System.out.println(meal);
        }
    }
}
```

Output from the program:

```
Serving meals from a HashSet (order can vary):
dinner
breakfast
lunch
Serving meals from a LinkedHashSet (always insertion order):
breakfast
lunch
dinner
```

Example 15.5 demonstrates set operations. It determines the following relationships between two sets of characters:

- Whether they are disjunct—that is, have no elements in common
- Whether they have the same elements—that is, are equivalent
- Whether one is a subset of the other
- Whether one is a superset of the other
- Whether they have a common subset

Given a list of words as program arguments, each argument is turned into a set of characters. This character set is compared with the set of all characters encountered so far in previous arguments.

The set encountered created at (1) accumulates characters as each argument is processed. For each argument, an empty set of characters is created at (2). This characters set is populated with the characters of the current argument at (3). The program first determines if there is a common subset between the two sets at (4)—that is, whether the current argument has any characters that were in previous arguments:

```
// Determine whether a common subset exists:                    (4)
Set<Character> commonSubset = new HashSet<>(encountered);
commonSubset.retainAll(characters);
boolean areDisjunct = commonSubset.size()==0;
```

Note that the retainAll() operation is destructive. The code at (4) does not affect the encountered and the characters sets. If the size of the common subset is zero, the sets are disjunct; otherwise, the relationship must be narrowed down. The subset and superset relations are determined at (5), using the containsAll() method.

```
// Determine superset and subset relations.                     (5)
boolean isSubset = encountered.containsAll(characters);
boolean isSuperset = characters.containsAll(encountered);
```

The sets are equivalent if both of the previous relations are true. If the relations are both false—that is, no subset or superset relationship exists, the sets only have the subset computed at (4) in common. The encountered set is updated with the contents of the characters set to accumulate all characters encountered so far. The addAll() method is used for this purpose at (6):

```
encountered.addAll(characters);                              // (6)
```

As we can see from the output, the program prints the contents of the sets in the standard text representation for collections.

- -

Example 15.5 *Using Sets*

```
import java.util.HashSet;
import java.util.Set;

public class CharacterSets {
  public static void main(String[] args) {

    // A set for keeping track of all characters previously encountered.
    Set<Character> encountered = new HashSet<>();            // (1)

    // For each program argument in the command line ...
    for (String argument : args) {

      // Convert the current argument to a set of characters.
      Set<Character> characters = new HashSet<>();           // (2)
      int size = argument.length();
      // For each character in the argument...
      for (int j = 0; j < size; j++)
        // add character to the characters set.
        characters.add(argument.charAt(j));                 // (3)

      // Determine whether a common subset exists:              (4)
      Set<Character> commonSubset = new HashSet<>(encountered);
      commonSubset.retainAll(characters);
      boolean areDisjunct = commonSubset.size()==0;

      if (areDisjunct) {
        System.out.println(characters + " and " + encountered + " are disjunct.");
      } else {
        // Determine superset and subset relations.              (5)
        boolean isSubset = encountered.containsAll(characters);
        boolean isSuperset = characters.containsAll(encountered);
        if (isSubset && isSuperset)
          System.out.println(characters + " is equivalent to " + encountered);
        else if (isSubset)
          System.out.println(characters + " is a subset of " + encountered);
        else if (isSuperset)
          System.out.println(characters + " is a superset of " + encountered);
        else
          System.out.println(characters + " and " + encountered + " have " +
                          commonSubset + " in common.");
      }

      // Update the set of characters encountered so far.
      encountered.addAll(characters);                         // (6)
```

```
        }
      }
    }
```

Running the program with the following arguments:

```
>java CharacterSets i said i am maids
```

results in the following output:

```
[i] and [] are disjunct.
[d, a, s, i] is a superset of [i]
[i] is a subset of [d, a, s, i]
[a, m] and [d, a, s, i] have [a] in common.
[d, a, s, m, i] is equivalent to [d, a, s, m, i]
```

15.5 Sorted Sets and Navigable Sets

Before reading this subsection, it is a good idea to review the Comparable<E> interface (§14.4, p. 761) for defining the natural ordering for objects, and the Comparator<E> interface (§14.5, p. 769) for defining a particular total ordering for objects.

The SortedSet<E> Interface

The SortedSet<E> interface extends the Set<E> interface to provide the functionality for handling sorted sets. Since the elements are sorted, iterating over the set using either the for(:) loop or an iterator will access the elements according to the ordering used by the set.

```
// First-last elements
E first()
E last()
```

The first() method returns the first element currently in this sorted set, and the last() method returns the last element currently in this sorted set. The elements are chosen based on the ordering used by the sorted set. Both throw a NoSuchElementException if the sorted set is empty.

```
// Range-view operations
SortedSet<E> headSet(<E> toElement)
SortedSet<E> tailSet(<E> fromElement)
SortedSet<E> subSet(<E> fromElement, <E> toElement)
```

The headSet() method returns a *view* of a portion of this sorted set, whose elements are strictly less than the specified element. Similarly, the tailSet() method returns a view of the portion of this sorted set, whose elements are greater than or equal to the specified element. The subSet() method returns a view of the portion of this sorted set, whose elements range from fromElement, inclusive, to toElement, exclusive (also called *half-open interval*). It throws an IllegalArgumentException if the fromElement is greater than the toElement.

Note that the views present the elements sorted in the same order as the underlying sorted set. Also, changes made through views are reflected in the underlying sorted set, and vice versa.

```
// Comparator access
Comparator<? super E> comparator()
```

Returns the comparator associated with this sorted set, or null if it uses the natural ordering of its elements. This comparator, if defined, is used by default when a sorted set is constructed, and used when copying elements into new sorted sets.

The NavigableSet<E> Interface

The NavigableSet<E> interface extends the SortedSet<E> interface with *navigation methods* to find the closest matches for given search targets. By navigation we mean operations that require searching for elements in the navigable set. In the absence of elements, these operations return null rather than throwing a NoSuchElement-Exception, as is the case for the methods in the SortedSet<E> interface.

The NavigableSet<E> interface replaces the SortedSet<E> interface and is the preferred choice when a sorted set is required. In addition to the methods of the Sorted-Set<E> interface, the NavigableSet<E> interface adds the following *new* methods:

```
// First-last elements
E pollFirst()
E pollLast()
```

The pollFirst() method removes and returns the first element and the pollLast() method removes and returns the last element currently in this navigable set. The element is determined according to some policy employed by the set—for example, queue policy. Both return null if the sorted set is empty.

```
// Range-view operations
NavigableSet<E> headSet(E toElement,   boolean inclusive)
NavigableSet<E> tailSet(E fromElement, boolean inclusive)
NavigableSet<E> subSet(E fromElement, boolean fromInclusive,
                       E toElement,   boolean toInclusive)
```

These operations are analogous to the ones in the SortedSet<E> interface (p. 810), returning different views of the underlying navigable set, depending on the bound elements. However, the bound elements can be *excluded or included* by the operation, depending on the value of the boolean argument inclusive.

```
// Closest-matches
E ceiling(E e)
E floor(E e)
E higher(E e)
E lower(E e)
```

The method `ceiling()` returns the least element in the navigable set greater than or equal to argument e. The method `floor()` returns the greatest element in the navigable set less than or equal to argument e. The method `higher()` returns the least element in the navigable set strictly greater than argument e. The method `lower()` returns the greatest element in the navigable set strictly less than argument e. All methods return `null` if the required element is not found.

```
// Reverse order
Iterator<E> descendingIterator()
NavigableSet<E> descendingSet()
```

The first method returns a reverse-order iterator for the navigable set. The second method returns a reverse-order view of the elements in the navigable set.

The `TreeSet<E>` Class

The `TreeSet<E>` class implements the `NavigableSet<E>` interface and thereby the `SortedSet<E>` interface. By default, operations on a sorted set rely on the natural ordering of the elements. However, a total ordering can be specified by passing a customized comparator to the constructor.

The `TreeSet<E>` class maintains non-`null` elements in sort order, and iteration is also in the same sort order.

The `TreeSet<E>` implementation uses balanced trees, which deliver excellent (logarithmic) performance for all operations. However, searching in a `HashSet<E>` can be faster than in a `TreeSet<E>` because hashing algorithms usually offer better performance than the search algorithms for balanced trees. The `TreeSet<E>` class is preferred if elements are to be maintained in sort order and if fast insertion and retrieval of individual elements is desired.

The `TreeSet<E>` class provides four constructors:

`TreeSet()`

The default constructor that creates a new, empty sorted set, according to the natural ordering of the elements.

`TreeSet(Comparator<? super E> comparator)`

A constructor that takes an explicit comparator for specific total ordering of the elements.

`TreeSet(Collection<? extends E> collection)`

A constructor that creates a sorted set based on a collection, according to the natural ordering of the elements.

TreeSet(SortedSet<E> set)

A constructor that creates a new set containing the same elements as the specified sorted set, with the same ordering.

Example 15.6 illustrates some selected navigation operations on a TreeSet<E>. Keep in mind that the Unicode values of uppercase letters are less than the Unicode values of lowercase letters—that is, the former occur before the latter in the Unicode standard.

The set is created at (1), and populated by calling the Collections.addAll() method at (2). The elements are maintained according to the natural ordering for Strings—that is, the one defined by the compareTo() method of the Comparable<String> interface implemented by the String class. The subset-view operations at (3) show how the bounds can be inclusive or exclusive. Note also how the closest-match methods at (4) behave. A sorted set with the reverse order corresponding to the natural ordering is created at (5). The methods pollFirst() and pollLast() remove the element that is retrieved—that is, they change the set structurally.

The following code shows how we can create a sorted set with a specific total ordering, by supplying a comparator in the constructor call:

```java
NavigableSet<String> strSetB = new TreeSet<>(String.CASE_INSENSITIVE_ORDER);
Collections.addAll(strSetB, "strictly", "dancing", "Java", "Ballroom");
System.out.println(strSetB);            // [Ballroom, dancing, Java, strictly]
```

Example 15.6 *Using Navigable Sets*

```java
import java.util.Collections;
import java.util.NavigableSet;
import java.util.TreeSet;
import static java.lang.System.out;

public class SetNavigation {
  public static void main(String[] args) {

    NavigableSet<String> strSetA = new TreeSet<>();                           // (1)
    Collections.addAll(strSetA, "Strictly", "Java", "dancing", "ballroom"); // (2)
    out.println("Before: " + strSetA);      // [Java, Strictly, ballroom, dancing]

    out.println("\nSubset-views:");                  // (3)
    out.println(strSetA.headSet("ballroom", true));  // [Java, Strictly, ballroom]
    out.println(strSetA.headSet("ballroom", false)); // [Java, Strictly]
    out.println(strSetA.tailSet("Strictly", true));  // [Strictly, ballroom,
                                                      //  dancing]
    out.println(strSetA.tailSet("Strictly", false)); // [ballroom, dancing]
    out.println(strSetA.subSet("A", false, "Z", false )); // [Java, Strictly]
    out.println(strSetA.subSet("a", false, "z", false )); // [ballroom, dancing]

    out.println("\nClosest-matches:");                // (4)
    out.println(strSetA.ceiling("ball"));             // ballroom
    out.println(strSetA.floor("ball"));               // Strictly
    out.println(strSetA.higher("ballroom"));          // dancing
    out.println(strSetA.lower("ballroom"));           // Strictly
```

```
        out.println("\nReverse order:");                  // (5)
        out.println(strSetA.descendingSet());  // [dancing, ballroom, Strictly, Java]

        out.println("\nFirst-last elements:");
        out.println(strSetA.pollFirst());                 // Java
        out.println(strSetA.pollLast());                  // dancing

        out.println("\nAfter: " + strSetA);               // [Strictly, ballroom]
    }
}
```

Output from the program:

```
Before: [Java, Strictly, ballroom, dancing]

Subset-views:
[Java, Strictly, ballroom]
[Java, Strictly]
[Strictly, ballroom, dancing]
[ballroom, dancing]
[Java, Strictly]
[ballroom, dancing]

Closest-matches:
ballroom
Strictly
dancing
Strictly

Reverse order:
[dancing, ballroom, Strictly, Java]

First-last elements:
Java
dancing

After: [Strictly, ballroom]
```

15.6 Queues

In this section we look at the different types of queues provided by the Java Collections Framework.

The Queue<E> Interface

The Queue<E> interface extends the Collection<E> interface to specify a general contract for queues. A *queue* is a collection that maintains elements in *processing order*. An implementation of the Queue<E> interface provides the queue policy for yielding the next element for processing. A *head* position in the queue specifies where the next element for processing can be obtained. A basic queue usually maintains its elements in FIFO (*first in, first out*) ordering, but other orderings are also quite common: LIFO (*last in, first out*) ordering (also called *stacks*) and priority ordering (also called *priority queues*). The order in which elements of a queue can be retrieved for processing is dictated either by the natural ordering of the elements or by a comparator. A queue can be *unbounded* or *capacity-restricted*, depending on its implementation.

The Queue<E> interface extends the Collection<E> interface with the following methods. A summary of these methods is presented in Table 15.4.

```
// Insert
boolean add(E element)
boolean offer(E element)
```

Both methods insert the specified element in the queue. The return value indicates the success or failure of the operation. The add() method inherited from the Collection<E> interface throws an IllegalStateException if the queue is full, but the offer() method does not.

```
// Remove
E remove()
E poll()
```

Both methods retrieve the head element and remove it from the queue. If the queue is empty, the remove() method throws a NoSuchElementException, but the poll() method returns the null value.

```
// Examine
E element()
E peek()
```

Both methods retrieve the head element, but do *not* remove it from the queue. If the queue is empty, the element() method throws a NoSuchElementException, but the peek() method returns the null value.

Table 15.4 *Summary of Methods in the Queue Interface*

Operation	Throws exception	Returns special value
Insert at the tail	add(e) *can throw* IllegalArgumentException	offer(e) *returns* true *or* false
Remove from the head	remove() *can throw* NoSuchElementException	poll() *returns head element or* null
Examine element at the head	element() *can throw* NoSuchElementException	peek() *returns head element or* null

The PriorityQueue<E> and LinkedList<E> Classes

Both the PriorityQueue<E> and LinkedList<E> classes implement the Queue<E> interface. Unless bidirectional iteration is necessary, other queue implementations should be considered, and not the LinkedList<E> class. (The LinkedList<E> class is also eclipsed by the introduction of the ArrayDeque<E> class when it comes to implementing deques, as we will see shortly.)

As the name suggests, the PriorityQueue<E> class is the obvious implementation for a queue with priority ordering. The implementation is based on a *priority heap*, a tree-like structure that yields an element at the head of the queue according to the priority ordering, which is defined either by the natural ordering of its elements or by a comparator. In the case of several elements having the same priority, one of them is chosen arbitrarily.

Elements of a PriorityQueue<E> are *not* sorted. The queue only guarantees that elements can be *removed* in priority order, and any iteration using an iterator does *not* guarantee to abide by the priority order.

The PriorityQueue<E> class provides the following constructors:

```
PriorityQueue()
PriorityQueue(int initialCapacity)
```

The default constructor creates a new, empty PriorityQueue with default initial capacity and natural ordering. The second constructor creates a new, empty PriorityQueue with the specified initial capacity and natural ordering.

```
PriorityQueue(Comparator<? super E> comparator)
PriorityQueue(int initialCapacity, Comparator<? super E> comparator)
```

Both constructors create a new, empty PriorityQueue where the ordering is defined by the specified comparator. The priority queue created by the first and the second constructors has the default initial capacity and the specified initial capacity, respectively.

```
PriorityQueue(PriorityQueue<? extends E> pq)
PriorityQueue(SortedSet<? extends E> set)
PriorityQueue(Collection<? extends E> c)
```

The first and the second constructors create a new PriorityQueue with the ordering and the elements from the specified priority queue or sorted set, respectively.

The last constructor creates a new PriorityQueue containing the elements in the specified collection. It will have natural ordering of its elements, unless the specified collection is either a SortedSet<E> or another PriorityQueue, in which case, the collection's ordering will be used.

Example 15.7 illustrates using priority queues. The example shows how priority queues maintain objects of the Task class. The natural ordering of the objects in this class is based on the *task number* (Integer). This natural ordering will result in the priority queue yielding its elements in *ascending* order of the task numbers—that is, tasks with *smaller* task numbers will have *higher* priority.

In Example 15.7, the main() method in the class TaskExecutor creates an array with some tasks at (1). The method essentially creates empty priority queues with different priority orderings, at (2) through (7), and calls the testPQ() method at (8) to execute tasks passed in the array using the supplied priority queue.

```
private static void testPQ(Task[] taskArray, PriorityQueue<Task> pq) {     // (8)
    ...
}
```

The testPQ() method at (8) loads the queue at (9) from the array of tasks. It calls the offer() method to insert a task in the priority queue. The method then calls the peek() method at (10) to examine the task at the head of the queue. The tasks are executed by removing them one by one at (11) by calling the poll() method. The output shows the order in which the tasks are executed, depending on the priority ordering.

The priority queue pq1 at (2) has its priority ordering defined by the natural ordering of the tasks.

```
PriorityQueue<Task> pq1 = new PriorityQueue<>();                           // (2)
```

Note that the text representation of the queue in the output

```
Queue before executing tasks: [100@breakfast, 200@lunch, 300@dinner, 200@tea]
```

does *not* reflect the tasks in priority order. It just shows what tasks are in the queue. The text representation of the queue is generated by the print method running an iterator over the queue. The iterator is under no obligation to take the priority order into consideration. The output also shows that the task with the highest priority (i.e., the smallest task number) is at the head of the queue:

```
Task at the head: 100@breakfast
```

The call to the poll() method in the while loop at (11) removes tasks in priority order, as verified by the output:

```
Doing tasks: 100@breakfast 200@tea 200@lunch 300@dinner
```

Since two of the tasks have the same priority, the queue selects which one should be chosen first. The queue is empty when the peek() method returns null.

The priority queue pq2 at (3) has its priority ordering defined by the reverse natural ordering returned by the static method reverseOrder() of the Comparator<E> interface:

```
PriorityQueue<Task> pq2 = new PriorityQueue<>(Comparator.reverseOrder());
```

Both priority queues pq3 and pq4 use reversed ordering based on the *task name*. This ordering is defined for pq3 and pq4 by a lambda expression at (4) and by methods of the Comparator<E> interface at (7), respectively. The latter implementation is obviously to be preferred:

```
PriorityQueue<Task> pq4 = new PriorityQueue<>(                             // (5)
    Comparator.comparing(Task::getTaskName).reversed()
);
```

The static method comparing() extracts a comparator that uses the getName() method of the Task class, and the default method reversed() reverses this comparator.

The priority queues pq5 and pq6 use total ordering based on multiple fields of the Task class: on the task number, followed by the task name. This ordering is defined for pq5 and pq6 by a lambda expression at (6) and by methods of the Comparator<E> interface at (7), respectively. The latter implementation first extracts a comparator based on the task number, and chains it with one based on the task name:

```
PriorityQueue<Task> pq6 = new PriorityQueue<>(                          // (7)
        Comparator.comparing(Task::getTaskNumber)
            .thenComparing(Task::getTaskName)
);
```

We leave it to the reader to verify that the output conforms to the priority ordering of priority queues at (3) through (7).

- -

Example 15.7   *Using Priority Queues*

```
/** Represents a task. */
public class Task implements Comparable<Task> {
  private Integer taskNumber;
  private String  taskName;

  public Task(Integer tp, String tn) {
    taskNumber = tp;
    taskName   = tn;
  }

  @Override
  public boolean equals(Object obj) {// Equality based on the task number.
    return (this == obj)
        || (obj instanceof Task other
              && this.taskNumber.equals(other.taskNumber));
  }
  @Override
  public int compareTo(Task task2) { // Natural ordering based on the task number.
    return this.taskNumber.compareTo(task2.taskNumber);
  }
  @Override
  public int hashCode() {                   // Hash code based on the task number.
    return this.taskNumber.hashCode();
  }
  @Override
  public String toString() { return taskNumber + "@" + taskName; }

  public String  getTaskName()   { return taskName; }
  public Integer getTaskNumber() { return taskNumber;}
}
```

- -

```
import java.util.Arrays;
import java.util.Comparator;
import java.util.PriorityQueue;
import static java.lang.System.out;
```

```
/** Executes tasks. */
public class TaskExecutor {

    public static void main(String[] args) {
        // Array with some tasks.                                                (1)
        Task[] taskArray = {
            new Task(200, "lunch"), new Task(200, "tea"),
            new Task(300, "dinner"), new Task(100, "breakfast"),
        };
        out.println("Array of tasks: " + Arrays.toString(taskArray));

        out.println("Priority queue using natural ordering (task number).");
        PriorityQueue<Task> pq1 = new PriorityQueue<>();                         // (2)
        testPQ(taskArray, pq1);

        out.println("Priority queue using reverse natural ordering.");          // (3)
        PriorityQueue<Task> pq2 = new PriorityQueue<>(Comparator.reverseOrder());
        testPQ(taskArray, pq2);

        out.println("Priority queue using reversed ordering"
            + " on task name (lambda expression).");
        PriorityQueue<Task> pq3 = new PriorityQueue<>(                           // (4)
            (task1, task2) -> {
                String taskName1 = task1.getTaskName();
                String taskName2 = task2.getTaskName();
                return -taskName1.compareTo(taskName2);
            }
        );
        testPQ(taskArray, pq3);

        out.println("Priority queue using reversed ordering"
            + " on task name (extracted comparator).");
        PriorityQueue<Task> pq4 = new PriorityQueue<>(                           // (5)
            Comparator.comparing(Task::getTaskName).reversed()
        );
        testPQ(taskArray, pq4);

        out.println("Priority queue using total ordering based on task number,"
            + "\nfollowed by task name (lambda expression).");
        PriorityQueue<Task> pq5 = new PriorityQueue<>(                           // (6)
            (task1, task2) -> {
                Integer taskNumber1 = task1.getTaskNumber();
                Integer taskNumber2 = task2.getTaskNumber();
                if (!taskNumber1.equals(taskNumber2))
                    return taskNumber1.compareTo(taskNumber2);
                String taskName1 = task1.getTaskName();
                String taskName2 = task2.getTaskName();
                if (!taskName1.equals(taskName2))
                    return taskName1.compareTo(taskName2);
                return 0;
            }
        );
        testPQ(taskArray, pq5);
```

```
      out.println("Priority queue using total ordering based on task number,"
         + "\nfollowed by task name (extracted comparators).");
      PriorityQueue<Task> pq6 = new PriorityQueue<>(                          // (7)
         Comparator.comparing(Task::getTaskNumber)
                   .thenComparing(Task::getTaskName)
      );
      testPQ(taskArray, pq6);
   }

   // Runs tasks.
   private static void testPQ(Task[] taskArray, PriorityQueue<Task> pq) {     // (8)
      // Load the tasks:                                                      (9)
      for (Task task : taskArray)
        pq.offer(task);
      out.println("Queue before executing tasks: " + pq);

      // Peek at the head:                                                    (10)
      out.println("Task at the head: " + pq.peek());

      // Do the tasks:                                                        (11)
      out.print("Doing tasks: ");
      while (!pq.isEmpty()) {
        Task task = pq.poll();
        out.print(task + " ");
      }
      out.println();
      out.println();
   }
}
```

Output from the program:

```
Array of tasks: [200@lunch, 200@tea, 300@dinner, 100@breakfast]
Priority queue using natural ordering (task number).
Queue before executing tasks: [100@breakfast, 200@lunch, 300@dinner, 200@tea]
Task at the head: 100@breakfast
Doing tasks: 100@breakfast 200@tea 200@lunch 300@dinner

Priority queue using reverse natural ordering.
Queue before executing tasks: [300@dinner, 200@tea, 200@lunch, 100@breakfast]
Task at the head: 300@dinner
Doing tasks: 300@dinner 200@tea 200@lunch 100@breakfast

Priority queue using reversed ordering on task name (lambda expression).
Queue before executing tasks: [200@tea, 200@lunch, 300@dinner, 100@breakfast]
Task at the head: 200@tea
Doing tasks: 200@tea 200@lunch 300@dinner 100@breakfast

Priority queue using reversed ordering on task name (extracted comparator).
Queue before executing tasks: [200@tea, 200@lunch, 300@dinner, 100@breakfast]
Task at the head: 200@tea
Doing tasks: 200@tea 200@lunch 300@dinner 100@breakfast

Priority queue using total ordering based on task number,
followed by task name (lambda expression).
Queue before executing tasks: [100@breakfast, 200@lunch, 300@dinner, 200@tea]
```

```
Task at the head: 100@breakfast
Doing tasks: 100@breakfast 200@lunch 200@tea 300@dinner

Priority queue using total ordering based on task number,
followed by task name (extracted comparators).
Queue before executing tasks: [100@breakfast, 200@lunch, 300@dinner, 200@tea]
Task at the head: 100@breakfast
Doing tasks: 100@breakfast 200@lunch 200@tea 300@dinner
```

15.7 Deques

In this section we look at *deques*—that is, linear collections that allow processing of elements from both ends.

The Deque<E> Interface

The Deque<E> interface extends the Queue<E> interface to allow *double-ended queues*. Such a queue is called a *deque*. It allows operations not just at its *head* as a queue, but also at its *tail*. It is a linear unbounded structure in which elements can be inserted at or removed from *either* end. Various synonyms are used in the literature for the head and tail of a deque: front and back, first and last, start and end.

A deque can be used as a *FIFO queue*, where elements added at the tail are presented at the head for inspection or removal in the same order, thus implementing FIFO ordering. A deque can also be used as a *stack*, where elements are added to and removed from the *same* end, thus implementing LIFO ordering.

The Deque<E> interface defines symmetrical operations at its head and tail. Which end is in question is made evident by the method name. A *XXX*First() method and a *XXX*Last() method process an element at the *head* and at the *tail*, respectively. Below, equivalent methods from the Queue<E> interface are also identified. The push() and pop() methods are convenient for implementing stacks.

```
// Insert
boolean offerFirst(E element)
boolean offerLast(E element)              Queue equivalent: offer()
void addFirst(E element)
void addLast(E element)                   Queue equivalent: add()
void push(E element)                      Synonym: addFirst()
```

Insert the specified element in the deque. They all throw a NullPointerException if the specified element is null. The addFirst() and addLast() methods throw an IllegalStateException if the element cannot be added, but the offerFirst() and offerLast() methods do not.

```
// Remove
E removeFirst()                              Queue equivalent: remove()
E removeLast()
E pollFirst()                                Queue equivalent: poll()
E pollLast()
E pop()                                      Synonym: removeFirst()
boolean removeFirstOccurence(Object obj)
boolean removeLastOccurence(Object obj)
```

Remove an element from the deque. The removeFirst() and removeLast() methods throw a NoSuchElementException if the deque is empty. The pollFirst() and pollLast() methods return null if the deque is empty.

```
// Examine
E getFirst()                                 Queue equivalent: element()
E getLast()
E peekFirst()                                Queue equivalent: peek()
E peekLast()
```

Retrieve an element from the deque, but do not remove it from the deque. The getFirst() and getLast() methods throw a NoSuchElementException if the deque is empty. The peekFirst() and peekLast() methods return null if the deque is empty.

```
// Misc.
Iterator<E> descendingIterator()
```

Returns an iterator to iterate over the deque in reverse order—that is, from the tail to the head.

Table 15.5 summarizes the methods provided by the Deque<E> interface, showing which operations can be performed at the head and which ones at the tail of the deque. Each row indicates the runtime behavior of the methods in that row, whether they throw an exception or not. Any method whose name starts with either "offer", "poll", or "peek" does not throw an exception. Counterpart methods inherited from the Queue<E> interface are marked by an asterisk (*) in the table.

Table 15.5 *Summary of Deque Methods*

Insert at the head	Insert at the tail	Runtime behavior on failure
offerFirst()	offerLast(), offer()*	*Returns* false *if full*
addFirst()	addLast(), add()*	*Throws* IllegalStateException
Remove from the head	**Remove from the tail**	**Runtime behavior on failure**
pollFirst(), poll()*	pollLast()	*Returns* null *if empty*
removeFirst(), remove()*	removeLast()	*Throws* NoSuchElementException

Table 15.5 *Summary of Deque Methods (Continued)*

Examine at the head	Examine at the tail	Runtime behavior on failure
peekFirst(), peek()*	peekLast()	*Returns* null *if empty*
getFirst(), element()*	getLast()	*Throws* NoSuchElementException

The ArrayDeque<E> and LinkedList<E> Classes

The ArrayDeque<E> and LinkedList<E> classes implement the Deque<E> interface. The ArrayDeque<E> class provides better performance than the LinkedList<E> class for implementing FIFO queues, and is also a better choice than the java.util.Stack class for implementing stacks.

An ArrayDeque<E> is also an Iterable<E>, and iteration is always from the head to the tail. The class provides the descendingIterator() method for iterating in reverse order. Since deques are not lists, positional access is not possible, nor can they be sorted. They are also not thread-safe, and null values are not allowed as elements.

The ArrayDeque<E> class provides the following constructors, analogous to the ones in the ArrayList<E> class:

```
ArrayDeque()
ArrayDeque(int numOfElements)
```

The first constructor creates a new, empty ArrayDeque with an initial capacity to hold 16 elements.

The second constructor creates a new, empty ArrayDeque with initial capacity required to hold the specified number of elements.

```
ArrayDeque(Collection<? extends E> c)
```

Creates a new ArrayDeque containing the elements in the specified collection. The ordering in the ArrayDeque is determined by the iteration order of the iterator for the collection passed as an argument.

The LinkedList<E> class provides constructors that are analogous to the first and the last constructors.

Example 15.8 illustrates the methods for inserting, examining, and removing elements from a deque. The program output shows how each method affects the deque when inserting, examining, and removing elements from either the head or the tail of a deque.

Example 15.8 *Demonstrating Deque Operations*

```
import java.util.ArrayDeque;
import java.util.Deque;

public class DequeOperations {
  public static void main(String[] args) {
```

```java
    Deque<String> deque = new ArrayDeque<String>();
    System.out.println("After creating the deque: " + deque);

    // Insert elements:
    deque.offerFirst("A (H)");              // Insert at the head
    System.out.println("After inserting at the head: " + deque);
    deque.offerLast("B (T)");               // Insert at the tail
    System.out.println("After inserting at the tail: " + deque);
    deque.push("C (H)");                    // Insert at the head
    System.out.println("After inserting at the head: " + deque);
    deque.addFirst("D (H)");                // Insert at the head
    System.out.println("After inserting at the head: " + deque);
    deque.addLast("E (T)");                 // Insert at the tail
    System.out.println("After inserting at the tail: " + deque);

    // Examine element:
    System.out.println("Examine at the head: " + deque.getFirst());
    System.out.println("Examine at the tail: " + deque.getLast());
    System.out.println("Examine at the head: " + deque.peekFirst());
    System.out.println("Examine at the tail: " + deque.peekLast());

    // Remove elements:
    deque.removeFirst();                    // Remove from the head
    System.out.println("After removing from the head: " + deque);
    deque.removeLast();                     // Remove from the tail
    System.out.println("After removing from the tail: " + deque);
    deque.pollFirst();                      // Remove from the head
    System.out.println("After removing from the head: " + deque);
    deque.pollLast();                       // Remove from the tail
    System.out.println("After removing from the tail: " + deque);
    deque.pop();                            // Remove from the head
    System.out.println("After removing from the head: " + deque);
  }
}
```

Output from the program:

```
After creating the deque: []
After inserting at the head: [A (H)]
After inserting at the tail: [A (H), B (T)]
After inserting at the head: [C (H), A (H), B (T)]
After inserting at the head: [D (H), C (H), A (H), B (T)]
After inserting at the tail: [D (H), C (H), A (H), B (T), E (T)]
Examine at the head: D (H)
Examine at the tail: E (T)
Examine at the head: D (H)
Examine at the tail: E (T)
After removing from the head: [C (H), A (H), B (T), E (T)]
After removing from the tail: [C (H), A (H), B (T)]
After removing from the head: [A (H), B (T)]
After removing from the tail: [A (H)]
After removing from the head: []
```

Example 15.9 illustrates using an ArrayDeque both as a LIFO stack and as a FIFO queue. Elements from an array are pushed onto the stack at (3), and then popped from the stack at (5). The call to the isEmpty() method in the while loop at (4) determines whether the stack is empty. The output shows that the elements were popped in the reverse order to the order in which they were inserted—that is, LIFO ordering.

Similarly, elements from an array are inserted at the tail of a FIFO queue at (8), and then removed from the head of the FIFO queue at (10). The call to the isEmpty() method in the while loop at (4) determines whether the FIFO queue is empty. The output shows that the elements were removed in the same order they were inserted—that is, FIFO ordering.

Note that in Example 15.9 the stack grows at the head of the deque, but the FIFO queue grows at the tail of the deque.

Example 15.9 *Using Deques as a LIFO Stack and as a FIFO Queue*

```java
import java.util.ArrayDeque;
import java.util.Arrays;

/** Executes tasks. */
public class TaskExecutor2 {

  public static void main(String[] args) {
    String[] elementArray = {"sway", "and", "twist", "stacks", "tall"};     // (1)
    System.out.println("Array of elements: " + Arrays.toString(elementArray));

    // Using ArrayDeque as a stack:                                         (2)
    ArrayDeque<String> stack = new ArrayDeque<>();
    for (String string : elementArray)
      stack.push(string);                                  // (3) Push elements.
    System.out.println("Stack before: TOP->" + stack + "<-BOTTOM");
    System.out.print("Popping stack: ");
    while (!stack.isEmpty()) {                              // (4)
      System.out.print(stack.pop() + " ");                 // (5) Pop elements.
    }
    System.out.println("\n");

    // Using ArrayDeque as a FIFO queue:                    (6)
    elementArray = new String[] {"Waiting", "in", "queues", "is", "boring"};// (7)
    System.out.println("Array of elements: " + Arrays.toString(elementArray));
    ArrayDeque<String> fifoQueue = new ArrayDeque<>();
    for (String string : elementArray)
      fifoQueue.offerLast(string);                         // (8) Insert at tail.
    System.out.println("Queue before: HEAD->" + fifoQueue  + "<-TAIL");
    System.out.print("Polling queue: ");
    while (!fifoQueue.isEmpty()) {                          // (9)
      String string = fifoQueue.pollFirst();               // (10) Remove from head.
      System.out.print(string.toUpperCase() + " ");
    }
    System.out.println();
  }
}
```

Output from the program:

```
Array of elements: [sway, and, twist, stacks, tall]
Stack before: TOP->[tall, stacks, twist, and, sway]<-BOTTOM
Popping stack: tall stacks twist and sway

Array of elements: [Waiting, in, queues, is, boring]
Queue before: HEAD->[Waiting, in, queues, is, boring]<-TAIL
Polling queue: WAITING IN QUEUES IS BORING
```

 Review Questions

15.1   Which statement is true about the following program?

```java
import java.util.*;
public class RQ400A100 {
  public static void main(String[] args) {
    int sum = 0;
    for (int i : makeCollection()) {
      sum += i;
    }
    System.out.println(sum);
  }

  static Collection<Integer> makeCollection() {
    System.out.println("A collection coming up.");
    Collection<Integer> collection = new ArrayList<>();
    collection.add(10); collection.add(20); collection.add(30);
    return collection;
  }
}
```

Select the one correct answer.

(a) The program will print
     A collection coming up.
     60

(b) The program will print
     A collection coming up.
     A collection coming up.
     A collection coming up.
     60

(c) The program will fail to compile.

(d) None of the above

15.2   Given the following code:

```java
import java.util.*;
class Fruity {
  private String fName;
  Fruity(String fName) { this.fName = fName; }
```

```
          public void setName(String newName) { this.fName = newName; }
          public String toString() { return fName; }
          public boolean equals(Object other) {
            if (this == other) return true;
            if (!(other instanceof Fruity)) return false;
            return fName.equalsIgnoreCase(((Fruity)other).fName);
          }
        }

        public class RQ400A50 {
          public static void main(String[] args) {
            Fruity apple = new Fruity("Apple");
            Fruity orange = new Fruity("Orange");
            List<Fruity> list = new ArrayList<>();
            list.add(apple); list.add(orange); list.add(apple);
            System.out.println("Before: " + list);

            // (1) INSERT CODE HERE

            System.out.println("After:  " + list);
          }
        }
```

Which code, when inserted at (1), will result in the following output from the program:

```
        Before: [Apple, Orange, Apple]
        After:  [Orange]
```

Select the two correct answers.

(a)
```
    for (Fruity f : list) {
        if (f.equals(apple))
          list.remove(f);
    }
```

(b)
```
    int i = 0;
    for (Fruity f : list) {
        if (f.equals(apple))
          list.remove(i);
        i++;
    }
```

(c)
```
    for (int j = 0; j < list.size(); j++) {
        Fruity f = list.get(j);
        if (f.equals(apple))
          list.remove(j);
    }
```

(d)
```
    Iterator<Fruity> itr = list.iterator();
    while (itr.hasNext()) {
        Fruity f = itr.next();
        if (f.equals(apple))
          itr.remove();
    }
```

15.3 Which statement is true about the following program?

```java
import java.util.*;
class AnotherListIterator<T> implements Iterable<T>{

  private List<T> lst;
  public AnotherListIterator(List<T> lst) { this.lst = lst; }

  public Iterator<T> iterator() {
    return new Iterator<T>() {
      private int next = lst.size() - 1;

      public boolean hasNext() { return (next >= 0); }
      public T next() {
        T element = lst.get(next);
        next--;
        return element;
      }
    };
  }

  public static void main(String[] args) {
    List<String> lst = List.of("Hi", "Howdy", "Hello");
    AnotherListIterator<String> rlt = new AnotherListIterator<>(lst);
    for (String str : rlt) {
      System.out.print("|" + str + "|");
    }
  }
}
```

Select the one correct answer.

(a) The program will fail to compile.
(b) The program will compile, but it will throw an exception when run.
(c) The program will compile and print |Hi||Howdy||Hello| at runtime.
(d) The program will compile and print |Hello||Howdy||Hi| at runtime.
(e) The program will compile and print the strings in an unpredictable order at runtime.

15.4 Which of the following statements are true about collections?
Select the two correct answers.

(a) Methods calling optional operations in a collection must either catch an UnsupportedOperationException, or declare it in their throws clause.
(b) A List<E> can have duplicate elements.
(c) An ArrayList<E> can only accommodate a fixed number of elements.
(d) A Set<E> allows at most one null element.

15.5 Which statement is true about the following program?

```java
import java.util.*;
public class Sets {
  public static void main(String[] args) {
    HashSet<Integer> set1 = new HashSet<>();
```

```
          addRange(set1, 1);
          ArrayList<Integer> list1 = new ArrayList<>();
          addRange(list1, 2);
          TreeSet<Integer> set2 = new TreeSet<>();
          addRange(set2, 3);
          ArrayDeque<Integer> deque = new ArrayDeque<>();
          addRange(deque, 5);
          set1.removeAll(list1);
          list1.addAll(set2);
          deque.addAll(list1);
          set1.removeAll(deque);
          System.out.println(set1);
        }
      static void addRange(Collection<Integer> col, int step) {
        for (int i = step * 2; i <= 25; i += step) {
          col.add(i);
        }
      }
    }
```

Select the one correct answer.

(a) The program will fail to compile, since operations are performed on incompatible collection implementations.

(b) The program will fail to compile, since no Comparator is supplied to the TreeSet constructor for sorting the elements.

(c) The program will compile. When run, it will throw an UnsupportedOperation-Exception.

(d) The program will compile. When run, it will print all primes below 25.

15.6   Which statement is true about the following program?

```
    import java.util.*;
    public class Iterate {
      public static void main(String[] args) {
        List<String> l = new ArrayList<>();
        l.add("A"); l.add("B"); l.add("C"); l.add("D"); l.add("E");
        ListIterator<String> i = l.listIterator();
        i.next(); i.next(); i.next(); i.next();
        i.remove();
        i.previous(); i.previous();
        i.remove();
        System.out.println(l);
      }
    }
```

Select the one correct answer.

(a) It will print [A, B, C, D, E].
(b) It will print [A, C, E].
(c) It will print [B, D, E].
(d) It will print [A, B, D].
(e) It will print [B, C, E].
(f) It will throw a NoSuchElementException.

15.7 Which of the following statements, when inserted independently at (1), will guarantee that the following program will print [1, 9]?

```java
import java.util.*;
public class RightOne {
  public static void main(String[] args) {
    // (1) INSERT DECLARATION HERE
    collection.add(1); collection.add(9); collection.add(1);
    System.out.println(collection);
  }
}
```

Select the four correct answers.

(a) Collection<Integer> collection = new HashSet<>();
(b) Set<Integer> collection = new HashSet<>();
(c) HashSet<Integer> collection = new LinkedHashSet<>();
(d) Set<Integer> collection = new LinkedHashSet<>();
(e) Collection<Integer> collection = new TreeSet<>();
(f) NavigableSet<Integer> collection = new TreeSet<>();

15.8 Which of the following statements, when inserted independently at (1), will result in program output that does not include the word "shell"?

```java
import static java.lang.System.out;
import java.util.*;
public class RQ400A400 {
  public static void main(String[] args) {
    NavigableSet<String> strSetA = new TreeSet<>();
    Collections.addAll(strSetA, "sea", "shell", "soap", "swan");
    // (1) INSERT STATEMENT HERE
  }
}
```

Select the two correct answers.

(a) out.println(strSetA.headSet("soap", true));
(b) out.println(strSetA.headSet("soap", false));
(c) out.println(strSetA.tailSet("soap", true));
(d) out.println(strSetA.tailSet("soap", false));
(e) out.println(strSetA.subSet("sea", false, "soap", true));
(f) out.println(strSetA.subSet("sea", true, "soap", false));

15.8 Maps

A *map* defines *mappings* from keys to values. The *<key, value>* pair is called a *mapping*, also referred to as an *entry*. A map does not allow duplicate keys; in other words, the keys are unique. Each key maps to one value at most, implementing what is called a *single-valued map*. Thus there is a *many-to-one* relationship between keys and values. For example, in a student-grade map, many students (keys) can be awarded the same grade (value), but each student has only one grade. Replacing the value that is associated with a key results in the old entry being removed and a new entry being inserted.

Both the keys and the values must be objects, with primitive values being wrapped in their respective primitive wrapper objects when they are put in a map.

The Map<K,V> Interface

A map is not a collection, and the Map<K, V> interface does not extend the Collection<E> interface. However, the mappings can be viewed as a collection in various ways: a key set, a value collection, or an entry set. A key set view or an entry set view can be iterated over to retrieve the corresponding values from the underlying map (p. 844).

The Map<K, V> interface specifies some optional methods. Implementations should throw an UnsupportedOperationException if they do not support such an operation. The implementations of maps from the java.util package support all the optional operations of the Map<K, V> interface (see Table 15.2, p. 788, and Figure 15.3, p. 787).

The Map<K,V> interface and its subinterfaces SortedMap<K,V> and NavigableMap<K,V> provide a versatile set of methods to implement a wide range of operations on maps. Several examples in this section and subsequent sections illustrate many of the methods specified in these interfaces.

Basic Key-Based Operations

These operations constitute the basic functionality provided by a map. Many of the methods will be used in examples presented in this chapter.

```
V put(K key, V value)                              Optional
default V putIfAbsent(K key, V value)
```

The put() method inserts the <key, value> entry into the map. It returns the old *value* previously associated with the specified key, if any. Otherwise, it returns the null value.

The default method putIfAbsent() associates the key with the given value and returns null if the specified key is *not* already associated with a non-null value; otherwise, it returns the currently associated value.

```
V get(Object key)
default V getOrDefault(Object key, V defaultValue)
```

The get() method returns the value to which the specified key is mapped, or null if no entry is found.

The default method getOrDefault() returns the value to which the specified key is mapped, or the specified defaultValue if this map contains no entry for the key.

```
V remove(Object key)                                    Optional
default boolean remove(Object key, Object value)
```

The `remove()` method deletes the entry for the specified key. It returns the *value* previously associated with the specified key, if any. Otherwise, it returns the null value.

The default method `remove()` removes the entry for the specified key and returns true only if the specified key is currently mapped to the specified value.

```
default V replace(K key, V value)
default boolean replace(K key, V oldValue, V newValue)
```

In the first `replace()` method, the value associated with the key is replaced with the specified value only if the key is already mapped to some value. It returns the *previous* value associated with the specified key, or null if there was no entry found for the key.

In the second `replace()` method, the value associated with the key is replaced with the specified newValue only if the key is currently mapped to the specified oldValue. It returns true if the value in the entry for the key was replaced with the newValue.

```
boolean containsKey(Object key)
boolean containsValue(Object value)
```

The `containsKey()` method returns true if the specified key is mapped to a value in the map.

The `containsValue()` method returns true if there exists one or more keys that are mapped to the specified value.

Creating Unmodifiable Maps

Creating unmodifiable maps is analogous to creating unmodifiable lists (§12.2, p. 649) or unmodifiable sets (p. 804). The Map<K, V> interface provides factory methods to create *unmodifiable maps* that have the following characteristics:

- Keys and values in such maps cannot be added, removed, or updated. Any such attempt will result in an UnsupportedOperationException to be thrown. However, if the keys and values themselves are mutable, the map may appear to be modified.

- The null value cannot be used for keys and values, and will result in a NullPointerException if an attempt is made to create such a map with null keys or null values.

- Duplicate keys are rejected when creating such a map, resulting in an IllegalArgumentException.

- The iteration order of mappings in such maps is unspecified.

- Such maps are serializable if their keys and values are serializable (§20.5, p. 1261).

```
static <K,?V> Map<K,?V> of(K k1, V v1, K k2, V v2, K k3, V v3, K k4, V v4,
                           K k5, V v5, K k6, V v6, K k7, V v7, K k8, V v8,
                           K k9, V v9, K k10, V v10)
```

This method is overloaded, accepting any number of entries (k, v) from 0 to 10. It returns an unmodifiable map containing the number of mappings specified. It throws a `NullPointerException` if any key or value is `null`. It throws an `IllegalArgumentException` if there are any duplicate keys.

```
@SafeVarargs static <K,V> Map<K,V> ofEntries(
                Map.Entry<? extends K,? extends V>... entries)
```

This variable arity method returns an unmodifiable map containing an arbitrary number of entries. It throws a `NullPointerException` if a key or a value is `null`, or if the variable arity parameter entries is `null`. The annotation suppresses the heap pollution warning in its declaration and unchecked generic array creation warning at the call sites. See the method entry() below to create individual entries.

```
static <K,V> Map.Entry<K,V> entry(K k, V v)
```

This generic method returns an unmodifiable `Map.Entry` object containing the specified key and value. Attempts to create an entry using a `null` key or a `null` value result in a `NullPointerException`.

Each entry—that is, *<key, value>* pair—is represented by an object implementing the nested `Map.Entry<K, V>` interface. An entry can be manipulated by methods defined in this interface, which are self-explanatory:

```
interface Entry<K, V> {       // Nested interface in the Map<K, V> interface.
    K getKey();
    V getValue();
    V setValue(V value);      // Only if the entry is modifiable.
}
```

```
static <K,V> Map<K,V> copyOf(Map<? extends K, ? extends V> map)
```

This generic method returns an unmodifiable map containing copies of the entries in the specified map. The specified map must not be `null`, and it must not contain any `null` keys or values—otherwise, a `NullPointerException` is thrown. If the specified map is subsequently modified, the returned `Map<K,V>` will not reflect such modifications.

The code below shows that a map created by the `Map.of()` method cannot be modified. We cannot change or remove any entry in the map. Note that the `Map.of()` method allows up to 10 entries, and there is no variable arity `Map.of()` method. The map returned is also not an instance of the `HashMap` class.

```
Map<Integer, String> jCourses = Map.of(
                        200, "Basic Java",    300, "Intermediate Java",
                        400, "Advanced Java", 500, "Kickass Java");
// jCourses.put(200, "Java Jive");              // UnsupportedOperationException
// jCourses.remove(500);                        // UnsupportedOperationException
System.out.println(jCourses instanceof HashMap); // false
System.out.println(jCourses);
// {200=Basic Java, 400=Advanced Java, 300=Intermediate Java, 500=Kickass Java}
```

The `Map.of()` method does not allow duplicate keys, and keys or values cannot be null:

```
Map<Integer, String> coursesMap1
        = Map.of(101, "Java 1.1", 101, "Java 17");  // IllegalArgumentException
Map<Integer, String> coursesMap2
        = Map.of(101, "Java 1.1", 101, null);        // NullPointerException
```

The following code creates unmodifiable map entries, where both the key and the value are immutable:

```
//  Map.Entry<Integer, String> e0 = Map.entry(100, null); // NullPointerException
Map.Entry<Integer, String> e1 = Map.entry(200, "Basic Java");
Map.Entry<Integer, String> e2 = Map.entry(300, "Intermediate Java");
Map.Entry<Integer, String> e3 = Map.entry(400, "Advanced Java");
Map.Entry<Integer, String> e4 = Map.entry(500, "Kickass Java");
```

The variable arity `Map.ofEntries()` method can be used to create an unmodifiable map from an arbitrary number of unmodifiable entries.

```
Map<Integer, String> unmodCourseMap = Map.ofEntries(e1, e2, e3, e4);  // Varargs
// {300=Intermediate Java, 500=Kickass Java, 200=Basic Java, 400=Advanced Java}
//unmodCourseMap.replace(200, "Java Jive");     // UnsupportedOperationException
//unmodCourseMap.remove(500);                   // UnsupportedOperationException
```

The following code creates mutable course names that we will use in the next map.

```
StringBuilder mc1 = new StringBuilder("Basic Java");
StringBuilder mc2 = new StringBuilder("Intermediate Java");
StringBuilder mc3 = new StringBuilder("Advanced Java");
StringBuilder mc4 = new StringBuilder("Kickass Java");
```

The following code creates unmodifiable map entries, where the keys are immutable but the values are mutable:

```
Map.Entry<Integer, StringBuilder> me1 = Map.entry(200, mc1);
Map.Entry<Integer, StringBuilder> me2 = Map.entry(300, mc2);
Map.Entry<Integer, StringBuilder> me3 = Map.entry(400, mc3);
Map.Entry<Integer, StringBuilder> me4 = Map.entry(500, mc4);
```

We can use the variable arity `Map.ofEntries()` method to create an unmodifiable map, where trying to replace or remove a course results in an `UnsupportedOperation-Exception`:

```
Map<Integer, StringBuilder> unmodMapWithMutableCourses
        = Map.ofEntries(me1, me2, me3, me4);         // Varargs
System.out.println(unmodMapWithMutableCourses);
// {200=Basic Java, 500=Kickass Java, 300=Intermediate Java, 400=Advanced Java}

// unmodMapWithMutableCourses.replace(200, mc4); // UnsupportedOperationException
// unmodMapWithMutableCourses.remove(400);       // UnsupportedOperationException
```

However, the mutable values in the map can be modified:

```
StringBuilder mutableCourse = unmodMapWithMutableCourses.get(500);
mutableCourse.replace(0, 7, "Smartass");
```

```
System.out.println(unmodMapWithMutableCourses);
// {400=Advanced Java, 500=Smartass Java, 200=Basic Java, 300=Intermediate Java}
```

The code below shows how we can make a copy of a map. The `Map.copyOf()` method creates a copy of the map passed as an argument at (1). The map created is unmodifiable analogous to the maps created with the `Map.of()` or `Map.ofEntries()` methods. The code also shows that modifying the original map does *not* reflect in the copy of the map.

```
// Original map:
Map<Integer, StringBuilder> courseMap = new HashMap<>();
courseMap.put(200, mc1); courseMap.put(300, mc2);
courseMap.put(400, mc3); courseMap.put(500, mc4);

// Unmodifiable copy of the map:
Map<Integer, StringBuilder> copyCourseMap = Map.copyOf(courseMap); // (1)

// Modify original map:
courseMap.remove(200);
courseMap.remove(400);
System.out.println("Original: " + courseMap);
System.out.println("Copy: " + copyCourseMap);
```

The code above prints the contents of the maps, showing that the copy of the map was not modified:

```
Original: {500=Smartass Java, 300=Intermediate Java}
Copy: {300=Intermediate Java, 500=Smartass Java, 200=Basic Java,
       400=Advanced Java}
```

Advanced Key-Based Operations

The following methods for a map take a *function* (implemented by a lambda expression or a method reference) as a parameter to implement various scenarios that manipulate the value associated with a key.

```
default V merge(K key, V value,
                BiFunction<? super V,? super V,? extends V> remappingFunc)
```

If the specified key has no entry or is associated with a `null` value, the method associates the key with the specified non-`null` value. Otherwise, it associates the key with the result of applying the remapping two-arity function to the specified value and the currently associated value, or removes the entry for the key if the result is `null`.

Note that if the specified `value` is `null`, a `NullPointerException` is thrown at runtime.

Returns the new value associated with the key, or `null` if entry for the key is removed.

```
default V compute(K key,
                  BiFunction<? super K,? super V,? extends V> remappingFunc)
```

The remapping two-arity function is applied to the specified key and its currently associated value. If the result is non-null, it associates the key with the result. Otherwise, it removes any entry for the key.

Returns the computed value associated with the key, or null if the key is removed or is not associated with a value.

```
default V computeIfAbsent(K key,
                          Function<? super K,? extends V> mappingFunc)
```

If the value associated with the specified key is null or the key has no entry, this method applies the given function on the key, and the result is only associated with the key if the result is non-null.

Returns the current (existing or computed) value associated with the specified key, or null if the computed value is null.

```
default V computeIfPresent(K key,
                           BiFunction<? super K,? super V,? extends V> remappingFunc)
```

If the specified key is already associated with a non-null value, the method applies the specified remapping two-arity function to the key and its currently associated value. The result is only associated with the key if it is non-null; *otherwise, the key is removed.*

This method returns the current (existing or computed) value associated with the specified key, or null if the key is absent or removed.

Table 15.6 summarizes typical scenarios when using these advanced key-based methods. Given the value associated with a key and the resultValue returned by the remapping function if it is executed, the action performed and the value returned by each method are shown for each scenario.

Table 15.6 *Summary of Scenarios Using Advanced Key-Based Operations*

The value associated with key in the map	The resultValue returned by the remapping function	merge(key, givenValue, remapping-BiFunction) and (givenValue != null)	compute(key, remapping-BiFunction)	computeIf-Absent(key, mapping-Function)	computeIf-Present(key, remapping-BiFunction)
non-null	null	remove(key), *returns* null.	remove(key), *returns* null.	*No change. Returns* value.	remove(key), *returns* null.
non-null	non-null	put(key, resultValue), *returns* resultValue.	put(key, result-Value), *returns* resultValue.	*No change. Returns* value.	put(key, result-Value), *returns* resultValue.

Table 15.6 *Summary of Scenarios Using Advanced Key-Based Operations (Continued)*

The value associated with key in the map	The resultValue returned by the remapping function	merge(key, givenValue, remapping-BiFunction) and (givenValue != null)	compute(key, remapping-BiFunction)	computeIf-Absent(key, mapping-Function)	computeIf-Present(key, remapping-BiFunction)
null	null	put(key, givenValue), *returns* givenValue.	remove(key), *returns* null.	*No change. Returns* null.	*No change. Returns* null
null	non-null	put(key, givenValue), *returns* givenValue.	put(key, result-Value), *returns* resultValue.	put(key, result-Value), *returns* resultValue.	*No change. Returns* null.
No mapping	null	put(key, givenValue), *returns* givenValue.	*Not entered. Returns* null.	*Not entered. Returns* null.	*Not entered. Returns* null.
No mapping	non-null	put(key, givenValue), *returns* givenValue.	put(key, result-Value), *returns* resultValue.	put(key, result-Value), *returns* resultValue.	*Not entered. Returns* null.

In the code snippets to illustrate each method, an emergency telephone number map, etnMap, is loaded with the same entries. This map is a HashMap<Integer, String> that is used to map emergency telephone numbers (Integers) to countries (Strings) where they are used. (*Disclaimer*: There is no guarantee that the information provided below is correct.)

```
Map<Integer, String> etnMap = new HashMap<>();
etnMap.put(112, "Norway");
etnMap.put(999, "UK");
etnMap.put(190, null);
etnMap.put(911, null);
// {112=Norway, 999=UK, 190=null, 911=null}
```

In the code below, six method calls are made corresponding to the column for each method in Table 15.6. Each method call shows the value returned by the method as a comment in the call statement.

The merge() method executes as follows:

- If the key is associated with the null value in the map, as shown at (3) and (4), or has no entry, as shown at (5) and (6), the key is associated with the *non-null given value*.

- Otherwise, the remapping two-arity function is computed.
    - If the result is null, the entry for the key is removed, as shown at (1).
    - If the result is non-null, the key is associated with the result, as shown at (2).

```
// Before: {112=Norway, 999=UK, 190=null, 911=null}
etnMap.merge(112, "Mordor", (oVal, value) -> null);      // (1) null, removed
etnMap.merge(999, "Mordor", (oVal, value) -> "Uganda");  // (2) Uganda, updated
etnMap.merge(190, "Mordor", (oVal, value) -> null);      // (3) Mordor, updated
etnMap.merge(911, "Mordor", (oVal, value) -> "USA");     // (4) Mordor, updated
etnMap.merge(100, "Mordor", (oVal, value) -> null);      // (5) Mordor, inserted
etnMap.merge(110, "Mordor", (oVal, value) -> "China");   // (6) Mordor, inserted
// After: {100=Mordor, 999=Uganda, 110=Mordor, 190=Mordor, 911=Mordor}
```

The compute() method executes as follows:

- The remapping two-arity function is executed.
    - If this result is non-null, as at (8), (10), and (12), this result is associated with the key whether or not the key has an entry in the map.
    - If this result is null and the key has an entry in the map, the entry is removed, as at (7) and (9).
    - If this result is null and the key has no entry in the map, no action is taken, as at (11).

```
// Before: {112=Norway, 999=UK, 190=null, 911=null}
etnMap.compute(112, (key, oVal) -> null);       // (7) null, removed
etnMap.compute(999, (key, oVal) -> "Uganda");   // (8) Uganda, updated
etnMap.compute(190, (key, oVal) -> null);       // (9) null, removed
etnMap.compute(911, (key, oVal) -> "USA");      // (10) USA, updated
etnMap.compute(100, (key, oVal) -> null);       // (11) null, no action
etnMap.compute(110, (key, oVal) -> "China");    // (12) China, inserted
// After: {110=China, 999=Uganda, 911=USA}
```

The computeIfAbsent() method executes as follows:

- If the key is associated with a null value or has no entry in the map, the remapping function is executed.
    - If the result is non-null, as at (16) and (18), this result is associated with the key.

```
// Before: {112=Norway, 999=UK, 190=null, 911=null}
etnMap.computeIfAbsent(112, key -> null);       // (13) Norway, no change
etnMap.computeIfAbsent(999, key -> "Uganda");   // (14) UK, no change
etnMap.computeIfAbsent(190, key -> null);       // (15) null, no change
etnMap.computeIfAbsent(911, key -> "USA");      // (16) USA, updated
etnMap.computeIfAbsent(100, key -> null);       // (17) null, no action
etnMap.computeIfAbsent(110, key -> "China");    // (18) China, inserted
// After: {112=Norway, 110=China, 999=UK, 190=null, 911=USA}
```

The computeIfPresent() method executes as follows:

- If the key is associated with a non-null value in the map, as at (19) and (20), the remapping two-arity function is executed.
    - If the result is null, then the entry with the key is removed, as at (19).

- If the result is non-null, then the key is associated with the result, as at (20).

```
// Before: {112=Norway, 999=UK, 190=null, 911=null}
etnMap.computeIfPresent(112, (key, oVal) -> null);      // (19) null, removed
etnMap.computeIfPresent(999, (key, oVal) -> "Uganda");  // (20) Uganda, updated
etnMap.computeIfPresent(190, (key, oVal) -> null);      // (21) null, no change
etnMap.computeIfPresent(911, (key, oVal) -> "USA");     // (22) null, no change
etnMap.computeIfPresent(100, (key, oVal) -> null);      // (23) null, no action
etnMap.computeIfPresent(110, (key, oVal) -> "China");   // (24) null, no action
// After: {999=Uganda, 190=null, 911=null}
```

Bulk Operations

Bulk operations can be performed on an entire map.

```
int size()
boolean isEmpty()
```

Return the number of entries (i.e., number of unique keys in the map) and whether the map is empty or not, respectively.

```
void clear()                                  Optional
void putAll(Map<? extends K, ? extends V> map)    Optional
```

The first method deletes all entries from the current map.

The second method copies all entries from the specified map to the current map. If a key from the specified map is already in the current map, its associated value in the current map is replaced with the associated value from the specified map.

```
default void forEach(BiConsumer<? super K,? super V> action)
```

The specified action is performed for each entry in this map until all entries have been processed or the action throws an exception. Iteration is usually performed in entry set iteration order. The functional interface BiConsumer<T,U> is covered in §13.7, p. 711, where this method is illustrated. It is also used in Example 15.10, p. 844.

```
default void replaceAll(BiFunction<? super K,? super V,? extends V> func)
```

The value of each entry is replaced with the result of invoking the given two-arity function on the entry until all entries have been processed or the function throws an exception. The functional interface BiFunction<T,U,R> is covered in §13.9, p. 717, where this method is illustrated.

Collection Views

Views allow information in a map to be represented as collections. Elements can be removed from a map via a view, but cannot be added. An iterator over a view will throw an exception if the underlying map is modified concurrently. Example 15.10, p. 844, illustrates collection views.

```
Set<K> keySet()
Collection<V> values()
Set<Map.Entry<K, V>> entrySet()
```

Create different views of a map. Changes in the map are reflected in the view, and vice versa. These methods return a set view of keys, a collection view of values, and a set view of *<key, value>* entries, respectively. Note that the Collection returned by the values() method is not a Set, as several keys can map to the same value—that is, duplicate values can be included in the returned collection. An entry in the entry set view can be manipulated by the methods defined in the Map.Entry<K, V> interface.

Example 15.10, p. 844, provides an example of using collection views.

15.9 Map Implementations

Figure 15.3, p. 787, shows four implementations of the Map<K, V> interface found in the java.util package: HashMap<K, V>, LinkedHashMap<K, V>, Hashtable<K, V>, and TreeMap<K, V>.

The classes HashMap<K, V> and Hashtable<K, V> implement unordered maps. The class LinkedHashMap<K, V> implements ordered maps, and the class TreeMap<K, V> implements sorted maps (p. 845).

Table 15.7 *Map Implementations*

Map	null as key	null as value	Kind of map	Thread-safe?
HashMap<K,V>	*Allowed*	*Allowed*	*Unordered*	*Not thread-safe*
LinkedHashMap<K,V> extends HashMap<K,V>	*Allowed*	*Allowed*	*Key insertion order/ Access order*	*Not thread-safe*
Hashtable<K,V>	*Not allowed*	*Not allowed*	*Unordered*	*Thread-safe*
TreeMap<K,V>	*Not allowed*	*Allowed*	*Key-sort order*	*Not thread-safe*

While the HashMap<K, V> class is not thread-safe and permits a null key and null values (analogous to the LinkedHashMap<K, V> class), the Hashtable<K, V> class is thread-safe and permits only non-null keys and values (see Table 15.7). The thread-safety provided by the Hashtable<K, V> class comes with a performance penalty. Thread-safe use of maps is also provided by the methods in the Collections class (p. 856). Like the Vector<E> class, the Hashtable<K, V> class is also a legacy class that has been retrofitted to implement the Map<K, V> interface.

These map implementations are based on a hashing algorithm. Operations on a map thus rely on the hashCode() and equals() methods of the key objects (§14.2, p. 744, and §14.3, p. 753).

The LinkedHashMap<K, V> implementation is a subclass of the HashMap<K, V> class. The relationship between the map classes LinkedHashMap<K, V> and HashMap<K, V> is analogous to the relationship between their counterpart set classes LinkedHashSet<E> and HashSet<E>. The entries of a HashMap<K, V> (analogous to a HashSet<E>) are unordered. The entries of a LinkedHashMap<K, V> (analogous to a LinkedHashSet<E>) are ordered. By default, the entries of a LinkedHashMap<K, V> are in *key insertion order*— that is, the order in which the keys are inserted in the map. This order does not change if a key is reinserted because no new entry is created if the key's entry already exists. The elements in a LinkedHashSet<E> are also at (element) insertion order. However, a LinkedHashMap<K, V> can also maintain its entries in *access order*— that is, the order in which its entries are accessed, from least-recently accessed to most-recently accessed entries. This *ordering mode* can be specified in one of the constructors of the LinkedHashMap<K, V> class.

Both the HashMap<K, V> and the LinkedHashMap<K, V> classes provide comparable performance, but the HashMap<K, V> class is the natural choice if ordering is not an issue. Operations such as adding, removing, or finding an entry based on a key are in constant time, as these are based on hashing the key. Operations such as finding the entry with a specific *value* are in linear time, as these involve searching through the entries.

Adding, removing, and finding entries in a LinkedHashMap<K, V> can be slightly slower than in a HashMap<K, V>, as an ordered doubly linked list has to be maintained. Iteration over a map is through one of its collection views. For an underlying LinkedHashMap<K, V>, the iteration time is proportional to the size of the map— regardless of its capacity. However, for an underlying HashMap<K, V>, it is proportional to the capacity of the map.

The concrete map implementations override the toString() method. The standard text representation generated by the toString() method for a map is

$$\{key_1\text{=}value_1,\ key_2\text{=}value_2,\ \dots,\ key_n\text{=}value_n\}$$

where each key_i and each $value_i$, where $1 \mathrel{<=} i \mathrel{<=} n$, is the text representation generated by the toString() method of the individual key and value objects in the map, respectively.

As was the case with collections, implementation classes provide a standard constructor that creates a new empty map, and a constructor that creates a new map based on an existing map. Additional constructors create empty maps with given initial capacities and load factors. The HashMap<K, V> class provides the following constructors:

```
HashMap()
HashMap(int initialCapacity)
HashMap(int initialCapacity, float loadFactor)
```
Constructs an empty HashMap, using either a default or specified initial capacity and a load factor.

```
HashMap(Map<? extends K,? extends V> otherMap)
```
Constructs a new map containing the elements in the specified map.

The `LinkedHashMap<K, V>` and `Hashtable<K, V>` classes have constructors analogous to the four constructors for the `HashMap<K, V>` class. In addition, the `LinkedHashMap<K, V>` class provides a constructor where the ordering mode can also be specified:

```
LinkedHashMap(int initialCapacity, float loadFactor, boolean accessOrder)
```
Constructs a new, empty `LinkedHashMap` with the specified initial capacity, the specified load factor, and the specified ordering mode. The ordering mode is `true` for *access order* and `false` for *key insertion order.*

Example 15.10 prints a textual histogram for the frequency of weight measurements in a weight group, where a weight group is defined as an interval of five units. The weight measurements are supplied as program arguments. A `HashMap<Integer, Integer>` is used, where the key is the weight group and the value is the frequency. The example illustrates many key-based operations on maps, the creation of key views, and iteration over a map.

We have intentionally used a `HashMap<K,V>`. It is instructive to compare this with the solution in Example 15.11 that uses a `TreeMap<K,V>` that simplifies the solution further, when the entries are maintained in key-sort order.

The program proceeds as follows:

- An empty `HashMap<Integer, Integer>` is created at (1), where the key is the weight group and the associated value is the frequency.

- A `for(:)` loop is used at (2) to read the weights specified as program arguments, converting each weight to its corresponding weight group and updating the frequency of the weight group.

Each program argument is parsed to a `double` value at (3), which is then used to determine the correct weight group at (4). The call to the `merge()` method at (5) updates the frequency map:

```
// With method reference:
groupFreqMap.merge(weightGroup, 1, Integer::sum);                          // (5)

// With lambda expression:
groupFreqMap.merge(weightGroup, 1,
    (oldVal, givenVal) -> Integer.sum(oldVal, givenVal));
```

If the weight group is not in the map, its frequency is set to 1; otherwise, the method reference `Integer::sum` increments the frequency by the given value 1. In both cases an appropriate entry for the weight group is put in the frequency map. Note the arguments passed to the method reference and the lambda expression: `oldVal` is the current value associated with the key and `givenVal` is the specified value, 1, passed to the `merge()` method.

Generic types guarantee that the keys and the values in the map are of the correct type, and autoboxing/unboxing of primitive values guarantees the correct type of an operand in an expression.

Some other strategies to update the frequency map are outlined here, but none is more elegant than the one with the merge() method.

The straightforward solution below requires an explicit null check to determine whether the value returned by the get() method is null, or risks a NullPointer-Exception at runtime when incrementing the null value in the frequency reference.

```
Integer frequency = groupFreqMap.get(weightGroup);
if (frequency == null) frequency = 0;
groupFreqMap.put(weightGroup, ++frequency);
```

Below, the getOrDefault() method never returns a null value, since it returns the associated frequency value or the specified default value 0 depending on whether the weight group is found or not found in the map, respectively. No explicit null check is necessary.

```
Integer frequency = groupFreqMap.getOrDefault(weightGroup, 0);
groupFreqMap.put(weightGroup, ++frequency);
```

The putIfAbsent() method puts an entry with frequency 0 for the weight group if it is not found so that the get() method will always return a non-null value which can be safely incremented.

```
groupFreqMap.putIfAbsent(weightGroup, 0);
Integer frequency = groupFreqMap.get(weightGroup);
groupFreqMap.put(weightGroup, ++frequency);
```

The compute() method always updates the value associated with the key if the two-arity function returns a non-null value, which is always the case below. The null check is now done in the lambda expression.

```
groupFreqMap.compute(weightGroup, (k, v) -> v == null ? 1 : v + 1);
```

- The program creates a sorted set of keys (which are weight groups) from the groupFreqMap at (6). The Map.keySet() method returns a set view of keys, which is passed as an argument to a TreeSet<E> to create a sorted set—in this case, the natural ordering of Integers is used.

```
TreeSet<Integer> sortedKeySet = new TreeSet<>(groupFreqMap.keySet()); // (6)
```

- The histogram is printed by implicitly iterating over the sorted key set at (7). Since a sorted set is an Iterable<E>, we can use the forEach() method that takes a consumer to print the histogram.

```
sortedKeySet.forEach(key ->                                          // (7)
    System.out.printf("%5s: %s%n", key,
        String.join("", Collections.nCopies(groupFreqMap.get(key), "*"))))
```

For each key, the corresponding value (i.e., the frequency) is retrieved and converted to a string with the corresponding number of "*". The method Collections.nCopies() creates a list with an equal number of elements as its first argument and where each element is the same as the second argument. The elements of this list are joined to create a string by the String.join() method with the first argument specifying the delimiter to use between the elements, which in this case is the empty string.

Alternately, a for(:) loop can be used to explicitly iterate over the sorted set view of the frequency map.

Example 15.10 *Using Maps*

```java
import java.util.Arrays;
import java.util.Collections;
import java.util.HashMap;
import java.util.Map;
import java.util.TreeSet;

public class Histogram {
  public static void main(String[] args) {
    System.out.println("Data: " + Arrays.toString(args));

    // Create a map to store the frequency for each group.
    Map<Integer, Integer> groupFreqMap = new HashMap<>();                // (1)

    // Determine the frequencies:
    for (String argument : args) {                                        // (2)
      double weight = Double.parseDouble(argument);                       // (3)
      int weightGroup = (int) Math.round(weight/5.0)*5;                   // (4)
      groupFreqMap.merge(weightGroup, 1, Integer::sum);                   // (5)
    }
    System.out.println("Frequencies: " + groupFreqMap);

    // Create sorted key set.
    TreeSet<Integer> sortedKeySet = new TreeSet<>(groupFreqMap.keySet()); // (6)

    System.out.println("Histogram:");
    // Implicit iteration over the key set.
    sortedKeySet.forEach(key ->                                           // (7)
        System.out.printf("%5s: %s%n", key,
            String.join("", Collections.nCopies(groupFreqMap.get(key), "*")))
    );
  }
}
```

Running the program with the following arguments:

> **>java Histogram** 74 75 93 75 93 82 61 92 10 185

gives the following output:

```
Data: [74, 75, 93, 75, 93, 82, 61, 92, 10, 185]
Frequencies: {80=1, 185=1, 10=1, 90=1, 75=3, 60=1, 95=2}
Histogram:
   10: *
   60: *
   75: ***
   80: *
   90: *
   95: **
  185: *
```

15.10 Sorted Maps and Navigable Maps

The SortedMap<K, V> interface extends the Map<K, V> interface, and the NavigableMap<K, V> interface extends the SortedMap<K, V> interface. The two maps are analogs of the SortedSet<E> and the NavigableSet<E> interfaces, respectively.

The SortedMap<K, V> Interface

The SortedMap<K, V> interface extends the Map<K, V> interface to provide the functionality for implementing maps with *sorted keys*. Its operations are analogous to those of the SortedSet<E> interface (p. 810), applied to maps and keys rather than to sets and elements.

```
// First-last keys
K firstKey()                                        Sorted set: first()
K lastKey()                                         Sorted set: last()
```
Return the first (smallest) key and the last (largest) key in the sorted map, respectively, dependent on the key-sort order in the map. They throw a NoSuchElementException if the map is empty.

```
// Range-view operations
SortedMap<K,V> headMap(K toKey)                     Sorted set: headSet()
SortedMap<K,V> tailMap(K fromKey)                   Sorted set: tailSet()
SortedMap<K,V> subMap(K fromKey, K toKey)           Sorted set: subSet()
```
Return different views analogous to those for a SortedSet<E>. The views returned are a portion of the map whose keys are strictly less than toKey, greater than or equal to fromKey, and between fromKey (inclusive) and toKey (exclusive), respectively. That is, these partial map views include fromKey if it is present in the map, but toKey is excluded.

```
// Comparator access
Comparator<? super K> comparator()
```

Returns the key comparator that defines the key-sort order, or null if the sorted map uses natural ordering for the keys.

The NavigableMap<K, V> Interface

Analogous to the NavigableSet<E> interface extending the SortedSet<E> interface, the NavigableMap<K, V> interface extends the SortedMap<K, V> interface with navigation methods to find the closest matches for specific search targets. The NavigableMap<K, V> interface replaces the SortedMap<K, V> interface and is the preferred choice when a sorted map is needed.

In addition to the methods of the SortedMap<K, V> interface, the NavigableMap<K, V> interface adds the *new* methods shown below, where the analogous methods from the NavigableSet<E> interface are also identified. Note that where a NavigableMap<K, V>

method returns a `Map.Entry` object representing an entry, the corresponding `NavigableSet<E>` method returns an element of the set.

```
// First-last entries
// Remove
Map.Entry<K, V> pollFirstEntry()                    Navigable set: pollFirst()
Map.Entry<K, V> pollLastEntry()                     Navigable set: pollLast()


// Examine
Map.Entry<K, V> firstEntry()
Map.Entry<K, V> lastEntry()
```

The `pollFirstEntry()` method *removes* and returns the first *entry*, and the `pollLastEntry()` method removes and returns the last *entry* currently in this navigable map. The entry is determined according to the ordering policy employed by the map—for example, natural ordering. Both return `null` if the navigable set is empty. The last two methods only retrieve, and do not remove, the value that is returned.

```
// Range-view operations
NavigableMap<K, V> headMap(K toKey,                 Navigable set: headSet()
                   boolean inclusive)
NavigableMap<K, V> tailMap(K fromKey,               Navigable set: tailSet()
                   boolean inclusive)
NavigableMap<K, V> subMap(K fromKey,                Navigable set: subSet()
                  boolean fromInclusive,
                  K toKey,
                  boolean toInclusive)
```

These operations are analogous to the ones in the `SortedMap<K, V>` interface (p. 845), returning different views of the underlying navigable map, depending on the bound elements. However, the bound elements can be *excluded or included* by the operation, depending on the value of the `boolean` argument `inclusive`.

```
// Closest-matches
Map.Entry<K, V> ceilingEntry(K key)                 Navigable set: ceiling()
K               ceilingKey(K key)
Map.Entry<K, V> floorEntry(K key)                   Navigable set: floor()
K               floorKey(K key)
Map.Entry<K, V> higherEntry(K key)                  Navigable set: higher()
K               higherKey(K key)
Map.Entry<K, V> lowerEntry(K key)                   Navigable set: lower()
K               lowerKey(K key)
```

The ceiling methods return the least entry (or key) in the navigable map >= to the argument key. The floor methods return the greatest entry (or key) in the navigable map <= to the argument key. The higher methods return the least entry (or key) in the navigable map > the argument key. The lower methods return the greatest entry (or key) in the navigable map < the argument key. All methods return `null` if there is no such key.

```
// Navigation-views
NavigableMap<K, V> descendingMap()                    Navigable set: descendingSet()
NavigableSet<K> descendingKeySet()
NavigableSet<K> navigableKeySet()
```

The first method returns a *reverse-order map view* of the entries in the navigable map. The second method returns a *reverse-order key set view* for the entries in the navigable map. The last method returns an *ascending-order key set view* for the entries in the navigable map.

The TreeMap<K,V> Class

The TreeMap<K, V> class is the analog of the TreeSet<E> class (p. 812), but in this case for maps. It provides an implementation that sorts its entries in a specific order (see also Figures 15.2 and 15.3, p. 786).

The TreeMap<K, V> class implements the NavigableMap<K, V> interface, and thereby the SortedMap<K, V> interface. By default, operations on sorted maps rely on the natural ordering of the keys. However, a total ordering can be specified by passing a customized comparator to the constructor.

A key in a TreeMap<K, V> cannot have the null value, but the value associated with a key in an entry can be null.

The TreeMap<K, V> implementation uses balanced trees, which deliver excellent performance for all operations. However, searching in a HashMap<K, V> can be faster than in a TreeMap<K, V>, as hashing algorithms usually offer better performance than the search algorithms for balanced trees.

The TreeMap<K, V> class provides four constructors, analogous to the ones in the TreeSet<E> class:

```
TreeMap()
```
A standard constructor used to create a new empty sorted map, according to the natural ordering of the keys.

```
TreeMap(Comparator<? super K> c)
```
A constructor that takes an explicit comparator for the keys, that is used to order the entries in the map.

```
TreeMap(Map<? extends K, ? extends V> map)
```
A constructor that can create a sorted map based on a map, according to the natural ordering of the keys of the specified map.

```
TreeMap(SortedMap<K, ? extends V> map)
```
A constructor that creates a new map containing the same entries as the specified sorted map, with the same ordering for the keys as the specified map.

Example 15.11 illustrates using navigable maps. It also prints a textual histogram like the one in Example 15.10, but using a TreeMap<K, V>, and in addition, it prints some statistics about the navigable map. See also the output from running the example. Some remarks about Example 15.11:

- An empty `NavigableMap<Integer, Integer>` is created at (1), where the key is the weight group and the value is the frequency. The loop at (2) reads the weights specified as program arguments, and creates a frequency map, as described in Example 15.10.

- The method `printHistogram()` at (15) prints a histogram of the frequencies in a navigable map:

  ```
  public static <K> void printHistogram(NavigableMap<K, Integer> freqMap) {...}
  ```

  It is a generic method with one type parameter, `K`, that specifies the type of the keys, and the type of the values (i.e., frequencies) is `Integer`. It prints the map and the number of entries in the map at (16) and (17), respectively. The `forEach()` method is invoked on the map at (18) to iterate over the *entries* in order to print the histogram, as explained in Example 15.10.

  Printing the histogram at (3) shows the number of entries ordered in ascending key order and the size of the map:

  ```
  Group frequency map: {10=1, 60=1, 75=3, 80=1, 90=1, 95=2, 185=1}
  No. of weight groups: 7
  ...
  ```

- Calls to the methods `firstEntry()` and `lastEntry()` at (4) and (5):

  ```
  out.println("First entry: " + groupFreqMap.firstEntry());        // (4)
  out.println("Last entry: " + groupFreqMap.lastEntry());          // (5)
  ```

  return the following entries, respectively:

  ```
  First entry: 10=1
  Last entry: 185=1
  ```

- Calls to the methods `floorEntry()` and `higherKey()` with the key value 77 at (6) and with the key value 90 at (7), respectively:

  ```
  out.println("Greatest entry <= 77: "
              + groupFreqMap.floorEntry(77));                      // (6)
  out.println("Smallest key > 90: "
              + groupFreqMap.higherKey(90));                       // (7)
  ```

  give the following output, respectively:

  ```
  Greatest entry <= 77: 75=3
  Smallest key > 90: 95
  ```

- Calls to the methods `tailMap(75, true)` and `headMap(75, false)` at (8) and (9) with the argument 75:

  ```
  ...
  printHistogram(groupFreqMap.tailMap(75, true));                  // (8)
  ...
  printHistogram(groupFreqMap.headMap(75, false));                 // (9)
  ```

  return the following map views, respectively:

  ```
  Tail map (Groups >= 75): {75=3, 80=1, 90=1, 95=2, 185=1}
  ...
  Head map (Groups <  75): {10=1, 60=1}
  ...
  ```

- The call to the subMap() method at (10)

```
printHistogram(groupFreqMap.subMap(                           // (10)
    groupFreqMap.firstEntry().getKey(), false,
    groupFreqMap.lastEntry().getKey(), false));
```

  returns the map view with the first and the last entry excluded:

```
Frequency map (first and last entry excluded): {60=1, 75=3, 80=1, 90=1, 95=2}
...
```

- Polling of a navigable map is shown at (11). Polling is done directly on the navigable map, and the first entry in the map is always retrieved and removed by the pollFirstEntry() method at (12). A while loop is used to iterate over the entries in the map until the map is empty. For each entry, its key and its value is printed.

```
// Poll the navigable map:                                    // (11)
int sumValues = 0;
while (!groupFreqMap.isEmpty()) {
  Map.Entry<Integer, Integer> entry = groupFreqMap.pollFirstEntry();  // (12)
  Integer frequency = entry.getValue();
  sumValues += frequency;
  out.printf("%5s: %s%n", entry.getKey(), frequency);
}
```

  The number of weights—that is, the sum of the values in the map—is also calculated in the loop and printed at (13) and (14), respectively. After polling the map, the output shows that the map is empty.

- -

Example 15.11 *Using Navigable Maps*

```
import java.util.Collections;
import java.util.Map;
import java.util.NavigableMap;
import java.util.TreeMap;
import static java.lang.System.out;

public class HistogramStats {
  public static void main(String[] args) {

    // Create a navigable map to store the frequency for each group.
    NavigableMap<Integer, Integer> groupFreqMap = new TreeMap<>();    // (1)

    // Determine the frequencies:
    for (String argument : args) {                                    // (2)
      double weight = Double.parseDouble(argument);
      int weightGroup = (int) Math.round(weight/5.0)*5;
      groupFreqMap.merge(weightGroup, 1, Integer::sum);
    }

    // Print statistics about the frequency map:
    out.print("Group frequency map: ");
    printHistogram(groupFreqMap);                                     // (3)

    out.println("First entry: " + groupFreqMap.firstEntry());         // (4)
    out.println("Last entry: " + groupFreqMap.lastEntry());           // (5)
```

```
        out.println("Greatest entry <= 77: "
                    + groupFreqMap.floorEntry(77));                         // (6)
        out.println("Smallest key > 90: "
                    + groupFreqMap.higherKey(90));                          // (7)

        out.print("Tail map (Groups >= 75): ");
        printHistogram(groupFreqMap.tailMap(75, true));                     // (8)

        out.print("Head map (Groups <  75): ");
        printHistogram(groupFreqMap.headMap(75, false));                    // (9)

        out.print("Frequency map (first and last entry excluded): ");
        printHistogram(groupFreqMap.subMap(                                 // (10)
            groupFreqMap.firstEntry().getKey(), false,
            groupFreqMap.lastEntry().getKey(), false));

        // Poll the navigable map:                                          (11)
        out.println("Histogram (by polling):");
        int sumValues = 0;
        while (!groupFreqMap.isEmpty()) {
          Map.Entry<Integer, Integer> entry = groupFreqMap.pollFirstEntry();   // (12)
          Integer frequency = entry.getValue();
          sumValues += frequency;
          out.printf("%5s: %s%n", entry.getKey(), frequency);
        }
        out.println("Number of weights registered: " + sumValues);         // (13)
        out.println("Group frequency map after polling: " + groupFreqMap);  // (14)
      }

      // Prints a histogram for entries in a navigable map.
      public static <K> void printHistogram(NavigableMap<K, Integer> freqMap) { // (15)
        out.println(freqMap);                                              // (16)
        out.println("No. of entries: " + freqMap.size());                  // (17)
        freqMap.forEach((k, v) ->                                          // (18)
            out.printf("%5s: %s%n", k,
                       String.join("", Collections.nCopies(v, "*"))));
      }
    }
```

Running the program with the following arguments:

```
>java HistogramStats 74 75 93 75 93 82 61 92 10 185
```

gives the following output:

```
Group frequency map: {10=1, 60=1, 75=3, 80=1, 90=1, 95=2, 185=1}
No. of entries: 7
   10: *
   60: *
   75: ***
   80: *
   90: *
   95: **
  185: *
First entry: 10=1
Last entry: 185=1
```

```
Greatest entry <= 77: 75=3
Smallest key > 90: 95
Tail map (Groups >= 75): {75=3, 80=1, 90=1, 95=2, 185=1}
No. of entries: 5
   75: ***
   80: *
   90: *
   95: **
  185: *
Head map (Groups < 75): {10=1, 60=1}
No. of entries: 2
   10: *
   60: *
Frequency map (first and last entry excluded): {60=1, 75=3, 80=1, 90=1, 95=2}
No. of entries: 5
   60: *
   75: ***
   80: *
   90: *
   95: **
Histogram (by polling):
   10: 1
   60: 1
   75: 3
   80: 1
   90: 1
   95: 2
  185: 1
Number of weights registered: 10
Group frequency map after polling: {}
```

Review Questions

15.9 Which of the following statements are true about maps?
Select the two correct answers.

(a) The return type of the values() method is Set<V>.
(b) Changes made in the set view returned by the keySet() method will be reflected in the underlying map.
(c) The Map<K, V> interface extends the Collection<E> interface.
(d) All keys in a map are unique.
(e) All Map<K, V> implementations maintain the keys in some sort order.

15.10 Which of the following methods are defined by the java.util.Map.Entry<K, V> interface?
Select the three correct answers.

(a) K getKey()
(b) K setKey(K value)
(c) V getValue()

(d) V setValue(V value)

(e) void set(K key, V value)

15.11 Given the following code:

```
import java.util.*;
public class TripleJump1 {
  public static void main(String[] args) {
    NavigableSet<String> set = new TreeSet<>(Collections.reverseOrder());
    Collections.addAll(set, "Step", "Jump", "Step", "Hop");
    System.out.println(set);
  }
}
```

What is the result?

Select the one correct answer.

(a) [Step, Step, Jump, Hop]

(b) [Step, Jump, Hop]

(c) [Hop, Jump, Step, Step]

(d) [Hop, Jump, Step]

(e) The result is unpredictable.

(f) The code will throw an exception at runtime.

15.12 Given the following code:

```
import java.util.*;
public class TripleJump2 {
  public static void main(String[] args) {
    NavigableSet<String> set1 = new TreeSet<>(Collections.reverseOrder());
    Collections.addAll(set1, "Step", "Jump", "Hop");
    NavigableSet<String> set2 = new TreeSet<>(set1);
    System.out.println(set2);
  }
}
```

What is the result?

Select the one correct answer.

(a) [Hop, Jump, Step]

(b) [Step, Jump, Hop]

(c) The program will compile, but it will produce an unpredictable result when run.

(d) The program will throw an exception at runtime.

(e) The program will fail to compile.

15.13 Given the following code:

```
import java.util.*;
public class TripleJump3 {
  public static void main(String[] args) {
    NavigableSet<String> set1 = new TreeSet<>(Collections.reverseOrder());
    Collections.addAll(set1, "Step", "Jump", "Hop");
    NavigableSet<String> set2 = new TreeSet<>((Collection<String>)set1);
```

```
        System.out.println(set2);
      }
    }
```

What is the result?

Select the one correct answer.

(a) [Hop, Jump, Step]

(b) [Step, Jump, Hop]

(c) The program will compile, but it will produce an unpredictable result when run.

(d) The program will throw an exception at runtime.

(e) The program will fail to compile.

15.14 Given the following code:

```
import java.util.*;
public class TripleJump4 {
    public static void main(String[] args) {
        NavigableSet<String> set1 = new TreeSet<>(Collections.reverseOrder());
        Collections.addAll(set1, "Step", "Jump", "Hop");
        NavigableSet<String> set2 = new TreeSet<>((Collection<String>)set1);
        while (!set1.isEmpty()) {
          System.out.print(set1.pollLast() + " ");
        }
        while (!set2.isEmpty()) {
          System.out.print(set2.pollFirst() + " ");
        }
    }
}
```

What is the result?

Select the one correct answer.

(a) Hop Jump Step Hop Jump Step

(b) Hop Jump Step Step Hop Jump

(c) Step Jump Hop Step Jump Hop

(d) Step Jump Hop Hop Jump Step

(e) The program will throw an exception at runtime.

15.15 What will be the output of the following program when compiled and run?

```
import java.util.*;
public class MapModify {
  public static void main(String[] args) {
    NavigableMap<String, Integer> grades = new TreeMap<>();
    grades.put("A",  5); grades.put("B", 10); grades.put("C", 15);
    grades.put("D", 20); grades.put("E", 25);

    System.out.print(grades.get(grades.firstKey()) + " ");
    System.out.print(sumValues(grades.headMap("D")) + " ");
    System.out.print(sumValues(grades.subMap("B", false, "D", true)) + " ");
    grades.subMap(grades.firstKey(), false, grades.lastKey(), false).clear();
    System.out.println(sumValues(grades));
  }
```

```java
public static <K, M extends Map<K, Integer>> int sumValues(M freqMap) {
    return freqMap.values().stream().mapToInt(i->i).sum();
  }
}
```

Select the one correct answer.

(a) 5 50 35 30

(b) 5 30 35 30

(c) 5 30 25 30

(d) 5 30 35 75

15.16 Which code, when inserted independently at (1), will result in the following output from the program: {Soap=10, Salts=30}?

```java
import java.util.*;
public class Mapping {
  public static void main(String[] args) {
    NavigableMap<String, Integer> myMap
                    = new TreeMap<>(Collections.reverseOrder());
    myMap.put("Soap", 10); myMap.put("Shampoo", 20); myMap.put("Salts", 30);
    // (1) INSERT CODE HERE
    System.out.println(myMap);
  }
}
```

Select the three correct answers.

(a) for (Map.Entry<String, Integer> entry : myMap.entrySet())
        if (entry.getKey().equals("Shampoo"))
          myMap.remove("Shampoo");

(b) for (Iterator<String> iterator = myMap.keySet().iterator();
          iterator.hasNext();)
        if (iterator.next().equals("Shampoo"))
          iterator.remove();

(c) for (Iterator<String> iterator = myMap.keySet().iterator();
          iterator.hasNext();) {
        if (iterator.next().equals("Shampoo"))
          myMap.remove("Shampoo");

(d) for (Map.Entry<String, Integer> entry : myMap.entrySet())
        if (entry.getKey().equals("Shampoo"))
          myMap.remove(entry);

(e) myMap.subMap("Shampoo", true, "Shampoo", true).clear();

(f) myMap.compute("Shampoo", (k, v) -> null);

15.17 Which statement is true about the following program?

```java
import java.util.*;
public class Valuables {
  public static void main(String[] args) {
    NavigableMap<Integer, Integer> iMap = new TreeMap<>();
    iMap.put(100, 1); iMap.put(200, 2); iMap.put(300, 3);
    int sumVal = 0;
    iMap.forEach((k, v) -> sumVal += v);
```

```
        System.out.println(sumVal);
    }
}
```

Select the one correct answer.

(a) The program will compile and print 6 when run.

(b) The program will fail to compile because the forEach() method requires a Function<T, R> and not a BiFunction<T, U, R>.

(c) There is no method named forEach for maps, only for collections.

(d) The program will fail to compile because the syntax of the lambda expression in the argument to the forEach() method is not correct.

(e) None of the above

15.18 Which statement is true about the following program?

```
import java.util.*;
public class InitMap {
    public static void main(String[] args) {
        Map<Integer, NavigableSet<String>> etnMap = new TreeMap<>();
        etnMap.computeIfAbsent(911, key -> new TreeSet<>()).add("USA");
        etnMap.computeIfAbsent(911, key -> new TreeSet<>()).add("Canada");
        etnMap.computeIfAbsent(911, key -> new TreeSet<>()).add("Argentina");
        etnMap.computeIfAbsent(112, key -> new TreeSet<>()).add("Norway");
        System.out.println(etnMap);
    }
}
```

Select the one correct answer.

(a) The program will fail to compile.

(b) The program will compile, but it will result in a runtime exception from one of the calls to the computeIfAbsent() method.

(c) The program will compile and print the following when run:
{112=[Norway], 911=[Argentina, Canada, USA]}

(d) The program will compile and print the following when run:
{112=[Norway], 911=[USA]}

(e) The program will compile and print the following when run:
{112=Norway, 911=USA}

(f) None of the above

15.19 Given the following code:

```
import java.util.*;
import java.util.function.*;
public class Test13RQ13 {
    public static void main(String[] args) {
        Map<Integer, String> values = new HashMap<>();
        values.put(1, "ONE");   values.put(2, "TWO");
        values.put(3, "THREE"); values.put(4, "FOUR");
        values.replaceAll((k, v) -> {
            switch (k) {
                case 1: return "FIRST";
                case 2: return "SECOND";
```

```
        case 3: return "THIRD";
        case 4: return "FOURTH";
      }
      return "ZERO";
    });
    values.forEach((Integer x, String y) -> { System.out.print(y + " "); } );
  }
}
```

What is the result?
Select the one correct answer.

(a) ONE TWO THREE FOUR
(b) FIRST SECOND THIRD FOURTH
(c) 1 2 3 4
(d) The program will compile, but it will produce no result when run.
(e) The program will throw an exception at runtime.
(f) The program will fail to compile.

15.11 The Collections Class

The Java Collections Framework also contains two utility classes, Collections and Arrays, that provide various operations on collections and arrays, such as algorithms for sorting and searching, or creating customized collections. Practically any operation on a collection can be done using the methods provided by this framework.

The methods also throw a NullPointerException if the specified collection or array references passed to them are null.

The utility methods declared in the Collections *class are all* public *and* static; *therefore, these two modifiers will be omitted in their method header declarations in this section.*

Unmodifiable Views of Collections

Unmodifiable views of collections are created by the utility methods unmodifiable*Interface*() in the Collections class, where *Interface* can be any of the core interfaces in the Java Collections Framework. The name of these methods is a slight misnomer, as they create unmodified *views* of collections on the *underlying* or *backing collection* that is passed as an argument to the method.

```
<E> Collection<E>    unmodifiableCollection(Collection<? extends E> c)
<E> List<E>          unmodifiableList(List<? extends E> list)
<E> Set<E>           unmodifiableSet(Set<? extends E> set)
<E> SortedSet<E>     unmodifiableSortedSet(SortedSet<E> sortedSet)
<E> NavigableSet<E>  unmodifiableNavigableSet(NavigableSet<E> navSet)
```

Return an *unmodifiable view* of the collection passed as an argument.

Query operations on the returned collection are delegated to the *underlying collection*, and changes in the underlying collection are reflected in the unmodifiable view.

Any attempt to modify the view of a collection will result in an Unsupported-OperationException.

The view collection returned by the unmodifiableCollection() method does not delegate the equals() and the hashCode() methods to the backing collection. Instead, the returned view uses the corresponding methods inherited from the Object class. This is to safeguard the contract of these methods when the backing collection is a set or a list. However, the views returned by the other methods above do not exhibit this behavior.

```
<K, V> Map<K, V>          unmodifiableMap(Map<? extends K, ? extends V> map)
<K, V> SortedMap<K, V>  unmodifiableSortedMap(SortedMap<K, ? extends V> sm)
<K, V> NavigableMap<K, V>
                      unmodifiableNavigableMap(NavigableMap<K, ? extends V> nm)
```

Return an *unmodifiable view* of the map passed as an argument.

Query operations on the view of the map are delegated to the *underlying map*, and changes in the underlying map are reflected in the unmodifiable view.

Any attempt to modify the returned map will result in an Unsupported-OperationException.

An *unmodifiable view of a collection* should not be confused with an *unmodifiable collection*. They are both unmodifiable—that is, they are *read-only* collections. No operations that can change them *structurally* are permitted (the famous UnsupportedOperationException). However, an unmodifiable view of a collection is *backed* by an *underlying collection*, but that is not the case for an unmodifiable collection. In the case of an unmodifiable view of a collection, any changes to the underlying collection are reflected in the unmodifiable view.

Examples of *unmodified collections* include the following:

- Unmodifiable lists created by List.of() and List.copyOf() methods (§12.2, p. 649). See also the comparison of unmodifiable lists and *list views* that are created by the Arrays.asList() method (§12.7, p. 660).

- Unmodifiable sets created by Set.of() and Set.copyOf() methods (p. 804).

- Unmodifiable maps created by Map.of(), Map.ofEntries(), and Map.copyOf() methods (p. 832).

The code below creates an *unmodifiable view* of a map whose values are mutable.

```
// Mutable courses:
StringBuilder mc1 = new StringBuilder("Java I");
StringBuilder mc2 = new StringBuilder("Java II");
StringBuilder mc3 = new StringBuilder("Java III");
StringBuilder mc4 = new StringBuilder("Java IV");

// Backing map:
Map<Integer, StringBuilder> backingMap = new HashMap<>();
backingMap.put(200, mc1); backingMap.put(300, mc2);
backingMap.put(400, mc3); backingMap.put(500, mc4);
```

```
// Unmodifiable view of a map:
Map<Integer, StringBuilder> unmodViewMap
                = Collections.unmodifiableMap(backingMap);
```

As in the case of unmodifiable collections, the code below throws an Unsupported-OperationException when an attempt is made to structurally change the unmodifiable view of a map.

```
// UnsupportedOperationException at (1), (2), and (3):
unmodViewMap.put(100, new StringBuilder("Java Now"));
unmodViewMap.remove(400);
unmodViewMap.replace(200, new StringBuilder("First Java"));
```

However, changes to the backing map are reflected in the unmodifiable view:

```
backingMap.remove(200); backingMap.remove(400);
System.out.println("Backing map:       " + backingMap);
System.out.println("Unmodifiable view: " + unmodViewMap);
// Backing map:       {500=Java Complete, 300=Java II}
// Unmodifiable view: {500=Java Complete, 300=Java II}
```

Since the values in the unmodifiable view of a map are mutable, the code below shows that changing a value of an entry in the unmodifiable view is reflected in the backing map.

```
StringBuilder mutableCourse = unmodViewMap.get(500);  // Get the course.
mutableCourse.replace(5, 8, "Complete");              // Change the course name.
System.out.println("Backing map:       " + backingMap);
System.out.println("Unmodifiable view: " + unmodViewMap);
// Backing map:       {400=Java III, 500=Java Complete, 200=Java I, 300=Java II}
// Unmodifiable view: {400=Java III, 500=Java Complete, 200=Java I, 300=Java II}
```

Ordering Elements in Lists

In order to sort the elements of a collection by their *natural ordering* or by another *total ordering*, the elements must implement the Comparable<E> (§14.4, p. 761) or the Comparator<E> (§14.5, p. 769) interface, respectively.

The Collections class provides two generic static methods for sorting lists.

```
<E extends Comparable<? super E>> void sort(List<E> list)
<E> void sort(List<E> list, Comparator<? super E> comparator)
```

The first method sorts the elements in the list according to their natural ordering. The second method does the sorting according to the total ordering defined by the comparator.

In addition, all elements in the list must be *mutually comparable*: The method call e1.compareTo(e2) (or e1.compare(e2) in the case of the comparator) must not throw a ClassCastException for any elements e1 and e2 in the list. In other words, it should be possible to compare any two elements in the list. Note that the second method does not require that the type parameter E is Comparable<E>.

If the specified comparator is null then the natural ordering for the elements is used, requiring elements in this list to implement the Comparable<E> interface.

```
<E> Comparator<E> reverseOrder()
<E> Comparator<E> reverseOrder(Comparator<E> comparator)
```

The first method returns a comparator that enforces the reverse of the natural ordering. The second method reverses the total ordering defined by the comparator. Both are useful for maintaining objects in reverse-natural or reverse-total ordering in sorted collections and arrays.

The List<E> interface also defines an abstract method for sorting lists, with semantics equivalent to its namesake in the Collections class.

```
// Defined in the List <E> interface.
void sort(Comparator<? super E> comparator)
```

This list is sorted according to the total ordering defined by the specified comparator. If the specified comparator is null then the natural ordering for the elements is used, requiring elements in this list to implement the Comparable<E> interface.

This code shows how a list of strings is sorted according to different criteria. We have used the sort() method from the List<E> interface and from the Collections class.

```
List<String> strList = new ArrayList<>();
Collections.addAll(strList, "biggest", "big", "bigger", "Bigfoot");

strList.sort(null);                                    // Natural order
strList.sort(Comparator.comparing(String::length));    // length order
strList.sort(Collections.reverseOrder());              // Reverse natural order
Collections.sort(strList, String.CASE_INSENSITIVE_ORDER);// Case insensitive order
Collections.sort(strList,                              // Reverse case insensitive order
              Collections.reverseOrder(String.CASE_INSENSITIVE_ORDER));
```

The output below shows the list before sorting, followed by the results from the calls to the sort() methods above, respectively:

```
Before sorting:                          [biggest, big, bigger, Bigfoot]
After sorting in natural order:          [Bigfoot, big, bigger, biggest]
After sorting in length order:           [big, bigger, Bigfoot, biggest]
After sorting in reverse natural order:  [biggest, bigger, big, Bigfoot]
After sorting in insensitive order:      [big, Bigfoot, bigger, biggest]
After sorting in reverse insensitive order: [biggest, bigger, Bigfoot, big]
```

It is important to note that either the element type of the list must implement the Comparable<E> interface or a Comparator<E> must be provided. The following code sorts a list of StringBuilder according to their natural ordering, as the class StringBuilder implements the Comparable<StringBuilder> interface.

```
List<StringBuilder> sbList = new ArrayList<>();
Collections.addAll(sbList, new StringBuilder("smallest"),
               new StringBuilder("small"), new StringBuilder("smaller"));
Collections.sort(sbList);              // [small, smaller, smallest]
```

Below is an example of a list whose elements are not mutually comparable. Raw types are used intentionally to create such a list. Predictably, the sort() method throws an exception because the primitive wrapper classes do not permit interclass comparison.

```
List freakList = new ArrayList();                    // Raw types.
Collections.addAll(freakList, 23, 3.14, 10L);
freakList.sort(null);                                // ClassCastException
```

The comparator returned by the reverseOrder() method can be used with *sorted* collections. The elements in the following sorted set would be maintained in descending order:

```
Set<Integer> intSet = new TreeSet<>(Collections.reverseOrder());
Collections.addAll(intSet, 9, 11, -4, 1);
System.out.println(intSet);        // [11, 9, 1, -4]
```

The following utility methods in the Collections class apply to *any* list, regardless of whether the elements are Comparable<E> or not:

```
void reverse(List<?> list)
```
Reverses the order of the elements in the list.

```
void rotate(List<?> list, int distance)
```
Rotates the elements toward the end of the list by the specified distance. A negative value for the distance will rotate toward the start of the list.

```
void shuffle(List<?> list)
void shuffle(List<?> list, Random rnd)
```
Randomly permutes the list—that is, *shuffles* the elements.

```
void swap(List<?> list, int i, int j)
```
Swaps the elements at indices i and j.

The effect of these utility methods can be limited to a sublist—that is, a segment of the list. The following code illustrates rotation of elements in a list. Note how the rotation in the sublist view is reflected in the original list.

```
// intList refers to the following list:               [9, 11, -4, 1, 7]
Collections.rotate(intList, 2);       // Two to the right.   [1, 7, 9, 11, -4]
Collections.rotate(intList, -2);      // Two to the left.    [9, 11, -4, 1, 7]
List intSublist = intList.subList(1,4);// Sublist:              [11, -4, 1]
Collections.rotate(intSublist, -1);   // One to the left.       [-4, 1, 11]
                                      // intList is now:   [9, -4, 1, 11, 7]
```

Searching in Collections

The Collections class provides two static methods for finding elements in *sorted* lists.

```
<E> int binarySearch(List<? extends Comparable<? super E>> list, E key)
<E> int binarySearch(List<? extends E> list, E key,
                     Comparator<? super E> cmp))
```

These methods use binary search to find the index of the key element in the specified sorted list. The first method requires that the list is sorted according to natural ordering, whereas the second method requires that it is sorted according to the total ordering dictated by the comparator. The elements in the list and the key must also be *mutually comparable*.

Successful searches return the index of the key in the list. A non-negative value indicates a successful search. Unsuccessful searches return a negative value given by the formula -(*insertion point* + 1), where *insertion point* is the index where the key would have been, had it been in the list. In the code below, the return value -3 indicates that the key would have been at index 2, had it been in the list.

```
Collections.sort(strList);
// Sorted in natural order: [Bigfoot, big, bigger, biggest]
// Search in natural order:
out.println(Collections.binarySearch(strList, "bigger"));   // Successful:    2
out.println(Collections.binarySearch(strList, "bigfeet"));  // Unsuccessful: -3
out.println(Collections.binarySearch(strList, "bigmouth")); // Unsuccessful: -5
```

Proper use of the search methods requires that the list is sorted, and the search is performed according to the same sort order. Otherwise, the search results are *unpredictable*. The example below shows the results of the search when the list strList above was sorted in reverse natural ordering, but was searched assuming natural ordering. Most importantly, the return values reported for unsuccessful searches for the respective keys are incorrect in the list that was sorted in reverse natural ordering.

```
Collections.sort(strList, Collections.reverseOrder());
// Sorted in reverse natural order: [biggest, bigger, big, Bigfoot]
// Searching in natural order:
out.println(Collections.binarySearch(strList, "bigger"));   // 1
out.println(Collections.binarySearch(strList, "bigfeet"));  // -1 (INCORRECT)
out.println(Collections.binarySearch(strList, "bigmouth")); // -5 (INCORRECT)
```

Searching the list in reverse natural ordering requires that an appropriate comparator is supplied during the search (as during the sorting), resulting in correct results:

```
Collections.sort(strList, Collections.reverseOrder());
// Sorted in reverse natural order: [biggest, bigger, big, Bigfoot]
// Searching in reverse natural order:
out.println(Collections.binarySearch(strList, "bigger",
                          Collections.reverseOrder())); // 1
```

```
out.println(Collections.binarySearch(strList, "bigfeet",
                          Collections.reverseOrder())); // -3
out.println(Collections.binarySearch(strList, "bigmouth",
                          Collections.reverseOrder())); // -1
```

The following methods search for *sublists*:

```
int indexOfSubList(List<?> source, List<?> target)
int lastIndexOfSubList(List<?> source, List<?> target)
```

These two methods find the first or the last occurrence of the target list in the source list, respectively. They return the starting position of the target list in the source list. The methods are applicable to lists of *any* type.

The following methods find the maximum and minimum elements in a collection:

```
<E extends Object & Comparable<? super E>>
    E max(Collection<? extends E> c)
<E> E max(Collection<? extends E> c, Comparator<? super E> cmp)
<E extends Object & Comparable<? super E>>
    E min(Collection<? extends E> c)
<E> E min(Collection<? extends E> cl, Comparator<? super E> cmp)
```

The one-argument methods require that the elements have a natural ordering—that is, are Comparable<E>. The other methods require that the elements have a total ordering enforced by the comparator. Calling any of the methods with an empty collection as a parameter results in a NoSuchElementException.

The time for the search is proportional to the size of the collection.

These methods are analogous to the methods first() and last() in the SortedSet<E> class (p. 810), and the methods firstKey() and lastKey() in the SortedMap<K, V> class (p. 845).

Replacing Elements in Collections

Both the List<E> interface and the Collections class define a replaceAll() method to replace elements in a collection, but they operate differently.

```
// Defined in the List<E> interface.
void replaceAll(UnaryOperator<E> operator)
```

With this method, each element is replaced with the result of applying the specified operator to that element of this list. Unary operators are covered in §13.10, p. 720.

```
// Defined in the Collections class.
<E> boolean replaceAll(List<E> list, E oldVal, E newVal) // Collections
```

Replaces all elements equal to oldVal with newVal in the list; it returns true if the list was modified.

The following code snippet illustrates how the replaceAll() method of the List<E> interface can be used to apply a UnaryOperator to each element of the list. The lambda expression at (1a) is executed for each string in the list strList, replacing each element with an uppercase version of the string. Equivalent method reference is used for the same purpose at (1b).

```
// Before: [biggest, big, bigger, Bigfoot]
strList.replaceAll(str -> str.toUpperCase());      // (1a)
strList.replaceAll(String::toUpperCase);           // (1b)
// After: [BIGGEST, BIG, BIGGER, BIGFOOT]
```

In contrast, the replaceAll() method of the Collections class can be used to replace all occurrences of a specific value in the collection with a new value. In the list palindromes of strings, the occurrence of the string "road" is replaced by the string "anna" in the method call below.

```
// Before: [eye, level, radar, road]
Collections.replaceAll(palindromes, "road", "anna");
// After: [eye, level, radar, anna]
```

The majority of the methods found in the Collections class that replace the elements of a collection operate on a List, while one method operates on arbitrary Collections. They all change the contents of the collection in some way.

<E> boolean addAll(Collection<? super E> collection, E... elements)

Adds the specified elements to the specified collection. This is a convenient method for loading a collection with individually specified elements or an array. The method is annotated with @SafeVarargs because of the variable arity parameter. The annotation suppresses the heap pollution warning in its declaration and the unchecked generic array creation warning at the call sites.

<E> void copy(List<? super E> destination, List<? extends E> source)

Adds the elements from the source list to the destination list. Elements copied to the destination list will have the same index as in the source list. The destination list cannot be shorter than the source list. If it is longer, the remaining elements in the destination list are unaffected.

<E> void fill(List<? super E> list, E element)

Replaces all of the elements of the list with the specified element.

<E> List<E> nCopies(int n, E element)

Creates an immutable list with n copies of the specified element. The *same* reference value of the specified element is saved in the list for *all* references.

The addAll() method is a convenient method for loading an *existing* collection with a *few* individually specified elements or an array of small size. Several examples of its usage can be found in this chapter. The array passed should be an array of objects. Note also the autoboxing of the int values specified at (1) and (2). The addAll() method does not allow primitive arrays as a variable arity argument, as attempted at (3).

```
List<Integer> intList = new ArrayList<>();                  // []
Collections.addAll(intList, 9, 1, 1);                       // (1) Varargs
// After: [9, 1, 1]
Collections.addAll(intList, new Integer[] {1, 1, 9}); // (2) An array of Integers
```

```
// After: [9, 1, 1, 1, 1, 9]
Collections.addAll(intList, new int[] {1, 9, 1});      // (3) Compile-time error!
```

As we can see at (2), the collection returned by the Collections.addAll() method is *not* of fixed size as more elements can be added to it. This is in contrast to the list returned by the Array.asList() method (§12.7, p. 659). However, the addAll() method of the Collection<E> interface can be used for adding an arbitrary collection to an existing collection.

When using the Collections.copy() method to copy elements from the source list to the destination list, the elements are copied to the *same* positional index in the destination list as they were in the source list.

```
List<String> dest = new ArrayList<>();
Collections.addAll(dest, "one", "two", "three", "four");// [one, two, three, four]
List<String> src = new ArrayList<>();
Collections.addAll(src, "I", "II", "III");              // [I, II, III]
Collections.copy(dest, src);                            // [I, II, III, four]
```

All elements of a list can be replaced with the *same* element, as shown at (1):

```
List<String> strList = new ArrayList<>();
Collections.addAll(strList, "liberty", "equality", "fraternity");
// Before: [liberty, equality, fraternity]
Collections.fill(strList, "CENSORED");                 // (1)
// After: [CENSORED, CENSORED, CENSORED]
```

Earlier we saw usage of the Collections.nCopies() method in Example 15.10 and Example 15.11. The for(;;) loop below

```
for (int i = 0; i < 5; ++i)
  System.out.printf("%d %s%n", i, Collections.nCopies(i, "*"));
```

prints the following:

```
0 []
1 [*]
2 [*, *]
3 [*, *, *]
4 [*, *, *, *]
```

15.12 The Arrays Class

In this section we look at some selected utility methods from the java.util.Arrays class, in particular, for sorting, searching, and comparing arrays.

Creating *list views of arrays* using the Arrays.asList() method is covered in §12.7, p. 660, and can be compared with *unmodifiable lists* created using the factory methods List.of() and List.copyOf().

Using the overloaded static method Arrays.stream() to create streams with arrays as the data source is covered in §16.4, p. 898.

The utility methods declared in the Arrays *class are all* public *and* static. *Therefore, these two modifiers will be omitted in their method header declarations in this section.*

Sorting Arrays

Sorting implies ordering the elements according to some ranking criteria, usually based on the *values* of the elements. The values of numeric data types are compared and ranked by using the relational operators that define the *numerical order* of the values. Objects are typically compared according to their *natural ordering* defined by their class. The class implements the compareTo() method of the Comparable<E> interface. The ordering defined by this method is called the *natural ordering* for the objects of the class, where obj1.compareTo(obj2) returns the following result:

- A *positive value* if obj1 is *greater* than obj2
- The value 0 if obj1 is *equal* to obj2
- A *negative value* if obj1 is *less* than obj2

The wrapper classes for primitive values and the String class implement the compareTo() method (§8.3, p. 432), thereby giving their objects a natural ordering. Arrays with objects of these classes can readily be sorted as the sort algorithm can take advantage of their natural ordering.

The Arrays class provides enough overloaded versions of the sort() method to sort practically any type of array. The discussion on sorting lists (p. 858) is also applicable to sorting arrays.

```
void sort(type[] array)
void sort(type[] array, int fromIndex, int toIndex)
```

The permitted *type* for elements includes byte, char, double, float, int, long, short, and Object.

These methods sort the elements in the array according to their *natural ordering*.

In the case of an array of objects being passed as an argument, the *objects* must be *mutually comparable* according to the *natural ordering* defined by the Comparable<E> interface; that is, it should be possible to compare any two objects in the array according to their natural ordering without throwing a ClassCastException.

```
<E> void sort(E[] array, Comparator<? super E> cmp)
<E> void sort(E[] array, int fromIndex, int toIndex,
              Comparator<? super E> cmp)
```

These two generic methods sort the array according to the *total ordering* dictated by the comparator. In particular, the methods require that the elements are mutually comparable according to this comparator.

The subarray bounds, if specified in the methods above, define a half-open interval. Only elements in this interval are then sorted.

The Arrays class also defines analogous methods with the name parallelSort for sorting the elements in parallel.

The experiment with a list of strings (p. 858) is repeated in the following with an array of strings, giving identical results. An array of strings is sorted according to different criteria.

```
String[] strArray = {"biggest", "big", "bigger", "Bigfoot"};
Arrays.sort(strArray);                                           // Natural order
Arrays.sort(strArray, Comparator.comparing(String::length));    // Length order
Arrays.sort(strArray, Collections.reverseOrder());   // Reverse natural order
Arrays.sort(strArray, String.CASE_INSENSITIVE_ORDER);// Case insensitive order
Arrays.sort(strArray,                             // Reverse case insensitive order
            Collections.reverseOrder(String.CASE_INSENSITIVE_ORDER));
```

The output below shows the array before sorting, followed by the results from the calls to the Arrays.sort() methods above, respectively:

```
Before sorting:                                    [biggest, big, bigger, Bigfoot]
After sorting in natural order:                    [Bigfoot, big, bigger, biggest]
After sorting in length order:                     [big, bigger, Bigfoot, biggest]
After sorting in reverse natural order:            [biggest, bigger, big, Bigfoot]
After sorting in case insensitive order:           [big, Bigfoot, bigger, biggest]
After sorting in reverse case insensitive order: [biggest, bigger, Bigfoot, big]
```

The examples below illustrate sorting an array of primitive values (int) at (1), an array of type Object containing mutually comparable elements (String) at (2), and a half-open interval in reverse natural ordering at (3). A ClassCastException is thrown when the elements are not mutually comparable, at (4) and (5).

```
int[] intArray = {5, 3, 7, 1};                    // int
Arrays.sort(intArray);                            // (1) Natural order: [1, 3, 5, 7]

Object[] objArray1 = {"I", "am", "OK"};           // String
Arrays.sort(objArray1);                           // (2) Natural order: [I, OK, am]

Comparable<Integer>[] comps = new Integer[] {5, 3, 7, 1}; // Integer
Arrays.sort(comps, 1, 4, Collections.reverseOrder());// (3) Reverse natural order:
                                                  //      [5, 7, 3, 1]

Object[] objArray2 = {23, 3.14, "ten"};           // Not mutually comparable
//  Arrays.sort(objArray2);                       // (4) ClassCastException

Number[] numbers = {23, 3.14, 10L};               // Not mutually comparable
//  Arrays.sort(numbers);                         // (5) ClassCastException
```

Searching in Arrays

A common operation on an array is to search the array for a given element, called the *key*. The Arrays class provides enough overloaded versions of the binarySearch() method to search in practically any type of array that is *sorted*. The discussion on searching in lists (p. 861) is also applicable to searching in arrays.

```
int binarySearch(type[] array, type key)
int binarySearch(type[] array, int fromIndex, int toIndex, type key)
```

The permitted *type* for elements includes byte, char, double, float, int, long, short, and Object.

These methods search for key in the array where the elements are sorted according to the natural ordering of the elements.

In the case where an array of objects is passed as an argument, the *objects* must be sorted in natural ordering, as defined by the Comparable<E> interface.

These methods return the index to the key in the sorted array, if the key exists. If not, a negative index is returned, corresponding to −(*insertion point* + 1), where *insertion point* is the index of the element where the key would have been found, if it had been in the array. In case there are duplicate elements equal to the key, there is no guarantee which duplicate's index will be returned. The elements and the key must be *mutually comparable*.

The bounds, if specified in the methods, define a half-open interval. The search is then confined to this interval.

```
<E> int binarySearch(E[] array, E key, Comparator<? super E> c)
<E> int binarySearch(E[] array, int fromIndex, int toIndex, E key,
                     Comparator<? super E> c)
```

These two generic methods require that the array is sorted according to the total ordering dictated by the comparator. In particular, its elements are mutually comparable according to this comparator. The comparator must be equivalent to the one that was used for sorting the array; otherwise, the results are unpredictable.

An appropriate import statement should be included in the source code to access the java.util.Arrays class by its simple name. The experiment from p. 861 with a list of strings is repeated here with an array of strings, giving identical results. In the code below, the return value -3 indicates that the key would have been found at index 2 had it been in the list.

```
Arrays.sort(strArray);
// Sorted according to natural order: [Bigfoot, big, bigger, biggest]
// Search in natural order:
out.println(Arrays.binarySearch(strArray, "bigger"));   // Successful:    2
out.println(Arrays.binarySearch(strArray, "bigfeet"));  // Unsuccessful: -3
out.println(Arrays.binarySearch(strArray, "bigmouth")); // Unsuccessful: -5
```

Results are unpredictable if the array is not sorted, or the ordering used in the search is not the same as the sort order. Searching in the strArray using reverse natural ordering when the array is sorted in natural ordering gives the wrong result:

```
out.println(Arrays.binarySearch(strArray, "bigger",
                   Collections.reverseOrder()));  //  -1 (INCORRECT)
```

A ClassCastException is thrown if the key and the elements are not mutually comparable:

```
out.println(Arrays.binarySearch(strArray, 4)); // Key: 4 => ClassCastException
```

However, this incompatibility is caught at compile time in the case of arrays with primitive values:

```
// Sorted int array (natural order): [1, 3, 5, 7]
out.println(Arrays.binarySearch(intArray, 4.5));// Key: 4.5 => Compile-time error!
```

The method binarySearch() derives its name from the divide-and-conquer algorithm that it uses to perform the search. It repeatedly divides the remaining elements to be searched into two halves and selects the half containing the key in which to continue the search, until either the key is found or there are no more elements left to search.

Comparing Arrays

The java.util.Arrays class provides a rich set of static methods for comparing arrays of primitive data types and objects. In this section we only consider the basic methods for array equality, array comparison, and array mismatch. We encourage the curious reader to explore the Arrays class API for more flexible comparison of arrays.

Array Equality

The Arrays.equals() static method can be used to determine if two arrays are equal.

```
boolean equals(type[] a, type[] b)
```

The permitted *type* for elements includes all *primitive types* (boolean, byte, char, double, float, int, long, short) and Object.

Two arrays are considered *equal* if they contain the same elements in the same order—that is, they have the same length and corresponding pairs of elements are equal. Two array references are also considered equal if both are null.

Two primitive values v1 and v2 are considered *equal* if new *Wrapper-Class*(v1).equals(new *WrapperClass*(v2)),where *WrapperClass* is the wrapper class corresponding to their primitive data type.

Two objects obj1 and obj2 are considered *equal* if Objects.equals(obj1, obj2).

Given two arrays fruitBasketA and fruitBasketB of strings, shown below graphically, we can conclude that they are equal, since they have the same length and corresponding pairs of fruits are equal.

```
Index                 0       1       2     3
fruitBasketA ==> [oranges, apples, plums, kiwi]
fruitBasketB ==> [oranges, apples, plums, kiwi]
Equals: true
```

However, the arrays fruitBasketA and fruitBasketC below would not be considered equal. Although they have the same length and the same fruits, their corresponding pairs of fruits are *not* equal. The first index where this occurs is index 2.

```
Index                    0       1       2       3
fruitBasketA ==> [oranges, apples, plums, kiwi]
fruitBasketC ==> [oranges, apples, kiwi, plums]
Equals: false
```

Obviously, the two arrays fruitBasketA and fruitBasketE that have different lengths are not equal, as we can see below:

```
Index                    0       1       2       3
fruitBasketA ==> [oranges, apples, plums, kiwi]
fruitBasketE ==> [oranges, apples]
Equals: false
```

The following code demonstrates the examples provided above, where System.out is statically imported:

```
String[] fruitBasketA = { "oranges", "apples", "plums", "kiwi" };
String[] fruitBasketB = { "oranges", "apples", "plums", "kiwi" };
String[] fruitBasketC = { "oranges", "apples", "kiwi", "plums" };
String[] fruitBasketE = { "oranges", "apples" };
...
out.println("Equals: " + Arrays.equals(fruitBasketA, fruitBasketB)); // true
out.println("Equals: " + Arrays.equals(fruitBasketA, fruitBasketC)); // false
out.println("Equals: " + Arrays.equals(fruitBasketA, fruitBasketE)); // false
```

According to the equals() method, two null arrays are equal. However, the first statement below will not compile. The compiler issues an error, as the method call matches many overloaded methods named equals in the Arrays API. A cast is necessary to disambiguate the method call, as shown in the second statement.

```
out.println(Arrays.equals(null, null));                  // Ambiguous method call.
                                                         //    Compile-time error!
out.println(Arrays.equals((String[]) null, null));  // true
```

Array Comparison

The compare() method of the Comparable<E> interface allows two objects to be compared. The comparison relationship is generalized by the Arrays.compare() static method to *lexicographically compare* arrays.

```
int compare(type[] a, type[] b)
<T extends Comparable<? super T>> int compare(T[] a, T[] b)
```

The permitted *type* for elements includes all *primitive types* (boolean, byte, char, double, float, int, long, short).

These methods return the value 0 if the first and second arrays are equal; a value less than 0 if the first array is *lexicographically less than* the second array; and a value greater than 0 if the first array is *lexicographically greater than* the second array.

The second method only permits arrays whose objects implement the compareTo() method of the Comparable<E> interface.

Two null array references are considered equal, and a null array reference is considered lexicographically less than a non-null array reference.

Consider the case where the two arrays diceA and diceD that represent the result of rolling a dice a fixed number of times. The arrays have a *prefix* ([5, 2]) which is common to both arrays. At index 2, diceA[2] (value 6) is *greater than* diceD[2] (value 3). In this case, the compare() method returns a *positive* value to indicate that array diceA is *lexicographically greater* than array diceD. Note that the index 2 is equal to the length of the prefix [5, 2] and it is a valid index in both arrays. The prefix [5, 2] is called the *common prefix* of diceA and diceD.

```
Index        0  1  2  3
diceA ==> [5, 2, 6, 3]
diceD ==> [5, 2, 3]
Common prefix: [5,2]
Compare value: 1
```

In the example below, the compare() method returns a *negative* value to indicate that diceA is *lexicographically less* than diceE because diceA[1] (value 2) is less than diceE[1] (value 6), where the common prefix [5] has length 1.

```
Index        0  1  2  3
diceA ==> [5, 2, 6, 3]
diceE ==> [5, 6]
Common prefix: [5]
Compare value: -1
```

If the arrays share a common prefix, as in the examples above, the lexicographical comparison is determined by the corresponding pair of values at the index given by the length of the common prefix. The length of a common prefix is always greater than or equal to 0 and less than the minimum length of the two arrays. By this definition, the length of a common prefix can never be equal to the length of the two arrays. A common prefix of length 0 means that the elements at index 0 from each array determine the comparison result.

Where the prefix is equal to one of the arrays, we need to consider the lengths of the arrays:

- If the lengths are equal, as shown in the example below, the arrays must be lexicographically equal and the compare() method returns the value 0.

```
Index        0  1  2  3
diceA ==> [5, 2, 6, 3]
diceB ==> [5, 2, 6, 3]
Prefix: [5, 2, 6, 3]
Compare value: 0
```

- If the lengths are *not* equal, as shown in the example below, lexicographical comparison is based on the lengths of the arrays. The longer array (diceC, length 4) is *lexicographically greater* than the shorter array (diceD, length 3). The compare() method returns a *positive* value. Note that the length of the prefix, 3 in this example, is a valid index in the longer array, diceC, but not in the shorter array, diceD.

```
Index        0  1  2  3
diceC ==> [5, 2, 3, 6]
```

```
diceD ==> [5, 2, 3]
Proper prefix: [5, 2, 3]
Compare value: 1
```

In the example above, the shorter array diceD is a prefix for the longer array diceC. Such a prefix is called a *proper prefix*—that is, it is equal to one of the arrays, where the lengths of the arrays are different.

The following code can be used to demonstrate lexicographic comparison of arrays, where System.out is statically imported:

```
int[] diceA = { 5, 2, 6, 3 };
int[] diceB = { 5, 2, 6, 3 };
int[] diceC = { 5, 2, 3, 6 };
int[] diceD = { 5, 2, 3 };
int[] diceE = { 5, 6 };
...
out.println("Compare value: " + Arrays.compare(diceA, diceD)); // 1
out.println("Compare value: " + Arrays.compare(diceA, diceE)); // -1
out.println("Compare value: " + Arrays.compare(diceA, diceB)); // 0
out.println("Compare value: " + Arrays.compare(diceC, diceD)); // 1
```

Array Mismatch

The Arrays.mismatch() static method returns the *first* index where a mismatch occurs between two arrays. If there is no mismatch, the arrays are equal, and the value -1 is returned. The index returned is determined by the prefix of the arrays. The discussion on common and proper prefixes in the subsection on comparing arrays is highly relevant for determining mismatch (p. 869).

```
int mismatch(type[] a, type[] b)
```
The permitted *type* for elements includes all *primitive types* (boolean, byte, char, double, float, int, long, short) and Object.

This method returns the *index* of the *first* mismatch between two arrays, where $0 <= index <= $ Math.min(a.length, b.length). Otherwise, it returns -1 if no mismatch is found.

The method throws a NullPointerException if either of the arrays is null.

The examples below illustrate how the mismatch is determined.

The two arrays fruitBasketA and fruitBasketC have a *common prefix* [oranges, apples]. Mismatch therefore occurs at the index given by the length of the prefix (2). The elements fruitBasketA[2] and fruitBasketC[2] mismatch—that is, the element strings are not equal. The mismatch() method returns the value 2, the same as the length of the common prefix.

```
Index                 0       1       2     3
fruitBasketA ==> [oranges, apples, plums, kiwi]
fruitBasketC ==> [oranges, apples, kiwi, plums]
Common prefix: [oranges, apples]
Mismatch index: 2
```

In the following example, the common prefix is empty. Its length is 0. The elements at index 0, fruitBasketA[0] and fruitBasketG[0], mismatch. The index 0 is returned.

```
Index                   0     1      2      3
fruitBasketA ==> [oranges, apples, plums, kiwi]
fruitBasketG ==> [apples]
Common prefix: []
Mismatch index: 0
```

In the next example, the array lengths are equal and the prefix is the same as both arrays. There is no mismatch between the two arrays. The value -1 is returned.

```
Index                   0     1      2      3
fruitBasketA ==> [oranges, apples, plums, kiwi]
fruitBasketB ==> [oranges, apples, plums, kiwi]
Prefix: [oranges, apples, plums, kiwi]
Mismatch value: -1
```

In the example below, the arrays have a *proper prefix*, [oranges, apples], as the prefix is the same as one of the arrays and the arrays have different lengths. Mismatch therefore occurs at the index given by the length of the proper prefix (2) in the longer array, fruitBasketA. Index 2 is only valid in this array. The mismatch() method returns the index 2.

```
Index                   0     1      2      3
fruitBasketA ==> [oranges, apples, plums, kiwi]
fruitBasketE ==> [oranges, apples]
Proper prefix: [oranges, apples]
Mismatch index: 2
```

The following code can be used to demonstrate the index value returned by the mismatch() method in the examples above, where System.out is statically imported:

```
String[] fruitBasketA = { "oranges", "apples", "plums", "kiwi" };
String[] fruitBasketB = { "oranges", "apples", "plums", "kiwi" };
String[] fruitBasketC = { "oranges", "apples", "kiwi", "plums" };
String[] fruitBasketE = { "oranges", "apples" };
String[] fruitBasketG = { "apples" };
...
out.println("Mismatch index: "+Arrays.mismatch(fruitBasketA, fruitBasketC)); //2
out.println("Mismatch index: "+Arrays.mismatch(fruitBasketA, fruitBasketG)); //0
out.println("Mismatch index: "+Arrays.mismatch(fruitBasketA, fruitBasketB)); //-1
out.println("Mismatch index: "+Arrays.mismatch(fruitBasketA, fruitBasketE)); //2
```

Miscellaneous Utility Methods in the Arrays **Class**

The methods toString() and fill() (Example 15.10, Example 15.11) have previously been used in this chapter.

```
String toString(type[] array)
String deepToString(Object[] array)
```

Return a text representation of the contents (or "deep contents") of the specified array. The first method calls the toString() method of the element if this element is not an array, but calls the Object.toString() method if the element is an array—that is, it creates a *one-dimensional* text representation of an array. The second method *goes deeper* and creates a multidimensional text representation for an arrays of arrays—that is, arrays that have arrays as elements. The *type* can be any primitive type.

```
void fill(type[] array, type value)
void fill(type[] array, int fromIndex, int toIndex, type value)
```

In these methods, the *type* can be any primitive type, or Object. The methods assign the specified value to each element of the specified array or the subarray given by the half-open interval whose index bounds are specified.

The code below illustrates how the Arrays.fill() method can be used. Each element in the local array bar is assigned the character '*' using the fill() method, and the array is printed.

```
for (int i = 0; i < 5; ++i) {
  char[] bar = new char[i];
  Arrays.fill(bar, '*');
  System.out.printf("%d %s%n", i, Arrays.toString(bar));
}
```

Output from the for(;;) loop:

```
0 []
1 [*]
2 [*, *]
3 [*, *, *]
4 [*, *, *, *]
```

The Arrays.toString() method has been used in many examples to convert the contents of an array to a text representation. The Arrays.deepToString() method can be used to convert the contents of a *multidimensional* array to a text representation, where each element that is an array is also converted to a text representation.

```
char[][] twoDimArr = new char[2][2];
Arrays.fill(twoDimArr[0], '*');
Arrays.fill(twoDimArr[1], '*');
System.out.println(Arrays.deepToString(twoDimArr));    // [[*, *], [*, *]]
```

In addition to initializing an array in an array initialization block, the following overloaded setAll() methods in the Arrays class can be used to initialize an existing array.

```
<T> void setAll(T[] array, IntFunction<? extends T> generator)
void setAll(int[] array, IntUnaryOperator generator)
void setAll(long[] array, IntToLongFunction generator)
void setAll(double[] array, IntToDoubleFunction generator)
```

Set all elements of the specified array, using the provided generator function to compute each element.

The code below illustrates how each element of an existing array can be initialized to the result of applying a function.

```
String[] strArr = new String[5];
Arrays.setAll(strArr, i -> "Str@" + i); // [Str@0, Str@1, Str@2, Str@3, Str@4]

int[] intArr = new int[4];
Arrays.setAll(intArr, i -> i * i);       // [0, 1, 4, 9]
```

 ## Review Questions

15.20   Which statement is true about the following program?

```
import java.util.*;
public class WhatIsThis {
  public static void main(String[] args) {
    List<StringBuilder> list = new ArrayList<>();
    list.add(new StringBuilder("B"));
    list.add(new StringBuilder("A"));
    list.add(new StringBuilder("C"));
    list.sort(Collections.reverseOrder());
    System.out.println(list.subList(1,2));
  }
}
```

Select the one correct answer.

(a) The program will compile. When run, it will print [B].
(b) The program will compile. When run, it will print [B, A].
(c) The program will compile. When run, it will throw an exception.
(d) The program will fail to compile.

15.21   Which of the following statements are true about the following program?

```
import java.util.*;
public class InitOnly {
  public static void main(String[] args) {
    List<String> list1 = new ArrayList<>();
    Collections.addAll(list1, "Hi", "Hello");
    Collections.addAll(list1, "Howdy");
    System.out.println(list1);                       // (1)

    List<String> list2 = new ArrayList<>(list1);
    list2 = Arrays.asList("Hi", "Hello");
    list2 = Arrays.asList("Howdy");
    System.out.println(list2);                       // (2)
```

```
            List<String> list3 = new ArrayList<>();
            list3.addAll(list1);
            System.out.println(list3);                      // (3)

            List<String> list4 = new ArrayList<>(list2);
            System.out.println(list4);                      // (4)
        }
    }
```

Select the four correct answers.

(a) Line (1) will print [Howdy].
(b) Line (1) will print [Hi, Hello, Howdy].
(c) Line (2) will print [Howdy].
(d) Line (2) will print [Hi, Hello, Howdy].
(e) Line (3) will print [Howdy].
(f) Line (3) will print [Hi, Hello, Howdy].
(g) Line (4) will print [Howdy].
(h) Line (4) will print [Hi, Hello, Howdy].

15.22 Which of the following statements are true about the following program?

```
    import java.util.Arrays;
    public class GetThatIndex {
      public static void main(String[] args) {
        if (args.length != 1) return;
        printIndex(args[0]);
      }

      public static void printIndex(String key) {
        String[] strings = {"small", "smaller", "smallest", "tiny"};
        System.out.println(Arrays.binarySearch(strings, key));
      }
    }
```

Select the two correct answers.

(a) The largest value ever printed by the printIndex() method is 3.
(b) The largest value ever printed by the printIndex() method is 4.
(c) The largest value ever printed by the printIndex() method is 5.
(d) The smallest value ever printed by the printIndex() method is 0.
(e) The smallest value ever printed by the printIndex() method is -4.
(f) The smallest value ever printed by the printIndex() method is -5.
(g) The smallest value ever printed by the printIndex() method is -3.

15.23 Given the following code:

```
    import java.util.*;
    public class Q36 {
      public static void main(String[] args) {
        String s1 = "London";
        String s2 = "Bergen";
        String s3 = "Saratov";
        Deque<String> trip = new ArrayDeque<>();
```

```
            String r1 = trip.pollFirst();
            trip.offerFirst(s1);
            trip.offerFirst(s2);
            String r2 = trip.pollFirst();
            String r3 = trip.peekFirst();
            trip.offerLast(s3);
            trip.offerLast(s1);
            String r4 = trip.pollLast();
            String r5 = trip.peekLast();
            System.out.println(r1 + " " + r2 + " " + r3 + " " + r4 + " " + r5);
        }
    }
```

What is the result?

Select the one correct answer.

(a) An UnsupportedOperationException is thrown at runtime.

(b) A NullPointerException is thrown at runtime.

(c) null Bergen London London Saratov

(d) null Bergen Bergen London London

(e) Bergen London London Saratov

(f) Bergen Bergen London London

15.24   Given the following code:

```
        import java.util.*;
        public class Q37 {
          public static void main(String[] args) {
            Integer x = 1, y = 2, z = 3;
            Set<Integer> coordinates = new TreeSet<>();
            coordinates.add(x);
            coordinates.add(y);
            coordinates.add(y);
            coordinates.add(z);
            coordinates.remove(x);
            System.out.print(coordinates);
          }
        }
```

What is the result?

Select the one correct answer.

(a) [1, 2, 3]

(b) [2, 3]

(c) [2, 2, 3]

(d) [1, 2, 2, 3]

(e) The program will throw an exception at runtime.

(f) The program will fail to compile.

15.25   Given the following code:

```
        import java.util.*;
        public class Q38 {
          public static void main(String[] args) {
```

```
        List<Integer> prices = new ArrayList<>();
        prices.add(1);
        prices.add(2);
        prices.add(2, null);
        prices.add(3, 3);
        prices.add(2, 4);
        prices.set(2, 3);
        prices.remove(2);
        prices.add(2, 2);
        System.out.print(prices);
    }
}
```

What is the result?

Select the one correct answer.

(a) `[1, 2, null, 3]`

(b) `[1, 2, 3]`

(c) `[1, 2, 2, 3]`

(d) `[1, 2, 2, null, 3]`

(e) `[1, 2, null, null]`

(f) `[1, null, 2,  2, 3]`

(g) The program will throw an exception at runtime.

(h) The program will fail to compile.

Index

Index includes entries for Vol. I and Vol. II. References to pp. 879–1752 refer to items in Vol. II (Chapters 16–Appendices).

Symbols

J

M

W

X

Y

Z